BADEN-POWELL
The Two Lives of a Hero

BADEN-POWELL
The Two Lives of a Hero

by

WILLIAM HILLCOURT

with Olave, Lady Baden-Powell

G. P. PUTNAM'S SONS : NEW YORK

First American Edition, 1964

© WILLIAM HILLCOURT WITH OLAVE, LADY BADEN-POWELL, 1964

Fourth Impression

SBN 399-10068-7

*Library of Congress Catalog
Card Number: 64-24263*

MANUFACTURED IN THE UNITED STATES OF AMERICA

CONTENTS

ILLUSTRATIONS

LIFE NUMBER TWO: THE CHIEF SCOUT OF THE WORLD

With the exception of the silhouettes on page 11 and the cover
design by John Hassall on page 285, all the line drawings are by
Lord Baden-Powell

ACKNOWLEDGEMENTS

In writing this account of the two lives of Lord Baden-Powell—as a military hero and as a hero to the youth of the world—I have had the unstinted help of the three leading characters in the life of Baden-Powell—himself, his mother, and his wife—and the assistance of numerous other people.

Baden-Powell is, of course, the main source for any of his biographers. First in line of source material come his books and pamphlets (as enumerated on pages 421–2) and the hundreds of articles he contributed to newspapers and periodicals. But of unique importance are the more than two thousand letters he wrote to his mother over a period of thirty-eight years, from the day he set out on his military career in 1876 to his mother's death in 1914. The letters describe his activities, almost from day to day, but, unfortunately, give little insight into his sentiments and emotions. As a true Victorian, he was reticent about wearing his feelings on his sleeve. Baden-Powell was fundamentally a man of action. A book about him must therefore be mainly a book of action. His actions during his military career were dictated by the policies of his government at the time and must be evaluated accordingly. So that they might be better understood after so many years, I have described the background of each of them, basing my accounts mostly on contemporary reports.

I am deeply in debt to Baden-Powell's mother, Henrietta Grace. She did everything a determined mother could do to assist her son's prospective biographers by collecting and preserving as many significant mementoes as possible. She started this effort during her son's childhood by saving his earliest sketches and his first missives. She continued by gathering photographs and clippings relating to her son's career, and pasting them up in large scrapbooks. But more than anything else, she saw to it that the letters he sent her were kept intact. In the instance of this book, she is, further, the main source, through some of her letters and journals, for the first chapter. Henrietta Grace's writings, preserved by her son George, were generously placed at my disposal by George's son, Donald Baden-Powell, and his wife Jane.

My debt to Lady Baden-Powell cannot be adequately expressed. From the first moment that I broached the idea of writing a definitive biography of her late husband, she has given me her unqualified assistance and enthusiastic support. Without any reservation, she turned over to me all Baden-Powell's letters in her possession. She arranged for me to make use of B-P's invaluable sketchbooks and his appointment diaries. She permitted me to peruse and to quote from her own diaries and letters and from the large scrapbooks in which she so carefully had continued Henrietta Grace's tradition of keeping the mementoes from Baden-Powell's later years. In addition, she has given my wife and myself, as family friends, the privilege of being her guests on numerous occasions in her Grace-and-Favour Apartment at Hampton Court Palace, during which she has talked freely of her life with Baden-Powell. She has followed the development of the manuscript for this biography from its inception, has carefully reviewed every chapter in each of several drafts, and has written out numerous items that have found their way into the final manuscript.

Of other people who have helped in the preparation of this biography, I am particularly indebted to Eileen K. Wade, Baden-Powell's secretary for twenty-seven years; to her husband, Major A. G. Wade, one of Baden-Powell's Organizing Secretaries during the early years of Scouting; and to Col. John Skinner Wilson, B-P's right-hand man and, for many years, Camp Chief of Gilwell Park and Director of the Boy Scout International Bureau. Each of them has provided me with valuable source material and has been of great assistance in reading and re-reading the manuscript and checking it for accuracy.

In addition to those mentioned above, numerous other persons have helped me in my efforts. Rather than enumerating them here in a dry listing, I mention them and the specific help they have given me in the pages that describe my sources (pages 423–44).

The drawings by Baden-Powell that illustrate the text pages have been gathered from some of B-P's books, as well as from some of his sketchbooks. The photographs are almost all from the Baden-Powell scrapbooks, in which they were inserted without indication of origin. If I had been able to trace the photographers I would gladly have given them credit. Since this has not been possible I extend them my thanks through these lines.

When I undertook the writing of this book as a spare-time activity—in addition to my regular work as National Director of Program Resources of the Boy Scouts of America and Scoutcraft Editor of *Boy's Life* magazine—I had no idea that the research, writing and re-writing would occupy practically all the evenings and week-ends of myself and my wife, Grace, for close to five years. I owe a great debt of gratitude to her—not just for her understanding and willingness to forgo my company through the long, solitary hours of study and composition, but also for her encouragement and support and for undertaking the tedious and exacting task of copying, re-copying and re-re-copying my pages until the completed manuscript, in a clean copy, could be placed in the hands of my publishers for the tender mercies and expert editing of Harvey Ginsberg of G. P. Putnam's Sons, New York, and Derek Priestley of William Heinemann Ltd., London.   WILLIAM HILLCOURT

LIFE NUMBER ONE

THE HERO OF MAFEKING

[Baden-Powell was relieved at Mafeking in May 1900, after a siege of 217 days.]

IN those days B-P's fame as a soldier eclipsed almost all popular reputations. The other B.P.—the British Public—looked upon him as the outstanding hero of the [Boer] War. . . .

Millions who could not follow closely or accurately the main events of the War looked day after day in the papers for the fortunes of Mafeking, and when finally the news of its relief was flashed throughout the world, the streets of London became impassable, and the floods of sterling, cockney patriotism were released in such a deluge of unbridled, delirious, childish joy as was never witnessed again till Armistice Night, 1918. . . .

WINSTON S. CHURCHILL

The Seventh Son

Years: 1857–70   Age: Birth to 13

1

THE funeral had been a quiet affair. Only the immediate members of the family and a few close friends had been present at the graveside.

Now the thirty-five-year-old widow of the late Oxford professor was alone with the seven of her ten children who had survived infancy, and the two step-children left in her care out of the four from her husband's previous marriage.

A formidable task lay ahead for the young Henrietta Grace Powell in bringing up nine children to do credit to the man she had loved. From being the adored and protected wife of a genial professor she was forced into becoming an astute *materfamilias* of a large household, a financial administrator, a property manager, a firm overseer of her children as well as their imaginative director. For these roles she would need her intelligence, her sense of humour, her faith and her idealism.

Henrietta Grace had had a full, rich life. She was determined that the lives of her children should be equally full and rich. The older boys had had a great number of advantages while their father was alive. She wanted the younger children to have just as many advantages. She knew the importance of all the children going to the 'right' schools and meeting the 'right' people, of the whole family living in the 'right' neighbourhood and doing the 'right' things. She had no inclination to settle down into pinched respectability.

A part of her problem solved itself shortly after the funeral. Her two step-children left the family home, 21-year-old Charlotte Elizabeth to join an Irish branch of the Powell family in Dublin and 19-year-old Baden Henry to try his luck in the civil service in India. Remaining with their mother were Henrietta Grace's own children: Warington, aged 13 at the time of his father's death; George, aged 12; Augustus, aged 11; Francis, 9; Stephenson, 3; Agnes, a year and a half; Baden, 3 weeks.

Henrietta Grace was in a very strategic position for getting all the help and advice she might need for keeping her family afloat. She was an attractive widow 'of good family' and had been married to a man who had been both a professor and a clergyman—two positions of high esteem in the reign of Victoria. Strong men would feel stronger in helping and advising her. And since she was ambitious for her children and not for herself she was willing to undertake many a bold project that she might otherwise have shied away from. She would be forgiven for her enterprise and probably admired rather than criticized. But first she needed to find out the status of the family finances—she knew little about them; her husband had hitherto handled all money matters.

To her great dismay she discovered that the house in Stanhope Street in which they lived was not theirs. Her husband, on the other hand, had been the owner of Broom Hill, one of the Powell family estates, inherited from his father. This was left to Henrietta Grace with £2,000 worth of 3 per cent Great Western Debentures and £5,000 worth of other 3 per centers from the marriage settlement. She sold the Broom Hill property and invested the £6,200 it realized in numbers 1 and 2 Hyde Park Gate, which promptly became the new Powell address. Her mother, dying shortly after her husband, left her a small legacy. There would be other legacies in the future as old and ailing members of the professor's family and her own passed away. To all of this came an annual pension of £150 from the Civil List and a stipend of £200 per year allotted by her husband's spinster sisters, Susan and Eleanor Powell of Speldhurst.

She would manage somehow. As the older boys grew up, they would share their incomes with the younger, and later, all of them with Agnes and herself. The pattern for the children's development had been set by their father. It was for their widowed mother to carry it to fruition. The solidarity of the family had been established. It was for her to see that it never faltered. Her children would know that she loved them, but also that they would break her heart if they let her down in her expectations of them. And so Henrietta Grace tied her six sons and her daughter to her with firm strings—not apron strings keeping them close to home but strings of love allowing them a great deal of freedom, yet strings nevertheless.

2

The marriage fourteen years before had been a true May–September romance between a British naval officer's 21-year-old daughter and a 49-year-old professor.

Henrietta Grace had met Professor Baden Powell for the first time in 1839 when she was 15. She, her mother and younger sisters had stayed at Oxford on a journey from their home in Bedford to Cardiff in Wales, where her father, Commander William Henry Smyth, was supervising the maritime and mineral properties of the Marquis of Bute. One evening during their Oxford stay, the professor and his wife had invited Mrs Smyth and the girls for dinner. 'At that time', Henrietta Grace wrote in her journal later, 'the mere name of Professor Baden Powell filled me with reverence and I listened with the greatest attention for every word that should drop from the lips of so learned a man'. During the evening Baden Powell showed his guests 'some beautiful experiments in polarized light' and entertained them on the organ. The professor struck the young Miss Smyth most agreeably by his 'clever countenance and gentlemanly bearing'.

Six years passed before Henrietta Grace, grown to young womanhood, again met the now widowed Professor Baden Powell.

By 1845, Commander Smyth and his family had a house in London, in Cheyne Walk, Chelsea, the street of many other members of the British intelligentsia: Swinburne, Rossetti, George Eliot, Thomas Carlyle. The Commander's door was always open to his many friends in the Navy, to his literary neighbours and to a number of amateur and professional scientists who shared his interest in astronomy and physics.

Professor Baden Powell had paid the Commander a short visit in June when he was in London for the annual visitation ceremonies at Greenwich Observatory. He had chatted amiably with Henrietta Grace and had again impressed her most favourably. She was pleased, therefore, when one morning in December 1845 her father announced that he had offered the hospitality of their house to Professor Powell who was coming up from Oxford to give a lecture.

The professor made his appearance on Thursday, 11 December, was installed in the guest-room and left almost immediately afterward with the Commander for the Royal Astronomical Society.

> On Friday morning [according to Henrietta Grace's journal], Mr Powell came in long before Papa and Mamma were ready for break-fast and stood by the fire. We described the neighbourhood and advised him to see the Botanical and Chelsea Hospital Gardens whilst he was with us. Shall I reveal another fact! viz. that I was warming one of my feet at the fire when my blushes were suddenly called forth by observing this philosopher Mr Powell dart a glance at it, give a deep sigh and exclaim aloud, though evidently unconscious that it was heard—'Yes, perfect.'

The professor was not particularly interested in the sights of Chelsea when they were first explained to him but on Saturday he suddenly suggested 'a small walk'. Mrs Smyth immediately arranged for Henrietta Grace to accompany Mr Powell.

During their walk, the two carried on an animated conversation, first on scientific matters, then on education. 'It was', Henrietta Grace confessed to her journal, 'somewhat bold of me to express my opinion on such a subject to such a man. However, he only said in answer how much he wished that I could see his children'. The deeper they got in their discussion, the more agitated the professor became. He was amazed and elated to find that they shared the same advanced views on religious education.

On their second walk, on Sunday, 14 December, Professor Powell surprised the young Miss Smyth in the midst of another lively conversation by asking her to become his wife. Henrietta Grace, to her own astonishment, blurted out a delighted 'Yes!' She had no idea how her parents would view the marriage of a daughter of theirs to a man old enough to be her father, nor of their feelings about her marrying a widower with four children. The professor had been married twice before. His first marriage (to Eliza Rivas in 1821) had ended upon his wife's death after almost fifteen years of marriage 'without issue'. By his second marriage (to Charlotte Pope in 1837) he had had one boy and three girls of whom the two younger were adopted by an aunt on their mother's death in 1844.

Henrietta Grace's anxiety about getting her father's and mother's consent was quickly dissipated. The professor pleaded his cause successfully. The parents of his intended bride considered the match 'quite desirable'.

On Tuesday, 10 March 1846, on a bright but cold morning, Henrietta Grace Smyth became the wife of Professor Baden Powell at St Luke's Church, Chelsea. After the ceremony, the couple went to Paddington and from there by train to Oxford. In her new home, the third Mrs Powell received into her arms the two children of her husband who were living with their father: 7-year-old Charlotte Elizabeth and 4-year-old Baden Henry.

Upon her marriage, Henrietta Grace promptly settled down to be an Oxford professor's wife, to share her husband's interests, to manage his house, to entertain his numerous friends and to bear his children.

The couple's first offspring, a boy, arrived within eleven months of the wedding, on 3 February 1847. He was christened Henry Warington Smyth Powell, Henry for Henrietta Grace's father and youngest brother, Warington for her mother's family name, Smyth for her father's. All subsequent children were named Smyth in addition to their father's surname of Powell.

The second child, George Smyth, was born on Christmas Eve 1847, ten months after the firstborn. A third boy, Augustus Smyth, followed in May 1849, and a fourth, Francis Smyth, in July 1850.

With four boys in little more than four years of marriage, Henrietta Grace fervently prayed that her fifth child might be a girl. Her wish was answered with the arrival of Henrietta Smyth in October 1851. But her happiness was of short duration. The girl died before she reached her third birthday, as did the couple's next child, John Penrose Smyth, born in December 1852. A second daughter, Jessie Smyth, born in November 1855, succumbed within eight months.

After having lost three children in succession, Henrietta Grace, pregnant again, looked forward with a mixture of dread and joy to the arrival of yet another child. By this time, the family had moved from Oxford to London and had made its home at 6 Stanhope Street, Paddington, a four-storey house in a pleasant residential area just north of Hyde Park. Here, Professor Powell's twelfth child and Henrietta Grace's eighth was born on 22 February 1857. At the baptism, on 8 July, the boy was christened Robert Stephenson Smyth Powell. The first two names were in honour of his godfather, the son of George Stephenson, the designer of the first successful locomotive, and famous in his own right as an engineer and a bridge builder.

A few days before Christmas of the following year, Henrietta Grace's heart was gladdened by the arrival of a long-hoped-for daughter, Agnes Smyth. One more child completed the family: Baden Fletcher Smyth, born in May 1860.

In spite of his preoccupation with educational and scientific matters and his heavy schedule of lecturing and examining at Oxford, Professor Powell spent much of his time with his family. He instructed his children at home and on walks in nearby parks, read aloud to them and got them interested in reading. In his spare moments he played the organ or painted or sketched. He was particularly adept at drawing caricatures of his Oxford colleagues. He also managed to do a great deal of writing. Numerous articles and books flowed from his busy pen, on mathematics and physics, theology and philosophy.

In much of his theological writing, especially in his early books *Revelation and Science* (1833) and *Connection of Natural and Divine Truth* (1838), Powell had fought for the principle that an acknowledgement of the scientific advances of his day was completely compatible with a sincere acceptance of the tenets of the Christian religion. With the public furore

2

over Darwin's *Origin of Species by Means of Natural Selection* (1859), he again took up his pen and contributed an essay, 'On the Study of the Evidence of Christianity', to a volume with the unassuming title of *Essays and Reviews* (1860). The book, with essays by six other scientist-theologians, created only a slight stir on its appearance. But the stir became a storm shortly after when the book was violently attacked by Bishop Wilberforce of Oxford, the same Wilberforce who a few months before had secured enduring fame by attacking Darwin and his theories. Now the battle pro and con raged in the press and from the pulpits. The seven authors were denounced as having been inspired by the Evil One himself and were accused by their more orthodox colleagues of threatening the existence of the Anglican Church. Two of the authors were prosecuted before a clerical court and sentenced to be suspended, only to be reinstated promptly afterwards when they appealed to the Queen in Council and had their sentences reversed by a judicial committee set up to try their case.

But by then Professor Powell was in his grave.

3

As soon after the professor's funeral as etiquette permitted, Henrietta Grace resumed seeing old friends. She again invited guests to the kind of social gatherings that had always been part of her life.

Robert Browning had brought his wife to her father's home and had spent many evenings with the Powells after Elizabeth Barrett's death and his return to England to supervise his son's education. The young Robert Wiedemann Barrett Browning had become a close friend of the older Powell boys. William Makepeace Thackeray, with the popular successes of *Vanity Fair* and *Henry Esmond* behind him, was a regular visitor; so were John Ruskin, the art critic and author, at the peak of his career, and the Martineaus—James and his sister Harriet, the lady writer, 'the fabulous invalid'.

The guests from the scientific world were many and varied. Here was Thomas Hardy Huxley, the biologist and 'Darwin's Bulldog'; John Tyndall, the physicist; Dr William Huggins, the astronomer; Sir Joseph Dalton Hooker, the botanist; Alfred Russell Wallace, the naturalist. The scholars were mostly friends from Professor Powell's Oxford circle: Dr Alfred Acland, Dr Henry George Liddell, Dr Benjamin Jowett, Dean Arthur Penrhyn Stanley, always ready to swing into learned dissertations about modern trends in philosophy and religion.

And then, of course, there were the members of the immediate family, largely from Henrietta Grace's side: her brothers and their wives, her sisters and their husbands.

In these parties Henrietta Grace generally included her elder sons when they happened to be back from boarding school. To her, these social functions were part of their education, a valuable asset toward turning them into gentlemen able to take their places in the station to which they were born.

The three younger children, on the other hand, were sent to bed early in order not to disturb the proceedings.

4

It was at one of his mother's social functions that 3-year-old Robert Stephenson Smyth Powell, later to become Lord Baden-Powell, Baron of Gilwell, made his first 'public appearance'.

The boy, known within the family circle by the abbreviation of his second name to 'Stephe' or simply 'Ste', disliked being sent to bed when a party was to begin. Usually, a firm glance from his mother made him scamper upstairs not to appear again. Only once did the temptation prove too great.

The humming voices downstairs kept him awake. He got out of bed, sneaked out of the nursery in his nightdress and proceeded downstairs. Thackeray, sitting closest to the door, spotted him. Sensing trouble, the author held up a warning finger. He reached into his pocket, pulled out a shilling and slipped it into Stephe's hand, then pointed his thumb biddingly upstairs. Without a murmur Stephe went back to bed with the Thackeray shilling clasped in his fist.

Stephe's upbringing was in good hands. It progressed under the watchful eyes of his mother, the supervision of a German nurse, and the proddings of his elder brothers.

There was little formality to his early education except for a short period when he attended a dame's school in Kensington Square. His mother had made it a habit to spend much of her time with the children, teaching them the fundamentals of reading and writing and inculcating in them her own ideals of honour and duty, self-reliance and perseverance. When the weather was good, the children were encouraged to romp through nearby Hyde Park, to play and to learn about plant and animal life. In bad weather, they could get learning and amusement from their father's extensive library, his scientific instruments, his natural history specimens. They were also early impressed with the value and prudent expenditure of money. Instead of providing each of her children with a personal allowance, Mrs Powell had evolved the idea of a communal cash-box—a small metal box from which the family members could draw pocket money as they required it, depositing a note of the amounts they withdrew. In Stephe's case, these notes mainly amounted to 'Orange, £0/0/1'.

In addition to the members of the household, the numerous Powells and Smyths also played their part in the upbringing of Henrietta Grace's children.

5

Stephe, even more than his brothers and sister, grew up to combine in his characteristics and mental make-up to an extraordinary extent the talents and traits of the two families from which they all sprang: the Powells and the Smyths.

On his father's side, Stephe could trace the family back for four hundred years, beginning with a certain William Powle (or Polle) of Suffolk, born in the middle of the fifteenth century. It is known that he was seneschal or steward of the Manor of Mildenhall in the year 1501.

For more than two hundred years after William's death his male descendants made their living as yeomen in Suffolk. In 1712 David Powell broke with the family tradition and, at the age of 17, went up to London to make his fortune. He managed very well indeed as a merchant of Broad Street and had, among others, considerable dealings in Italy with Benjamin D'Israeli, the grandfather of the future Lord Beaconsfield. At 71, David Powell returned to his home county a wealthy man, purchased the estate of Wattisfield Hall and spent the remaining eighteen years of his life as lord of the manor. David's wife, Susannah, was responsible for bringing the Baden name into the Powell family, from her grandfather, one-time Mayor of Salisbury in Wiltshire.

David Powell's grandson, Baden Powell, was a successful gentleman farmer of Tunbridge Wells in Kent. He owned in succession five estates —Hollands, Broom Hill, Bentham Hill, Langton Manor and Speldhurst —and served his county as High Sheriff. He was active in other capacities as well and was, in 1822, Master of the Mercers' Company, the premier Guild of the City of London.

Baden Powell's eldest son, Baden—the Baden Powell who married Henrietta Grace Smyth—was born at his father's Speldhurst estate on 22 August 1796, in the thirty-sixth year of the reign of George III. This Powell—Stephe's father—unlike so many of his forebears, was not interested in being a gentleman farmer or a merchant. He had set his mind on becoming a clergyman. He persuaded his father to send him to Oxford where he entered Oriel College at 17. He received his M.A. degree in 1820, with first-class honours in mathematics. Soon after, he was made curate of Midhurst in Sussex, and in 1821 became Vicar of Plumstead in Kent.

During the six years of his vicariate, he combined his clerical duties with further studies of mathematics and with scientific research, particularly in the subjects of light and heat. As a result of these extra-curricular interests he was elected a Fellow of the Royal Society at 27 and in 1827, at the age of 31, was invited by the University of Oxford to occupy the chair of geometry founded and endowed by Sir Henry Savile in 1619.

Professor Powell entered into his new career with vigour and enthusiasm.

Old silhouettes (appr. 1780) of David Powell, 1695–1784; his son, David, 1725–1810; his grandson Baden (B-P's grandfather), 1767–1844.

He proved himself an eloquent and effective lecturer who 'did much', according to a contemporary account, 'by his popular addresses to create an appetite for science among the Oxford citizens'. He became associated with Herschel and Faraday and other scientific celebrities of that time. As a member of the Royal University Commission of 1850 he was instrumental in improving the education pursued at Oxford by securing a more prominent place for science in the curriculum of the university. His work made him a welcome Fellow of the Royal Astronomical and the Geological Societies.

The adventuresome qualities of Stephe's developing character reflected his mother's rather than his father's side of the family.

An early Smyth or Smith may have been among the first Scots to settle in America, on the 'Long Island' that stretched eastward from the harbour of New York town. But nothing is known of this early Smyth forebear.

The first authenticated Smyth—the early American Smyth's son?,

grandson?, great grandson?—was Benjamin Smyth of Walpack Township, Sussex County, Province of West New Jersey (now the northernmost
county of the State of New Jersey). He was born about 1700 and seems
to have been quite well off: he owned a farm, a grist mill, and a sawmill.
He was highly regarded by the people of his small community. He was
Town Clerk in 1735 and 1746, Overseer of Roads in 1749, and a member
of a committee established in 1754 'according to an act of Assembly . . .
for to divide the county into precincts'. By the 1760s Benjamin Smyth
had moved to Knowlton Township, Sussex (now Warren) County. Here he
died shortly after making his will on 14 July 1769, leaving his estate to his
wife Dority, his sons Benjamin, Henery, Abraham, John, Joseph and his
daughters Catharene and Nancy.

Joseph Smyth—or, to give him his full name, Joseph Brewer Palmer
Smyth—settled down to be a farmer and a miller like his father but ran
into difficulty at the start of the Revolutionary War in 1775.

Throughout the previous months, in heated debates with his neighbours, Joseph Smyth had taken the part of Parliament and King. Now,
with the threatened arrest and imprisonment of all loyalists he left all his
possessions behind him and fled northward through the woods into
Canada. Here he joined Sir John Johnston's Scottish regiment under
General Burgoyne. He became a lieutenant in January 1777 and served
on the Canadian border until November 1778 when he embarked from
Quebec with part of his regiment to reinforce the British army in New
York.

Joseph's previous troubles had been as nothing compared to the tribu-
lations of the odyssey on which he now found himself. His ship, the *Mary*,
was overtaken and boarded by the *General Sullivan*, an American privateer.
The American captain, finding Joseph Smyth to be an American loyalist,
stripped him of everything and threw him into the ship's hold in irons.
The *General Sullivan* sailed on and soon after captured the *Endeavour*,
a British privateer out of Glasgow. After some negotiation, the *Endeavour*
was ransomed and took on board the passengers and crew of the *Mary*
to bring them to England. Joseph Smyth landed at Falmouth in January
1779 'in a most forlorn condition', destitute and suffering from fever.
An attack of smallpox 'reduced him to the last extremity of weakness and
real want'. His appeal for help as a war refugee was answered by the Lords
of the Treasury with a grant of £100. The Royal Commissioners eventually
allowed him £60 a year in restitution for losses sustained because of
loyalty to the Crown.

The American period of Joseph Smyth's life was at an end. All his
efforts to regain his properties in New Jersey proved unavailing. He
established himself in England, married an English girl, Georgina Caroline

Pilkington, and raised a family of two, one of them a boy: William Henry Smyth, born 1788—Henrietta Grace's father.

In spite of Joseph Smyth's sad experiences at sea, his son decided to make the sea his career. He joined the British Navy at an early age, sailed in Indian, Chinese and Australian waters and saw action against the French fleet during the Napoleonic Wars. Because of his navigating skill he was given the task, after Napoleon's defeat, of making a scientific survey of the Mediterranean, charting its main waters and mapping its more important ports. The work occupied seven years (1817–24) and earned Commander Smyth the nickname of 'Mediterranean Smyth'. While stationed in Naples he wooed and wed Annarella Warington, daughter of Thomas Warington, the British Consul at the court of the newly restored King Ferdinand IV of Naples. Two of their sons were born in Naples, another son and three daughters in England.

Back at home again, William Henry Smyth did major service to the Admiralty as a hydrographer, investigating a number of British ports and making recommendations for their development. In his spare time, he pursued his interest in astronomy. He built himself an observatory at Bedford and studied 'nebulae, clusters, double stars and binaries, to the amount of 850'. A two-volume treatise of his findings, *A Cycle of Celestial Objects, for the Use of Naval, Military and Private Astronomers*, earned him the Newtonian Medal of the Royal Astronomical Society in 1845. He was for a period (1845–46) president of the Royal Astronomical Society as well as of the Royal Geographical Society (1849–50) of which he was one of the founders.

When at long last Smyth retired from the Navy (Rear-Admiral from 1853, Vice-Admiral 1858, Admiral 1863), he divided his days between his town house in Cheyne Walk in Chelsea, and his country house, St John's Lodge, at Aylesbury in Buckinghamshire, the patriarch of a prominent and prosperous family. Each of his children had met with success. His eldest son was now Sir Warington Wilkinson Smyth, the geologist. His second son, Charles Piazzi Smyth, had been appointed Astronomer Royal of Scotland. His third son, Henry Augustus Smyth, was a colonel in the British Army. His daughter Rosetta was the wife of Sir William Flower, the Director of the Natural History Museum. Ellen had married Captain Harry Toynbee, and Henrietta Grace, the renowned Professor Baden Powell.

6

Mrs Powell and her children loved to spend their holidays in the country visiting their relatives.

Some of these holidays they spent at Speldhurst, the Powell family estate near Tunbridge Wells in Kent, where the late Professor Powell's younger brother and his two spinster sisters lived. Here the children had miles of countryside to explore, trees to climb, even a small river to dam for a swimming pool.

They liked even better going to St John's Lodge at Aylesbury to stay with their only living grandparents, Admiral Smyth and Grandmother Annarella. The Lodge had even more attractions for the children than Speldhurst. They could roam the Tundal Woods that surrounded the grandfather's property, swim in the nearby lake in the summer holidays and skate on its surface in the winter. They could get the groom to saddle up ponies for rides along winding country lanes and over fields. They could use the Admiral's sextant in the daytime and look through one of his telescopes at night. They could spend rainy days in his library and among the mementoes from his years in the Mediterranean.

It was not always happy occasions that sent the children to St John's Lodge. When one or more of them came down with a childhood disease, the rest were shipped off to Aylesbury where the grandparents were ready to receive them with open arms. One such instance occurred in March 1863 when Stephe wrote home to his mother from Aylesbury:

> My dear Mama, I thank you very much for your kind note. I hope dear Gus is a little better. Agnes, Baden and I send our kind wishes to him. Your affectionate,
>
> R. S. S. POWELL

Stephe never saw 'Gus' again. Augustus, dead at 13 of consumption, was buried by the time the three younger children returned home.

When his older brothers were not on hand Stephe made his grandfather his main male confidant.

At St John's Lodge the Admiral had a terrace he called his 'quarter-deck'. It reminded him of his old days on H.M.S. *Adventure* when he marched his ten paces, turned about and marched back ten paces, up and down on the small space available on board ship. When visiting his grandfather, Stephe often joined him in walking the 'quarter-deck', running to fit the old man's pace, listening to his stories of adventures at sea and sharing some of his own thoughts with him.

From his home in London, Stephe was in regular correspondence with his grandfather from the moment he first learned to print the alphabet. The Admiral acknowledged each of his grandson's letters with full and respectful answers.

At the time of his eighth birthday, Stephe was concerned about the condition in which he found the world and felt that something needed to be done about the situation. So that he would not forget his intentions, he carefully wrote out for himself a set of

LAW'S FOR ME WHEN I AM OLD

I will have the poor people to be as rich as we are, and they ought by rights to be as happy as we are, and all who go across the crossings shall give the poor crossing sweepers some money and you ought to thank God for what he has given us and He has made the poor people to be poor and the rich people to be rich, and I can tell you how to be good, now I will tell you. You must pray to God whenever you can but you cannot be good with only praying but you must also try very hard to be good.

By R. S. S. Powell   26 February 1865

He rushed a copy of his 'law's' to his grandfather and shortly after received a reply from 'your aged correspondent, W. H. Smyth'.

The Admiral was, of course, pleased to receive his grandson's letter but was not persuaded to Stephe's laws: 'Oh Law!' he wrote back, 'Is not law like a country dance where people are led up and down in it till they can hardly stir their stumps, as Milton says, says he. Law is like physic, those wot take the least of it is best off'.

After the Admiral's death in 1865, the family's visits to Aylesbury became less and less frequent. Instead, Mrs Powell took the children elsewhere, visiting relatives and friends, or staying at seaside resorts or country places that had caught her fancy and were not too much of a drain on the pocket-book. The south of England became a favourite summer excursion area: St Leonard's in Sussex, Mousehole in Cornwall, the Isle of Wight. And Stephe had his first experience of travelling in a foreign country when one winter his mother took him and Frank to Biarritz and St Sebastian 'for their health'.

7

When Stephe was 8, Frank left for college. With Frank's departure the division of the Powell children into two separate entities became even more pronounced than it had been before. One was an older group, with all members away from home and with Warington the natural leader; the other was the younger group at home, with Stephe the eldest member and therefore the logical head.

Warington, Stephe's senior by ten years, had decided on a career in the merchant marine. After finishing at St Paul's School and completing three years' training in H.M.S. *Conway* with 'double extra certificate', he had left for Calcutta by way of the Cape on board the East Indiaman *Hotspur*, a sailing ship of the Smith Line. George (nine years older than Stephe) had also finished at St Paul's School and had also gone to sea on the India run. Frank (six years older) was at Marlborough College. Left at home were Stephe, with Agnes and Baden as his playmates and responsibilities.

Stephe enjoyed playing with his sister and younger brother and acting as their leader. He made up small plays in which all three of them could act, always with a fat part for the low comedian of the company: himself. He taught them things their older brothers had taught him—how to make playthings from boxes, how to make kites they could fly in Hyde Park, model boats they could sail on the Serpentine.

But he also found occasion to be alone, to concentrate on his own pursuits: his reading, his playing tunes on every odd instrument he could lay his hands on, his sketching, his painting.

From his earliest childhood, Stephe had liked to play with paper and pencil, crayons and water-colours. While his father had been interested mostly in drawing humorous caricatures, his mother was adept at water-colours and had encouraged all the children to draw and paint. But Stephe's technique bothered his mother. He had early picked up the habit of using both hands, shifting pencil or brush from his right hand to his left and back again indiscriminately and with little change in style. The idea that her boy was not 'normal' gave her concern. How was she ever going to 'cure' him of his left-handedness?

On one of John Ruskin's visits, she confided her dismay to her guest. The great art critic suggested: 'Let me see the boy at work'.

Mrs Powell led Ruskin up into the nursery where young Stephe was painting with a penny box of water-colours before him. After the customary courtesies of bowing and shaking hands, the boy went back to work. Ruskin studied the boy's busy hands carefully for a while and watched him painting with equal ease with either hand. He realized that here was a case of true ambidexterity. 'Let him draw as he likes', Ruskin advised the mother. She had no cause for alarm, he told her. On the contrary, she should be happy that her son possessed this rare ability.

To reassure her further, he invited her to bring Stephe for lunch at his Denmark Hill estate so that the young artist might see his art collection and get further inspiration for pursuing his hobby.

With the approval of his mother and Ruskin, Stephe's ambition grew.

He first looked in books for subjects to illustrate. An English translation of Alain-René Le Sage's rather saucy *Adventures of Gil Blas* among his father's books inspired him to produce a series of pen-and-ink drawings in the equivalent of a mid-Victorian 'comic-book' style. He then began writing small stories of his own and illustrating them himself. After all, if Thackeray was able to illustrate his own writings, certainly a son of Professor Powell should be able to do the same.

An attempt by Stephe, at nine, to illustrate one of Gil Blas's adventures.

His mother did everything to encourage the boy in his efforts. She looked to the future and saw Stephe following in the footsteps of his father as a literary man of great artistic ability. She carefully kept and collected Stephe's 'masterpieces'. Some day somebody else would appreciate those early attempts by a son of her beloved Professor Baden Powell.

Baden Powell. . . . But Stephe was not a 'Baden Powell'—only a Powell. So were all the other children except the youngest.

Mrs Powell made up her mind to have the family name changed to 'Baden Powell' to honour her husband, the children's devoted father, and to perpetuate his name. The family lawyer, Mr Arnold, undertook to have the double surname legalized. On 21 September 1869, by 'public notice', all members of the family became Baden Powells.

The new name sounded fine, except for the youngest child. Baden Baden Powell would just have to make the best of it. The situation was remedied somewhat when shortly afterwards a hyphen made its appearance. The family was now the Baden-Powells, with a rather fashionable double name, never again to appear in directories under P. It took a while for Mrs Baden-Powell to get friends and relatives to use the double name but they finally submitted. She had become so persistent that the family jokingly referred to her as 'Old Mrs Hyphen'.

So Stephe became Robert Stephenson Smyth Baden-Powell, soon after by his school mates, and eventually by the whole world, abbreviated to B-P.

8

At 11, the time had come for Stephe to leave home for his first 'real' schooling. For this his mother sent him to Rose Hill School, at Tunbridge Wells, a school near the Powell homestead, attended by his father almost sixty years before.

After the customary spell of homesickness of a new boy, Stephe settled down to his studies. In addition to regular school subjects he continued the piano lessons his mother had started at home. Stephe would much rather have taken drawing lessons, but this was yet another 'extra' and could not be afforded. To make up for the hoped-for lessons, he continued to teach himself drawing 'by studying and copying pictures by artists and noting how they got their effect'. His health at the time was not too good. He suffered from recurring colds and from a slight touch of anaemia for the cure of which the usual mid-nineteenth-century remedy was provided and duly charged on the school bill: 'Wine merchant—1 bottle of port at 5s.'

After two years at Rose Hill School Stephe was of an age to enter some public school for his further education. His conduct at Rose Hill had been 'painstaking and industrious'. He had done so well, in fact, that the school-mistress, Mrs Sarah Allpee, informed Mrs Baden-Powell that she would gladly have kept her son on without fees of any kind, 'so great was his influence on the moral tone of the school'.

Thirteen-year-old Stephe did not look forward to leaving his happy nest in the small school where he was a somebody to find himself 'a stranger and a worm under the foot of a mass of bigger boys in the big community' of a large school. But his mother made up his mind for him. She had, as a matter of fact, already started another of her periodic campaigns to secure yet another scholarship for a son of Professor Baden Powell.

The free schooling at St Paul's School that had been Warington's, George's and Frank's under their father's livery in the Mercers was available to Stephe as well. But something had gone awry. Mrs Baden-Powell had got it into her head that St Paul's School had become 'un-healthy'. She was taking no chances. She would have to find another school for Stephe, and to do so she busied herself in writing letters to the governors and trustees of some of the top public schools of Great Britain, pleading for a scholarship.

Through her efforts and, probably, through the influence of her brother, the Astronomer Royal of Scotland, she met with success at Fettes School, Edinburgh. Stephe dutifully went to Scotland for the 1–2 June 1870 examinations and was accepted as one of the forty-one boys by the trustees.

He had hardly returned home when a fatter plum than far-off Fettes fell into his cap, by courtesy of his mother and the Duke of Marlborough. The Duke, at Mrs Baden-Powell's urgings, had nominated Stephe for a scholarship as a Gownboy Foundationer at Charterhouse in London, with the hope 'that in thus exercising my trust as a Governor I may be doing it in a way to give full effect to the intentions of the founder of the Charity in establishing a seminary for sound learning and true Christian instruction in the doctrines of our Church'.

Stephe threw in his lot with Charterhouse, and never regretted it.

II

Charterhouse Boy

Years: 1870–76   Age: 13–19

1

ON 28 November 1870, during 'Oration Quarter', Stephe Baden-Powell, newly nominated Gownboy Foundationer, went to Charterhouse 'a boy of medium size with curly red hair, decidedly freckled, with a pair of twinkling eyes', as one of his school mates described him later.

With traditions of more than two hundred years behind it, Charterhouse was the school of Sir Richard Lovelace, of Sir Richard Steele and Joseph Addison, of John Wesley and Sir William Blackstone, of Dean Liddell of Oxford's Christ Church and William Makepeace Thackeray. It was situated in the heart of London, west of Aldersgate, with the great Cattle Market of Smithfield almost immediately outside its walls and the dome of St Paul's half a mile to the south.

The name 'Charterhouse' goes back more than nine hundred years, even beyond the day in 1086 when Bruno, a monk from Cologne, and his six followers were assigned a desolate spot for a life of silence and prayer in the mountains of Dauphiné near the village of Chartrouse (today: Chartreuse). Before long, more *maisons chartrouse* were established in France. The order reached England in 1178. In 1371, Sir Walter de Manny established a Carthusian monastery just outside the old walls of the City of London. By a process of simple etymology, the French 'Chartrouse' soon became the English 'Chart(e)r(h)ouse'.

When Henry VIII dissolved the monasteries of England in 1535 and confiscated their property, the monks of London Charterhouse stood strongly against him. Many of them were carried off to Newgate Gaol, chained upright to their dungeon walls and left to starve to death. The Prior was taken to the Tower. When he still refused to acknowledge Henry 'in all causes ecclesiastical as well as civil in those his Dominions supreme', he was 'draune from the Tower unto Tyborne and there hangyd, heddyd, and quartered'. The Charterhouse became Crown property and was, for a while, occupied by Queen Elizabeth I.

In May 1611, Charterhouse was purchased by a wealthy Lincolnshire merchant, Thomas Sutton. After his wife's death, the childless Sutton devoted his time and his fortune to charitable causes. Among other things, he decided to turn Charterhouse into 'a hospitall and a free Grammar Schoole'. On 1 November 1611, at the age of 80, Sutton signed the deed of gift. On 2 November, he made his will. On 12 December, his life ended—as all Carthusians know.

When the will was opened it was found to stipulate that the property was to be constituted a Foundation to provide for the souls and bodies of 'children not yet come to, and old men already past, helping of themselves'. Within two years, arrangements had been made to accommodate eighty old male pensioners (later called 'Codds') and forty boys. The boys, dressed in a picturesque, gown-like garment, became known as 'Gownboys'.

When Robert Stephenson Smyth Baden-Powell joined Charterhouse in 1870, it had a hundred and twenty pupils and was still located in London in the old Carthusian monastery buildings. Its reputation had grown to the point where many parents who could afford to pay considerable fees for their boys' education were sending them to Charterhouse. But the Founder's wish was respected, and free scholarships were still reserved for forty Gownboys—sons of 'poore men of gentle birth', one of them the son of a deceased Oxford professor.

2

On entry, Stephe was placed in the third form and housed in 'Gownboys', the middle block of the vast old monastery, under the popular housemaster, Frederick Kennedy Wilson Girdlestone. Here he soon began to move ahead in his schoolwork 'without gaining unpopularity by undue attention to his studies'.

Coming from a large family Stephe had no difficulty in adjusting himself to his new life and fitting himself into the 'fag system' of Charterhouse. He looked upon the older students in the same light in which he saw his older brothers: they were his elders, his 'uppers', hence his superiors. They had a right to expect obedience and a certain amount of servitude. The more cheerfully he accepted this status, the easier it would be for him to get along with them.

After the usual two-weeks' grace allowed a new boy, Stephe was assigned to an 'upper' and quickly discovered that being a 'fag' at Charterhouse was a sinecure compared to being the youngest member of Warington's crew at home.

Soon after Stephe's arrival at Charterhouse, John Hullah, the music master, collected all the newcomers to try their singing voices for the choir. Each boy after being tested was sent to one or another corner of the room. When it came to Stephe's turn he was put into a third corner, all by himself, and there he remained the solitary one, until all the boys present had been tried. It turned out later that one lot were likely singers for the choir, the other lot had either no voice or no ear, while Stephe was judged to have an excellent falsetto voice.

Stephe remained in the choir for six years. After his speaking voice broke he was still able to sing. It did not make any difference whether the part called for a soprano, an alto, a tenor or a baritone, Stephe managed them all with equal ease. 'I don't say I had a good voice in any of them', he acknowledged later, 'for I certainly had not, but I was just passable for general use.'

With his boundless energy, Stephe proved himself a great joiner. He had hardly entered the choir before he also joined the cadet corps as a bugler, the orchestra as a violinist and Mr Cousins's brass band as a player of the flugel horn.

But in spite of all his joining, there was always a certain aloofness to Stephe. According to E. H. Parry, his upper, the young Baden-Powell was 'cheerful, perfectly straight and clean in every way: with nothing whatever of the prig about him', but he 'was always rather unlike other boys who were often puzzled by him and never quite knew when he was joking and when he was serious. Generally popular, he never seemed to make any very close friends, and not being very skilful at either cricket or football, except later on in the latter game as a goal-keeper, the prestige he gradually acquired arose from his good humour, his powers of mimicry, and wonder at his many quaint antics, which to the ordinary boy marked him out as being gifted with an admirable species of madness.'

Stephe threw himself with gusto into all Charterhouse activities and absorbed, as if by osmosis, the traditions of the old school. He was particularly happy when activity and tradition joined hands—as in the yearly 'lemon-peel fight' and in the Founder's Day celebration.

On Shrove Tuesday, each boy received two lemon halves with his pancakes. But instead of using the lemon halves for the intended purpose, the boys ate their pancakes plain and put the lemon halves in their pockets. After dinner, the Gownboys took up their stand against the 'Oppidans', the pupils not on the Foundation, for the impending lemon-peel fight.

Someone rang the house bell, and immediately the air was filled with the missiles.

For one of these lemon-peel fights, Stephe appeared on the scene 'swathed from head to foot in tremendous padding, with nothing to be seen of his face save the bright, mischievous eyes peeping out of two slits.' He rushed in between the two lines with a piercing war-whoop, squatted on the ground and announced in a ringing voice, 'Let the battle commence!' The command was immediately obeyed, with Stephe the main target.

Founder's Day ceremony in Chapel on 12 December, just before the start of the Christmas holidays, was a solemn occasion.

At old Charterhouse in London the ceremony was not very different in Stephe's day from the ceremony described by an earlier Carthusian, Thackeray, in his novel *The Newcomes*:

> The Chapel is lighted, and Founder's Tomb, with its grotesque carvings, monsters, heraldries, darkles and shines with the most wonderful shadows and lights. There he lies, *Fundator Noster*, in his ruff and gown, awaiting the Great Examination day. . . . Yonder sit forty cherry-cheeked boys, thinking about home and holidays to-morrow. Yonder sit some three score old gentlemen pensioners of the Hospital, listening to the prayers and psalms. You hear them coughing feebly in the twilight. . . . A plenty of candles light up this chapel, and this scene of age and youth, and early memories, and pompous death. . . .

At the end of the ceremony and the oratory in praise of Thomas Sutton, Stephe joined in the singing of the Charterhouse hymn, pronouncing the Latin lines as clearly as he knew how.

Afterwards he marched round the grounds with the other Gownboys, carolling Sutton's praise with even greater enthusiasm in a less poetic but more pertinent ditty that ended in

> Then blessed be the memory
> Of good old Thomas Sutton
> Who gave us lodging—learning—
> As well as beef and mutton.

3

At Charterhouse, Stephe came under the influence of the Reverend Canon Dr William Haig Brown, who had come to the school as headmaster in 1863.

3

According to contemporary reports, Dr Haig Brown was far from being the strict disciplinarian, the firm-handed administrator of the Victorian school system. He believed in each pupil as an important entity that needed to be known and whose possibilities for growth should be furthered. He governed by example, by understanding, by his ability to inspire, by his keen sense of humour. He knew the importance of scholastic learning, but subordinated it to the growth of the spirit, to the character, to the initiative of those who came under his care. In the case of Stephe, he could therefore excuse and condone the boy's lack of enthusiasm for book learning. He knew that under the surface lay a natural intelligence, an unbounded enthusiasm.

It was under Dr Haig Brown that the young Baden-Powell received his first lesson in military tactics.

There was a standing rivalry between the boys of Charterhouse and the butcher boys of neighbouring Smithfield Market, a rivalry that often broke out into pitched battles.

> On this particular occasion [Baden-Powell wrote later], the Smithfield boys had taken possession of a waste piece of ground, 'Over Hoard-ings', adjoining our football ground, from which they attacked us with showers of stones and brickbats whenever we attempted to play. This was responded to from our side in like manner, with occasional sorties by strong bodies of us over the wall.
>
> With four or five other boys too small to take part in the actual fray, I was looking on at the battle when we suddenly found the head-master alongside us, anxiously watching the progress of the fight. He remarked to us:
>
> 'I think if you boys went through that door in the side wall you might attack the cads in the flank.'
>
> 'Yes, sir,' one of us replied, 'but the door is locked.'
>
> The worthy doctor fumbled in his gown and said: 'That is so, but here is the key.'
>
> And he sent us on our way rejoicing, and our attack was a complete success.

Stephe entered Charterhouse at a time when the old school was in a state of transition and upheaval.

From the moment Dr Haig Brown had become headmaster, he had realized that the kind of education he visualized would be impossible in the cramped and out-dated quarters of the ancient Carthusian monastery. If Charterhouse were to take its rightful place among the leading public schools of England it must move to modern and greatly expanded quarters, away from confining city walls and distracting city noises to an area where accelerated growth would be possible, not only for the institution but for the pupils as well.

Haig Brown had many obstacles to overcome before he saw his goal of moving in sight. The first obstacle, the Board of Governors, he cleared with little effort. The major obstacle was Parliament which would have to approve the transfer of the ancient Foundation to another place. The headmaster's argument eventually proved so effective that an Act of Parliament was passed in 1867 permitting the removal.

After a great deal of searching, Haig Brown and the Board of Governors chose for the new location a seventy-acre site thirty miles south-west of London, near Godalming in Surrey, the boyhood stamping ground of James Edward Oglethorpe, the founder of the thirteenth colony—Georgia —of what later became the United States of America. The site was bought at £60 an acre and the first sod turned on 12 December 1869, the anniversary of the death of Thomas Sutton 258 years before. The construction was begun on 29 June 1870. The main buildings were scheduled to be completed for use by the summer of 1872.

When the time finally came, nearly two years after Stephe had joined the school, for its removal from the old monastery in the heart of London to the new buildings on the high plateau overlooking the Wey Valley, he was ready and eager for the change. 'In the somewhat trying circumstances of this removal he proved most useful', Dr Haig Brown asserted years later. 'He showed remarkable intelligence and liberality of feeling—most boys are so conservative by nature—helping to smooth over the difficulties involved in the change to the new place; and taking up every school institution which was new.'

The expression 'trying circumstances' used by the good Doctor was something of an understatement. The removal of Charterhouse to Godalming took place amid a great deal of confusion.

On 16 May, at the closing of Long Quarter, Sutton's scholars cleared out of 'the hallowed and historic site'. While the old pensioners stayed behind, the boys were sent home with instructions to reassemble a month later, on Waterloo Day (18 June), at Godalming.

When the boys arrived to start school in the new quarters they found the outside of the buildings, three 'central or block houses' and 'Big School', completed. But the interiors were far from ready. Beds had been installed in the 'cubicles' of new Charterhouse, but all other furniture had somehow been delayed in transit. The gas for lighting was not yet turned on. The boys had to study by the light of candles stuck into ginger-beer bottles. The houses swarmed with earwigs and rats. Earwigs were being squashed by the thousand, and to get rid of the rats the boys were permitted to keep ferrets in their quarters. The cricket ground was laid and turfed but unfit for play. The future football ground was a wild tangle of gorse, yellow broom, and blue borage.

But nothing made much difference that first summer. The weather turned unusually hot and the boys spent most of their free time bathing in the River Wey that flowed through the school property.

Eventually the missing furniture—tables, benches, cupboards—turned up. The gas was 'laid on', but, for a long time after, had a way of suddenly going out altogether. After what seemed one long picnic of a summer, the students turned to their studies.

New Charterhouse settled down to academic pursuits.

4

In Stephe's case, the outcome of his 'academic pursuit' was far from impressive. He managed occasionally to be twelfth in a class of fifteen, but also once succeeded in being nineteenth out of nineteen students. Nevertheless, after a particularly bad report, Dr Haig Brown felt called upon to reassure Mrs Baden-Powell that 'Your son's ability is greater than would appear by the results of the quarter. I am well satisfied with his conduct, and I hope he will work enough to ensure himself against superannuation at 16.'

Stephe himself did not seem particularly worried about becoming 'superannuated'. His reports continued on the down grade through the following terms, with comments such as these:

In Classics: 'Seems to me to take very little interest in his work.'

In Mathematics: 'Has to all intents given up the study of mathematics.'

In Natural Science: 'Pays not the slightest attention, except in one week at the beginning of the quarter.'

When it came to Modern Languages, his French teacher Monsieur Buisson shook his head, mumbled 'Badden Povvell! It is in vain—it is not of use!' and wrote on Stephe's report card: 'Could do well, but has become very lazy; often sleeps in school.'

Of these reports, only Monsieur Buisson's was completely off the mark. If there was one thing of which young Baden-Powell could not be accused it was of being lazy. The trouble was that his exuberant energy had carried him into a multitude of activities that completely overshadowed his interest in school subjects.

Sports, for instance: Football in the winter was his favourite game, and in this he particularly shone as goalkeeper for reasons entirely in keeping with his character.

Stephe had an uncanny ability for knowing exactly where a ball would come streaking in and for preventing his opponents from scoring a goal. His peculiar behaviour was part of his strategy. When his goal was in danger, he would give off a blood-curdling Indian yell of defiance and challenge that would momentarily paralyse the forward about to shoot and cause him to miss his kick, giving Stephe a chance to drive the ball far upfield. For the rest of the play, Stephe's ringing voice, carrying over the entire football field, could be heard encouraging his team-mates. And during half-time he would make a special ceremony out of taking off his boots and changing into another pair—not for luck, as was generally assumed by the crowd of admiring youngsters gathered around the goal-posts, but because two of his aunts had each presented him with a pair of football boots and he did not want to disappoint either of them in not wearing her gift.

Rifle shooting occupied another considerable part of his time. Soon after the removal to Godalming he helped in the formation of a Rifle Corps and became one of its most eager members.

In 1874, when Charterhouse competed for the first time at Wimbledon in the Public Schools' Match for the Ashburton Shield, the Charterhouse team hit the targets seventy-seven times and missed them altogether seventy-seven times. The only bright spot was that 'Private R. S. S. Baden-Powell' shot the only bull's-eye scored during the whole competition—a fact which his mother proudly reported in her letters to friends and relatives.

Yet another activity encroached, and encroached heavily, on Stephe's time: Amateur theatricals.

Dr Haig Brown 'looked upon play-acting as a useful means of education for certain intellects among the boys, and so he encouraged, in fact almost ordered, theatricals among us'. Later, Baden-Powell credited his acting at Charterhouse with much of his success in life.

Stephe's first stage appearance was in a short comedy entitled *To Parents and Guardians*, played just before Charterhouse's removal to Godalming. During the following years, as Stephe's grades went down, the number of his histrionic activities went up.

He appeared in *The Area Belle* and in Charterhouse pensioner John Maddison Morton's *Whitebait at Greenwich*, but his major success was as Cox in *Cox and Box*, the little masterpiece by Arthur Sullivan, later of Gilbert and Sullivan fame, based on Morton's farce, with F. C. Burnand's libretto. Stephe's clear, resonant voice filled the role to perfection and Cox became his favourite stage part. Long afterwards he estimated that he had played it on twenty-six occasions.

Dr Haig Brown himself appreciated Stephe's ability as an actor and an impromptu performer and more than once called on the boy to save the situation.

> On one occasion [the headmaster recalled many years afterwards], when a school entertainment was in progress, a performer 'scratched' at the last moment. The boys were beginning to get somewhat impatient at the long pause—so I said to Baden-Powell, who was sitting next to me, 'We must do something—cannot you fill the gap?' He immediately consented and, rushing to the platform, gave them a bit of his school experience. Fortunately, the French master was not present, for he described a lesson in French with perfect mimicry. It was inimitable. It kept the boys in perfect roars of laughter.

It was inevitable that Stephe should eventually find himself a charter member of a secret social club made up of twelve students of the Upper School. The first meeting was held in Oration Quarter, 1873, and was occupied in the election of officers, framing of rules, and selecting a name for the club. The name decided on was 'The Druids'—not for any patriotic reverence for early British history but for the less romantic reason that the name of the head monitor and first club president was W. W. Drew.

At the meetings, held on Saturday nights, 'The Druids' gathered round the table in Hall with 'gowser' mugs of beer before them—beer was liberally provided at Charterhouse in those days—and each member in turn regaled the others with a speech, with all of them joining in singing such English old-timers as 'Hearts of Oak' and 'Weel May the Keel Row'.

'The Druids' prospered for two years, then died a lingering death as the interest of the members shifted elsewhere, but left behind a number of pages of minutes, all extensively decorated with pen-and-ink sketches by the Honourable 'Lord Bathing Towel', as Stephe had been dubbed by his fellow 'Druids'.

5

The multitude of activities into which Stephe threw himself gave him an outlet for his gregarious exuberance. But there was another facet to his character. From time to time he found himself in urgent need of solitude —of being completely alone, completely unattached. He found the perfect locale for this in The Copse, an untouched belt of woodland wilderness stretching for a mile or so along the steep hillside below the playing fields and having the added appeal of being out of bounds.

The Copse was a dense stand of hazel, chestnut, beech and oak, with an undercover of bracken and brambles, and with a few narrow trails occasionally patrolled by a vigilant schoolmaster or monitor. The bird life was prolific. The animal life was varied, with foxes, and an occasional fallow deer.

> It was here [the grown-up Stephe explained] that I imagined myself a backwoodsman, a trapper, and an Indian scout. I used to creep about warily looking for 'sign' and getting close-up observations of rabbits, squirrels, rats and birds.
>
> As a trapper I set my snares, and when I caught a rabbit or hare (which wasn't often) I learned by painful experience to skin, clean and cook him. But knowing that Redskins were about, in the shape of masters looking for boys out of bounds, I used a very small non-smoky fire for fear of giving away my whereabouts.
>
> Incidentally, also, I gained sufficient cunning to hide up in trees when danger of this kind threatened, since experience told me that masters hunting for boys seldom looked upward. The Greeks made a bloomer when they styled man *anthropos*, or 'he who looks up', since in practice he generally fails to look above his own level. . . .

Stephe learned a great number of outdoor skills in The Copse, but The Copse gave him far more than skills:

> What I picked up in The Copse was both a preparation and a pursuit. The Copse lore . . . went beyond the development of health of body and mind—it helped me as a youngster to find my soul. It was an elemental way, but that solitary creeping and 'freezing' in observation of the birds and the beasts and the butterflies made one a comrade instead of an interloper in the family of nature, it brought some realization of the wonders that surround us, and it revealed too, through open eyes, the beauties of the woods and the sunsets.

6

During his Charterhouse years, Stephe received another kind of training that was important to his development. This training, achieved at the hands of his older brothers, taught him teamwork, resourcefulness, and courage, and helped to mould his body into sinewy toughness.

These three boys, like himself, were all lovers of the open-air life. Warington, George and Frank had already spent many adventuresome holidays together on land and sea. When Stephe could be considered able to take care of himself, he joined in with them. Agnes, being a girl, had to remain with her mother, and Baden was still the baby of the family.

With the three older boys Stephe saw much of his country on tramping expeditions during some of his school holidays, 'each of us carrying a bag on his back and sleeping out at night wherever we might happen to be'. On these tramps the brothers would generally call at a farm and buy some milk, eggs, butter and bread, and ask permission to sleep in a hay-loft if the weather was bad. When the weather was good they would sleep in the open alongside a hedge or haystack.

In 1872, when Stephe was 15, his mother arranged to spend the summer holidays in the Wye Valley of Wales. A reporter from *The Times* had offered her the loan of his house, The Falls, near Llandogo. Mrs Baden-Powell left by train with Frank, Agnes and Baden. Warington had insisted that he, George and Stephe should go by boat and by boat they went— or rather, by canoe: the self-same craft that Warington had previously paddled across Sweden by canal and lake. They went up the Thames 'till the river became a stream and finally a brook that was too small to float us.' They portaged over the watershed, dipped their craft again in the waters of the Wiltshire–Somerset Avon and continued downriver through Bath and Bristol, rowing, sailing, poling or towing, as the circumstances required. At Avonmouth they turned north-eastward along the left bank of the Severn, crossed the river to Chepstow and proceeded north- ward on the Wye into Wales. They carried tents and cooking pots with them and camped out every night.

But it was the open sea that held the greatest attraction for the boys.

Warington, after four years of sailing to India with the P & O, had been given the chance to study at Oxford where George and Frank had already entered Balliol. He left the Merchant Service, submerged his sea ambitions and set out to become a barrister. By pooling the family money, the boys managed to acquire a 5-ton cutter, the *Diamond*. It was built to Waring-ton's own design and berthed most of the time at Shanklin, the small seaport on the Isle of Wight. They used it for two years, then replaced it with a 10-tonner, the *Kohinoor*, also of Warington's design.

Whenever the brothers could get together they took off for days at sea in the Channel, fishing in spring, cruising in summer, racing in autumn, wildfowling in winter. They formed an efficient crew under Warington's strict discipline and 'learned not only navigation and boat handling, but also about bending the sails, rigging and painting the ship, deck-scrubbing, cleaning and carpentering. Also, of course, we all had to be able to cook and most important of all, perhaps—to swim'.

As the youngest of the four, Stephe was unanimously, by the others, elected cabin boy and cook and crockery washer. His first attempt at pea soup proved somewhat of a failure, due partly to a smoking fire and a scalded pot, and partly to the fact that he had not realized that some form of meaty ingredient was desirable. Warington's verdict of Stephe's cooking was quickly forthcoming: 'Frank will sit by and see that you eat the whole of that muck yourself!'

" Exam " R.S.S. Baden Powell. 1875.

A Charterhouse exam, sketched by Stephe at the age of seventeen.

Portsmouth Harbour, the British naval base, became a favourite haunt. But the boys also went farther afield. They investigated the harbours of Southampton, Bournemouth and Weymouth, streaked by Brownsea Island into Poole Harbour, sailed up Christchurch Bay and almost came to grief off Torquay once when beating down the Channel against a rising gale from the south-west.

7

By the time Stephe was 18 he was in the sixth form and had become second monitor of Girdlestone's house. The number of Charterhouse pupils had quadrupled to almost five hundred since the removal from London and the office of monitor had gained in significance.

The younger boys found it easy to act as fags to Stephe. They were intrigued by his unconventional ways and his astonishing ability to dash off recognizable portraits of school personalities, now with the right hand, now with the left, now two at a time with a pencil in each hand. Stephe, for his part, thought of the younger boys in terms of Baden, his 'baby brother', who had joined him at Charterhouse as yet another Gownboy: they needed his encouragement, his help, his understanding. He would expect a certain amount of deference but was, himself, expected to treat them with fairness.

He had become a frequent and lively contributor of articles and art to the newly established school magazine, *The Carthusian*, and had joined the new Debating and Literary Society as a very active debater. This society had started in a rather tame fashion with a debate on the motion 'That the band is beneficial to the school' but had soon taken up national and international questions.

There were plenty of such questions to debate during the early 1870s. Europe had just been through the collapse of the French Empire and the rise of the German. In England, Gladstone had been defeated and Disraeli had re-emerged as Premier. The purchase of Army commissions had been abolished and England had secured an interest in the Suez Canal. Small wars were taking place in many parts of the globe. The whole world was a proper subject for debate by the Charterhouse Debating and Literary Society.

There was a debate in the Baden-Powell household as well. This was Stephe's last year at Charterhouse. Some thought had to be given to his future. Any hankering on Stephe's part to become an actor or an artist was turned down as not even worthy of discussion. There was time to settle on a career after he had been to the university.

Consequently, in April 1876 when his Charterhouse days drew to a close, Stephe went up to Oxford for the necessary entrance examinations.

He was turned down by Dr Jowett of Balliol as being 'not quite up to Balliol form'. He tried at Christ Church and suffered the same ignominy there. His examiner in mathematics, Professor Charles Lutwidge Dodgson, better known as Lewis Carroll, the author of *Alice in Wonderland*, 'found out what I could already have told him, but what I hoped he would not discover for himself, that it was a subject about which I knew little or nothing'. For the time being Stephe was signed up as *scholares non ascripti*, non-attached student.

There was general consternation in the Baden-Powell household when the reports reached it that Stephe had failed his examinations. How was it possible that a Baden-Powell could have failed at Oxford? Hadn't Stephe's father made a brilliant career at the University? Hadn't his brother George just won the Chancellor's Prize? Wasn't Frank going through Balliol on a well-earned scholarship?

And now this! What was to become of Stephe? Stephe himself took a Micawberish attitude. Something would turn up.

One morning he came upon the announcement of an Open Competitive Examination for commissions in Her Majesty's Army for ninety appointments in the Infantry of the Line and ten in the West India Regiments as well as for thirty commissions in the Cavalry.

He had not previously given much thought to a military career. But why not? There was no tradition on his father's side of anyone having chosen the service life. But there was ample precedent on his mother's side. Stephe's grandfather, the Admiral, had made the most of a naval career. His uncle, Colonel Smyth, was doing well in the Army. If they had succeeded why couldn't he?

He investigated the requirements. His age was right. Candidates had to be between 17 and 20 and he was 19. The 'preliminary examination' consisted of simple arithmetic and geometry, French or some other modern language, writing English correctly, geography, geometrical drawing, with marks allotted in geometrical drawing only. The 'further examination' called for a choice of four subjects out of eight: mathematics, English composition, Latin, Greek, French, German, experimental sciences, geography—plus free-hand drawing.

The same examinations counted for Infantry and Cavalry, so why not sign up for both branches of the service? There was little time for cramming. Stephe had to depend on his general knowledge and his mother wit to carry him through most of the subjects. Where he had a choice, he had to choose with care.

For twelve days during the period 3–17 July 1876, Stephe sweated out his future within the walls of the severe and forbidding London University building in Burlington Gardens. He came out of the examinations with fair optimism.

While waiting for the result of the Army examination, Stephe went on holiday with the family to the Isle of Wight.

One morning when he and his brothers were cruising in the *Kohinoor* through the Solent, the strait between the island and the mainland, they were hailed from the *Gertrude*, a yacht belonging to Dr Alfred Acland, the old friend of the family. Stephe boarded the yacht to pay his respects. One of the guests on board was the Dean of Christ Church, Dr Liddell. The Dean accosted Stephe with the news that, according to the newspaper, a namesake of his had passed his exam for the Army. 'And there, in black and white, was my own name!'

Out of the 718 'gentlemen examined', Stephe had been placed fifth for Infantry, second for Cavalry, with 5,350 marks out of a possible 11,300.

The jubilation in the Baden-Powell family was great. Here was proof that Mrs Baden-Powell's faith in her red-haired, freckled son had been justified. Her motherly pride knew no bounds. She couldn't help herself. She had to write to those people at Oxford to inform them of the opportunity they had missed in turning down her Stephe. She gloried when she received the abject apologies from the people who had 'misjudged' her son.

> I assure you it was not my doing that your son was not admitted at Christ Church [Dean Liddell wrote her]. The mathematical Examiner, through whose lectures all young men must pass, thought it necessary to examine him in the common subjects, and his report of your son's answers was such that it was absolutely impossible for me to overrule him. . . . I regret, and hereby express my regret, that we have not Stephenson's name on the books of our House. I think they must have the same feelings at Balliol.

They had. The Master of Balliol wrote to Mrs Baden-Powell to express his happiness over Stephe's success but added a reasonable alibi for having turned him down: 'It makes me almost think that he cannot have tried to do his best when he came up here. . . . I am sorry that he did not come again unless (as I dare say) he likes his present place better than anything Oxford could offer him.'

In the general jubilation in the family over Stephe's success the financial problem involved was not lost sight of. Officers' commissions in the 1870s were sought mostly by the sons of at least fairly well-to-do families. The pay was small and the expenses heavy.

Stephe's older brothers met with his mother in family council. It was decided that Stephe should accept the commission he had earned and that the other members of the family would help him to carry through. On these conditions he might as well pick the Cavalry commission. It would involve greater expense but also had greater glamour.

On 11 September 1876, Stephe received his commission in the British Army. Ordinarily, successful candidates were drafted first to the Royal Military College, Sandhurst, for a two-year course of instruction before actually joining the Army, but in this particular instance the first six were excused this preliminary and were at once gazetted to regiments, Stephe to the crack 13th Hussars.

Within a couple of weeks, Stephe's orders arrived at 1 Hyde Park Gate South addressed to 'Sub-Lieutenant R. S. S. B. Powell'. Mrs Baden-Powell turned the envelope over in her hands. 'Stephe is actually and really in the Army!' The orders commanded Stephe to proceed forthwith to India where his regiment was stationed.

Less than a month to sailing time! The household was thrown into happy yet melancholy uproar. There were uniforms to be fitted, equipment to be bought. Agnes joined Mrs Baden-Powell in getting everything ready, in checking that everything that Stephe needed was packed. At the last moment the new sub-lieutenant included in his luggage a box with the texts of all the plays in which he had appeared at Charterhouse.

On 30 October 1876, the family said good-bye as Stephe boarded the *Serapis* in Portsmouth Harbour. He left England on the eve of a memorable event: the proclamation of Victoria Regina as 'Imperatrix' and 'Kaisar-i-Hind' of all India.

III

A Subaltern in India

Years: 1876–78   Age: 19–21

1

THE 5,000-ton *Serapis* was considered a magnificent ship in her day. She was a propeller-driven steamship able to average nine knots under favourable conditions. She was prepared for any eventuality, even for the complete breakdown of her engines, by being fitted with masts and sails. She was scheduled to reach India in a month with a complement of 1,150 men and officers, including 19-year-old Stephe Baden-Powell.

The ship had hardly left Portsmouth Harbour before the exuberant Stephe teamed up with a companion who had ranked third in the Army examination, Frederick Stevens 'Tommy' Dimond. The first night out the two conspirators busied themselves around midnight 'swinging all the fellows in their hammocks to make them sick'. The episode was duly recorded in one of the earliest of thousands of letters to his mother in which Stephe was to detail his doings over a period of more than forty years. What the 'fellows' did to the two companions Stephe failed to note.

The Atlantic made the ship roll a good deal, but the Bay of Biscay was on its best behaviour. After following the Portuguese coast, the *Serapis*, under full steam, passed among numerous large sailing ships lying becalmed off Cape St Vincent, then sped through the Strait of Gibraltar with all sails set before a fresh breeze that sprang up from the west. Stephe exulted in a letter home: 'Have you ever heard of the blue water of the Mediterranean? If you don't believe in it just come here and look at it, and you will see a blue there's no mistaking!'

After a day at Malta and an overnight halt at Port Said, the *Serapis* steamed through the seven-year-old Suez Canal over which Benjamin Disraeli had obtained control for Britain only the year before. In spite of the 'flocks and flocks of millions of flamingoes' flying overhead, Stephe was not impressed. He found the Canal a 'dreary scene: low banks of mud, and beyond these, on one side a sandy desert, on the other a lagoon stretching away to the horizon'.

The *Serapis* had been out from England only a few days when a committee of officers was formed to provide entertainment for the passengers during the long journey. One of the officers was given the job of interviewing the available talent.

The young Baden-Powell volunteered his services. 'I told him what I could do—so he put me down to act in some theatricals. Then he said he did not know what to act—so I got out my boxful of plays and gave them to him to read.' Baden-Powell suggested the farce *The Area Belle* for a start. The committee accepted not only the young subaltern's recommendation but also his eagerness to work. Stephe painted playbills, helped rig up a stage on the poop, assisted in directing. On the night of the performance, he spoke a prologue written for the occasion by the captain, acted in the play and sang a couple of humorous songs.

The evening's success made Baden-Powell, actor, one of the most popular young officers in the ship. And Baden-Powell, artist, had the satisfaction of having the captain ask to keep one of the playbills he had painted. The ship's newly formed dramatic group put on more of the plays in which he had acted at Charterhouse: *Cox and Box, Whitebait at Greenwich, Ici On Parle Français*—with B-P playing parts of his own choosing.

Beyond Aden the weather turned 'roaring hot' and Baden-Powell started out on 'a new way of living'. 'I get up at about 5.30, have a cup of tea and a biscuit, walk or run a mile on deck in my pyjamas, have a bath, lie on deck and read a novel, then at 8.00 go below and get on uniform. At 8.30 a light breakfast. 10.30 parade, then loaf about till lunch at 12. From 12 to 4 do various odd jobs. Then dress for dinner at 4.30. Eat as little as possible—dance till tea at 8. From 8 to 11, write, draw and smoke, and then to bed.'

The *Serapis* at last dropped anchor in Bombay Harbour on 6 December 1876. The officers on board celebrated their arrival in India by parading on deck in full regalia—then turned to the task of getting their men disembarked and the equipment and supplies unloaded.

Stephe and his friend 'Tommy' Dimond did their utmost to hurry their baggage off the ship but it was evening before they succeeded. They had been rather satisfied with themselves in their dashing uniforms early in the day, 'but as hour followed hour in that soggy heat we seemed to melt into the thick tight-bound cloth, and we wished we had something more sensible to wear. By nightfall we were dog tired and our pride had all leaked out, and under the cover of darkness we willingly climbed up onto a pile of baggage on a bullock-cart and allowed ourselves to be ignominiously carried through the back streets of Bombay to Watson's Hotel'.

The next day the detachment of officers and men set out on the long rail journey across half India via Jubbulpore to Lucknow where the 13th Hussars were stationed in one of the largest British cantonments in India.

2

Lucknow, in 1876, was far from being the 'noble, walled city' that Baden-Powell had expected. The Indian quarter was 'no regular town with streets, except where you come on a bazaar . . . and that is an arrangement of mud hovels'—but only 'miles and miles of broad, dusty roads with trees at each side' along the River Gumti winding its way towards its juncture with the Ganges at Benares nearly two hundred miles to the south-east.

The British section of Lucknow still showed signs, almost twenty years later, of the Indian Mutiny of 1857 when the Bengal troops had gone on a murderous rampage against the armies of the British East India Company and Britons in general. The headquarters building, the Residency, still stood in the pock-marked ruins to which bombardment and fire had reduced it. So did the Surgeon's House by the Baillie Guard-gate where Lucknow's commander, Sir Henry Lawrence, had died of his wounds and where the officers' wives had been sheltered in the underground rooms during the eighty-seven-day siege.

Stephe threw himself whole-heartedly into his life as a soldier. He was proud of his regiment. For more than two hundred years it had played a part in the wars of Europe—originally as the 13th Light Dragoons but after 1861 as the 13th Hussars. It had fought against Napoleon. It had formed the right flank in the luckless 'Charge of the Light Brigade' at Balaclava during the Crimean War. It had emerged from this *débâcle* to become a crack regiment once more under the command of Colonel John Miller.

Upon arrival Baden-Powell was assigned to the regiment's Troop B under Captain Pryce and was provided with bungalow quarters and a Government pony. He further found himself the master of a British officer's usual complement of seven Indian servants: a bearer (valet), a *khidmutgar* (cook and waiter), a *dhobi* (washerman), two *syces* (grooms), and two grass cutters (for securing forage for his horse). It was a new experience for Stephe to be waited on hand and foot. He quickly learned to appreciate and like his servants but kept aloof from other Indians around the garrison. They struck him as overdoing their saluting of any European who crossed their path, to the point of cringing.

Baden-Powell had reached Lucknow at a time of great excitement. The regular routine of the regiment was completely disrupted by the preparation for the big events immediately ahead, the regimental Christmas celebration, the Imperial Durbar in Delhi on 1 January 1877—the State reception at which Queen Victoria was to be proclaimed Empress of India—and the Race Week, the first week of the New Year, with its balls, its sports, parties and theatricals.

Captain Pryce and a number of his fellow officers were picked to represent the 13th Hussars at the Durbar. When the captain left, he put Sub-Lieutenant Baden-Powell, with only two weeks of active service, in sole command of Troop B.

Baden-Powell took on the assignment with his usual optimistic self-confidence and managed surprisingly well during Pryce's absence. A lucky incident the day after he joined the regiment had established him in the eyes of his men as an officer with a level temper, a sense of humour, of evident fairness, young in years but deserving of their respect.

Troop B had been ordered to parade in double rank and Baden-Powell had been directed to inspect the men to see that each of them had on his 'cholera belt'—a band of heavy flannel round the waist intended to ward off cholera, but hot, uncomfortable and highly unpopular.

B-P had inspected the front rank and was turning at the end of it to walk up the rear rank when, out of the corner of his eye, he noticed a movement at the other end of the troop, of a man stepping from the rear rank into the front rank. It happened to be the only man B-P knew by name. He was the soldier who had been detailed to bring him his horse the day before.

Without saying a word, Baden-Powell moved along the rear rank, inspected each man in turn, debating in his own mind what to do. When he had finished the inspection, he faced the troop. 'Private Ramsbotham,' he called out, 'step to the front. Are you wearing your cholera belt?'

There was a confused reply of 'No, sir' followed by a roar of jeering laughter from the troop.

With all the gruffness he could muster the new sub-lieutenant admonished the culprit: 'Take care you don't let it happen again, Private Ramsbotham. You will wear two belts until further notice.'

B-P's simple handling of his first disciplinary problem met with his men's general approval. They accepted his command.

With the big celebrations over, B-P settled down to 'a continued round of drill and duty from morn to dewy eve': cavalry instruction and parades, sword exercises and carbine practices, inspections and orderly service. He shared his 'early miseries of riding school, garrison class, and elementary

4

drill' with 'Tommy' Dimond but soon made other friends among the young officers.

Stephe's early interest in horses grew into a passion. Under John Watson's tuition he soon developed into a daring horseman, but the hours spent in cavalry training were not enough horsemanship for him. He made up his mind to join the polo-playing set of the regiment. But the regimental horses were not available for inexperienced players to practise on. To play polo he would have to get a horse of his own.

It was generally expected in the British Army of 1870–80 that an officer in the Hussars, even a subaltern, would be a 'gay blade'. Many of Baden-Powell's companions lived up to this traditional picture. Most of them came from families of means and could well afford strings of horses and extravagant mess bills. They had picked a military career for pleasure rather than from any deep-seated conviction that Her Majesty's Forces really required their services.

Stephe was in a different category. He was convinced that the British Empire depended upon him and others like him to keep up her traditions and expand her influence. He was deeply dedicated to the career he had chosen. He was different also in having little money of his own. From time to time, his mother arranged to send him a few pounds from the communal funds at home. And occasionally he received a couple of hundred rupees from his half-brother, Baden Henry, who had been in India since 1860 and was stationed in Lahore as a member of the Chief Court of the Punjab. For the rest, B-P was determined to make his own small pay of £10 a month go as far as possible:

> I have altogether given up smoking [he wrote to his mother]. It saves a big item in the mess bill. . . .
>
> At dinner I drink very little—a bottle of soda with a glass of sherry in it. Most people take great silver cups full of claret, etc., but I feel much healthier after a little drink, although I am thirsty enough to drink a dozen cups full—and you can imagine the expense comes somewhat different in the end. . . .
>
> Last month mine was the lowest mess bill, being 175 rupees. Dimond's was the next lowest, 275 rupees.

A good polo pony was expensive. If he was to have one of his own he would have to buy it cheap and train it himself.

He found what he sought in Hercules, the first pony he ever owned.

He purchased Hercules from a man who had made his living by cutting grass and selling it for horse fodder. 'Hercules had to carry the load of grass every day to the market and the load was as big as himself—that was how he got the name of Hercules. . . . My word, he was ugly! A little, thin, red chestnut pony, with a head like a fiddle and hip bones sticking up like hat pegs—a miserable-looking rat of a thing.'

Man and horse learned to play polo together. 'While I learned to hit the ball as we galloped along, Hercules learned that it was his business to take me wherever the ball was going as fast as he possibly could. He got to be quite quick at seeing the ball and trying to follow it. Very often his sharp eyes would find it through a cloud of dust before I saw it for myself, and away he would go carrying me to it.'

By careful budgeting, B-P slowly built up the string of horses he desired. He got them partly by buying them with the money he saved through his frugal living and partly by purchasing run-down horses, training them and selling them at a profit.

3

Ordinarily, there was a great chasm between the senior and the junior officers in a British garrison. The senior officers tolerated the younger men but made sure to keep them in their place. It was an unusual subaltern who could break this invisible barrier. But then—Baden-Powell was an unusual subaltern. He was no bumptious youth or sophisticated dandy. He was a straight-forward young man full of life, excited by the newness of his surroundings and the fascination of India and not ashamed of showing it.

Stephe's talent as an actor and his abilities as a mimic helped him immensely in breaking the barrier. One of the first questions asked him by his regimental adjutant, Lieutenant Christie, on his arrival was: 'Can you act—or sing—or paint scenery?' Christie was gratified to learn that Baden-Powell could do all three, but Stephe was disappointed in the question. He had expected the first thing asked him would deal with his ability to drill, to ride, to shoot. He soon discovered the importance of his talents in the theatrical line, not only to himself but to the whole regiment.

The two main enemies of the soldiers of the Queen's Army garrisoned in India were disease and boredom. Dysentery and typhoid were prevalent, and cholera might strike suddenly and unaccountably. Heat and fever lowered·the men's energy and morale, but ennui was an even greater depressant. To overcome it, each regiment went in heavily for amateur theatricals and musicals and anyone with abilities in these lines was in great demand.

Stephe began as a scene-painter and did very well indeed. The speed with which he worked exceeded any previous accomplishment in this field for the simple reason that he was the first ambidextrous scene-painter the regiment had ever had. 'The quality may not have been good,' he admitted afterwards, 'but the quantity was there!'

He quickly graduated to the stage itself as an actor in each of the plays he had brought to India with him in his barracks box. And for the first time he saw his name in print in an Indian paper, the *Lucknow Times* of 10 February 1877: 'Mr Powell as John Small in the farce *Whitebait at Greenwich* could not have been better. The corps is to be congratulated on receiving into its ranks this talented young comedian.'

After a performance in the regimental theatre it was customary for the officers and their ladies to attend a ball at the General's residence or at Government House. At one of these balls, B-P went to the refreshment buffet for ices for himself and his partner. He was having trouble making the Indian waiter understand what he wanted when a stranger, a short man with a soldierly figure standing beside him, gave the order to the man in Hindustani.

'Young fellow,' said the helpful stranger, 'you will make your life happier here if you learn a bit of the language. Who are you and where are you staying?'

Stephe thanked the stranger, gave him his name and thought nothing further of it. But the next day he received a little note giving the name of a local teacher of Hindustani. It was signed 'F. S. Roberts'.

It was Baden-Powell's first encounter with Sir Frederick Sleigh Roberts —an officer for whom he was to gain the highest respect as their paths crossed and recrossed.

4

In spite of his many extra-curricular activities, Baden-Powell progressed satisfactorily in his training as an officer.

At the end of July 1877, he passed his first examination and was specifically complimented on the way in which he had 'shouted out the words of command very clearly' during a number of field tests. As a result of the examination, B-P was pronounced professionally fit to become a lieutenant, making him eligible for the eight-month garrison course from which he would become educationally fit for the promotion.

During the summer a severe famine hit India. The situation among the native population grew desperate. The British authorities worked assiduously to alleviate the suffering but with relatively little success. With the famine growing steadily worse in southern India during the autumn, officers were called on to volunteer their services to help direct the relief work in Madras.

Baden-Powell tried to sign up but was turned down. One of the requirements was the ability to speak Hindustani fluently, and so far he had only picked up the rudiments of the language. It was back to the classroom and field exercises for him.

He started his garrison course in October with great confidence. He found it fairly easy to pursue his studies during Lucknow's rather cool winter, but when the heat set in by the middle of April and hit a temperature in early May of 116 degrees in the shade, daytime study became virtually impossible. To get his work done he was forced to use the night hours and often sat up working until 2 a.m., trying to master military law and administration, his two toughest subjects.

To complicate matters further he had a 'sharp go' of fever at the beginning of exams in June 1878, and tried to shake it off with his customary cure: 'At dinner eat little, drink a lot of good champagne; before going to bed have twenty minutes boiling hot bath, with cold stream on the head—then a dose of castor oil and go to bed in flannel clothes; next day lie down, and take quinine, and then the fever goes.'

It didn't this time. B-P went up to the final examinations with his head fizzing and came away certain that he had failed. He had in fact received a total of 1,724 points out of a possible 2,500 and was certified First Class. In addition, he had taken a 'star' in surveying—the only 'star' that year, not only at the Lucknow garrison but in all India. He was promoted to lieutenant with his commission antedated two years because of the First Class rating he had earned.

As soon as the exams were over, Baden-Powell was granted a one-month leave to recuperàte. He wrote to Baden Henry in Lahore and asked if he might pay him a visit. By return mail he got an invitation from his half-brother to join him in the mountain resort of Simla in the lower Himalayas, the summer headquarters of a number of Government departments, including Baden Henry's, and the summer residence of the Viceroy.

B-P reached Simla after a two-day horse-cart journey. He was greatly impressed with his half-brother's quarters. The house was large and comfortable and perched rather precariously on the edge of a precipice with a magnificent view to the mountains. The Simla weather was perfect, cool and pleasant after the heat of Lucknow.

In Simla, Baden-Powell ran into a number of officers he had already met and made new friends among the Government officials to whom Baden Henry introduced him as 'my half-brother and the young fellow who does so much acting in Lucknow'.

The Simla season was in full swing with almost daily balls and entertainments. Baden-Powell was invited to several of them but yearned to take a more active part in the *divertissements*. He suddenly got his chance.

The Simla Amateur Dramatic Club had been rehearsing a play, *Walpole* by Bulwer Lytton—the first Lord Lytton and author of *Last Days of Pompeii*. A few days before the performance, one of the actors was unexpectedly recalled to his regiment and Baden-Powell was asked to step into the breach. He jumped at the opportunity, crammed for his part, and had the satisfaction of performing before the Commander-in-Chief of the British Forces in India and before the Viceroy himself—Bulwer Lytton's son, the second Lord Lytton.

During the next weeks, Baden-Powell was asked to take other parts and still others. He telegraphed to Colonel Miller asking to have his month's leave extended by an extra week because of the theatricals. The permission was granted. But when he telegraphed later to ask for four more days, the Colonel's reply was 'Absolutely not!' An answer that was quickly changed into an affirmative 'Certainly!' when the Commander-in-Chief himself interceded and telegraphed to Miller.

The leave in Simla had buoyed up Stephe, but not for long. On his return to Lucknow he was plagued again with headaches and fever and was steadily losing weight. 'I have had to have my pantaloons taken in,' he informed his mother, 'but', he added hopefully, 'I shall pick up again in the cold weather all right'.

But the weather did not co-operate. It turned 'queer: one day wet and cool, the next cloudy and muggy, always steamy.' Several Lucknow townspeople came down with cholera. One of the men of the 13th Hussars died of it. Another regiment stationed at Lucknow had three fatal cases.

Baden-Powell was on a steady diet of 'liver medicine every day, quinine from time to time, diarrhoea medicine now and then. . . . I never feel fit or well now . . . existence is like a bad dream'. The glamour of military life in India faded. For the first time in two years Baden-Powell yearned for home.

> I am getting to dislike India so [he wrote to his mother]. I do wish I could get home. . . . The only regret I should feel would be that of leaving the regiment—for I am so at home in it now, and not only like all the officers, but also have a lot of friends among the men.

In November, a severe attack of diarrhoea sent Baden-Powell to the hospital. His general condition was so poor that the regimental doctor decided to have him examined by a medical board. The board convened on 28 November and found their patient suffering from 'hepatic symptoms, loss of weight, instant nausea, distaste for food, increasing diarrhoea, pyrexia at frequent intervals, slight enlargement of the spleen, occurrence of dyspepsia after every meal and a general malaise'.

On the basis of the board's finding, the staff surgeon of the 13th Hussars certified Lieutenant R. S. S. Baden-Powell as being 'in a bad state of health'. He decreed that 'a change of air' was 'essentially necessary' and recommended that B-P be returned to England on sick leave at public expense.

Before leaving for home, Baden-Powell paid a farewell call, as was the custom, on the commanding general of the Lucknow garrison. The general greeted him kindly, and then, to B-P's surprise, invited the recently promoted lieutenant into his inner sanctum. Here the general brought out a large scrapbook, placed it on the table and opened it.

B-P gaped while the general laughed. Pasted into the scrapbook seemed to be all the doodles and sketches, most of them caricatures of his officers, that B-P had drawn during the tedious hours in the classroom. 'I thought your illustrations rather good,' the general explained, 'so I got the orderly who swept up the lecture room, to save any pictures you discarded and bring them to me for my collection.'

With his spirits somewhat raised Stephe left Lucknow for Bombay to board the ship for home.

> Mark the coincidence [he wrote to his mother on leaving]: I landed in India from the *Serapis* on 6 December 1876, and shall embark in the *Serapis* on 6 December 1878. Ta-ta!

IV

The Hussar in Action

Years: 1879–84   Age: 22–27

1

STEPHE BADEN-POWELL came back to England to a new home. During his two-year absence, his mother, with his older brothers, had managed to consolidate some of the family finances and had bought 8 St George's Place, Hyde Park Corner. It was a larger and better house than any other the family had ever had, with a great number of high-ceilinged rooms. Each family member had a spacious room, Warington one in which to keep his law books and the mementoes of his days in the merchant marine, George for his books on Colonial affairs and treasures from his Australian tour of duty, Frank for his easels and canvases, Stephe for his scrapbooks and Indian souvenirs, Baden for his kites and balloon models, Agnes for her embroidery frames, her dried flowers and her beehives. And here was ample space for Mrs Baden-Powell's thoroughly Victorian teas, dinners and evenings-at-home, as well as quarters for a housekeeper and cook, kitchen maid and two housemaids.

The new home was the culmination of Mrs Baden-Powell's hopes and ambitions for the family. For the first time in many years all her surviving children would be under one roof. Soon again the boys might scatter and leave only Agnes and herself behind, but the Baden-Powell family would go on. And so would their communal way of sharing—the system she had built up over the years and had used to govern the lives of herself and her children, a system she proudly challenged her five sons never to forget:

> When you are old you will boast of it [she wrote in an extraordinary document that she had each of the boys initial] and so remarkable a distinction will it be that men will then scarce believe it. They will deem it impossible that you and we—seven of us living in the world,

46

not shutting ourselves up, five young men at the very ages to be tempted to spend on yachts and horses and books and pictures and wines and dinners and carriages and clubs—should yet all join in one purse that all can cheerfully agree to arrange the expenditure to suit the very limited income—that each and all as they earn or receive money add it to the public purse, without one murmur, without any

" An Awkward Team to drive through the World "

Stephe agreed with his mother's description of the Baden-Powell children as 'an awkward team', with W keeping a steady pace, G needing to be held back, F to be urged forward, and S and B not yet broken to harness.

slightest jealousy. Nay, rejoicing to see each other allowed the expense desirable towards each one's special prospects.

This is a state of union and self-restraint which seems to you all so natural you little imagine the wonder it would seem to the world in general.

I really think one of you should keep this letter to remind you of it in your old age. For alas! I suppose we must stop this purity and virtue when any one of you marries, and tie each one down to the selfish ordinary life of earning and spending for himself alone.

Ever your loving

MOTHER

The sea journey and the cool weather that greeted Stephe on his return to England helped bring back his health. His mother's and his sister's care did the rest. Within a couple of months he had become his usual light-hearted self. His weight had again reached his customary 10 stone (140 lb). The colour had returned to his cheeks, the sparkle to his eyes.

But his red hair, bleached sandy under the tropical sun, was already showing signs of thinning.

After he had recuperated somewhat, Stephe found himself in an almost daily round of visits to close and distant family members. The Powells and Smyths and Flowers and Toynbees all wanted to see the young Hussar who had just returned from India. Stephe had also many other social obligations. He had promised several of his Lucknow officer friends to give their greetings to their families on his return to England. Everywhere he presented himself he was made most welcome, and was invited for speedy return visits.

There were trips to Charterhouse to see Dr Haig Brown and Mr Girdlestone and the other masters, as well as old school friends—especially the 'Skakers', a small coterie of Carthusians, each of them a survivor of the Gownboys of Old Charterhouse, who met periodically for refreshment and fun.

Although Stephe enjoyed the hours with family and friends, he was never happier than when he could spend the evening in a London music hall or a theatre where there was operetta or light comedy. He had a serious purpose in mind: he was bent on increasing his stock of songs and recitations. Besides, he had agreed to send his friend Christie, the Lucknow adjutant, anything new in the theatrical line that might be used to keep the garrison entertained.

He spent several nights at the Opera Comique where Gilbert and Sullivan's *H.M.S. Pinafore* was packing in the crowds and at the Folly Theatre where Planquette's *Les Cloches de Corneville* was a great hit. The songs he learned became a part of his repertoire. The sketches he made of costumes and scenery, he mailed off to India with the published musical scores. And when finally, after 700 performances, *H.M.S. Pinafore* was taken off, the new attraction by the same team in the same theatre proved of even greater interest to Stephe: he could see himself staging *The Pirates of Penzance* in Lucknow, with himself in a leading part.

2

As the weeks passed by, Stephe began to miss his officer friends in the 13th Hussars. He missed his horses, his polo—even the daily routine in the regiment. He missed especially the excitement of being close to the latest war front.

Soon after he left for home, the relations between Britain and Afghanistan had blown sky-high. The trouble had started over the *rapprochement* between Russia and the Afghan Amir. Russia, in 1873, had assured Britain that she considered Afghanistan outside her zone of influence; nevertheless, in July 1878 she sent a mission to Kabul, the Afghan capital. Amir Sher Ali received the mission in state—while at the same time turning back a British mission at the Khyber Pass. After several protests, the British Government demanded an apology by a certain date for what it considered a public affront. If this was not forthcoming, Sher Ali would be considered a declared enemy of Britain. The day came and went with no reply from the Afghan Amir. And so, late in 1878, British forces under Major-General Sir Frederick Roberts were sent into Afghanistan. They quickly overwhelmed the Amir's troops. Sher Ali, with the members of the Russian mission, fled to Turkestan. His son, Yakub Khan, took over the government and signed a peace treaty with Britain. In June 1879, a British mission was received by the new Amir and settled in Kabul. With peace re-established, Britain withdrew her forces to India.

But they did not stay away very long. On 3 September 1879, a mob of mutinous Afghan soldiers stormed the residence of the British mission, massacred the staff and set the buildings on fire. Roberts was again ordered into Afghanistan and again beat down the Afghan forces. On 9 October, he occupied Kabul. Amir Yakub Khan abdicated and was shipped off to India. Roberts was promoted to Lieutenant-General and charged with the government of Afghanistan until a new Amir could be found and installed.

An illusory peace settled over the country.

By then, Lieutenant Baden-Powell had entered the School of Musketry at Hythe in Kent for a course in small arms. A pass certificate would enable him to become musketry instructor to his regiment if he were to return to India, and would bring him an allowance of 100 rupees a month in addition to his regular pay. While he was at it, he decided that he might as well take up military signalling; a certificate would have no financial advantage but might help him in his ambition to get a staff appointment.

In the summer of 1880 the lid again blew off the Afghan kettle.

A number of dissident Afghan chiefs had assembled with their warriors in the mountain areas three hundred miles north-west of Kandahar, Afghanistan's second-largest city. They had placed themselves under the leadership of Ayub Khan, Yakub Khan's younger brother, and had induced him to proclaim a *jahad*, a holy war, against the infidel British invaders. In mid-July, Ayub Khan moved towards the city with his army of mountain tribesmen and fanatical *Ghazis*. The main part of the British force stationed at Kandahar was sent out to check the advance.

The two armies clashed at Maiwand on the morning of 27 July. By four o'clock in the afternoon it was all over. The British force was completely routed by the numerically superior Afghan army. What remained fled back towards Kandahar with many of the men succumbing to thirst and exhaustion along the way. Only the inertia of the Afghans in taking up the pursuit kept those who were left from annihilation. Of the 2,476 engaged at Maiwand on the British side, 934 were killed, 177 missing.

When the news of the *débâcle* reached London, Britain clamoured for quick retribution. Roberts in Kabul immediately set about forming a powerful army to march against Ayub Khan who was now investing Kandahar. On 11 August, Roberts led a force of close to ten thousand men out of the Afghan capital on the trek across mountain ranges, through valleys, over barren desert stretches towards Kandahar. Twenty days later, after a strenuous 313-mile journey that gained world renown, Roberts and his men reached their destination 'in famous health and spirits'. The following day, 1 September, Roberts threw his force against Ayub Khan's army and defeated it completely. The beaten Ayub Khan fled westward with a few of his followers.

At home in Britain, the names of Roberts and Kandahar were on everyone's lips. Queen Victoria combined them in conferring upon the victorious general the title 'Lord Roberts of Kandahar'.

Baden-Powell and his officer friends at Hythe were aflame with excitement about the happenings in distant Afghanistan. All Stephe's disenchantment with life in India had vanished. His whole desire was focused on getting back as quickly as possible. In garrison school in India he had learned Wellington's dictum, 'In Afghanistan, when the military difficulties are over, the real difficulties begin'. Roberts might have saved the day, but there would be plenty of trouble ahead and, sooner or later, the 13th Hussars would be involved.

Stephe went on to pass the Hythe musketry course First Class with 'Extra' certificate. A short while after, to his delight, he received his orders: he was to present himself on board the *Serapis* in Portsmouth Harbour on 3 October for shipment to India.

3

While Baden-Powell's first trip to India had been rather uneventful, his second had its exciting moments.

In the Bay of Biscay, the *Serapis* ran into a 'regular good buster': '... one boat was stove in ... a bit of bulwark broken ... bowsprit shrouds carried away ... the cover of a hawsepipe hole was washed away and the sea poured in so that the troop deck was flooded up to the men's waists . . . the steering wheel "took charge" and half-killed a bluejacket . . . in the saloon, furniture and crockery were smashed . . . and all the time, I and Gordon, the only other fellow who was not sick, were in a continual state of enjoyment.'

The 'state of enjoyment' he had felt evaporated as the ship ploughed through the Red Sea: 'Awfully warm . . . thermometer at 96 degrees at dinner . . . four or five children died . . . several ladies ill . . . worst of all: all the cooks got so ill they had to go to hospital, and now a lot of soldiers do the cooking under a steward.'

When the *Serapis* arrived in Bombay, several days late, B-P learned that his regiment had been ordered to Kandahar and had started from Lucknow that very day. He enquired at the brigade office about his orders and was told to proceed immediately to Lucknow. To his utter disgust he was to remain at the garrison in charge of the quartermaster depot and the sixty men of the 13th Hussars who had been left behind.

He had hardly assumed his task before his orders were changed: he was to secure two chargers and to proceed to Kandahar forthwith. While he was getting himself ready, a new doctor for the regiment turned up and reported to B-P as the only officer present. He was accompanied by a youth who looked about 14. Baden-Powell persuaded the doctor to join him on his journey to overtake the regiment. 'But what will you do with the boy, your son?' he asked.

'My son? That's not my son,' said the doctor, 'that's an officer who has come to join the 13th!'

The youth turned out to be Lieutenant Kenneth McLaren who because of his appearance was fated ever after to be known as 'The Boy'.

Two days later, the small party was *en route* by train, via Lahore and Multan, to the Baluchi town of Sibi, the base of supplies for Afghanistan. A few miles out of Sibi the temporary railway came to an abrupt end at the foot of the mountains. 'No station or anything—we simply got out of the train, saddled our horses and rode away to camp a little way off where ponies were supplied to us.' The next morning the group rode northward. It took them a 'march' of eight days through mountain gorges and over sandy desert to reach Quetta. Here Baden-Powell learned that he had missed his regiment by three days. He picked up a dozen stragglers and continued with his small command towards Kandahar, with the worst part of the journey ahead.

After Quetta, the men had to proceed over the Kojak range between British Baluchistan and Afghanistan with revolvers at the ready. Marauding bands of *Ghazis* had been discovered in the mountains, friendly Afghans had been waylaid and wounded in fights with the fanatics, and reports had it that the regiment, on the way up, had found three men with their hands tied and their throats cut.

Baden-Powell and his group reached Kandahar on 17 December. It was 'a strange place to see' but not as large as he had expected. It was a city of flat-roofed houses and narrow alleyways enclosed by huge grey walls with towers. 'The sandbags are still up on the ramparts and everywhere you see signs of the fighting. The citadel is all covered with shot marks received during the siege of Ayub. There is a rough gallows outside the main gate where they string up Afghans every few days.'

Baden-Powell had been lucky during his formative school years in having for his headmaster William Haig Brown. He was equally lucky during his formative years as a young officer in having for his superior Colonel Baker Creed Russell who had succeeded 'Old' Miller during B-P's absence in England.

Baker Russell had already made a name for himself as a fighting man before taking over command of the 13th Hussars, soon after nicknamed 'The Baker's Dozen'. He had fought in the Indian Mutiny in 1857 and had served under Garnet Wolseley in the Ashanti War of 1873–74 and in South Africa in 1879. He was, according to B-P, 'a character and no mistake! He was a fine figure of a man and a soldier, standing well over six feet, with the piercing eye of a hawk, a big, black moustache, and a stentorian voice like a bull. He was the sort of man you would think twice before trifling with, and you would be right!'

But the trait in his colonel's make-up that had the greatest appeal to Baden-Powell was that Baker Russell was not an 'orthodox' colonel: 'He was in no way guided by the drill book, and knew little and cared less for the prescribed words of command. But he had a soldier's eye for the country and for where his men ought to be in a fight, and he led them there by his own directions rather than by formal formations as laid down in the book.'

Baker Russell had an uncanny ability for bringing out the intelligence and initiative and the self-reliance of his men. He promptly decided that B-P fitted his ideas of what a young British officer should be and gave him all possible opportunity to use and develop his qualities.

Baden-Powell's first important chance, under his new colonel, to prove his skill in one of his specialities arose less than two weeks after his arrival in Afghanistan. A reconnoitring squadron was to be sent to the battlefield of Maiwand to make reports and maps to be used in the court martial convened to determine the responsibility for the *débâcle*. B-P reminded Baker Russell of the 'star' he had received in surveying, and had his application to be sent with the squadron approved.

As far as B-P was concerned, the reconnaissance, with General Wilkinson, Colonel Oliver St John 'and several other swells', turned into an exciting three-day outing. The squadron covered every foot of the battlefield, left by the fleeing British soldiers five months before: 'Any amount of dead horses, lines of cartridge cases, wheel tracks and hoof marks quite clear, dead men in heaps—most had been hurriedly buried, and dug up again by jackals—clothes and accoutrements all over the place.'

Lieutenant Baden-Powell had his own ideas about the *débâcle*. In a letter to George, he placed the main blame for it on the poor musketry of the British soldiers: they had been firing with the sights too high. 'The enemy were within three hundred yards of them and we found bullets two miles off—Martini-Henry bullets—spent ones.' The rest of the blame was quite obviously with the general in command: 'I consider now that he ought to be shot—more or less don't you know—rather more than less tho'!'

B-P prepared nine different maps showing the positions of the various troops in the battle and revealed by the tracks left. One set of his maps was used at the court martial, another was submitted to the Commander-in-Chief of the British Forces in India, Sir Frederick Haines. And Baker Russell used the occasion to boost his young lieutenant by mailing a set to London to his old friend and companion-in-arms, Sir Garnet Wolseley, now Quartermaster-General of the British Army and at the point of assuming responsibility for officer's training.

B-P was thoroughly content with the life he was leading in Afghanistan. 'I enjoy this business awfully, there is always something to do', he wrote home.

One day B-P would be sent out with his troops to make a show of force to frighten certain tribes who were preventing others from sending supplies into Kandahar; another day his troop would ride up into some mountain pass to clear it of bands of robbers waylaying the caravans. Still other days he would be reconnoitring with his troop, bringing back sketch maps and reports, or enjoying a picnic 'as if war were a thing unheard of'.

Many of his nights he spent on vedette, mounted sentry duty. 'At dusk we go out of camp a mile—post vedettes about, and send out patrols every hour all night to examine the neighbourhood. We take tents with us, but keep dressed, with horses saddled, all ready to turn out. At daybreak we patrol a pass five miles off and then come back to camp. . . .' On these expeditions during the Afghan winter it often got so cold at night that instead of putting up the tents the men preferred to roll themselves up in them to keep warm.

The young lieutenant was also given by his colonel the responsibility of 'concocting a programme' of entertainment for the regiment. B-P set out to find the best talent the 13th had to offer. The officers and men he gathered built a stage and put on a concert of songs and sketches.

At the end of the interval in the middle of their first performance, there was a stir at the back of the hall. A visiting general, grey-haired and grey-moustached, entered from the rear of the audience and walked down the aisle calling out in a genially considerate tone, 'Sit down, men, sit down!', which, of course, made them all look round and jump to their feet in salute. Baker Russell offered the general a seat in the front row, but the general would have none of it. 'Oh no,' he told the astonished colonel, 'I have come to help entertain the men.' He mounted the stage and broke into song:

> I am the very model of a modern Major-General.
> I've information vegetable, animal and mineral.
> I know the Kings of England and I quote the fights historical,
> From Marathon to Waterloo, in order categorical. . . .

It was only when the officer was well in the middle of the major-general's song from *The Pirates of Penzance* that the audience realized that he was Baden-Powell and broke into enthusiastic applause. B-P had made certain in advance that Colonel Baker Russell had not yet met the general who was coming to inspect the regiment and had persuaded the general's aide-de-camp to lend him the uniform.

The Saturday night concerts arranged by Baden-Powell became a regular feature in the life of the 13th Hussars. Then he decided to stage the whole opera of *The Pirates of Penzance*. There were no indoor facilities for rehearsing so all rehearsals had to be held outdoors, 'but there was always the danger of fanatical tribesmen rushing down on us at any moment with their nasty great knives. So each performer brought his sword with him to rehearsals, and those weapons we stuck up in the ground to mark the boundaries of our stage, and they were at the same time handy in case of an attack.'

The three performances of *The Pirates* became the main social event in the spring-of-1881 season of the Kandahar garrison.

General Roberts, after his victorious march from Kabul to Kandahar, had been ordered home to be fêted for his great military exploit. Before leaving Afghanistan, he had arranged, with the approval of the home Government, for Abdur Rahman, an older brother of Sher Ali, to take over the Amirship. At the same time Roberts had assured the new ruler that the British Army would be withdrawn as soon as the country had settled down peacefully. When the Amir's troops entered Kabul, the British forces were pulled out of the Afghan capital. Shortly after, the forces in the Khyber Pass left.

The turning over of Kandahar to the new ruler of Afghanistan took place on 15 April 1881 with great ceremony. As the British flag was lowered, a British escort commanded by Lieutenant Baden-Powell fired a salute, whereupon the British forces marched off towards India.

The troops had hardly passed out through the gates of the walled city before B-P remembered something: a coloured print from the *Graphic* of John Everett Millais's *Cherry Ripe* had been left behind in the Kandahar mess. 'I somehow did not want it to fall into the hands of the Afghans, so I rode back and fetched it away with me, and for a long time afterwards it decorated my tent and bungalow. And so, accidentally, I was the last Britisher to leave Kandahar.'

During the return march to India, the regiment was repeatedly troubled by Afghan thieves who sneaked into camp at night and stole horses, arms, and other valuables. One night in the Kojak Pass Baden-Powell resolved to catch one of them. He had noticed a logical spot for a horse thief to enter. 'After mess I went to my tent to get my revolver out—examined it previous to loading it to see if it was properly oiled and if the trigger worked all right—and by jove, it did!'

While in Kandahar, B-P had lent this revolver to his soldier servant as nobody was allowed to go about unarmed. When the soldier returned the gun he had failed to remove the cartridges. As B-P touched the trigger, there was an explosion, and a bullet went in at the top of his left calf, continued down inside the leg and settled in the thin part of the heel.

The result of the accident was that, instead of marching with his men to Quetta, B-P had to ride ignominiously in a covered stretcher carried by a couple of Afghan porters. He was disgusted about his mishap but pleased with the attention he was getting: 'The Colonel has been awfully kind,' he informed his mother, 'and the General sent over a kind message yesterday and our Brigadier-General came himself to see me.' And when the regiment arrived in Quetta, Colonel St John, the chief political commissioner with whom Baden-Powell had reconnoitred the Maiwand battlefield, invited him to stay at his place.

While laid up Baden-Powell kept himself busy. He took Hindustani lessons and polished up his French, wrote articles and drew sketches and sent them off to the *Graphic* whose editor paid him a guinea each for them; he practised new songs and monologues and planned new theatricals for the regiment.

Six weeks after his accident, the doctors finally cut out the bullet. One month later B-P was on horseback again.

Quetta was an unhealthy spot. Many officers and men came down with dysentery and enteric fever; a number of them died ('We are getting to know the "Dead March" just as well as "Stable Call" '). But the regiment was forced to stay on. Another disturbance had broken out in Afghanistan. On the anniversary of the battle of Maiwand, Ayub Khan had reappeared on the scene with a large force, had defeated the Amir's army and had taken Kandahar. But his luck quickly turned. Abdur Rahman's men re-entered the city less than two months after.

The British forces stayed on in Quetta until peace had again descended on Afghanistan, then prepared to move south. On 3 November B-P could note that 'the long-prayed-for moment had arrived and I heard "Boots and Saddles" sound for marching out of Quetta and I stood by the trumpeter while he sounded, and drank it all in.'

The 13th Hussars marched over the Bolan Pass to Sibi where they embarked for the four-day train journey to Jullundur. From here the regiment marched the nearly four hundred miles to its new headquarters at Muttra.

By Christmas, Baden-Powell and his friend, 'The Boy' McLaren, had established themselves comfortably in Muttra in a nine-room bungalow with a good stable and a large garden, quickly dubbed 'Bloater Park' ('as "Bloater" is what "The Boy" calls me').

4

The three years that Baden-Powell spent in Muttra were happy ones. He liked his command, his work and his colonel. He became adjutant to Baker Russell and was promoted to captain at the age of 26.

The work kept him jumping. Over and above his office duties, he was musketry instructor, riding master, director of the regimental theatre and manager of the band. As if this were not enough, he took on a class of non-commissioned officers for instruction in reconnaissance and scouting.

His interest in horses was shared by his friend McLaren and by two other officer comrades, Lieutenant 'Ding' MacDougall and Captain 'Pa' Braithwaite. The four made an almost unbeatable polo team that carried honours back to the 13th Hussars from the inter-regimental matches in Meerut and Agra.

But there was yet another activity involving horses from which Baden-Powell received an even greater joy and fulfilment than he got from polo: it was the hazardous sport of pigsticking.

To the uninitiated, this might seem a rather tame occupation. The pig involved, however, is not an ordinary pig but the wild Indian boar—a born fighter, the only animal reported to have the courage to share a water-hole with a tiger. The 'sticking' consists in running down the pig on horseback and felling him with a six-foot lance.

Muttra had excellent territory for pigsticking. The flat, low-lying ground along the River Jumna abounded in dense growths of reeds and cane, tall tiger grass and tamarisk bushes—perfect cover for wild boar.

Baden-Powell had his first try at the rough sport of pigsticking early in January 1882. Pigsticking soon occupied every Saturday he could manage to get away from his regimental work. It so completely engrossed him that the next year he did not even take the usual annual leave to the hills in the hot weather. He simply could not tear himself away from what he considered the 'sport of rajahs'.

In 1883, Baden-Powell entered three horses in the competition for the top prize in pigsticking, the famed Kadir Cup (named for the *kadir* or river-bed country where it was run) put up by the Meerut Tent Club, the leading pigsticking club in India. He went off to Meerut and proved his mastery of the sport by riding two of his horses—Hagarene and Patience— through to the final heat. Fortunately, the rules of the meet were such that B-P could ride one of his horses himself and could run his second by 'putting up a weight not less than his own'.

B-P mounted Hagarene; his friend 'Ding' MacDougall, Patience. With two other finalists, they lined up, ready for the starting signal.

> Such excitement! [B-P wrote to the family] Twenty elephants with onlookers, fellows up in trees, others riding with us to see the fun.
>
> Away goes a great pig. 'Ride!'—and away we go. Hagarene soon gets away from the rest—the pig dashes into thick grass jungle—but I am pretty close to him and can just see him every now and then. Great tussocks of grass six feet high. Haggy bounding through them —then twenty yards of open ground, then into a fresh patch of jungle thicker than the others. Suddenly a bright green sort of hedge appears in front. As the pig disappears through it, Haggy leaps it and there, eight feet below it, is a placid pond—the pig goes plump under the water and Haggy and self ditto almost on top of him— right down we go to any depth—a deal of struggling—striking out —hanging on to weeds, etc. And I emerge on the far bank—and see

Haggy climbing out too—and away she goes for camp—and the pig I can see skulking away in some weeds. Up come the other three men and look over the hedge at me. I point out the pig and away they go and MacDougall gets first to him and so wins the cup for me!

And a funny object I look when all the fellows come up to congratulate me—covered with mud and garlanded with weeds.

In India, Baden-Powell threw himself energetically into the dangerous sport of pigsticking—wild-boar hunting on horseback.

5

Baden-Powell was already well known in officer circles throughout northern India as an actor and entertainer. Now, with the winning of the Kadir Cup, his repute was further established.

But this did not satisfy B-P. Whatever 'fame' he had gained was of the fleeting kind as compared to what his older brothers had achieved. All of them were doing well in their chosen professions and were making their marks in public life. Three of them had broken into print. Baden Henry, the Lahore judge, had had five books published on Indian affairs, the first when he was 27. Warington had a book out on canoe travelling written when he was only 24. George had three books to his credit, the first published after his tour of Australia when he was 25. Frank was making a name for himself as a marine painter. Even Baden was beginning to be noticed for his experiments with man-carrying kites and his interest in military ballooning.

B-P felt himself falling behind his brothers in the keen competition within the family. He had had a number of drawings and short articles published by the *Graphic*. Something more impressive needed to be accomplished. He wrote to George for advice. George encouraged his younger brother to get the lectures on reconnaissance he had given his men into shape for publication. He also suggested that some English journals might be interested in an article on pigsticking.

The timing was excellent for a book on reconnaissance. A new general order had just been issued directing garrison instructors 'to give lectures in reconnaissance to the N.C.O.s and men of regiments in or near their stations'. Since in many regiments, in B-P's estimation, 'the officers appear unable to do so themselves to the required extent', a book of lectures 'ready to their hands' seemed bound to become popular. But the sales and possible profits from the book were the least of his considerations: 'Even if it did not sell more than twenty copies it would be a grand advertisement for me—because I could send copies to all the boss quartermaster-generals, Wolseleys, etc., asking if they approve of it. . . .'

Baden-Powell immediately set about revising and rewriting his reconnaissance lectures.

> If you think the book can be published [he wrote to George], I'll hatch out some more. I've got a lot of powder boxes, which I call my 'incubators'—I chuck into them anything that turns up from day to day on their particular subject. . . .
>
> Your scrap of paper suggesting an article on pigsticking started a new incubator which is now half full of information. I have the framework of three articles and the main idea for a book on the subject. . . .

George had no problem finding a publisher for his brother's first book effort. It was accepted by William Clowes & Sons, Limited, and published (in 1884) under the title of *Reconnaissance and Scouting* as a neat booklet, bound in red cloth, with a dozen map sketches prepared by the author.

But there were still other ways of getting to be better known.

Baden-Powell began 'grouping events', as the family called its system for 'getting on', for making one thing lead to two others—such as drawing a series of sketches of pigsticking and sending them to the art exhibition in Simla where they would be seen by the 'right' people; such as buying horses, breaking them in, getting the Baden-Powell name into the papers because of the quality of the stable; such as sending for new songs and monologues from home and performing them at regimental concerts.

Chance came to B-P's assistance in 'grouping events' to his advantage, far beyond his expectations.

In the autumn of 1883 the third son of Queen Victoria, Prince Arthur, Duke of Connaught, was appointed Divisional General at Meerut. The 32-year-old Duke brought out to India with him his young Duchess, the former Princess Louise Margaret of Prussia. They were accompanied by Lord Downe, the Duke's aide-de-camp, and Lady Downe.

The regiments under the Duke's command left their stations for Meerut for divisional parades and manoeuvres. Colonel Baker Russell was put in charge of a brigade of cavalry and made Baden-Powell his temporary brigade major.

The divisional parade was highly commended by His Royal Highness. So was the field day a few days later during which Baker Russell took occasion to inform the Duke that the maps used had been prepared, after thorough reconnaissance in the field, by his adjutant, Captain Baden-Powell. And afterwards, when the Duke dined with the 13th Hussars, B-P had further occasion to be pleased when 'his' string band played at dinner and 'his' glee club sang afterwards and his Kadir Cup was brought out for the Duke's inspection.

'Events' continued 'grouping' without any effort on Baden-Powell's part.

The 13th Hussars had hardly started the return march to Muttra when B-P was recalled to Meerut. The Gaiety Company of actors had lost a player through illness and needed his services for a performance 'under the Distinguished Patronage of Their Royal Highnesses The Duke and Duchess of Connaught'. B-P was at his very best in his old roles as Slimmer in *Whitebait at Greenwich* and Cox in *Cox and Box*.

He returned to Muttra on 15 February just in time to learn that His Royal Highness had decided to inspect the 13th Hussars the following week and had expressed a desire to test his riding skill at pigsticking. And what could be more appropriate than for the most recent winner of the Kadir Cup to introduce the Duke to the sport?

Baden-Powell had a thrilling twenty-seventh birthday on 22 February 1884, the day that he, McLaren and 'Tommy' Dimond took the Duke of Connaught pigsticking, with the Duchess watching from the back of an elephant.

We had one splendid run [B-P reported] after a young and speedy boar, who led us a tremendous dance at a great pace through rather tricky country full of clumps of thorn bushes, which were continually

delaying us at the critical moment, so that the boar kept getting a
fresh start every time we were gaining ground on him. Eventually,
feeling himself done, he turned in a ravine and stood at bay. The
Duke was the first to come up with him . . . and delivered a thrust
which secured him the honours of 'first spear'; the others on the
field then closed in and gave the boar his quietus.

The next month Baden-Powell returned to Meerut for a month's proba-
tionary training in the adjutant-general's office 'so that the general can
report whether he considers me likely to make a good staff officer.'
   Lady Downe took the young captain under her wing and insisted that
he join the Downe household. The result was that Baden-Powell was
seeing the Duke every day and had dinner regularly with the royal couple.
B-P reached the pinnacle of his association with the Duke of Connaught
when he was assigned to the Duke's office to take over Lord Downe's
work for a few days while the aide-de-camp was away.

The arrival of Their Royal Highnesses had set Meerut society whirling.
Every day had its social event in honour of the Duke and Duchess. Baden-
Powell found himself pulled into a great number of them and managed
to combine them with his busy office schedule.
   Up to this time, there had been little occasion for the young B-P to
have much to do with members of the opposite sex. At Meerut, the
situation was different. The British colony contained a large number of
unattached young ladies eager to make the acquaintance of young officers
—particularly when they were as well known as Captain Baden-Powell
of the 13th Hussars and were socially acceptable to the Duke of Connaught.
   Now, at almost daily social events—tennis, picnics, dinners—the young
captain was thrown into close contact with female companions. He
enjoyed being with them, but had no intention of getting serious about
any of them, not even when, as happened, one of them proposed to him.
'I had a quiet talk with her,' he informed his mother, 'and gave her some
advice, and I made her smile on a chap who loves her better than I do
so it is all right; but she is very pretty and awfully lively.'
   He had his own cynical philosophy on how to deal with young ladies
and impressed it on his brothers at home: 'As soon as you get to know
them tell them that you are not going to ask them to marry—you're simply
there as a friend and will help them in any way you can. That's what I
do and the matter being thus defined the girl confides in you and you have
much better fun.'
   A *billet-doux* he received from a young lady ('Unmarried!! Beautiful
voice!') he sent to his sister with the note, 'What do you think of this from

a young lady? I had told her I would take her for a ride on an elephant to see a big native fair—only she must be prepared for jeers from the Artillery mess as we went by and also she must get Mrs A. to chaperone me. I warned her that if she attempted to make love to me I should immediately get off the elephant and walk home with Mrs A.'

But so that his mother might not become concerned about the attention he was getting, he did his best to allay her fears: 'All right, Ma, don't feel nervous. I accept it all with the grace for which I am so renowned and behind my sleeve I grin the grin which only I can grin. . . .' And as a final clincher: 'I'm going to wait until I'm a major and then it will be a £50,000 girl at home.'

6

After thirty-three months of regimental work without a break and with the pigsticking season at an end and the heat of summer approaching, Baden-Powell requested and got the three months' leave to which he was entitled. He packed up his camping outfit and his 'incubator' and went forth, determined to find some spot in the foothills of the Great Himalayas to write his projected book on pigsticking.

He found the place forty miles north of Simla at an altitude of 9,400 feet with a view that was 'one of the most beautiful that can be got anywhere.' He settled down in a small bungalow and was soon deep in work. 'But—pigsticking—my wig—I didn't know there was so much in it to write about. I can go on by the hour.' By the time his leave was up he had written two of the five parts he had planned and had outlined the rest in detail.

He did not find time to finish his book when he got back to Muttra. The regiment had received orders to embark early in November at Bombay for England. The 13th Hussars were leaving India after ten years' service there.

Baden-Powell had his hands full during the remaining days at Muttra, not only with extra office work but with the disposing of his stable of horses at a fair profit, shipping off his souvenirs of India to 8 St George's Place, and packing his personal effects.

I am beginning to feel quite sorry to leave this place [he wrote home]. I have just got together a perfect set of horses and what is harder, of grooms—and pigsticking is such grand sport. . . . I shall be glad of a spell in England—though I shan't be the millionaire there that I am here. It will be quite strange being reduced to two or three horses after having seven or eight—but then, of course, they are not so useful or necessary as they are here.

The long train journey across half of India to Bombay proved a tedious ordeal. The regiment travelled by night to interfere as little as possible with the ordinary traffic, and the men were detrained into rest camps by day.

The leisurely jogging of the train got the better of Baden-Powell. The thought struck him that although he was the godson of the son of the man who had invented the first practical locomotive, he did not know how to drive one. 'No opportunity like the present,' he decided, 'so I got on terms with the driver and took my place on the footplate, and was very soon, in my own estimation, quite a capable driver.'

It was only later that B-P was told what his explosive colonel had said when he woke up in the middle of the night and realized 'that the train had suddenly exchanged her demure progress for a new life, and was rocking and tearing along at seventy miles an hour!'

V

Service in Africa

1

ON 13 November 1884, the ship carrying the 13th Hussars, again the *Serapis*, steamed out of Bombay.

But not for England!

Just before sailing time, orders reached the regiment to land at Durban in Natal. There was trouble with the Boers of South Africa.

This was not the first time a problem had arisen between the British and the Boers.

The Boers (from the Dutch word for farmer) were the descendants of the Dutch settlers who had first landed in Table Bay in 1652. These early colonists ruled Dutch South Africa until 1797 when Governor Sluysken was forced to hand over the country to the British Major-General Craig who had arrived with eight ships and four thousand men 'to protect the colony against an invasion of the French'. When Great Britain made peace with Napoleon in 1802, the Cape Colony was returned to Dutch rule. But only for a short interlude. Britain and France were again at war in 1805 and a British force again took over the South African colony. The development of Britain's possessions in India had turned the Cape into an important military station too valuable to be relinquished.

During the years that followed, the British Government introduced a number of reforms that displeased the Boers: English was decreed the official language, law courts and local governments were reorganized, slavery was abolished. When finally some of the land settled by the Boers was ordered to be restored to the Kaffirs from whom it had been taken, the Boers had had enough. In 1836 a large number of Dutch *Voortrekkers* (pioneers) set out northward on the 'Great Trek' in long wagon trains drawn by innumerable oxen. Most of them settled in the area about the

River Vaal. Only a few crossed the Drakensberg Mountains into the east coast area of Natal.

When more and still more Dutch Boers had moved up from the south, Britain agreed to grant independence to the two States established by the settlers: the Transvaal north of the River Vaal (1852) and the Orange Free State south of the Vaal (1854). Natal, on the other hand, was made a British colony (1856).

The Boers soon found themselves in deep trouble. They had hoped to lead a peaceful life on their new land but their hope was of short duration. They had fled from 'British tyranny' only to run into the savagery of the fierce Matabele to the north, the Basutos to the south and the Zulus to the south-east. In numerous raids, naked African warriors massacred hundreds of Boers with spears and clubs and were, in turn, massacred by the thousands by skilfully used Dutch rifles.

But the Boers' main troubles were self-created. Unwilling to be governed by Britons, they were equally unwilling to be ruled by their own people. Rivalries arose among various Boer factions. Political and religious cleavages developed. Payment of taxes failed, public revenues dropped, paper money fell to a fraction of its supposed value, bankruptcy was imminent.

Things had come to such a pass after twenty-five years of Boer self-rule that the British Government felt called upon to step into the situation. Lord Carnarvon, Secretary of State for the Colonies, sent Theophilus Shepstone, an expert on South African affairs, to Pretoria, the Transvaal capital, to straighten things out. If this seemed impossible, Shepstone was authorized to declare the Transvaal annexed by the British Government.

After conferring with the Transvaal President and *Volksraad* (parliament), Shepstone decided that the situation was beyond repair. On 12 April 1877, he issued a proclamation declaring the country annexed by Great Britain. On Her Britannic Majesty's fifty-eighth birthday, 24 May 1877, the Union Jack was hoisted at Pretoria.

By annexing the Transvaal Great Britain assumed all the country's problems and added yet another to the burdens she had chosen to bear: the resentment of the Boers on being deprived of their independence and right of self-determination.

One of the first problems that Britain needed to solve was that of securing the south-eastern border of the Transvaal against the Zulus. This required disarming the Zulu army and deposing Cetywayo, the bellicose Zulu chieftain. On 12 January 1877, the first of many British columns crossed the River Buffalo from Natal and entered Zululand. Ten days later, the column was overrun by a savage horde of some twenty thousand screaming Zulus. In a few hours of ferocious hand-to-hand fighting eight hundred British soldiers and almost five hundred native troops were slaughtered—only six escaped. The Zulu losses were equally staggering —close to three thousand of them lay scattered over the battlefield, killed by British bullets and bayonets.

After three disastrous months of fighting with heavy casualties on both sides, the Natal command, reinforced with troops from England, turned the tide and pushed the Zulus back. The Zululand invasion took on the aspects of a major campaign with more than twenty thousand British troops in the field. In a decisive battle at Ulundi on 4 July the Zulus were routed and Cetywayo deposed.

Pax Britannica had come to Zululand and to the Transvaal border, but not to the Transvaal itself.

During the next three years more and more Boer voices spoke up against British domination, more and more Boer patriots demanded restoration of their independence. Their hopes rose when Disraeli's Government fell and Gladstone took over the reins—the new Prime Minister in his campaigning had criticized severely the annexation of the Transvaal and the Government's determination 'to transform republicans into subjects of a monarchy'. But the Boers' hopes were dispelled after the election. After once having assumed power, Gladstone's tune had changed. It was now his view 'that the Queen cannot be advised to relinquish her sovereignty over the Transvaal'. The Boers rose in armed revolt, proclaimed the Transvaal once more an independent republic (16 December 1880) and beleaguered detachments of British troops within its borders.

In quick succession, the British troops suffered defeat upon defeat. Part of a detachment marching to the relief of Pretoria was slain, the rest captured. A force of a thousand under the command of General George Pomeroy Colley, Governor of Natal, attempting to enter the Transvaal over the Drakensberg Mountains, was repulsed with heavy losses at Laing's Nek. And when Colley returned to the attack and occupied Majuba Hill, the hill was stormed by the Boers. The British force was routed with severe casualties and Colley himself was killed. Colley's successor entered into negotiation with the Boer Commandant, Piet J. Joubert. On 3 August 1881, the Convention of Pretoria was signed granting the Transvaalers 'complete self-government, subject to the suzerainty of Her Majesty'.

But this was not the end. Some of the Boer leaders began to suffer from 'expansion fever'. Before long, parties of *Vrijbuiters* straggled across their own borders into surrounding British territories. The incursions of the Boer freebooters into Bechuanaland and their attempts to carve up lands of the Barolong tribe around Mafeking became so persistent that the British Government decided to stop them by a show of force. General Sir Charles Warren was sent into Bechuanaland with an army of four thousand men to cover the eastern border towards Transvaal. Other British troops were ordered to Natal in readiness to march into Transvaal from the south if the need should arise.

On 29 November the 13th Hussars, newly arrived from India, joined some of these other regiments in camp at Pinetown, a scattering of a few cottages an hour's railway journey from Durban.

2

Baden-Powell, young and eager for advancement, had looked forward to actual fighting in South Africa. Instead he found himself caught in a daily round of office work, lecturing and drill. Only the expectation of impending action against the Boers buoyed him up.

But the action was not forthcoming. Sir Charles Warren's Bechuanaland expedition had bogged down in tedious negotiations with the Boer representatives.

As week upon weary week passed by with regimental routine and no prospect of fighting, B-P longed to join his younger brother for active service in Egypt where Baden, an officer in the Camel Corps, was involved in the war against the Mahdi, the religious fanatic Mohammed Ahmed, and his Arab tribesmen. But there was no way for B-P to get to Egypt. He had to curb his impatience and console himself with the tasks immediately before him. 'It's no good wishing,' he wrote home, 'the only thing is to try and work it somehow—but how, I don't know as the apes seem to think we are on service here!'

To pass the time, B-P occupied himself when off duty with writing and sketching. He kept working tenaciously on his pigsticking book until he reached the point where he needed the help of the reference books in the Reading Room of the British Museum at home to continue, then swung into another writing project.

The mild success of his *Reconnaissance and Scouting* spurred him to pursue the same general line of military writing. A second book was almost writing itself. All he had to do to produce it was to expand his notes for the cavalry training he was giving the men of his regiment and turn them into chapters for 'A manual for the use of Officers conducting a course of military Instruction in accordance with General Order No. 30 of 1884.'

By following the routine he had established for himself in India, of getting up early in the morning and doing most of his work before breakfast, he completed the manuscript in three months. He mailed it off to

England hoping that a publisher would accept it but instructing the family that 'if no publisher cares to publish it please have it printed—because I am certain it will sell, particularly if brought out as soon as possible'.

He had no cause for concern: his manuscript was accepted by the firm of Harrison & Sons and rushed into print in the form of a pocket-size manual of 280 pages entitled *Cavalry Instruction.*

'All work and no play. . . .' But the kind of 'play' B-P hankered for was not readily achieved around Pinetown, Natal. First of all, there was no pigsticking. There were no pigs. There was no polo. The fields were 'too hilly and broken'. And there were no paper chases. The ground was 'too mined by ant-eaters'. Furthermore, 'being in an unsettled state as to when we may be ordered home none of us has more than two horses or ponies at the outside'.

He and some of his officer comrades did contrive to have one bit of exciting sport. One day in the officers' mess they were discussing a newspaper report of a riding feat of a hundred miles in ten hours performed by a group of Austrian cavalry officers. They made up their minds to find out what British officers could do. If Austrians could do it in ten hours Britons should be able to do it in less. Seven of them, including B-P, McLaren and Dimond, started out one morning on a hundred-mile ride. They covered the fifty-six miles from Durban west to Pietermaritzburg in 4 hours 28 minutes, rested for two hours and rode the remaining distance of forty-four miles on their return journey in 4 hours 10 minutes. 'At the end of it we felt quite ready to go on for another hundred miles,' B-P boasted proudly afterwards. 'So that ride of the Austrian cavalry officers was nothing very wonderful.'

Another bit of excitement followed shortly after for Baden-Powell alone.

From the day the regiment arrived in South Africa, Colonel Baker Russell had been concerned over the incomplete information that was available on the mountain passes leading from Natal into the Transvaal and the Orange Free State. He had full intelligence about the two main passes that were firmly held by the Boers but needed to know of other passes that could be used if he were required to move to the attack. He decided to give Baden-Powell a mission that would produce the needed information and at the same time would keep his restless captain occupied for a while. He ordered B-P on a solitary reconnaissance into the Drakensberg Mountains, emphasizing the necessity of absolute secrecy.

This was an assignment to Baden-Powell's liking. Now at last he would get some of the action he craved. He grew a straggly beard, put on worn civilian clothing and disappeared into the mountains with two horses, one for riding, the other for carrying his blankets and rations.

For three weeks, from 31 March to 21 April 1885, he traversed the mountains, averaging thirty-three miles a day and keeping himself going on simple army rations. Some of the nights *en route* he unrolled his blankets and slept under the open sky. At other times he stopped at a farm for the night and used as his excuse for travelling about in this fashion that he was a newspaper correspondent seeking information 'with a view to recommending the country for immigration'. He met a number of Boer farmers on his journey and got on friendly terms with them. Even the usually taciturn Boers opened up to him. B-P developed a great admiration for the average Boer but found it difficult to get close to him. 'There was a certain dignity about him which would resent any familiarity.'

While surveying and sketching the territory, B-P discovered that the maps he had brought with him were inaccurate in many respects. He made the necessary corrections as he went along, concentrating on those that were of value from a military point of view. He also studied the area from a tactical angle, and came to the conclusion, among other things, that 'in the event of our column from Natal being driven back in its effort to advance northward, it should fall south of the Tugela, and not attempt to hold Ladysmith'—advice not heeded by British forces fourteen years later, with calamitous results.

Baden-Powell came back to his regiment well pleased with his accomplishment and in perfect health after his 600-mile ride. He wrote out his field notes into a complete report, turned his rough sketches into finished maps and delivered them to his colonel on 5 May after sitting up the last night drawing the final map by candlelight.

By then the difficulties in Bechuanaland had been reconciled without the firing of a single shot. Sir Charles Warren, with Baden-Powell's brother George as his political adviser, had reached an agreement with President Paul Kruger of the Transvaal. The border question had been settled, the British Government had formally proclaimed Bechuanaland a British protectorate, and a military government had been established to run it.

3

When rumours began to circulate that the 13th Hussars would soon be returned to England, Baden-Powell became determined to satisfy one of his ambitions: he wanted a taste of big-game hunting before leaving Africa, perhaps never to return. He obtained a leave at the time when the South African big-game hunter, Reuben Beningfield, was getting ready to leave on a two-months' safari into Portuguese East Africa. B-P signed up with the experienced Beningfield. So did four of his officer friends.

The six proceeded northward by boat from Durban on 10 July, and disembarked at Inhambane, an old slave port on the east coast of Africa. They spent the first few days getting their safari organized ('Our party consists of 6 English, 95 carriers, 7 servants, 2 hunters, 2 cooks, and 30 escort—total 142'), then travelled inland for three days to their base of operation, a Kaffir kraal standing 'inside the bush on the edge of a wide grass plain dotted with dwarf palms'. The following days the hunters went out in pairs to shoot. They found numerous tracks of wildebeest and koodoo, of impala and sable antelope, but saw surprisingly little game beyond a few reedbuck.

One morning Baden-Powell went off to a lake near the kraal. By nightfall he had earned a new name for himself.

He had previously seen spoor of hippo along the muddy shore. This morning he found half a dozen hippo submerged in the lake. At about two-minute intervals, the six little black dots representing each hippo—nostrils, eyes, ears—appeared above the surface long enough for the animal to take a full breath. Then they sank out of sight, to break the surface again a couple of minutes later.

Baden-Powell focused his attention on one set of black dots. To get his hippo he would have to hit him in the eye—anywhere else a bullet would simply glance off the tough hide.

> I did not dare to risk a shot from the shoulder when he bobbed up—it would be too hurried for accuracy. So I lay down on my back as the steadiest position for shooting.... When the hippo put up his head I took careful aim, in the two short seconds available, at his eye—but I didn't fire. I kept that aim steadily on the spot where his eye had been and when he came up again I made sure that it was directed straight on his eye—but again I didn't fire. The instant he appeared for the third time I pressed the trigger.... The hippo sank below the surface.

Had he hit it? He wouldn't know for several hours. A hippo when killed usually sinks to the bottom, then later floats to the top, buoyed up by the gases forming in the body.

That evening an excited runner sprinted into the kraal to tell the party that B-P's hippo had risen to the surface. As Baden-Powell arrived at the lake he was cheered by the safari's Kaffir carriers already busily flenching the carcass. They greeted him by the name they had given him: *M'hlalapanzi*—literally 'The-man-who-lies-down-to-shoot', but also, metaphorically, 'the man who lays his plans carefully before shooting them into practice'.

During the rest of their safari the hunters roamed farther and farther afield from their 'standing camp' on two- or three-day excursions. The results were disappointing. Outside of a dozen reedbuck, their bag came to just one impala, one steinbok and a few brace of pheasant for the pot. Only once were they within sight of a lion and then at too great a distance to overtake it.

His technique in hippopotamus hunting earned Baden-Powell the nickname of M'hlalapanzi—'*the man who lies down to shoot*'.

As far as sport was concerned, the expedition had been a failure. But it had had a profound influence on Baden-Powell. It had turned him into an ardent devotee of the rough and ready 'flannel-shirt life' of the African veld. It had given him a greater confidence in his ability to take care of himself in the outdoors. But also, the experience had started him off on a new writing habit: of interspersing his diary entries with occasional 'how-to' asides on various aspects of outdoor living that might come in handy some day—who knows?—for use in some kind of 'instruction book'.

The expected orders finally arrived for the 13th Hussars to proceed to England.

By 5 November 1885 the regiment was quartered at Norwich, the county town of Norfolk.

6

On Both Sides of the Channel

Years: 1886–87   Age: 29–30

1

BADEN-POWELL had been adjutant to his regiment for four years. While the adjutancy had had a certain attraction under Baker Russell in India and Natal, back in England under a new colonel he found it of little appeal. He had always liked to work with men, to guide them and stimulate them and to be himself stimulated. He wished to get back again to dealing directly with men and sent in his request to be permitted to resign his adjutancy. His request was granted and he was given command of a detachment of the 13th Hussars at Colchester in Essex.

B-P threw his efforts into creating a crack troop and took on a great deal of the men's training himself. For drilling he invented a way of using hand signals instead of shouted commands. He knew from experience in Afghanistan the importance of being able to move troops forward silently in the proximity of the enemy.

When the commanding general, Sir Evelyn Wood, came to inspect the 13th Hussars he requested a demonstration of Baden-Powell's silent system. It turned out to be a cold, clammy day with a thick fog, with just enough visibility for Baden-Powell's men to see their captain. They reacted quickly and efficiently to his signals.

> Then I drew the General's attention to the noise being made by the regiment in the distance, where the officers were shouting their words of command, which told one exactly what the regiment was doing, what direction it was moving in, and in what formation. . . . Sir Evelyn, in spite of his deafness, did not fail to hear the noise made by the regiment, and galloping forward with me he made me lead my squadron on and catch the regiment in the flank from an unexpected quarter, by silently working round it. The manoeuvre came off quite successfully. . . .

2

The invention of smokeless powder in 1884 had created a complete revolution in the design of firearms. No longer were weapon makers at the mercy of the uncontrollable whim of black powder in its multitudinous mixtures and its varying ingredients. The new propellant burned at an even, controllable rate, and the recoil could be put to use. Instead of hand-cranked machine-guns it was now possible to produce guns that reloaded automatically. The world's weapon manufacturers took up the challenge of designing the most effective new weapons based on the latest firearms principles.

Baden-Powell's innate curiosity did not permit him to sit back and wait for the day the new arms would be issued to his detachment. He wanted to know what was happening every step of the way. He got himself invited to visit Sir W. Armstrong's works where he saw all the processes in the manufacture of machine-guns. He studied the latest reports of experiments in England and on the other side of the Channel. But this was not enough for him. He had to know from personal investigation.

The German Army had boasted of a new machine-gun, had announced its calibre and had even made pictures of it available to the press of Europe. But nothing was known about the speed of firing and the efficiency of this new gun. Other items of military importance were being developed on the Continent. Germany and Russia were both experimenting with new types of military balloons, and the Russian Army was testing a new kind of searchlight that was reported capable of lighting up a whole battlefield.

Baden-Powell resolved to spend his 1886 leave on the Continent and to take part, uninvited and unofficially, in the autumn manoeuvres of the Russian Army. He was well aware of the risks involved. If caught, he might be taken for a foreign spy and might, if lucky, get off with a few years' imprisonment. But the risks added extra attraction to the project. He fancied the idea of matching his cunning against the wits of some unknown adversary in the exhilarating game of spying. He inveigled his younger brother into going with him. Baden had become an officer in the Scots Guards and had been dubbed the 'balloonatic' within the family for his interest in balloons.

The morning after the two brothers arrived in Berlin, in August 1886, Baden got wind of where the balloon experiments were to take place and went out to have a look. B-P went to the military camp at Spandau. He quickly located the rifle range but couldn't get near enough to suit him. The range was surrounded by a belt of trees and wooden boarding that was guarded by pacing sentries.

As the firing started on the range, Baden-Powell worked out a strategy. He lay down on the grass and pretended to fall asleep. But he was listening and counting and glancing at his watch. He soon knew the rate of fire at which the machine-guns were working and calculated their accuracy from the pings against the iron targets when the bullets hit the mark.

But besides hearing, B-P wanted to see. He had noticed a slight break in the boarding. Now he used the opportunity, while the sentry's back was turned, to saunter casually up to it and peer through it. By a fluke, the sentry turned before he reached the end of his beat. He saw a stranger apparently disobeying the regulations against approaching the area and came up quickly, 'looking uncomfortably firm'.

B-P was prepared. He did a slow twist, turned his back to the approaching sentry, pulled a small bottle of brandy out of his pocket and sprinkled half of it over his clothes 'to give the right atmosphere'. By the time the German sentry reached his intended victim, he was confronted by a staggering 'drunk' reeking of brandy and insisting on sharing the bottle with him. The soldier took the 'drunk' by the arm, gently pushed him off and advised him to disappear—which Baden-Powell did forthwith.

The Russian army manoeuvres took place outside the capital, at Krasnoe Selo. The brothers put up at an inn not far from the railway station and for the next few days went on long walking tours, shadowing troops and watching them at work.

But they had come to see searchlights and balloons—not just marching soldiers. For this they needed to get into the area where the experiments were being made. There was a ring of notice boards round this area stating that nobody was allowed within this circle of notices. So the brothers 'argued that if once we were inside, any sentry or detective would suppose we had leave to be there. We tried the idea, and it worked splendidly.' They walked in as if with a set purpose and knowing their way perfectly. They saluted anybody whom everybody saluted and strolled past sentries without a question being asked them. They studied the gondola of a *ballon captif* while the guards were away having dinner. They stayed far into the evening to watch the searchlights and found them far less effective than they had anticipated.

Their Russian adventure almost ended in grief for B-P.

On the last night of the manoeuvres, Czar Alexander III himself was to be present. Baden-Powell had arranged with Baden to observe the scheduled 'attack' on Fort Nikolina from the outside while he went inside to watch the 'defence'. When he entered he found the place teeming with extra large numbers of staff officers and police and thought it wiser to clear out—which he did. As he walked back along the road in the dark he was suddenly caught in the beam of lights of the first carriage of the Czar's entourage. Involuntarily, instead of coming to attention, he turned his head to avoid being recognized. The officers in the carriage got suspicious, seized him and pulled him inside and drove on without checking the progress of the rest of the carriages.

At Fort Nikolina, B-P was questioned about his identity and the reasons for his presence. He explained that he was an Englishman, that he had lost his way to the station and would appreciate being directed to it. Instead he was taken to St Petersburg in 'open arrest': he was permitted to live in an hotel under surveillance but was not allowed to leave town until further notice.

Baden-Powell managed to get hold of his brother. Together they decided on a bold stratagem for getting away: 'We found out when the steamer sailed [for Copenhagen] and then gave out in the hearing of the hotel detective that we were going by the 10.50 train—and off we went to Kronstadt and nipped on board [the *William Bailey*] and got passed out by the police officer there. . . .'

3

The Baden-Powell brothers had hardly returned home from their 'spying' adventure before another incident set B-P dreaming of being off again.

All Europe was agog over the 'war crisis' that had suddenly burst upon an unsuspecting world. It was a purely manufactured 'crisis' invented by Germany's Chancellor to outwit the German *Reichstag*. To get his army bill approved Bismarck raised a general cry of having secret knowledge that France was preparing for *revanche* (revenge) for its 1870–71 defeat; that the French Minister of War, General Georges Boulanger, was getting the armed forces of France ready for quick mobilization.

The Continent awaited further developments with increasing trepidation.

B-P had his own ideas about the situation. He doubted that war was imminent yet decided to get himself in readiness in case the unforeseen should happen. He thought that only Germany and France would be involved in a shooting war, that Great Britain would remain aloof. But the British populace would want to know what was going on; the British papers would need a number of alert and daring reporters and he would be one of them. But to be among the chosen it was imperative for him to be familiar with the areas where the battles would be fought.

He arranged for a three weeks' leave in January 1887. His timing was perfect. Just before his departure for the Continent, Bismarck made another inflammatory speech, the German *Reichstag* was dissolved, and the call went out for the election of a new and more willing one to defend the 'threatened' *Vaterland*.

B-P's trip this time would not be a 'spying' expedition but rather a reconnaissance in depth. Since there was no outstanding quarrel at the time between Great Britain on the one side and France or Germany on the other he decided that the simpler way of proceeding would be better. He would be on his own some of the time and for the rest would act the part of a British officer paying a courtesy visit on his German and French colleagues.

He stopped first at Antwerp and walked round the fortifications. He criss-crossed the Waterloo battlefield from one end to the other on foot. He took a fifteen-mile walk over the battlefield of Colombey ('Waterloo ridiculously small field compared with this') and spent the whole day tramping through the snow in a fresh breeze over the grounds of St Privat and the Gravelotte defile.

In Metz he made his first contact with a German officer, Prince Waldeck, and was taken on a tour of the Plappville barracks ('Saw drills going on. Noticed sentry-boxes have electric bells to guardroom'). Then still more battlefields: Stiringen, Saarbrucken, Wörth. And still more contacts with German officers at Strasbourg where he was treated like a long-lost brother by the chief of staff of the Uhlan regiment stationed there.

After Alsace-Lorraine, Baden-Powell went into France and was well received by the French commander at Nancy. The general asked him to lunch and dinner 'but could not let me see the regiment without an order from the War Minister'.

In Paris B-P learned of military preparedness exercises going on outside the city. He went to Vincennes and roamed through the woods in a swirling fog. Twice the sound of bugle calls led him to places where conscripts were being put through their paces. When the fog lifted he spied some special activities coming his way. He sat down on a bench and promptly 'fell asleep'. Through half-closed eyes he watched as 'two batteries mounted and four squadrons dismounted of Artillery were inspected and marched past by General Boulanger'—the cause of Bismarck's tirades, *Général Revanche* himself.

Baden-Powell came home with a clear picture of the various battlefields in his mind and with numerous notes and sketch maps. But his dream of becoming a war correspondent was soon blasted. Bismarck won the German election and his coalition *Reichstag* approved his army bill on 11 March 1887. The 'war crisis' was put in mothballs.

4

In May 1887, the command of the 13th Hussars was shifted to Manchester. Baden-Powell's detachment was ordered to Seaforth, near Liverpool, and was soon involved in the preparations for a Grand Military Tournament to be held as part of the country-wide celebrations of the Golden Jubilee of Queen Victoria's reign.

The large audience that witnessed the event was especially impressed by the last act: '*The Bivouac*—a military scene, giving the incident of a reconnaissance by a cavalry patrol in an enemy's country. Arranged by Captain Baden-Powell. Carried out by non-commissioned officers and men of the Seaforth Detachment, 13th Hussars.' *The Bivouac* was a highly dramatic show winding up with an impressive cavalry charge across the field and the complete routing of 'the foe'. Baden-Powell had included among the props one of the new machine-guns under trial for use in the Army. He had made the acquaintance of Torsten Nordenfelt, the inventor of the Nordenfelt machine-gun, and had persuaded him to lend him a gun on a 'galloping carriage' for the occasion.

Baden-Powell's interest in the machine-gun had far-reaching effects. One day shortly after the tournament, his sergeant rushed into his quarters to tell him that the Adjutant-General of the British Army was in the barracks square and wanted to see him. B-P went down in no particular hurry, wondering who would be trying to pull his leg. It wasn't customary for an Adjutant-General to come calling on a captain. But when he got down to the square he found Lord Wolseley himself, in plain clothes, waiting to see him.

Wolseley had heard that Baden-Powell had used a machine-gun here. What did he think of it? Was it possible to use it with cavalry in rough country?

It certainly was, Baden-Powell assured him. He had the gun brought out, harnessed up the horses and started out of the barracks gate with Wolseley sitting on the gun, himself on one of the horses. Off they went over the sand dunes in 'a real up-and-down switchback performance' that made the Adjutant-General 'hang on tight to the handstraps even if it didn't make his hair stand on end'.

By the end of September, the Nordenfelt machine-gun had been adopted for the British Cavalry and the first men were being trained in its use, but apparently not to Wolseley's satisfaction, for on 31 October 1887 he wrote to B-P:

> Dear Captain Baden-Powell, A recent inspection of the handling of the machine-guns attached to the several regiments of Cavalry at

Aldershot was anything but a success, attributable apparently to the defective training of the detachments. I am anxious that this defect be remedied, and I wish you, as one of the few officers of the Army who have the requisite knowledge, to do so. It will be necessary for you to be at Aldershot for about a fortnight, and I want you to let me know when it will be convenient for you to go there.

Yours truly,
WOLSELEY

Baden-Powell was delighted with this chance to go to Aldershot where his old colonel, Baker Russell, was second in command under General Drury Lowe. He found the latter part of November 'convenient'. He developed a training plan and instructed a group of officers in it. He also devised a quick-release harness to replace the gear issued by the Ordnance Department. The new harness was patented in B-P's name. It brought him a commendation from the War Office and eventually an award of £100, which just about covered his expenses in getting the harness made to his specifications.

Back again with his squadron at Seaforth, Baden-Powell was suddenly confronted with a major opportunity for change. His uncle, now General Henry A. Smyth, had been made G.O.C. (General Officer Commanding) South Africa. He offered his nephew the position as his aide-de-camp.

Four years before, General Smyth had extended a similar offer to his nephew, only to have it turned down. B-P at the time was enjoying himself too well in India with excellent chances for 'pay, promotion, pig-sticking and polo'. Furthermore, to him, being an A.D.C. 'is not soldiering, so doesn't as a rule lead to better things on its merit, although of course you meet with swells whose interest may get you on'.

But his uncle's offer this time was something different.

Now it was Africa calling! Just being in Africa was enough for B-P to overcome all his disinclination for office work. He quickly accepted his uncle's offer.

When the day for his departure from Seaforth arrived, the men of his squadron lined up for parade. Although testimonials from men to officers were strictly forbidden, Baden-Powell's men decided to defy regulations. They presented their popular captain with an illuminated address printed on white satin on which they tendered their best good wishes for his success.

On 30 December 1887, B-P was on the high seas once more, bound for South Africa.

VII

Africa Again

Years: 1888–89   Age: 31–32

1

AT the Cape Baden-Powell soon had his notion confirmed that an A.D.C.'s berth 'is not soldiering'. He became an office commuter. He lived with his uncle, the General, and his Aunt Constance at the Government country house at Wynberg ('an English house in a large garden . . . without exception the most beautiful and charming place I have ever been in') and caught the 10.25 train for Cape Town every weekday morning in time to be at his desk in The Castle at 11. The office work, as far as he was concerned, was 'merely waiting in case of being wanted. Awful waste of time—which I can't get used to'. At three the train took him back to Wynberg. 'Then we take a walk, ride, or go calling till dinner. After dinner chess between Aunt C. and self and then early to bed.'

Aunt Connie got her nephew involved in various social activities: theatricals in the ball-room of The Castle, musical evenings, dances, programmes of sports including horse-racing for the men and rifle shooting for the ladies. In addition there were the dinners for any number of 'swells' moving in and out of Government House where Sir Hercules Robinson, the High Commissioner, was a generous and popular host— 'a typical Colonial Governor, very British, a diplomatist and a sportsman, and managed to look all three'.

B-P's only real excitement was an occasional buck shoot and his two afternoons of polo a week. He became secretary of the Polo Club, second whip of the Cape Foxhounds and a member of the Tandem Club, the most exclusive men's club of Cape Town. But what he was doing was emphatically not soldiering! His main anxiety all the time was that a war would start somewhere and he would not be in it.

As always when he had a problem he turned to his brother George for help. George had stood successfully for election the previous autumn as

Member of Parliament for Liverpool and had been made the first 'Sir' in the Baden-Powell family for his work for the Crown in various parts of the Empire. George, he decided, should be able to use his political pull somehow to get his younger brother recalled for some kind of active duty if war should break out somewhere.

But there were no wars in sight. Baden-Powell would have to settle for something less than a full-fledged war.

By June he got a sample of what he wanted.

2

One morning an alarming telegram arrived at The Castle. It was from Sir Arthur Havelock, Governor of Natal and Zululand. There had been an uprising in Zululand of the Usutu, the followers of the late Chief Cetywayo. Immediate military assistance from the Cape was urgently required.

There had been no let-up in the trouble in Zululand since the battle of Ulundi in 1879 that broke the resistance of the Zulus and destroyed the power of Chief Cetywayo.

At the conclusion of the Zulu War, Sir Garnet Wolseley, as Commander and High Commissioner, had divided the country into thirteen artificial 'provinces', twelve of them with Zulu chieftains as their heads, one of them with a white chief—John Dunn, a Scottish trader who had lived among the Zulus since his boyhood and had been one of Cetywayo's chief advisers.

This division had not ensured peace. On the contrary, the more belligerent of the thirteen chiefs were soon invading the others' territories, burning their kraals, raiding their cattle herds. Civil war became the order of the day throughout Zululand. The Usutu lined themselves up behind Dinizulu, Cetywayo's son, and the young chieftain called on a number of well-armed, mounted Transvaal Boers to come to his assistance. With this Boer help, Dinizulu quickly rose to power over the neighbouring tribes. But the hour of reckoning struck. Dinizulu had promised his Boer helpmates land in return for their military aid. Now he was confronted with the demands of eight hundred Boers for adequate remuneration for their services adding up to 2,260,600 acres. As a 'generous' compromise they were willing to settle for the whole northern area of Zululand plus a wide strip of land down to the eastern shore of Africa 'with the right to establish there an independent republic to be called the New Republic'.

In his desperation over the prospect of losing a major part of his country to his Boer 'friends', Dinizulu turned to Great Britain for help. The British

Government succeeded in contesting the Boers' drive to the sea on the basis of previous treaties but could do little about the rest. The New Republic of Vrijheid came into being. To prevent further Boer encroachment on Zululand, Great Britain annexed what remained of the country and placed the responsibility for its administration in the hands of the Governor of Natal, Sir Arthur Havelock.

At the ceremony of annexation three of the leading chiefs were notable by their absence: Dinizulu and his two uncles. Annexation by Britain had been far from Dinizulu's mind when he asked for British help. Before long it was discovered that the three were intriguing together and had gathered an army of about four thousand war-hungry Usutu. Early in 1888 Dinizulu and his warriors broke into open defiance of the British authorities by raiding the domain of one of the loyal chieftains and killing some of his men.

Sir Arthur demanded that Dinizulu stop his provocations and disperse his army. When Dinizulu paid no attention to the Governor's demand, Sir Arthur issued a warrant for his arrest and sent a force of two hundred Zululand police and British troops to execute it. The force was attacked by Dinizulu's Usutu and compelled to withdraw with several casualties.

The news of Dinizulu's successful routing of the British police and soldiers spread throughout Zululand. Several of the other Zulu tribes went on the rampage. They attacked and looted mission stations, stores and traders' wagons and killed more than two hundred native and European men, women and children. At Umsinduze, Pretorius, the resident magistrate of the area around the mouth of the River Umfolozi, was besieged by a couple of hundred Europeans and three hundred native allies.

The situation had become critical. Sir Arthur sent off his appeal for help to Cape Town and General Smyth made ready to leave in command of an army of two thousand British soldiers. Colonel Frederick Carrington was to mobilize a levy of loyal Zulus and Captain Baden-Powell would accompany his uncle as acting military secretary in place of Smyth's former secretary who was on his way to England for re-posting.

General Smyth and his staff arrived in Durban on 26 June 1888, went by special train to the rail terminus at Verulam and pressed on from there by mule wagons north to the single white settlement in Zululand— Eshowe, the spot designated as headquarters.

One of the first orders of urgent business was the relief of Umsinduze. News had arrived of attacks and counter-attacks in which Pretorius had lost forty killed. Major McKean of the 6th Royal (Inniskilling) Dragoons was placed in command of a relief force of four hundred mounted men and two hundred native police. He picked as his staff officer Captain Baden-Powell, and for another member of his staff a young captain by the name of Edmund H. H. Allenby who had returned just in time from a leave in England.

On their second day out, this flying column of McKean's was joined by John Dunn, the white chief, and his impi (army) of close on two thousand Zulu warriors—'fine strong muscular fellows', wrote B-P, 'with cheery handsome faces . . . their brown bodies were polished with oil and they looked like bronze statues.'

> I heard a sound in the distance [he recalled many years later] which at first I thought was an organ playing in church and I thought for a moment that we must be approaching a mission station over the brow of the hill. But when we topped the rise we saw moving up towards us from the valley below three long lines of men marching in single file and singing a wonderful anthem as they marched. Every now and then one man would sing a few notes of a solo which were then responded to by an immense roar of sound from the whole impi, of deep bass voices and higher tones singing in harmony.

Baden-Powell jotted down the tune and the words as far as he could make them out:

> *Eengonyama Gonyama! Invooboo!*
> *Ya-boh! Ya-boh! Invooboo!*

He asked John Dunn what the words meant. The Scot laughed as he translated the Bantu words: 'He is a lion. Yes, he is better than a lion: he is a hippopotamus!'

After covering fifty miles in two days, the flying column slowed down to proceed with greater care through the enemy-held territory. When it reached Umsinduze after shaking off a number of hostile Zulu scouts, it found Pretorius and his men in good spirits. The soldiers of the relief force immediately set about rebuilding and strengthening the fortifications and earthworks. Baden-Powell, as the best-trained first-aider of the force, attended to the wounds from spears and bullets that had been suffered by the besieged and had not been properly dressed.

McKean left a small garrison to protect Pretorius's fort, then returned to headquarters with the remainder of the column in the soggiest weather B-P had ever experienced. The column had seen no sign of Dinizulu.

General Smyth instructed his acting military secretary to establish an intelligence department to secure exact information about Dinizulu's whereabouts. B-P organized a small group of Zulu spies and located a skilful interpreter. Within a short while, he had gathered complete information about Dinizulu's movements and about the size and disposition of his army which was hidden in the fastnesses of the Ceza, a mountain spread with a jumbled mass of broken rock and boulders and scarred with a number of thickly wooded ravines running up into a jungle of trees and bush near the summit.

On the basis of Baden-Powell's reports, General Smyth moved his headquarters to N'Konjeni within twenty miles of Ceza, set up a semi-circular line of posts and prepared for the attack. It was a difficult area, partly because of its topography, but also because of the way it straddled the border of the New Republic which, the year before, had been incorporated into the Transvaal. An ill-timed or delayed movement and Dinizulu would be gone, into Boer territory where he could not be followed.

Just as everything was ready for starting the hunt, a telegram arrived from Sir Arthur Havelock telling General Smyth not to attack without the Governor's explicit approval. Although Sir Arthur had turned to Cape Town for military help after his civilian police had failed to stop the insurrection, he was jealous of his prerogative as Governor and Commander-in-Chief of Zululand.

The General fumed. So did his whole staff. Baden-Powell considered Sir Arthur's order 'silly'. How could a person sitting in an arm-chair in Pietermaritzburg a hundred miles away know what should be done or when?

Five days went by before the permission to go ahead arrived from Sir Arthur. Baden-Powell moved into the Ceza bush in command of a column of dragoons, mounted troops and part of Sir Frederick Carrington's levy of friendly Zulus.

As he and his men climbed up over one of the ridges leading to their destination they spied a number of Usutu scurrying off into refuge in the caves of an opposite ridge. In a short, fierce skirmish four hiding Usutu warriors were killed and a hundred head of cattle rounded up.

The next night, B-P led his troops forward in the dark deeper into the Ceza bush. At daybreak they climbed the mountain side and combed the brush and rock heaps of the plateau above. They clambered in among little forts built of piled-up stones and numerous huts, many of them burned, all of them deserted but indicating clearly the size of the impi that had occupied them. In one of the forts Baden-Powell found a number of weapons and trinkets left behind, among them a long string of quaintly carved wooden beads such as only a chief would have worn. There was no doubt in his mind that this had been Dinizulu's own hide-out.

But the bird had flown across the border into the Transvaal, and with him about two thousand of his followers. The delay in attacking had been costly indeed.

Since there was nothing further to be accomplished in the Ceza bush, B-P returned with his men to headquarters to report the result of their expedition. The day after, General Smyth removed the headquarters back to Eshowe.

With Dinizulu out of the way, the resistance of the remaining rebel chieftains collapsed. For the rest, it was simply a matter of sending out troops of police and soldiers to round up the scattered bands of Usutu that roamed the countryside and persuade them to surrender. This meant days and weeks of office work, of orders and reports for Baden-Powell, the acting military secretary, although he did go out on two mopping-up expeditions before it was all over.

At the end of August, the campaign was concluded. On 12 September General Smyth and B-P were back in Cape Town.

Although the objective had been achieved—to put down the rebellion —Baden-Powell considered the campaign as a whole 'another example of the futility of divided authority between civil and military authorities when once the military force has been called in'. Nevertheless, personally, he had gained a great amount of valuable experience. For the first time in his military career he had been responsible for deploying men and columns and had had occasion to work with native levies and native spies. He had become thoroughly familiar with the skills involved in primitive warfare by actual practice in the bush and on the veld. He had learned the Zulu ways of living and of fighting.

Throughout it all he had kept an exhaustive diary, jotting down experiences and tips for future reference. He had added materially to his store of information for the booklet on 'scouting' he might some day write.

3

And now he was back at the daily office routine. Life had become a little simpler: The General and Mrs Smyth had moved into The Castle and had arranged for B-P to take over the quarters ordinarily assigned to the military secretary—a string of spacious rooms with a magnificent view across Table Bay.

He had the rooms and the work of 'Milit. Sec.', but not the title. The General had asked the War Office, in June when the position became vacant, to confer this title on Baden-Powell, but this had been refused. To become a military secretary an applicant must be a field officer. Now, well satisfied with B-P's work as acting military secretary during the

Zululand campaign, General Smyth again remonstrated with the War Office. This time he met with success. A telegram from London informed him that the Commander-in-Chief 'has been pleased, in recognition of the good service lately performed by Captain R. S. S. Baden-Powell, 13th Hussars, to make an exception in the case of this officer and to approve his appointment as Assistant Military Secretary . . . from 21 June last'.

It was as 'Assist. Milit. Sec., South Africa' that Baden-Powell sent off to England the completed manuscript of his book on pigsticking for George to handle. It was accompanied by a score of full-page illustrations, the best water-colours B-P had so far painted.

The manuscript was accepted first time out, by Harrison & Sons, London. Baden-Powell's first major book, entitled *Pigsticking or Hog-hunting*, was published early in 1889 as a high-grade piece of book printing with a hard cover embossed in gold. It was dedicated 'by kind permission' to the Duke of Connaught—'the First Prince of Royal Blood Who Has Taken a "First Spear" '.

The reviews of it were uniformly good, although the reviewers generally agreed that the book would be of greater interest to military personnel and civil servants stationed in India than to the general public. It eventually attained the distinction of becoming a classic and the undisputed authority on the sport of pigsticking.

While hard at work as assistant military secretary and *primus motor* in many of Aunt Connie's social projects, B-P, in his eternal restlessness, looked about for new worlds to conquer. He turned his eyes northward. It had come to his attention, he wrote his brother George, that 'the Government here is most anxious to have proper information as to the navigability of the River Zambesi and the truth as to how far Portuguese influence really extends there'.

Baden-Powell worked himself into a high state of excitement about an expedition to explore the Zambesi. He wrote to his hunting friend, Reuben Beningfield, urging him to join him and to send the steam launch he had at Delagoa Bay up to the river. He asked Warington to have a collapsible boat sent out from England for him to use in the rapids.

But the moment he broached his idea to his uncle, General Smyth promptly squashed it. Word had reached him that Sir Hercules Robinson, the High Commissioner, would return to England on 1 May and that a new Governor was to be appointed. In that case General Smyth would become Administrator during the interregnum and would not be able to spare his military secretary for the length of time a Zambesi trip would take. He suggested, however, that Stephe should take a couple of weeks off for an elephant hunt at Knysna.

With an officer friend and a local big-game hunter Baden-Powell criss-crossed the elephant grounds round Knysna on foot for several days without luck. Finally, on the next-to-last day the hunters saw a herd on the other side of the valley. They struggled through a dense jungle to get to them, but by the time they arrived the elephants had disappeared. 'What we should have done had they been there I don't know,' he commented in his diary, 'but I imagine it would have depended chiefly on the good feeling of the elephants themselves.'

4

Sir Hercules and Lady Robinson left on 1 May 1889, and General Smyth, as expected, became Administrator. He moved into Government House with his wife and his staff, including Robert S. S. Baden-Powell, military secretary and senior aide-de-camp, and entered into a period of hectic official and unofficial functions: opening the Cape Parliament, parade of troops on Queen Victoria's birthday, luncheons and dinners, balls and theatricals.

In the middle of it all, Baden-Powell was incapacitated by a carbuncle on the neck, that had developed into a major inflammation. He had been miserable for more than a month, with intense pain, poor appetite and lack of sleep, not able to lie down in his sick-bed, but sitting up night and day. The doctor prescribed 'patience and poultices' and a two-month leave to recuperate.

General Smyth blamed it on his nephew's living habits: 'We think this attack came on him because he would work himself physically too hard,' he wrote to his sister, B-P's mother, 'and breakfast on a chocolate sweet-meat, or the like—a kind of training to hard work and endurance which cannot go on forever.' But whatever the cause, the General reluctantly approved the doctor's decision to send the patient home—with the hope that his nephew would 'come back in two months all right and ready to take breakfast like a Briton'.

Without advising his mother, Baden-Powell arrived in London. He never saw her during the two weeks he was at home—Mrs Baden-Powell and Agnes had gone off to the Continent. But he did see George who got him stirred up about an important South African project that was in the wind: Sir George had heard that Sir Francis de Winton was going to Swaziland as a Royal Commissioner to help to straighten out the muddled affairs of this troubled country.

B-P immediately went to see Sir Francis. Using his most convincing arguments, he persuaded the Royal Commissioner to apply to the Colonial

Office for Captain Baden-Powell to accompany him to Swaziland as his secretary—subject, of course, to General Smyth's approval.

After returning to the Cape, while waiting for Sir Francis' arrival, Baden-Powell used his spare moments to prepare a résumé of the Swaziland question—past, present and future. As soon as Sir Francis arrived, on 24 October, B-P boarded his ship and placed his résumé in the Commissioner's hands. 'We put him up at Government House and he at once applied to the General for me—and, apparently without much difficulty, got me.'

5

The Swaziland excursion would not be as exciting as the Zululand expedition, of that Baden-Powell was certain. The problem here was a matter for negotiation, not for military action. It nevertheless promised to be of some interest, and would at least get him away from his office routine for a while.

The trouble that needed to be settled in Swaziland, a small upland territory in South-east Africa wedged in a corner between the Transvaal and Zululand, had been caused to a great extent by the weakness of the ruling chieftain, King Umbandine. The fertile land and the promise of mineral wealth had attracted a great number of white settlers and prospectors. Umbandine's sketchy habit of selling grazing rights and mineral rights of the same piece of land to several people in succession had made the white settlers unruly and Umbandine himself uncomfortable. The Governments of the Transvaal and Great Britain had both come to the conclusion that something must be done to straighten matters out. The two countries agreed to send a joint commission to Swaziland to attempt to settle the country's future status.

The situation in Swaziland became further complicated while Sir Francis, representing Britain, was on his way to the Cape. King Umbandine died after a short illness and his mother, Queen Usibati, took over the government of the country as regent for her grandson, Bunu, still just a boy.

Sir Francis and his newly appointed private secretary sailed from Cape Town to Durban on 26 October. At Pietermaritzburg they picked up the other two members of the British commission, Advocate William P. Schreiner, the legal adviser, and Colonel Richard Martin, and continued by rail to Ladysmith. Here the party, now including a couple of servants, changed into travelling kit and set off for Pretoria in a coach with ten horses.

After four days of journeying they reached Johannesburg. During a short stay Baden-Powell roamed the streets of this flourishing centre. 'It is a wonderfully big city of thirty thousand inhabitants,' he noted in his diary, 'and has only been invented within the last three years. All the bigger buildings and offices are brick or stone with zinc roofs. But in spite of its richness and good buildings the town is still unpaved and unlighted at night. The streets are therefore always ankle deep in either dust or mud. Mud had it while we were there.'

The next day the party travelled in another coach the thirty-five miles to Pretoria. 'We had three changes of horses *en route*, so went at a rattling pace.' They were greeted six miles out of town by General N. J. Smit, Vice-President of the Transvaal, and by the famous Piet J. Joubert, the Commandant-General, who had commanded the Boer forces in the attack on Majuba Hill in 1881. The travellers were brought into the capital in style and put up as guests of the State in the town's leading hotel.

After changing into formal dress and donning their top hats, the members of the British Commission went to pay their respects to the Transvaal's President Paul Kruger. They found him living in a long, low, single-storeyed villa in a quiet side street. After passing a lounging sentry at the garden gate, they were taken into the drawing-room, 'a little-used room with at least three Bibles on its three tables'. Here they were received by the President, 'a big, heavy man, with a flabby, heavy face, a big mouth and a big nose, but a small forehead'. At first, 'Oom Paul' struck B-P as being extremely shy, suspicious and silent, 'but Sir Francis was a mass of tact and gradually drew him out on his two favourite topics—lion hunting and the Bible—and before we parted we were the best of friends'.

The British party stayed in Pretoria for ten days, getting instructions from the President, conferring with their Boer co-commissioners, agreeing on the general conduct of the commission, meeting a number of Boers at dinners and informal gatherings.

Baden-Powell used the opportunity to learn as much as he could about the Boer character and about the Boers' attitude to themselves and others. An evening he spent with a group of young Boers who called themselves the Young Afrikanders, proved a particularly good eye-opener: 'They are a well-educated lot with large ideas about their country and very small ones about their present government. These Afrikanders are, of course, dead against English rule, but their idea is apparently a general federation of all the South African states, assisted by England.'

At last the hour came for the departure of the combined party of the British and Boer commissioners for Swaziland.

We said our final good-bye to the President and he came out into his garden and gave us his blessing, praying that our mission would be successful and bring peace and happiness to a torn land. He evidently felt, and must almost have believed, what he was saying, for tears were in his eyes.

He had always been a great hero to me, and I looked upon him as a second Cromwell. But he never did rise higher in my estimation than when he wished us Godspeed at his garden gate.

He rose higher still some time later when I discovered that this impressiveness on his part was put on.

B-P's sketch of Jokilobovu, the Swazi Queen's executioner, is an excellent example of his skill in handling pen and ink.

For nine days the party travelled by ten-mule coaches across the wide, undulating veld towards Swaziland, stopping for a short outspan in the middle of the day, pitching camp in the late afternoon and spending the night under the stars.

To Baden-Powell the long journey was a thoroughly pleasurable experience. Instead of wearing the formal uniform of the Cape, here he could revel in the casual 'undress' outfit he had come to like: flannel shirt and shorts, broad-brimmed Boer hat, puttees, socks, and shooting boots.

B-P made particularly good friends with Advocate Schreiner and the two Boer generals, Smit and Joubert, all of them good huntsmen. Morning after morning *en route* one or the other joined the early rising B-P for shooting—snipe, partridge, duck, springbok, depending on the area—except on Sundays ('No shooting, travelling, or any other occupation allowed by the Dutch today').

The representatives from the two Governments went directly into the heart of Swaziland, to the King Kraal at Embekelweni, near Bremersdorp. Here they were met by the Swazi Queen-Regent and close to a hundred Swazi chiefs. In the beginning very little headway was made but eventually, after a week of conferring under the adroit chairmanship of Sir Francis de Winton, an agreement was reached: the independence of the Swazi nation was acknowledged by Great Britain and the Transvaal, the boy-king was recognized as successor to Umbandine with Queen Usibati as regent, and three delegates, British, Boer and Swazi, were appointed to help the Queen. On 16 December the Queen-Regent proclaimed her acceptance of the proposals of the joint commission. On 20 December the British and Boer commissioners set out on their return journey.

The trip into Swaziland in company with a group of trained statesmen—Britons and Boers—was an important element in Baden-Powell's education. It taught him that not everything is solved by a show of arms, that differences can be overcome and agreements worked out when men of goodwill skilled in the art of negotiating get to work.

6

Back in Natal after an 'unprecedently short journey' from Swaziland ('We had good mules and fine weather and came along at a tremendous pace, doing in thirteen days what would usually take about twenty or more'), Sir Francis and his party stayed at Newcastle. Here a letter in a Government House envelope was delivered to Baden-Powell. It was from his uncle, the General:

My dear Stephie, Changes arrive fast and furious. On the morning of 13th last as we awaited the landing of Sir Henry Loch for Governor, a telegram arrived from the C.-in-C. offering me Malta. Looking at it as a distinct professional advancement, I accepted before five minutes had passed, after receiving my wife's sanction, and just as the salute from H.M.S. *Raleigh*, in Table Bay, commenced on the arrival of Sir Henry Loch's ship.

Now comes a personal matter. Would you like to come with me to Malta, as Milit. Sec. and A.D.C.? I suppose it will follow as a matter of course, if wished by us both. But I have some provisos to lay down—viz. if you come, you will have to look to my work only, for your career, and to fitting yourself for that work, for your employment, whilst with me; and you will have to give up the expectation of leave for extraneous objects, whether political, sporting, or exploratory, unless only for a few days, or unless I be going on leave myself. . . .

If, however, you should be disinclined to such a limited sphere of motion, and prefer rather to attach yourself to the development of South African progress, now's the time to speak. . . .

Your affectionate Uncle,

H. A. SMYTH

B-P read the letter twice, then proceeded to the Newcastle telegraph office to send off a telegram accepting his uncle's offer and agreeing to observe his provisos. Then immediately wondered: 'Did I do rightly?'

VIII

Mediterranean Interlude

<hr>

Years: 1890–1895   Age: 33–38

1

ON 27 February 1890, the newly knighted Sir Henry Smyth made his entry into the San Antonio Palace of Valetta, Malta, accompanied by his wife, Lady Smyth, and his military secretary and A.D.C., the recently promoted Brevet Major Baden-Powell.

The position Sir Henry had accepted was by no means a sinecure. A new constitution, strenuously fought, had just been approved for Malta after the final details had been worked out by a committee with B-P's brother George a 'joint commissioner'. A new legislative council had been established and the questions of taxation, of laws respecting mixed marriages, of the status of the Italian language as against the English and Maltese, hung heavily in the air. It would take all of Sir Henry's skill—aided by his command of Italian—to govern Malta and the other Maltese islands.

The beginning was auspicious. Sir Henry's welcoming levee attracted four hundred prominent men, Lady Smyth's reception a crowd of seven hundred and thirty.

Baden-Powell had his hands full. As military secretary he was responsible for the liaison with the five regiments stationed on Malta as well as for the official English mail, incoming and outgoing. As senior A.D.C. he was in charge of the Governor's and Her Ladyship's multitudinous social occasions, not just for the British, Maltese and Italian communities on the island, but also for the senior personnel of visiting flotillas of the French, German, and Italian fleets. He also had to attend to the entertainment at the Palace of members of British and Continental society calling at Malta in their private yachts on their winter cruises in Mediterranean waters.

B-P knew what he had let himself in for, but he could not help dreaming himself away, from time to time, from the routine of office work and social affairs to a real soldier's life. Once, at a Palace afternoon 'At home', when he was handing a cup of tea to one of the lady guests—'an old dowager, who bridled up in a mantle with bugles and beads'—his perceptive Aunt Connie noticed that his face wore an absent look. After the guests had gone she asked her nephew where his thoughts had been at the time. 'I could only reply,' as he admitted later, 'that my mind was a blank, with a single vision in it, lower half yellow, upper half blue—in other words, the yellow veld of South Africa, topped with the blue South African sky. Possibly the scent of the tea had touched some memory chord which connected it with my black tin billy steaming among the embers of a wood fire. . . .'

It didn't help his peace of mind when George sent him a letter he had received from Sir Francis de Winton:

> My dear George, This latest news from Uganda seems to point to some active service, one that might be an additional incentive to Stephen. Of course, I cannot promise a war but we shall have to retake Uganda and replace Mwanga.
>
> Yours,
> DE WINTON

Baden-Powell was immediately aflame. But Sir Henry would hear none of it. 'The family,' he wrote to George, 'may rest easy about Stephe for the present, as I haven't the slightest idea of lending him to Sir F. de Winton or anybody else away from his office here.'

B-P gave vent to his disappointment at not joining Sir Francis in a doleful letter to his mother: 'You can't picture that "camp sickness" (as I should call it) that gets hold of one—a sort of hunger to be out in the wilds and away from all this easy-going mixture of office, drawing-room, clerk and butler. . . .'

But it was not just the 'camp sickness' that had made B-P want to join Sir Francis. He was thinking further ahead than to an excursion into Uganda. He was thinking of his whole future in the British Army. For his longed-for advancement he would either have to go to Staff College for two years of study, of theory, of mainly sedentary life, or he would have to be 'qualified for staff work without going through Staff College' by doing actual service in the field, in an engagement such as the one Sir Francis might encounter.

With his chance to go to Uganda vetoed by his uncle, Staff College would probably have to be the answer. Half-heartedly B-P wrote his brother to send him books on arithmetic, algebra, and Euclid. 'I propose to work for Staff College again.'

2

Baden-Powell also took up Italian, so essential for communication with a great part of Malta's population. He became deeply interested in the island's long past and induced his Aunt Connie to join him in explorations. Together they visited some of the prehistoric caves and some of the monumental limestone buildings scattered over the countryside. They tried their hands at archaeological excavation, with amazing luck— one of the old Phoenician rock tombs which they helped to dig out produced some of the best artefacts discovered up to that time on the island.

But B-P did not have to travel far to step back into history. The Palace in which he lived had been built more than three hundred years before by the Grand Master of the Knights of Saint John—the same Jean de Vallette who had given his name to the town of Valetta. Among the treasures of the Palace was a large store of armour that clamoured for cataloguing and arranging. After several attempts at finding a local person familiar with armour and its history Baden-Powell finally invited an armour dealer from Rome to visit Malta to value the swords and halberds, helmets and body armour: 'He told us there were a lot of excellent pieces in the collection—one such he valued at £8,000.' With the help of some of his officer comrades and a few Maltese, Baden-Powell got the collection into fairly satisfactory condition for public display.

It was not just the things of the past that occupied B-P's mind. He was seriously concerned with the welfare and morale of the British troops on Malta.

The health condition of the garrison was fair. Malta had no cholera or typhus such as Baden-Powell had encountered in India. The notorious Malta fever, transmitted mostly by goats' milk, was of little consequence to the British soldiers. They were not interested in milk: they preferred to swill their mugs of lukewarm beer in their poorly provisioned canteens. But, as in India, the main disturbing element among the soldiers was boredom.

B-P set about remedying the matter. He persuaded the regimental bands to take turns at weekly entertainments. He arranged programmes, rehearsed actors, made sandwich boards and handbills, and stage-managed smoking concerts for the soldiers in the Valetta Gymnasium. He created a mixed ensemble and introduced it as The Magpie Minstrels. He resurrected *Cox and Box* with himself playing Cox one week, Box the next. 'Week after week,' the *Malta Times* reported, 'the spacious hall was crowded to its utmost capacity, with delighted audiences, enjoying the liberal programmes, in which the name of Major Baden-Powell invariably appeared.'

The smoking concerts did not always come off according to schedule. But the audience never knew when a calamity had occurred and had been hastily surmounted by the indefatigable impresario. When an actress once failed to show up for a performance of the currently popular high-kicking 'skirt dance' Baden-Powell himself put on the voluminous pleated skirt and after a few rehearsals performed a 'skirt dance' such as had never been seen before, or since, on Malta.

Although, ordinarily, such concerts would have been free of charge for the soldiers, B-P insisted on a token admission fee—he had a long-term objective in mind. By the time two years were up, Baden-Powell's entertainment committee had sufficient funds on hand to rent, for a whole year, a vacant hospital and turn it into a soldiers' and sailors' club for non-commissioned officers and men.

Once started, the club paid for itself, 'not only financially but in a moral sense as well'. Certain protests were raised against it. Most of these came from local public-house proprietors at losing the soldiers' patronage, but some were voiced by the chaplains who complained about the club's location in the worst part of town. Baden-Powell met the chaplains and innocently asked, 'Well, if you had an infected place where would you put the poultice?' There was a moment's pause, then the chaplains saw the point and dropped their objections. But the name stuck. Baden-Powell's club became aptly known as The Poultice.

Outside the formal and informal entertainments at the Palace and in the Club, Malta had little to offer in the form of recreation.

Baden-Powell had hoped for a great deal of polo but the facilities were unsatisfactory: the polo ground was solid rock in most places. A hard-hit ball would ricochet off the ground with terrific force. If a person were hit by a ball or had a fall, dangerous contusions, concussions and cuts often resulted.

The shooting, similarly, was not without danger. When the woodcock arrived on their annual migration every hunter on the island took to the fields. But 'the fields' were 'tiny enclosures between five-foot stone walls and when birds were about there was a sportsman with a gun in almost every other field—they fired in any direction and their shot striking the walls glanced off at all angles'.

During the first summer of his stay on Malta Baden-Powell bought a £1 ticket in a raffle for a local charity. To his astonishment he won first prize: a pony and cart and the harness to go with them. He thought at first of getting another pony and turning his cart into a tandem, as was customary among the Malta *élite*. But then he had a better idea: He bought two more ponies and harnessed his cart into a *troika*. With his team of three ponies abreast he drove through the streets of Valetta and into the surrounding countryside, often with a pretty girl at his side.

B-P enjoyed these excursions with his female companions but brushed aside, as he had done in India, any onset of budding affection. 'Lord R.'s daughter,' he reported home, 'is great friends with me (even more so than I with her).' 'There is a nice electrical engineer and his daughter here— she is a good sort of girl—plain but pleasing.' 'As for Lady S., I am sorry to say she is already engaged, and even if she were not I fear she is not at all what I want.' But also, to offset any rumours that might reach London: 'I hear from friends that I am engaged to be married: it's great fun. I shall be getting a lot of wedding presents soon! What I want to know is, can one get damages out of a person for spreading such a report?'

3

Luck again stepped into the picture to provide B-P with a measure of excitement. The intelligence officer to the headquarters staff completed his tenure. Sir Henry recommended his A.D.C. for the position although he feared that the lack of Staff College training might make his nephew ineligible. To the surprise of both uncle and nephew the Adjutant-General approved the Governor's selection. There was no pay attached to the duty, 'but it is still a good thing to have held'.

As intelligence officer for the Mediterranean area, Baden-Powell was in charge of gathering and submitting to the War Office information on the disposition of troops and ships of the different countries, their armament and other items of military value.

He first turned his eyes south and decided to go 'snipe hunting' in Tunis and Algeria. On his first trip to these North African countries, both of them French regencies, Baden-Powell focused his attention on Bizerta.

During the late 1880's the French Government had commissioned two of the largest contractors in France to expand this Tunisian port. The work was started in 1890, the same year that B-P arrived on Malta. A few weak voices in England suggested that France was intending to establish a naval depot at Bizerta, but the British military 'experts' pooh-poohed this idea. 'Bizerta is only 244 miles from Toulon,' they argued, 'and to defend two such places, France must considerably increase her fleet. French naval men would much rather see Bizerta as a port of refuge.'

B-P took a room in Bizerta overlooking the canal and the lake and spent several days roaming the town and the surrounding area, ostensibly looking for birds in the snipe bogs. When he had gathered all the data he considered pertinent he went inland with a guide, an interpreter, and a couple of beaters, for an honest-to-goodness snipe shoot at a farm owned by a British settler, near Mateur.

Back in Malta, Baden-Powell wrote up his report and sent it to the War Office in London. He received an appreciative reply from Lord Wolseley himself. But even Wolseley seemed to underestimate what was going on at Bizerta, for he closed his letter with the comment: 'With their enormous military budget the French find it hard to spare vast sums of money for outside ventures.'

On other trips to North Africa, the inquisitive Baden-Powell covered the area from Nemours in French Algeria to Tripoli, the capital of Turkish Tripoli, by sea, by railway, by diligence, on horseback and on foot. He visited Oran and Algiers, Constantine and Biskra, Tunis and Kairouan, Sousse and Gabés. He went 'snipe shooting' and snipe shooting, watched the manoeuvres of Spahis and Chasseurs d'Afrique, witnessed the obvious growth of the harbour of Bizerta into a major French naval base—and sent reams of reports and scores of sketches and maps off to England.

When 'snipe shooting' was inappropriate as an excuse, B-P adopted some other subterfuge—'butterfly hunting', for instance. It was as an avowed entomologist that he went to Dalmatia to investigate the surroundings of Cattaro, the capital. Cattaro (present-day Kotor) had had a tumultuous existence. At various times it had been occupied by Turks, Venetians, Spaniards, Austrians, Italians, Russians. Napoleon held it for six years until it was taken, in 1813, by the Montenegrins aided by the British fleet. But the Montenegrins were deprived of the coveted port a year later. The Congress of Vienna turned it over to Austria, and Austria made it one of the most heavily fortified ports on the Dalmatian coast. How heavily fortified? That was what Baden-Powell was interested in finding out.

With his usual thoroughness, he prepared himself by taking along all the paraphernalia of a butterfly hunter. He also brought a sketch-book in which he had already sketched a number of butterflies, some of them finished, others in outline only.

After arriving by boat at Cattaro, at the head of the long fiord, he climbed up into the barren Krivosi heights behind the town and started using his eyes—committing certain details to memory, others to the pages of his sketch-book.

Whenever he ran into an Austro-Hungarian military guard or officer, he put on a good show of actual butterfly hunting. Then 'with my sketch-book in hand, I would ask innocently whether he had seen such-and-such a butterfly in the neighbourhood, as I was anxious to catch one. Ninety-nine out of a hundred did not know one butterfly from another—any more than I did—so one was on fairly safe ground in that way, and they thoroughly sympathized with the mad Englishman who was hunting insects.'

The officers looked admiringly at Baden-Powell's colourful sketches of Red Admirals and Painted Ladies and other *Lepidoptera* but failed to scrutinize the sketches closely enough to notice that the delicately drawn veins of the butterfly wings were exact delineations of their own fort and that the spots on the wings denoted the number and calibre and positions of their guns.

In Austria for the autumn military manoeuvres in 1891, B-P took on the semblance of what he actually was on this occasion: a 'military correspondent' accredited to the London *Daily Chronicle*.

By adding the intelligence he picked up to the official *communiqués* that were passed out he came to the conclusion that the main battle of the manoeuvres would take place in a certain area near Schwarzenau. He rolled a spare flannel shirt, a pair of socks, soap, a toothbrush and a towel, into his overcoat, strapped it up, slung it over his shoulder horseshoe fashion and took the train from Vienna to Schwarzenau. He intended to spend the night in the nearby woods to be on hand at the expected scene of the battle at daybreak.

After shopping for bread, sausage and apples in the village, he proceeded in the darkness along the road to the woods. *En route* he heard the men of an outpost of the Southern Army talking and knew he was close to a sentry. He sneaked past without being detected and indulged for a fleeting moment in one of his mannerisms: of rubbing his hands together and chuckling to himself when he was particularly satisfied with what he had done or triumphant over a stunt he had pulled. This time he did it prematurely: he suddenly heard a rough voice demanding '*Wer ist da?*' and found himself confronted by three Austrian soldiers of a second sentry post. He quickly explained that he was an English tourist on his way to his inn, whereupon the soldiers let him go. B-P continued up the road, then plunged into the dark shelter of the pine woods and made himself comfortable for the night.

The next morning, after walking about four miles, he noticed small groups of cavalry on reconnaissance and the distant movement of troops and concluded that the Northern Army was advancing to attack the Southern Army. He climbed a hill and had a perfect view of the battle being enacted below him. He had the most conclusive proof imaginable that he had picked the right spot for observing this major battle of the Austro-Hungarian manoeuvres: from a position only a couple of hundred feet below him, the show was witnessed by Emperor Franz Joseph himself and his guests, Kaiser Wilhelm of Germany and the King of Saxony.

Baden-Powell—the 'artist' this time—arrived at the Italian manoeuvres in August 1892 by the back door: by the simple expedient of walking over the Saint Bernard Pass from Bourge St Pierre in Switzerland to St Rhemy in Italy. A fly brought him to Villeneuve, a little village swarming with soldiers billeted there for the manoeuvres.

From information he had picked up B-P decided that the main battle would be fought in the vicinity of Mourge, so he left by diligence for that Alpine village. Here he found a brigade of Alpinis.

With some difficulty, he located a bed for the night in a small inn ('I had to share it with another, but, as the landlord expressed it, he was quite *comme il faut*'). He didn't have much sleep, however. He was up in the morning at three to find his way in the dark up the mountainside to a good vantage point. When he got to the top of the ridge he was startled by the view of Mont Blanc at sunrise: 'At the height I was it looked enormous, and quite close—and the wonderful red light on the mountain was reflected on the surface of the glaciers although they themselves were still in the greeny-blue stage. It was grand!' Out came his sketch-book and his water-colours. He painted hurriedly, in an effort to put the effect on paper in a couple of sketches.

He was in the midst of his work when an Alpini soldier appeared in the landscape before him, seemingly out of nowhere, and disappeared again. B-P looked about him and saw two long, snaky lines of soldiers coming towards him. Some of the officers spotted him. 'There was no escape, so I just sat tight and said "Good morning".'

Before any of the officers raised any questions, B-P showed off the sketches he had just made of 'Dawn among the Mountains'. He was soon on the best of terms with the Italian officers. He expressed a mild interest in what they were doing and 'the less interest I showed, the more keen they seemed to be to explain matters to me, until eventually I had the whole of their scheme exposed before me, illustrated by their own sketch maps of the district, which were far more detailed and complete than anything of the kind I had seen before'.

In the middle of their exchange of civilities a signal sounded and the column marched off for the advance. Baden-Powell watched the soldiers descend into the valley and then, in an incredibly short space of time, saw them climb the opposite mountain. He had seen what he came for: 'the special troops, their guns, their supply and hospital arrangements, their methods of moving in this apparently impassable country, and their maps and ways of signalling.'

On yet another intelligence trip, this time to Turkey, Baden-Powell made the acquaintance of an American lady living in Constantinople. She insisted on showing him the sights of the city. When they had visited the main attractions she asked him if there was anything else he wanted to see.

B-P told her that he had heard of interesting forts along the Bosporus. He airily wondered whether there was any possibility of getting to see one. There certainly was, the American lady assured him. An old acquaintance of hers, Hamid Pasha, was the commandant of the most important of these Bosporus fortifications. She would arrange an invitation for Baden-Powell and herself.

Hamid Pasha proved a charming host. He gave them an excellent tea, then took them round the fort pointing out its ancient and modern devices for defence.

Towards the end of their tour of inspection they arrived before two large canvas-covered guns pointing threateningly out over the Strait of Bosporus. B-P's excitement grew intense. He whispered to his companion to try to persuade Hamid Pasha to allow them to look at the guns. Their courteous guide acquiesced. With a grin he pulled off a canvas cover and displayed a gun to his two visitors.

Baden-Powell immediately recognized the gun as a model that was not very new or very powerful. Before he could say anything, Hamid Pasha gave away the reason for all the secrecy: 'These are the same old guns that have been here for years, but we thought it advisable, in view of some moves by a certain neighbouring power, to let them suppose that we had re-armed ourselves with something very new and very formidable.'

On his return from Constantinople to Malta, B-P hoped to learn something about the defences of the Dardanelles. He managed to do this quite easily by taking passage on the tramp steamer S.S. *Wallachia*, under Scottish Captain Croskery, carrying grain from Odessa. He had a good view from the ship of the Boulair Lines, 'a strong line of earthworks across the isthmus', but he was more interested in the fortifications at the entrance to the Dardanelles.

As the ship stopped at Chanak (present-day Çanakkale) to send its papers on board the Turkish guard-ship, Baden-Powell had a boat lowered so that he could do a bit of fishing while the S.S. *Wallachia* was at anchor. Several patrol boats from the forts called at the ship to tell the captain to clear out, but each time their orders were drowned by a loud hammering in the bowels of the ship. Captain Croskery informed the patrol boats 'that his engines had broken down, and as soon as these were mended he would gladly get on his way again—meantime could they advise his nephew in the boat yonder what was the best bait to use for fish?'

And all the while the 'nephew' was busy 'fishing'—'fishing' for information, sketching and taking the angles of the embrasures and the facets of some of the main fortifications protecting the Dardanelles.

4

After three rather pleasant years on Malta—in spite of occasional flare-ups of 'those beastly Maltese politics'—Sir Henry's term as Governor approached its end.

The closer the final day, the more concerned the 36-year-old Baden-Powell became about the future. He hadn't saved any of his meagre pay at Malta. His writings and drawings had brought him a fair amount of publicity but little in the way of remuneration. He had tried for the Staff College nomination but had been refused for lack of an active service record. He had applied to get in on several small campaigns—in the Sudan, in Mashonaland—but had met with no success.

He had a heart-to-heart talk with his uncle about his prospects for the future. 'Go back to your regiment in Ireland,' Sir Henry told him. 'Regular regimental service will tell better than anything else in your future career: the War Office looks askance at an "office man" for high billets—but a soldier who has also done office work (e.g. military secretary) is the man they want for many billets. Moreover England is the place to serve in, being under the eye of the head people—and Ireland combines that with less expense.'

He wrote to his old colonel, Sir Baker Russell, for advice. Sir Baker recommended that B-P resign as military secretary and return to his regiment in time to take part in the spring training. Sir Henry agreed and sent off his A.D.C.'s resignation to London.

The War Office's telegram accepting B-P's resignation contained a bouquet for his work as Intelligence Officer in the form of a grant of £40 for a side trip on the way home, for 'snipe hunting' in Algeria.

After a boisterous send-off in his completed pet project, the Soldiers' and Sailors' Club, Baden-Powell left Malta with the appreciation of the garrison ringing in his ears: 'Everyone in the Army and out of it here,' the *Malta Chronicle* wrote, 'will be sorry at his departure, for we feel that he had the highest interests of the soldier very much at heart. . . . We wish all happiness and success, wherever he may be, to THE MAJOR!'

B-P returned home by way of Tunis, Bizerta, Constantine, Algiers, Oran, Marseilles, and Paris. On his arrival in London on 28 May 1893, he was met at Victoria by George, married just seven weeks before.

George had become the first of the five brothers to break the communal bonds of the Baden-Powell family—the first to tie himself down, as Mrs Baden-Powell had feared, nine years before, might happen, 'to the selfish ordinary life of earning and spending for himself alone'.

B-P had no misgivings on that score. He had received the news of

George's forthcoming wedding with real joy: 'The more I think of Old G's goings-on, the more I like them,' he had written home. 'I think it's a rare good thing for him, and I hope the example will not be set in vain to the rest of the family (always excepting me—I'm too young yet!).' He had missed being in England for George's Whitsuntide wedding. Now, at last, he was to meet his brother's bride.

He approved of what he saw. Although tiny next to her imposing-looking 45-year-old husband, Frances Baden-Powell had her own quiet way of asserting herself. She fitted well into the Baden-Powell family. And Mother Baden-Powell's fear of the 'selfish ordinary life' that a son of hers would enter into, married, did not come to pass, to a great extent because Frances was the favourite daughter of a wealthy and generous father, Charles Wilson of Cheltenham, formerly of Australia.

5

Baden-Powell rejoined the 13th Hussars at Ballincollig in County Cork, Ireland. In spite of his three-year absence from the regiment he was made to feel as if he had never been away—especially by his old friend McLaren. B-P took over the command of his old squadron and was soon back in the swing of activities—not just of military duties but also of arranging entertainments for the whole regiment.

He staged his first variety show in the regimental theatre within two weeks of his return. The hall was filled with an expectant crowd. When B-P came on stage to sing his first song his colonel arose in the audience and shouted out 'B-P, old chap, we're glad to have you back!' The men jumped up on the benches, yelling and cheering. The row lasted for almost five minutes. 'It was so jolly unexpected, too. I felt like a fool.'

Most of Baden-Powell's time was taken up with the training of his squadron. He put his men through an intensive musketry course. He took a veterinary course himself and taught the skills he had learned to his men. He instructed them in precision riding to such a point that the whole squadron could perform a 'musical ride' to the accompaniment of the regimental orchestra.

The special conditioning Baden-Powell had given his squadron showed in the way it acted during the yearly summer manoeuvres of the British Forces in Ireland round the Curragh in County Cork, under Lord Wolseley as General Officer Commanding.

An episode during these manoeuvres threatened for a moment to get out of control but turned out profitably in the end. During the fighting, B-P and the squadron were watching for an opportunity to get a dig at the 'enemy'. If he could only capture that battery.... But how? There was little cover among the Irish hills for his squadron to approach the gun position unseen. Success could only be attained by first drawing away the defending cavalry.

The weather had been unusual for Ireland—a prolonged hot spell. The fields were as green as ever but the roads were dusty. Baden-Powell worked out a ruse: He sent half a dozen men at a fast pace down a long dusty lane, each towing a tree branch behind him. 'This raised a great cloud of dust, rapidly moving, with here and there a Hussar visible among the dust.'

The illusion was perfect. Only a whole squadron of horsemen could possibly raise that much dust. The bait was too strong for the enemy's guarding cavalry. Off it went. And as soon as it was well away B-P dashed in with his squadron and captured the battery.

While the umpire was in the middle of telling the gunners that they were put out of action, a horseman arrived on the scene: 'The G.O.C. wants to know the name of the officer who played this trick.' B-P gave his name. 'You had better come along with me,' suggested the horseman, 'and explain the action yourself.'

As B-P followed him he saw in his mind's eye an irate General greeting him with a 'You are not here to play the fool, sir, but to soldier!' But to his amazement, 'there was Lord Wolseley, very calm and cheery, asking me quite easily what I had done. When I got through with my explanations he thanked me and said he liked to see an officer use his wits and not always feel tied down by Drill Book regulations.'

In 1895 the 13th Hussars were transferred to Dundalk and, later to Belfast.

By then Baden-Powell had reconciled himself to the kind of future that lay before him: 'I am afraid the Staff College is beyond me now,' he wrote George. 'I think I am over-age and I am certain I can't afford a crammer —nor can I learn the required mathematics. Nor would it be much good to me now, whereas if I can only manage to stick on for the next six years in the regiment I shall then get the command—just as we go to India— and so come on very good pay, with a fair pension four years later.'

But in the meantime, how was he to pay a cavalry officer's expenses on fifteen shillings a day? He simply had to increase his income. And as far as he was concerned that could only be done by writing and sketching.

When off duty he wrote and sketched, sending his production to English newspapers and magazines. In one two-month period he submitted eleven articles and twenty drawings of which three articles and eight drawings were accepted, two articles and five drawings held for further consideration, six articles and seven drawings declined. 'The money has not all come in yet but I expect it will run to about £16 or £17. Well, it's not much to boast of, is it?—but it's better than a poke in the eye with a sharp stick.'

He was wondering how he could improve his average of acceptances and, as usual, turned to George for suggestions. George told his ambitious brother to aim his contributions more directly at specific publications instead of sending them off indiscriminately. By following George's advice, Baden-Powell managed to raise his income for the year from his journalistic and artistic efforts to £47. 'I hope to double it next year.'

The chance of doing this doubling suddenly appeared promising.

B-P was shooting in Norfolk at the home of an officer friend in November 1895, when a telegram arrived from the *Graphic*. The editor had heard that Baden-Powell was on leave and desired his services. He wanted him to go to Constantinople to cover the tense situation in Turkey where thousands of Armenians had been massacred. The *Graphic* would pay all expenses plus thirty shillings a day.

B-P wired back his acceptance and started to pack. He had hardly gathered his gear together before another telegram arrived. This one was from the War Office:

> You are selected to proceed on active service. . . . You are assigned to the Staff of Sir Francis Scott. . . . You will proceed to the Gold Coast 23 November. . . .

The telegram bore the name of the aide to Lord Wolseley—Lord Wolseley of the long memory: remembering a young officer surveying at Maiwand, demonstrating a machine-gun at Seaforth, reporting on the fort at Bizerta, playing a trick on his 'enemy' at the Curragh. Lord Wolseley, just promoted to Commander-in-Chief of the British Army upon the retirement of the Duke of Cambridge, required an officer of a special calibre for a job of a special character.

Here at last was the 'field service' and the 'small war' B-P had longed for! He rushed up to London to present himself to the Commander-in-Chief and to receive further orders.

'You will raise a native contingent and command it as a scouting and pioneering force for our Ashanti expedition,' Lord Wolseley told him, 'not that this is a cavalry service', he apologized to the Major of the 13th Hussars, 'but rather one in which you will have the opportunity to make full use of your wits'.

IX

Ashanti Expedition

Years: 1895–96   Age: 38

1

GOLD COAST! Ashanti! Here were names to conjure with! And only ten days available for Baden-Powell to read up the country in the handbooks of the United Service Institution, to learn the background for the impending expedition, to find out the scope of the undertaking, to receive briefings in the War Office.

The Gold Coast along the southern shore of the westward-jutting bulge of the African continent—now part of the country of Ghana—had had a stormy history for more than five hundred years, from the days in 1366 when French traders from Rouen settled there for the purpose of digging in its river beds and panning out the alluvial gold from the forest muck and ore-bearing sand. They found it mostly in the form of dust but occasionally also as nuggets—the largest, according to legend, heavy enough to tether a horse to.

The French had been followed by the Danes and the Dutch, the English, the Portuguese and the Swedes. All of them built trading posts and fortresses along the shore and all of them prospered. Especially after they had discovered that the hinterland contained another kind of gold in even greater demand than the yellow metal: the glistening black gold of human bodies, of slaves for the plantations of the western hemisphere.

White traders and black kings connived together. War-like tribes like the Ashanti raided the kraals of peaceful natives—killing the children and the weak, chaining the fit together and driving the wailing hordes through the tropical forest to the coast where slavers were waiting to carry their cargo of human despair across the ocean. Until suddenly, in the early years of the nineteenth century, the market collapsed because of the

British Government's abolition of the slave trade, a turnabout completely inexplicable to the native kings.

The Ashanti would have none of it. Slaves might be off the market as items of trade, but they had other uses: they were required for human sacrifices. And so the Ashanti, living in the area beyond the River Prah, the natural northern boundary of the Gold Coast Colony, continued their assaults on neighbouring tribes and regularly penetrated on savage raids into the British colony itself.

The British went to war. In 1824 they sent a force of five hundred native troops and eight white officers under Sir Charles McCarthy against the Ashanti. Within a few days the force was wiped out. Sir Charles fell into an ambush and was slain. The Ashanti followed up their victory by completely subjugating the neighbouring tribes. Their raids into the Gold Coast Colony became yet more frequent—until newly introduced war-rockets drove the Ashanti out of the British territory and, in 1831, forced them into a treaty by which they renounced their pretended suzerainty over all other tribes and agreed to abolish human sacrifices.

In spite of the treaty the Ashanti soon resumed their raids on their neighbours and continued their human sacrifices.

In 1863 another British punitive expedition set out for Kumasi, the Ashanti capital. Again the British suffered a major military disaster, mainly due to the fact that the operations were undertaken at the wrong season of the year, with the resulting terrible ravages of malaria and dysentery among the troops.

For a while the Gold Coast Colony languished under the resolution of withdrawal adopted by the House of Commons in 1865: 'All further extension of territory or assumption of government or new treaties offering any protection to native tribes would be inexpedient. . . .'

This 'Little Englander' resolution proved completely impracticable. Every trend was in the opposite direction. And so, in 1873, the British again were at war with the Ashanti, this time with forces under Sir Garnet Wolseley. Unlike his predecessors, Wolseley did not underestimate the strength of the enemy. With an army of fourteen hundred British soldiers he executed a series of brilliant actions and marches, captured and burned the Ashanti capital on 4 February 1874.

King Kofi Karikari—known to the British as King Coffee—fled into the jungle but was eventually persuaded to sue for peace. Again, the Ashanti pledged themselves by the Treaty of Fomena, to abolish human sacrifices, to keep a trade road open between Kumasi and Prahsu, the British outpost on the River Prah, and to pay a war indemnity of 50,000 ounces of Ashanti gold. Whereupon the British retired, 'imagining in our folly', as B-P's brother George put it, 'that a nation steeped to the lips in barbarism and savagery would abide by and carry out the terms of a paper convention'.

The outcome was inevitable. It was further aggravated by a decimating civil war among the Ashanti and the 'enstooling' in 1888 of King Kwaku Dua III—a youth of 16 better known under his nickname of Prempeh— on the Golden Stool of Ashanti.

For several years the British watched this young ruler break every obligation of the 1874 treaty. For every breach the Ashanti committed unpunished their reputation among surrounding tribes increased while British prestige suffered. At last the British Government had had enough. The time had come to break the power of Prempeh, to destroy the influence of the Ashanti once and for all.

The time was 1895—and Wolseley, the officer who had been in charge of the 1873 expedition into Ashanti, was Commander-in-Chief of the British Army. Of all people, he knew best the difficulties inherent in an expedition into malaria-ridden West Africa, the minimum strength and material required.

In the briefings of the staff that was to accompany Sir Francis Scott to the Gold Coast, Lord Wolseley told the officers of the refrain of the war song chanted by the Ashanti going into battle:

> If I go forward I die;
> If I go backward I die;
> Better go forward and die.

As a military man, Baden-Powell was intrigued by the chant's apparent sentiment of boldness and bravery. But he was surprised and somewhat amused when he learned the actual meaning as interpreted by Wolseley: 'If in battle the Ashanti turns to flee, there are men on the look-out close behind him who have positive orders to kill him without quarter. If these men in the second line fail to do their duty in this respect, their superiors in the third line will kill both them and the run-away coward. . . .' and so on, for several lines the whole way back to Kumasi. Forward or backward, the Ashanti knew that he might die in battle. No wonder the Ashanti warriors had shown themselves fierce fighters.

The expedition to which Baden-Powell was assigned promised to be an interesting and difficult one. After his preliminary study of the situation on the Gold Coast and in Ashanti, B-P felt himself in complete agreement with the statement made in Parliament by Joseph Chamberlain, the Secretary of State for the Colonies: 'The duty of this country in regard to all these savage countries over which we are called upon to exercise some sort of dominion is to establish, at the earliest possible date, *Pax Britannica*, and force these people to keep the peace among themselves.' B-P had only disdain for the voices raised by Members of Her Majesty's Government's Loyal Opposition, to the effect that Chamberlain's decision to make the Ashanti fulfil their 1874 treaty obligations at this particular time might have been influenced by the doings of the French in their military territories to the west and north of Ashanti and of the Germans in their Togoland colony to the east.

Prempeh, in the opinion of B-P and numerous other Britons, had stood in the way of civilization and trade long enough and should be 'put a stop to'. It was a matter of sufficient men and matériel and a bold strategy. It was a matter of sending out advance troops to help the local authorities to enrol native workers to get the road northward through the Gold Coast Colony in condition for an onrushing army. It was a matter of shipping out, and providing for, a British force of two thousand men.

Since pack animals—horses and mules—could not be employed because of the tsetse fly and the absence of forage, the army had to depend on the time-honoured method of traversing a wilderness: the use of porters. Close to twelve thousand native carriers would be needed, computed on the basis of one carrier per soldier plus ten thousand others for bringing up the necessary supplies of arms, ammunition, food, medicines, stretchers for the sick, telegraph and bridge-making equipment, and a hundred other items. In addition, about five hundred other natives were required for Baden-Powell's command.

2

On 13 December 1895, the British troopship S.S. *Bathurst*, with Baden-Powell and Sir Francis Scott's two-thousand-man detachment on board dropped anchor off Cape Coast Castle.

Instantly, the ship was surrounded by scores of large open boats, each manned by a crew of twelve. Officers and men clambered into the boats and were sped through the surf by dark-skinned boatmen, sitting on the gunwales and wielding their three-pronged paddles in time to a native chant. As the boats neared the beach, a rush of naked helpers took over and ran them well up onto the sand. The British force stepped ashore, dry-shod, at the Castle water-gate. A short delay for the customary official reception by His Excellency the Governor, W. E. Maxwell—then to work.

In answer to a telegram from Sierra Leone, the local authorities had assured Baden-Powell that preliminary arrangements had been made to obtain the personnel he needed for his African levy. It was now up to

B-P and his helper, Captain Graham of the 5th Lancers, to rally their men and establish their command.

The two officers immediately got in touch with the headmen. King Matikoli of the Krobos ('1 king at 10s. *per diem*') solemnly promised to have three hundred and fifty of his men ('At 9d. *per diem*') ready to march. Chief Andoh ('1 chief at 7s. 6d. *per diem*') who had been an interpreter for Wolseley in 1873 agreed to bring twenty-five of his Elmina warriors. Chief Brew of the Mumfords would provide a hundred men. The Krobos and the Elminas were known as warlike tribes. They would make good fighting men if necessary. The Mumfords, on the other hand, were coast fishermen with 'iron sinews but hearts of mice'. Their main value would be as labourers.

After two days of further palavering—'alternate cajoling and threatening'—king and chiefs arranged to have their men assembled on the parade grounds outside the Castle at noon on 16 December, ready for departure. The men were divided into companies and 'uniforms' distributed: a red fez for each man, 'but it gives as much satisfaction to the naked warrior as does his first tunic to the young hussar'.

Late that afternoon the levy marched out of Cape Coast Castle. Its first function was to proceed as quickly as possible to Prahsu and there await the arrival of Sir Francis's main force, which would follow as closely behind as conditions would permit.

The first day B-P and his men covered thirteen miles, most of them along a hard gravel path that ran through a labyrinth of small, brush-covered hills. The next day, the column entered a dense tropical jungle of palms, giant ferns, trees of many different kinds, with occasional huge shafts of silk-cotton and bombax trees piercing the foliage overhead. Some of the tree trunks were covered for fifty feet with delicate ferns, wax-flowers and orchids. But the rule seemed to be: the prettier the spot, the more noxious the air—reminding Baden-Powell of the smell 'that meets you near old cabbage plots in England'.

B-P's levy pressed on through the jungle along the road originally opened up during the 1873–74 campaign and now in process of being put back in shape and widened by work groups of the advance party. On 20 December, the levy marched into Prahsu.

While waiting for Sir Francis Scott's main force to move up, Baden-Powell established a more complete organization of his levy, installed officers, distributed arms and trained the men in the pioneering skills of axemanship and rope work that would be required in their advance towards Kumasi. He further mobilized a hundred Adansi hillmen, some of them to accompany the levy and act as sentries, others to reconnoitre ahead to ascertain every move made by the Ashanti.

At three o'clock on Christmas Eve, Baden-Powell received the order to move off. By five the levy had been ferried across the yellow, slow-flowing Prah in large dug-out canoes.

The preliminaries were over. Now for the main task.

3

B-P's levy was required to proceed as a scouting force through enemy territory and, at the same time, clear the road for the British troops coming up behind it and prepare shelters for the men, from the River Prah to the Ashanti capital, seventy-four miles to the north. Two white officers were responsible for getting this task done, with five hundred Africans willing enough to march but most unenthusiastic about working.

In the beginning, Baden-Powell found the levy hard to deal with and progress exceedingly slow. Again and again he had to curb his impatience —nothing would have been gained by showing it. He had been told that 'A smile and a stick will carry you through any difficulty'—but he discovered that another Gold Coast proverb was even more to the point: 'Softly, softly, catchee monkey'. He quickly arrived at the firm conviction that 'no man acting on any other principle could have organized a native levy on the West Coast of Africa—and lived'.

Eventually, by dividing the levy into small companies of from twenty to thirty men, each under a 'captain', and making the headmen responsible for the conduct of their own tribesmen, the work began to progress more smoothly.

Day in and day out, the levy moved northward with slashing machetes and whacking axes cutting through brush and fallen trees; laying corduroy roads over swampy places, bridging streams, building camps. And every day, after the usual infuriatingly slow start, the routine was the same:

On through the deep, dark aisle, still foggy with the morning mist and wet with the dripping dew. Twisting and turning, now up, now down, clambering over giant tree roots, splashing through the sucking mud—all in moist and breathless heat, till, tired and dripping, we reach the site for camp. Two hours' rest for mid-day chop, and then parade. More delays, more excuses, and at last every company has its work assigned to it. . . .

Further delays and further excuses throughout the afternoon. . . .

But the bush comes down nevertheless, and, what is more wonderful, by sunset there is an open space where this morning there was nothing but a sea of bush jungle, and large palm-thatched sheds have sprung up in regular lines. . . .

*Baden-Powell's responsibilities in Ashanti, 1895–96, included the building
of a great number of pioneering bridges.*

It was exhausting work for the men and a 'pretty powerful exercise, both
mental and physical', for Baden-Powell. 'By the end of the day', he
confessed to his diary, 'one wants but little here below but to drink and
to lie down and sleep or die, you don't care which.'

But there was no halting. The next day it was forward again in the
intense heat and oppressive humidity, with greater and greater care the
farther the levy penetrated into Ashanti.

From time to time, now, silent forms, naked except for a few discoloured
rags, sneaked up to the column. They were Adansi scouts bringing

reconnaissance reports of doings in Kumasi, the more 'promising' the closer the levy got to the Capital. The reports had it that King Prempeh had ordered a council of war; that most of his chiefs had attended it, but that a few had not; that the ceremony of 'taking fetish' (the oath to fight) had been carried out; that eight thousand warriors were gathered in Kumasi and in outlying villages.

On 3 January 1896, Baden-Powell got his first real excitement. On that day two breathless messengers brought him an urgent request from Bekwai: the king desired to be placed under the British flag forthwith. He was one of the chiefs who had disobeyed Prempeh's order to come to Kumais for the war council and now realized the need for protection before Prempeh's wrath could reach him.

But how get help to Bekwai in time? Bekwai was off to the west of the direct route to Kumasi and the Ashanti were reported to have an outpost force at Essian Kwanta where the trail for Bekwai turned off from the Kumasi trail. There was only one solution for the problem to Baden-Powell's mind: he would send off a small party of scouts to Essian Kwanta to divert whatever enemy force might be there and take the rest of the levy on a secret night march through the jungle directly towards Bekwai. In this way he would bring the Bekwai king the desired assistance and would, at the same time, outflank the Ashanti outpost.

To confuse any Ashanti spies who might be about, he ordered the levy to halt and prepare to settle down for the night. But as dusk fell, Baden-Powell gave out secret orders for a parade at moonrise, a quarter to nine. Then the column moved off into the deep, dense gloom of the jungle.

At three in the morning the column reached the village of Heman, well within Bekwai country. It had been a hard journey: 'Only nine miles in six hours, and everybody fagged!' Four hours' sleep and a light breakfast, and the column was again on the move. Ten more miles, easier because of the daylight, and Bekwai was reached.

Baden-Powell was received at the royal 'palace' by the king in council and tendered the royal thanks for the prompt arrival of the protecting force. The British flag was raised over Bekwai with elaborate ceremony, to the cheers of a vast crowd of several thousand Bekwaians. At a business palaver following the ceremonial palaver, Baden-Powell, in return for British protection, asked for Bekwai warriors for the final onrush towards Kumasi, for more workers and more porters. After an interminable argument he finally got what he wanted.

While B-P was still in Bekwai, the scouts he had sent toward Essian Kwanta brought him the news that the Ashanti outpost had made off towards Kumasi. The main route was clear for the British troops moving up and Bekwai was safe for the time being. B-P and his levy continued northward, back at their work of road clearing.

At Ordasu, a few miles from Kumasi, Baden-Powell halted while the main force caught up with him. Here plans were laid for the final push towards the Ashanti capital: Baden-Powell was to send two flanking parties along the by-ways to Kumasi while moving up with the rest of his men on the central road. Sir Francis Scott's force was to march up immediately behind B-P's columns.

All kinds of rumours reached the advancing troops—that the enemy meant to make a firm stand against the British Army at the very gates of Kumasi, that Ashanti columns were approaching from all directions, that if the Ashanti were beaten the city would be blown up.

Suddenly a weird sound filled the air: the throbbing and booming of drums. It sounded as if a swarm of bees in a hive were being disturbed. There was a certain cadence to the sound. The drums were making 'drum talk'. Baden-Powell moved his men warily forward.

The jungle ahead thinned. And after three weeks, on 17 January 1896, B-P's levy moved out of the dark, soggy depths of the jungle into the open sunshine. 'There lay before us a clear space like a parade ground, a quarter of a mile wide; and beyond it, on a gentle slope in a hollow, a mass of thatched roofs stretched away into the jungle beyond.' Kumasi!

4

Yes, Kumasi at last. And what a disappointment! The 'gates to the city' that they had heard about were non-existent. The 'city' itself was a clutter of the usual African wattle-and-daub huts. The 'King's Palace' was a collection of larger huts with high walls, high-pitched roofs and endless courts connected by narrow entries. There was nothing imposing about any of it—yet this was the place with a long and lurid history, the key to a vast hinterland.

Baden-Powell marched his main column directly into the open space and brought it to a halt. A few moments later, his flank detachment arrived.

The drumming that B-P had heard before reaching the town grew louder. A roar of voices began to fill the air as a band of drums and elephant-tusk horns marched into the square. It was followed by a number of coloured umbrellas that danced and bobbed above the heads of a surging crowd of natives: King Prempeh and his chiefs had arrived to watch the entry of the British troops. Their brass-nailed chairs were lowered to the ground. And there they sat until five in the afternoon, Prempeh looking very bored, yet regal, with a black and gold tiara on his head, with strings of large golden beads and nuggets round his neck and arms and with a peculiar nut-shaped charm between his clenched teeth to keep his mouth from uttering 'the wrong word'.

While waiting for the main force to enter Baden-Powell did some reconnoitring. So did his second-in-command, Captain Graham. As the Captain approached a small grove of huge owa-owa trees B-P noticed a sudden wave of excitement spreading among the head Ashanti. The thought struck him that the Captain might be walking into an ambush. He called to Graham to halt and sent a number of scouts to investigate the grove. They returned with the highly interesting information that Graham had stumbled on the Ashanti fetish grove. The ground under the huge trees was littered with the skeletons of decapitated bodies and loose skulls, all of them with the jaw-bones missing. Within an hour of their arrival, B-P's men had secured confirmation that human sacrifices were still frequent in Ashanti.

All day long, Sir Francis Scott's force came marching in: two thousand British soldiers interspersed with twelve thousand native carriers—column after column after column, a winding snake nine miles long, quickly split up on entering the square as billeting officers led the groups out to their camp sites.

Late in the afternoon, Sir Francis Scott and his staff seated themselves in a semicircle on the parade ground. There had been some guesswork among the officers as to what Prempeh might do when asked to come down from his throne to meet the commander of the British troops. Would that be when the trouble would start?

The answer was surprising. Without a word, the Ashanti king left his chair and approached the British general. His meeting with Sir Francis lasted a moment only. He was informed that he would have to make his submission to the Governor who would arrive in Kumasi a few days later and that he would be expected, on that occasion, to pay in full the indemnity prescribed in the 1874 treaty.

There was not a flicker of change in the expression on Prempeh's face. He waited until Sir Francis had had his say, then turned, reseated himself on his throne and was carried off the square.

Did Prempeh mean this apparent surrender? B-P had his doubts. He made up his mind to keep the king and his chiefs under close surveillance, and to do some reconnoitring of his own.

In investigating the surroundings of the royal 'palace' B-P discovered that the palace enclosure adjoined the bush at the back, that the fencing round it had a hidden exit, that a secret footpath led from this point into the forest beyond. It was an easy route for a person desiring to escape.

Without asking royal leave, B-P put some of his men to work with machetes clearing a space round the palace enclosure so broad that no person could cross it unnoticed. As a further precaution, B-P placed a twenty-four-hour guard of hidden sentries about the whole area.

For a couple of days and nights nothing suspicious happened.

On 19 January 1895, His Excellency the Governor arrived from the coast. Final arrangements were made for Prempeh's submission the following day. If anything was to upset the plans, Baden-Powell decided, it would have to take place this last night.

As night fell one after the other of Prempeh's chiefs approached and went into the palace. Late in the evening, they were all assembled within the royal enclosure. Baden-Powell wondered what was up. Would Prempeh's chiefs, after their palaver, try to slip away to join up with their adherents in the jungle for an attack on the Britons from all directions? Would Prempeh himself make an attempt to flee before the final submission, as his uncle, 'King Coffee' had fled? B-P was determined that none of this should happen.

The hours moved by. Midnight came and went. A thick wet mist covered the whole area.

Some time after three o'clock, B-P, from where he lay near the path, saw a figure approaching, outlined against the mist, one of Prempeh's chiefs. He let the man pass, then gave a soft whistle, a prearranged signal to his men behind him., There was the sound of a brief struggle, of much gasping and grunting, then again silence. At intervals during the night other quietly moving men passed close to Baden-Powell only to fall into the hands of his men, to be gagged and bound.

Finally the last of Prempeh's visitors came down the path so silently that Baden-Powell did not know of his presence until he was alongside him. Suddenly the Ashanti stopped. He stood perfectly still for a few moments as if sensing an ambush, then seemed on the point of turning to rush back to the palace to give warning. Baden-Powell rose from his hiding-place, got his arms around the Ashanti's neck and his knee in the small of his back and tumbled over with him. In their struggle B-P realized that his adversary was swinging a gun towards him. He grabbed for it, and the old flint-lock came apart in his hand. At that moment B-P's orderly joined the fight. Between them the man was quickly subdued. Another prisoner had joined the rest.

At long last reveille began to sound in one camp after another round the town. The mist grew lighter overhead. The night watch was over. Any notion that Prempeh or his chiefs might have had of escaping had been thwarted. Everyone supposed to be on hand for the day's doings would be there.

Later that morning, British troops marched into the parade grounds and planted themselves in a closed square. The people of Kumasi, curious and apprehensive, formed a solid wall behind the soldiers.

Shortly before the hour for Prempeh's public submission, Governor Maxwell and Sir Francis Scott entered the square and seated themselves on a dais. After a long wait, booming drums announced the approach of Prempeh and his retinue. The line of British soldiers opened to admit the Ashanti king, the queen mother, and the head chief, then closed again, keeping out all the royal attendants.

Through an interpreter, the Governor informed Prempeh that the British expedition had arrived in Kumasi for the sole purpose of ensuring that the Treaty of Fomena was finally kept. He told the Ashanti king that the British Government did not intend to depose him and the queen mother, provided they made their submission at once 'in accordance with the native form and custom' and paid the indemnity.

Silently and slowly Prempeh removed the gold circlet from his head and slipped out of his sandals. Barefooted, he and his mother moved up to the dais, knelt before it and embraced the knees of Governor Maxwell. A shocked sigh went through the crowd that surrounded the British troops. Never before had a King of Ashanti humiliated himself like this!

Prempeh arose. 'I now claim the protection of the Queen of England,' he said.

But Maxwell was not done. He pointedly apprised Prempeh of the fact that there was yet the matter of the indemnity to be paid—50,000 ounces of gold. The king insisted that no such amount was available in Ashanti. He offered to pay 680 ounces immediately, the rest later.

The Governor was adamant. The payment was due at once. Since it was obviously not forthcoming he declared Prempeh, the queen mother and the leading Ashanti chiefs under arrest. They would be taken to Cape Coast Castle as prisoners, as security for the payment of the indemnity.

Maxwell's unexpected move had an instant demoralizing effect on the Ashanti. They were stunned by what must have seemed to them a high-handed act of treachery. 'The nation is now like a flock of sheep without a leader,' Baden-Powell noted immediately after the event. He was convinced that 'had the people even guessed beforehand what the result of the coup was to have been . . . they would have fought to prevent it'.

Governor Maxwell was certain that Prempeh had lied, that the Ashanti gold for paying the full indemnity was actually on hand. Baden-Powell was ordered to make a search for it.

B-P, with members of his levy, looked for it first in the royal palace.

He found 'piles of the tawdriest and commonest stuff mixed indiscriminately with quaint, old and valuable articles'. But a large number of treasures known to belong to the king had disappeared, among them his golden hat, his golden chair of state, and, above all, the Golden Stool that contained the *sunsum* or soul of the nation and on which Ashanti kings were 'enstooled'.

Baden-Powell had no more luck finding gold in the sacred fetish houses of Bantama, the burial place of the kings of Ashanti. As he and his men broke open the sealed entrance they found the nine coffins of the departed rulers in seemingly perfect order. But when the lids were removed the coffins were empty. The royal bones and the gold supposedly buried with them had disappeared—presumably, B-P thought, carried into the jungle for safe concealment by the fleeing guardian priests.

Nevertheless, Baden-Powell did not leave Bantama empty-handed. After burning down the fetish houses, as per instructions, he was making ready to return to Kumasi when some of his men came up to him and asked him to follow them. They led him to a find they had made: a large bowl of beaten brass, about four feet across and eighteen inches deep. B-P was enthusiastic: it was just the tub he needed—he hadn't had a decent bath since Cape Coast Castle.

But B-P never had his bath in it. When the bowl was brought to Kumasi he was surprised at the great attention it received. It was only then that he learned that his trophy was the famous fetish bowl of the Ashanti used to collect the blood that welled from the necks of decapitated slaves, to be used by the king for the ceremony of 'washing the bones' of his forebears. As B-P studied closely the inside of the bowl he saw a 'high-water mark' and completely lost his desire to use the bowl for a bath-tub.

5

The 'conquest' of Kumasi and the overthrow of the Ashanti king had been a disappointing affair to Baden-Powell. He had expected a hard fight, not this abject surrender. But although the campaign had been bloodless it had not been without casualties.

What King Prempeh had failed to do, King Fever had accomplished.

Fifty per cent of the white soldiers had come down with dysentery or malaria. Among the officers the fever had struck even harder—80 per cent were ill. Scores of men and officers had succumbed, among them Prince Henry of Battenberg who had volunteered for the post of military secretary to Sir Francis Scott.

B-P's second in command, Captain Graham, had been ill with fever.

So had his replacement—and yet another. Baden-Powell himself had succeeded in keeping well.

He had been told: 'Keep your shirt on.' He did. It got soaked quickly from perspiration in the torrid atmosphere, but B-P had a way of taking care of the situation. He carried a dry shirt across his back, tied by the sleeves around his neck. When the shirt he was wearing got wet, he put on the dry shirt.

'Keep your head covered.' He had brought along the wide-brimmed Boer hat he had used during the Zulu uprising in Southern Africa. It came in handy. He had the tender skin of most people with freckles—his skin sunburned instead of tanning. The wide brim protected his face and neck far better than the colonial helmet. But also, it gave protection against branches and vines as he ploughed through the bush. The broad-brimmed hat had became so much a trademark for B-P that the natives had called him *Kantankye*—'He-of-the-big-hat'.

Lord Wolseley had given him advice: 'Use a tent with double netting— and smoke it up with tobacco smoke when you turn in.' B-P tried to follow this advice but with little success. His tobacco, already adulterated with dried eucalyptus leaves 'against the fever', turned mouldy—the taste was awful. He stopped smoking and never took it up again.

The return of the British troops to the coast began on 22 January.

Rumours had reached Sir Francis Scott that an attempt would be made on Prempeh's life on his way to Cape Coast Castle, either by the Ashanti to prevent the disgrace to their nation or by the Bekwai to pay off old scores. Consequently, every effort was made to prevent the rumours from becoming reality. Baden-Powell and his levy, on their return march, were ordered to search the bush between Kumasi and Essian Kwanta. They flushed out a number of Ashanti but they proved to be mostly runaway slaves rather than would-be assassins.

After Essian Kwanta, the levy was released from further duty. Where- upon B-P marched it off to the coast at the rate of twenty miles a day ('not a bad pace in such a climate') and reached the Castle at daybreak on 29 January.

After paying off his men, B-P had himself rowed out to the hospital ship *Coromandel* lying at anchor off the coast, in the hope of 'cadging' a good breakfast. 'When I got on board they all thought I was an invalid from my appearance. I sat down in a chair and fell fast asleep till somebody woke me up for lunch. Then I made no bones about it—I got into bed and slept and slept till next morning—and got up an entirely different being.'

The Ashanti campaign was over. It closed in the docks of London with an ironical blunder.

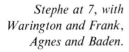

The Rev. Professor Baden Powell,
F.R.S. Born 1796, died 1860.

Mrs Henrietta Grace Powell, née
Smyth. Born 1824, died 1914.

Stephe at the age of 4, in typical
Victorian boy's garb.

Stephe at 7, with
Warington and Frank,
Agnes and Baden.

Stephe at Charterhouse, aged 17.

The Wimbledon rifle team, 1874 (Baden-Powell third from left).

Lieutenant Baden-Powell, aged 21.

Promoted to Captain in 1883, aged 26.

Impeesa *in South Africa, 1896.*

*B-P and the Ashanti scout (illustra-
tion in 'Downfall of Prempeh').*

Capt. Villiers, Major B-P, General Carrington, at Bulawayo, 1896.

The Baden-Powell family in 1897. Standing: Baden, Agnes, Frank, Frances (George's wife), Robert. Seated: Sir George, Mrs Baden-Powell with George's daughter Maud on her lap, Warington.

Colonel B-P made up for his part as Wun-Hi in 'The Geisha', 1897.

B-P inspecting the improvised armoured car before start of war.

Baden-Powell's lookout on roof of Mafeking lawyer Minchin's office.

'The Hero of Mafeking'. A photograph of B-P taken during the siege.

The Mafeking Officers. Standing: Major Panzera, Capt. Ryan, Capt. Greener, Major Lord Edward Cecil, Capt. Gordon Wilson, Capt. Hanbury-Tracey, Capt. Cowan. Seated: Major Godley, Major Vyvyan, Magistrate Bell, Col. B-P, Major Whiteley, Col. Hore, Dr Hayes. On the ground: Lieut Moncrieffe.

The Mafeking Cadet Corps and the siege stamps used for the local mail.

CLIMAX ONE

The climax event of Baden-Powell's first life—the relief of the siege of Mafeking—was celebrated throughout Britain. On Mafeking Night, 18 May 1900, Piccadilly Circus became a surging mass of humanity.

B-P (*left*) escorted the Joseph Chamberlains through South Africa.

B-P in S.A.C. uniform (*from a painting by Harold Speed*).

The Inspector-General with his staff inspecting British Cavalry, 1904.

As the ship bringing home the expedition entered the dock, another big ship cut in ahead of it. As she did so a large posse of general and staff officers from the War Office formed on the red carpet to receive her and a band on the wharf struck up 'See the Conquering Hero Comes'.

Then Baden-Powell noticed a commotion in the ranks: 'As our ship was warped in to the opposite side of the dock the band suddenly ceased playing and the bandsmen, together with the generals and staff, scuttled round the dock, hastily leaving the first ship to come round and welcome us.'

The ship that had cut in proved to be the transport that was bringing back to England as prisoners Dr Leander Starr Jameson and the men implicated with him in the Jameson Raid that had turned South Africa into a hornets' nest and had brought the Transvaal and the British Empire to the point of war.

X

The Matabele Rising

Year: 1896   Age: 39

1

DURING the first days after his arrival home from Ashanti, Baden-Powell was kept busy in the War Office—there were reports to be made. But one day he dropped into the office of the *Graphic* and was greeted with open arms. He had already received £150 in payment for sketches he had sent home from the campaign. Now the editor had another task for him: would he be interested in taking part in the Dongola Expedition into Anglo-Egyptian Sudan as correspondent for the *Graphic* and at his own terms? B-P would, indeed, but unfortunately, would not be able to: there would be no possibility of getting the necessary leave.

He was received with even greater enthusiasm when he went to see the editor of the *Daily Chronicle*. And well he might have been: he had provided the *Chronicle* with the main newspaper scoop to come out of the Ashanti campaign. The day he reached Kumasi with his levy, B-P had immediately transmitted the news by field telegraph to the coast from where it was relayed to the *Chronicle* office in London. It was the first and only intimation that the press had of the event for two days. A sudden tropical storm cut the telegraph line just after Baden-Powell's dispatch had passed over it.

Baden-Powell had been considering turning the articles he had sent home from Ashanti into a book and had already been approached by a publisher interested in the project. But with the *Graphic* and the *Chronicle* both clamouring for articles, he was forced into a reconsideration of his writing programme. After debating the issue with himself, he made up his mind to forget the book and concentrate on article writing. It was easier and would earn him more money.

B-P might have given up the book idea, but his potential publishers had not. The publishing house of Methuen & Co. approached him with an offer of £100 down and a tempting royalty arrangement.

B-P weakened. 'The lucre was offered, my debts stared at me, and I fell,' he wrote to his Aunt Connie. He went over his Ashanti material: the articles he had sent home to the papers, his letters to his mother, his diaries, his staff reports. All that was needed was some logical arrangement, some editing, a few more drawings, an 'apology to the reader' by himself, and a short political analysis as an epilogue by his brother George—and the job would be done. 'On Sunday I got the offer, and on Thursday I sent off the manuscript of the book. . . . It will, I hope, be out by the end of the month, under some such title as *The Downfall of Prempeh*.'

For his services in the Ashanti campaign, B-P was awarded the campaign medal and promoted to Brevet Lieutenant-Colonel. But this was by no means 'enchanting news' to him. He wanted action, excitement, and, in his estimation, the main drawback to a promotion was 'that, the higher one's rank, the less is one's chance of being employed on these many little expeditions which I do dearly love'.

But it took events less than a month to prove his concern utterly unfounded.

On 28 April 1896, he received War Office orders informing him that passage had been provided for him in the S.S. *Tantallon Castle* leaving for Cape Town on 2 May. He was to be the Chief of Staff of Sir Frederick Carrington in the operations against the rebelling tribes of Rhodesia's Matabeleland. His services had been expressly requested by Sir Frederick who had had a chance to assess B-P's abilities on General Henry Smyth's expedition to Zululand eight years before.

Baden-Powell heaved a great sigh of relief. He had rejoined his squadron of the 13th Hussars, now stationed in Belfast. 'Such a place to station cavalry in! Half the squadron in barracks in the centre of that big city with its miles of stone-paved streets; the other half quartered in the tramways stables out in the Falls Road suburb.' That was what he had had to look forward to. No wonder that he jumped at the chance to get off to Africa again, and to the part of Africa he had come to like so much.

The *Tantallon Castle* arrived at Cape Town at four in the morning of 19 May. At nine that same evening, Baden-Powell was aboard the northbound train rattling off for three nights and two days and nine hundred miles to Mafeking, the terminus of the Cape Colony railway—a small town consisting of 'a few low-roofed tin (corrugated iron) houses'.

In Mafeking B-P caught up with General Carrington. The next day, the

General and he, with two other members of the staff, embarked on the 557-mile journey to Bulawayo in the centre of Matabeleland. They travelled by coach—'a regular Buffalo-Bill-Wild-West-Deadwood affair hung by huge leather springs on a heavy, strongly built undercarriage, drawn by ten mules', with two drivers, three soldier-servants and baggage on the roof, and inside, the staff officers, each in his own corner.

For ten days and nine nights the passengers were 'rocked and rolled and pitched and scended' in the creaking, groaning coach along the deep, dusty wagon ruts of the open, waterless veld. They stopped from time to time to cook a meal from provisions brought from Mafeking, outspanned at night at some wayside station or some kraal of friendly natives, continuing after a halt of a few hours with 'new' but equally weak mules.

The journey was tedious, the sun was hot, the flies were 'as thick as dust'. And daily, they came upon evidence of the ravages of the dreaded rinder-pest—the infectious cattle plague that was sweeping through South Africa. They passed wagons that had been abandoned because the dray oxen had fallen dead in their harness. They travelled through an area where the ground was littered with the carcasses of dead oxen and mules ('Three thousand two hundred beasts dead at this one place!'). The stench of putrid flesh was so strong that 'one could lean against it'. And, one day, one of their own mules died 'on the march'.

But in spite of everything, B-P was content. To him, all the discomforts and inconveniences were 'compensated for by the splendid climate, the starry nights, and the "flannel-shirt" life'.

As the coach approached its destination, the landscape changed from open veld to a mass of fantastic, rock-strewn hillocks—kopjes—separated by high-grass valleys. Up through the Mangwe Pass at the tail of the Matopo Hills and on to the open downs of the Matabele plateau, past small forts six to eight miles apart. And finally into Bulawayo at one in the morning of 3 June.

2

General Carrington and his staff had arrived for a task which, in its most naked terms might be described as pulling Cecil Rhodes's—the Empire Builder—smouldering chestnuts out of the African bonfire and salvaging Rhodesia for Rhodes and his British South Africa Company.

Cecil Rhodes, the son of an English clergyman, had come to South Africa for his health in 1870, at the age of 17. He arrived at the height of the diamond fever and immediately set off for the Kimberley diamond fields. By the time he was 20, he had made a fortune. By the time he was 27, he was a multimillionaire, the founder and director of the De Beers

Mining Company. That year he stood for election and became a member of the Cape Colony Legislature. At 28 he was back in England, studying at Oxford and taking the B.A. degree his poor health had previously denied him. At 33, back in South Africa, he made a killing in gold that culminated in the organization of the Consolidated Gold Fields Company with himself the director.

Rhodes had the Midas touch. But his tastes were different from those of King Midas. He did not covet gold for the sole purpose of filling his coffers. To him, wealth meant power. And only by power could he accomplish the dream that had built up in him: to make all Africa British, to link the domain 'from Cape to Cairo' into a British Colony.

And why not? The race for the partitioning of Central and South Africa was in full swing. The Belgians were in the Congo, the French in the Cameroons, the Portuguese on both sides of the dark continent, the Germans wherever they could manage to get a toehold. And the Boers were entrenched in the Transvaal. There was no time to lose. Rhodes looked northward. Bechuanaland would be the first step.

The young millionaire-politician rose in the House of the Cape Colony Parliament and demanded backing for his scheme of expanding the Colony, of bringing 'civilized government' to Bechuanaland.

At this stage, the President of the Boer Transvaal, 'Oom Paul' Kruger himself, unwittingly came to Rhodes's assistance. Kruger had long had his eye on Bechuanaland. Now he sent a force of Boer freebooters into the area. This was too much for Britain. Within a year, she formally annexed Bechuanaland.

From Bechuanaland Rhodes again looked north, towards the land of the Matabele, a vast territory rich in minerals. The Matabele—a branch of the Zulus—had been pushed out of South Africa by the Boers about forty years before. They had moved north under the leadership of their king M'silikatsi, had overpowered the unwarlike Shona tribes and taken their land.

Rhodes had no luck persuading the Cape Colony Parliament to take over Matabeleland. But there were other ways of skinning this cat. What could not be done by a cautious government might be done by a bold private concern.

In 1887 Rhodes sent agents of his company to Lobengula, M'silikatsi's successor. They succeeded in perpetrating what was probably the sharpest real estate deal since the day in 1626 when Peter Minuit bought an island off the American mainland from the Manahatin Indians for sixty Dutch guilders' worth of trinkets. Lobengula agreed to give Rhodes's company 'complete and exclusive charge over all metals and minerals in my kingdom, principalities and dominions, together with full power to do all things that they may deem necessary to win and procure the same and to collect and enjoy the profits and revenues, if any, derivable from the said metals and minerals'.

And what was Lobengula to receive in return for these rights in an area of some seventy-five thousand square miles? A princely monthly stipend of £100, a thousand Martini-Henry rifles, a hundred thousand cartridges, and —by a brilliant inspiration of Rhodes—an armed steamboat on the River Zambesi!

On the basis of this brazen deal, Rhodes—now the Prime Minister of the Cape Colony—established the British South Africa Company which promptly applied for, and received, a Royal Charter.

But why stop at Matabeleland when Mashonaland to the north was still awaiting its white 'deliverers'? Why indeed? Whereupon the Chartered Company sent a group of pioneers north under the professional big-game hunter Frederick Courtney Selous. At a suitable spot—graciously named Salisbury for Lord Salisbury, the British Prime Minister who had signed the company charter—the Union Jack was raised on 13 September 1890. Rhodes placed his good friend, Dr Leander Starr Jameson, over Mashonaland as its Administrator.

Before long Lobengula discovered that he had been duped. He was not particularly concerned about the minerals. He was mainly worried about the miners who had poured in by the thousand to extract them from his lands and the thousands of settlers who had followed in their wake. The King of the Matabele voiced his complaints to his royal colleague, Queen Victoria, but received little satisfaction from Her Majesty's Colonial Secretary:

> The Queen [Lord Knutsford wrote] advises Lobengula not to grant hastily concessions of land or leave to dig, but to consider all applications very carefully. It is not wise to put too much power into the hands of men who come first, and to exclude other deserving men. A king gives a stranger an ox, not the whole herd of cattle, otherwise what would other strangers have to eat?

Rhodes and the Chartered Company had the mineral rights. Now they coveted the actual land from Lobengula. 'Incidents' developed along the frontier between Mashonaland and Matabeleland. In 1893, Jameson decided that the time had come to strike. With a small force of Chartered Company troops he moved into Matabeleland. Hundreds of Matabele, fighting with spears and outdated rifles, were killed. Lobengula fled into the bushland to the north. Two months later he was dead of smallpox.

Rhodes had 'had his way and his war'—as Kruger said. The Matabele had been cowed. Rhodes's British South Africa Company took over the vast area and ruled it as a sovereign power, subject to the approval of the British Government.

The newspapers in Cape Colony and in England had been calling the combined areas of Matabeleland and Mashonaland 'Rhodesia' in honour of the man who had 'liberated' them for the white settlers. By 1895 the name became official and Rhodes and his friend, Dr Jameson, looked about for new lands to conquer.

Jameson, particularly, was getting impatient. He looked east, towards the Transvaal where some of Kruger's non-Boer *Uitlanders* were showing increasing resentment against 'Oom Paul'—a feeling that had been building steadily for ten years. These *Uitlanders* were the 'Outlanders'—the British, Colonial, European prospectors, workers, traders and businessmen—who had streamed into the Transvaal after gold had been discovered in the Witwatersrand, to get their share of the newly found wealth. They had been largely responsible for the growing prosperity of the Boer republic through their work and managerial skill. Kruger had been perfectly willing for the *Uitlanders* to pay most of the country's taxes but had no intention of permitting them to become naturalized and enfranchised. The time was quickly approaching when the *Uitlanders* would outnumber the Transvaalers and would be able to take over the country if they had the vote. Time and time again the *Uitlanders* had petitioned the *Volksraad*— the Transvaal parliament—to be granted the right to vote. Each time they were turned down. Some of the *Uitlanders*—the 'Reformers'—were particularly outspoken. They held to the old tenet of 'no taxation without representation' and began to plot against the Government.

Doctor Jameson developed a plan: the 'Reformers' were to rise in Johannesburg . . . they were to appeal for help from the other side of the border . . . Jameson would move into the Transvaal with a force of fifteen hundred men . . . the Transvaal Government would be held at bay . . . Rhodes would rush up from Cape Town to re-establish peace . . . a compromise would be made. Result: more territory would be added to Rhodesia.

But everything that could go wrong went wrong in the Jameson Raid. The 'Reformers' did not co-operate, Doctor Jim did not raise the necessary force, old màn Kruger knew every detail of the plot better than the widely scattered plotters themselves. Jameson, with five hundred men, had hardly crossed the border on 29 December 1895, before he ran into trouble. On 1 January 1896, he and his raiders surrendered to superior numbers of Boers.

The year that had just opened became the darkest in Rhodes's life. In the investigations that followed, it was proved beyond doubt that Rhodes had been implicated in Jameson's plot. He was forced to resign as Prime

Minister of the Cape Colony. He was forced out as managing director of the Chartered Company. The terribly contagious rinderpest struck 'his' Rhodesia and killed the cattle. Drought destroyed the grain. The Matabele rose in fury against their white overlords to reconquer the land which they had originally stolen themselves.

Since losing their king the Matabele had been like a body without a head. They had feared the might of the white man. With Jameson defeated and shipped off to England for trial they realized that the white settlers were not as all-powerful as they had thought them. They turned again to the M'limo, their god, who for generations past had guided them in their emergencies.

The M'limo spoke to his people through an oracle in the caves of the Matopo Hills. He ordered the Matabele to rise on a certain night, make their way to Lobengula's old town of Bulawayo—'the place of killings'— and massacre the white people who had usurped it. After that they were to spread out and murder the individual white settlers on their farms.

The plan miscarried because of the impatience and blood lust of some of the Matabele warriors. They started killing off farmers while on their way to Bulawayo. But they were not thorough enough. Some of the farmers managed to escape. They sped into Bulawayo and gave warning of the impending attack. The townspeople moved their wagons into the market square and formed a strong defensive laager and organized themselves into fighting units.

When the Matabele hordes arrived in the night the town was dark and unnaturally quiet. The warriors did not dare to enter. Instead they contented themselves with burning outlying farms and killing any stray white men, women and children they came upon.

The next day the news reached Salisbury where Rhodes had just arrived. He collected a force of Mashonaland residents and set out for Bulawayo. At the same time, Colonel Herbert Plumer sped northward from the Cape Colony with a relief force of eight hundred British soldiers. But still more troops were needed, and more leaders. And so General Sir Frederick Carrington was sent to Bulawayo—and with him, his Chief of Staff, Brevet Lieutenant-Colonel Robert S. S. Baden-Powell.

3

Within a few hours of their arrival in Bulawayo, General Carrington went into the first of numerous conferences with the local officials—Sir Richard Martin, the Imperial Commissioner; Earl Grey, the Administrator of the Chartered Company; Cecil Rhodes, no longer managing director but very much in evidence; as well as a number of others. Baden-Powell, as chief of staff, set to work 'to evolve some kind of order out of chaos'.

The problem was formidable. It involved military operations over an area the size of Spain, France and Italy combined, much of it mountainous—without railways, without proper roads, ordinarily depending on oxen and mules for transport but now, because of the onslaught of rinderpest, beset with daily-mounting logistic complexities. The Matabele, with the neighbouring Mashonas rising to join them, were estimated to number twelve thousand against the two thousand men the British were moving into the field.

The work of quelling the rebellion in the whole vast territory was to be managed from Bulawayo, the military headquarters, using the troops that had been brought up to the town for keeping the immediate area free of rebels and using the telegraph for directing the operations of other columns throughout the rest of Matabeleland. Sir Frederick's immediate plan was to send strong columns simultaneously to the north-east, north, and north-west to clear that country of rebels and prevent their re-assembly at their centres. The southern part of the country—the Matopo Hills— was afterwards to be tackled by the combined forces on their return from the north.

Baden-Powell had hardly settled down to the feel of his office chair before he had his first chance of excitement.

Late in the evening of 5 June, two horsemen galloped up, dismounted and rushed into the office; they were Sir Charles Metcalfe, consulting engineer of the Chartered Company, and Frederick Russell Burnham, an American scout employed by the Company. They had been on a ride out on the Salisbury road and had seen camp fires on the other side of the River Umgusa about three miles from Bulawayo. They had set out to investigate and had found themselves confronted by a large impi—an armed force— of Matabele encamped along the river. They had escaped by making their way home at a gallop by a detour through the bush.

Baden-Powell sent out patrols to investigate further. The report was correct. And so, in the early morning hours, B-P gathered some two hundred mounted men and moved to the attack.

At the river, Baden-Powell formed his men into a cavalry line, then ordered them forward. It took them only a few moments to ford the Umgusa and to break into the impi before them.

The Matabele had behaved in a most peculiar fashion during the fording. They had stood silently watching as if mesmerized while the British soldiers crossed the river. It was only after the horses had breasted the slope on their side of the stream that they reacted. 'The pop-pop-pop, ping-ping.

As they blazed away at us we charged right through them and away they went in a great hurry. After them we went zigzagging among the bushes, our men jumping off to fire a shot and then up again till they saw another chance—and they hardly ever missed!'

Baden-Powell was surprised at the blood-thirsty rage with which some of his men took after the fleeing Matabele, but then, he had not, as they had, seen the mutilated bodies of European men, women and children left behind after a merciless Matabele attack on some isolated farm.

At last B-P called a halt to the pursuit. The horses were spent, the Matabele scattered. Several of the British soldiers were wounded, but only three seriously.

Baden-Powell found out from some surrendering rebels that the Matabele impi had consisted of close to twelve hundred men from all the main tribes. Two hundred had been killed during the fight, among them fifteen headmen. What was even more important was that the Matabele's belief in the M'limo, their god, had been badly shaken. The M'limo had instructed the warriors to take up a position close to Bulawayo to draw out the British garrison and trick it into crossing the Umgusa. He had promised them that the river would open up and swallow the soldiers—whereupon the impi could walk into Bulawayo and cut up the white women and children at leisure. Somehow the M'limo's magic had miscarried.

Baden-Powell went back into his office to become enmeshed 'from morn till night without intermission' in a hundred details: handling men, handling supplies, handling reports in quadruplicate.

Some of these reports indicated that more and more Matabele impis were taking refuge in the Matopo Hills. It became evident that the almost inaccessible kopjes of the Matopos would become the main theatre of war for the operations against the Matabele. For the tasks ahead of driving them out, guides would be needed, and maps. Few people knew the Matopos as well as Burnham, the American scout, who had spent several years of his life in the area. But Burnham would be leaving shortly for another assignment.

Before losing Burnham's services, Sir Frederick decided that the American should take his chief of staff into the Matopos to acquaint him with the territory.

Their reconnaissance turned into a three-day expedition on horseback during which Burnham and Baden-Powell climbed in among the kopjes that commanded a view of the enemy's positions and of the Matopos in general ('Awful country—weird, jumbled mass of bush and boulders and jagged mountains'). Baden-Powell spent much of the time drawing maps and making panoramic field sketches of the landscape, indicating enemy caves and strongholds. For the rest, he picked up from Burnham a number of scouting tricks the American had used in the 1893 war against the Matabele and as a U.S. Army scout fighting in the Apache Indian wars.

The two men found they had much in common and struck up a firm friendship. For hours they shared their experiences and innermost thoughts as they lay, after a day's reconnaissance, beside a tiny concealed camp fire

The kopjes of the Matopo mountains, riddled with caves and underground passages, made the Matabele War of 1896 a difficult campaign.

under the stars of the African sky, before turning in for a few hours' sleep on what B-P considered the best of beds: 'the veld tempered with a blanket and a saddle'.

Baden-Powell had hoped to do much further scouting with Burnham but never had the chance. Within a few days B-P was back at his desk and Burnham had left for his special assignment.

4

By the middle of June, the rebellion had spread into Mashonaland to the north. Carrington and his staff worked 'literally from daylight till—well, long, long after dark. Not a scrap of exercise, no time to write a letter home.' More troops were requisitioned from the Cape but only to the extent of a thousand since 'every nerve will have to be strained to feed even these'.

With the tempo of the war increasing, General Carrington realized the need for speedier and more exact information on the enemy's movements. Of his staff officers only Baden-Powell had the skill, the audacity, the alertness, the deductive ability required of an army scout. He transferred the office duties to another officer, Captain Courtenay B. Vyvyan, and assigned Baden-Powell to reconnaissance and scouting.

B-P had the great luck to find the perfect companion for his expeditions in Jan Grootboom, a tall, muscular, brown-skinned Zulu somewhere in his twenties. Jan had lived much among the white settlers and had served them as a hunter and a guide. He spoke English and had taken to wearing the ordinary clothes of the white man. He had the reputation of being a clever scout and an intrepid spy.

In Baden-Powell's reconnaissance he would depart with Grootboom at dusk, spend the night riding into enemy territory, then stop for a short sleep until dawn. During the day, from their advanced position, B-P would study the territory through field-glasses, sketch out enemy positions, attempt to gain information about numbers, supplies, and the whereabouts of the women and cattle. As night came on again, the two scouts retired from their position and returned to headquarters.

One night during B-P's early association with Grootboom the two men had ridden to the vicinity of one of the enemy camps and were lying in hiding, waiting for the dawn when the Matabele would give away their location by lighting their fires for cooking their morning meal. At last one fire blazed up, then another, and yet another. But before half a dozen had been lighted B-P heard Grootboom growling under his breath: 'The swine! They are laying a trap for us!'

He heard Grootboom's whisper, 'Wait here. I'll go and look.' He turned his head towards his companion. The Zulu was stripping off his clothes. In a moment Grootboom stepped from the white man's world into the world of the naked African. His copper-brown skin glistened in the dim light. Then he was gone.

B-P looked after him with misgiving. 'The worst of spying', he acknowledged later, in relating the incident, 'is that it makes you always suspicious, even of your best friends'. So, as soon as Grootboom was out of sight, Baden-Powell hid himself among some rocks in such a manner that he would be able to slip away in case Grootboom intended to betray him and returned with some Matabele. For more than an hour he lay there until he saw Grootboom creeping back, alone. Ashamed of his doubts, he got out of his hiding place and joined the Zulu who was again putting on his clothes.

Grootboom had been right. He had found a large party of Matabele lying in ambush in the grass by the track he and B-P would have followed in getting closer. What had made him suspicious was the fact that the fires, instead of lighting up all over the hillside at different points at about the same time, had been lighted in succession, as if by a single man going round doing it.

B-P had had his object lesson in regard to Grootboom's loyalty and had, at the same time, learned a useful strategic tip.

He was particularly impressed by Grootboom's ability one day when, riding across an open grass plain, they came upon a few down-trodden blades of grass that led them on to footprints in a sandy patch of ground. They were those of women (judging from size and shape) on a long journey (they wore sandals), going towards the hills.

Grootboom looked about him and suddenly gave a 'How!' of attention. A few yards off the tracks he picked up a leaf and sniffed it. It was the leaf of a tree that did not grow in the area but some ten or fifteen miles distant. It was damp and smelt of Kaffir beer.

From his observations Grootboom worked out his deductions: It was evident that women had been carrying beer from the place where the tree grew (the Matabele stop up the mouths of their beer pots with leaves) and had passed this way at four in the morning (a breeze had blown at that time strong enough to carry the leaf for several yards). This would have brought the women into the Matopos about five o'clock. The men would have drunk the fresh beer before it turned sour and would, by this time, be 'very comfortable if not half-stupid'.

On the strength of the evidence given them by bruised grass, a few footprints, and a damp leaf, B-P and Grootboom set off into the Matopos. They returned with the information of yet another impi hiding place.

It was a thrilling but dangerous game that B-P was playing among the granite boulders of the Matopos. He knew that the slightest inattention on his part might result in a Matabele bullet or spear piercing his body—or, even worse, that he might fall alive into an ambush and be exposed to some of his enemy's more refined forms of torture. But the danger added the necessary spice to make these adventurous days, 'the best days of my life' —as Baden-Powell still remembered them forty years later.

In some of his boldest reconnoitrings it was inevitable that he would be detected by the Matabele. But somehow he always managed to evade even the fastest pursuers, once by applying the high-stepping 'skirt dance' agility he had practised for his theatrical performance at Malta five years before. The enemy never knew where B-P might turn up, or from what direction. He seemed to be about night and day as if he were some extraordinary creature who could hunt forever without rest. They came to call him *Impeesa*—'The-wolf-that-never-sleeps'. He considered this nickname one of the highest compliments ever paid him.

For almost three weeks Baden-Powell and Grootboom were at work. The large number of maps and panoramic sketches Baden-Powell brought back from his expeditions were lithographed by a Bulawayo printer and distributed among the British officers.

The preparations were now completed for smoking the Matabele out of their mountain retreats. The task would be tough. It would involve fighting in a tract of cragged country, containing a jumble of granite-bouldered mountains and brush-grown gorges, extending for some sixty miles in length, twenty miles in depth.

5

During the first weeks of July the columns that General Carrington had sent northward returned to Bulawayo. They had effectually broken up the Matabele to the north and had scattered the rebels.

Carrington now turned his attention towards the Matopos that Baden-Powell had so thoroughly reconnoitred and mapped. The General directed Colonel Henry Plumer, in command of the special Matabele Relief Force raised in Cape Town, to take on the operations. Plumer, in turn, as one of his first actions, requested the services of Baden-Powell. Carrington again released B-P from office work and placed him on Plumer's staff.

Plumer moved his force into camp below the Matopos and prepared to attack the central area. The first of these attacks took place on 19–20 July and was directed against Babyan, the most important of the Matabele *indunas* (chieftains).

Late on the night of 19 July, Plumer's force paraded 'without noise or trumpet call' and moved off in the moonlight into the Matopos with Baden-Powell as its guide. At dawn, Baden-Powell took charge of a special advance command consisting of two corps of Cape Boys—English-speaking natives and half-castes from the Cape Colony—plus two hundred friendly Matabele and twenty mounted white scouts. Close behind him came Colonel Plumer's main body of about a thousand white troops.

With extreme caution, B-P advanced with his men into a broken, bushy valley, surrounded on every side by rough, rocky cliffs. Ahead of them, thin streamers of smoke began to rise. Through his field-glasses he could see the enemy camp with large numbers of Matabele warriors milling about. He sent a dispatch back to the main body to move the guns into position at certain designated points. Shortly after, shells were exploding 'with beautiful accuracy' in the rebel camp, causing a terrified scramble.

While Plumer's guns shelled the Matabele impi Baden-Powell led his men in a circling movement round part of the enemy stronghold and found a perfect site for his machine-guns. Using this point as a base, he ordered his command in small, detached, attacking parties up over the mountain. At every point the rebels were cleared out and driven into flight or killed in their caves.

With his mission accomplished, B-P returned with his men towards the main body attempting, at the same time, to draw what was left of the enemy after him. Plumer, watching B-P's manoeuvre, sent his main body into action. The rebels, caught between two fires, broke up in hurried flight, leaving behind them a number of 'dusky bodies dead among the yellow grass'.

By two o'clock in the afternoon the operation was completed. Although practically only Baden-Powell's advance command had been engaged, the action had been a success. Babyan's impi had been broken up, his force dispersed, his stronghold cleared. The defeat of King Lobengula's most trusted *induna* would have a great moral effect on the remaining rebel chiefs.

The attack of 19–20 July had shown the feasibility of forcing the Matabele out of their established kraals and of inflicting casualties on them. But the Matopos was an impossible area from a military point of view: 'One could have lost an army corps in it', Baden-Powell felt. When an impi was driven from one place, it simply went farther into the mountains and re-established itself, somehow eking out a half-starving existence. Occasional large-scale operations would be in order. For the rest, attacks by flying columns appeared a more expedient practice.

Baden-Powell was on almost continuous service as officer in charge of groups of about a hundred soldiers and a score of native scouts. He wound up each of his skirmishes against the enemy by establishing a fort from which a small force of armed men with a single Maxim gun could control the surrounding area and keep it clear of Matabele.

On 4 August, on 'a delightful patrol' with Jan Grootboom and N. C. Richardson, his interpreter, B-P's small party surprised two women walking along with loads on their heads. The older woman was caught at once but the younger one ran off and disappeared in the reeds along the bank of a stream.

Baden-Powell brought the old woman back to camp for interrogation. With her dark-brown skin, her wrinkled face, her arms and hands like dried-up tree branches, her flabby breasts, the ancient crone looked unreal, inhuman. Her age was uncertain. She might have been 100 but looked older.

Her appearance was against her, but she proved to be 'a charming old thing . . . a very well informed and a very communicative lady when we gave her lots of beer'. Yes, she belonged to Umlugulu's kraal. Yes, Umlugulu was still in the mountains and so were many other *indunas* with their impis. Yes, the rebels were getting tired of war. It had cost lives and property, had caused misery and starvation and, if continued into the African spring, would prevent the sowing of next year's crop and result in further suffering.

And who was she? She was Umzava, one of the wives of the mighty M'silikatsi, step-mother of Lobengula, mother of Chief Inyanda—a lady of importance, high in rank among the Matabele.

Baden-Powell ordered her to be well taken care of. The seed of a 'dodge' for ending the fighting in the Matopos had taken root in his mind. But the time was not ripe. There would have to be yet more fighting first.

On 5 August Plumer mounted another major attack against the Matabele. Again, Plumer used Baden-Powell as a guide for his column, and again, B-P took personal charge of an advance force and led it on to the initial assault.

The battle between five allied Matabele impis totalling an estimated four thousand men and a British force of seven hundred and sixty lasted from sunrise to one o'clock in the afternoon. It resulted in the complete routing of the Matabele with a loss of more than two hundred Africans killed against five British soldiers killed and fifteen wounded.

Vere Stent, the *Cape Times* correspondent, expressed great admiration for Baden-Powell's part in the Matopos operations: 'Every time we went out he led us to where he had located the lurking impis of the Matabele. And, every time, we found the impi where we expected it.' In Stent's estimation, 'Baden-Powell planned the Matopos campaign—Colonel Plumer carried it out.'

Plumer himself admitted as much in his book about the campaign, *An Irregular Corps in Matabeleland:*

> The success of the various operations in the Matopos Hills was unquestionably due to his [Baden-Powell's] able reconnoitring and the wonderful knowledge he had acquired of all the intricacies of the fastnesses of the hills. . . . To me personally, he had rendered the most cordial co-operation and assistance for which I can never be sufficiently grateful.

6

One after the other, the Matabele chieftains and their impis were driven farther up into the mountains. One after the other, their kraals were destroyed, their huts burned to the ground, what remained of their herds was captured. And one after the other, tribes of homeless, starving Matabele—men, women and children—were surrendering.

From the reports that reached the British camp through native scouts and through the interrogation of prisoners, Baden-Powell became convinced that the Matabele still pinned down in the Matopos were ready to give up. The time had come for him to put his 'dodge' to the test—the 'dodge' involving Umzava, Inyanda's ancient mother.

B-P explained his idea to the two men who had been present when the old crone was taken prisoner: Grootboom and Richardson. They both thought the idea feasible and agreed to carry it out. But more helpers would be needed. They found them in two friendly Matabele, James M'kima and John Sail, who 'volunteered' their services at £25 each.

With everything arranged, Baden-Powell mounted his horse and 'rode thirty miles into Bulawayo during the night, in order to report to the General that the enemy in the Matopos were now completely broken up, and probably willing to surrender if we gave them a chance'. He laid the 'chance' he envisaged before his commanding officer.

Without knowing it, Baden-Powell had written the script and set the stage for Cecil Rhodes's come-back.

On 11 August, a small procession arranged for by B-P left Plumer's camp for the mountains. Directed by Richardson, the two friendly Matabele carried old Umzava on a stretcher into the general vicinity of the spot where Inyanda's kraal had stood. There the men built a hut for her, gave her a supply of corn and meat, and provided her with an old half-witted woman to attend her. They hung a big white flag above the hut, then left her to be called for. As they went off, they shouted to the rebels up on the hill that if they wanted peace they should come down and talk to the old lady. She would have all the information. The rebels would have four days to make up their minds. During that time no fighting would take place, no move would be made by the British.

By dawn the next day the two women and the flag had disappeared.

Grootboom and Richardson hung around waiting for developments— one day, two days, three. On the morning of the fourth day, 15 August, the white flag waved again from the spot where it had been placed originally as an intimation that some, at any rate, of the Matabele wished to surrender.

The following day, Grootboom and the two friendly Matabele went into the mountains to attempt to make contact with the *indunas*. They returned in the evening. They had had an *indaba* (council) with two of the chieftains, Inyanda and Sikombo. Both the chiefs had seemed willing to surrender but had asked for a delay of two more days during which they expected to have word from the other chiefs by messengers they had sent into the mountains.

On 18 August two Matabele arrived in Plumer's camp. They brought the message that the *indunas* were willing to meet 'the white chief' three days later to talk surrender.

B-P's 'dodge' was working.

But: 'the white chief'—there was the rub! There was no single 'white chief'. There was a whole string of them. Baden-Powell enumerated them at the time:

> Virtually, of course, the General [Sir Frederick Carrington, representing the Imperial Army] is the head while active operations are in progress, but he has to cut his cloth according to the style of the Deputy Commissioner [Sir Richard Martin, representing the High Commissioner], according to the expense sanctioned by the Administrator [Earl Grey, representing the Chartered Company], and according to the general design required by the High Commissioner [at Cape Town, representing the Crown], while not totally disregarding the local experience of Mr Rhodes and others.

Baden-Powell had hoped to take part in the negotiation that was to open as the result of his 'dodge', but he was *hors de combat*. To his dismay, Carrington had seemed less concerned with the plan than with the health of his staff officer. He called in the regimental doctor who immediately put B-P on the sick-list and ordered him to bed for fever, dysentery, exhaustion from overwork.

While B-P fumed in his hospital room, Carrington summoned 'all the heads of affairs' to decide who was to carry out the negotiations with the Matabele *indunas*.

Of those involved, Cecil Rhodes had most to gain and most to lose. Although the military operations for stopping the Matabele rebellion were in the hands of the Imperial Army, the British Government was not footing the bill—Rhodes's British South Africa Company was, to the tune of £4,000 a day. The first Matabele War in 1893 had cost the company millions of pounds which had just been paid off by the issue of new shares. Before the end was reached, the current campaign might cost as much as five million pounds, not including the losses incurred by the rinderpest and the continued suspension of all mining operations. The Company would be ruined unless the fighting was stopped promptly.

Rhodes came up with an offer—an offer not without danger. He had shown abundant mental courage in his business transactions. But here was a case where physical courage was required. Rhodes had that, too. It might have been born of desperation, but it was sired by his pride and self-respect.

He offered to go into the Matopos unarmed and, by using his past reputation among the Matabele, attempt to persuade them to give up their fight and surrender. He might have no official status as far as the British Government was concerned, but he was still looked upon by the Matabele as the head of the white men—'The-big-brother-who-eats-up-countries-for-his-breakfast' as Lobengula had called him years before.

Baden-Powell was not convinced of the wisdom of letting Rhodes handle the situation. He felt that the *indunas* might not understand why they were not dealt with by the Army which had been fighting them and which was now apparently being held in the background, while untrained men tried to persuade them to give up their weapons. Would the Matabele chieftains not think that this was a ruse, that as soon as they laid down their arms the Army would let loose on them again to wipe them out? Would they not procrastinate and further delay the inevitable day of surrender? He suggested 'that we give them till the new moon to make up their minds and if they don't give in by then, we go in and smash them'.

In spite of military doubts, Rhodes's offer was accepted. If he could manage to get the Matabele to agree to stop fighting, fine. If he couldn't, nothing would be lost. The fighting would resume.

Several members of Rhodes's staff wanted to accompany him. Carrington offered him a military escort. But Grootboom had received specific instructions from the Matabele: only four white negotiators would be acceptable.

After further discussion, the four were decided on: Cecil Rhodes; Johann Colenbrander, interpreter and confidant of the late Lobengula; Dr Hans Sauer, Rhodes's manager of the Rhodesia Exploration Company; Vere Stent, correspondent of the *Cape Times*, to represent the press.

On 21 August, the four men, accompanied by Grootboom, rode into the Matopos. They dismounted on the spot agreed upon. Grootboom disappeared into the hills and shortly after re-appeared, followed by about thirty *indunas*—Inyanda, Babyan and Sikombo among them. The chieftains sat down in a semicircle before Rhodes who had seated himself on a defunct ant-hill.

The fabled *indaba* of the Matopos commenced. The first step had been taken towards what came to be known as 'Rhodes's Peace'. There were many more to follow.

The news of the Matopos *indaba* spread quickly. To Rhodes's admirers, his action was a further proof of the man's greatness. To his detractors, it was a theatrical stunt that again proved Rhodes's ability to dramatize everything he undertook.

To Colonel Plumer, it was something between these two extremes. 'It was, undoubtedly, a very plucky thing to do,' he wrote. 'There was every reason, it is true, to believe that the *indunas* were in earnest and anxious for peace; but even if this were so, and no treachery intended, which was by no means certain, there was always the chance that the temptation of killing the big white chief might be irresistible to some of the younger and more excitable warriors.'

While the lengthy discussions were going on in the Matopos, Matabeleland to the north and the south was 'clear and peaceful'. It was only in outlying districts to the east and north-east that bodies of rebels were still on the warpath.

And throughout it all, Baden-Powell remained on his back, limp and washed out, thin as a rail from violent attacks of dysentery—in spite of the care of a competent nurse, who, by a quirk of fate, had had her training in the home of the Powells of Dorking, B-P's cousins in England.

7

As the days passed, Baden-Powell felt more and more discouraged, unable to shake off his illness. He was especially downcast when, on 26 August, an expedition which he was to have led to the River Shangani had to leave without him. 'I never felt so down on my luck,' he wrote in his diary.

It was not until twelve days later that General Carrington gave him 'a better tonic than any which the combined medical faculty of Bulawayo could devise'. Carrington had received the doctor's reluctant approval to return B-P to active service. Baden-Powell could still have the command of the Shangani column if he felt himself well enough to undertake it.

He emphatically did. Here was his opportunity, as the commander of a flying column, to root out and destroy the Matabele impis still harassing the northern districts, to track down Uwini and M'qwati and Wedza and drive them from their hiding places. And here was his chance, as well, for more of the life of the open veld that he so thoroughly enjoyed. He arranged for horses and provisions and rode off with three companions to catch up with his column, now about a hundred miles away.

During this ride, on 11 September 1896, Baden-Powell celebrated his twentieth anniversary of joining Her Majesty's Service ('I always think more of it than of my birthday'). He could not picture a more enjoyable way of celebrating the occasion than riding across the African veld with three good companions.

When Baden-Powell reached his command, he learned that a small patrol from it had just captured Uwini after wounding him and following his bloody trail through a labyrinth of caves. It was an important catch. Uwini was not only a rebel leader who, as one of the M'limo's high priests, had aroused his people to open rebellion, he had also caused the burning of numerous homesteads and the murder of several European men, women and children. He had himself, according to reliable reports, killed two white settlers. B-P ordered him to be tried before a field general court-martial.

The court gave Uwini a long hearing during which he practically confessed to all the charges against him. He was found guilty on all counts and sentenced to be shot. The warrant was brought to Baden-Powell who signed it reluctantly ('I felt sorry for him; he was a fine old blackguard').

Late in the afternoon all the natives in camp—refugees as well as prisoners—were paraded to witness Uwini's execution. He was taken to an open place in the centre of what had formerly been his stronghold so that any of his people still holding out in the kopjes could see what was going on. They knew, of course, that nothing could befall Uwini. Uwini was invulnerable, as the M'limo had said. The British bullets would turn to drops of water on hitting him.

The firing-squad lined up. 'Fire!' Uwini fell to the ground without a sound.

The effect of the execution followed almost immediately. While a number of the hiding Matabele fled to the north in the night, the majority stayed behind and came into camp the next morning to give themselves up.

The case of Uwini was closed. At least Baden-Powell thought so.

Baden-Powell sped north with his flying column on the hunt for yet another Matabele *induna* and his impi. This time the quarry was M'qwati, another high priest of the M'limo, reported to have sought refuge in the Somabula Forest, 'an easy place to lose your way in, and an unpleasant one on account of want of water'.

B-P divided his command of a hundred and sixty men—Hussars and Mounted Infantry—into three hunting parties and sent them off in different directions to track down the rebels and drive them out of the forest. He took personal charge of one of them.

Several times during the week that followed, Baden-Powell's party came upon enemy camp sites. But the Matabele always seemed to have sensed danger. They fled, leaving behind them cooking pots, clubs and spears, in one place a signal horn made from the twisted horn of a koodoo, and, in a couple of instances, loot of men's and women's clothing, axes, saws, tinned provisions—the spoils from the farms of murdered whites.

Deeper and deeper into the Somabula Forest. And harder and harder the going. The horses began to falter from the effect of hard work and want of proper fodder and water. Their only forage was the withered, parched grass, and watering places were few and far between. The men themselves were not much better off than their animals. Food was getting scarce. They had expected to use fresh game for meat, but instead of scaring up startled, fleeing game they found only the wasted carcasses of koodoo, dead of rinderpest.

The onward movement turned into night marches, with a brilliant moon showing the way. And then, on the seventh night, the party struck the River Shangani that had eluded them because of their poor maps. 'I was glad', Baden-Powell admitted to his diary. 'All my anxiety was over. We camped then and there on a tree-shaded, rocky knoll overlooking the river. I boiled up my last spoonful of cocoa, and after a nugget of rock-like bread and a fid of horse, I am going to bed WITH MY BOOTS OFF! I do not care for Matabele now; I am going to try for a good sleep—and I will see that I get it!'

Two days later the three sections of Baden-Powell's command were re-united. The Somabula Forest had been criss-crossed in all directions. The Matabele who had been there had fled north into Mashonaland.

The impi of Uwini and M'qwati had been put to flight, but with Wedza and his impi still to be subjugated, Baden-Powell and his command turned south-eastward towards Wedza's stronghold in the Belingwe district, travelling through a territory that had already surrendered to the British. 'It is a new sensation to see natives walking across the veld and not to hunt them, to see fresh spoor and not to let your heart jump with joy.'

At last, after trekking with weary, half-starved animals over more than a hundred and twenty miles of veld, B-P's party arrived at the foot of Wedza's mountain stronghold. It was the Matopos all over again, and nobody knew better than Baden-Powell how to overcome an enemy impi hiding among Matopo-like kopjes.

He estimated that Wedza's people, scattered throughout his stronghold in eight large kraals, would number something like sixteen hundred, with six or seven hundred of them fighting men. B-P had a hundred and fifteen men now but imagination for five times that number. With the right amount of bluff thrown in, the strength of the two forces should be about even!

He sent a group of mounted infantry up to occupy the 'neck' that joined Wedza's mountain to the range of mountains to the north. There were only twenty-five men but they were to act as if they were two hundred and fifty by moving from bush to bush and shooting from time to time. As soon as they were established, B-P gave the order to bombard Wedza's central position and, at the same time, sent off parties of Hussars to threaten the enemy's left flank and rear.

Throughout the day Baden-Powell's men played their game of deception. And when night fell, Wedza's Matabele warriors, looking down into the valley, saw a hundred British camp fires quietly burning. They could not know that B-P was using against them a trick he had learned from other Matabele in the Matopos, that the many fires were tended by only a few British soldiers moving from one to the other.

At daybreak, Baden-Powell's command began hammering away again with their single seven-pounder cannon, their two Maxims, and their solitary Nordenfelt, then advanced for the main attack. The Matabele fled out of their burning kraals into protecting caves, only, when these were also shelled, to steal away through bush and among rocks. At day's end the stronghold was a stronghold no longer. It had become a flaming beacon proclaiming Wedza's downfall as far as the gleam of the fire penetrated the night.

Three more days of the same tactics and Wedza's people were harried into submission. Wedza gave himself up to the British authorities.

With the surrender of Wedza, the principal remaining hold-out, the second Matabele War was virtually at an end. Baden-Powell's assignment was accomplished.

He rode off for an appointment in Gwelo.

8

Just before the attack on Wedza's stronghold, B-P had received a dispatch from his commanding general. General Carrington wrote to inform him that Lord Rosmead, the High Commissioner at Cape Town, had learned of Uwini's trial and execution and had become highly incensed that the *induna* had been tried by a court-martial instead of being turned over to a civil court. He had telegraphed ordering Baden-Powell's arrest, an order which the General had respectfully declined to carry out with the comment that 'Colonel Baden-Powell should be spared the indignity of arrest as an officer who had done so much excellent service.' Instead, Carrington had arranged a court of inquiry to assemble at Gwelo to question B-P 'as soon as you have finished your operations against Wedza'.

The inquiry took place on 30 October. Baden-Powell's defence was simple. He confined himself mainly to the legal point that, according to military law, he had the power to exercise his own judgement if he were over a hundred miles from a superior authority. He pointed out that no civil court existed in the area and contended that the summary punishment of Uwini in the presence of his own people had crushed their belief in the M'limo and had gained their surrender, in this way saving a great many lives, British and Matabele, alike.

The court of inquiry, after having taken all the evidence in the case, found Baden-Powell 'Not guilty' and forwarded its findings to General Carrington. Sir Frederick sent them on to Cape Town with his personal comment:

> I am of the opinion that the military exigencies of the circumstances in which Lieut.-Colonel Baden-Powell found himself at the time of Uwini's capture were such as to call for strong measures, and subsequent events have, to my mind, clearly proved that the prompt punishment at his own stronghold of Uwini, as a powerful and notorious instigator of crime and rebellion, exercised a very wholesome influence on the surrounding district and undoubtedly expedited its final pacification.

9

On 12 November, Baden-Powell joined General Carrington and the other staff members at Enkeldoorn, whereupon the whole party proceeded on horseback to Salisbury.

The town was full of interesting celebrities and the ten days in Salisbury became a round of social events: dining with Earl and Lady Grey; reminiscing with the Public Prosecutor, an old Carthusian; talking with Cecil Rhodes who had come out of the Matabele *mêlée* with renewed fame as the great *Umlanulang Mkngi*—'The-bull-that-separates-the-fighting-bulls'—after his success in finally arranging peace terms with the Matabele in the Matopos on 13 October.

His discussions with Rhodes about the Empire Builder's future plans for Rhodesia were of special interest to B-P.

> He is always thinking or doing what you don't expect [Baden-Powell wrote in his diary]. In talking over ways and means or plans of campaign, he almost invariably throws quite a new light on the subject, and has a totally different plan, and one which is often the best

*On a ride in 1896, Cecil Rhodes explained to Baden-Powell his dream of a
telegraph line from the Cape to Cairo.*

of the lot, especially from the Chartered Company's point of view, as
far as ultimate results go, not present expenditure—that is the point
that often makes us pause, but he never seems to think of it, for he
looks to the better economy in the end. And while he talks he doesn't
sit still, but he'll be sprawling all over the sofa one minute, the next
he'll have his legs crossed under him, *à la Turc*—full of restlessness
and energy.

Rhodes was at his expansive best and invited General Carrington and
Baden-Powell to stop on their way to England at his beautiful country
estate Groote Schuur near Cape Town.

After several delays, caused by drenching downpours at the start of the
South African spring, General Carrington's staff moved off, leisurely,
eastward towards the coast where they were to board the Cape Town
steamer for the first lap of their homeward journey.

Half way towards the coast they were overtaken by Cecil Rhodes's
party.

Rhodes was apologetic. 'I am sorry to find that I shall not be able to give you accommodation at my house,' he said. He had just been informed by telegraph that Groote Schuur had burned to the ground. 'It is a great pity, because there were some old things there that could not be replaced. I liked my house.'

'Providence has not been kind to me this year,' he added. 'What with Jameson's Raid, rinderpest, famine, and now my house burnt, I feel rather like Job, but, thank God, I haven't had sores yet. Still, there remains some of the year, and there is yet a chance for me to develop some totally new kind of boil. That would be the height of evils, to have a boil called after one. Fancy being the inventor of the "Rhodes boil"!'

After entering Portuguese East Africa, the party went by rail to the coast. They boarded their ship at Beira and steamed south along the African coast.

Their stops at British ports turned into triumphal receptions for Cecil Rhodes. The welcome at Cape Town was especially impressive. Large crowds were waiting for Rhodes's arrival. He was greeted with cheers and shouts of welcome—a tribute to his peace work among the Matabele— where less than a year before he had been booed for his complicity in the Jameson Raid.

And then the party was on board the S.S. *Dunvegan Castle* bound for England. 'A most interesting shipload,' Baden-Powell called it in his diary. Most interesting indeed!

General Carrington was there with a number of other British officers, ready to tell their fellow passengers all the details of the successfully completed campaign. Cecil Rhodes, Sir Charles Metcalfe and other officials of the Chartered Company were there, willing to extol the virtues and excuse the shortcomings of the Company to anyone who cared to listen.

But also on board were S. C. Cronwright-Schreiner and his famous wife, Olive Schreiner, perhaps South Africa's greatest writer and Rhodes's most outspoken critic. She was bringing with her to England in her steamer trunk the manuscript of her new book *Trooper Peter Halkett of Mashona-land*—the strongest condemnation yet of the Chartered Company and its machinations. Many efforts were made to get her to speak to Rhodes, but she refused absolutely. . . .

XI

A Command in India

Years: 1897–1899   Age: 40–42

1

WHEN Baden-Powell rejoined his regiment at the Marlborough Barracks in Dublin, he found himself in an anomalous situation. He had been awarded a brevet of full colonel for his part in the Matabele campaign but here, in the 13th Hussars, he still figured as major—below the lieutenant-colonel in command and the senior major. The War Office solved the dilemma in a truly Solomonic fashion: it offered B-P the command of the 5th Dragoon Guards in India.

Baden-Powell hated the idea of leaving the 13th, his home for twenty years—yet, as he told his mother, 'the departure would have to come some day, and I should not get command here for another seven years. So of course I must accept, for my own good.' There was one consolation: he would again be under his old colonel who now, as Sir Baker Russell, had been promoted to General and Commander-in-Chief in Bengal. He would also be able to renew his friendship with 'The Boy' McLaren, who was back in India as military secretary to Sir Baker.

B-P decided to make 'the big wrench' of leave-taking as easy as possible for all concerned. He would slip away before breakfast on the day of departure. He asked his orderly to arrange to have a cab at the rear of his quarters in the early morning, with his luggage loaded.

On an agreed-upon signal B-P sneaked out the back door. The cab was there, all right. But so was something else. The regimental sergeant, sitting in the driver's seat, raised his baton and the regimental band, gathered around the cab, struck up a marching tune. The men of B-P's squadron, harnessed in long ropes attached to the cab, were ready to start pulling. The rest of the regiment was lined up to see its popular officer out of the barrack gate. 'And off we went, the most choky experience I ever had.'

His last glimpse of the barracks was one of 'blankets being waved from every window, and all through the streets of Dublin went this mad procession which finally landed me at the station with a farewell cheer'.

Baden-Powell's return to the great military station at Meerut was like another home-coming: 'It almost feels as if I had been away from it for twelve months instead of twelve years.' He found the 5th Dragoon Guards in fair shape only. He had a good group of officers and non-commissioned officers to work with. The men were a varied lot—much as he had expected them. A great amount of effort would be needed to bring the regiment up to the standard he envisaged for it. But he remembered the saying he had learned in Ashanti: 'Softly, softly, catchee monkey.' That would be his slogan.

In the meantime he set about solving some pressing problems dealing with the health of his men. Enteric fever was playing havoc with the regiments stationed in Meerut. B-P gave strict orders to have all possible sanitary precautions taken as far as the 5th was concerned. The barracks were scrubbed and disinfected, the water supply checked, the cook-houses made spotlessly clean. Everything was done according to the most advanced knowledge of the time—but the cases of enteric did not diminish.

Baden-Powell became convinced that his men contracted the scourge from the food and drinks they bought in the bazaars of Meerut. He did not want to issue a general order declaring the bazaars out of bounds. Instead he paraded the regiment, explained the situation to his men and suggested they all try together to learn the correctness or fallacy of his theory. It could be proved or disproved quite easily: by everyone staying out of the bazaars for a two-week period.

The men gave him their unqualified co-operation. The incidence of enteric dropped. The experiment showed Baden-Powell that he was on the right track. But he knew that he couldn't beat something with nothing. If he were to keep the men away from the bazaars he would have to provide them with something better.

He opened up a club for temperance men and a refreshment room for the others. He inaugurated a regimental bakery under a sergeant who had been a pastry-cook before becoming a soldier. He established a mineral-water factory for making ginger-beer, lemonade and other carbonated beverages. He started a dairy to produce pasteurized milk and to make butter under scrupulously sanitary conditions.

Baden-Powell was fortunate in all these efforts for his men's welfare in having the whole-hearted support of his immediate superior, General Sir Bindon Blood, commanding the Meerut Garrison. Sir Bindon watched with interest the results of B-P's experiments and saw to it that the other regiments picked up some of the ideas introduced in the 5th Dragoon Guards.

2

B-P was getting himself well established in command of the 5th. He liked his task as regimental commander and looked forward to the future with equanimity. Soldiering in India, he felt, was soldiering—although he wouldn't mind a few diversions.

On 10 June 1897, a British political officer and his escort were attacked in the Tochi Valley on the North West Frontier and a number of Britons were killed. It seemed an isolated occurrence quickly quenched—but it proved otherwise. At the end of July a full-fledged frontier war got under way with a rising in the Swat Valley. A force of ten thousand fanatical mountain tribesmen staged a determined night attack on Malakand. Luckily, the British garrison of three thousand men had been warned in time. The enemy were routed with heavy losses.

British reinforcements were ordered to the Frontier. The Malakand Field Force of eight thousand men was organized and shipped north under the command of General Sir Bindon Blood. Baden-Powell tried desperately to have his regiment included in the Field Force, but Blood had made other dispositions. There would be no war for B-P this time.

But at the Frontier the war continued. The rebels attacked again and again, up and down through the wild mountain passes—the Khyber, the Alachi, the Sangutti. They lost men by the thousand while the British lost them by the hundred. By the end of September, the enemy were dispersed, the leaders put to flight. But guerilla fighting continued.

B-P's determined efforts to get to the Frontier in one capacity or another eventually met with success. Sir Bindon had used cavalry successfully on several occasions to rout the rebels. He came to the conclusion that it might be worth while for the colonel of the 5th Dragoon Guards to come up to the North West Frontier as an observer in case his regiment should later be called into action in the area.

Early in January 1898, the General sent off a telegram to B-P:

> We are having a pheasant shoot on the 7th. Hope you will join us.
>
> BINDON BLOOD

Baden-Powell, reading between the lines, hastened to avail himself of Blood's invitation. He took the train to Newshara, then went the last fifty miles of the six-hundred-mile journey in 'a ramshackle tonga [a two-wheeled buggy] drawn by a horse and a scrap of a pony'. He reached Sir Bindon's camp at Sanghao on the evening of 6 January.

The next morning—'a clear, frosty, iced-champagne-sort-of-morning', as B-P described it, the British troops moved into position for the attack on the Buner country, 'divided from our territory by a precipitous range of mountains only passable (by difficult tracks) at three or four places'. The main assault was against the Tungi Pass.

Baden-Powell joined General Blood and his staff in climbing a stony scrub-grown hill in front of the enemy's positions. From the top of the hill the officers had an excellent view over the whole area. Before them spread a narrow valley, faced by a steep rocky ridge, some two thousand feet high. Along the crest of it they could see hordes of tribesmen with their banners awaiting the British attack. 'They had built little stone forts or *sungars* along the top, which afforded beautiful targets for our guns. These kept shelling them heavily while our troops made their attack and scaled the heights at different points.'

As B-P trained his field-glasses on one of the stone forts under bombardment, he saw a man rushing out of it, down the hill towards the British forces, with a glittering sword in his hand and his loose blue clothing flying out behind him. B-P followed the man's descent:

> He springs rapidly from point to point—still coming downwards. At first it seems as if he were making for a big rock to roll it down— but he passes it. He comes to a bit of a precipice and stops a moment to find a way down. Then carefully creeping down, once more he takes up his running, leaping pace. Meantime spurts of dust keep jumping up near him: our men are firing at him but it does not seem to affect him in the least. Suddenly he stops and goes a bit slower— he is hit—but still he comes on waving his sword, eager to get down to where our troops are. It is a grand and pathetic sight to see this one plucky chap advancing single-handed to attack the whole British force. But he suddenly tumbles forward and rolls over a rock, and lies in a huddled heap—dead.

It was a sight that Baden-Powell never forgot. For the rest of his life he considered that solitary, undaunted mountain tribesman, courting death for his faith, 'the bravest man I ever saw'.

But in those days of his military career and at that point in history, he could not afford to be sentimental. To him and to his army colleagues, the kind of war being fought on the North West Frontier was exactly the kind that was necessary for the realistic instruction of the British Army:

> We as a nation [he wrote in *Indian Memories*] are exceptionally fortunate in having a valuable training ground for our officers in the North West Frontier of India, with real live enemies always ready to

oblige in giving us practical instruction in the field in tactics and strategy, transport and supply, sanitation and ambulance work, and general staff duties. If Waterloo was won on the playing fields of Eton, there are many victories before us that will have been won in the more practical fields of the North West Frontier.

The result of the day's fighting was foreordained. Heavy shelling by the British artillery cleared the mountain ridges of the poorly armed tribesmen, and waves of infantry did the rest.

3

Baden-Powell had had some of the excitement he craved. He was satisfied to settle down for a while to the routine of regimental life—that is, to the B-P kind of regimental 'routine'.

He was keenly aware that one of his main tasks, in addition to running the regiment, was to turn the young recruits who came out to India from England into cavalry soldiers. They came to him with a reasonable amount of schooling, with a fair knowledge of the three R's, 'but without individuality or strength of character, utterly without resourcefulness, initiative or the guts for adventure'.

He had his own ideas about the kind of training that would achieve in them what he wanted. It should, first of all, be enjoyable to the men. It should be done in small groups. It should encourage self-discipline and provide opportunity for accepting responsibility. Hitherto, as a subordinate officer, he had had to follow the training procedures as laid down by his regiment. Now, as regimental commander, he had almost complete freedom in applying his theories and practising his ideas.

He had long held the opinion that scouting and reconnaissance were not only of supreme value in cavalry work but were also activities in which men and officers took the liveliest interest. His previous use of them and the popularity of the small handbook he had written on them fourteen years before had proved it to him. Now he developed a new syllabus of instruction centred on these two subjects, but with special emphasis on scouting. He started giving lectures on his pet subjects to just a small group of volunteers. But the group grew larger and larger. He was a vivid lecturer, thoroughly familiar with his subject. He spiced his tales with anecdotes and samples from military history, with joking reminders and challenging suggestions.

When the instruction was completed B-P put his trainees 'through practical work in varied scouting exercises over the varied country, in pairs and individually'. The men who satisfactorily passed the tests he had laid down were honoured by the designation 'scout' and were given a distinguishing arm badge: a fleur-de-lys or north-point—based on the design used to indicate north on a map and on a compass.

Baden-Powell's unorthodox training methods resulted in a higher morale

Scouts of the 5th Dragoon Guards on manoeuvre. Notice First Class badge on the right sleeve of the top-most figure.

and a stronger pride in the 5th than it had ever had before. There were greater efficiency and better performance on parade and off.

It had meant lots of work for the men who had taken the instruction, but it had been purposeful work understood by all. 'Our colonel does work us hard', as one of the men had confided to a regimental nurse, 'but the worst of it is we don't knock up but are all the better for it. . . .'

4

While managing his regiment effectively, Baden-Powell also succeeded in indulging in some of his favourite hobbies: acting, pigsticking, polo.

The first summer of his new term in India as a regimental commander, he was invited by the Simla Amateur Dramatic Club to come to the

Indian summer capital to play a part in the fifth play of the Simla season: *The Geisha*—the operetta by Sidney Jones, with libretto by Owen Hall and Harry Greenbank, that had pulled in the audiences at London's Daly's Theatre for the past year. The invitation was a flattering proof that his histrionic abilities were still appreciated in India.

The Geisha was a great success. The review in the *Simla News* was highly complimentary. The reviewer was especially impressed with B-P's performance: 'The antics of his Wun-Hi were indescribably funny, and he was the life and soul of the piece. . . .' The operetta played for eleven performances to full houses and was attended by the Commander-in-Chief, the Adjutant-General, the Quartermaster-General, the Inspector-General of the Cavalry, but not by the Viceroy—he was away at the time. Truly, acting at Simla had its advantages: 'You may think it an awful waste of time on my part,' B-P confided to his mother, 'but there was a lot of nasty cool calculation underlying my taking the part—and briefly the net result is that three weeks ago I was a total stranger to the authorities and everybody, now I am on the best of terms with all of them.'

The rumour-mongers in Simla had been busy. B-P and a friend of his had been seen much in the company of two of *The Geisha*'s leading belles. They had had the ladies to dinner and had been entertained in the home of one of them. Baden-Powell had seemed particularly interested in the operetta's Molly Seamore. The two had been observed, on several occasions, riding on Jakko Hill—the eminence of the spur of the lower Himalayas on which Simla is built. And when a gentleman takes a young lady on Jakko Hill three times it has only one meaning: his intentions are serious—everybody in Simla knows that!

Everybody, it seemed—except Baden-Powell. . . .

Back in Meerut B-P had occasion once again to take up pigsticking.

He was actually jittery before his first pigsticking meet in thirteen years— he didn't know whether he still had the nerve of his youth to be any good at it. But when the yells of the beaters suddenly burst into a chorus of *Wuh jata hai! Bara dant wallah!* ('There goes he! A big tusker!') he found himself galloping after the boar as confident as ever. 'We got five pigs among six of us and I got two of them! Not so bad for an old man.'

In addition to weekly pigsticking meets, B-P was also soon again involved in the polo games of the Meerut garrison. He bought two beautiful Arabs and discovered that he was playing better than he had ever played before. He took his place on the regimental team and handled the arrangements for the Inter-Regimental Tournament of North India held in Meerut early in 1898.

Although his team did not win, the tournament was a joyous occasion.

The visiting teams made use of the mess of the 5th Dragoon Guards and guests and hosts quickly formed one very large and happy family.

Their fellowship reached its zenith on the evening after the final tie had been decided, when the 5th gave a grand dinner to signalize the event. The health of the winning team and of the losers was drunk collectively and individually with all honours, far into the night, with each member of each team in turn tendering his thanks to the assembled company.

When at last all the speeches, harping on the one topic of polo, had been finished, a member of the 4th Hussars' team jumped to his feet. 'Now, gentlemen,' he said, 'you would probably like to hear me address you on the subject of polo?'

There were immediate cries of 'No we don't! Sit down!' But the young officer disregarded all objections.

> With a genial smile [as B-P told the story afterwards] he proceeded to discourse on the subject, and before long all opposition dropped as his honeyed words flowed upon our ears, and in a short time he was hard at it expounding the beauties and possibilities of this wonderful game. He proceeded to show how it was not merely the finest game in the world but the most noble and soul-inspiring contest in the whole universe. Having made his point he wound up with a peroration which brought us all cheering to our feet.
>
> When the cheering and applause had died down one in authority arose and gave voice to the feelings of all when he said: 'Well, that's enough of Winston for this evening!'
>
> The orator was taken in hand by some lusty subalterns and placed underneath an overturned sofa upon which two of the heaviest officers were then seated, with orders not to allow him out for the rest of the evening. But very soon afterwards he appeared emerging from beneath the angle of the arm of the sofa, explaining:
>
> 'It's no use sitting upon me, for I am india-rubber—and I bounce!'

Winston Spencer Churchill, at 23, had demonstrated one of his most important and enduring characteristics.

5

Of all his various activities during his third stay in India B-P got his greatest thrill out of a two-month trip to Kashmir during August and September 1898, a trip he had dreamed of making for years.

He went by train to Rawalpindi and then by tonga for the hundred and sixty miles up into Kashmir. At Baramoola he boarded the *doonga* he had rented for a month, for a leisurely 'loaf' up the Vale of Kashmir. 'My *doonga* is like a long Thames punt—six feet in beam, fifty-six feet long, with a grass mat roof. Divided by curtains into rooms: dining-room, bedroom, bathroom, verandah, with crew's quarters in the stern. A crew of four punt, paddle or tow as the occasion requires. A smaller boat carries servants, kitchen, stores, etc.'

He had struck his ideal of a 'good time'. He dined on the *doonga* or had his little table set up on shore. He slept on board or in a bed put up 'on the velvet turf on the bank under a gigantic chinar tree'. He did a bit of reading (Henderson's *Strategy and Its Techniques*, Colonel French's *Cavalry Manoeuvres*, and Whinfield's translation of Omar Khayyam's *Ruba'iyat*) but spent most of his time sitting on the verandah of his *doonga* watching the view continually changing and filling sketch-book after sketch-book with scores of water-colours. The people he saw on shore or passing in boats he found 'hopelessly picturesque'. The vistas of the valley and the mountains in the background were magnificent. He reached an important conclusion: 'I ought to be married! I feel the want of a wife— one who can do landscapes at which I am no good.'

After two weeks of mountain hiking around Kunbul, the port of Islamabad, B-P was ready for his return journey to India but instead of going back by the water route by which he had come, he decided to hike the Jammu trail over the mountain passes out of Kashmir. He took fourteen carriers along on the hundred-and-twenty-mile trek, to transport his gear and to act as beaters in case a bear should cross his path. They took their time, marching over one pass after another, at a steady rate of a dozen miles a day. This gave them a chance, almost daily, to drive for bear.

One day, after a long climb and a long beat, Baden-Powell got his bear: 'Just as he plunged into the jungle I changed his plunge into a dive with a shot from behind—and he fell dead a few yards farther on. When I got down to where he lay, with the beaters jabbering round him, he looked like a respectable gentleman who had for once imbibed too freely—and was lying in the gutter in his glossy black clothes with a ribald crowd jeering round him. I instinctively looked for his tall hat and for a hansom to take him home.'

There was only one thing that B-P disliked about bear hunting: the long waits while the beaters were getting to their places. With his obsessive compulsion for work it occurred to him that he might use the time while waiting 'to write a book about scouting. So during these waits I've jotted down in my notebook first heads for chapters, and finally subjects of paragraphs. Today [4 September 1898] I finished it all ready for my shorthand clerk (I have one in the regiment) to take down from dictation.' He gave his projected new book the tentative title of *Cavalry Aids to*

Scouting. He could not know at the time what effect this little volume, so casually conceived, would have on his life.

6

B-P came back from Kashmir to a great amount of work. Before leaving he had been told that the 5th Dragoon Guards were to take up a new station, at Sialkote, in the Punjab, and was to march there following the winter manoeuvres around Delhi. There were hundreds of details to be arranged before the departure of his brigade.

In the midst of his work the editor of the Meerut newspaper brought him sad news. A telegram had just been received from London announcing the death on 20 November 1898, of Sir George Baden-Powell, K.C.M.G., M.P.

It was not unexpected. George had been in failing health for more than a year. And yet, in a letter B-P had received from his brother only two months before, George had seemed improved in health and in good spirits. And now it was all over. He would miss his brother greatly. 'Poor George —he always took me under his wing—and I cannot yet realize that he is gone.'

On 14 December Baden-Powell and his brigade left for the manoeuvres at Aligahr to join the other brigades of the Southern Division.

The two forces—Northern and Southern Divisions—came in collision ten miles before Delhi. 'We easily defeated their cavalry and artillery and also cut off their only line of retreat to Delhi—but the infantry held on to the last.' The mock battle almost turned into bloodshed when the 'enemy'— a Pathan regiment of native infantry—got excited, and not only fired point-blank into the faces of their 'adversaries' but also heaved stones at them. 'For a few minutes, before we could stop them, it was something more than the mere "image of war".' The Southern Division won every fight in which it was engaged. In scouting, manoeuvring, parade movements, assault at arms, condition of horses, B-P's regiment had come out best of all the twelve regiments participating.

The 5th Dragoon Guards set out in high spirits for Sialkote—men, officers, and horses fit and well and the weather splendid. When they marched into their new quarters forty days later, they found them ready and in excellent condition.

This was B-P's doing. On his way back to Meerut from Kashmir he had stopped at Sialkote and had learned that the station had just been vacated. He immediately put local craftsmen to work getting the buildings into shape. When the regiment arrived the men were greeted by clean barracks, new kitchens, a bakery, a dairy, a mineral-water factory, and two supper clubs—all the comforts of home that the 5th Dragoon Guards had learned to appreciate at Meerut.

After settling his regiment, laying out its summer programme and demonstrating the efficiency of the 5th in its new quarters before the Inspector-General of Cavalry, Baden-Powell made ready to start for England for a long leave.

He left India for home on 6 May 1899. He would be back again with his regiment in Sialkote before the end of the year unless something completely unexpected should occur.

XII

The Start of the Boer War

Year: 1899   Age: 42

1

ON the first Monday of July 1899, only a couple of weeks after his return from India, Baden-Powell was lunching at the Naval and Military Club in Piccadilly when George Gough, A.D.C. to Lord Wolseley came over to his table.

'I thought you were in India,' Gough said. 'I have just cabled to you to come home—the Commander-in-Chief wants to see you.' B-P finished his lunch quickly, then proceeded to Whitehall.

At the War Office, Wolseley came directly to the point. 'I want you to go to South Africa,' he said.

'Yes, sir!' B-P answered.

'Well, can you go on Saturday next?'

'No, sir!' B-P replied without a moment's hesitation.

The Commander-in-Chief was not accustomed to 'No sirs'—he looked up sharply. 'And why not?' he barked.

'There's no ship on Saturday,' Baden-Powell informed him. 'But I can go on Friday.' With all the rumours in the air caused by the recent breakdown of the conference between the British Government and the Transvaal Republic, he had had a suspicion of what his next appointment might be and had checked the sailings of the ships for South Africa.

Wolseley burst out laughing, then, serious, told Baden-Powell what he was expected to do: he was to go to Rhodesia to raise two regiments of mounted infantry and to organize the defence of the Rhodesia and Bechuanaland Protectorate frontiers towards the Transvaal, in preparation for a possible war. If war should come, he was to keep the troops of the enemy occupied in this direction away from their main forces.

After giving him his instructions, Lord Wolseley took B-P into the office of Lord Lansdowne, the Secretary of State for War, who accorded

him the high-sounding title of Commander-in-Chief, Rhodesian Frontier
Force.

B-P left the War Office elated. This was the greatest challenge that had,
so far, been given him. He knew the area involved and the conditions he
would meet and could readily imagine the arrangements he might have to
make. Before the day was over, he had formulated in his mind his
general plan for accomplishing the task.

His innate impatience gave him no peace while he waited for Friday to
come. He was filled with his usual apprehension before a major undertaking that something might happen to prevent him from going. He was
'nervous as an old lady crossing a street for fear of being run over'. He
'clung to the rail in going downstairs' in dread of slipping and spraining
his ankle.

In spite of his concern he managed to get round to make his farewells to
friends and relatives without becoming a casualty. He also paid a visit
to his old headmaster at Charterhouse. 'I hope they'll give me a warm
corner,' he said as he gripped Dr Haig Brown's hand in good-bye.

He was apprehensive to the last. He left for South Africa with the
fervent hope that 'we shan't hear at Madeira that Kruger has given in'.

Kruger hadn't.

2

Ever since the Jameson Raid in 1896, the Transvaal British *Uitlanders* had
found their position increasingly intolerable. They had had no satisfaction
in getting redress for their grievances, and their enfranchisement was as far
away as ever. Finally, in desperation, in March 1899, some twenty thousand British subjects prepared a 'humble petition' stating their complaints
and sent it, not to Kruger, but through the British High Commissioner of
the Cape Colony, Sir Alfred Milner, to Her Britannic Majesty, Queen
Victoria. The petition was placed in the lap of Joseph Chamberlain, the
Colonial Secretary, for him to accept as coming within the scope of British
obligations or to reject. Chamberlain decided to accept it. He suggested
that negotiations be started forthwith.

A conference was arranged at Bloemfontein at the end of May 1899,
between Sir Alfred Milner and President Kruger. Milner held that any
British subject who had resided in the Transvaal for five years should be
entitled to vote and suggested that these *Uitlanders* should be guaranteed a
certain fixed minimum of representation. Kruger showed reluctant willingness to accede to a seven-year residence but tied any consideration of
granting a franchise to the abolition of the British suzerainty over the
Transvaal that had been a thorn in the side of the Boers since it was

imposed on them in 1881. Milner was persistent; Kruger was adamant. The two viewpoints were irreconcilable and the Bloemfontein Conference ended in complete failure.

The British Government had committed itself to helping the *Uitlanders*. British popular opinion was stirred into a frenzy. There would have to be other negotiations, of course—but in the meantime: better be prepared for any eventuality.

During his sea voyage, Baden-Powell developed his campaign in further detail and had everything ready when his ship touched at Madeira. He posted his plans to the corps officers at home for approval and telegraphed instructions to the Cape. For a while he had nothing further to do but 'fold my hands in peace and possess my soul with patience till the ship reaches the Cape'.

He found excellent use for his patience—not just for the remainder of the sea journey but even more so on his arrival in South Africa. At Cape Town he learned that nothing had been done to fill his requirements.

3

The military situation in Cape Colony bordered on the incredible.

Sir William Butler, the G.O.C. (General Officer Commanding) South Africa, was at odds with the High Commissioner. Butler had on occasion taken the part of the Boers against the British *Uitlanders* in the Transvaal and was, in Milner's opinion, 'a violent Krugerite' and therefore hardly the right commander for preparing the country for a possible conflict with the Boers. As if this were not enough, the Parliament of the Cape Colony had a Dutch majority, and the Premier of the Cape Government, William P. Schreiner, B-P's hunting companion on the Swaziland excursion, was an Afrikaner—a British subject, but one who had blood ties with the Boers.

Baden-Powell had expected to run into difficulties, but not to the extent of what seemed to be in the offing. But he had no inclination for fretting. During the two days he spent in Cape Town he conferred with Rhodes who was certain that Kruger would give in when British forces embarked for South Africa and equally certain that there would be no native rising in Rhodesia. He also laid the foundation of a co-operation between himself and the High Commissioner's military secretary, Colonel John Hanbury Williams.

A journey of five days—as compared to fifteen days in 1896—brought Baden-Powell to Bulawayo, the centre of his Rhodesian domain. It was an entirely different Bulawayo from the one he had known only three years before: 'On arrival then I slept on a *stoep* and tubbed in the street, but today it is the Grand Hotel with rooms upstairs, electric lights, and bath-rooms with water laid on. . . . The only touch that still lingers of the old days and customs is the going about, and even lunching at the club, in shirt sleeves: long may it reign!'

In Bulawayo, Baden-Powell was joined by the other officers who had been assigned to his Frontier Force and had a happy reunion with his friend from Matabeleland, Colonel Herbert Plumer, and his still older friend Captain 'The Boy' McLaren.

The more he considered the five-hundred-mile-long frontier that his force was to protect the clearer it became to Baden-Powell that this protection could not be provided by establishing a single headquarters and spreading the men thinly along the whole vast line. He decided upon the bold strategy of forming two separate entities: one regiment to be re-cruited in Rhodesia, with headquarters at Bulawayo and a frontier post at Tuli on the River Limpopo, and another to be based on Ramathlabama and made up of volunteers from the Bechuanaland Protectorate and, he hoped, of others streaming in from the Cape Colony. He turned the task of raising and commanding the Rhodesia regiment over to Colonel Plumer with McLaren on his staff. The leadership of the Protectorate regiment he entrusted to Colonel C. O. Hore who had just arrived in South Africa after seeing service in Egypt.

B-P knew very well that Mafeking, rather than the tiny railroad stop of Ramathlabama, twenty miles to the north of it, was the logical base for his second regiment. But he also knew that a military build-up in Mafeking would be out of the question. Anything he did there would be viewed with alarm by the Boers of the Transvaal. Besides, since the town was within the borders of the Cape Colony, he would be stymied every step along the way. In Ramathlabama, on the other hand, he would be under the direct control of the British Colonial Office which meant that he would have a comparatively free hand securing supplies and recruiting volun-teers. He nevertheless made arrangements with Cape Town to use Mafeking for his general supply centre. It was the only place where adequate storage facilities were available.

For the next two months—August and September—Baden-Powell was on the road continually between Bulawayo and Mafeking, supervising the raising, organization and training of the two regiments, securing their supplies of horses, food, guns, ammunition, and keeping up a barrage of correspondence with the Cape.

The enlisting of the volunteers proved a harder task than he had ima-gined. The men were reluctant to give up their jobs for a military service whose length was contingent upon a war that so far was only in the threatening stage. However, the volunteers were slowly forthcoming. Plumer and Hore lined up a number of good men who, in turn, recruited others, but with exasperating slowness. 'The volunteers keep havering and changing their minds every day,' B-P reported to Hanbury Williams. 'It is maddening. . . . I burst with rage but have to whistle to myself "Wait till the clouds roll by". Fuming does no good—one has to be, or pretend to be, patient.'

Supplies were another of Baden-Powell's great concerns. Matériel to the extent he felt necessary would cost money—lots of money. And money was not forthcoming—General Butler refused to authorize any for the purpose of building up stores in Mafeking for a war that, in his opinion, was not likely to happen. Fortunately, the town was well stocked. Earlier in the year the Government had decided to levy a new customs duty on all goods shipped into Rhodesia after a certain date, with the result that some of the major Cape Colony firms had shipped large consignments to Mafeking. The local branch of the firm of Julius Weil & Co. alone was reported to have provisions on hand valued at £30,000.

In spite of all difficulties, things were moving forward so well that B-P, on 10 September, could drop his mother an optimistic note: 'I have nearly completed my task. . . . It has involved a lot of work but all has gone well so far—and my two regiments are raised, mounted, equipped and fed for three months to come. I have just been visiting them and found them already really well in the field.'

His main frustration now was that he still could not make use of Mafeking as headquarters for himself and for Colonel Hore's regiment.

After a number of conferences between the British and Boer Governments, the Transvaal *Volksraad* had finally passed a Franchise Bill, only to withdraw it again when it was branded as completely unacceptable by Britain. Her Majesty's Government suggested another conference but was rebuffed. It was evident to all concerned that the situation was leading to a military show-down: while the conferences had been going on, modern weapons from Krupp's, in Germany, and Creusot's, in France, had been pouring into the Transvaal by the shipload by way of Lourenço Marques, the Portuguese East Africa port.

Britain was also preparing. Ten thousand British soldiers from various overseas stations, mainly India, were sailing for South Africa. The War Office replaced Sir William Butler, the General Officer Commanding, by General Sir F. Forestier-Walker. At long last, the military supplies and provisions B-P had wanted began to move more freely up the railway towards Mafeking.

On 15 September a telegram from the High Commissioner granted

Baden-Powell permission to send an armed guard into Mafeking to protect the accumulated stores. B-P interpreted the permission liberally: 'As the strength of that guard was not stipulated I moved the whole [Bechuanaland Protectorate] regiment into the place without delay.' He would make Mafeking a tough nut to crack in case the Boers should get the notion to attack it.

But, unfortunately, with the situation still officially under Colonial Office control, he was not yet able to act as the military commander of Mafeking. He and the members of his staff had to move about in civilian clothes and do what should be done in a *sub rosa* manner so as to give no offence to the Afrikaner majority in the Cape Colony Parliament.

He could not call for volunteers, for instance, or arm the citizens, distribute ammunition or inquire into the supplies of the local police openly—but he did these things nevertheless, secretly, with the connivance of Mafeking's British Mayor and Resident Commissioner. He could not fortify Cannon Kopje, a height overlooking the town, but did it anyway under the pretence of building a rifle range. He could not requisition sandbags for fortifications, but collected all empty grain sacks usable for the purpose. He could not ask to have a couple of armoured trains sent up from Cape Town, but had two constructed clandestinely in the railway yard in Mafeking by walling up long 'bogie trucks' with steel rails.

He went over the local artillery with the colonel in charge of the British South Africa Police and found a rather discouraging collection of weapons. The town's armament consisted of two seven-pounder M.L. guns, one one-pounder Hotchkiss, one two-inch Nordenfelt, and seven .303 Maxims—all of them of old vintage.

B-P wrote and telegraphed Cape Town for more guns, and wrote and telegraphed again. Finally, a telegram informed him that two FOGBELLS—code name for 5.7 Howitzers—were on their way. He revised his scheme for defence accordingly and was on hand at the railway the day the guns were expected. So was most of the garrison. The men flocked to the station to greet the two 'monster guns' that were to repel any attacker.

When the train pulled in B-P saw no outward sign of the guns. Oh, yes, the guns were there all right, the guard assured him as he opened the van. But instead of the two FOGBELLS B-P had expected, he was faced with two guns with the code name FOLKRIGHT: two obsolete seven-pounders similar to the two he already had, one of them an old-timer that had seen service in Matabeleland under the affectionate name of 'Crooked-tail Sal'.

B-P sent off an indignant telegram asking for an explanation and demanding that the Howitzers be shipped immediately. He got no satisfaction, beyond a letter of apology which arrived after it was too late to remedy the situation.

But fortunately and unexpectedly, a few days later, four Maxims arrived in town to add to the meagre artillery.

4

Baden-Powell had accomplished two of the tasks Lord Wolseley had sent him out to South Africa to do: he had raised the two regiments of Mounted Infantry and had organized the defence of the frontier towards the Transvaal. But if he were to perform the third task—keeping the enemy occupied in that area in case of war—he needed a larger mobile force. B-P visualized the war he knew to be imminent as a war of movement. The Boers were excellent horsemen. They would move quickly and strike suddenly, and, if repulsed, would reorganize and return for another strike. Only cavalry would have a chance to cope with them. And so Baden-Powell requested Cape Town to send up two squadrons of cavalry, preferably from his own 5th Dragoon Guards, now moved to South Africa from India. 'Two hundred cavalry,' he wrote, 'are better than four hundred infantry. Offensive action is a far better safeguard against attack and infinitely better for our prestige than sitting down to be invested.'

But the Cape didn't quite see it that way. B-P was advised that it was not deemed feasible to add cavalry to the force already gathered in Mafeking.

Mafeking. . . . Mafeking. . . . All that B-P was hearing now was Mafeking. But he had not been sent to South Africa for the purpose of defending Mafeking. He wrote to Sir F. Forestier-Walker asking to have the situation clarified: 'The Protectorate Regiment,' he reminded the general, 'was raised under War Office instructions to protect the border and to make diversions later when necessary; but under present circumstances, owing to there being no efficient garrison at Mafeking it is tied there to protect its stores.' B-P wanted to know 'if this departure from instructions is approved by the General Officer Commanding'.

In answer, General Forestier-Walker informed B-P that he was well aware that the employment of the Protectorate Regiment as a garrison for Mafeking was not in accordance with the object for which it had been raised. But no other force was available to defend Mafeking. Baden-Powell would have to make the best of the situation.

As October arrived with reports of the further deterioration of the position between the British and the Transvaal Governments, the War Office finally reacted: B-P's force was transferred from the Colonial Office to the direct command of the G.O.C., South Africa. Baden-Powell at once ordered his men into uniform and assumed full command of the preparations for the defence of Mafeking.

It was his idea to protect Mafeking with an outer circle of small independent forts manned by the trained troops, and with an inner line of defences on the edge of the town manned by the town guard. He put all available men to work with pick and shovel to create a system of sixty sandbag forts along a perimeter of nearly six miles. Some members of his staff expressed concern about the length of the perimeter but B-P knew what he was about. He felt certain that the Boers would bring up modern, long-range guns. The farther away from the town he could keep them, the poorer would be their aim.

For his headquarters, Baden-Powell acquired the offices of Spencer Minchin, Mafeking's lawyer. He put up a look-out tower on top of the building, and had a hole cut through the roof for a speaking tube. Through this tube he could communicate with his underground telephone exchange below, which, in turn, could connect him with each of the outlying forts. From his perch, B-P could see not only all his defence works but also any the Boers might throw up if they should surround the town.

A short distance from his office and look-out, Baden-Powell established a bomb-proof shelter for himself and his staff. It was 'a queer dark hole in which an officer was always on duty. The earthen roof was covered with a tarpaulin to prevent it getting soaked and over-heavy in the tropical rains that fell. The front door was protected from bullets by some bales of hay'.

To man the forts and outworks he could count on close to seven hundred and fifty men of the Bechuanaland Protectorate Regiment, the British South Africa Police, the Cape Police, and the Bechuanaland Rifles, a volunteer corps. To garrison the town itself he enrolled three hundred able-bodied townsmen, all good shots. In addition to this trained personnel, he employed about three hundred local natives as cattle guards, watchmen and police in the native part of Mafeking.

In preparing for the defence of the town, Baden-Powell was energetically and ably assisted by his staff: 'His officers,' according to the *Official History of the War in South Africa*, 'were men after his own heart, keen and adventurous, and like himself animated by that disciplined unrest which not only leads men out of the beaten path, but empowers them to beat out paths of their own.' The roster of his staff must, as a matter of fact, have gladdened the heart of Baden-Powell's mother who had striven so valiantly over so many years to ensure that her children met and associated with the 'right' people. The list sounded like a page from *Burke's Peerage, Baronetage and Knightage:* Major Lord Edward Cecil, his chief of staff, was the fourth son of Lord Salisbury, the Prime Minister. His intelligence officer, Lieutenant the Hon. Algernon Hanbury-Tracy, was the son of Lord Sudeley, and his aide-de-camp, Captain Gordon Wilson, the son-in-law of the Duke of Marlborough. Captain Charles Fitzclarence was a descendant of William IV and one of his ten children by the Irish actress Dorothea Jordan during their twenty-year liaison. Captain the Hon. Douglas H. Marsham was the son of the Earl of Romney, and Lieutenant Lord Charles Cavendish-Bentinck, the half-brother of the Duke of Portland.

In spite of their titles and their ancestry, these men were all down-to-earth, dedicated officers. They all performed their duties expertly. So did the un-titled members on B-P's Mafeking staff—specifically Lieutenant-Colonel Hore of the Protectorate Regiment, Major Alexander Godley, second in command of the Protectorates, Major F. W. Panzera of the Royal Artillery, and Major Courtenay B. Vyvyan of the Royal Engineers, who had served with B-P in Matabeleland.

When the fortifications were completed, Baden-Powell gave them a minute inspection. They were as good as could be expected, but he knew that fortifications alone were not enough. For further protection, Mafeking would need to be surrounded by a mine field.

He promptly had notices distributed throughout the town:

NOTICE

DEFENCE MINES

The inhabitants are warned that mines are being laid at various points outside the town in connection with the defences. Their position will be marked, in order to avoid accidents, by small red flags.

Cattle herds and others should be warned accordingly.

Mafeking: Dated this 7th day of October, 1899.

There was plenty of dynamite in town. But, unfortunately, it was in the form of charges for use in the mining works up north. It had been shipped up from the Cape and had become stranded in Mafeking. It was unsuited for defence mines.

But this did not deter Baden-Powell. He had his own philosophy in regard to mines and his own idea about making them. He placed Major Panzera in charge of a secret 'laboratory' for making mines, each of them to be enclosed in a wooden box. When completed the mines were carried to their locations, with the greatest care, by natives who had been warned against the disastrous explosion that would follow if they should drop one of them. The little black boxes—hundreds of them—were buried at different points along the front line and connected by wires to the central observation post.

To give proper effectiveness to his ruse, Baden-Powell notified the population of Mafeking that, on a certain day between noon and 2 p.m., a trial would be made to see that the mines were in working order. People were warned to stay away from the east front during the trial period.

> With everybody safely indoors, Major Panzera and I went out and stuck a stick of dynamite into an ant-bear hole. We lit a fuse and ran and took cover until the thing went off—which it did with a splendid roar and a vast cloud of dust!
>
> Out of the dust emerged a man with a bike who happened to be passing, and he pedalled off as hard as he could go for the Transvaal, eight miles away, where he no doubt told how by merely riding along the road he had hit off a murderous mine.
>
> The boxes were actually filled with nothing more dangerous than sand!

The news spread all over town of the formidable ring of mines that B-P had established. The loyal townspeople perked up. The spies and traitors—of whom there were many in Mafeking—sent off dire warnings to their Boer friends.

Next in importance to the defence of Mafeking was the provision of shelters for the town's women and children for protection against shell fire. For this a large underground gallery was constructed. No such shelter was required for the native women—the Boers would not think of attacking their part of the town. This would be a 'white man's war'. In addition to this main shelter, trenches were dug through all the streets, in back yards, and criss-crossing the Market Square. They had a double purpose: to protect the population against shells and to slow down the enemy if he should succeed in penetrating the town. To harass the enemy further, trek wagons were piled up as barricades across the roads leading in from the veld.

5

In the middle of his busy schedule, Baden-Powell took a couple of hours off to read galley proofs of the small book he had written based on the training sessions he had given his men in the 5th Dragoon Guards.

Immediately on arriving home from India he had sent the manuscript to the firm of W. Thacker & Co., the main distributor of books on military subjects used in India. The firm had turned it down. The publisher himself had written to B-P declaring that he did not foresee a large enough sale to justify the publication of *Aids to Scouting* as B-P had finally dubbed his book.

After this refusal, B-P had left the manuscript with his brother Frank to handle for him. Frank sent it to Gale & Polden Ltd. at Aldershot, the publishers of a popular *Military Series*, who without hesitation accepted the book and offered to pay the author 'a royalty of £5 on each thousand copies sold after the first two thousand copies had been disposed of'.

In August, Frank dropped a letter to his brother telling him the good news. B-P wrote a quick note back: 'I would like to see the proofs before it is published.'

The proofs arrived at the end of September. To B-P's relief, the material read rather well. He felt that he had covered the subject of military scouting adequately and in an interesting fashion, quite different from most military manuals. He had included scores of anecdotes and examples, dozens of field games and contests.

He caught a couple of errors and revised a chapter, then wrapped the proofs in the same paper in which he had received them and shipped them off to England with the casual notation 'Publish it'.

6

In the daytime, Baden-Powell's hours were occupied in planning with his staff and in conferring with contractors and suppliers.

Much of what he did depended upon exact information about the Boers, their numbers, their artillery, their intentions, their plans for attack. The telegraph kept him informed on the day-by-day development in the renewed British-Boer conferences. Natives returning from the Transvaal brought him reports of a large number of Boers assembling and talking among themselves of capturing Mafeking or shelling it to ruins. Reconnoitring parties and scouts brought him further information about what was happening on the other side of the border.

But he needed to know further details. He needed to be positive. And the only way he knew to be positive was to find out for himself.

And so, B-P again became *Impeesa* as the Matabele had called him: 'The-wolf-that-never-sleeps'. He rode off in the dark of night for the Transvaal. A short distance within the border he located two large laagers. From the number of camp fires and wagons he estimated that these alone contained about six thousand Boers, and there were other laagers to the south, with yet more.

7

On 9 October 1899, President Kruger threw aside all semblance of negotiation on the *Uitlander* issue. Confident in Boer invincibility, in the vast store of arms he had accumulated and in the expected support of Germany and Russia, he dispatched an ultimatum to the British Government. In it he demanded that all British troops near the Transvaal border be instantly withdrawn, that all recently arrived reinforcements be removed from South Africa, that the troops on the sea should not be landed. He gave Britain forty-eight hours to provide a satisfactory answer.

The answer was forthcoming before the time was up. It was, as could be expected, a flat rejection by Her Majesty's Government.

And so, at five o'clock on the afternoon of 11 October 1899, with the expiration of Kruger's ultimatum, the Transvaal and Great Britain were at war. The first Boer commandoes crossed their own borders. It was 'Oom Paul's seventy-fourth birthday.

The next morning, Baden-Powell posted a proclamation throughout Mafeking:

> In consequence of the Armed Forces of the South Africa Republic having committed an overt act of war in invading British territory, I give notice that a state of war exists and that the Civil Law is for the time being suspended and that I proclaim Martial Law from this date in the Mafeking District and Bechuanaland Protectorate, by virtue of a power granted to me by His Excellency the High Commissioner.
>
> Mafeking, 12 October 1899,
>
> R. S. S. BADEN-POWELL, Colonel Commanding Frontier Force.

The 'Colonel Commanding' had a busy day. He had hardly finished a staff meeting before he was on hand in the Market Square to inspect the Town Guard, a motley but determined lot of men who cheered wildly for the Queen and as wildly for their commander. B-P ended a brief speech to them with a ringing 'All you have to do is to sit tight, and when the enemy comes shoot straight—and you will soon send these fellows to the right-about. Take my word for it, if you act as I fully expect you will act, the Boers will never enter Mafeking!'

Then on to the railway station to say good-bye to some two hundred women and children being sent south to Kimberley for safety in a train piloted by one of B-P's precious armoured trains, manned by fifteen colonial volunteers under Lieutenant Nesbit.

As soon as the passenger train was well out of town, B-P returned to his headquarters. He opened his diary and added a footnote to the day's activities: 'Telegram today from Military Secretary that Imperial Government will not pay railway fares of women and children. Nor will I!'

He had expected the armoured train to get back the next day. It never returned. He soon learned the reason. After escorting the passenger train safely to Kimberley, it had started on the return trip. About fifty miles south of Mafeking, Nesbit was informed that Boers had been reported on the line a few miles farther on. Instead of first reconnoitring to make certain that he could get through, Lieutenant Nesbit had ordered full speed ahead, with the foreseeable result: at Kraaipan the train was derailed and shelled by the Boers under Commandant J. H. (Koos) de la Rey. Nesbit was forced to surrender with all his men, some of them wounded.

Nesbit's foolhardy action had given the Boers the war's first victory. The first British blood had been shed, the first British prisoners taken. And B-P had lost an important piece of ordnance.

While waiting for the first reports of the advance of the large Boer force he had spied on, B-P was told by an excited official that the railway yard still harboured two railway trucks containing twenty-two tons of dynamite. If hit by a Boer shell the havoc would be tremendous.

After some discussion, one of the engine drivers, a young Irishman from County Kildare named Ferry, together with his stoker boarded his engine and rattled north pushing the two dynamite cars before him.

Not quite half an hour later, a terrific explosion shook the windows of Mafeking. People rushed out of their houses and gathered in the streets. A huge, balloon-shaped cloud soared into the sky away to the north.

Shortly afterwards, Engine 123 came speeding down the rails with its bass whistle sounding full blast. Ferry brought it to a halt, jumped off and made his report.

About six miles out of town he had come upon a large group of Boers tearing up the tracks. He had stopped his train, dismounted, uncoupled the engine and had steamed toward home, leaving the dynamite trucks behind. A mile away he had stopped to watch what would happen. The Boers had obviously mistaken the trucks for an armoured train and had started to fire on it. Suddenly the 'armoured train' had gone skyward with a roar.

Baden-Powell sent a reconnoitring party to look over the scene of the explosion. Later he jotted down their findings in his diary: 'No Boers hurt, bodily, by the explosion of the dynamite trucks—but they were much hurt in their feelings at having what they thought was a dirty trick played on them.'

During the afternoon, scouting patrols reported the steady advance of the Boers. The enemy was moving in on Mafeking—slowly, inexorably. From the north, from the south, from the east, and, after a flanking movement, from the west.

By nightfall on 13 October 1899 the town was completely surrounded and cut off from the rest of the world.

The siege of Mafeking had begun.

XIII

The Siege of Mafeking

Years: 1899–1900   Age: 42–43

1

MAFEKING—'the place of stone'—wasn't much of a place, although it was the largest town in north Cape Colony. 'It had', according to J. Emerson Neilly, correspondent to the *Pall Mall Gazette,* 'the appearance of a place which has been planned and partly built upon, but has not had time to more than half grow.'

It lay shimmering in the African sun, at an altitude of 4,190 feet in the midst of a bare prairie landscape. Around it the stony veld spread in all directions, dipping slightly from the edge of town, rising slightly again towards the horizon, with occasional scattered hills a couple of hundred feet high: Cannon Kopje a mile to the south-east, Signal Hill about four miles to the north. And here and there, the monotony broken by a solitary acacia or gum tree, a feature so rare that each tree had a name: Jackal Tree, Game Tree.

Mafeking was, in reality, a dual town—part white, part black. The white section was laid out like a draught-board, about a thousand yards square, with wide streets at right angles to each other and with a large open market square in the centre. The walls of the buildings were built from unbaked adobe bricks made from the reddish clay in the Brickfields east of town. The roofs were of corrugated tin, and clattered like a hundred-piece drum corps whenever a tropical downpour hit the town. The buildings around Market Square housed the shops, the bank, the local printing-shop, the public library, Dixon's Hotel, and Minchin's law office in which Baden-Powell had established his headquarters. The population of the white section amounted, according to a census taken by Baden-Powell, to 'white men, 1,074; white women, 229; white children, 405—a total of 1,708'.

To the north of the town, a quarter of a mile away, were the hospital and the convent of the Sisters of Charity, an Irish sisterhood. To the west lay the barracks of the BSAP—the British South Africa Police—and west of these spread the native kraals: a *stad* of hundreds of circular, reed-thatched wattle-and-daub huts that housed about 7,500 natives of the local tribe, the Baralongs, under their chief, Wessels Montsica.

The sluggish River Malopo—'an uncertain stream of no greater importance in dry weather than a Buckinghamshire ditch'—flowed in from the east through the Brickfields, passed south of the white town, then continued through the native *stad* in its westward meanderings. The railway swung in from the south-west, crossed the iron bridge over the Malopo and turned straight north between the native *stad* and the white quarter, past the Mafeking station with its engine house and well-equipped workshops. Half a dozen dusty roads, all of them emerging from Market Square, spread out across the veld towards the north and the south, the east and the west.

No, Mafeking wasn't much of a place, but in Baden-Powell's opinion it was the most important point in the domain he had been ordered to defend —for several reasons, some strategic, some sentimental, others political.

Strategically, Mafeking was the outpost for Kimberley and Cape Town to the south, for Bechuanaland Protectorate and Rhodesia to the north. It threatened the weak flank of the Transvaal Republic only eight miles to the east. It was the chief town of the large native districts of north-west Cape Colony, with their more than 200,000 inhabitants. It contained valuable railway stock and workshops, and large food and forage supplies.

But also, Mafeking had long been a thorn in the side of the Boers. It had seen the stand of Sir Charles Warren in 1884 and had been the head-quarters of the Jameson raiders planning their dash towards Johannesburg in 1895, therefore its reduction was sentimentally imperative to the Boers. By taking it, and taking it quickly, the Boers would wreak the vengeance they craved and simultaneously prove to the natives of South Africa their superiority over the British.

As if this were not enough, rumour had it that the fall of Mafeking would be the signal for all the Cape Dutch to rise in arms and spread the war south to the very waters of Table Bay.

From the moment Baden-Powell knew that the Boers were on the march towards Mafeking he was itching to 'have a go' at them. He considered it a great compliment that Kruger had sent 'The Lion of the Transvaal'— General 'Honest Piet' Cronje, with an estimated force of nine thousand men to take Mafeking.

The Boers, with their superior force, might decide to rush the town and take it in a single bloody attack. Some of the remarks of their leaders had

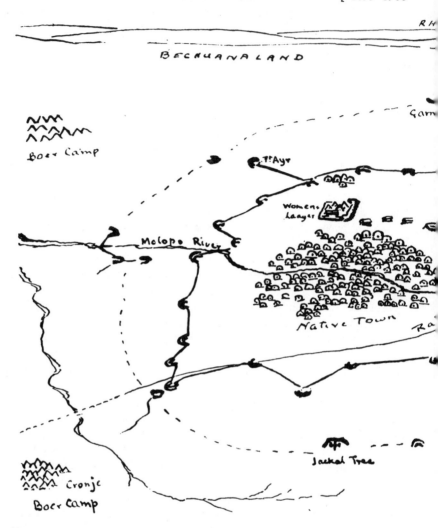

indicated this: 'We'll eat them up as crows do lice off a cow's back.' Nevertheless, B-P, with his knowledge of the Boers, could not quite see the careful, slow-moving Dutch burghers acting in this fashion. They would be more apt to approach carefully, feeling their way and then, after knowing the lie of the land, attempt to take the town at as small a cost in casualties as possible. He could imagine the Boers, under Cronje, establishing a blockade and starting a bombardment before attempting open battle.

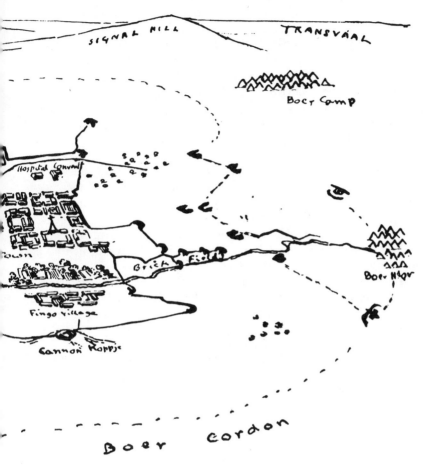

A bird's-eye view of the siege of Mafeking.

He decided to counter the Boer's probable course with two specialties of his own: bluff and boldness.

He set the pattern for what was ahead in the Standing Orders to his men:

> Bluff the enemy with show of force as much as you like but don't let yourself get too far out of touch with your own side without orders, lest you draw them into difficulties in their endeavour to support you. Lend a helping hand to your side whenever you see a chance.

Do not always wait for an order, if you see the situation demands action.

Don't be afraid to act for fear of making a mistake—'a man who never made a mistake never made anything'. If you find you have made a mistake carry it through nevertheless with energy. Pluck and dash have often changed a mistake into a success. . . .

B-P had already started his strategy of bluff. Now he was ready for his first show of boldness: Mafeking would hit the enemy before the enemy had a chance to strike.

At dawn the morning after the Boers had ringed the town, Baden-Powell sent out reconnaissance patrols to find out the disposition of the widely spread enemy forces. The patrol to the north brought back the report of the approach of a strong party of Boers.

B-P ordered out the remaining armoured train at once, with instructions to rush the Boers and pour a heavy fire into them. 'I want', he told his men, 'the first blow felt by them to be a really hard one'.

The armoured train, and a squadron of seventy men of the Protectorate Regiment supporting it, quickly found themselves under hot enemy fire. The Boers spattered lead over the steel sides of the train and threatened to encircle the British squadron.

In spite of the danger that the Boers might use this diversion to attack the town from another direction, in the hope of finding Mafeking 'denuded of defenders', B-P sent more of his slender force into action. His boldness paid off.

The first engagement at the gates of Mafeking lasted four hours and resulted in a vastly outnumbered British detachment driving back the Boers with 'a spirit and dash worthy of highly trained troops'. The British casualties had been four killed and sixteen wounded. The Boer losses had been many times larger. They were afterwards found to have been fifty-three killed and close on a hundred and fifty wounded.

Baden-Powell had struck hard and unexpectedly and had succeeded, so early in the game, in instilling apprehension in the minds of the Boers—first through the highly publicized 'minefields', then the explosion of the 'armoured train', and now this.

Confidently, B-P jotted in his diary: 'This smartly fought little engagement will have a great and lasting moral effect on the enemy.'

Baden-Powell had warned the population that shelling could be expected at any moment on any day. The first of these shellings began at 9.50 on the morning of 16 October. During the next three hours sixty-three shells fell on Mafeking. The shelling ceased at 1.05 p.m.

Shortly after, a Boer messenger approached the British outposts under a white truce flag. He was conducted to Baden-Powell. He had come with the demand from General Cronje that the Mafeking garrison surrender immediately and unconditionally.

Baden-Powell looked at the messenger in mock surprise. 'And why should we?'

'To avoid further bloodshed.'

'But we haven't had any yet!' B-P said.

The Boer emissary was regaled with beer and sent on his way back to his own forces.

The effect of the first shelling had been slight indeed. The range had been bad, the shrapnel of poor quality. Some of the town roads had been ploughed up and Market Square was littered with shrapnel. The only two shells that had taken effect had hit the convent and the hospital, although both were flying Red Cross flags, without inflicting any damage beyond knocking out a bit of masonry and ripping up a few floor-boards. No casualties had resulted.

The shellings the following days were equally ineffective. So much so that Baden-Powell scribbled a scornful note and sent it to the north during the night by a native runner through the Boer lines:

'All well. Four hours' bombardment. One dog killed.'

The message was meant solely for the reassurance of Colonel Plumer and the men of the Rhodesia Regiment. B-P had no idea that Plumer would telegraph it on to England where it was grasped with eagerness as a proof of the Mafeking commander's indomitable spirit.

The effect of Baden-Powell's bluff and boldness was quick in showing itself.

A few days after the attack by the armoured train, two natives, taken prisoner by the Boers, escaped and brought news into Mafeking. They reported that General Cronje had called a mass meeting of his burghers and had told them 'that he intended to take Mafeking but that he did not want his burghers shot down like dogs by the "steam fort" which had murdered them on Saturday; that the place was surrounded by dynamite traps like the one which was exploded on the railway; that Mafeking was not worth the risk of so many valuable lives. He had therefore sent to Pretoria for a big gun which would level the town to the ground from a safe distance'.

Baden-Powell soon received official confirmation of the natives' report. An emissary arrived from the Boer lines under a white flag, bringing a letter addressed to *Den Wel Ed Gertr. Heer Bevelvoeder von Mafeking—* The Well-born Honourable Commander of Mafeking. The missive was from General Cronje himself:

Wel Ed Heer, Aangezien het mij thans blikjkt dat er geene endere
bestaat om Mafeking in bezit te nemen dan door een bombardment
moet ik tot mijm leedwezen daartoe overgaan. . . .

Or, in English translation:

Honourable Sir, Since it appears to me that there is no other way of
taking Mafeking than by means of a bombardment, I have to adopt
that course with regret. I shall allow you forty-eight hours to prepare
your people, black and white. You have to see that non-combatants
leave Mafeking before the expiration of that time. If you do not
comply with this I will not be answerable for the result. . . . The time
allowed to you is from Saturday, 21, at 6 a.m. till Monday, 23, at the
same hour.

I have the honour to be, sir, your obedient servant,

P. S. CRONJE, General W.C.

Baden-Powell answered the letter the following day in the same polite vein:

To His Honour Piet Cronje, commanding the Z.A.R. Forces near
Mafeking.

Sir, I am sorry that you have to confess yourself unable to take
Mafeking without bombarding it. But this course you are quite at
liberty to take if you imagine it will help you. . . .

I am much obliged to you for giving warning to the non-combatants
to move away from Mafeking; but they do not propose to avail
themselves of it. In return for your courtesy I wish to warn your
people that I have had the ground at a distance around Mafeking
prepared with dynamite defence mines. . Some of these are self-acting;
the others are fired from observation points. I am loath to make use
of the n except when special reasons of defence demand it. . . .

Though obliged to take the measures I above indicate, I beg you
will understand that I am indebted to you for the courteous manner in
which you have carried on communication with me.

I have the honour to be, sir, yours most obediently,

R. S. S. BADEN-POWELL, Commanding H. M. Forces, Mafeking.

The correspondence was kept up throughout the siege, at times with as
many as four messages a day going back and forth under the white truce
flag. The pleasant tone was always kept—ponderous from the Boer side,
courteous from B-P's side but often teasing and subtly derisive.

A native runner sneaking into Mafeking during the night brought news
that seemed to indicate that Cronje's intention to level Mafeking with

siege guns was no empty threat: 'In Zeerust the Boers talk of the big gun that is coming from Pretoria to blow Mafeking to bits. It is drawn by sixteen black oxen. Its shell takes four men to lift.'

2

Monday, 23 October, the town awakened in deep anxiety.

Today, according to Cronje's ultimatum, was the day when the big bombardment was to start. Today the shells from a big siege gun would be exploding throughout the town. With what effect? How many houses would be laid in smoking ruins? How many broken bodies would be lying in the streets? How many lives would be wiped out before the day was done? And what would the Boers do to the survivors when they stormed the shell-pocked town?

The firing started at daybreak. The townspeople listened—incredulously. Those 'pops' could not possibly be from the dreaded siege gun.

They were not. Baden-Powell had again decided to strike first. He had aimed his own guns against the enemy positions—specifically against the Boer location near Jackal Tree where unusual activity seemed to be taking place, but where no big gun was as yet in sight. The townspeople all agreed with J. Angus Hamilton, the reporter for *The Times*, that 'it was a pleasant surprise to find that the bombardment of Mafeking by the Boers had been converted into the bombardment of the Boers by Mafeking'.

The day went by and the night.

Early the following morning, a reconnaissance patrol reported that the Boers were drawing a big gun towards Jackal Tree. The morning passed. Noon.

At 1.30 p.m. there were indications that the enemy was ready to fire.

A sharp ringing of the headquarters phone. The look-out at Cannon Kopje reporting: 'The big gun is being loaded. She is now elevated and pointing at the town.' 'Bang, bang, bang,' goes our gong—at once answered by the railway iron hung up in the hotel verandah and taken up by bells about the town. The people in Market Square and in the streets dive for cover into the nearest shelter or behind buildings. And 'Boom—scre-e-e-ech—bang and crash!' comes a shell—with a cloud of red dust flying from the garden of a house out yonder.

The 'big gun'—or 'Marguerit', as the Dutch had called her and which had quickly degenerated to 'Gretchen' and 'Grietje' and had finally become anglicized into 'Creaky'—kept up for two and a half hours, firing twenty-three rounds at seven-minute intervals, then ceased her shelling. Shell fragments and an unexploded shell told Baden-Powell the kind of weapon Mafeking was up against: a ninety-four-pounder Creusot siege gun.

In the evening, B-P totalled the casualties: 'One trooper, Protectorate Regiment, leg broken by fragment of shell; one native, scalp wound from splinter of shell.' He checked the damage done: 'Damage by shell fire in town very small. Riesle's Hotel struck twice. Weil's store struck by live shell that went through the wall but was stopped effectively by his corned beef.'

Baden-Powell was proud of the low rate of casualties. He credited this partly to the extended area over which the town was distributed and partly to the completely bomb-proof cover that had been provided for the defence and for the women and children. The small property damage could also be traced to the way Mafeking was laid out, with widely scattered buildings, but even more clearly to the building material. The unbaked clay bricks used for the walls crumbled when hit. A shell simply made a hole right through the wall. If the walls had been built of burned bricks that scatter on impact, the destruction would have been vast.

And so, regularly, day in and day out—with the exception of Sunday—Mafeking was exposed to a savage barrage of exploding shells from weapons of German Krupp and French Creusot manufacture. Old 'Creaky' eventually proved less of a terror than expected—mainly because of the time lapse between its firing and its hitting. People obeying the warning bells could get under cover and stay there till the burst of the shell was over.

While it was comparatively easy to get the adults into the bomb shelters, it was almost impossible to keep the Mafeking boys underground. The boys were the last in the shelters when the alarm was given and the first out after a shell had burst, racing to pick up the fragments often long before the 'All Clear' signal had sounded.

Lord Edward Cecil agreed to attempt to harness the boys' exuberant energy for the benefit of the whole town. The men of Mafeking were needed for the firing line. The more of them who could be released from other duties by boy power, the better.

Ned Cecil announced the formation of a cadet corps for boys 9 years old and upwards and found the boys eager to join. He started with a group of eighteen—one sergeant-major, one sergeant, two corporals, and fourteen privates. He scrounged special khaki uniforms for them to wear, with forage caps or wide-brimmed 'smasher' hats with yellow pugarees. He taught them drill and discipline and gave them a thorough training for their various tasks by means of games and competitions.

Before long, Ned Cecil had his boys adequately trained to carry military messages, deliver civilian mail, act as orderlies, take turns at look-out posts. His Mafeking Cadet Corps was eventually recognized as an official part of the Mafeking defences.

On 25 October, the shelling started early and was particularly heavy. Baden-Powell foresaw a possible full-scale attack on the town and alerted his whole command. The red Alarm flag was hoisted to the top of the flagpole of the headquarters building.

At noon the shelling stopped.

In the lull, the outposts looking across the veld began reporting to B-P by telephone: 'Eight hundred enemy moving in from the south-west with three guns'—'Two hundred Boers against north-east of town'—'Six hundred men with two guns advancing against Cannon Kopje from south-west'—'Troop of enemy approaching at a gallop towards west position.' Baden-Powell gave his orders. 'Keep under cover. Reserve your fire for close distances.'

The shelling resumed. The enemy moved closer and closer.

When the Boers were within comfortable range, the British opened fire with rifles and machine-guns. The firing had a surprising immediate effect. 'So soon as our volleys and Maxims commenced the enemy stopped their advance and began to withdraw at all points. Casualties on our side were one man wounded, two horses and eight mules wounded. The Boer losses unknown—enemy ambulances picking up for over an hour.' Why had the Boers retired so precipitously? Had they actually felt themselves beaten? Or had they lacked the spirit to attack? B-P and his Mafeking defenders began to think that there might be some truth to the report that while Kruger had ordered the capture of Mafeking he had forbidden any action likely to result in more than fifty casualties.

The next attempt of the enemy to break into Mafeking followed soon after. But instead of a frontal attack the Boers went over to trench warfare. They had early cut the supply pipes from the waterworks east of town and had established themselves in trenches in the surrounding fields— the Brickfields. Working at night, they were now moving the trenches up to within two thousand yards of the Brickfields defence posts and were apparently intent on working up to an even closer range. B-P arranged a night attack on the Boer trenches and entrusted the task to a squadron under Captain 'The Devil' Fitzclarence.

As night fell, Fitzclarence gathered his men 'with magazine charged, but no cartridges in the chamber, the order being to use the bayonet only'. A line of red lanterns were hung up on posts to make it possible for the men to find their way back into town in the darkness—they simply had to strike homeward in line with the lights.

The force crept off noiselessly behind their leader, reached the flank of the advanced Boer trench without a shot being fired, wheeled into the trench and cleared it with the bayonet. The whole action took a matter of minutes only—whereupon the squadron dispersed and the men retreated individually as silently as they had come, making for the guiding lanterns back into Mafeking.

But this was not the end of the skirmish. The Boers in the advance trench, taken by surprise, had tried to defend themselves. Shots rang out. Men shouted and howled, then fled to the rear. The Boers in the rear trenches mistook their fleeing comrades for attacking Britons and opened fire. The volleys continued long after the British had regained their own lines.

The Boer's casualties, B-P heard on reliable authority, 'amounted to forty killed and wounded with the bayonet, sixty killed and wounded by rifle fire. Our casualties were six killed, nine wounded, two missing.'

The Boers had never, themselves, attempted a night attack in any previous engagement with the British forces, and had never before been exposed to one. After this attack, they were always on 'night alert', fearing a repetition.

B-P took advantage of their dread. He learned that the Boers had connected the attack with the red lanterns that had been strung up. Now, whenever he wanted to give the Boers something to worry about at night, all he had to do was to perpetrate another bluff by putting up a string of red lanterns somewhere on the outskirts of town.

This was not the only time during the siege that B-P made use of special lighting effects.

One day, a Mr Walker, the agent for the South African Acetylene Gas Company, came to see Baden-Powell. He had become stranded in Mafeking at the outbreak of the war and had been wondering how he might be of service. He informed B-P that a couple of drums of carbide were stored in Mafeking and proposed that it might be used to produce the acetylene for a couple of searchlights. B-P told him to go ahead. With the help of a local tinsmith, using metal from large biscuit tins, the headlight from a locomotive, and a surveyor's tripod, Walker constructed a passable searchlight.

On the next dark night, the new searchlight was set up at one of the outermost forts. The acetylene was turned on and ignited. A strong beam of brilliant white light shot out over the veld and lighted up an enemy installation several hundred yards distant. The British soldiers could see the Boers caught in the light diving into cover. Then the light was turned off. The night was as velvety black as it had been just a few minutes before.

A short while after, the beam of an acetylene searchlight shot across the veld eastwards, towards the Brickfields trenches. Later in the night, the enemy's southern breastwork was brilliantly illuminated.

The Boers quickly reached the conclusion that Mafeking was now surrounded by a ring of searchlights to discourage night attacks. They did not know that only one had been made. Walker and a couple of Protectorate soldiers had spent the night rushing it back and forth among the British outposts.

In the trenches of Mafeking during a heavy Boer bombardment.

Unfortunately, the searchlight dodge did not last long. Shortly after its successful debut a torrential downpour struck Mafeking. The place where the carbide was stored was inundated—and the released acetylene gas mingled in the breeze that swept across the veld.

One Boer peculiarity gave Mafeking's defenders a weekly respite and allowed the townspeople on occasion 'to come out from their dug-outs and enjoy the fresh air and each other's society'. The Boers were 'strict Sabbatarians'. They might shell a town and kill non-combatants and soldiers alike on weekdays—but certainly not on the Sabbath!

Baden-Powell employed the Sundays effectively. He used them to keep up the morale of all the besieged in Mafeking and announced in General Orders 'that Sunday would be observed up till twelve o'clock, and after that hour as Saturday'.

The Sunday in Britain might be dull. But not the Sunday in Mafeking. The townspeople went to church in the morning and in the afternoon enjoyed 'sports, baby shows, concerts, theatricals, and fooleries of every kind'. B-P's old histrionic skills again came to the fore. He spouted some of his favourite monologues, sang selections from Gilbert and Sullivan, played the piano as 'Signor Paderewski', dressed up as a circus ring-master to run the sports events to the great entertainment of the townspeople.

During one of these Sunday frolics, B-P noticed that the Boers, on their part, were taking advantage of the Sabbath to stretch their legs by climbing through the wire entanglements round their trenches into the no man's land between the two lines. He could not actually see the wire but he could see the posts on which it was stretched. Furthermore, the way the men stepped over or crawled under the wire showed that it was there.

That gave him an idea. He, too, would put up wire entanglements. He had no wire. But that didn't bother him. If he couldn't see the Boer wire even through his field glasses, they wouldn't be able to see his—which meant that he wouldn't need any. During the following week, he gathered all the posts that Mafeking held—poles, garden fences, saplings. The next Sunday a forest of posts was put up around Mafeking and 'wire' stretched among them. The men were given strict instructions when entering or leaving their forts to clamber laboriously over this imaginary wire or to creep carefully under it. Mafeking's 'wire entanglements' added greatly to the Boer's respect for the strength of the town's fortifications. They never discovered that the wire was non-existent.

On 30 October, Baden-Powell's signallers intercepted a heliograph message that was flickering between Cronje's camp to the south-west and the Boer camp to the north: 'What is there in the little red fort?'

B-P alerted his men in the 'little red fort'. He had expected an early attack on his 'little red fort'—his outpost on Cannon Kopje, strategically the most important position near Mafeking. From the tall tower on the kopje a look-out could watch every movement of the enemy to the south and the south-west.

The attack came the following morning. It started with a heavy, concentrated shell fire directed against the kopje. For a while little harm was done beyond knocking down parts of the parapet and smashing the iron supports of the look-out tower. Most of the garrison was entrenched about a hundred yards to the rear of the fort.

After half an hour's steady and accurate artillery fire, a large force of

Boers began to advance in extended order on Cannon Kopje from three sides at once. They were backed up by supporting parties. Altogether an estimated eight hundred Boers were on the move. Baden-Powell sent part of his forces, with Maxims, to a position from which the enemy's left flank might be hit, another force with a seven-pounder to another position where the enemy's right flank might be reached. Simultaneously, the Cannon Kopje garrison moved up from its trenches and manned the parapet.

As the enemy line neared the fort, steadily, confidently, it was suddenly exposed to crackling gun fire from each flank, a blistering rifle fire from the front. The line wavered. 'The enemy hesitated—and in spite of the efforts of the mounted commandant they turned and ran . . . the firing slackened. Enemy sent out two ambulances under Red Cross flags picking up men about the field. Losses evidently fairly heavy. . . . Our casualties: six killed, five wounded.'

The Boers had again acted the way they did five days before and had retired before their mission was accomplished. 'If the Dutchmen had come on, the kopje was theirs,' Neilly of the *Pall Mall Gazette* wrote. 'But they always flunked the last six hundred yards, and went back. They did it on this occasion and threw away their chance because they did not care to lose more men.'

Throughout the first month of the siege, Baden-Powell had had little intelligence about what was happening outside the Mafeking line. He had learned that Kimberley, with Colonel R. G. Kekewich and Cecil Rhodes vying for command, and Ladysmith, under General Sir George White, had been invested by the Boers at the same time that Mafeking was surrounded and were still holding out. His knowledge of the number and whereabouts of the British forces that had arrived in South Africa was very meagre and unreliable. It consisted of occasional rumours and tidings brought in by native runners. From what little he knew it would be a long time before help would arrive in Mafeking.

So, 'seeing that we could not be relieved for many weeks, if not months, I took over into our own management all details such as hospital, municipality, police, treasury, post and telegraph, railway, native affairs, water supply, ordnance shops, etc., and put everybody on rations'.

With the South African summer at hand, he encouraged all the townspeople to plant gardens. The alternate spells of tropical downpours and hot sun would produce a good supply of fruit and vegetables.

Cronje, B-P learned, was getting impatient. The Boer general had reached the conclusion that he was wasting his time and expending the energies of a large force needed elsewhere on a stubborn town under a stubborn commander, who didn't seem to realize that he had not the slightest chance of holding out against the might of the Transvaal.

After having lost a month before Mafeking, Cronje gave up the idea of taking the place by storm. He moved off south with six thousand men and half a dozen guns, leaving General J. P. Snijman and Commandant J. D. L. Botha to do the job of finishing off Baden-Powell with the remainder of the Boer force—about three thousand men with ten guns, including the ninety-four-pounder Creusot siege gun and two fourteen-pounder quick-firing Krupps.

Baden-Powell had only disdain for General Snijman. 'Snijman,' he wrote later, 'was a cowardly creature who shelled the hospital, convent, the women's laager, but had not the pluck to lead an attack.' Commandant Dantje Botha, on the other hand, B-P described as 'a fine type of Boer—a dour, stolid man who took up his country's causes with a whole heart, and went through the campaign to the bitter end. . . .'

3

It wasn't a particularly happy Christmas in Mafeking that year. The people did what they could to provide a bit of cheer for the children and gathered for some entertainment of their own on 24 December which fell on a Sunday. As the Boers decided to make Christmas Day another Sunday, Mafeking had an extra day of quiet. Some of the townspeople went to church, others roamed about town in search of Christmas gaiety. Rationing was suspended for the day.

And in the evening as many as could get in crowded a stable near one of the defences for a show, which, according to Neilly, proved to be 'a screamingly jolly entertainment in which took part singers who could not sing, and Christy Minstrels who could not Christy Minstrel, and speech-makers who could not remember their points. . . . We wanted to laugh—we had not laughed in two months—and to us that performance, which would not have been tolerated on the sands at home, was as welcome as the best comedy that ever brought down a house. . . .'

But Baden-Powell's thoughts were far away from the 'screamingly jolly entertainment' that was being played out before them and which he could not have kept from attending without causing wonder about his absence.

Just before the Christmas holiday, he had received news that Plumer was moving south with his Rhodesia regiment and hoped to join forces with British troops to the south. Plumer had asked for orders.

B-P considered the situation carefully. If the juncture could be made, the combined force would be able to clear Bechuanaland of Boers; it could reopen the railway and communication to Bulawayo; it would restore the confidence of the natives. He sent word to Plumer to go ahead. Meantime, in Mafeking, he would make sorties to relieve the pressure.

For his first sortie, B-P settled on the enemy's fort at Game Tree.

Game Tree Fort had long needed taking. The silencing of its guns was getting more and more imperative. The shelling had become very erratic. Many shells had hit the hospital and the convent and had caused numerous casualties. Game Tree Fort commanded the best grass land around Mafeking; if it were taken it would be possible to secure grazing for the half-starved cattle and in this way improve the meagre rations. And Game Tree Fort should not be too hard to take. B-P's scouts and reconnoitring patrols all reported that it was poorly constructed, poorly defended.

Baden-Powell had consulted his staff. The officers were eager to strike. They were getting impatient from their enforced idleness. Tactics were decided on, commands distributed. The attack, scheduled for dawn, 26 December, was only hours away. In the meantime: 'Merry Christmas'.

At two in the morning of what was to become known as 'Black Boxing Day', Baden-Powell watched his attacking force move off. He then took up position in the outermost 'dummy' fort north-west of town, within a mile of the Boer-held Game Tree Fort straight to the north. Several staff members huddled with him, and one of the war correspondents: Vere Stent of Reuter's Agency.

The night was cool but the day ahead promised to be hot and sultry. It was midsummer in South Africa.

Exactly on schedule, Baden-Powell and his companions heard the armoured train, under Major Godley, steam up toward its planned position half a mile beyond Game Tree Fort, to the fort's rear flank—slowly, to keep the clickety-clacks of its wheels from resounding across the veld. Only, somehow, as B-P followed it through his field-glasses, it seemed to halt before reaching the point decided on. . . .

Shortly after dawn, Major Panzera's two seven-pounders and his Maxim opened a frontal attack against Game Tree Fort to attract the attention of the Boers in his direction. With covering fire from Godley to the right and Panzera to the left, Captain Vernon and his men began their attack on Game Tree Fort, with Fitzclarence's squadron following right behind. The men moved steadily forward in short rushes, 'by alternate troops in extended order'.

From their advanced position, B-P and the men with him could see the khaki-clad troopers rise from the tall grass that had hidden them and rush forward. They disappeared out of sight in among the scrub in front of the fort. The firing for a while was furious. Then followed an ominous lull.

Suddenly a staff officer next to Baden-Powell said, 'Our men are coming back!'

The British were falling back, turning to fire again and again. Then they again disappeared, getting under cover in a hollow in the ground.

A pause. An aide-de-camp came galloping up to Baden-Powell with a message from Major Godley. 'Captain Vernon has been repulsed, sir,' he said. 'The position is practically impregnable to infantry. Major Godley advises against further action.' Something had gone wrong.

Vere Stent, standing at B-P's side watched the defender of Mafeking: 'For a moment the Colonel hesitated, and we could see that the question as to whether he should not again attempt to carry the enemy's position was being weighed in his mind. Then he turned round to the C.O. and said, "Let the ambulances go out." That was all. The battle of Game Tree was over.'

The ox-drawn ambulance wagons moved out under the Red Cross flag. The Boers came out of their stronghold to help in the loading. The loss was the heaviest the garrison had suffered in more than three months of siege: Twenty-four killed, twenty-three wounded, three missing, presumed taken prisoners.

Something had indeed gone wrong.

As Baden-Powell pieced the reports together afterwards, it became evident that the Boers had received advance information of the intended attack. Somehow the plans had leaked out. Dutch spies or traitors in Mafeking had informed the Boers. The enemy had quickly, and in great secrecy, strengthened the fort, sent in reinforcements, torn up the rails in front of Game Tree Fort. The supposed 'surprise attack' had been no surprise to the Boers.

Captain Vernon, leading his men into the ditch of the salient, had been killed firing his revolver into enemy loop-holes. Half of the squadron had been shot down, the rest forced to fall back. As the supporting squadron joined in the attack, Fitzclarence fell wounded. His men charged on—only to find the leading squadron decimated and no entrance available. They tried to work to the opposite flank of the fort but found it hopeless and took cover a few hundred yards from the fort until ordered to retire.

The failure of the mission and the loss of his men had been a severe blow to Baden-Powell. Some of the officers killed had been 'the very soul of the defence'. His sublime confidence was shaken—but only momentarily. He exorcised all doubts from his mind by accepting full responsibility: 'If blame for this reverse fall on anyone it should fall on myself, as everybody concerned did their part of the work thoroughly well, and exactly in accordance with the order I had issued. Both officers and men worked with splendid courage and spirit.'

During the days that followed, the sky was sombre. A canopy of leaden clouds covered the veld, brightened from time to time by flashes, of lightning. With the thunder rolling it was almost impossible to distinguish the Boer cannons from the heavenly artillery.

The clouds opened up in tropical deluges. The rain roared in sheets over the clayey ground, rushed in muddy rivulets along every crack in the ground, poured into dug-outs and ground shelters. The downpours kept everybody huddled in shell-torn houses and clammy forts and trenches. Native runners made use of the weather to sneak through the Boer lines into Mafeking.

The reports they brought were as gloomy as the weather. Within a single week, the British forces to the south and to the east had been thrown back with severe losses at Stormberg, had suffered hundreds of casualties at Magersfontein, had met a major defeat at Colenso. The 'Black Week' of December 1899 had been one of the most humiliating in British military history.

Inwardly, Baden-Powell's mood reflected the weather.

'Outwardly,' Hamilton commented, 'he maintains an impenetrable screen of self-control, observing with a cynical smile the foibles and caprices of those around him. He seems ever bracing himself to be on guard against a moment . . . in which by a word, by an expression of face, by a movement, or in turn of phrase, he should betray the rigours of the self-control under which he lives. Every passing townsman regards him with curiosity not unmixed with awe. Every servant in the hotel watches him, and he, as a consequence, seldom speaks without a preternatural deliberation and an air of decisive finality. . . .'

Almost nightly now, B-P disappeared into the veld on silent espionage excursions of his own to the Boer lines to gain personal, intimate information about the disposition of the opposing forces. On his return he would lie awake hour after hour planning how he could forestall the Boer moves, which, unknown to the enemy, he had personally watched.

New Year's Eve, like Christmas Eve, fell on a Sunday. And the Boers would be keeping the Sabbath as usual.

During the afternoon, B-P staged a special sports event with races for the children, riding and mule-driving for the men. As always, the races created a great deal of excitement and set the tone for the day.

In the evening, as the discussion continued about whether this last day of December 1899 was just the turn of another year or whether it was the end of a century, as proclaimed by the Boers' best friend, Kaiser Wilhelm II of Germany, many of the townspeople gathered for midnight services in the churches of Mafeking. But very few troopers attended. There was no telling what the Boers might do when the Sunday truce ended at mid-night.

Baden-Powell spent the last evening of the year moving from fort to fort in a drizzling rain. 'At 11 p.m. the Boers on the east front fired a few volleys perhaps a false alarm or possibly in honour of the New Year.'

At midnight the singing of the National Anthem and *Auld Lang Syne* floated over the veld. Glasses and canteens were raised for a toast to 1900. But no church bells rang in the New Year—the bells were reserved for warning of enemy attack.

The Boers opened the New Year at 10 a.m. on New Year's Day with a barrage that lasted for six hours. It was a particularly vicious shelling that caused a great deal of damage, killed three people and wounded many others.

The New Year promised to be 'hot'.

4

Mafeking, in January, was a miserable sight. It had, according to Hamilton, 'that general appearance of destruction which marks the path of a cyclone' with houses 'shattered, gaping holes in the walls of buildings, furrows in the roads, broken trees, wrecked telegraph poles. . . .'

Baden-Powell tried to think of ways he had not used before of forcing the Boers back, of re-establishing communication with the outside. But all his considerations came up against the fact that the Boers had modern guns with which they could shell the town at will while his own artillery reached only half way to the Boer lines. He had tried to breach the distance by bold sorties, but he could afford no more direct attacks and loss of men.

If only he had a gun with which he could strike back! And suddenly he had one.

Major Godley, on a morning inspection ride, passed the entrance to a farm within the Mafeking line. He noticed a peculiar-looking gate-post and got off his horse to investigate. It was an old brass cannon, two-thirds buried and almost completely hidden behind a bush.

The Major reported his find to Baden-Powell who ordered that the gun was to be dug up and put in working order. It proved to be an old muzzle-loading sixteen-pounder ship's carronade in good condition. There was neither crown nor cipher on it to denote a Royal Navy origin—this was obviously a privateer's cannon—but in the cleaning of it several numerals and letters made their appearance, among them the year it was cast: 1770. But the most astonishing thing about the gun was the fact that it carried the initials 'B.P.' This was a good omen, the Mafeking defenders felt. Some-one suggested that it must have belonged to Baden-Powell in a former incarnation. 'It didn't really,' B-P commented drily. 'These initials stood for Bailey, Pegg & Co.—the founders—of Brierley Foundry, Staffordshire.'

How had the gun ended up in Mafeking? Some old inhabitant remembered hearing that two Germans had brought it in about 1860, and had sold it to the chief of the local tribe for twenty-two oxen, to aid them in their fight against the Boer freebooters. And here it was, forty years later, to aid the British against the self-same Boers. But could it be used?

The gun was mounted on a carriage and tried out. It worked! It carried a ten-pound shot with fair accuracy into the Boer lines two thousand yards away.

'Lord Nelson'—as the gun was dubbed because of its ancient naval connexion—became an important part of the Mafeking defence.

Major Panzera, developing ammunition for the 'new' gun and studying it in action, began to wonder. If that piece of antique junk was usable why shouldn't it be possible for him and the men in the railway workshop to make a workable gun of their own?

No harm in trying. Panzera's men improvised a furnace by lining an old iron cistern with fire-brick, then proceeded to lap and weld a number of red-hot iron bars together round a ten-foot length of four-inch steel pipe until they had surrounded the pipe with an iron casing. They cast trunnions and a breech in the railway foundry, added sights and mounted the gun on a carriage made from the chassis of an old threshing machine.

After making shells and mixing powder the men rolled the new piece of artillery into the fields for trial. 'She was loaded and set ready for firing, and then the gun crew and onlookers lay down under cover in case she should prefer to burst rather than send out the shell. But she didn't burst. She seemed to know what was wanted of her, and banged out the shell with a tremendous burst of smoke and flame! It was a grand success, and considerably astonished the Boers who thought that we must have had a new gun sent to us unknown to themselves.' With home-made ammunition, the gun managed to throw an eighteen-pound shell for a distance of four thousand yards.

And so, not long after the debut of 'Lord Nelson', another gun added its roar to the Mafeking defence. It was named 'The Wolf' from Baden-Powell's Matabele nickname.

By late January, the British situation in South Africa began to brighten.

The news reached Mafeking by a native runner that B-P's military idol, Field-Marshal Lord Roberts, had been appointed to supreme command

and had already arrived in Cape Town with Major-General Lord Kitchener of Khartoum as his chief of staff. British soldiers by the tens of thousands were pouring into South Africa from Great Britain and the Colonies.

The hope of early relief for Mafeking soared—but was quickly dashed. On 8 February, another runner sneaked into town with a two-week-old message from the new Commander-in-Chief. There was little hope, Lord Roberts wrote, of relief reaching Mafeking before well into May. Roberts asked the garrison to make supplies last that long.

B-P took the news calmly. He re-checked available stocks. The prospects were not particularly rosy. But, somehow, he would manage to hold Mafeking for another hundred days—until, say, 18 May. He sent a native runner off with a message to that effect and set about keeping his promise.

The food stocks he had commandered early in the siege had seemed more than adequate under the ration system he had then set up. But as the months had gone by without relief, the rations had been steadily reduced. Now B-P gave further orders to have every scrap of edible material put to use.

He had read somewhere about the meat-packing companies of Chicago utilizing every part of a slaughtered animal. 'In Mafeking', he noted with pride, 'we were not far behind Chicago, except perhaps in cleanliness.' Until late January 1900, there had been enough beef to fill the meat ration, but in February horse became an accepted part of the diet. 'The meat was cut off and minced; the interior arrangements were cut into lengths and used as skins for the mince; the hide, after having the hair scalded off, was boiled with the head and hoofs to make brawn; the bones were collected and pounded into dust and used for adulterating the flour; the manes and tails were used to fill the mattresses at the hospital—so that the summing up of the Chicago industry applies equally well to ours, namely, "Everything pertaining to the animal is utilized except the squeal".'

To feed the townspeople with the least waste, B-P set up four big soup kitchens to provide wholesome—if not appetizing—meals at low cost. The soup recipe was simple: 'Half a horse, 250 pounds; mealie meal, 15 pounds; oat husks, 47 pounds. This makes 132 gallons of soup the consistency of porridge.'

The oats that had been shipped in for horse fodder before the siege began became an important part in the feeding, especially of the natives. The kernels were ground into flour for bread, the husks fermented and made into 'sowens', a kind of porridge that had the appearance and taste of 'bill-sticker's paste' but was nourishing. Toiletries, such as *poudre de riz*, perfumed oatmeal, violet face powder were tried for making desserts, with fair results—especially the violet powder which made a pudding that tasted to B-P like 'scented baby'.

An influx of locusts 'thick as fleas on Margate sands' provided a welcome variety on the menu. The Baralong tribesmen and children went at them in a rush and swept them into heaps before they had a chance of flight. The white population just as eagerly stored up 'the heaven-sent delicacies'. Fried locusts were not too bad—they had 'all the aroma and subtlety of chewed string'—but curried locusts, B-P remembered from India, were better and, fortunately, Julius Weil & Co. still had a small supply of Indian curry powder.

5

It was not only the food supplies that were running low. The currency was getting short. People were holding on to their coins and notes not knowing how long and how far their money would have to stretch.

There was only one solution to the dearth of ready money: to print some. Baden-Powell looked up his army regulations but found no information in them on the theory and practice of counterfeiting. He challenged his chief paymaster, Captain H. Greener, to produce suitable bank-notes.

There was no special problem about making vouchers for 1s., 2s., and 3s., and notes for 10s. The local printing shop did an acceptable job of producing them. But for the £1 notes something better was needed.

Greener turned to Baden-Powell for a suitable design and B-P made a drawing symbolizing the defence of Mafeking, showing 'The Wolf' surrounded by determined-looking defenders. The design was photographed onto a glass plate and printed on blue-print paper made by the local chemist.

What could be done with bank-notes could be done with stamps as well, the Mafeking postmaster, J. V. Howat, decided. He, too, was running out of supplies.

The official Cape of Good Hope stamps with the figure of Britannia and the Bechuanaland stamps with Queen Victoria's head were needed for regular mail being sneaked through the Boer lines by native runners, for transmission to all parts of South Africa and to England. But the runners were expensive. They valued their lives and their efforts creeping through the enemy lines under cover of darkness at £15 per trip. The postmaster overcame the extra cost by overprinting his regular stamps with the words MAFEKING BESIEGED and adding a surcharge—increasing the ½d. stamps to 1d., the 1d. stamps to 3d., the 3d. stamps to 6d., and the 4d. and 6d. stamps to 1s.

Town mail was another matter. There just weren't enough regular postage stamps to go round, and stamps were necessary for the local mail carried so effectively by the boys of the Cadet Corps.

The Postmaster took his problem to B-P's chief of staff, Lord Edward Cecil, who, in turn, called in Major Godley and Captain Greener. The four men quickly decided that it would be *lèse majesté*, and probably illegal as well, to put the Queen's picture on home-made stamps that would not carry a letter further than 'from one hole to another'. But nobody could object to the use of the head of Mafeking's commanding officer on the 3d. stamps needed for letters between the town and the various outposts.

Without consulting Baden-Powell, the four conspirators secured a good likeness of him, and Greener made up a suitable design. The local photographer, D. Taylor, copied the design, made a dozen prints, pasted them on a large piece of ruled cardboard, re-photographed them in reduced size onto a glass negative and made blueprints of them. The sheets were gummed and perforated by a 12-gauge single-line perforator by Townshend & Son, the printers of the *Mafeking Mail*.

Ned Cecil and Captain Greener proudly brought the first finished sheet to their commanding officer.

'Why my head?' asked B-P. 'Why not the Queen's?'

The men explained their reason for omitting the Queen's head. Baden-Powell agreed with their argument on this score but questioned the use of his own head. The paymaster began to fret. The stamps were being printed. To remake them with a new design would mean a loss of time and a waste of money.

'Well,' said B-P, 'as you have them all ready, carry on.' He turned from such a trifling item to far more pressing matters at hand. But inwardly, he was rather pleased. In a letter sneaked through the Boer lines on 30 March 1900, he told his mother:

> You would be amused if you could drop in and see us here. We are quite a little republic and I am a sort of tyrant or president—making my own laws and orders on all points. . . . I have drawn and issued a bank-note of my own. . . . Today we are making a new issue of stamps—one with *my* head on it instead of that of the Queen or of Paul Kruger! That, I think, is the proof of our being an independent republic in Mafeking!

The design for another stamp—the 1d. stamp for letters carried within the limits of the town proper—was quickly decided on. Since the boys of the Cadet Corps were doing the job of delivering the mail, why not put a picture of one of them on the stamp?

Baden-Powell had followed Lord Edward Cecil's work with the Cadet

Corps with earnest attention. He had been amazed at the eagerness with which the boys had accepted responsibility and the thoroughness and lack of fear with which they had carried out their assigned tasks. 'I said to one of these boys on one occasion when he came through rather heavy fire: "You will get hit one of these days riding about like that when shells are flying." And he replied: "I pedal so quick, sir, they'll never catch me."

The Cadet Corps of Mafeking, organized by Major Lord Edward Cecil, did messenger service throughout the siege.

These boys didn't seem to mind the bullets one bit; they were always ready to carry out orders, though it meant risk to their lives every time.'

The photographer took a photograph of the leader of the Mafeking Cadet Corps, 13-year-old Sergeant-Major Warner Goodyear, seated on his bicycle, and got Dr Will Hays to draw a design for the stamp. Within a few days, the 1d. stamps, gummed and perforated, were on sale—to the pride and joy of every member of the Cadet Corps.

6

By March, the war between Snijman and Baden-Powell had become mostly a 'sit-down' affair. The Boers continued their daily bombardment but the British returned the fire only when necessary. B-P had to watch the expenditure of ammunition. It was running dangerously low.

Although the majority of the Boers were doing little but 'sitting', their sappers had resumed work digging trenches closer and closer to the British fortifications and to the town itself. From their trenches in the Brickfields to the east, Boer sharpshooters were able to spray the streets of Mafeking with rifle bullets. They had killed a number of burghers.

The British also resumed digging, and eventually got to a point where they were only thirty yards from the enemy. But here they were stuck for lack of bombs or hand-grenades.

It was again Major Panzera who came to the rescue, this time with ammunition. The Boers had German-made hand-grenades they could toss into the British trenches. The British had none—until Panzera made them 'out of old potted-meat or jam tins filled with dynamite or powder with a fuse attached'. The chief honour for delivering the home-made bombs into the Boer trenches went to Sergeant Page, who in his younger days had done bait-casting off the rocks of East London. He soon could 'cast' Panzera's bombs from the end of a 'whip-stick' over a distance of sixty yards. He quickly taught his companions the same trick. Between British sharpshooters and bomb 'casters' the Boer trenches became untenable.

During the night of 23 March, B-P received reports that there was unusual activity in the enemy lines. 'We heard the Boers making a considerable noise, calling out to each other to retire, and we could hear them making their way through their communication trench, evidently vacating their front line. My men were wild with joy and eager to rush in to take possession, but I stopped them.'

Why should the enemy be leaving noisily, when one would expect them to creep away quietly? he wondered. Their behaviour was highly suspicious.

B-P sent two of his men out to investigate. They came back and reported that the Brickfields trenches had indeed been evacuated by the Boers. But B-P was not satisfied. He had the trenches searched. The search turned up a number of wires. The wiring was cut and the trenches occupied. B-P's caution saved his men. The wires were connected to a 250-pound dynamite mine. 'And while we sang, "God Save the Queen", the Boers were probably touching the button at the other end of the wire with considerable impatience at the failure of their fireworks.'

During March, Colonel Plumer, with his forces to the north, established almost daily contact with Mafeking with the help of native runners. For the first time Baden-Powell got regular news of what was happening outside his restricted corner of the world. And for the first time the news was encouraging—of the British finally taking the lead, of Kimberley being relieved on 15 February, of his old adversary General Cronje surrendering with his whole force at Paardeberg on 27 February, of Ladysmith being relieved on 28 February, of a relief force from the south moving closer and yet closer to Mafeking.

On 31 March, Plumer attempted to reach Mafeking in a daring plunge. He did not succeed. The Boers sent a superior force against him and tried to surround him and his men. He extricated himself by a clever manoeuvre but was forced to retire to his starting point at Ramathlabama after suffering severe casualties.

The news of the attempt and the subsequent withdrawal reached B-P. He took the disappointment with the same cool reserve that he had shown in so many other cases, until he was informed that his long-time friend 'The Boy' McLaren had been killed in action.

Within a few days his anguish turned to joy when he learned that McLaren, seriously wounded, was a prisoner in the Boer laager. Baden-Powell wanted to rush to his friend's side under the white truce flag, but his staff officers refused to let him go. If he were recognized, they argued, the Boers would hold him and Mafeking would be lost. B-P acknowledged the validity of their argument. He confined himself to sending special greetings to his friend, using the opportunity to tell the Boers, who were certain to read his missives, of the ineffectiveness of their shelling: 'You need not feel alarmed about us when you hear the shelling—we really enjoy it and never have any casualties. . . .'

B-P had written weekly letters home and had sent them off by runner but had heard nothing from England in return. He had wondered about his mother's health, how Agnes and Frank were getting along, about Warington, whether Baden had been sent to South Africa with his regiment.

At last, during the night of 10 April, a runner from the south stole into Mafeking with a dispatch-case full of mail. B-P spent much of the day opening letters from home, four, five, six months old.

The letters were bursting with pride. These were the first real reports he had received of the reaction of people at home to the siege of Mafeking.

> Everybody is talking of you [Agnes wrote]. You are the hero of the day. All the papers describe your many-sided talents. . . . They speak of 'the courage and daring of that small force under one of the most distinguished officers we have.' . . . Your photo is in all the shops now, and on inquiring they say yours is first favourite, then Roberts, Buller, White, etc., but yours sells best. . . .

B-P was particularly pleased with what she had to say about the fate of *Aids to Scouting*, the book he had completed just before the siege:

> I have got your book and very delightful it is. Several papers published an account of your having corrected the proofs at Mafeking

and since then the books have sold like a house on fire. Numbers of civilians, too, have told me how delighted they are with the ingenuity and the clever stories in it. One said it is as good as a good novel! And perhaps you don't know that *Aids to Scouting* has been translated into German and the order given to give a copy to every trooper in the German Army. . . .

B-P did not have long to enjoy his mail from home. On 11 April the Boers opened fire at dawn and that day gave Mafeking the heaviest shelling of the siege. Over a period of four hours 'Creaky' dropped seventy ninety-four pound shells on the town. Seven other guns and two Maxims joined in. And in the middle of the shelling, the Boers made 'an advance in skirmish' towards the town. The Mafeking defenders held their fire until the enemy was within range, then dropped five of the advancing Boers with a single volley. The enemy retired.

The big bombardment proved to be the swan song of 'Creaky'—a special farewell salute. In the darkness of the following night the big siege gun was withdrawn—rumour had it to prevent it from falling into the hands of the advancing British troops. It was a good riddance. During the almost six months it had been outside Mafeking, it had peppered the town with fifteen hundred ninety-four pound shells. It had caused numerous casualties but had not succeeded in breaking the determination of the besieged.

The joy with which the defenders of Mafeking greeted the news of the departure of 'Creaky' soared even higher later the same day when Baden-Powell made public a greeting that had been sneaked into town in the night. It was from Queen Victoria herself:

> I continue watching with confidence and admiration the patient and resolute defence which is so gallantly maintained under your ever resourceful command.   V.R.I.

The news from the outside again turned bleak with reports of new British setbacks. B-P had confirmation of them in another message from Lord Roberts, smuggled into Mafeking. It asked B-P to make his supplies last longer than originally suggested 'as matters have turned out somewhat unexpectedly and there may be some delay in dispatch of relief expedition'.

The situation was already one of extreme gravity. 'The quality of the food now supplied to the garrison,' Reuter's Vere Stent reported, 'is below the standard of what is required to support the strength of men already weakened by sickness. Heavy rains have caused an increase in the number of cases of fever and dysentery, while cases of enteric, typhoid, and malaria are numerous.'

Baden-Powell talked over the situation with his staff, then for a long, disheartening day debated within his own mind whether the time had actually come that he must withdraw the garrison from Mafeking, whether starvation had finally accomplished what the Boer guns had failed to do, whether all had been in vain.

He had another check made of the remaining food supplies. Breadstuffs of ground oats and mealie meal could be made to last to the middle of June, he estimated, 'without allowing for wastage, mice, etc'. The 'sowens' would hold out until 15 July. Oxen, calves, sheep, horses, donkeys, mules, in reduced rations, would provide meat for ninety days. He worked out a new ration scheme. Mafeking would hold out!

The last day of April, a British patrol inspecting the railway line to the south-west found an envelope addressed to Baden-Powell.

B-P read the contents with a sardonic smile. It was from the recently arrived young commandant of the Johannesburg Commando, ambitious Sarel Eloff, one of President Kruger's thirty-five grandsons at the fighting front:

> *Dan Kolonel* Baden-Powell, I see in the *Bulawayo Chronicle* that your men in Mafeking play cricket on Sundays and give concerts and balls on Sunday evenings.
>
> In case you would allow my men to join in the same it would be very agreeable to me as here outside Mafeking there are seldom any of the fair sex and there can be no merriment without their being present. . . . .
>
> Wishing you a pleasant day, I remain your obliging friend,
>
> S. Eloff, Commandant, Johannesburg Commando.

B-P sent his answer to the Boer line under a white flag:

> Sir, I beg to thank you for your letter of yesterday, in which you propose that your men come and play cricket with us.
>
> I should like nothing better—after the match in which we are at present engaged is over. But just now we are having our innings and have so far scored 200 days, not out, against the bowling of Cronje, Snijman, Botha, and Eloff: and we are having a very enjoyable game.
>
> I remain, yours truly,
>
> R. S. S. Baden-Powell.

7

At four in the morning of 12 May, Baden-Powell was awakened by an explosive bullet striking the ground under his verandah bed. He heard heavy fire to the east of town. He sounded the alarm and rushed up on his look-out. The night was dark. The moon had just set.

'Is this a feint,' he wondered, 'or is it the real thing?'

The enemy fire slackened, then started again, this time to the west, beyond the native *stad*. There was an urgent message over the telephone. 'A force of about three hundred Boers are advancing up the Malopo valley. They have broken through our pickets. They are in the *stad!*'

B-P stared into the darkness. And then, suddenly, the darkness was dark no more. The western sky was brilliantly lighted by orange flames leaping up from the thatched Baralong huts in the western part of the *stad*. The smell of burning straw and wood hung on the breeze.

B-P quickly surmised what had happened: A force of Boers had broken through the weak outer rim of the western defence line, had rushed up the Malopo valley and was attempting to take the whole of Mafeking through the breach.

He began snapping out orders and found, to his relief, that all the telephones were working. Part of his force he ordered to the western posts to prevent other Boers from joining those who had already entered. Another force was sent to close the breach in an effort to contain the Boers who had penetrated the Mafeking defence line.

Not knowing what was happening in their rear, the Boer's invading force moved deeper into the native *stad*, setting fire to still more huts, driving the terrified Baralongs before them as a shield—then surrounded the British South Africa Police fort manned by a score of men under Colonel Hore. In the darkness, the British mistook the Boers for their own men retiring and let the Boers get to within two hundred yards before firing. The Boers, more than two hundred of them, rushed the fort and made the British their prisoners.

From B-P's look-out post, the situation was unclear. For a while there was no reply to his urgent telephone calls to the fort. When the phone was finally answered it was in a gruff Dutch voice. The Boers were in possession of the fort. Baden-Powell instantly threw a wide cordon round the fort and sent an emissary to the Boers to tell them they were surrounded and to order them to surrender. 'They sent back declining, thinking apparently that they had taken Mafeking. I ordered the town defenders to open fire on them which they did with good effect, driving them to take refuge in the B.S.A.P. fort.'

While directing the counter-attacks of his men, Baden-Powell was also watching the Boer lines and was receiving telephone calls from the out-lying forts indicating feverish activity in the Boer laagers. The enemy was shelling Mafeking with bursts of rapid fire. B-P had every reason to think that this was a prelude to a direct attack on the town in support of the force that had breached the defence line. General Snijman was probably awaiting some signal from inside Mafeking before moving into action.

The situation called for yet another bluff. B-P wrote a letter to McLaren and sent it off to the enemy line under a white flag. The orderly carrying it was instructed to inform any interrogating Boer accepting it 'that we had killed a large number of Boers and had surrounded such as were not already prisoners and they were surrendering'. The letter itself was to add credence to the story. It was written to this effect:

> Dear Boy, I hope you were not too disturbed by heavy firing in the night, but the Boers made an attack on us and we have scuppered the lot. Let me know if you want any clean pyjamas or any books. . . .

The bluff worked far beyond Baden-Powell's expectations. Shortly after the white flag had reached the Boer laager 'strings of men were seen emerging in their hundreds from various ravines and hollows from both sides of the place, and returning back sullenly to their camps'.

With one group of Boers bottled up in the fort, the town defenders set about the 'scuppering' that B-P had pretended was already accomplished: rounding up the scattered Boers or driving them out of Mafeking and closing the defences after them.

As night fell, B-P again turned his attention on the police fort where the main part of the Boers had held out for twelve hours with their score of British prisoners, without water and exposed to a steady sniping fire from the outside. He ordered his troops to close the circle around the fort.

Before the circle was completed a number of Boers rushed out of the fort, dispersed and ran for the River Malopo. Some of them fell wounded by British bullets but several of them escaped. Suddenly the door of the fort swung open and a British voice cried out, 'Stop firing! The Boers have surrendered to me!' The voice was Colonel Hore's. The Boers had given themselves up to their own prisoners. The siege within the siege was over.

The firing died down. The Boers streamed out of the fort, arms in air. First the commander: Sarel Eloff, Kruger's grandson. Then his assistant commandants—a German, a Frenchman and two Boers—and finally his men: a total of sixty-eight.

The surrendered officers were taken to B-P's headquarters. Baden-Powell greeted them with a pleasant smile.

'Good evening, Eloff,' he said. 'You're just in time for dinner.'

14

The most dangerous attack against Mafeking in seven months had turned into a complete Boer fiasco.

By the middle of May, Baden-Powell had full information through runners and carrier pigeons that a relief column approaching from the south under Colonel Bryan Mahon had passed Vryburg, seventy miles below Mafeking, and was attempting to· join hands with Colonel Plumer's forces to the north.

On the afternoon of 16 May, the sound of guns to the west indicated to Baden-Powell that the relief force was moving to the attack of the Boer line.

> Some of us climbed up on the high engine sheds of the railway works for a better view. We could see the dust and smoke of the bursting shells in the distance, and even mounted men hurrying about from point to point. At last came the flick-flick of a heliograph through the haze:
>
> 'FROM X COLONEL X MAHON X HOW X ARE X YOU X GETTING X ON?'
>
> Then there was a pause for a long time. Again the flicker went on:
>
> 'WE X ARE X FIGHTING X HARD X BUT X GETTING X ON X WE X ARE DFH X AND ...'
>
> And that was the end of the message—evidently the enemy interfered with their position. However, it was good enough for us. With a small party of men, who volunteered themselves as fit to march five miles, and a gun, we moved out to the front of Fort Ayr and made a diversion against the rear of the Boers who were barring the advance of the relief force—and the Boers cleared away from being between two fires ...
>
> Soon after dark a messenger from the relief column reached us to say they were camping for the night where they were, five miles outside, and would enter in the morning.
>
> So I went to bed!

But B-P's first unworried sleep in seven months was of short duration.

At three in the morning of 17 May, someone grasped him by the shoulders and shook him. He woke up abruptly and turned on the scoundrel who had broken his rest, and looked into his brother's grinning face. Major Baden Baden-Powell had come up as Intelligence Officer of the Relief Force. He had been sent into Mafeking in the middle of the night to tell his brother that Mahon and Plumer had changed their minds. Instead of entering in the morning they had decided to do so in the dark.

B-P jumped out of bed. His tiredness had evaporated completely. He was wide awake. He quickly put on his uniform and walked out towards Fort Ayr. Here he found a whole crowd of men coming along in the darkness. It was the relief column at last! And in a few minutes Mahon and Plumer and a host of other officer friends were gathered over a cup of hot cocoa in the old police fort that only a few days before had been in enemy hands.

After a siege of 217 days, Mafeking had been relieved!

The news sped to all corners of the world: Baden-Powell, the Hero of Mafeking was freed at last! And the British Empire went on an emotional spree bordering on delirium!

Climax One

London, 18 May 1900

It had been an unusually pleasant May day in the British capital. The slight drizzle of the day before had given way to a clear, rain-washed morning. The good weather seemed to have brought out into the streets more than the usual number of Londoners. In the heart of the vast city the pavements were filled with tail-coated gentlemen and long-skirted ladies, slow-moving window-shoppers and hurrying messengers. Hansom cabs and broughams, horse-drawn buses and vans passed and re-passed each other, only occasionally overtaken by one of those new-fangled motor carriages spewing off foul-smelling exhaust gases.

In Whitehall people stopped for a moment in front of the War Office to read the latest bulletin. But there was nothing there—only a small poster at the entrance with the simple, characteristic announcement 'No news'.

On this, the 220th day of the South African War, the stories in the newspapers had dealt mainly with Mafeking and they had been quite confusing. The telegrams from Cape Town were reassuring. They told of Colonel Baden-Powell still holding out, after more than seven months, in the beleaguered town of Mafeking in the middle of the African veld. He had even recently captured a small Boer force attempting to penetrate his defence line. The telegrams from Pretoria, the enemy capital, on the other hand, were ominous. They told of the Boers repulsing the British relief force advancing towards Mafeking from the south. If the Boer information was correct it would mean that Lord Roberts commanding the British Army in South Africa had failed in his promise to relieve Mafeking by this very day.

But things in general were looking up. After all the agony of the first four months of the war, with defeat upon defeat at the hands of the Boers, the tide had turned. The enemy was being pushed further and further north. Roberts was marching towards Pretoria. Ladysmith and Kimberley had been relieved.

Now if only that glorious town of Mafeking could be reached . . . if only the gallant B-P could be freed . . . if only the relief force could get there in time before the defenders were starved into submission. . . .

The afternoon papers proved disappointing. They contained nothing new about Mafeking and little else worth reading beyond the fact that the Russians were again stirring up trouble in Korea, beyond a juicy story out of Sweden of a sailor on a canal boat who had gone berserk, had killed seven passengers and had escaped in a life-boat.

With night coming on, London's offices emptied, its shops closed. The street vendors turned their barrows homewards. The pavement strollers thinned out. The lamplighters set out on their rounds to fill the streets with the soft glow from thousands of gas lights. Club members took to their clubs, diners to their restaurants. A crowd bent on entertainment in spite of the sombreness of the times surged into the West End's theatres and music halls.

The quiet of a spring evening enveloped London until a bulletin on the Mansion House broke the calm with shattering force and turned the night into the most tumultuous one in the history of the British capital.

Eleven short words did the trick:

MAFEKING HAS BEEN RELIEVED.

FOOD HAS ENTERED THE GARRISON.

ENEMY DISPERSED.

The bulletin had hardly been posted before a crowd formed in front of it, of boisterous young men becoming even more boisterous, of shy young ladies forgetting their shyness, of sedate elderly people forgetting their sedateness.

And then: 'Hurray for Mafeking!' 'Three cheers for B-P!'

Men who had never met before shook hands wildly. Women who did not know each other embraced in the street.

More and more people rushed up. The mass of them quickly spilled from the pavement onto the roadway. Buses and cabs came to a halt in the midst of the milling crowd. 'What is going on?' The drivers, informed, forced their vehicles through the throng, hurried the horses up Ludgate Hill, shouted out the tidings as they went. A few minutes later the police were forced to divert all City traffic to the side streets. The whole space between the Mansion House and the Royal Exchange had become a surging crowd of people waving flags, shouting themselves hoarse, cheering Mafeking and Baden-Powell, calling for the Lord Mayor to step out on his balcony to give official word to their feelings. When he did, he was greeted with a vociferous outburst.

'I wish,' he shouted at the top of his voice, *'that the music of your cheers could reach Mafeking.'* Loud hurrahs! *'We never doubted what the end would be.'* Tremendous cheering. *'British pluck and valour when used in the right cause must triumph.'* Deafening outburst of shouting.

The rest of His Lordship's speech was drowned in enthusiastic cheering and in the singing of *'God Save the Queen'*, then *'Rule Britannia'*, then *'Soldiers of the Queen'*, while more and more and yet more people poured into the crowded space.

There was pandemonium at Ludgate Circus soon after the Mansion House. From all the side-streets people were streaming into it. The shouts of the Fleet Street newsboys of *'Extra! Extra! Special pi-per!'* had become the great rallying cry of the Metropolis.

By ten o'clock the Strand was an endless procession of pedestrians singing and cheering for Baden-Powell. A surging flood of people moved from the City into the West End to be met by thousands of others moving in the opposite direction. A clamour of *'Send her victorious'* was greeted by an equally enthusiastic chant of *'Britons never shall be slaves'*.

Trafalgar Square became a sea of exultant faces, of waving Union Jacks. Flags sprouted everywhere—in every window, on every bus top, on every cabman's whip. The magic initials of B-P blazed out in red, white and blue lights from the façades of a score of buildings.

Pall Mall was packed with a jubilant mass of cheering and singing humanity. Piccadilly Circus was a churning crush of people wheeling around the Eros fountain, the crush growing denser and denser by the minute as more and yet more people emptied into the circle from half a dozen side-streets, singing, cheering.

'Long to reign over us—God save the Queen! Hip-hip-hip: Hoo-o-o-o-ray!'

'Hurrah for Mafeking!' the cry of a silk-hatted gentleman from the top of a hansom cab. *'Three cheers for Baden-Powell!'* the shout of a be-pearled costermonger. *'And don't forget his mother!'* the appeal of a thought-ful old woman—a suggestion that caused part of the crowd to move off towards Hyde Park Corner, to gather under the balcony of Baden-Powell's home at St George's Place for a thousand-tongued serenade to the hero's mother.

The din in the streets reached into the crowded West End theatres and music halls. The dull roar from without, louder than usual, made heads turn to-wards the doors.

At the Tivoli, a reporter from the Daily Telegraph brought the news backstage. The manager rushed onto the stage just as one of the acts was coming to an end. He held up a hand for attention.

'Ladies and gentlemen,' he said, 'I think you will pardon an interruption. I have great news: Mafeking has been relieved.'

Like a multi-headed Jack of a jack-in-the-box, the audience sprang to its feet, cheering, shouting, waving hats, handkerchiefs, programmes, with delirious delight, then swung into a wild chorus as the orchestra struck up the National Anthem.

At Covent Garden the curtain had just fallen on the second act of Lohengrin when a jubilant cry of 'Mafeking relieved!' sounded in the amphitheatre where an evening paper was being passed from hand to hand. Wagner and the new tenor were forgotten. There were cheers for Mafeking and Baden-Powell and an a capella rendering of 'God Save the Queen'—the conductor and his orchestra had unfortunately just left their places. It was sung with special fervour by the Prince and Princess of Wales entertaining the King of Sweden in the Royal Box.

At Wyndham's Theatre, Charles Wyndham, as Cyrano de Bergerac, was pleading with Mary Moore's Roxane for a kiss when a shout from the outside of 'Mafeking relieved!' made the audience break into a wild outburst of enthusiasm. For a moment, Wyndham stepped out of his role as a noble-souled Gascon duellist and poet and became an Englishman as elated as his audience. 'The news for which we have waited so long has arrived,' he said, and added 'Thank God!' Rule Britannia—then back to the balcony scene and the rest of Rostand's play.

In most of the music halls, the remaining acts of the programme were shifted to patriotic songs and tableaux. Only in the houses of legitimate drama were the plays carried to their final curtains, with the stalls and boxes and galleries singing in chorus between the acts to voice their excitement—at Her Majesty's Theatre where A Midsummer Night's Dream was playing, at the Lyceum where Eleonora Duse was trying to breathe life into Dumas's La Princesse Georges, at the Garrick Theatre where Mrs Leslie Carter was appearing in David Belasco's version of ZaZa, at the Royalty where Mrs Patrick Campbell neared her hundredth performance of Suderman's Magda. The audiences poured out into the streets to merge with the hundreds of thousands of others who were filling the night air with a continuous roar of cheering that sounded like the surf breaking against a rocky shore.

Big Ben boomed out the midnight hour but there was no let-up in the rejoicing.

More and more people converged on the West End, by foot across the Thames bridges, by Underground and train from the suburbs, to join in the spontaneous orgy of thankful revelry, to give vent to their long-pent-up enthusiasm for the Defender of Mafeking who had captured the heart of the nation and the Empire.

In Piccadilly Circus traffic had now come to a complete halt as a milling mass of humanity jolted and jostled good-humouredly and bellowed itself hoarse in national songs and in the latest patriotic refrains. Street hawkers were doing tremendous business selling trumpets and 'squakees', rattles and shawms and 'ladies' tormentors'. Ear-splitting sounds emerged from every sort of raucous instrument. An enterprising organ-grinder dispensed 'It's the Soldiers of the Queen, My Lads' and was showered with pennies as the throng around him took up the chorus in singing and whistling.

A wreath-crowned banner with a portrait of Colonel Baden-Powell bobbing over the heads of the crowd brought forth cheer upon cheer upon cheer. Half a dozen soldiers ready for the front were shouldered high and vociferously acclaimed. The same fate overtook half a score of sailors from Her Majesty's Navy. And all the while policemen by the hundred stood by, powerless and smiling but alert to trouble that never came.

And everywhere and rising above every other sound until the morning sun gilded the dome of St Paul's and sent night revellers home, two great shouts repeated again and again and followed each time by clamorous cheering and the waving of thousands of Union Jacks:

'Hurray for Mafeking!'

'Three cheers for Baden-Powell!'

The End of a War

Years: 1900–03   Age: 43–46

1

BADEN-POWELL got no further sleep the first night of the relief of Mafeking. By dawn he was at his usual look-out studying the Boer position through his field-glasses. The enemy appeared still to occupy the two laagers to the east of Mafeking and the trenches in the Brickfields. Boer flags were still flying over Game Tree Fort and near Snijman's headquarters. There was so little activity evident that B-P reached the conclusion that the Boers 'meant to stay for the day'. He had no intention of letting them.

He called out his garrison and went to the attack while the relief forces shelled the Boer positions with the guns that had been brought into Mafeking during the night. 'As soon as the shells began to fall into the laager, the Boers made off for the Transvaal as hard as they could go.'

B-P and his men entered the Boer lines. The main laager had been hastily evacuated. Pots and kettles containing the burghers' breakfast were still boiling on the fires. Several wagon-loads of foodstuffs had been left behind. Snijman's field office was strewn with a mass of papers and telegrams. Baden-Powell moved on to Game Tree Fort. The Boer flag was pulled down and the Union Jack went up to wild cheering. And in the field hospital beyond the Boer lines Baden-Powell had a happy reunion with Captain McLaren. 'The Boy' and thirty other wounded British soldiers were in good enough shape to be taken to the town hospital.

With the mopping-up completed, the troops returned to Mafeking. When they reached the town they found Market Square milling with people waiting to receive them. The moment they entered, the cheers rolled around them. 'It was a sight that will ever be remembered by those who saw it,' J. Emerson Neilly wrote, 'this wild joy on the hunger-stricken faces of the recently beleaguered ones, the tears that flowed unbidden from the eyes of dozens of those who spent the time in alternately cheering and choking down sobs. . . . It was evident that the gallant B-P himself was not unmoved. There were visible signs of the emotion that was within him as he sat on his horse and witnessed the wild outburst of the people he had worked so well to protect. His eyes, too, were within an ace of over-flowing. . . .'

The next morning Baden-Powell went round and thanked each unit of the relief force for its work and each corps of the garrison for its share in the defence, then held a parade of the whole garrison for a thanksgiving and memorial service. Although the casualties during the siege had been numerically small, they had been proportionately large. Among the 1,019 combatants, there had been 326 casualties, with 92 men killed outright or dying from their wounds. The eight thousand non-combatants had suffered 487 casualties, with 333 dead from enemy bullets and shells.

As soon as all formal and informal ceremonies had been taken care of, all available manpower went into action. The town was cleared of its barricades. The bomb-proof shelters were dismantled—their roof beams were needed for the function for which they were originally intended: railway ties. One work force set out to re-establish the telegraph line towards the Cape, another to restore the railway to the north and to the south.

The moment the telegraph line was open, an avalanche of more than five hundred telegrams poured into Mafeking and kept the operators working night and day. One of the earliest of those messages was in-stantly rushed to Baden-Powell. It had a familiar address of origin: Windsor Castle.

> I and my whole Empire [Queen Victoria telegraphed] greatly rejoice at the relief of Mafeking after the splendid defence made by you through all these months. I heartily congratulate you and all under you, military and civil, British and native, for the heroism and devotion you have shown.
>
> V.R.I.

A few days later another telegram arrived, this one from the War Office: Her Majesty had been pleased to approve the promotion of Colonel Robert S. S. Baden-Powell to the rank of Major-General. At 43—and without having taken Staff College!—B-P had not only gained the advance-ment he coveted but had become the youngest Major-General in the British Army.

But it was not until the railway line to the south was restored and the trains started to pull in that B-P got the full effect of what the siege had meant to the people of Great Britain. Every train arriving at the Mafeking depot spewed forth mailbags with letters by the thousand, most of them addressed to the spontaneously proclaimed 'Hero of Mafeking'. B-P's brother Baden, staying on for the time being, undertook to handle the voluminous mail. He organized a volunteer force for opening and sorting the letters.

Without exception the letters expressed the deepest admiration for Baden-Powell's feat in holding Mafeking and the highest delight in each of the bluffs he had pulled on his besiegers. It seemed as if all Britain had hung on the messages that had emanated at rare intervals from the beleaguered town, from B-P's frivolous 'Four-hours-bombardment one-dog-killed' telegram in the early days of the siege to his assurance to Lord Roberts towards the end that Mafeking would hold out.

The letters had come from all classes of British people—from dukes' palaces and servants' quarters, from generals and soldiers, from farmers and clerks, from housewives and actresses, from school children and pensioners. There was no way of estimating from the letters how many proud fathers and mothers had named their offspring for the Hero of Mafeking, nor how many animal pets had suffered the same fate. Scores of young ladies proposed marriage to the highly eligible bachelor and youngsters of all ages expressed their hope of joining their hero in his future exploits.

The Commander-in-Chief of the British Army joined in the chorus:

> You did splendidly, and it was indeed one of the pleasantest things I had to do in the war when I recommended within a few hours of the news being received of Mafeking being relieved, that the Queen should promote you.
>
> You now have the ball at your feet, and barring accidents greatness is in front of you. That you may win the goal is earnestly wished you by yours very sincerely,
>
> WOLSELEY

But it was not just in Mafeking that letters for B-P were piling up. The same was happening at home in London at 8 St George's Place:

> Azzie˙and I [his mother wrote] devote every day to answering hundreds and hundreds of letters and poems full of the 'admiration of the whole world'. So many ask questions, so many send humble presents, and so many send carefully laboured gifts. Small busts of you, small trinkets with your portrait, china mugs and loving cups—all dedicated to the Hero of Mafeking. A German has sent a pair of vases. An Australian sent a grand medal in your honour in solid gold. Brooches innumerable. . . .

In conversation, Plumer and Mahon brought Baden-Powell up to date on the war.

It seemed that the first stage—of repeated reverses for the British forces, of defeat upon defeat, of bungling and vacillation—had ended with the replacement of Sir Redvers Buller by Lord Roberts of Kandahar as Commander-in-Chief for South Africa. Roberts, immediately upon his arrival at Cape Town on 10 January 1900, with Lord Kitchener of Khartoum as his Chief of Staff, had set about creating an effective field army and planning his campaign. While keeping the Boers occupied with minor demonstrations of force, he had gathered his forces between the Orange and Modder rivers.

The second stage of the war had started on 11 February with Roberts's army advancing into the Orange Free State which was fighting at the side of the Transvaal. A cavalry division had been sent northward under General French to break the siege of Kimberley. B-P's antagonist in the early days of the siege of Mafeking, Piet A. Cronje, had been defeated at Paardeberg on 27 February and had surrendered with four thousand men. Buller's fifth attempt at relieving Ladysmith had met with success. On 13 March, Roberts had entered Bloemfontein, the capital of the Orange Free State, in spite of being harassed by Boer commandos under Commandant Christian de Wet.

The tide of the war had changed. It was running favourably at last for the British cause.

There had been a long enforced delay for Roberts at Bloemfontein. The railway communications to the south, repeatedly broken by Boer saboteurs, had to be re-established, and supplies and reinforcements had to be brought up. The situation had been further aggravated by a severe outbreak of enteric fever among the British troops. The delay had worked to the advantage of the enemy: the Boers, in spite of the illness and death of their popular Commandant Piet Joubert on 28 March, had recovered their initiative and had returned to the attack.

It was while waiting in Bloemfontein that Roberts had ordered General Archibald Hunter to send a flying column under Colonel B. T. Mahon northward from Kimberley to the relief of Mafeking. Then, at long last, on 11 May, Roberts had resumed his advance. He was now continuing northward through Johannesburg to Pretoria. He was confident that the Boers would sue for peace and the war would be over.

2

Roberts moving to Pretoria! After having been a virtual prisoner for seven months within the confines of Mafeking, Baden-Powell was yearning to spread his wings, to do the kind of real soldiering he loved, across the African veld, to join the force moving onward to the ultimate victory.

His wish was granted in a matter of weeks. At the end of May, when he returned the control of Mafeking to the civilian government, he was given command of the Marico, West Lichtenburg and Rustenburg districts of the Transvaal.

On 30 May, President Kruger fled his capital by train to the east taking with him the Transvaal state archives and all available funds. On 5 June, Roberts entered Pretoria.

By then, Baden-Powell was moving eastward from Mafeking into the Transvaal with a force of eight hundred men. During his two-week onrush he took an area of a hundred by two hundred and fifty miles, accepted the surrender of a thousand Boers and collected more than two thousand rifles and large stocks of ammunition. He installed magistrates over the districts under his command and subdued bands of marauding natives bent on looting farms deserted by their Boer owners.

He reached Rustenburg on 14 June and took it without a fight. He had expected violent resistance. To his surprise there was none.

Rustenburg was an important plum in the conquest of the Transvaal. It was the birthplace of 'Oom Paul' Kruger himself and the stronghold of the old 'Dopper' Boers, the most old-fashioned and bitterest of their people. Many of the farms around Rustenburg, reportedly the best farming land in the whole of the Transvaal, were owned by members of the Kruger family. Piet Kruger, the president's son and himself a Rustenburg farmer, had been busy until the night before B-P's entry trying to line up a force to oppose the approaching Britons but without success. The next morning he was among the first of Rustenburg's burghers to surrender.

At Rustenburg, B-P was within seventy miles of Lord Roberts's headquarters at Pretoria. But he was still without instructions from the Commander-in-Chief and without telegraphic communication—the lines had been cut. Baden-Powell decided to ride to the Transvaal capital to get his orders directly from Roberts. With a small escort of half a dozen men he rode off from Rustenburg. Somehow, the report of his coming preceded him: he was met near Wolhuters Kop by a column of troops sent out to convoy him into town and take him directly to the Residency.

B-P was flabbergasted at his reception in Pretoria. His was a triumphant entry and an indication of what might be in store elsewhere for the Hero of Mafeking. Thousands of people cheered him along the streets. A teeming mass of friends and strangers surrounded him in the square near Government House. And when he arrived at the Residency, Lord Roberts himself with members of the High Command greeted him from the steps.

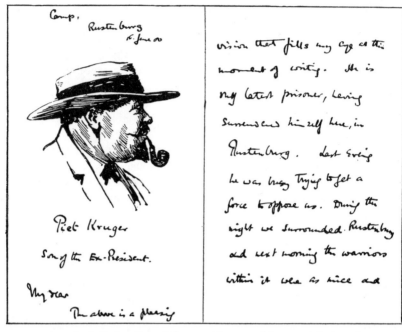

A typical Baden-Powell letter, illustrated by a quick sketch.

'It was awfully embarrassing,' B-P confided in a letter to his mother. 'I felt as if I were the Queen—and didn't know whether to grin or bear it—so did both.'

The two days B-P spent in Pretoria being briefed he was the guest of the Governor in a 'beautiful elaborately furnished house belonging to some local millionaire'. He breakfasted with General French and the Cavalry Division, lunched with Lord Downe and all the foreign attachés, dined with Lord Roberts and Lord Kitchener, and for the first time in eight and a half months undressed to go to bed. 'It was a luxury! But I do look forward to my blanket on the veld under the stars after one night's taste of a bright modern bedroom and sheets!'

Before leaving Pretoria, Baden-Powell was interviewed by the war correspondent for the London *Morning Post*, a young man he had met previously in India. The two men rode for more than an hour, while the reporter listened intently to the story of the Mafeking siege told him by the general. Before dispatching his story, he submitted the manuscript to B-P. 'He read it with concentration and some signs of embarrassment', the reporter recalled afterwards, 'but when he finished he handed it back to me saying with a smile, "Talking to you is like talking to a phonograph".'

Through his exclusive interview with the fabled Hero of Mafeking, the reporter, Winston Spencer Churchill, scored yet another scoop for his paper.

Baden-Powell had received his orders. Now he proceeded to carry them out. Working out of Rustenburg he occupied salient points along the Rustenburg—Mafeking road to the north of the Magaliesberg range, and started the preparation for a projected move northward. To hold his line of communication and the vast areas to the north and the south of it he had at his disposal a force of two thousand men.

During the rest of June and the first week of July everything was peace and quiet in the Magaliesberg range; but it was the quiet of sitting on a box of firecrackers while someone was lighting the fuse.

On 11 July, the first firecracker went off. The Boer commandant, de la Rey, moved in from the north-west with a force of more than a thousand burghers, attacked a mountain pass a few miles from Pretoria, then turned and closed in on Rustenburg. For a week Baden-Powell was hard put to it to keep his line of communication open. He had begun to make the preparations for another siege when Lord Methuen's forces came up from the south, drove back de la Rey's commandos and then, after making heliograph contact with the Rustenburg garrison, marched south again.

Less than two weeks later, the next firecracker exploded. On 30 July, the Orange Free State forces suffered a major defeat at Brandwater Basin— more than four thousand Free Staters surrendered, but fifteen hundred mounted men under Commandant Christian de Wet escaped and rode north-westward to link up with de la Rey. The Rustenburg area abruptly became the storm centre of the war, and Baden-Powell's task, figuratively speaking, turned into a matter of plugging up the mouse-holes (the passes over the Magaliesberg range) while the British generals in the field (Lord Methuen, Sir Ian Hamilton, Lord Kitchener) chased the mouse (de Wet).

Roberts in Pretoria realized that strong measures were required. He ordered General Hamilton to proceed towards Rustenburg from the east. At the same time he sent word to General Carrington to dispatch a force from the west, from Mafeking, to rout a Boer commando under de la Rey that was laying siege to Baden-Powell's outpost at Brakfontein—an outpost of five hundred men commanded by Colonel Hore who had been Sarel Eloff's prisoner in the police barracks of Mafeking less than three months before.

While waiting for Hamilton to arrive, Baden-Powell sent a detachment of three hundred men out to assist Carrington's move. They were halted by a numerically superior enemy force ahead of them but heard gun fire that gradually shifted westward. It appeared from the sound that the

Brakfontein outpost was being successfully withdrawn towards Mafeking according to instructions. Satisfied that Hore and his men had been relieved—but unaccountably, without reconnoitring the situation—B-P's detachment returned to Rustenburg.

Baden-Powell was elated that Hamilton's forces were coming to his aid: now, he felt, he would finally have the necessary number of soldiers to thwart any Boer attacks in the districts under his command. But Hamilton had not come to reinforce Baden-Powell. On the contrary, he had arrived with orders from Lord Roberts to bring B-P and his men safely back towards Pretoria. The Commander-in-Chief had decided to give up the Rustenburg area as being 'too far away to be anything but a source of weakness'.

Orders were orders. Very much against his will B-P on 6 August evacuated Rustenburg and moved his troops eastward to occupy Commando Nek although—as he couldn't help mentioning in a letter to Roberts—'I considered (and still do) that the importance of holding Rustenburg and its passes was very great'.

And then, to B-P's distress, the news reached him that Hore and his men had not been relieved after all. Carrington's force had been driven back by the Boers before reaching Brakfontein. What Baden-Powell's detachment had heard was the skirmishing as Carrington's men returned towards Mafeking without having accomplished their mission. It was officially announced that Colonel Hore's post had surrendered. But it hadn't. It had dug itself in and had held out with extraordinary energy and ingenuity against twice as many Boers. Its plight was finally discovered and a flying column sent to the rescue. After a siege of eleven days Colonel Hore and his men were free once more.

3

The great manhunt for de Wet and his commandos—one of the most extraordinary features of the whole South African War—was in full cry through south-western Transvaal. Time and time again, British troops found the trail of the Boer general and almost caught him. But time and time again de Wet succeeded, by some manoeuvre, in evading his British pursuers, winning for himself extraordinary credit as a guerilla leader. It was a credit that Baden-Powell considered to a great extent undeserved: 'I say "undeserved" because it was largely through our own fault that he continued his "tip and run" raids for so long. Columns were sent after him by telegraphed orders from General Headquarters with the usual result that they arrived at a given spot, sometimes colliding with each other, a few hours after he had departed elsewhere. Had two or three column leaders been told simply to go and catch de Wet it would have been done without very special difficulty—but on telegraphic instructions from Headquarters it was hopeless.'

Baden-Powell's contention was never better illustrated than on 14 August when Methuen pursued de Wet northward toward Oliphant's Nek, one of the main passes over the Magaliesberg range. Now at last de Wet was trapped, for forces under Hamilton had just occupied the pass. Except that they hadn't. Hamilton, misled by telegraphic information from Pretoria, did not reach the Nek until the evening of the day that de Wet had slipped over it.

Three days later de Wet arrived on the north side of Commando Nek held by Baden-Powell and started warily into the pass. To ascertain the strength of the British forces holding it, he sent off a note in Dutch under a white flag demanding the immediate, unconditional surrender of the 'Officer in Command British Troops' to 'prevent bloodshed'.

Baden-Powell spelled himself through the Boer commandant's letter. Why should de Wet have sent such a message? Obviously as a blind to cover some other move of his. What other move? A breakthrough to the south? But why should he want to go south when he had just escaped to the north? There could be only one answer: safely across Commando Nek, de Wet would be able to sweep eastward along the valley for a raid on Pretoria only twenty miles away. B-P told his staff officer to write an answer to the Boer leader:

> To de Wet, Your note has been received but I am not able to trans-
> late it. One of my men says it means you desire to surrender to me.
> Another says it means I am to surrender to you. Will you kindly
> make it clear to me which you mean.

With his bluff called, de Wet moved northward with his commando. Baden-Powell followed him.

From a couple of Boer prisoners he had captured B-P learned that de Wet's intention now was to swing north to Pretoria to join Louis Botha's army in east Transvaal. By forced marches Baden-Powell moved northward parallel to de Wet's commando, hugging its right flank, keeping it from turning east. On 20 August he overtook a British force under General Paget, then continued northward, still holding de Wet's commando toward the west. He raced the enemy to Warmbaths and headed it off before it could reach the Buiskop Pass. Three days later he turned the flank of the Boer commando and on 26 August marched into and occupied Nylstroom. 'Being now in rear of the enemy I hoped General Paget would be able to attack him from the front.'

But it didn't work out that way. Paget had just received telegraphic

orders to retire towards Pretoria and had already sent some of his infantry
back in that direction. 'Having no further supplies and in consequence
of General Paget's message I now withdrew my force by the same route
by which we came and rejoined General Paget the following day at
Warmbaths.'

His ten-day action had not ended the way Baden-Powell had hoped.
de Wet had again slipped away into the African bush with a few of his
men, leaving his main force to fend for itself. But B-P at least had the
satisfaction of having prevented the de Wet commando from turning
eastward to join Louis Botha.

4

What next? The answer to B-P's unspoken question was already on its
way. It arrived in the form of a telegram dated August 29:

> Major-General Baden-Powell, I want you to see me without delay
> regarding formation of Police Force for Transvaal, Orange River
> Colony, and Swaziland,
>
> ROBERTS

Accordingly, 'without delay', B-P handed over his command to his right-
hand man, Colonel Plumer, and left for Lord Roberts's new headquarters
at the eastern Transvaal village of Belfast.

Lord Roberts was in the midst of the last part of his campaign—the march
along the Delagoa Bay railway line to the border between the Transvaal
and Portuguese East Africa, the march that would, he now confidently
believed, end the war. His troops had captured every station along the
line with little difficulty, driving Botha's commandos and President
Kruger's special railway carriage before them. The British army, almost
20,000 strong, was converging on Belfast where Roberts had arrived on
26 August to take charge of the final onslaught.

The last pitched battle of the Boer War—the Battle of Bergendal—
opened the morning of 27 August with a tremendous artillery barrage.
At noon the infantry went into action. By early afternoon the Boers were
in flight. The British had 'won' another battle. But Botha had escaped
and his army of seven thousand burghers, undefeated, had split into
three groups disappearing to the north and the south of the railway
line.

Yet as far as Lord Roberts was concerned this was the end. The war
was over. The time had come to take steps for placing the country under
peace-time control. And as a first step the police force envisaged by Sir

Alfred Milner, the High Commissioner, needed to be established at the earliest possible moment.

Sir Alfred had been pleading for more than three months for his idea of a police force for South Africa. On 10 May, he had written to Lord Roberts suggesting that

> The policing . . . of the country . . . should be entrusted to mounted marksmen of the Cape Mounted Rifles or Cape Mounted Police type. Indeed I should like to see one body of police of this kind (at least two thousand strong) take over the whole of the country work in the Transvaal and Orange Free State. . . .

On 27 June he had placed his idea before Joseph Chamberlain.

Both Roberts and Chamberlain had agreed to Milner's point of view. But who was there to organize such a force in such a short time?

Roberts indicated his preference in the matter in a letter to Milner on 4 July:

> For head of the military police and of any local troops that may be raised, Baden-Powell is far and away the best man I know. He possesses in quite an unusual degree the qualities you specify, viz. 'energy, organization, knowledge of the country, and a power of getting on with its people'. As a member of the Government you would find Baden-Powell most useful. . . .

And so, with Milner's assent, Roberts telegraphed for Baden-Powell.

B-P arrived at Lord Roberts's headquarters on 31 August and went immediately into conference with Roberts. On his way to Belfast he had roughed out on a half-sheet of paper his ideas about a police force, computing its strength according to the area, population, cities and mining centres involved. After receiving Roberts's general approval of his scheme B-P left for the Cape to discuss his views with Milner, while back in Belfast Lord Roberts proclaimed the annexation of the Transvaal to the Queen's dominions.

As his train steamed into Cape Town with a couple of Union Jacks on the engine Baden-Powell was greeted by loud cries of 'Hurrah' from a large group of officials gathered on the railway platform. Before he knew what was happening to him a couple of men had grabbed him from the back and had lifted him to their shoulders. Outside the station a huge crowd cheered vociferously as Baden-Powell's bearers carried their captive through their midst the half mile to Government House and deposited him at Sir Alfred's front door.

But this was only the minor demonstration that Cape Town had planned for its visiting hero. The major ones occurred five days later and took the form of a torch-light parade in front of the Town House.

When Baden-Powell mounted the dais of the grandstand at exactly eight o'clock the crowd of more than twenty thousand people jostled forward in a surging, struggling mass. B-P was the first to recognize that a dangerous situation was developing. He immediately took charge, raised his stentorian voice urging those at the back to hold off. Within a few moments he had the situation under control. He then sat down to the crowd's cheering, ready to listen to the formal speeches of welcome.

At the end of the speeches thousands of torch-bearers threw their torches into one big bonfire in the centre of the square and the ceremony ended in wild disorder. Flames shot up dangerously near an electric light cable. . . . The local fire superintendent realized the terrible consequences that might ensue if the fire severed the cable. . . . He instructed his men to turn on a hose . . . a huge jet of water went hissing into the air . . . the great pressure of the water made the firemen lose control of the hose . . . hundreds of people were caught in the drenching shower bath and scattered in all directions. And the band struck up 'God Save the Queen'.

Although Baden-Powell had put up a good front before the people of Cape Town he was concerned about what had happened. He did not like the adulation and did not want it.

> I do wish they would not make me their hero [he wrote to his mother, telling her of his experiences]. I don't deserve a word of it for one thing, and for another I hate the publicity. And it quite prevents me from venturing home for some time to come. . . . If it is like that here what would it be like at home. . . .
>
> If I get any leave I shall slip off to Kashmir for a bit until they have forgotten me and I can come home and have some fun.

Baden-Powell spent close to three weeks at Cecil Rhodes's Groote Schuur —now completely rebuilt after the devastating fire of 1896—preparing the final plans for the new police force, writing a manual of instruction for the men, travelling to Cape Town for conferences with Milner at Government House. He had been toying with the idea of taking a leave as soon as he got his plans down on paper but the more he discussed the situation with Milner the more he was convinced that whatever was to be done must be commenced at once.

The English press had clamoured for Baden-Powell to come home for a hero's welcome, his family had expected him for months, his mother had urged him to join her in the Canary Islands so that she might help him write the book on the Siege of Mafeking for which the publishing house of Methuen & Co. had offered him a substantial advance payment. But to B-P the creation of his new force came first. He decided to forgo a leave to get the job done and invited his mother and his sister to pay a visit to Cape Town at his expense instead.

At the end of September Baden-Powell travelled north to Pretoria to lay his plans before Lord Roberts at his re-established headquarters in the Transvaal capital. He had everything ready for final approval when Milner arrived on 15 October.

There were numerous things to be settled. Lord Roberts had just received word from London that he had been appointed Commander-in-Chief in England to succeed Lord Wolseley whose term of office had expired. At his recommendation Lord Kitchener had been made his successor in South Africa, much against Kitchener's wishes: he had his mind set on becoming Commander-in-Chief in India. The turning-over of command had to be accomplished, military and civilian dispositions had to be made.

Now that peace was at hand one of the most urgent of the civilian arrangements was the official establishment of Baden-Powell's police force. It took several long conferences and 'a considerable fight' to settle the matter, with Milner on one side wanting to limit the number to six thousand, Roberts and Kitchener on the other side holding out for twice as many, and B-P caught in the middle.

Eventually all points were cleared up. Baden-Powell's plans were approved and Milner's figure accepted for the time being. The South African Constabulary came into existence with Baden-Powell as its Inspector-General by Lord Roberts's Proclamation No. 24 of 1900, dated 22 October, 'to act as a police in and throughout the Transvaal and Orange River Colony for preserving the peace and preventing crimes, and apprehending offenders against the peace; and also as a military force for the defence of the Colonies'. It was to be ready by June 1901, under the orders of Sir Alfred Milner as High Commissioner.

On 28 October, at a short ceremony before his return to the Cape, Milner had the great satisfaction of inaugurating the first small contingent of Baden-Powell's South African Constabulary. The following day Kitchener took over the command of the army in South Africa, and Lord Roberts left for England to be created an Earl and a Knight of the Garter for his services to the Empire.

Baden-Powell spent the next two months—November and December 1900 —getting his staff assembled and his force organized. It was more difficult than he had expected.

In the belief that South Africa would soon settle down to peace and that much of the army would be released and shipped home Roberts had agreed to hand over to Baden-Powell a proportion of officers, non-commissioned officers and men, up to 20 per cent of each corps, with horses, saddlery, arms and transport. Roberts's successor quickly learned that the war was far from over: every defeat had made the Boers more determined to fight on, every disaster had spurred them to new life. But instead of maintaining a couple of large armies to fight pitched battles against the British on a couple of major fronts, the Boers had split their forces into hundreds of guerilla bands for hundreds of commando raids on hundreds of small fronts. Kitchener could spare neither the personnel nor matériel from his army but, on the contrary, had to appeal to England for more men, more supplies as the war went on and on and on.

Baden-Powell had to fend for himself. Foiled in his efforts to get the officers he needed from the Army he turned to an army camp near Cape Town that had recently added a word to the English language: to be 'stellenbosched', to be relegated to a position in which little harm could be done. With Milner's blessing he went to secure some of his officer material at Stellenbosch—'a sort of purgatory in which officers were placed who had been responsible for any "regrettable incident" in the campaign'. He took the view that 'these men had made their mistakes and were therefore all the more likely not to do so in the future'. His faith proved justified.

A goodly number of Britons in South Africa enrolled in B-P's force but many more were needed, particularly since Kitchener early in December secured Government agreement to increase the size of the Constabulary to ten thousand. B-P established recruiting offices in Cape Colony and Natal and called for recruits from overseas. Eventually, he and his staff 'raked in men and officers wherever we could get them, from all over the Empire—stock-riders from Australia, farmers from New Zealand, Northwest Mounted Police constables and cowboys from Canada, planters from India and Ceylon, Royal Irish Constabulary constables from Ireland, and yeomen from England'.

Since the Army in the circumstances was unable to provide the promised equipment and horses and other transport, and was incapable of meeting the force's medical, veterinary and building needs, Baden-Powell had to organize his own departments in each of these fields and find officers and men to run them.

There were other things with which B-P had to concern himself—a suitable uniform for his men, for instance.

He designed it himself. He wanted it to look different from the Army uniform and to be not only smart but comfortable. Thinking of his own pleasure in the 'flannel-shirt life', he developed an informal camp dress of khaki shirt with a soft collar in place of the stiff military stand-up collar. To this he added a plain khaki coat for more formal wear. For headgear he settled on his own favourite broad-brimmed hat, known in the trade as the 'Boss of the Plains' or 'B.P.'—a coincidence in initials that brought about the mistaken notion that the hat had been designed by B-P himself.

The uniform of the South African Constabulary, designed by B-P.

With what seemed to him excruciating slowness the South African Constabulary took shape—but only because of his astonishing capacity for work. For days and weeks on end he was 'head over ears in work, starting work at 5.30 a.m. and not leaving the office until 8 p.m., with an average of two hundred letters and telegrams a day'.

'He is an awfully jolly sort of fellow', one of his men wrote of him at the time, and added, 'but his notions of how much sleep you want are hazy'.

In the midst of his work, Baden-Powell had to hurry off to the Cape. His mother and sister had taken him up on his invitation to visit him in South Africa. They arrived on 17 December in the 'worst south-easter for the past thirty years'. The gale kept the ship hove to in Table Bay for nearly forty-eight hours, cutting by two days the week's leave B-P had been able to scrape together.

The three made the most of the time they had. 'Stephe' took his mother and Agnes on visits all over the Cape, introduced them to many of his friends and regaled them with stories of the siege. They told him among other things of their experiences in London the night the news reached the capital of the relief of Mafeking and of their efforts to keep up with his mail. They could also tell him more about the success of *Aids to Scouting*. The book had sold close to a hundred thousand copies and was appearing at that moment in a new magazine for boys, *Boys of the Empire*, as a serial under the rather intriguing title of 'The Boy Scouts'.

When his week was up, Baden-Powell went back to Johannesburg. He left his mother and sister behind at the Cape to enjoy the South African sunshine for a while longer before they returned to their dank English winter.

In the first days of 1901 Baden-Powell established his headquarters for the South African Constabulary at Zuurfontein and his central training depot in a dynamite factory at nearby Modderfontein, between Johannesburg and Pretoria. Here he and his staff started training the men in groups as they arrived by a 'patent short-cut method', following lines explicitly laid down in the manual he had written, *Notes and Instructions for the South African Constabulary*.

This small book of a hundred pages, with an additional fifty-four pages of appendices, expresses more clearly than any other of Baden-Powell's writings his philosophy as a military man. It was written directly for each man, telling him of his duties and his privileges, of the work that was needed and the satisfaction that would accrue from performing it.

> I appeal to the British spirit already ingrained in you [B-P wrote], of 'playing the game', that is, of doing your duty just as thoroughly when you are away from the eye of authority as when under it—not from fear of punishment for neglect to do it, but simply because it is 'the game' and is expected of you as a man of honour. Recruited from every portion of the Empire, ours is the first truly Imperial corps and once imbued with this spirit, it is going to be the finest corps in the world.

The men of the force quickly caught the spirit of their Inspector-General. They chose for their slogan 'Be Prepared'—partly because it bespoke their readiness to take on any kind of duty at any time, partly because of its play on their commander's initials.

At Modderfontein the recruits went through an intensive course of riding and musketry, drills and tactics. They learned to build huts and dig trenches, put up barbed-wire entanglements and lay mines. The method used in the training was remarkably effective although frowned upon by old-time disciplinarians as being highly unconventional. B-P knew from his previous experiences that it would work. It was based on his belief in decentralized responsibility and his trust in his men to live up to his expectations of them. He subdivided each of his five divisions into four districts, each district into troops, each troop into patrols consisting of a squad of six men—every subdivision with its own responsible leader.

On 23 January 1901, word reached the British forces in South Africa that their Queen had died at Osborne the night before. One of the last things she had asked, just before drifting into unconsciousness, was 'What news is there from Lord Kitchener?'

The news from Kitchener was not good. Boer commandos had been on the rampage throughout December and January and had inflicted some humiliating, although insignificant, defeats upon the British. Roberts's policy of burning the farms of the rebel Boers had proved a serious mistake, as had the severely criticized concentration camps for surrendered burghers and their families. Some new scheme was required for fighting this new kind of war.

Kitchener evolved a plan and started to put it into effect towards the end of January. His idea was to fence off large areas of the Transvaal and Orange River Colony with long chains of blockhouses, connected by barbed wire, and to mop up the Boer commandos within each area by concentrated drives of large numbers of British troops. For this kind of warfare more and still more men were needed, including every man of Baden-Powell's South African Constabulary.

Although the S.A.C. properly speaking was an Imperial civil force under the High Commissioner it saw no police duty while the war lasted. Milner lent it to Kitchener for use as a military contingent.

As quickly as Baden-Powell could get his men trained and equipped they were sent into active duty, some of them to man blockhouses, some of them to take part in the cross-country drives. B-P himself was everywhere, rushing back and forth among his scattered divisions, spending untold hours at his headquarters and at his training depot, seeing his Constabulary blossom into a well-knit, well-trained, highly regarded unit.

By the end of June the Constabulary was within reach of the ten thousand men projected for it. But while the force was growing stronger and stronger every day, it's commanding officer wasn't.

Staying at Johannesburg on one of his exhausting inspection trips, B-P fell ill. The army doctor sent him to bed and convened a medical board.

It took the board only a few minutes to reach its decision: it ordered Baden-Powell home on leave and would hear nothing of his protests— the South African Constabulary was so firmly established that it could get along for a while without its Inspector-General. The army doctor, Lieutenant-Colonel W. Beevor, was very explicit in accounting for the reasons for the decision:

> I have long hoped he would not work so hard: he would get fever of a severe enough type to lay most men up in hospital, but would go on working. Doubtless this is a modification of the Ashanti fever, and it always remains in the system for years. It is a very depressing type; and no man affected with it should be overworked. What our General went through at Mafeking was again enough to lay most men up for some considerable time; and all this on top of the organization of such a corps as this, ten thousand strong, was more than human endurance could stand.
>
> About a month ago an undoubted attack of influenza came on; it was followed by bronchitis; so I would not take the responsibility, and was only too glad to have a medical board, and recommend the General for six months' leave. Of course he didn't think he required so long; but although his brain power is phenomenal, his body cannot go on at full tension for ever! So I trust he will not worry himself by inaction. . . .

5

B-P turned his command over to his Chief-of-Staff, Lieutenant-Colonel John T. Nicholson, and started for home.

On stopping at Madeira, the captain of his ship brought Baden-Powell disconcerting news: a telegram just received informed him that a civic reception in honour of the Hero of Mafeking was being prepared at Southampton. B-P cabled to have it cancelled. To no avail: when the ship docked an immense flag-waving, cheering crowd lined the pier and the mayor stepped forward in all his finery to deliver his speech of welcome.

In the midst of the Southampton celebration B-P was told that a similar reception awaited him in London. He appealed to the mail authorities. His entreaty was heeded. 'They tacked a carriage for me on to the engine and vans which took the mails ahead of the boat-train to London, and gave orders to the driver to stop and let me out at Woking.' He spent a couple of days near Woking at the home of 'The Boy' McLaren who had been invalided to England because of his wounds. From here B-P slipped off for a quiet week with his mother and sister at Hindhead in Surrey, where they were staying for the summer. Mrs Baden-Powell had her hero-son safely at home at last.

The next couple of months Baden-Powell rested in various parts of the British Isles, staying with old friends at their country homes or at out-of-the-way hotels and inns under the name of 'Colonel Nicholson'.

When at last he felt strong enough to approach London he soon got himself involved in some special activities.

Charterhouse had shown its affection for its old Gownboy by collecting thousands of pounds for the Mafeking Relief Fund. Now Dr Haig Brown called on Baden-Powell to lay the foundation stone for the Memorial Cloister being erected in honour of the Old Carthusians who had fallen in the war.

Another function he could not evade was a luncheon given him by members of the Powell family once or twice removed. Altogether 167 'cousins' showed up for the event and presented their famous relation with a gold chronometer. B-P himself had trouble getting in to his own luncheon. A policeman at the door had received strict orders to admit guests with tickets only. When a gentleman appeared without one, the policeman stopped him. 'My dear fellow,' said the gentleman, 'you can't have a funeral without the corpse.' But it took Baden-Powell several minutes to persuade the policeman as to his identity.

On yet another occasion, at a reception at the Imperial Institute, South Kensington, Joseph Chamberlain paid B-P an elaborate tribute and presented him with a handsome gold-mounted Sword of Honour from his admirers in Australia.

Back at 8 St George's Place Baden-Powell finally started to skim through the voluminous mail that had accumulated for him and had been neatly sorted out for him by his mother and sister. A new wave of letters was pouring in now that it had become known that B-P was back in England.

One of the letters needed instant attention. It was a command invitation from his new sovereign, King Edward VII, to join him and the Queen at Balmoral for the week-end. B-P left London by the night train. The next afternoon, Colonel Davidson, the King's Equerry took him to His Majesty's study.

> Had a long sit-down talk alone with him [Baden-Powell wrote his mother that night]. Then he rang and sent for the Queen, who came in with the little Duke of York—and we had a long chat, chiefly about my Police . . . present state of the war, Colonials as troops, etc. as well as about Mafeking (of course).

The King handed me C.B. [Companion of the Order of the Bath] and South African Medal.

Davidson had told me before that in kissing hands with the Queen I would be lucky if I got my kiss 'home'—and he was right, she jerked her hand away at the critical moment—and I kissed my own hand (more or less).

In London Baden-Powell had a quiet time, reading, writing, sketching, visiting, going to the theatre a couple of times a week to catch up on plays and operettas. Beerbohm Tree gave him a dinner at which many of his actor friends were present. Cyril Maude gave him another. And two famous artists painted his portrait: Sir Herbert von Herkomer for the Cavalry Club, George Frederick Watts for Charterhouse.

But winter was coming to England—and there was summer in South Africa and work to be done. Baden-Powell appealed to the Army's medical board to be permitted to return to his job. After having refused an appeal two months before, the board this time agreed to let him terminate his sick leave a month ahead of schedule.

6

Arrived in Johannesburg where the South African Constabulary had finally been provided with a permanent headquarters B-P found that Colonel Nicholson had handled the force with high efficiency during his absence: 'We—the S.A. Constabulary—are now quite a power in the land,' B-P could report, 'doing excellent work in every direction. And all is going very well with the war, much better than people at home realize.'

It seemed that Kitchener's blockhouse plan was finally paying off. Every week the 'drives' of the army, assisted by members of the S.A.C., netted a 'bag' of a couple of hundred Boers—although the leaders invariably escaped. Peace was in the air. If only. . . .

If only the Boers would give up. If only de la Rey would surrender his commando in West Transvaal and Botha his in East Transvaal. If only de Wet would stop his sabotage in the Orange Free State and Jan Christian Smuts his exasperating raids into the Cape Colony. They all knew very well that they had lost the war. And yet they fought on in their vast country—'not for victory', as Winston Churchill pointed out, 'but for honour'. They fought on to make the British victory as dearly bought as possible and caused the British Army a number of final defeats—the most humiliating of all the routing in March of Lord Methuen's column by de la Rey, killing two hundred men and capturing six hundred, among them the wounded general himself.

Another loss threw a dark pall over Britain towards the end of the same month. The heart of Cecil Rhodes gave way. The 'Empire Builder' died at 49 without experiencing the conclusion of the war—'So little done; so much to do.'

But the end was near. The Boers could not go on much longer in the devastated land. Their commanders requested safe-conduct passes from Kitchener so that they might meet and discuss the situation. Kitchener acceded. Thirty representatives from the Transvaal and thirty from the Orange Free State met to confer at Veereeniging. Kitchener laid before them a proposal drafted by Milner and himself in conformance with directives from the Cabinet at home.

After two weeks of agonized haggling the Boers gave up. On the afternoon of 31 May 1902, they voted to accept the British terms. That same night they went to Pretoria and signed the terms in the dining-room of the British Headquarters in the presence of Kitchener and Milner. The terms contained ten articles:

1. The Boers in the field were to lay down their arms immediately and acknowledge King Edward VII as their lawful sovereign.
2. All prisoners, on making the same acknowledgement, were to be returned to their home.
3. The Boers surrendering or returning were not to be deprived of their personal liberty or their property.
4. There would be no civil or criminal prosecution of Boers except for certain acts 'contrary to usages of war'.
5. The Dutch language would be taught in public schools where parents desired it and used in courts of law when necessary.
6. Possession of rifles would be allowed for personal protection.
7. Military administration would be replaced by civil government, and eventually with self-government 'as soon as circumstances permit'.
8. The question of granting franchise to natives would not be decided until after self-government had been established.
9. No special war tax would be imposed.
10. District commissions would be appointed to assist the restoration of the Boers to their homes and the resumption of their normal occupations. The British Government would provide the sum of £3 million for this resettlement work, as well as loans free of interest for two years.

After two years and eight months 'the unnecessary war' had come to an end. Soon, Kitchener left for England to be created a Viscount and to be granted his heart's desire of becoming Commander-in-Chief in India.

7

The Boer War was over. The main work of the South African Constabulary, with Baden-Powell at its head, was at hand.

On 8 June 1902, the South African Constabulary was released from its Army work to become an arm of the civil government directly responsible to Milner, who had been recently raised to the peerage.

It was the moment that Baden-Powell had looked forward to ever since Roberts and Milner had entrusted him with the task of raising a police force more than nineteen months before. During the years B-P had spent in South Africa at different times prior to the war, he had formed many friendships among the South African Dutch. Now he was relieved from further fighting against them and would have the opportunity of making 'some sort of reparation' to his Boer friends by helping them re-establish their lives.

B-P issued orders to his troops—now numbering 10,016 officers and men—to take up posts over the whole face of the new colonies, an area more than three times the size of England.

Everywhere newly appointed 'resident magistrates' hurried out to their respective districts and started to administer civil justice from the tents or shanties or farm ruins that served them for offices. For every three or four of these districts a complete mounted mobile troop of South African Constabulary moved in to maintain order. By the end of July more than two hundred S.A.C. stations had been established. This rapid policing of the country made the speedy repatriation of the burghers possible.

The Constabulary was called on to perform a multiplicity of tasks: They delivered the mail and collected customs. They vaccinated babies and inoculated cattle. They stopped the traffic in illicit liquor and foiled the smuggling of arms. They went in for locust destruction and traced stolen cattle. They controlled gold rushes and took on general town policing. 'A fairly catholic kind of service for us officers', as B-P put it, 'but all the more interesting for that'.

As soon as the distribution of the S.A.C. was accomplished Baden-Powell's chief responsibility consisted of inspecting each of the police posts scattered in a vast network over the country from east to west, from the Orange river to the Limpopo. It was only by frequent inspection, he felt, that he would be able to judge the effectiveness of his troops and keep in personal touch with the officers and men of the widely scattered stations.

He set about performing this inspection by train and by horse, accompanied by his personal staff officer, Captain Harvey Kearsley. At the end of a year, Kearsley estimated that the two of them had travelled a distance of 13,503 miles by train and had covered 2,306 miles on horseback at an average of thirty-four miles a day.

While on one of his extended inspection trips a letter from his mother caught up with Baden-Powell to inform him that his brother Frank, the artist-barrister, had become engaged to a New Zealand girl, Florence Watt.

With Frank soon to be married, he looked to the future: 'Now it only remains for W[arington] to get married, and it will be my turn—and I shall have no excuse for evading it. But I don't see how I am ever to get a chance of finding a lady at this rate. The work goes on as heavily as ever: the one great point is that every day shows progress.'

Frank's engagement was of short duration. There was no reason for waiting if he was to have a reasonable share of wedded bliss—he was 52 already. The couple married and left for a leisurely honeymoon trip to New Zealand to visit the bride's family and called at South Africa on the way. Stephe arranged to take a leave and met them at Kimberley as the train pulled in after the long journey from Cape Town.

Baden-Powell carried through a full three weeks' programme with them. He eventually waved them good-bye from the pier at Durban, and returned to Johannesburg.

Ever since the peace agreement had been signed Lord Milner had urged Joseph Chamberlain to come to South Africa. He asserted that it was of extreme importance for the Secretary of State for the Colonies to find out about conditions in the colonies by personal inspection. 'Pushful Joe' of the monocle and orchid finally arranged his affairs so that he could be away from England for three months and sailed for South Africa with his wife. After spending Christmas and the New Year in Natal the Chamberlains arrived in Pretoria in January 1903 for a one-month tour of the Transvaal and the Orange River Colony.

In addition to his regular work, Baden-Powell had been busy preparing for Chamberlain's visit: the South African Constabulary had been given the responsibility of arranging the tour and B-P himself had been assigned the task of accompanying the Colonial Secretary and his wife.

The visit of the Chamberlains to the new colonies had a spectacular beginning at the big public banquet in Pretoria, attended by some of the top Boer commandants: Botha, de la Rey and Smuts. Chamberlain was in perfect form—his speech was such an oratorical masterpiece that even the Boer leaders could applaud.

Part of the touring that followed under B-P's direction was done by train but where no railway line existed it was necessary for the party to cross the open veld by 'trekking'—travelling in covered wagonettes, Cape carts, spiders, or riding on horseback. The baggage and servants followed by mule wagons.

During the first day's trek of thirty miles out of Potchefstroom the party ran into a violent South African thunder-storm. At Witpoort it stopped at a hotel where 'the dining-room just held seven people besides the tea-kettle which was a rather full-sized one'. Wentersdorp was all flags and cheers for Chamberlain—his open-air address to the inhabitants was well received and 'very audibly punctuated by a beery admirer who kept calling to the audience at intervals "How's now? Ain't he a daisy?" '

At Lichtenburg—the home of the main De la Rey commando that prided itself on never having surrendered—the reception was completely different. There were no flags or cheers to welcome the Chamberlain party. Only the local British inhabitants and a small group of sullen, curiosity-driven Boers were on hand. But Chamberlain did an astute thing: he spoke over the heads of the Britons directly to the burghers. He complimented them on the way they fought for their cause, called them the 'bravest of the brave'. Baden-Powell listened with admiration to the statesman's speech: when Chamberlain finished 'he had the whole lot cheering him as if that was what they had come for'.

In Mafeking Chamberlain and his party were regaled with a gala reception by the Mayor and—since they had now entered the Cape Colony—by the Governor and the Premier who had come up from Cape Town. Then a rail trip to Kimberley for another civic celebration and a further trek of three days across the veld by wagons and on horseback to Bloemfontein.

Before Chamberlain left for Cape Town, Baden-Powell staged a private parade of the Constabulary for him. The Colonial Secretary walked along the lines, interviewed a number of the men and expressed his great satisfaction at the work of the force as a whole—a satisfaction to which he gave public utterance in the House of Commons upon his return to England.

8

Baden-Powell had enjoyed the tour with the Chamberlains. But his thoughts had been far away from what was happening around him.

In the midst of the Chamberlain visit he had received a letter from the War Office offering him the post of Inspector-General of Cavalry for Great Britain and Ireland, with responsibility also for the cavalry in Egypt and South Africa.

B-P had immediately communicated the news to Lord Milner:

> The question as to whether I accept rests rather with your S.A.C.—
> and so I put myself in your hands. . . .
>   The appointment offered me is beyond what I had ever expected
> but I am not so ambitious as to want to leave my present work unless
> you can easily spare me—and if I do go it will be with sincere regret
> for it has been a real pleasure to me to have a share, however small,
> in the big work here which you have directed.

Lord Milner urged him to accept the post—the Blue Riband of the Cavalry
Service. 'The principal advantage,' he told Baden-Powell, 'is that you are
brought back into the main stream of the Imperial Service. . . . The S.A.C.
while a good show, is a side show. . . .'

The creation of the South African Constabulary from scratch into an
effective force of ten thousand men, trained for war and for peace, was
always afterwards, to B-P, the greatest accomplishment of his military
career. 'To have seen the whole thing from the very start to the final
incident of Chamberlain's visit and his instructions for the future of the
country was a grand and satisfactory experience for me.'
    After a round of farewell parades and dinners, B-P left for home with
mixed feelings of elation and regret. His regret was tempered somewhat
by the kindly farewell messages he received, not only from members of
the Constabulary but from civil and military friends, British and Boer
alike—among them one from one of his S.A.C. officers that pleased him
especially:

> Your extreme get-at-ableness stands out in bold relief. That rather
> awkward fence which generally surrounds a General has been non-
> existent with you, and I know there are many like myself who have
> appreciated to the full the freedom from strict convention that you
> have given.

XV

Inspector-General

Years: 1903–07   Age: 46–50

1

As on a previous occasion, twenty-four years before, Baden-Powell returned to England to a new home. The house at 8 St George's Place had fallen before the onrush of civilization to make room for Hyde Park Corner station of the 'awful Tuppenny Tube'—the London Underground. Mrs Baden-Powell and Agnes had moved to 32 Princes Gate, S.W. It had been hard for his mother to leave the old place, but B-P had tried to console her by pointing out that its real use was over, that 'No. 8 had done its work for the family and had fairly launched us all'.

Baden-Powell established himself in his own spacious room in the new family house. He decorated it with a few of his water-colours and with a large array of his big-game trophies. His London home was an excellent base of operations although he was to make little use of it—his work and his travels gave him few chances to spend his time at home.

On 9 March 1903, Major-General Baden-Powell presented himself at the War Office.

He had become Inspector-General of Cavalry at a propitious time. The Boer War had been a great eye-opener to the British public and to the high command of the British Army. A comparatively small number of Boers, untrained in military drill, under voluntary leaders, had held at bay for almost three years a much larger army of supposedly well-trained soldiers, under a great number of professional officers; obviously something was wrong and obviously, also, changes were in order.

The War Office was willing to listen to new voices and to new ideas. Baden-Powell was given the chance to express himself, to impose on the whole British cavalry the methods he felt would prove most effective.

His responsibility was great. So were his misgivings. Because of his numerous absences in various parts of the Empire he had only served intermittently with the cavalry in England and consequently felt himself 'a bit out of touch with the men and measures of the day at home'. He had not been through Staff College and had only a 'scrappy' knowledge of strategy and military history. On the other hand, he had seen active service with mounted troops in India and Africa, had commanded a cavalry regiment and a brigade overseas, had had experiences outside purely regimental work at several army manoeuvres. He had the necessary background, although he could not claim to be 'a strictly orthodox cavalry officer'. His main need was to get himself educated in up-to-date cavalry methods.

For this purpose he arranged to visit cavalry centres and military manoeuvres abroad, anticipating that these visits would provide him with the necessary knowledge and ammunition for his efforts to improve the cavalry of England.

He left on the first of these trips less than a month after his return. Accompanied by his A.D.C., Major Harvey Kearsley, whom he had brought with him from South Africa, he set out from Bremerhaven for the United States and Canada on the four-funnelled S.S. *Kronprinz Wilhelm*, after paying a short and rather disappointing visit to the German Cavalry School at Hanover.

2

Baden-Powell had a special reason for going to America first. He had been raised in the *arme blanche* tradition of the cavalry where the stock in trade was the violent galloping charge with slashing swords, to the accompaniment of shrill trumpet blasts. In actual 'civilized' warfare he had seen little use of this melodramatic performance although it had been effective on a couple of occasions against the Zulus and the Matabele. The Americans, during their Civil War, had used their cavalry differently: the mounted charge had been somewhat of a rarity while the speedy movement of the cavalry, the scouting and screening and the dismounted attack had become the order of the day. Confederate General J. E. B. ('Jeb') Stuart had used these tactics in supporting General 'Stonewall' Jackson's corps; Union General Philip Sheridan's highly mobile cavalry had been one of the causes of the defeat of Lee's army.

At the War Office of the United States Army in Washington, D.C., Baden-Powell was received by Elihu Root, Theodore Roosevelt's Secretary of War, and introduced to the American generals in charge of cavalry and officers' training. After a long and very satisfactory session on methods and problems, one of his new officer friends drove B-P to Fort Myers, a few miles outside the capital, for 'a stunning display' of precision riding by a cavalry squadron.

During the next week Baden-Powell and Kearsley proceeded in a leisurely way through the main battlefields of the American Civil War. B-P had read up carefully on the history and strategy of each battle. Visiting the spots made each action come vividly alive to him.

At the U.S. Military Academy at West Point, New York, the super-intendent showed the British Inspector-General all possible honours. During a busy day he visited all the buildings, witnessed a riding display and a cavalry drill, and was regaled with a *bona fide* American baseball game between West Point and Harvard University.

Before returning home, B-P made a five-day trip into Canada. He stopped at Niagara Falls, Toronto, Ottawa, Montreal, Quebec, and met Canadian military leaders to 'talk over cavalry and colonial army matters'.

B-P's trip to the United States had repercussions. They were mostly of his own making, caused by his insistence on travelling incognito for the sake of dodging reporters. His aliases of 'Colonel R. Stephenson' in New York and Washington, 'Horace Peel' in Montreal and 'Mr Harvey' in Quebec were quickly penetrated. In each city the newspapers carried full accounts of his comings and goings, including his aliases, although no reporter ever caught up with him.

But on the last day of his stay in New York he ran into trouble. He had already packed and had sent his luggage on board the S.S. *Kaiser Wilhelm II*. He had been talking on the telephone in his hotel room to one of his friends and had omitted to ring off when the telephone began 'working' again. It was a reporter asking the hotel manager if General Baden-Powell was in and whether he was to sail by the afternoon boat. 'So I took on myself to answer him as I would have wished the manager to do—i.e. put him on the wrong scent altogether.'

B-P dodged the reporter but the reporter was not so easily dodged. His 'interview' with the British General appeared in his paper the next day and created a considerable stir.

Baden-Powell was purported to have told the reporter that 'as a whole the American cavalry arm does not come up to the high-water mark of the British branch of the service . . .'; that 'the physique of the men is below the standard of the British cavalrymen . . .'; that 'the food which your cavalrymen are given each day is far too highly seasoned and too much coffee is drunk . . .', and so on, for a solid newsprint column of fabricated 'quotes'.

Newspapers throughout the United States picked up the story and expressed their criticism editorially of 'General Baden-Powell's reported unfavourable comment on the American cavalry'.

B-P himself was unaware of the commotion as he was on the high seas. But soon after his return to England the original article and the criticism caught up with him. He immediately made the trans-Atlantic cable hot with his denials and sent off letters to Washington, Fort Myers, West Point and to the offending newspaper.

General Henry C. Corbin who had made the arrangements for him in the United States was not perturbed: 'I have caused your cable and your letter to be widely published. ... But my dear Powell—why give it a thought? ... I assure you that our people will understand from your denials how free you have been from offending any one. ...'

But the editor of the newspaper was profoundly chagrined. He ran a public apology in his paper and closed a personal letter to Baden-Powell by saying: 'I may add that the reporter is an Englishman and we could not imagine that he would try in any way to misrepresent a British officer.'

The incident was closed. But the effect lingered on in Baden-Powell's stiffened attitude towards newspapermen.

3

Baden-Powell spent the spring and summer of 1903 finding out about the condition of the cavalry at home. From early May to late August he was on the move continuously inspecting the cavalry and yeomanry centres of England and Wales, Scotland and Ireland, visiting more than a score from Dorset to Inverness-shire, from Kent to County Kildare. For the long stretches between centres he made use of the railway but for shorter distances he preferred the new-fangled motor-car that was slowly gaining favour.

He was as unorthodox in his inspecting as he was in many other military matters. He did not follow the time-honoured procedure of infecting the officers for weeks in advance with 'inspection fever' and sticking to a short formal programme during the inspection. Instead, B-P preferred to come unannounced and to stay for a couple of days with each regiment, living with it in its camp or its barracks, seeing it at work and at play, watching the way the officers handled their men, the way the men responded to their officers. He did not believe in the old-fashioned superficial approach. He was not interested in 'spit and polish' appearances but in finding out the efficiency of his regiments.

After a couple of inspections each week, B-P tried, as far as possible, to keep the week-ends for himself for visits in the area he was inspecting at the time. It was not just his old friends he visited—the Nobles, the Grants, the Greaves, the Baker Russells and many others. Wherever he went for an inspection, invitations were extended to him to stay overnight at nearby country houses and castles, to stop for fishing or shooting. He was enthusiastically welcomed. As a conversationalist and entertainer he was unsurpassed. He had not only retained but greatly enlarged his wealth of interesting stories, his repertoire of songs and skits. And as a celebrity he was eagerly sought: everywhere he went his Boer War fame went with him—unobtrusively as far as he was concerned, but definitely there in the minds of all the other guests.

There were further invitations the 'Hero of Mafeking' could not refuse: requests for him to present medals to veterans of the South African War or to inspect various youth groups, calls for him to appear to accept the freedom of different cities, with the accompanying parades, receptions, dinners and speeches.

Nor could he turn down an invitation from the King of Saxony for the Inspector-General of Cavalry of the British Army to attend the German autumn manoeuvres at the end of August 1903.

4

B-P had previously attended foreign army manoeuvres clandestinely. Now he was to witness one as an official guest representing his country.

He reached Zeithain near Dresden the day after leaving London. A carriage with a soldier orderly met him and took him to the cantonments where the officers were at dinner. He was greeted with profuse courtesy by the Crown Prince of Prussia and by von der Planitz, General of Cavalry. The next day he was supplied with a horse and taken out by his A.D.C. to the drill grounds four miles away.

All morning long he watched the divisional movements with a critical eye: 'Six schemes carried out. Minor drill very good, major evolution often poor.' He was, of course, particularly interested in the manoeuvres of the cavalry under von der Planitz. He wasn't especially impressed: 'Although their officers were good and strictly trained, they made quite glaring mistakes in the field and lacked initiative.'

But he was impressed by the two-hour march past a couple of days later of the thirty-four thousand men of the XII (Saxon) Army Corps before the Emperor of Germany and his staff, the King of Saxony with his entourage, and thousands of spectators. 'Quite a wonderful sight for uniformity and good drill. Infantry excellent. Cavalry ditto—especially Prussian Cuirassiers in white tunics and steel cuirass and helmets, with black and white lances.'

After the parade the royalties and their guests proceeded to the station to take their places in the special train that was to take them to Dresden for the evening's gala dinner. As B-P was hustling along to his carriage someone behind him called his name in an English voice. He turned and found himself face to face with Kaiser Wilhelm II.

The German Emperor was in his most genial mood. He chaffed Baden-Powell about the beauty of his full-dress uniform as compared with his South African Constabulary outfit, then asked him how he liked the parade—particularly, what did he think of the Uhlans' lances?

'The parade was magnificent,' B-P told the Emperor. 'But as for the lances I consider them too long for practical use.'

'And where could one get experience in the practical use of the lance?' Kaiser Wilhelm wanted to know.

'You could go in for pigsticking,' Baden-Powell suggested helpfully.

That might be very well for war purposes, the Kaiser agreed, if the 'pigs' were available, but in peace-time he found the lance of greater use for another purpose: 'For every inch you put onto the height of the lance,' he said, 'you add two feet to the lancer's self-esteem—and spirit is the thing to breed in peace-time.'

Kaiser Wilhelm became expansive. He made his British military confrère listen to his stories about his 'Uncle George' (the Duke of Cambridge) and about his 'Grandmama' (Queen Victoria). 'The way he did it tickled me considerably,' Baden-Powell reported later, 'and I couldn't help laughing'—particularly when the Kaiser confided to him with a straight face that he had had a scheme drawn up by his own staff for the use of the British reserves, but his 'Cousin Edward' (King Edward VII) had apparently felt disinclined to adopt it.

5

By the end of 1903, Baden-Powell had formulated his scheme for the reorganization and improvement of the British cavalry. He submitted it for their comments to the Duke of Connaught (now in line to become the Inspector-General of the whole British Army), Sir Evelyn Wood, John French (who commanded the cavalry division during the Boer War), Douglas Haig (who had just been appointed B-P's opposite number as Inspector-General of Cavalry in India) and other high-ranking officers. After receiving general approval of his suggestions he called a conference of officers representing the various branches of the cavalry to formulate detailed plans for the future.

During the next four years, through his untiring efforts, Baden-Powell saw a great number of his suggestions take effect.

A major step towards efficiency was the replacement of the pre-Boer

War skeleton establishment of cavalry regiments on the home roster with three effective cavalry brigades in England and one in Ireland under brigade generals—among the first-appointed were Allenby and Byng.

Baden-Powell arranged to get a Cavalry School established at Netheravon, Wiltshire, for training selected officers and N.C.O.s, and founded the *Cavalry Journal*—a monthly publication 'for the circulation of information concerning cavalry matters in our own and other armies. . . .'

For the proper training of the cavalry as B-P visualized it, the cavalry training manual of the day was completely inadequate. It had grown into a very portly volume and was badly out of date. Baden-Powell himself undertook to 'recompile' it, reducing its bulk by half and changing its high-faluting language into more common-place terms.

His men's quarters were of great concern to B-P. In his inspections he had found many cavalry barracks totally unfit for occupation. He sent in regular reports on barracks conditions to the War Office and followed them up vigorously until improvements were made. In addition to major improvements Baden-Powell also accomplished a great many minor ones. Among other things, he managed to get officers' expenses reduced and instituted mobilization practice in all regiments. He arranged to have better quality horses purchased and put horse-training on a new footing.

One big result of his many efforts was that the spirit of the British cavalry rose to a height it had seldom reached before in its long history.

6

In spite of his many busy hours at the War Office, his inspections and his participation in manoeuvres, Baden-Powell still found time to go abroad on occasion to continue his study of the cavalry and the cavalry training in other countries.

In France he visited the French Cavalry School at Saumur and was struck by the good all-round training. He was intrigued with the badge in the form of a star that he saw on the arm of some of the officers and enquired about its meaning. 'But, monsieur,' he was told, 'it is your badge, indicating the trained scout—except that we cannot use the fleur-de-lys because of its political significance in France and therefore have replaced it with a star.'

At the French manoeuvres at Bar-le-Duc he had a chance to compare the performance of the French cavalry with the work of the German that he had witnessed the year before. 'I had no shadow of doubt as to the superiority of the French, both in horsemanship and for practical work in the field and I told them so.' But the morale was at a low ebb. 'It is not Germany we are afraid of', a highly placed French officer told him.

'It is our own people. We do not know where we stand with one another.'
The debate in the French assembly over the bill to separate Church and
State had split the country into two factions, and the army was further
compromised as the last sordid act of the Dreyfus affair was being played
out on the public stage.

On other trips he took to the continent, the armies of Austria, Belgium
and Italy opened the doors of their cavalry establishments to the famous
British general. Invariably, B-P found some item of special interest that
might be adapted for use by the cavalry at home. The Belgian long-
distance riding competition was a case in point: 'It was a revelation to
see the great distances which could be accomplished without injury to the
horses by men who knew how to nurse them—and who could therefore
instruct and lead their men on long reconnaissances.'

7

As expected, the Duke of Connaught was appointed Inspector-General of
the Army and immediately entered upon a heavy schedule of inspections
of army units in Britain and overseas. In the autumn of 1906 he suggested
to Baden-Powell that it would be appropriate for B-P, in his capacity of
Inspector-General of Cavalry, to accompany him to South Africa for the
purpose of inspecting South African cavalry units while the Duke made
an official tour of the colonies.

B-P spent Christmas and New Year on a leisurely seventeen-day ocean
journey to Cape Town. He renewed his old friendship from India with
the Ducal couple and met several new friends—among them Rudyard
Kipling who was on a trip to South Africa with his wife and children.
After participating in the formal reception of the Duke of Connaught in
Cape Town, B-P was on his own. He went up-country by train for his
cavalry inspections.

He was back on the veld again, back again in the land that held so many
memories for him. There were still signs of Boer War days visible from
the train: 'The earthen mounds along the line mark the foundations of
blockhouses since removed; here and there parts of the wire entanglement
still stand with their old meat tins hanging to ring the alarm when stumbled
on at night; a broken girder in a spruit shows where a culvert had been
destroyed.' And every temporary slowing-up made him instinctively
think, 'Boers on the line!'

The next three weeks were busy weeks, 'nothing but hard work inspecting
from early morning till night', and train journeys over the veld to get
from one garrison to another. He inspected the cavalry units at Middel-
burg and Johannesburg, Pretoria and Potchefstroom, Bloemfontein and

Kimberley and got to Mafeking on 30 January, one day ahead of His Royal Highness.

He arrived unannounced at four in the morning and took a walk. 'At that hour of the morning it was exactly as if I were back in the siege again—in fact when an early market cart rattled over some stones I thought for the moment that it was musketry fire going on as of old. But when one comes to look for signs of the siege there are not many to see: all the defence works have been pulled down and trenches filled in. The damaged roofs and walls have all been repaired—and the streets have been improved and trees grown up so that it looks quite a neat, very respectable little country town now.'

As soon as Baden-Powell had established himself at the home of an old comrade-in-arms, visitors by the score began to arrive. Among them was a strapping young man of 19 whom B-P was particularly happy to see: he was the young Warner Goodyear who, at 13, had been the Sergeant-Major of the Mafeking Cadet Corps.

The tour of Mafeking the following day by the Duke and Duchess of Connaught was marred by a drenching mid-day downpour. But the Duke insisted on carrying out his programme nevertheless. He lunched with the town fathers, walked over the defence areas with B-P, dropped in at the hospital and inspected the garrison. On a visit to the Convent he chatted with the Sisters, all wearing their war medals with their bright ribbons on their sombre habits. In one of the main rooms of the Convent the Duke noticed a number of pockmarks in the wall, each of them marked by the word 'shell'.

'You must have had a hot time in this room during the siege,' he commented.

'Yes, Sir,' the Mother Superior agreed. 'It would have been quite to the point if the painter had omitted the "s" from that word in this room.'

With the reception at Mafeking Baden-Powell's duties were over until he should rejoin the Ducal party in British East Africa for the journey back to England. He left by train for Bulawayo and did in twenty-seven hours what had taken him ten days and ten nights by mule-wagon the first time he made the journey.

As he continued, he stopped for a look at the Victoria Falls. For years he had wanted to see these immense falls. A distant relative of his, William Cotton Oswell, had been the first white man to learn about them and to mark them on a map, in 1851. He spent a couple of days at the Falls sketching, trying to capture the overwhelming spectacle in his water-colours.

Salisbury was a different kind of revelation. When B-P was there about ten years before, 'the only signs of a town were a number of pickets driven into the ground, some spit-locked lines, and a few notice boards.' Now Salisbury was a flourishing town—the headquarters of the Government of Rhodesia.

On to Beira on the coast of Portuguese East Africa and north by steamer. At Mombasa he stepped ashore to join his brother Frank and his sister-in-law for a week of big-game safari in British East Africa, near Nairobi. He fell in love with the area and promised himself to return some time. 'This country is really most delightful—and though we are practically on the Equator it is not a bit hot. It consists of open plains of grass varied by thickly wooded hills and mountains . . . numerous streams and lakes . . . game abundant . . . delightful climate all the year round . . . wonderful views over the plains to the bold snowpeak of Mount Kenya.'

The three Baden-Powells went by train to Nakuru, then marched seven miles into the country accompanied by a long string of carriers, 'supplied by a contractor at a cost of about £35 per month in pay and £5 in food, for about forty men, including headmen, gun-bearers, cook, etc'. They had a successful shoot: zebra, hartebeeste, gazelle and a single impala buck.

After an excursion across Lake Victoria to Uganda, Baden-Powell rejoined the Ducal party at Mombasa for the homeward trip by way of the Suez Canal.

On his return to England, B-P received several generous offers from British publishers eager to publish a book on his recently completed trip to Africa. His popularity as a national hero was still high—a new book of his would have a good sale, especially if it contained the defender's own account, never before published, of the Siege of Mafeking.

B-P got busy, adding a heavy spare-time schedule of writing, sketching and painting to his already crowded military activities.

On 13 August, he could report to his mother that 'I've finished half my book about the African trip'. A month later he handed over to the publishers the completed manuscript together with the art work for the book and was paid 'enough to purchase my first automobile, a 45-h.p. Daimler—with £25 to spare'.

The publishing house of Smith, Elder & Co. did itself proud. *Sketches in Mafeking and East Africa* is the most spectacular of all Baden-Powell's books, with its full-colour plates of almost a dozen of his best water-colours, black-and-white reproductions of seventy more, and eighty line drawings. The text, on the other hand, leaves much to be desired. It is probably B-P's least inspired writing. It reflects clearly the hurried deadline conditions under which the book was written.

8

Baden-Powell's tenure as Inspector-General of Cavalry was drawing to a close. There was one major duty he still had to perform: he had to inspect the cavalry units of Egypt—they were part of his responsibility. His previous experiences in Egypt had amounted to quick passages through the Suez Canal, on the way to or from India or South Africa, with short stops at Port Said and Cairo.

Egypt had always held a fascination for him as a land of antiquity and mystery. His interest had been fanned by his mother's brother, Piazzi Smyth, the Astronomer Royal of Scotland, who in the early 1860s had become excited over John Taylor's theories about the Great Pyramid at Khufu—that its dimensions showed that the early Egyptians had solved the problem of 'squaring the circle', that its design had been divinely revealed to its constructor and held the key to the history of mankind. Although ridiculed by 'academic archaeology', Smyth became so inflamed with Taylor's theories that he went to Egypt himself to re-survey the Great Pyramid and to re-ascertain all its outside and inside measurements. He returned home after four months' work convinced of the correctness of Taylor's theories and with a number of theories and deductions of his own. His three-volume opus on the subject, *Life and Work at the Great Pyramid* (1867), caused a flurry of excitement. It became the forerunner of a number of books expounding extravagantly on the 'mysteries' of the Great Pyramid and using its measurements to prophesy the fate of the world. These prophecies persisted even after W. M. Flinders Petrie, the British Egyptologist, in 1881 had arrived at 'the ugly little fact which killed the beautiful theory'—the fact that previous proportionate measurements had been founded on a wrong assumption in regard to the base of the pyramid.

The first week that Piazzi Smyth's nephew spent in Egypt was a hectic one: 'Wednesday I called on all officials. Thursday, Friday and Saturday I have been inspecting from early morning till evening. . . . Monday and Tuesday more inspections.'

He did manage to get out to the Pyramids on the Sunday and here met the untiring Professor Flinders Petrie who was in charge of the latest excavations.

It was from Petrie that B-P learned that his very existence had depended on a quirk of fate: Petrie's father, William Petrie, had courted Baden-Powell's mother before her marriage to Professor Powell but had found no favour with the girl's parents. Before his infatuation had grown into a romance, Mrs Smyth had spirited Henrietta Grace off to visit friends in Cambridge and William had found another love in one of Henrietta Grace's best friends.

On his way up into Egypt, B-P stopped for a few days at Luxor ('Tourists are in crowds here . . . the large proportion Americans and Germans. Most of them maiden ladies of a certain age'). He rode on a 'trotting donkey' to the ruins of Karnak and spent a whole day sketching the temple and the two Colossi of 'Memnon' rising in majestic grandeur outside Thebes.

The Colossi of Amenophis—a sample of the pen-and-ink sketches with which Baden-Powell illustrated his travel diaries.

After stopping at Aswan to see the 'enormous modern dam' just then under construction, B-P went by steamer up the Nile for two days and continued by train across the open desert to Shendo. Here he inspected squadrons of Egyptian and Sudanese cavalry 'at home in their sandy cantonments with drill on the desert'.

His visit to Khartoum turned into a 'sentimental journey'. Every moment was a reminder of General 'Chinese' Gordon's ill-fated mission and his tragic end.

Khartoum was 'very much what I had pictured it from reading of Gordon's defence of it—but now enormously modernized'. The steamer that took him across the river to the steps of the palace was 'the same one which waited at those steps for Gordon to escape in—which he could have done when the palace was stormed, but he would not go'. B-P's room was located almost at the spot where Gordon had had his look-out. And the place where Gordon was killed, at the top of the stairs, was 'just below my bedroom door'.

Baden-Powell was entertained royally at Khartoum by Slatin Pasha, the Austrian-born Rudolph Carl von Slatin, Inspector-General of the Sudan. Slatin Pasha himself had been caught up in the holy war that engulfed Gordon and his men. He had been a prisoner of Mohammed Ahmed for twelve years until he finally made his escape with the help of a member of the Egyptian intelligence department.

Slatin Pasha accompanied his honoured guest to the field manoeuvres of the Sudanese infantry and artillery. He walked him all over the Mahdi's capital and showed him the mud hut in which he had been a prisoner in chains on the fateful morning of 26 January 1885 when Khartoum fell and the Mahdists showed him General Gordon's severed head as proof of their victory.

Of even greater interest to Baden-Powell was his visit with Slatin Pasha to the remains of Gordon's fortifications. B-P, on the basis of his own familiarity with the holding of a town, could not help but wonder about the dispositions that had been taken at Khartoum: 'Why did Gordon spread out his defence over such a very long single line with distant outposts at Omdurman Tutu and Elephant's Trunk [the point of the peninsula where the White and the Blue Nile meet]? A small circle of independent forts with short lengths of obstacle between should have done it better.'

Baden-Powell had hardly returned from his trip to Egypt before he was off to various parts of England and Ireland for further cavalry inspections —one a week for each of the six weeks that remained of his military stint.

On 5 May, 1907, his term as Inspector-General of Cavalry came to an end. The occasion was celebrated at a sumptuous dinner with close to a dozen British generals present, among them Sir Douglas Haig, Edmund Allenby, Julian Byng.

The next day, Baden-Powell handed the duties of his office over to his successor and was lauded by the Duke of Connaught. 'B-P,' the Duke said, 'had done more than any other Inspector-General for the cavalry.' On 10 June, he was advanced to Lieutenant-General and placed on the Reserve at half pay pending his next appointment.

After thirty years in the Army, Baden-Powell was a free man at last, with no military responsibilities for the time being. He could indulge in any fad that struck his fancy.

And the fad was there ready for him to give it his full attention.

LIFE NUMBER TWO
THE CHIEF SCOUT OF THE WORLD

How lucky for B-P that he was not in the early years of the century taken into the central swim of military affairs, and absorbed in all those arduous and secret preparations which ultimately enabled the British Expeditionary Army to deploy for battle at Mons!

How lucky for him, and how lucky for us all! To this he owes his perennially revivifying fame, his opportunity for high personal service of the most enduring character; and to this we owe an institution and an inspiration, characteristic of the essence of British genius, and uniting in a bond of comradeship the youth not only of the English-speaking world, but of almost every land and people under the sun.

WINSTON S. CHURCHILL

The Genesis of an Idea

Years: 1904–07   Age: 47–50

1

At four o'clock on the afternoon of Saturday, 30 April 1904, Baden-Powell rode on to Yorkhill Drill Ground in Glasgow, Scotland. Dressed in his general's uniform, mounted on a lively black charger and escorted by a party of the 17th Lancers, he made a spectacular entrance. He had come to Scotland to inspect the Lancers and had arranged to combine this task with another: to act as Inspecting Officer of the Annual Drill Inspection and Review of the Boys' Brigade on the occasion of the organization's coming-of-age. Almost a year before, in May 1903, he had presided in the Albert Hall, London, over the largest indoor gathering of the Brigade ever assembled. Now he was to witness the Brigade's activities in an outdoor setting.

The Boys' Brigade had been started in Glasgow in 1883 by a Scottish merchant, William Alexander Smith, a lieutenant in the 1st Lanark Rifle Volunteers and a dedicated Sunday school teacher. 'Finding', according to the *Glasgow Weekly Herald*, 'that some of the unruly, unwashed boys belonging to his Sunday school were entirely beyond the range of ordinary methods of discipline, Lieutenant Smith became inspired with the idea of turning the lads into young soldiers. So he put uniforms on their backs and rifles in their hands. The result was so marvellous, and the transformation in the manners, morals, and discipline of the lads so striking, that Lieutenant Smith's example was followed far and near.'

The declared purpose of the Boys' Brigade was: 'The advancement of Christ's Kingdom among Boys, and the promotion of habits of Obedience, Reverence, Discipline, Self-respect, and all that tends towards a true Christian Manliness.' Smith's organization met with success in Great Britain and in several other countries. On its twenty-first birthday it

17

could pride itself on a membership of fifty-four thousand boys in the British Isles alone.

The Drill Inspection and Review was an impressive affair, with seven thousand youngsters going through their 'evolutions' before eleven thousand 'ticket-holder onlookers'. Time and again the audience broke into enthusiastic applause over the boys' manoeuvring. The loudest applause followed the main feature of the drill when, as reported in the *Glasgow Evening Citizen*, 'the youthful soldiers, many of whom were hardly as tall as the toy guns they carried', marched past the inspecting officer 'in quarter column, the boys keeping almost perfect step, carrying their heads erect, and maintaining a well-balanced line as they crossed the field before the inspecting officer'.

The enthusiasm of the boys and their leaders opened Baden-Powell's eyes to two important facts: 'that boys would come eagerly in their thousands of their own accord to be trained where the training had its attractions for them . . . that hundreds of adults were willing to sacrifice time and energy in the service of training these boys.' But the programme bothered him: the playing at being soldiers—the marching, the drilling, the uniforms, the imitation arms, the military aspects of the bands. In working with men in the Army, he had moved further and further away from formal drill to a programme for developing individual pluck, intelligence, initiative, a spirit of adventure. Yet here, in the training of boys, formal military drill was being used.

As the boys marched off the field, Baden-Powell turned to Smith who had been at his side on horseback during the march past. He congratulated the Boys' Brigade founder on the turn-out but added 'chaffingly' that the Brigade, to his way of thinking, should have many more members than it had—and would have ten times the number with more variety and attraction in the training.

Without a moment's hesitation, Smith agreed—and instantly challenged Baden-Powell to develop a programme that would provide that added 'variety and attraction'. He specifically suggested that it might be done through a boys' version of B-P's small book, *Aids to Scouting*.

The two men rode off the Drill Ground, and found themselves engulfed in a mass of boys and adults wildly cheering the 'Hero of Mafeking'. It took the concentrated effort of all B-P's escorting Lancers to open a path for him and his companion and to conduct them off the ground.

Back at his headquarters Baden-Powell wrote out a report of the review and sent it off to Smith. After complimenting the boys and their leaders and summing up the results of his inspection as 'most satisfactory', B-P presented his first suggestions for the Brigade:

Boys should try to do everything to make themselves strong and healthy so as to become good, able-bodied citizens when they grow up. A great step towards this would be to encourage the practice of free gymnastics or physical exercises more frequently on parade, and also on every opportunity at home.

Something might, I think, also be done towards developing the boy's mind by increasing his powers of observation, and teaching him to notice details. I believe that if some form of scout training could be devised in the Brigade it would be very popular and could do a great amount of good. Preliminary training in this line might include practice in noting and remembering details of strangers, contents of shop windows, appearance of new streets, etc. The results would not only sharpen the wits of the boy, but would also make him quick to read character and feelings, and thus help him to be a better sympathizer with his fellow-man.

2

Baden-Powell had come home in the spring of 1903 to an England he didn't know. Except for a few short leaves, he had been away from home for close on ten years—removed from an awareness of the social changes that were taking place.

He had left an England that was steeped in conservatism. Queen Victoria, with her fixed principles in regard to her exalted position, had been the steadying influence through the 'industrial revolution' that had changed Britain from an agricultural country to the most highly industrialized nation in the world. Lord Salisbury, Her Majesty's Prime Minister and the leader of the Conservative Party, had upheld and perpetuated the Victorian creed that the success of Britain as a world power was due to a properly qualified ruling class guiding the British democracy. People knew their 'places'. The 'higher classes' considered themselves the upholders of tradition and continuity, the defenders of Church and State. And the 'lower classes' acquiesced to the point of voting Conservative— or, at the very most, Liberal—rather than striking out politically on their own. Victoria's Empire had carried on with tranquillity at home and in 'splendid isolation' towards the rest of the world.

B-P had returned to a different England—a country that was no longer tranquil and no longer truly conservative.

The staid decorum of the sombre court of the 'Widow of Windsor' had given way to the gay sociability of her son, King Edward VII. Outwardly, the early Edwardian age was an era of festivity, of a fabulously wealthy high society taking the spotlight—and getting the headlines in the halfpenny press, the *Daily Mail* and the *Daily Express*. Next to a juicy murder, nothing seemed of greater interest to the general populace than some extravagant society affair. But below the glittering surface, a great number of currents were running.

Politically, the country was in turmoil. Chamberlain had come home from his trip to South Africa with a dream of economic unity for the Empire. In a speech at Birmingham on 15 May 1903 he threw British politics into an uproar by a demand for a tariff system that would place a tax on foodstuffs and merchandise from foreign countries while providing special financial concessions to imports from the British dominions and colonies. It was his contention that such a system involving 'Imperial preference' would strengthen the bonds of Empire by tying the overseas realms more closely to the mother country. His Tariff Reform proposal split his own Conservative party from top to bottom. The Liberals—out of office for almost twenty years except for the three embarrassing years of 1892–95—were jubilant. Here they finally had an issue that could be understood by the electorate: Chamberlain's protective tariffs would mean 'dearer food' while the continuation of the doctrine of Free Trade that had been a corner-stone of British policy for more than fifty years would guarantee the 'big loaf of bread'.

The political waves kept surging higher and higher. The Conservative Prime Minister, Arthur Balfour—Lord Salisbury's nephew—fought to keep his party on an even keel. But it was obvious that the Conservative Party was losing its popularity. Less than three years after Chamberlain's pronouncement the Liberals swept the Conservatives out of office in the greatest electoral upheaval since 1833—a landslide of 397 Liberals against 157 Conservatives. Sir Henry Campbell-Bannerman took over as Prime Minister. He brought into his cabinet H. H. Asquith, Sir Edward Grey, R. B. Haldane, D. Lloyd George—and, incidentally, gave the office of Under-Secretary of State for the Colonies to a promising young politician by the name of Winston Churchill.

It was not just the Liberals who gained by the general election of 1906. A brand-new party—the Labour Party—came into being. For a number of years different labour groups—trade unions, the Social Democratic Federation, the Fabian Society, the Independent Labour Party—had gone their own various ways. It was not until the turn of the century that they effected a political coalition and set out to establish a distinct working-class party. Their concerted effort in the campaign was a success. Twenty-nine Labour members were swept into parliament on the tide that engulfed the Conservatives.

But beyond the doings of high society and the debates of politicians there were things that were causing great concern to thoughtful people.

Although the South African War had ended, its effects lingered on. The slackening of morals that always accompanies a major war persisted and deepened. The artificial prosperity of the war days had been followed by a general depression of trade. Wages had dropped. Unemployment had risen, aggravated by the return of reservists from the war. There was a daily procession of unemployed, many of them youths in their teens, carrying collection boxes in the London streets.

A report of conditions in the British capital, just published after exhaustive study, revealed the shocking fact that 30 per cent of the population of London—a city that prided itself on being the richest in the world—were suffering from malnutrition. Another report showed that of more than two million school boys, only about a quarter of a million were under any kind of 'good' influence after school hours. The terrible consequences of life in the slums of the larger British cities were becoming more and more evident. Crime and drunkenness were on the upsurge. Vandalism and vice were rampant—particularly among the younger generation. Hooliganism was becoming a cause of public anxiety. Special places of detention for youths—among them Borstal in Kent—were filled to overflowing.

As Baden-Powell travelled round Britain, he found great poverty in the midst of extravagant affluence. He had seen barefooted, ragged waifs begging in the streets. He had witnessed the decrease of active participation in sports and a vast increase in 'spectatoritis', with mobs of youngsters turning out simply to watch. His heart sickened at seeing these 'thousands of boys and young men, pale, narrow-chested, hunched-up, miserable specimens, smoking endless cigarettes, numbers of them betting.'

And all this at a time when Britain needed to be stronger than ever before—at a time when a surge of anti-British feeling was rampant in Europe; when Germany, the leading member of the powerful Triple Alliance, was reaching out for greater and yet greater empire status by strengthening her army and building a navy second only to Britain's; when France was expanding her influence in Africa and Russia hers in the Far East.

The challenge of Smith at the time of the Boys' Brigade Drill Inspection —to provide a programme of activities for boys—had struck home.

Was this challenge, Baden-Powell wondered, the answer to a question he had asked himself a thousand times since the—to his mind—'unexpected, unearned, and unsought notoriety' occasioned by the defence of Mafeking had been thrust upon him? 'Could there be some higher purpose underlying it? Was it a call to me? Could it be utilized to some good end? If so, in what way would I act up to it?'

B-P had marvelled at the way in which the holding of Mafeking had caught the imagination not only of the adults but also of the youth of the Empire. While he was still in Africa engaged in guerilla fighting and in establishing the South African Constabulary, he had received letters by the score from boys and girls asking for advice, and letters by the dozen from various youth organizations requesting 'messages' for their members. He had religiously prepared longhand answers to all the letters, trying to reply to the letter-writers' questions and adding a bit of inspiration and philosophy of his own. In these answers he had repeatedly held up as valuable assets for successful living some of the old-fashioned virtues that had been inculcated in him in his childhood—the virtues of obedience ('One thing you must learn before you can be a good soldier', he had written to one boy, 'and that is to be obedient to your superior officer'), preparedness and devotion to duty ('Be prepared to take such place as duty directs'), cheerfulness ('Be happy—for "cheeriness is next to Godliness" '), helpfulness ('Make up your mind to do at least one "good turn" to somebody every day').

He had expected that the obvious idolatry that shone through the letters sent to him would disappear as the glitter of his 'notoriety' wore off, that the excitement of seeing the 'Hero of Mafeking', of getting near him, of shaking his hand would soon lose its appeal. This had not happened. Three years, four years seemed to have had little diminishing effect on the hero worship. It had had one of its most extravagant expressions at the Drill Inspection and Review of the Boys' Brigade.

Smith's challenge stayed with him for two busy years, during military inspection trips, manoeuvres in England and Ireland, France and Italy, during the establishment of the Cavalry School at Netheravon and the birth pangs of starting the *Cavalry Journal*. And it went with him on his trip to South Africa with the Duke of Connaught.

Only after he got back home in the middle of April 1906 did he find time to sketch out some of his preliminary thinking. He sent a copy of his programme suggestions—which he called 'Scouting for Boys'—off to William A. Smith. To find out whether he was on the track of something worth while, he mailed other copies to a number of men whose opinions he valued.

One of the first of these men to answer him was his old idol, Lord Roberts. On 1 May 1906, Roberts sent his reactions to Baden-Powell—and used the opportunity to give B-P a couple of realistic pointers:

Dear Baden-Powell, I am much obliged . . . for sending me your paper on training boys in scouting. I like the idea and think it may have good results. Boys are very receptive and would enjoy the delights of such training if it were carried out in a satisfactory manner. Good instructors would be needed, and I suppose a certain amount of financial assistance would be required. . . .

Hoping that your scheme may be given a fair trial—Believe me—

Yours sincerely,

ROBERTS

William A. Smith thought enough of the 'paper' Baden-Powell had sent him to forward it to the editor of *The Boys' Brigade Gazette*. But the material was so entirely different from the usual articles in the *Gazette* that the editor was somewhat confounded. He had an article in hand from one of the most famous of Britons—yet much of what the author had to say ran counter to the traditional organization and activities of the Brigade. What should he do? The *Gazette* editor solved his dilemma by cutting B-P's material to the bone and prefacing it with a couple of paragraphs of rather condescending editorial comment.

The article, published in the June 1906 issue of the *Gazette*, suggested a number of activities that boys might undertake in city parks and in the country. But instead of employing the company formation used in the Boys' Brigade for some new kind of semi-military drill, B-P's recommendations were for things that a boy could do alone or in a small group: observation and deduction, first aid and distance judging. Instead of formal callisthenics as practised in the Brigade for physical fitness, B-P suggested using the skills of hiking and camping: tracking and swimming, fire lighting 'using two matches only', cooking 'without the help of cooking utensils', competing in a 'scouting race' involving the use of compass.

This first published version of Baden-Powell's ideas of 'Scouting for Boys' had little effect. There was nothing particularly exciting about it, especially not in the *Gazette* editor's condensed version. Nevertheless, the article presented a series of outdoor skills that might very well fit into a version for boys of *Aids to Scouting*. It also contained a first attempt at lining up a series of qualifying tests in outdoor skills.

3

Smith was not the only one who had seen the educational values of *Aids to Scouting*. B-P had learned, after coming home from the Boer War, that a number of educators had actually made use of his book as a supplementary teaching aid.

His old friend General Allenby had told him of one of these uses which he had learned about in a rather special way. One day as the General

was riding home from parade, he had been startled by a shout. It was
his small son Michael calling to him: 'Father, you're shot! I ambushed
you. You didn't see me!'

Now Allenby looked up: his son was sitting on a branch high above
him. But to the General's amazement the boy's governess, Miss Katarina
Loveday, was sitting on another branch even higher up.

'What on earth are you doing up there?' the General asked the governess.

'Oh, I am teaching him scouting,' Miss Loveday said.

Yes, she explained after climbing down from the tree, she was teaching
Michael scouting in accordance with *Aids to Scouting*. B-P's book had
been one of her textbooks at Miss Charlotte Mason's Teachers' Training
College at Ambleside where she had been trained as a governess. It had
been Miss Mason's contention that practice of observation and deduction
was a vital point in modern education and that Baden-Powell's small
volume was the best book on the subject.

B-P hadn't looked at his small military manual for a couple of years.
Now the more he studied the pages the more he realized the difficulty of
turning *Aids to Scouting* into a book that would serve the purposes of the
Boys' Brigade and other existing boys' organizations. All army references
would have to be taken out—all mention of army procedures and war
conditions. The only parts suitable for a book for boys were some of the
games and practices, some of the anecdotes about tracking and stalking.
The whole basis of the book was wrong. This was a book for training
men for war. What was needed was a book for training boys for peace.

The further Baden-Powell delved into the subject, the more evident it
became to him that in writing the book that was slowly evolving in his
mind, he would have to go beyond merely lining up the attractive activities
that Smith had asked for. To get boys to undertake a more exacting
programme they would need a more appealing reason than that proclaimed by the Boys' Brigade. Also, to make the training of the individual
boy more effective, an organization different from the Brigade's companies
of twenty to thirty boys or more would have to be devised.

Having gone so far, B-P decided to go all the way and consider the
whole problem of training boys for citizenship.

He turned for help to the books that crowded the bookshelves of 32
Princes Gate—some of them books from his father's library that had
influenced him as a youngster, many of them books he had gathered over
the years on subjects ranging from history to outdoor living, from nature
to health, from civics to adventure in outposts of the Empire.

He went back two thousand years to Epictetus's philosophy of character
and conduct and of methods of instilling them in youth, and to Livy's

ideas about voluntary associations of boys for improving their physique and developing their patriotism. He got Frazer's *Golden Bough* down from the shelf and studied its descriptions of the manhood training methods of primitive peoples—Zulus and Polynesians, Australian aborigines and American Indians—and consulted other books describing the training of boys in Sparta and old Japan, in Ancient Britain and Ireland. He pored over Kenelm Henry Digby's *Broadstone of Honour or The True Sense and Practice of Chivalry* with its detailed accounts of the training of the medieval page, squire and knight, and the code by which they lived.

He studied the works of Johann Friedrich Ludwig Jahn, the father of German gymnastics, and looked into the methods of dealing with boys of John Pounds, the old shoemaker of Portsmouth who had originated the 'ragged schools', and of Johann Heinrich Pestalozzi, the Swiss educational reformer. He investigated thoroughly the rules and regulations and administration of existing youth organizations—the Boys' Brigade, the Church Lads' Brigade, Lord Rodney's Cadets, Forbush's Knights of King Arthur and several others.

And finally, he consulted military and civilian leaders he knew were concerned with the coming generation—Lords Roberts and Grey, Rodney and Strathcona; Stephen Gwynne and Quintin Hogg, Jr.; as well as several officials of the London Polytechnic and of the Y.M.C.A.

In the midst of all these studies, he suddenly received help from an unexpected source.

4

At the end of July 1906, a small book arrived in the mail. Its title: *The Birch-bark Roll of the Woodcraft Indians*. Its author: Ernest Thompson Seton, a British citizen living in the United States.

Ernest Thompson Seton was born in 1860 at South Shields, Durham, England, as the eighth of ten sons of a Scottish shipowner. In 1866, after serious reverses had almost wiped out his father's business, the whole family emigrated to Canada. Ernest spent his early boyhood in the primitive backwoods around Lindsay, Ontario, and came to know and to love the wild animals and their ways. In 1872, the family moved to Toronto. Here, in 1879, Ernest received a gold medal from the Ontario Art School for his sketches of Canadian wild life. As a result, his father decided to send him to London to study art. His artistic ability was so well developed that he obtained a welcome scholarship at the Royal Academy School of Painting and Sculpture.

Called back to Canada in 1881, the young Seton accepted the position of naturalist for the provincial government of Manitoba. Almost immediately, a steady stream of illustrated articles about North American wild life began to flow from his pen. By 1883, Seton had made up his mind to make writing and illustrating his lifework. He went to New York where he knew that he would have his greatest chance of success. Soon after, Seton's animal stories made their appearance in American magazines of a wide editorial range.

In 1898, Charles Scribner's Sons published Seton's first book, *Wild Animals I Have Known*, illustrated by more than two hundred of the marginal pen-and-ink drawings that became a Seton trademark. The book, an instantaneous hit, made Seton popular as a naturalist-artist-writer. It was followed by the equally successful *Biography of a Grizzly* and *Lives of the Hunted*.

Because of the great appeal of Seton's writings to youngsters, the *Ladies' Home Journal* asked him to prepare a series of articles for a 'New Department on "American Woodcraft" for Boys'. The first of these articles appeared in the magazine in May 1902 under the title of 'Ernest Thompson Seton's Boys'.

By the time the series of seven articles on woodcraft and Indian lore had run its course, a number of tribes of 'Seton's Indians' or 'Woodcraft Indians' had sprung up across America. Numerous requests arrived at the office of the magazine for reprints. Seton accommodated his readers by collecting the articles into a pamphlet, *How to Play Injun*, and reprinting it in several editions as the need arose. Finally in 1906, he arranged with the publishers of his books to bring out the fifth edition of his material in the form of a small book under the title of *The Birch-bark Roll of the Woodcraft Indians*.

In addition to his success as an author and illustrator, Seton had become a popular lecturer. He had lectured in England in 1904 and was planning a return visit in the autumn of 1906. In arranging for the tour, he decided to send copies of *The Birch-bark Roll* to persons in England who had been reported to him as interested in work with boys. One of them went to Baden-Powell.

On receiving Seton's book, Baden-Powell sent a letter to the author thanking him for his kindness.

> It may interest you to know [he added] that I had been drawing up a scheme with a handbook to it, for the education of boys as scouts —which curiously runs much on the lines of yours. So I need scarcely say your work has a very special interest for me.

Each man was eager to meet the other, Seton to secure the co-operation of the 'Hero of Mafeking' in extending his Woodcraft Indians in Great Britain, Baden-Powell to find out from the well-known author how his ideas about the training of boys differed from his own. And so, on 30 October, the 46-year-old naturalist-writer and the 49-year-old general lunched together at the Savoy Hotel and struck up an easy friendship.

B-P was intrigued with what Seton told him of his Woodcraft Indians and of the scouting practices of the American Indian. Although he doubted whether Seton's 'Red Indian Boys' Scheme' would appeal to the English boy, he found certain aspects of it worth noting in his diary:

> Each 'camp' ruled by its own council. Each boy begins with a scalp which he loses if he fails to do something—and can only redeem by payment. He gains feathers and badges by qualifying in various subjects (all outdoor)—no competition, only qualifying. Scouting practices good.

The day after their meeting, Baden-Powell sent Seton his *Aids to Scouting* and a copy of the material he had prepared earlier that year regarding his ideas on 'Scouting for Boys'. In an accompanying letter he wrote:

> You will see that our principles seem practically identical—except that mine do not necessarily make their own organization; they are applicable to existing ones. If we can work together in the same direction I should be very glad indeed—for I'm sure that there are great possibilities before us.

During the next two months, the two men made several efforts to meet again—but each time, a Seton lecture or a Baden-Powell inspection tour kept them apart. They got together by correspondence only—through which Seton secured B-P's promise of assistance in revising the Campcraft section of *The Birch-bark Roll* for the sixth printing and Baden-Powell got Seton's permission to use some of the games of the Woodcraft Indians in his programme.

Whereupon the two men went off in different directions: Seton back to America, Baden-Powell to Africa for his last task as Inspector-General of Cavalry.

5

It was Baden-Powell's firm intention, during his inspection trip to the Egyptian Sudan to work out a more comprehensive draft of his Boy Scouts scheme. He finished a résumé of it eleven days out from London, just before his ship reached Port Said on 5 February 1907.

BOY PATROLS.

(in response to a number of reps)

The following is the outline of a scheme which I offer for the consideration of officers of Boys' Clubs, Brigades, Cadet Corps as other such organizations for boys, masters of schools of all denominations, members of YMCA, clergymen, County Settlements, and others interested in our rising future, whether at home or in the colonies.

OBJECT (Big type) — To help in making the rising generation, of whatever class or creed, into good citizens or useful colonists.

REASONS — This idea has been prompted by:
The existing urgent need of development among the rising generation of the many qualities tending to good citizenship in our Nation;

The want of attractiveness in some of the existing organizations for boys.

The want of novelty felt in all such organizations for keeping up the boys' interest. Numerous requests made to me for suggestions.

METHOD — By giving, under the name of "Scouting", a novel as attractive form of training in manly qualities.

It can be applied to any existing organization or where such does not exist it can without difficulty be run on its own lines.

Applicable to town or country, at home or in a Colony.

Might also be extended to the training of girls.

Inexpensive, easy, as interesting for the officers.

SUBJECTS — Instruction in Scoutcraft including observation, tracking, deduction, woodcraft, watermanship, life saving, health, thrift, self-sacrifice, discipline, responsibility, chivalry & patriotism.

GAMES — For further practice as for maintaining interest in these a number of games as competitions have been devised, with certain "Honours" attaching to them.

HANDBOOK — An inexpensive illustrated handbook, "Scouting for Boys", is being drawn up, containing (giving all details as) progressive course of lessons which will enable an untrained instructor, though untrained himself, to teach his boys;—or it can be put in the hands of a boy for his own self-instruction. Any profits from the sale of the work will be devoted to organization of the Boys Patrols.

Baden-Powell's attempt, in February 1907, at further developing his Scouting scheme.

The title of the résumé—'Boy Patrols'—indicated clearly Baden-Powell's conviction that the training of boys for citizenship could best be done in small groups, with the boys themselves, as far as possible, responsible for their training: a bold new approach never before attempted in an organized youth movement.

In the résumé, B-P for the first time spelled out explicitly his aim in undertaking work with boys ('Object: To help existing organizations in making the rising generation, of whatever class or creed, into good citizens or useful colonists'), the activities he intended to promote ('Subjects: Instruction in Scoutcraft including observation, tracking, deduction, woodcraft, watermanship, life-saving, health, thrift, self-sacrifice, discipline, responsibility, chivalry, and patriotism'), and the organization he planned to use ('Organization: A "Patrol" is formed of six boys under a senior boy as "Patrol Leader". From four to ten patrols form a "Troop" under an officer as "Scoutmaster" ').

Back in England, his tenure of the post of Inspector-General of Cavalry completed, Baden-Powell had the time, at last, to devote himself to his new project.

First—and of primary importance—was the task of getting his ideas more sharply defined in a prospectus he could use to interest people in his cause.

He revised his early résumé of 'Boy Patrols' and prepared an accompanying statement that would explain the needs of his scheme and asked for suggestions or criticisms. To lead off this statement he chose the words of a prominent contemporary British politician, George Wyndham:

'The same causes which brought about the downfall of the Great Roman Empire are working today in Great Britain.'

These words [B-P continued] were spoken the other day by one of your best known democratic politicians, and their truth is practically admitted by those who have studied and compared the general conditions of both countries.

The main cause of the downfall of Rome was the decline of good citizenship among its subjects, due to want of energetic patriotism, to the growth of luxury and idleness, and to the exaggerated importance of local party politics, etc.

Personally I am not pessimistic enough to think with some people that we are already so far on the downward grade as to be hopeless: on the contrary, I think we are only near to the parting of the ways where it becomes incumbent upon every one of us who has the slightest patriotism in him to earnestly help, in however small a way, to turn the rising generation on to the right road for good citizenship.

To this end the following scheme is offered as a possible aid towards putting on a positive footing the development, moral and physical, of boys of all creeds and classes, by a means which should appeal to them while offending as little as possible the susceptibility of their elders.

It is intended to be applicable—and not in opposition—to any existing organization for boys, such as schools, boys' brigades, messengers, cadet corps, etc. or it can supply an organization of its own where these do not exist. . . .

Finally satisfied, he sent his drafts off to be printed in the form of two four-page circulars—*Boy Scouts, A Suggestion* and *Boy Scouts, Summary of Scheme*. He left instructions with the printer to mail the finished circulars to a number of his friends and left for the fishing holiday he had promised himself upon stepping down from the Army to the Reserve.

On the way he stayed the night at Sheffield on 9 May to inspect the local Boys' Brigade, according to a promise previously made, and used the opportunity that evening to expound his ideas by giving a 'lecture on scouting to a very big audience including a hundred members of the Young Men's Christian Association—and I am glad to say that though entirely unrehearsed and unprepared, the lecture was a complete success and lasted an hour and a half!' This was the first of hundreds of such lectures recorded in his diary.

After two weeks, pleasurably fishing in Ireland, B-P returned to London to find in his mail a number of enthusiastic endorsements of his scheme. Several writers expressed their happiness that B-P was interesting himself in teaching boys good citizenship and patriotism. They all encouraged him to go ahead with developing his scheme further and placing in the hands of the boys of Britain, as promised in the prospectus, the 'small handbook which is intended to serve either as a textbook for instructors or as a self-educator for individual boys'.

As soon as Baden-Powell realized that the handbook would have to be a brand-new book rather than a rewritten *Aids to Scouting*, he had started to use the same incubator system that had worked so successfully before in developing ideas for articles and in writing his book on *Pigsticking*. He brought out his old tin dispatch-box and began putting into it, in old envelopes and spring book-covers, anything that he thought might have a bearing on the subject: suitable anecdotes, suggestions for games and practices, ideas for enticing boys to take up scouting.

He considered in turn each of the publishing houses that had published his previous books: Methuen, Gale & Polden, Heinemann, Smith & Elder. Any one of them would probably be interested in publishing the book he had in mind. But he would require more than a book publisher this time. He needed someone who, in addition to publishing the proposed book at the lowest possible price, had the means of publicizing and promoting the whole Boy Scouts scheme. He came to the conclusion that C. Arthur Pearson Ltd. might be the publishing house best suited and that C. Arthur Pearson might be his man.

6

Cyril Arthur Pearson, in 1884, as an 18-year-old apprentice, had accepted a clerkship at £100 a year in the office of *Tit-Bits*, one of the highly popular George Newnes papers. Within two years he was the manager of *Tit-Bits* and, three years later, of Newnes's *Review of Reviews* as well.

But the young Pearson's dream went much further than managing someone else's property. In 1890 he borrowed £3,000, persuaded a couple of colleagues from *Tit-Bits* to join him and set out on his own publishing career with *Pearson's Weekly*—a magazine intended 'to interest, to elevate, to amuse'. In 1900, he jumped into the daily newspaper field by buying the *Morning Herald*—a title soon changed to the *Daily Express and Morning Herald*—a halfpenny paper in competition with Alfred C. W. Harmsworth's *Daily Mail*. Shortly afterwards he added the *Standard* and the *Evening Standard* to his stable and, in rapid succession, half a dozen Midland papers.

The largest of the Pearson papers used 'yellow journalism', reaching great circulations—partly because of their breezy journalistic style, partly by their use of competitions and free insurance policies for their readers. One of their more altruistic promotions was The Pearson Fresh Air Fund which, every summer, gave thousands of slum children from the big cities a health-giving holiday far from the crowded streets.

Baden-Powell had spent a week-end in July 1906 as a guest of Pearson at the publisher's country estate at Frensham Place in Surrey. The expansive Pearson had made it a habit during the summer months to invite parties of statesmen, military men, authors, and members of the publishing profession to spend the week-ends at his home. B-P's stay there had been filled with interesting conversation and excellent food, and he had had a chance to see the human side of Pearson when the publisher had invited him to join him for a motor ride to the Guildford Crippled Children's Hospital—one of Pearson's 'causes'.

It was to this man—publisher, philanthropist, and politician—described by Joseph Chamberlain as 'the greatest hustler I have ever known'—that Baden-Powell turned for the publishing of his book and the promotion of his scheme.

He arranged to meet Pearson for dinner on 5 June 1907, and quickly convinced the publisher of the value of the Boy Scouts scheme. It was obvious to both of them that, to speed the scheme into reality, the handbook envisaged by Baden-Powell should be made available at an early date. But how? To assure the greatest possible dissemination it might be advisable to print it first in several parts for sale through all the country's bookstalls. If published in this way by, say, Horace Cox who did much of Pearson's printing, the parts could be distributed by Messrs C. Arthur Pearson Ltd. through their regular outlets. It was equally obvious that, once the scheme was launched, Baden-Powell would have to keep in touch with his followers. A weekly newspaper—a vigorous magazine for boys in which the General could further explain and promote his scheme— might prove an acceptable addition to Pearson's line of weekly publications.

Before committing himself, Pearson suggested that Baden-Powell get some of the chapters for his proposed book into shape for printing. In the meantime he would consult his associates.

B-P was ready at last for some concentrated writing on his projected handbook on scouting. There was little chance of working without disturbance in London. But he knew a perfect place for getting work done —and for doing a bit of fishing as well. On 15 June, he packed up his tin dispatch-case, took the train for the Midlands, put up at the Izaak Walton Hotel in Dovedale near Ashbourne in Derbyshire, and started writing.

While at Dovedale, B-P got qualms about throwing his lot in with Pearson—not Pearson the publisher, but Pearson the politician. What would be the effect on the scheme if it appeared to have political connotations? What would happen to it if it were used as a promotion stunt for a magazine? Remembering that Seton had launched his Woodcraft Indians through an American magazine, he dropped a note asking for his opinion. After receiving Seton's assurance that the proposition seemed feasible, B-P was satisfied. From then on, his diary became filled with notations such as: 'A. Pearson for breakfast,' 'Lunch with A. Pearson', 'Pearson—dinner'.

It had been his plan to continue working on his book in Dovedale, but he had a number of appointments scheduled in London. Since Dovedale was too far away, he accepted an invitation to come to Wimbledon and make use of the Mill House—a cottage belonging to Mrs R. S. Fetherstonhaugh, the widow of an officer B-P had met in Malta. The cottage was situated next to Wimbledon Windmill, a famous landmark in the midst of the thousand-acre expanse of Wimbledon Common on the south-western outskirts of London.

The book was taking shape in these pleasant surroundings, but things were not moving fast enough to suit Pearson. After a breakfast conference on 18 July, Pearson sent two shorthand writers out to help him. Baden-Powell 'yarned' to each of them in turn and triumphantly reported to his mother: 'I hope to finish my book on Tuesday [23 July].'

He managed to have a first draft in shape, and not a moment too soon. Another deadline was staring him in the face from the pages of his appointment book: 'Go to camp 29 July.' He had decided to try out his scheme in camp with a score of boys before putting his manuscript into final form.

Just before the camp deadline, after a number of further conferences, Baden-Powell and Pearson reached a tentative arrangement. B-P, 'subject to consent of army authorities', agreed to write a manual with regard to the Boy Scouts not to exceed a length of a hundred thousand words, and C. Arthur Pearson Ltd. agreed to arrange for the publication of this book 'in four weekly parts, each the same size as thirty-two pages of *Pearson's Magazine* with cover'. The parts were to be sold at fourpence each. The complete book, to appear in March 1908, was to sell for 1/6d. To promote the scheme, Baden-Powell was to 'arrange to lecture on the Boy Scouts at the leading public schools and institutions throughout the Kingdom'. The expense of these lecture tours and of the organization generally was to be borne by Messrs. C. Arthur Pearson Ltd. 'up to the sum of £1,000 . . . to be expended in consultation with Messrs. C. Arthur Pearson Ltd.' B-P further agreed 'to make a weekly publication issued by Messrs. C. Arthur Pearson Ltd. the official organ of the Boy Scouts', and 'to devote as much time and attention as possible to the organization of the Boy Scouts', and also 'to permit the association of his name with the paper which represents its [the organization's] interests'.

After having bound Baden-Powell to this extent, Messrs. C. Arthur Pearson Ltd. allowed the General to leave for his experimental camp.

XVII

The Island Adventure

Year: 1907   Age: 50

1

BADEN-POWELL was determined to give his Boy Scouts scheme a thorough test before he developed the final details. Since one of its main characteristics was to be adventuring outdoors the only way of doing this testing was by camping with a group of boys. This, in itself, was a revolutionary idea at the time. Hitherto, camping had been reserved almost exclusively for the military at home and abroad, and for explorers and sportsmen overseas. Now, for the first time, it would be made generally available to British boys on their home ground on a year-round basis.

The first problem that faced B-P was to find a suitable camping site where he and the boys could work undisturbed. He knew from past experience that if he were to take a group of boys camping at a place that was easily accessible, reporters and photographers by the score would dog his steps. The privacy he coveted could best be obtained on a desert island. But, alas, desert islands were few and far apart along the coast of England. If an island, it would have to be one that was inhabited. Did any of his acquaintances happen to own an island suitable for his purpose? One of them did.

During his fishing holiday in May 1907, at Knocklofty in Ireland, Baden-Powell had met a charming couple in their late forties—Mr and Mrs Charles van Raalte. They had a home in London and another on Brownsea Island, Dorset. The van Raaltes had insisted that the General must visit their island some time. It was less than a three-hour run from London by train to Poole, where their steam launch could be waiting at the quay to take their guest across the harbour to the island. B-P knew the spot. As a boy he had sailed into Poole Harbour with his brothers and had passed the island. He had seen its pine-crowned Spy-glass Hill from the water. His brothers and he had clandestinely landed on its

264

beaches. Brownsea Island would be excellent: of irregular oval shape, about a mile and a half long by three-quarters of a mile wide at its widest part: five hundred and sixty acres of undulating land, thickly wooded in spots, open in others, with two small lakes.

B-P wrote to van Raalte and explained that he would like to bring a score of boys to the island for a week's camping during the August holidays to try out a scheme he was working on. He received an immediate, favourable reply. At the same time, van Raalte sent him a recently published monograph about Brownsea and its history, written by himself and illustrated with a dozen full-colour reproductions of island landscapes from water-colours painted by his wife.

The more B-P found out about Brownsea Island the more certain he became that he had picked the most suitable place in England for his experimental camp. Not only did the fields and woods of the island lend themselves magnificently to camping, but Brownsea and the waters round it had a colourful history that would excite the imagination of the boys.

Lying as it does, as the guardian of the entrance to Poole Harbour, Brownsea early became of strategic importance for the defence of the towns and lands beyond. Roman triremes and Danish longships used it as a base. King Canute was reported to have stored some of the spoils from attacks on Dorset and Somerset on Brownsea. And in the fifteenth century, one of England's most daring buccaneers, Harry Page of Poole, better known to the French as 'Arrypaye', made it his refuge.

When buccaneering waned, smuggling took its place. The smugglers of Poole Harbour were among the most notorious along the Channel coast, until about 1520, when Henry VIII decided to put a stop to the smuggling. He accomplished this by the simple expedient of grabbing Brownsea and building a fortified blockhouse on its easternmost tip. From this point six guardsmen could watch the comings and goings of all ships using the harbour. In 1581 the fortifications were further strengthened against the threatened Spanish invasion.

For a couple of centuries Brownsea remained Crown property. Then it was sold to private owners and changed hands a number of times. One of its owners attempted to turn the island's plentiful deposits of 'tolerably pure clay' into a lucrative pottery business but went bankrupt in the process. Other owners expanded Henry VIII's simple fortifications into an impressive residential 'castle' with towers and turrets. These buildings were almost completely destroyed by fire in 1896. Yet another castle, even more imposing, rose from the ashes. It became the home of the van Raalte family in 1901 when Charles van Raalte, the wealthy stockbroker son of a Dutch immigrant father, bought the island.

2

Baden-Powell had his camping site. Now he went after the boys.

He wanted to see how far his scheme would interest boys of different upbringing and education and therefore recruited his campers from various walks of English life. He invited some of his army comrades to send their sons or nephews—pupils of large public schools such as Eton and Harrow. He issued an invitation to the Bournemouth Boys' Brigade company to pick six of its members, and the Poole Boys' Brigade three of its boys to join him—secondary school boys, farm boys, sons of working-class families.

The letters of invitation were very explicit. B-P explained in detail the purpose of the camp and the instruction he intended to give the boys. He gave the day's routine and assured the parents that 'wholesome food, cooking, sanitation, etc. will be carefully looked to'. He included a list of camp kit and clothing. He asked that each boy come to camp thoroughly practised in using three simple knots—the reef knot, the sheet bend, and the clove hitch—and provided sketches of the knots for those who might not know them. He further informed the parents that 'the camp will be open to receive boys from 29 July. The course of instruction begins on the morning of 1 August and ends with evening of 8 August. Boys return home 9 August.'

The invitations to go camping with the 'Hero of Mafeking' were accepted with alacrity. B-P had originally planned to take eighteen boys but twenty-one accepted his invitation. As an afterthought, and after some prodding by the boy's mother, he agreed to take along his 9-year-old nephew Donald, the son of his late brother George. To help him run the camp, B-P persuaded his old friend, 'The Boy' McLaren, to join the expedition.

Baden-Powell's next concern was the equipment for the camp. He sent off another letter to the captain of the Bournemouth Boys' Brigade, Henry Robson: 'Perhaps you could give me some advice as to whether I could hire bell tents and flooring in Bournemouth or Poole, for that week, and at what price. Also whether I can get a contractor to cater for feeding and cooking.'

Robson agreed to help in any way possible. The equipment he would handle himself. For the catering and cooking, he would get his friend, G. W. Green, the captain of the 1st Poole Boys' Brigade, to secure a professional cook and make arrangements to ship the food out to the island—it should be a simple matter: Green's firm was in the baking and catering business.

B-P sent Robson a complete list of what was needed: tents and bedding, cooking gear, boats and other special equipment. The Boys' Brigade captain managed to deliver everything in time for the camp opening—but not without difficulty. He found some of B-P's requests rather hard to fill. 'Harpoons, which Baden-Powell wired for on the eve of camp,' Robson said later, 'were not readily obtainable in a small seaside town.' He finally arranged to have a local blacksmith make them.

3

On 29 July 1907, Bill Harvey, one of the local boatmen, was waiting at the Customhouse Steps in Poole to take Baden-Powell, his nephew, and some of the boys from London out to Brownsea. They boarded his motor boat *Hyacinth* and set out on the two-mile crossing to the island. Bill Harvey landed the party on Seymour's Pier on Brownsea and returned to Poole, while Baden-Powell and the boys made their way the half mile along the island shore to their camp site.

The camp site was everything B-P could have hoped for. It was a level spot at the south-western shore of Brownsea, with a view across the water and tidal flats towards distant Purbeck Ridge, and the imposing ruins of Corfe Castle in a cleft in the hills. The ground was dry, hard clay—the spot was an old pottery site—with heather, bracken, and patches of spiny furze aflame with yellow flowers. On one side of the site were a couple of boggy ponds, with oozy banks of rust-red mud overgrown with rushes and sedge. At the other side was a deserted, half-ruined two-storey building—the old pottery pay-house—which would come in handy for storage. A grove of Scotch pines and pinastic firs would provide fuel and wood for camp construction. The shore directly below the camp was littered with shards of tiles and broken bricks, and unsuited for bathing —but the beach to the east was excellent, with soft, white sand.

B-P and the boys with McLaren who had preceded them the day before went to work pitching tents and establishing camp. The tents were bell tents, each of them large enough to sleep five campers on paillasses. B-P had a tent of his own; so did McLaren. An army marquee tent was set up to serve as dining-room and kitchen and as a gathering place in inclement weather. In the middle of the site, a flag pole was erected from which the Union Jack was to fly from morning till night. Near his own tent, B-P pushed into the ground one of his pigsticking lances from India with the flag that had waved over his Mafeking headquarters fastened just below the spearpoint.

By nightfall on 30 July, the camp was ready and twelve boys had moved in—the rest arrived on 31 July. All the boys were in their Sunday best on arrival but quickly changed into the 'camp clothes' they had brought —shorts and flannel shirts for those who had them. Baden-Powell had managed to secure a number of soft-brimmed 'donkey hats' for dressing-up purposes. With the brims pinned up rakishly on one side they made the boys look like fair replicas of the men of the South African Constabulary.

B-P himself wore one of his old South African flannel shirts with collar and tie. As a new feature for this occasion, he pinned a long white streamer to the left shoulder seam of his shirt. His shorts were not particularly short—they came well below his knee-caps and almost touched the tops of his golf stockings. For headgear he alternated between a sixpenny cap and a soft trilby hat. He disappointed the boys by not wearing the broad-brimmed hat that had become his distinctive trade mark. He had a reason: he was experimenting with a cloth hat that could be rolled up and stuck in the pocket.

As darkness fell on 31 July, the boys gathered round their first camp fire. B-P was the camp fire leader, the song leader, the story-teller. He told them tales of India and Africa and explained some of the details of the programme for the days ahead. He was at his very best. During the past few years he had associated with many groups of boys and had spoken before their gatherings. But this was different. These boys were his— his for a week, to work with, to play with, to learn from, and, if his ideas were right, to guide, to influence, to mould. . . .

As the embers faded, the boys rose for prayers, then turned in for their first night under canvas. Baden-Powell sat up a little longer, talking over the next day's schedule with McLaren. Then General and Major went to their camp-beds. Lights out. Silence in camp—with the waves sighing along the shore and the night-jars burring among the trees.

The next morning Baden-Powell formed the twenty-one boys who were to test his scheme into four patrols, one of six boys and the other three of five boys, each patrol with a name from the animal kingdom—the world's first Boy Scouts in the world's first Boy Scout patrols in the world's first Boy Scout camp:

> *Curlews.* Musgrave C. ('Bob') Wroughton, patrol leader; Cedric I. Curteis; John Michael Evans-Lombe; Percy Arthur Medway; Reginald Walter Giles; Simon Rodney.
> *Ravens.* Thomas Brian Achton Evans-Lombe, patrol leader; Arthur Primmer; Albert Blandford; James H. B. Rodney; Marc Noble.

Wolves. George Rodney, patrol leader; Herbert Watts; J. Alan Vivian; Terence Ewart Bonfield; Richard Grant.

Bulls. Herbert Emley, patrol leader; Ethelbert James Tarrant; Herbert Collingbourne; William Rodney; Humphrey B. Noble.

(B-P's nephew Donald Baden-Powell was designated 'adjutant'.)

Each boy was provided with a shoulder-knot, a long streamer of brightly coloured tape, to indicate the patrol to which he belonged: yellow for the Curlews, red for the Ravens, blue for the Wolves, green for the Bulls. The patrol leaders each sported a short staff with a white flag with a picture of the patrol animal painted by B-P. They had the further distinction of wearing a fleur-de-lys badge on the front of their hats—the badge that B-P had used for his army scouts and which, soon, slightly modified, would become known the world over as the Scout badge.

4

On 1 August, the camp woke up to a brilliant English summer day with a blue sky and a soft breeze, exactly what B-P had wished for his new campers. The weather continued fair all through the camp, except for a couple of insignificant showers.

To the boys, the Brownsea camp became a thrilling adventure. They were having fun and excitement. They were not aware of the significance of what was happening—that their working and playing together would eventually result in millions of other boys sharing in the same game. To them, everything was new and something to be treasured: the experience of camping in itself, the friendships they made in their patrols, the scout-craft skills they learned, the camp fires, the tenting at night.

The day began at 6 a.m. when Baden-Powell roused the camp with weird notes from the long, spiral horn of an African koodoo—the war horn he had picked up on his expedition into the Somabula Forest during the 1896 Matabele Campaign.

A quick wash, a cup of hot cocoa, a short demonstration of 'the subject of the day' that had been introduced at the camp fire the night before. A brief session of physical drill with B-P himself leading it. Then the flag was hoisted, prayers said and breakfast eaten. Afterwards it was full speed ahead on 'scouting exercises', with practices, games and competitions in the day's subject, which might be campcraft or observation, woodcraft or life-saving or some other phase of scoutcraft.

Baden-Powell found the triple way he had devised of presenting and practising each subject highly effective:

> For example, take one detail of the subject 'Observation'—namely tracking:
> 1. At the camp fire overnight we would tell the boys some interesting instance of the value of being able to track.
> 2. Next morning we would teach them to read tracks by making foot marks at different places, and showing how to read them and to deduce their meaning.
> 3. In the afternoon we would have a game, such as Deer Stalking. . . .

Deer Stalking proved one of the most popular scoutcraft practices in camp. But there were many others: Spot the Thief, Lion Hunting, Bang the Bear, Dispatch Running, Old Spotty-face. And, of course, Whale Hunt which B-P had 'cribbed' (by his own admission) from Ernest Thompson Seton's *Birch-bark Roll*—the game for which Baden-Powell had requisitioned the harpoons that Robson had so much difficulty procuring, and which was played from two boats.

Most of the time B-P introduced the day's subject and handled the games and competitions. While watching the reactions of the boys, he enjoyed himself immensely. He had the chance to demonstrate to them all the tricks he had learned during his military scouting career and on his many hunting expeditions—and even during his Charterhouse days and his experiences with his brothers. For demonstrations in first aid and firemanship, he called in the Chief Officer of the Coast-Guard at Sandbanks, William Stevens.

The night work was a source of added adventure to the Brownsea campers.

> Each night [as B-P explained it], one patrol went on duty as night picket, i.e. drew rations of flour, potatoes, meat and tea, and went out to some indicated spot to bivouac for the night. Each boy carried his greatcoat and blankets, cooking pots and matches.
> On arrival at the spot, fires were lit and suppers cooked, after which sentries were posted and bivouac formed. The picket was scouted by patrol leaders of other patrols and myself some time after 11 p.m. After which the sentries were withdrawn and the picket settled down for the night, returning to camp next morning in time for breakfast.

The cooking on these night picket expeditions was of a primitive kind. The baked potatoes turned out fair—but the bread. . . . 'I remember,' Arthur Primmer of the Raven Patrol reported long afterwards, 'cooking some flour balls, using the inside of my jacket for mixing the dough. I am afraid they would not have passed muster with the camp cook—but to us boys it was great fun.'

The boys on sentry duty during night picket took their jobs seriously—and well they might: there were 'enemies' about.

One night, for instance, the van Raalte's young son and daughter decided to 'invade' the camp. They were 'arrested' and sent on their way home. Another night, a party of ladies and gentlemen—visitors at Brownsea Castle—were intercepted during a twilight stroll.

Even Baden-Powell himself became the victim of a night picket sentry on one of his attempts to 'scout' a patrol. He was spotted by his nephew, Donald, hanging on for dear life to a tree limb overhead.

The patrol overnight camps with the patrols away from the main camp on their own and under the leadership of their own boy leaders were of special concern to B-P. They were to show him whether one of the corner-stones of his Boy Scouts scheme—the patrol system—was sound or not, whether it could be depended upon to work.

The system worked beyond Baden-Powell's expectations:

> The organization of dividing the boys into patrols of five, with a senior boy in each as patrol leader was the secret of our success [he reported after the camp]. Each patrol leader was given full responsibility for the behaviour of his patrol at all times, in camp and in the field.
>
> The patrol was the unit for work or play. . . . The boys were put on their honour to carry out orders. Responsibility, discipline, and competitive rivalry were thus at once established and a good standard of development was ensured throughout the troop.

In spite of all the other excitement in camp, the evening camp fires with Baden-Powell as camp fire leader proved the high spots of the experience.

The flickering flames lit up the circle of boys gathered around them—and carried B-P back in his memory to the camp fires on the open veld of Africa. He had never told his stories to a more appreciative audience.

Then a quick change of mood from the serious to the playful, with B-P teaching the boys the *Eengonyama* chorus, the Zulu marching chant that had thrilled him almost twenty years before. His clear, resonant voice led off with *Eengonyama!* and the boys joined in a resounding chorus of *Invooboo! Ya-boh! Ya-boh! Invooboo!* And then these English boys, not quite knowing what this was all about, yet caught by the thrill of the night and the camp fire, jumped up and swung into line behind their famous leader for a wild dance. Until finally, exhausted but laughing, they dropped to the ground to sit again in an enchanted circle, firing questions at B-P, listening solemnly to his closing story, before they were sent off to turn in.

The last day of camp, 8 August, was a very special sports day.

B-P had intended it to be the 'proof-of-the-pudding' occasion and had invited the parents of the boys, the van Raaltes and their guests, and all the islanders to come to Battery Hill to witness the boys putting on a display of the skills they had learned. Percy W. Everett, editorial manager for C. Arthur Pearson Ltd., came down from London on behalf of his firm to find out how well Baden-Powell's experimental camp had succeeded.

The show became an extraordinary performance—completely boy-planned, boy-led and boy-executed. It was a mixture of games and competitions, of demonstrations of first aid and firemanship, of mat weaving and ju-jutsu. It ended in a tug-of-war between the 'birds' (the Curlews and the Ravens) and the 'beasts' (the Wolves and the Bulls), won by the 'birds'.

Time and again the audience broke into appreciative applause. And when the show was over, the van Raaltes invited the whole camp to Brownsea Castle for a banquet-like tea in the beautiful dining-room, with a brass band from Poole playing on the terrace outside. At the call of one of their number, the boys gave three cheers for 'the best General in the world' and three more for their hosts, then returned to their tents and to the sad task of beginning to strike camp.

The last camp fire. The last singing of the *Eengonyama* chant. The last story by B-P. The last night under canvas.

The next morning the experiment was over. As the boys sailed for Poole in the *Hyacinth* their good-bye cheers carried back across the water to Brownsea. B-P and his nephew stayed behind for breakfast with the van Raaltes, then they also departed.

The Brownsea camp was history. The island returned to normal.

5

As soon as he got back to London, Baden-Powell wrote out a report of the camp and arranged to have it printed in a four-page leaflet, as a companion piece to his two previous leaflets, *Boy Scouts, A Suggestion* and *Boy Scouts, Summary of Scheme*. He called it *Boy Scouts, A Successful Trial*. It contained a résumé of what happened on Brownsea and wound up with B-P expressing his wish 'to be able to organize the wider distribution of this scheme and to issue a handbook or "self-educator" such as will assist schoolmasters, officers of Boys' and Church Lads' Brigades and cadet corps, and all others interested in boys, in the development of manliness and good citizenship among the rising generation, by an adaptable and inexpensive means which is not only popular and attractive

A popular activity during the first Boy Scout camp at Brownsea Island, in 1907.

to the boys, but is also intensely interesting to the instructors themselves'.

B-P himself considered the camp a success. It had shown him the soundness of his patrol system. It had demonstrated the appeal of camping and outdoor activities to boys of all classes. It had established that the most effective way of learning scoutcraft was through practices and games. It had proved that, when put 'on their honour', boys would do their very best.

Within a few days of his return B-P began to receive letters from the boys and their parents. The boys all expressed themselves enthusiastically. They had had a marvellous time. The reactions of the parents were of the greatest importance to Baden-Powell. They had trusted their boys to his care for an experiment. Had the camp benefitted the boys? The parents seemed to think so. Their boys had not only picked up useful knowledge but had become more resourceful and more independent.

Some of the parents enclosed in their letters an extra pound note and a few words to the effect that B-P could not possibly have managed a ten-day camp on £1 per boy.

He hadn't. The camp ended with a deficit.

Saxton Noble, the father of Humphrey and Marc, was among those who volunteered financial assistance. Baden-Powell was happy to receive this evidence of support and wrote back:

> It was awfully kind of you to offer to help me in the matter of expenses—I am afraid they may come a bit higher than I had at first estimated—but I always intended to spend something on this experiment myself as a necessary step towards getting the scheme perfected. So as the camp was in this way partly for the benefit of the scheme I thought it right that the boys whom I was using in the experiment should merely defray some of the cost—i.e. the bare expenses of their food, etc.
>
> But unexpected expenses have cropped up. . . . So that a little help would probably be very acceptable indeed.

Baden-Powell worked out the account of the camp and sent a copy of it off to Saxton Noble:

	£	s.	d.
Expended	55	2	8
Receipts:			
From thirteen boys at £1 for messing . .	13	0	0
From nine town boys at 3/6 do. . . .	1	11	6
Donations to date	16	0	0
	£30	11	6

Leaving £24 11s. 2d.

Most great movements have had small beginnings. Compared to others, the cost of £55 2s. 8d. for the actual start of the Boy Scout movement can hardly be considered extravagant.

XVIII

The Making of a Best Seller

Years: 1907–08   Age: 50–51

1

AFTER his successful island adventure, Baden-Powell found himself in the position of a juggler trying to keep six balls in the air at one time—to write a book, arrange a lecture tour, reach a final agreement with Pearson, plan a weekly paper, organize his Boy Scouts scheme and secure Army consent to carry it out.

He decided to make the last item the first order of the day. If he were to make a success of his scheme he would have to give it a great deal of time. He had to be certain that he would have the time available.

He sent a copy of his circular, *Boy Scouts, A Suggestion*, to R. B. Haldane, the Secretary of State for War in Campbell-Bannerman's Liberal Cabinet, with a letter asking 'whether there would be any Army objection to my carrying it out, and if there was any likelihood of the Army wanting my services shortly and so interrupting me in the starting of the Scouts'.

In answer, Haldane requested that B-P come to Cloan, his home in Scotland, in order to discuss a 'project' on which he was working.

Haldane's 'project' was his plan, in connexion with his Army reorganization, of enlisting and training a Territorial Army of three hundred thousand volunteers, to be closely related to the regular Army. The plan had been widely discussed in the press and in military circles—with Sir Ian Hamilton joining Haldane in promoting a voluntary corps, with Lord Kitchener strongly disapproving the idea and with Lord Roberts insisting that only conscription of the young men of Britain would provide the necessary defences. At the moment, Haldane did not know for certain whether the plan would be approved but, in case it was, he wanted B-P 'to take up the training of a force of some forty thousand men to give a system and a standard for others to train on'. Haldane had no objection to Baden-Powell going ahead with his scouting scheme in the meantime but asked him to be available for anything that might come up in regard to the Territorial Army.

Two months later, Baden-Powell again heard from Haldane. The Territorial and Reserve Forces Act had been passed by Parliament. Haldane offered B-P the command of the Northumbrian Division of the Territorials, to take effect 1 April 1908. It would be a new challenge for his special abilities, even greater than the South African Constabulary. It would also mean going back on full pay rather than getting along on half pay in the Reserve.

With Haldane's blessing and with half a year ahead of him before resuming active duty in the Army, Baden-Powell went ahead with the further development of his scheme and the completion of his handbook.

He already had most of the manuscript describing the activities of 'peace scouting' to the boys in shape. Now, in October 1907, he concentrated on writing the section that was to explain the philosophy of his scheme, and his proposed method of instruction, to the young men who, as 'instructors', were to help boys become Scouts.

It was B-P's intention that this section, 'Notes to Instructors', should be the first part of his book and should be published in advance of the other parts. But Pearson thought otherwise. To secure a large sale of the parts they should, he felt, appear at regular and short intervals—not with one part for instructors in October and the others a couple of months later. If the material for instructors was needed at an early date for answering requests for information, the solution would be to publish it as a separate pamphlet, independent of the book for the boys.

Baden-Powell accepted Pearson's advice. He had the material for instructors printed as a thirty-two-page pamphlet. It went on the bookstalls priced at twopence. The pamphlet, entitled simply *Boy Scouts Scheme*, carried on its cover a reproduction of Baden-Powell's first drawing of a Boy Scout in full uniform, including shorts, neckerchief and broad-brimmed hat.

The text of B-P's pamphlet concluded with the writer's invitation to his readers to take up his scheme or to act as local honorary secretaries in all parts of the country, 'in communication (but not in bondage) with me at the Central Office at Goschen Buildings, Henrietta Street, London, W.C.' The office was one made available by Pearson for handling the influx of letters expected as a result of Baden-Powell's forthcoming lecture tour. B-P had wanted his younger brother to become manager of this first Boy Scout headquarters, but Baden had other plans for the future. B-P next prevailed upon his old friend and Brownsea assistant, Major McLaren, to take the post.

Throughout the autumn, Baden-Powell was making steady progress on the manuscript of the handbook that was to instruct the boys in scouting. Because he was shooting on 1 November 1907 on the estate of an Army friend in Yorkshire, the boys of Guisborough, including the local Church Lads' Brigade, became the first to be exposed to his lecture expounding his Boy Scouts scheme and telling of the Brownsea adventure. During the next six weeks he continued his lecturing on a tour of Britain that carried him from Llanelly in the west to Scarborough in the east and from Exeter in the south to Edinburgh in the north.

With this first part of his projected lecturing concluded at Christmas-time, he was ready to settle down for some concentrated work on his manuscript. He again asked Mrs Fetherstonhaugh for permission to take over the Mill House on Wimbledon Common and 'went into residence' in it on 26 December. To expedite the job of getting *Scouting for Boys*—as the forthcoming book had been dubbed—to press, Pearson assigned Percy W. Everett to work with Baden-Powell.

2

Baden-Powell's attempts to reach a final agreement with C. Arthur Pearson had run into a snag. At the end of October Pearson had gone angling for a much larger fish than B-P's scheme for boys promised to be: the management of the most respected paper in the Empire, *The Times*.

The Times had fallen on lean days. For several years the paper had been losing money. It had tried to stave off disaster by various book publishing schemes but, by the autumn of 1907, the day of reckoning was at hand. The eighty or more proprietors clamoured for a reorganization to protect their investments.

Pearson got news of the situation and moved into the fray. He had to proceed warily. If it was rumoured that a newspaperman from the 'popular journalism' field was angling for *The Times*, the fish would be snatched out of reach. The negotiations became so involved and so time-consuming that Pearson hardly had time for his own business, much less for Baden-Powell's. He turned the job of coming to terms with the General over to one of his managers, Peter Keary, the author of several successful self-improvement books.

Keary exhibited little of Pearson's altruism. To him, the dealings with Baden-Powell were very strictly confined to a business footing. He considered his task to be mainly to secure an agreement with Baden-Powell that would be of the greatest advantage to the company of C. Arthur Pearson, Ltd., and for his company to secure a firm hold in whatever might come out of B-P's scheme.

Baden-Powell soon found himself so much at variance with Keary that he felt called upon to appeal to Pearson directly. On 19 November he wrote to the publisher:

> In coming to a formal agreement with you as regards the Boy Scouts scheme the form now proposed seems to me to put us on a different footing than that originally planned. It tends to form your staff and myself into a committee of management of the Boy Scouts. Well— I am afraid I could never work with a committee. Could you?

As Baden-Powell understood their original discussion, Pearson and he were each to have a definite part in fostering the scheme, and the agreement between them was to be a personal one. To such an agreement B-P would heartily subscribe:

> I, on my part, undertake to:
>> Plan and organize the Boy Scouts scheme and be responsible for its development under a manager of my own selection.
>> Explain it in the chief towns of England before the end of March.
>> Write and publish a handbook in January and February.
>> Devote the proceeds of such book to the furtherance of the scheme.
>> Give my name to an article in each number of *The Scout* newspaper as long as our agreement lasts.
>> Be consulted about the proper expenditure of your contribution of £1,000.
> You, on your part, undertake to:
>> Find £1,000 for the first twelve months—renewal of such contribution being optional.
>> Run a newspaper (*The Scout*) in connexion with the scheme, in which I can publish any orders or information for the Boy Scouts. All the profits to go to you.
> This agreement to stand for one year after which it may be cancelled at one month's notice on either side.

Pearson, in his answer, conceded most of B-P's points but vigorously opposed the one-month cancellation notice. His firm, he informed the General, could not possibly agree to this after having put its money, energies, skill and experience into the project. The agreement, he felt, should last so long as the Boy Scouts organization should continue to be in existence..

To Baden-Powell, this point was of tremendous importance. Looking

to the future of the Boy Scouts scheme he felt that it should be permitted
to develop freely, without any permanent connexion with a commercial
enterprise:

> I am very sorry [he wrote to Pearson on 29 November] but I cannot
> bind myself or my scheme to Pearsons Ltd. for an indefinite time and
> I think as it [the cancellation clause] now stands it is fair to both of
> us since we can separate at any time that we may wish after the
> contract has been completed, viz. of twelve months' work on my part
> for £1,000 on Pearson's part, by which both of us have our schemes
> started: you, Pearson, your newspaper; I, my Boy Scouts.

Pearson realized that he might have driven Baden-Powell a bit too far.
To settle matters amicably, he arranged a meeting between himself and
Baden-Powell on 3 December. B-P came away partly mollified but still
feeling that what they had worked out was 'a bit one-sided'. After further
talks and correspondence he gained practically all his points. His own
part was to be exactly as proposed by him, with an added agreement 'to
contribute a signed article' to each issue of *The Scout*. Pearson, on his
part, agreed to a modified terminal clause: 'After the first twelve months
Lieutenant-General Baden-Powell may terminate this agreement at any
time on his being ordered abroad or accepting any appointment incon-
sistent with his obligations under this agreement; or either party may
terminate it on three months' notice at any time after twelve months.'
      After more than six months of discussion, Baden-Powell had an agree-
ment that closely resembled his original ideas. He signed it on 1 January
1908. It was signed, on behalf of Messrs C. Arthur Pearson Ltd., by Peter
Keary.

On the same day that Baden-Powell signed his agreement with C. Arthur
Pearson Ltd., C. Arthur Pearson himself, in great secrecy, signed the
preliminary papers for the incorporation of *The Times*, Limited. The
editorial character of *The Times* would remain unchanged, but the business
management would be reorganized by Pearson, 'the proposed managing
director'.
      The following Sunday, 5 January, one of Pearson's competitors leaked
the story: 'It is understood that important negotiations are taking place
which will place the direction of *The Times* newspaper in the hands of a
very capable proprietor of several popular magazines and newspapers.'
      The lid was off. The eighty-odd proprietors of *The Times* clamoured
for an explanation. The 'Pearson Scheme' was placed before them.
Slowly in the beginning, but quickly gathering momentum, objections to

the choice of Pearson as 'the man who would save *The Times*' poured in. The objections turned into a storm of protest. Other schemes for the payment of a better price than Pearson was willing to pay were brought forward in opposition. On 14 February, Pearson withdrew from the negotiations. The fish had been torn off his hook in spite of all his efforts.

On 16 March, the sale of *The Times* was revealed. Ironically, it proved

Baden-Powell's earliest known drawing of a Boy Scout.

to be Lord Northcliffe, the former Alfred C. W. Harmsworth, Pearson's rival in the 'popular journalism' field, who had pulled in the catch.

3

Baden-Powell had managed to get the first two parts of *Scouting for Boys* into final form and off to the printers by the end of December 1907. But as the new year rolled round he had to continue his interrupted lecture tour. His itinerary for the next two months had been carefully planned. Local Y.M.C.A.s, Boys' Brigade companies and various citizens' groups had agreed to sponsor his appearance, and Henry Shaw, working from the offices of C. Arthur Pearson Ltd., had done a thorough job of advertising them.

B-P's lecture tour during January and February 1908 was literally a *tour de force*. Only a man with Baden-Powell's stamina, determination and enthusiasm could possibly have carried out a programme that called for almost daily luncheon engagements, afternoon meetings and evening lectures in city upon city, with the further hardship of much travelling by night during the bleakest months of the year. In seven weeks, B-P gave forty lectures before approximately twenty-five thousand boys and men in thirty population centres. And between his lecture engagements he was doing the final writing and revising of the remaining parts of *Scouting for Boys*, keeping just one jump ahead of the printer.

4

Part I of *Scouting for Boys* appeared on the bookstalls on Wednesday, 15 January 1908.

There was no mistaking the name of the author. The letters B-P dominated the top right-hand corner of the cover—with a parenthetical Lieut.-Gen. Baden-Powell, C.B. below them. The cover drawing by John Hassall was exciting to a youngster of 1908. It showed a boy lying hidden behind a large rock above a sandy shore watching the landing of a party of smugglers(?) or pirates(?) from a mysterious ship. The boy wore the shorts that were soon to be one of the marks of a Boy Scout. Next to him lay his broad-brimmed hat and his staff soon to become just as familiar.

The booklets were snatched off the shelves with astonishing speed at fourpence each. B-P's lectures had proved to be excellent publicity. So had Shaw's press campaign. Boys—and girls, too, it proved—were waiting to find out what the 'Hero of Mafeking' had to say. Now they had their chance.

There was nothing in the format, the printing and the literary style of this first part to suggest that here was the beginning of a book that would bring into being a new youth movement—a movement whose influence would be felt in practically every civilized country in the world for years to come. Today's reader might, with fair accuracy, compare the seventy-two-page Part I of Baden-Powell's *Scouting for Boys* to a boy's version of a copy of the *Reader's Digest*: it was a compendium of a great number of short features. One of these features was a piece of autobiography

('Mafeking Boy Scouts'), another, a book condensation (Kipling's *Kim*), still another, a murder story with a boy detective ('The Elsdon Murder'). The booklet further contained an article on famous men and women in English history, about a dozen games, and even a short play (*Pocahontas or The Capture of Captain John Smith*) accompanied by a 'do-it-yourself' article on making the costumes.

But under this 'sugar coating' were the items that really counted: a summary of the meaning of being a Scout, with a promise of adventure in the outdoors and with a challenge to the boy's sense of honour, his willingness to help other people, his endurance, his patriotism; a description of the boy-type of organization that scouting called for: 'To become a Scout you join a patrol . . . or . . . raise a patrol yourself by getting five other boys to join. . . . One boy is then chosen as Patrol Leader to command the patrol, and he selects another boy to be the corporal or second in command. Several patrols together can form a Troop under an officer called a Scoutmaster.'

The other serious articles were a delineation of the ideals behind scouting—the Scout Oath that the boy was to take on joining, the Scout Law 'which you swear to obey when you take your oath as a Scout', and the Scout Motto, 'Be Prepared'; the tests for earning the Scout badge (none for tenderfoot, five for second-class Scout, seven more for first-class Scout), as well as for earning three Badges of Honour, suggested by Seton's Woodcraft Indian 'Honors' and forming the germ of the proficiency or merit badge programme which, later, was to become an important feature of Boy Scouting. Finally there were the special trimmings that Baden-Powell knew would appeal to a boy's heart—the Scout salute, the Scout uniform, patrol calls and secret signs.

This jumble of seemingly unrelated subjects, written in simple language, was not divided into the usual chapters of an ordinary book. Instead, it was presented in a series of Camp Fire Yarns. This was not a book to be read in a stuffy room. It was meant to be talked about, dreamed about round a camp fire. It was meant to stir the imagination, to challenge the reader to action.

The next four parts of *Scouting for Boys*, appearing on the bookstalls every other Wednesday during January, February and March 1908, were similar to Part I in their structure and appeal. They contained anecdotes, games and practices in a wide variety of subjects: observation and deduction; tracking and stalking; getting to know animals and birds, trees and plants; pioneering and camping; pathfinding and signalling; physical fitness and chivalry; first aid and life-saving; patriotism and duties as citizens.

The last part—Part VI—was quite different from the preceding five. It was addressed directly to 'young men of all kinds . . . each training a few boys'. It was an urgent appeal to all Britons to become 'instructors', to take up the cause of 'peace-scouting' and to teach it to boys.

The youngsters of Great Britain took *Scouting for Boys* to heart. A great number of their elders realized the value of Baden-Powell's Boy Scouts scheme. Even the newspapers found the General's book of sufficient news value and importance to open their columns for reviews.

The Times allotted almost two solid columns of its editorial page to comment on the book, but viewed it mainly as a book on outdoor skills. *The Spectator* ended a review of the book with the statement that 'It is very unconventional, and whether the boyish fancy will be captured by the precise mixture of seriousness and madness which it prescribes as a working rule of life we cannot undertake to say. Let us hope it will.' Several other papers expressed the same sentiment, among them the Glasgow *Evening Citizen*: 'One hopes that a scheme of so much practical promise may justify the characteristic optimism of its promoter.'

Of all the papers, the *Daily Graphic* seems to have been the most visionary. It ended its review by stating that 'All can help. . . . This is a kind of "snowball" organization to which nobody could object.'

On 1 May 1908, *Scouting for Boys* was published in book form by Horace Cox at 2s. a copy, cloth-bound.

The 'snowball' picked up speed.

XIX

A Scheme Becomes a Movement

Years: 1908–10   Age: 51–53

1

SPURRED by Baden-Powell's enthusiasm and personal magnetism, Boy Scout patrols had started to appear in each of the communities in which the General had stopped on his country-wide tour to describe his Boy Scouts scheme. Now, with the publication of *Scouting for Boys*, patrols by the thousand sprang up throughout the British Isles. By the time the sixth and final part of the book had made its appearance at the end of March, Boy Scouting had swept like a tidal wave across the length and breadth of the United Kingdom.

Small bands of boys in broad-brimmed hats, with brightly coloured scarves round their necks, roamed through the countryside. Mothers were pressed into cutting knickers and trousers into shorts, while the boys bravely folded down their long, black stockings to expose their pale knees to the harsh English winter—according to Baden-Powell's drawing of what the well-dressed Scout should wear. Hardware stores had a run on broomsticks to be used as Scout staves. In almost every British town and village, houses and pavements became decorated with long chalk arrows to indicate to stragglers that 'I have gone this way' or chalk circles with a prominent centre to proclaim that 'I have gone home'. Shrill whistle signals broke the silence of practically every English park. The chop-chop of tomahawk-shaped axes resounded in woods throughout the land, and the swirling smoke from thousands of camp fires rose over the tree tops.

What was there in Baden-Powell's scheme and in his book that had so stirred the boys' imagination? There can be little doubt that the prime factor was B-P himself. The boys of Britain had all heard of the Hero of Mafeking from their fathers' lips, and the young adults, just out of boyhood, remembered vividly the excitement of Mafeking Night. Here was a 'man' in the best sense of the word—a man who had seen a lot of life and a lot of fighting, a man who knew what he was talking about when he spoke of life in the outdoors, of courage and self-discipline, of loyalty and chivalry. Here was a man's man who was devoting himself to becoming a boy's man. Here was a man whom boys would willingly follow. The fact that he beckoned them on with an enticing programme of activities made his appeal that much stronger.

B-P's programme, as it emerged from the pages of *Scouting for Boys*, carried a promise of gay adventure under the open sky—of white tents

Part I of Scouting for Boys, *with cover design by John Hassall.*

and red camp fire flames, of hut-making and bridge-building, of finding the way by night and day, of following the tracks of wild animals, of living the life of explorers and backwoodsmen, hunters and pioneers, brown Zulus and Red Indians. It was a programme that appealed to the love of action and to the inherent idealism of boyhood.

'I am going to show you how you can learn scoutcraft for yourself and can put it into practice at home,' Baden-Powell told the boys of Britain. 'You can best learn by joining the Boy Scouts.'

Boys by the tens of thousands took him at his word, and men with the spirit of the boy within them and a desire to serve boys joined the ranks.

Baden-Powell had included in *Scouting for Boys* a note to the effect that 'further information or advice' would be readily given on application to The Manager, Boy Scouts, at the Goschen Buildings in Henrietta Street, London.

The small office was deluged with letters. They came in great numbers from boys who wanted to find out where to get uniforms, cooking pots, staves, haversacks, tracking irons, whistles, knives and the many other appurtenances of scouting. But there were also letters by the hundred from schoolmasters, retired army officers, clergymen requesting further information. Baden-Powell himself and his small office staff of Major McLaren and their secretary, Miss Margaret MacDonald, tried valiantly to keep up with the mail—but the letters kept coming in a flood.

To alleviate the situation, work was rushed forward on the publication of the first issue of *The Scout*—the weekly newspaper that was to be Baden-Powell's mouthpiece and was to contain, as far as possible, the further information the boys asked for.

The wheels were turning with extraordinary speed. Pearson wanted the first issue of the new weekly to be on the bookstalls within a fortnight of the appearance of the last part of *Scouting for Boys*. He assigned one of his editors, Herbert Shaw, already a well-known author of boys' books, to edit the new publication, with Henry Holt, another Pearson man, as his assistant. Authors and artists were called in. Stories and articles and illustrations were chosen.

The deadline was met. The new weekly, *The Scout*, dated 18 April, appeared on the bookstalls on 14 April 1908. For the time in which it was born, *The Scout* was a creditable publication. It contained stories by popular British writers in the boys' field. It carried a couple of inspirational features: 'The Secret of Success', and 'Why All Scouts Must Keep Fit'. It began a series of short items, 'Things All Scouts Should Know', and brought the first announcement of a contest for the readers, with the prizes being the chance to spend 'A Fortnight in General Baden-Powell's Camp—The Most Fascinating Holiday Ever Offered—Thirty Boys Invited'.

But the most prominent feature of the first issue of this new weekly was Baden-Powell's own contribution, 'How I Started Scouting'. It was the first of more than fifteen hundred articles, faithfully contributed. It was the first weekly batch of words which were, eventually, to reach an estimated volume of 1,700,000, contributed by B-P himself to the paper he had started.

The Scout became as popular as the six parts of *Scouting for Boys* had been. The early issues were sold out within a couple of days of publication. By the end of its first year *The Scout* had reached a circulation of 110,000 copies a week.

The appearance of *The Scout* resulted in the formation of many more patrols and troops throughout Britain. But instead of alleviating the work of the Goschen Buildings office, it further increased the number of letters pouring into the Boy Scouts headquarters from all parts of the British Isles—and soon from the British dominions and colonies overseas as well. But by then, B-P had left London to take up his task in connexion with the organization of Haldane's Territorial Army.

2

Baden-Powell had hardly assumed command of the Northumbrian Division of the Territorials—covering Northumberland, Durham, and North and East Yorkshire—when he found himself in trouble.

On 2 May 1908, he delivered a speech before a large gathering of commissioned and non-commissioned officers assembled at St George's Drill Hall at Newcastle, on the subject of 'The Territorials as a Fighting Force'.

In his usual direct manner he presented the main object in the training of the 'Terriers': to be ready to resist an enemy invasion at any moment. By whom? One hundred years ago, he said, the enemy was the French; fifty years ago it was Russia. Now, he suggested, Germany was the enemy: 'Germany wants to develop her trade and commerce, and must, therefore, get rid of England.' Where would Germany strike? Not London which was only the capital of England in a geographical sense, but the strategic capital that consisted of the great industrial centres of the north Midlands. And when might Germany strike? On some day when the British people were least prepared and when British communications were temporarily disorganized, some year on an August Bank Holiday, for instance.

After this introduction, the speaker went on to describe the kind of training he envisaged for the Territorials. He closed his speech by challenging the officers present to turn their men into the kind of fighting force that was required for the protection of the country.

The speech was given on a Saturday. On the following Monday, B-P found it reported in complete detail in the *Newcastle Daily Journal* although no reporter was supposed to have been present at a purely military gathering. He immediately realized the uproar the newspaper account might produce. He took the night train to London, lunched with Haldane the next day, explained the situation and returned to Newcastle.

The storm over B-P's 'war speech' was not long in breaking.

On 13 May William P. Byles, Liberal M.P. for Salford North, rose in the House of Commons and asked the Secretary of State for War 'whether his attention has been called to a public lecture lately delivered in

Newcastle by Lieut.-Colonel [sic] Baden-Powell of an alarmist character and couched in language likely to be offensive to a friendly power; and whether he will do anything to restrain such utterances by senior officers of His Majesty's Army'.

Haldane replied that Baden-Powell 'was lecturing to a uniformed meeting of the Territorial Force and was given to understand that no reporters were present. He prefaced his remarks with a few words on the German Army in view of its special standard of efficiency which was a natural object of attention on the part of all keen soldiers. These remarks could not be construed as in any way offensive to the German nation, and it is to be regretted that any one present should have made such a report to the papers.'

'Was he justified', J. M. Robertson, M.P. for Northumberland, Tyneside, wanted to know, 'in speaking of Germany as a natural enemy of this country and in predicting a desperate and bloody war between the two countries?'

Haldane evaded answering the question by saying 'I do not think he said that. Certainly he did not tell me about it.' He closed the debate by telling the House that it did not seem to him worth while 'to enter upon the laborious investigation which I should have to enter upon before I could be sure of having reached the true view of the merits of the controversy'.

Baden-Powell went ahead developing his division of the Territorials, with headquarters at Richmond in Yorkshire. He transformed his motor-car into a vehicle that combined the means of transportation with bedroom and office quarters and toured his territory continually, getting in personal touch with every unit and studying the local conditions under which it had to work. He found excellent material available and was particularly happy over the quality of the men from the mining districts: 'They were pretty rough but hearty sportsmen and brave fellows.'

He knew that for men like these, 'barracks square drill was worse than useless and yet it was what we had hitherto imposed upon them.... We had had as our adversaries in the Boer War men who had never had a day's drill in their lives and yet were effective in the field against our trained troops through their individual intelligence, pluck, and will to succeed. So it was on this line that I tried to develop our training in my Division.'

3

During the spring and summer of 1908, *The Scout* had promoted its 'voting' contest (based on the number of subscriptions secured) to select thirty boys to go to summer camp with B-P. The contest had been a huge success, in spite of the fact that neither the 'when' nor the 'where' of the camp was ever fully explained. Time and place had to be kept vague until the very last moment—both of them had to fit into Baden-Powell's obligations to his Territorials.

One week before the closing of the contest, the dates were finally settled and a suitable location found near Humshaugh (pronounced humz-off). The camp site, on the side of a gently sloping hill, overlooked the Northumbrian moors and dales, with a view towards the Roman Wall.

The winners of the contest, the 'Gallant Thirty', gathered on the evening of 22 August and settled into camp under the guidance of B-P's 'manager'. Every portion of the United Kingdom was represented. The boys had come from Scotland, Ireland, Wales and all parts of England.

Inspection of three separate week-end encampments of his Territorials prevented Baden-Powell from being present for the Saturday opening of his Boy Scout camp, but he did succeed in arriving in time for the camp fire on Sunday night. The weather the next four days was atrocious, but B-P carried through the programme nevertheless, including hikes to the Wall and to nearby castles. Then the skies cleared over the week-end for Sunday service at Hexham Abbey and the great sports day.

The first camp of trained Scouts under Baden-Powell's direct personal leadership came to a close on 4 September. A year had made a great difference: the thirty Boy Scouts taking part in the Humshaugh camp were well acquainted with the scouting programme from practising it in their patrols at home. B-P had little to do but give general guidance and inspiration.

Baden-Powell had his hands full in his double capacity of an Army General and the founder of a new movement. Every place he went on Territorial business, he attempted also to inspect the local Scouts, to give public talks on scouting, to meet prominent men for the purpose of interesting them in helping boys of their communities become Scouts. In addition to these direct personal contacts, he had to prepare his weekly articles for *The Scout* and answer numerous letters on scouting matters sent up to him by McLaren from the London office.

As more and more boys and men joined up, he came to realize that he had made several miscalculations in opening up his Pandora's Box of scouting.

He had underestimated the enthusiasm of boys in following his lead. He had expected, and indeed intended, the boys to join existing organizations, such as the Boys' Brigade, which would give them the scouting they craved. He had not planned to start a new organization. But he had not counted on the boys themselves. They had no intention of being Boy Scouts plus something else; they wanted to be Boy Scouts and nothing else. So instead of joining existing groups of other established societies and clubs, for the purpose of getting a taste of scouting, they had made up their own patrols and started scouting straight off.

He had overestimated the ability of existing youth organizations to adapt his Boy Scouts scheme to their programme. The Boys' Brigade and the Church Lads' Brigade had made half-hearted attempts to establish a scouting branch within their organizations, but with little success. And while Baden-Powell had taken for granted that the leaders of these organizations would provide whatever controls would be needed to give guidance to the boys wanting to take up scouting, he found in practice that this was the case in a few instances only—that, on the contrary, the self-proclaimed Boy Scouts either roved the countryside without adult supervision or had subjected themselves to self-appointed scoutmasters who, in many cases, had neither the necessary qualifications nor character required for giving leadership to a group of eager youngsters.

For every day that passed, the situation was getting more and more acute. To protect the good name of scouting, some kind of supervision and control became imperative.

After pondering the question, Baden-Powell acted. In late September 1908, he sent out a letter addressed to all interested adults whose names were on file in the headquarters office.

After admitting 'that the want of discriminating supervision in the appointment of scoutmasters, and in the bestowal of Scout badges, is leading to confusion and misunderstandings', he proposed to extend a 'system of advisory committees to every city where gentlemen will be so good as to serve upon them'.

These local advisory committees would, as Baden-Powell visualized them, get in touch with all patrols and troops within their districts, register them, and appoint scoutmasters who were found 'fit and proper men to teach the lads'. They would also award the badges of classification to Scouts, make arrangements for camps and parades, and generally help in the matter of establishing troops and in outfitting boys with equipment. Two 'travelling inspectors'—W. B. Wakefield for the North of England and Eric Walker for the South of England and Wales—would visit, free of charge, any centre requiring their services 'to give advice and suggestions, to conduct tests, and generally to regulate administration up to a recognized standard'.

Wakefield and Walker did yeoman work. Through their efforts, combined with Baden-Powell's own work, a network of local Boy Scout committees began growing throughout Britain.

4

Early in December, Baden-Powell learned that his old regiment, the 5th Dragoon Guards was returning from India. He decided to go to Southampton to be on hand to receive it. The ship was delayed. The weather turned foul. A blizzard swept across southern England. In the midst of it all, Baden-Powell was walking along the docks when, in passing some of the warehouses, he noticed 'a very delightful aroma'. His curiosity led him to investigate. The aroma emanated from a shipment of coffee and spices from Brazil. 'I made up my mind there and then to take a ticket for Brazil, whether I could afford it or not.'

With the exception of a number of week-ends for shooting and fishing Baden-Powell had had no real holiday since returning from Egypt almost two years before. He felt himself in desperate need of a break, especially one that could take him away from the dismal English winter into sunshine. Now he finally arranged for a leave. But his exchequer was low; he could not afford the trip, unless perhaps. . . .

He went to the offices of the Royal Mail Steam Packet Company. After some bargaining he came away with a free ticket for a return trip to South America. In return for his passage he would write and illustrate an article on his trip for the *Graphic*, to be published afterwards in pamphlet form by the shipping company as part of its advertising.

He sailed on 19 February 1909 on the S.S. *Aragon* 'in a very nice cabin in a good ship in good company'. Because of a delayed arrival in Rio de Janeiro he did not get to see much of Brazil's capital, although what he saw intrigued him: 'Rio was better than anything I had expected. It was not unlike Cape Town at its very best magnified about twice, and put down on the shores of the Bosporus (together with Table Mountain and the Lion).'

In Buenos Aires B-P was completely overwhelmed by the reception he received as the 'Hero of Mafeking'. Not only the British colony but also the Argentine Government was on hand to do him honour. For a week, he was fêted and dined, taken on excursions and on military inspection trips and then, 'when they heard I wanted to go to Chile, the railway company gave me a free pass, the Minister of the Interior gave me his own saloon, and the War Office sent an ADC to attend me on my journey'.

The railway took Baden-Powell to the Andes, then up and up and onto a narrow-gauge track through 'bare, dry hills—all exactly like the Bolas Pass in Baluchistan'. At the end of the line, where a tunnel was under construction, Baden-Powell was met by the superintendent of the Chilean railway line with horses and mules and escorted on the zigzag ride over the top of the pass, at an altitude of 12,400 feet, and down to the railhead on the Chile side of the Andes, where he was received as warmly as he had been in the Argentine. When he left after a stay of three days, the population turned out to see him off at the station and two military bands played 'God Save the King' for half an hour without stopping. 'I never saw such people!'

5

The day after his arrival home, Baden-Powell went to the new Boy Scouts Headquarters at 116–118 Victoria Street, Westminster S.W., to confer with his new managing Secretary, J. A. Kyle.

Before leaving for South America, B-P had renewed his arrangement with C. Arthur Pearson for another year. But he had insisted that 'the office must be separate from that of C. Arthur Pearson Ltd., if we are to get the right men as vice-presidents and managers'. He found a suitable office in Victoria Street and, on McLaren's decision to retire because of ill health, secured the services of Kyle, until that time organizing secretary of the South-west London District.

Baden-Powell had made an excellent choice. Kyle was an efficient organizer and a dedicated enthusiast. B-P had nothing to worry about in going back to his 'Terriers' after his South American jaunt.

This year *The Scout* again ran a 'voting' contest with prizes being 'A Fortnight at General Baden-Powell's Camp'—this time not for thirty boys, but for a hundred. B-P decided to make use of an invitation extended to him by C. B. Fry, the famous cricketer, who had recently established a training school for boys. Part of his school's curriculum consisted of seamanship practice on his training ship *Mercury*. Fry offered to make the *Mercury* available for a fortnight for Baden-Powell's camp. But only fifty of the scheduled hundred boys could be accommodated on board. Baden-Powell worked out a double attraction: half of the boys would live for a week on the ship, the other half in camp on land; the second week, the boys would change places. For the 'land group', he found a camp site at Buckler's Hard in Hampshire, on the estate of Lord Montagu of Beaulieu. The camp site had historical significance—on this spot had been the slipways from which many of Admiral Nelson's ships had been launched.

The 'sea camp' was handled by members of Fry's staff. The 'land camp' had three scoutmasters, one of them Percy Everett of Pearson's. One other adult took part in the adventure: H. Geoffrey Elwes, a Colchester solicitor, who was to report to the Archbishop of York his views on the possibility of The Church of England Men's Society endorsing the Scout movement.

The camp period—7 to 21 August—fell at the most inopportune time for Baden-Powell. He had a heavy summer schedule inspecting the camps and manoeuvres of his 'Terriers'. He paid a flying visit to his Scout camp on its first Sunday, then rushed back to London to catch the night train to Durham. The second Sunday he started off by motor-car from York at 4.20 a.m. and arrived at the camp that night at 8 p.m. It was a proud accomplishment: 'Total 250 miles in 13 hours—19 miles an hour, excluding stoppages for meals, but including repairs and towns totalling 40 minutes—or 20 m.p.h.'

Each time Baden-Powell came down from London, he brought rain with him, but none as heavy as on the last day of camp when a long programme of water sports and a Scout play were scheduled. The sports had to be abandoned, and the play given up in favour of an indoor sing-song. 'After this had continued for some time', Geoffrey Elwes reported at the time, 'we settled down for our last stories, and the General talked on—stories of hair-breadth escapes and stories of amusing adventures—till it was long past post. Then came his last solemn words to the boys, and they were very still. . . .'

Elwes returned from camp impressed with what he had seen and completely converted to scouting. Baden-Powell also had been converted—to the idea of making sea scouting part of his programme.

6

The Buckler's Hard camp had been a sound success—but the Crystal Palace Rally two weeks later became the major event up to this time of the fledgling Scout movement.

The suggestion had reached Baden-Powell from many sources to attempt to bring together the Scouts, not only of London but of the whole British Isles, for an event in the capital 'to demonstrate to the public the aims and progress of the movement, and its stupendous growth since its initiation in the summer of 1907'. He agreed to try out the idea and drew up a programme of various scoutcraft competitions. The plan was to run elimination contests in scoutcraft throughout the country and to stage the finals in London.

On 4 September, in spite of unsettled weather, with rain threatening at any moment, Scouts in their thousands poured onto the cycle track adjacent to the Crystal Palace and set out to prove their skills. The scout-craft display was almost over when a deluge forced Baden-Powell to order the Scouts into the shelter of the Crystal Palace for the rest of the programme. As B-P, in his general's uniform, mounted the platform inside the vast structure, he was greeted by a tumultuous roar of young voices.

Thousands of Scout hats were swung aloft on thousands of upraised Scout staves—a special kind of greeting that became a unique Scout tradition.

At a signal, the cheering died down and the Chief Scout spoke. 'I have a telegram', he began, 'from His Majesty the King. I will read it to you: "Please assure the boys that the King takes the greatest interest in them, and tell them that if he should call upon them later in life, the sense of patriotic responsibility and the habits of discipline which they are now acquiring as boys will enable them to do their duty as men should any danger threaten the Empire." '

After renewed cheering, Baden-Powell commended the boys on the skills they had shown in the day's competitions and presented the prizes to the winners. He finally sent the boys on their way with a ringing challenge to them to live up to their Scout Oath and their Scout Law, and as they marched past him out of the Crystal Palace he stood to attention, giving them the Scout salute. 'It would be difficult' [*Public Opinion* reported], 'to convey an adequate sense of the moving significance of the scene, far more uplifting in its genuine emotionalism and meaning than any other one could think of. It was far more than mere empty pageantry as rank after rank . . . marched on with set and earnest faces under the banner of the Empire. One felt instinctively how much less indifference our present generation of men and women might have been guilty of could they have been subjected to a similar influence in the days that are past.'

To Baden-Powell, the rally had been a stirring experience. He was highly satisfied with the turn-out—nearly eleven thousand at the final count—but he was even happier because of the spirit that had been evident. The boys' self-imposed discipline had made it an easy matter to carry out the programme. He had every reason to be proud of the way his teaching had taken effect.

The Crystal Palace Rally had several far-reaching results.

Baden-Powell, in walking among the Boy Scouts during the competitions, had come upon a small group of seven girls dressed in white blouses, blue skirts and long, black stockings. They wore Scout hats and Scout scarves and carried Scout staves.

'Who are you?' he asked them.

'We are the Girl Scouts', said their spokeswoman, a pert little 11-year-old. They were the first members of a possible feminine counterpart to the Boy Scouts to make a public appearance.

Baden-Powell realized that the time had come for guiding girls in their desire to have the same kind of fun they saw their brothers having. More than six thousand girls had already registered as Boy Scouts at the office in Victoria Street. Numerous other letters had arrived, asking for advice, among them a rather pathetic missive from a young lady:

> Dear Sir, If a girl is not allowed to run, or even to hurry, to swim, ride a bike, or raise her arms above her head, can she become a Scout? Hoping that you will reply. Yours sincerely,
>
> A WOULD-BE SCOUT

B-P knew very well that in certain circles in those Edwardian days it was still considered extremely undignified for any young lady 'to run, or even to hurry'. Any attempt to involve girls in boyish activities would most assuredly, in the mind of large sections of the public, serve to deprive them of their expected maidenly modesty, take them out and away from their duties at home, teach them uncouth manners or none at all, turn them into tomboys. Looked at from the angle of the 11-12-13-year-old boys, girls taking up scouting would turn the boys' game into 'sissy-stuff', and they would have none of it!

The girls, B-P felt, would have to have some kind of scheme expressly designed for them, with the same aim as Boy Scouting—character development and citizenship training—but with activities centred on 'home-making and mother-craft' rather than in robust outdoor adventuring. He would also insist that a girls' movement should stand on its own feet, should not attempt to capitalize on the term 'scouting'.

What to call the girls, then? Baden-Powell picked the name Girl Guides—from a famous corps of guides he knew of in India, 'distinguished for their general handiness and resourcefulness under difficulties, and their keenness and courage . . . a force trained to take up any duties that are required of them, and to turn their hand to anything'. The name also had a symbolic value as implying that guides know the way and lead others in the right direction.

B-P discussed his view on Girl Guiding with his mother and sister. Mrs Baden-Powell proved a valuable critic and adviser. Agnes, the 50-year-old spinster-companion of his mother, was enthusiastic over the possibilities. All three agreed that to get Girl Guiding off to a good start, Baden-Powell himself must be closely associated with its development. The problem was where would he find the time.

There was a simple solution. B-P challenged his sister to take on the development of Girl Guiding, to form a committee to assist her and to re-write *Scouting for Boys* into a handbook for girls.

Agnes accepted. As the sister of the founder of the Boy Scout movement she was the logical choice for president of B-P's new movement for girls. She was also the best guarantee to the mothers of Great Britain that they need have no fear that their daughters, in becoming Girl Guides, would turn into tomboys. 'Anyone', as one of her friends wrote later, 'who had come in touch with her gentle influence, her interest in all womanly arts, and her love of birds, insects, and flowers, would scoff at the idea of her being the president of a sort of Amazon Cadet Corps.'

There was another important outcome of the Crystal Palace Rally. It eventually provided the answer to the main criticism that had been raised against Baden-Powell's Boy Scouts.

Although the majority of the people of the United Kingdom had accepted the scouting idea as 'a good thing', both extreme pacificists and ultra-militarists raised violent objections.

The pacifists accused Baden-Powell of having created a monstrous propaganda machine for indoctrinating the boys of Britain with militaristic ideas. 'It is all a part of a deep scheme', one of them wrote in a Leeds newspaper, 'to foster the military spirit and pave the way ultimately for universal conscription, when these generals, colonels, and other officers hope to be considered of more importance to the nation than statesmen and reformers.' *Scouting for Boys* was condemned by pacifists for its militaristic tendencies: 'The cloven hoof of the military alarmist seeking to embroil the British nation in a bloody war with her neighbour seems to underlie the whole book.'

The militarists, on the other hand, blamed Baden-Powell for muffing his chance to instil a firm military spirit into the youth of the country and for his bungling attempt to turn army life into a game for school children.

Baden-Powell tried to reassure each group but met with little success. To his distress, some of the pacifists set up a splinter group, the National Peace Scouts, while some of the militaristically inclined people established the British Boy Scouts and the Empire Scouts as an answer to his uncompromising stand against including military drill in his scheme. Fortunately for the future of the Scout movement these organizations soon fell apart while the parent movement—popularly referred to now as B-P's Scouts—continued to prosper.

Other attacks against B-P's scheme came from Socialists and a number of trade unions. They accused Baden-Powell of being 'anti-Socialist' and 'anti-union' and 'proved' their point—at least to their own satisfaction—by quoting various paragraphs from *Scouting for Boys* out of context and by harping upon the second point of Baden-Powell's Scout Law: 'A Scout is loyal to the King, and to his officers, and to his country, and to his employers. He must stick to them through thick and thin against anyone who is their enemy, or who even talks badly of them.' A Conservative, arguing the opposite point of view, 'proved' in like fashion that Baden-Powell was a Socialist. B-P, he held, was advocating 'the essence of true Socialism' in the fourth point of his Scout Law: 'A Scout is a friend to all and a brother to every other Scout, no matter to what social class he belongs. . . .' Baden-Powell had even gone so far in *Scouting for Boys* as to insist that 'We are all Socialists . . .'—although he had modified this statement by continuing '. . . in that we want to see the abolition of the existing brutal anachronism of war, and of extreme poverty and misery shivering alongside of superabundant wealth, and so on; but we do not quite agree as to how it is to be brought about.'

Even Ireland joined in attacking the Scout movement. A political faction put up posters and distributed handbills warning the boys of Erin that 'The Baden-Powell Scouts are established in Dublin to tempt Irish boys to betray their country by swearing to be loyal to England's King and to train Irish boys to fight England's battles.' The posters bid the boys: 'Be true to Ireland and do not join the Baden-Powell Scouts.' The effect of the posters was the opposite of what was intended. To many Irish boys, this was their first intimation that such a thing as Boy Scouts existed. And the very fact that they were commanded not to join was the spur they needed for becoming Scouts.

But the major criticism of the Boy Scouts scheme was its supposed lack of religious purpose. Until the advent of scouting, practically every movement for boys had had a church background and religious instruction had been a part of its programme. Now a new movement had appeared on the scene, one without definite church affiliation, one that seemed to pay scant attention to religion. Only two pages of the more than three hundred pages of its handbook, *Scouting for Boys*, dealt with the subject 'Duty to God'.

It made no difference to his critics that Baden-Powell insisted that he had not meant to establish a new movement but had simply intended his scheme and his book to provide a programme of activities for already existing organizations, practically all with a strong church background. The fact remained that a new movement was in being. Letters to the Editor, critical of scouting's religious approach, made their appearance in ever-increasing numbers in *The Times* and other newspapers. The point was even raised on the floor of the House of Commons. The criticism needed to be answered by a clearly formulated policy acceptable not only to church people and the general populace but also to all Scout leaders.

Baden-Powell placed the problem before the hundred participants at the Scoutmasters' Conference that had been convened at the Crystal Palace in conjunction with the rally. He called on H. Geoffrey Elwes to address the gathering on the subject of the attitude of scouting towards religion. As the result of Elwes's clear-cut presentation, the scoutmasters present passed a resolution to the effect 'that the leading representatives of the various denominations should be invited to a conference to discuss methods by which a common and practical religious ideal should be imparted to the movement'.

After this Crystal Palace conference, Baden-Powell and Elwes met with representatives of the major religious denominations. Their efforts resulted in the formulation of a religious policy for the Boy Scouts satisfactory to the heads of all denominations.

Unaffected by the bickerings of their elders, the boys of Britain continued to become Scouts by the thousand. They proudly donned the Scout uniform and stoutly withstood the ridicule to which they were often exposed from boys of the same age who had not caught the scouting 'bug'.

A patrol or troop of Scouts marching down the street in those early days of scouting could generally expect to be accompanied by a horde of jeering hooligans, yelling their contempt, 'Go 'ome and wash your knees!' or bawling

> Here come the Brussel Sprouts,
> The stinking, blinking louts. . . .

Only when the hooting was accompanied by a hail of horse dung did the Scouts turn against their tormentors and scatter them by brandishing their Scout staves.

7

Within a month of the Crystal Palace rally Baden-Powell received an envelope containing a piece of stiff cardboard with some writing surmounted by the royal insignia:

> The Master of the Household is commanded by His Majesty to invite Lieutenant-General R. S. S. Baden-Powell to stay at Balmoral from Saturday the 2 October until Monday the 4 October.

For a couple of anxious days it had seemed as if B-P would have to call off a scheduled appearance before a large gathering of more than five thousand Glasgow Scouts, but by special arrangement of the Master of the Household his arrival at Balmoral was deferred from Saturday to Sunday.

He arrived in style. He was met at Ballater by a royal carriage and pair and driven to the castle. He reached Balmoral just in time for dinner. After being greeted by a large group of guests—mostly military, with Haldane among them—he went to his room to dress.

Almost immediately things began to happen and continued happening until midnight when an exhausted but exhilarated Baden-Powell sat down to add a postscript to a letter he had written to his mother on embossed Balmoral Castle stationery:

> P.S. Just before dinner the King sent for me. The equerry, Col. [H. C.] Legge, took me to his [the King's] room and while outside the door took off my miniature medals and pinned two safety pins on the outside of my coat, and ordered a footman to take in a cushion: it was very like preparation for an execution.
>
> Then he walked in. The King in Highland costume shook hands and kept hold of my hand while he told me that for all my past services and especially my present one of raising Boy Scouts for the country he proposed to make me Knight Commander of the Victorian Order. Then he sat down and I knelt in front of him. The equerry handed him a sword and he tapped me on each shoulder; then hung the cross round my neck and hooked the star of the Order on my coat, and gave me his hand to kiss. And then told me that his valet would put the ribbons right for me, and off I went!
>
> So that's all right, and I hope satisfactory to you, my dear Ma. . . .

When Baden-Powell got back to the drawing-room the whole party of guests was awaiting him, with those possessing the Victorian Order lined up as a guard of honour to shake his hand. 'It was all very embarrassing —and very jolly.' But he found it strange to have people address him as Sir Robert: 'I didn't realize at first who they were alluding to when they said "Sir Robert" does this or that.'

B-P had wondered about the peculiar haste with which he had been made a Knight. He learned the reason as he sat down to dinner: The place card on the table before him carried the legend Sir Robert. The staff officer in charge of seating had assumed that B-P would have been knighted the previous day; it was to make the card correct that the King had had to do the knighting without delay.

After dinner King Edward called the new Knight aside and sat him down on the sofa; the King wanted to learn more about the Boy Scouts from the mouth of the founder. Their conversation lasted for more than half an hour. The King agreed to Baden-Powell's suggestion that boys who passed special tests for efficiency should be ranked as King's Scouts. And Baden-Powell, in turn, agreed to his King's suggestion that he should bring his Scouts to Windsor, some time the following year, for a royal review.

Back in London piles of congratulatory telegrams and letters awaited him. The stream finally abated but only to start again the following month when there was a further announcement that it had pleased His Majesty to make B-P a Knight Commander of the Order of the Bath.

8

Until far into 1909 Baden-Powell had hoped that his Boy Scouts scheme might be the common bond that would bring the existing youth organizations into close touch with each other 'even if the desirable consummation —namely, amalgamation of the whole into one big "combine"—were not possible'. By the autumn of the year his hand was forced: whether he liked it or not his Boy Scouts had become a separate movement clamouring for adequate organization.

All his military life, Baden-Powell had believed that if organization was necessary it should be with as little red tape as possible. A method of decentralization and delegation of responsibility had worked in the South African Constabulary; B-P had every reason to believe that a similar system might work in England for his Boy Scouts scheme. It would be a matter of letting the local committees work within their individual communities and of establishing national committees to give them help and mild supervision from a central headquarters in the British capital.

Baden-Powell went to see an army colleague from his days in India, Lieutenant-General Sir Edmond Roche Elles, G.C.I.E., K.C.B., an outstanding administrator and, like B-P himself, a firm believer in the effectiveness of decentralization. He also discussed his ideas with Sir Herbert Plumer, his old comrade-in-arms from Matabele and Boer War days, and with Colonel Ulick G. C. de Burgh.

Since the Boy Scouts was a voluntary movement, it should, B-P felt, be governed by volunteers. For such volunteers to do an effective job, they should be men of influence with the necessary time at their disposal. He eventually worked out a plan whereby a Governing Council of prominent Britons would be responsible for the association as a whole, while an Executive Committee of this Council would take on specific responsibilities as they arose. To perform the day-to-day work, there would be a Headquarters Staff of volunteers, with salaried secretaries to handle the office routine.

Baden-Powell sent out personal letters to the men he thought best qualified to make up his Governing Council—representatives of existing youth organizations, public schools, physical education institutions, the Services and the Colonies, and of various religious bodies. He explained what he had in mind and invited them to support him in his efforts. Almost all the men whom Baden-Powell invited to serve accepted his invitation. The Governing Council was convened on 10 December

1909, and formed the first Executive Committee of the Boy Scouts Association.

Sir Edmond Elles, as Chief Commissioner, agreed to undertake the task of completing the formation of the country's local associations and nominating local commissioners. Colonel de Burgh, Deputy Chief Commissioner, was to supervise the administration of the Headquarters Staff. Sir Herbert Plumer, Vice-Chairman, agreed to head a department to deal with kindred organizations. Francis W. Pixley, a barrister-at-law in the Middle Temple, accepted the position of Treasurer. Baden-Powell himself was, as a matter of course, Chairman of the Committee.

One of the earliest difficulties to be overcome by the new committee was that of financing the young movement. Up to this time, the financial responsibility of the Boy Scouts scheme had rested exclusively with Baden-Powell. For running the headquarters, he had contributed the income from his book, *Scouting for Boys*, and had made use of the £1,000 provided by Pearson in return for publishing the official organ of the Boy Scout movement and receiving a weekly article from B-P's pen. The deficit the first two years had been paid from private contributions by some of Baden-Powell's friends—a method which obviously could not go on for ever.

Fortunately, the Executive Committee contained a number of hard-headed businessmen. They immediately saw the inequity of the Pearson arrangement and moved to remedy the situation. They formed a Finance Sub-Committee to work out a new agreement. In the discussions that followed, C. Arthur Pearson Ltd. were granted a five-year contract instead of the ten-year contract they had sought. For publishing *The Scout* and using B-P's weekly feature the company was to pay £500 cash and 10 per cent of the profits of the paper. For publishing *Scouting for Boys*, Pearson's would pay a straight 20 per cent royalty—a royalty which Baden-Powell insisted on contributing to the Boy Scouts treasury.

The immediate expenses for running the greatly enlarged headquarters were assured, but still more money was necessary to provide for expansion. The Executive Committee turned to the British public in an appeal for extra funds through annual subscriptions. With the help of some of the newspapers, particularly the *Daily Telegraph*, the sum of £6,000 was raised.

The new movement could look to the future with confidence. With the creation of the Executive Committee, the distribution of the ever-increasing responsibilities and financial backing assured, it was possible for Baden-Powell to concentrate on the things at which he excelled. He would be free to travel round the country to get public support for the movement and to meet the boys themselves; he would be able to keep in touch with

Scouts and leaders alike through the columns of *The Scout* and the newly established *Headquarters Gazette*, through up-to-date, revised editions of *Scouting for Boys*, and through future books on scouting that he hoped to write.

9

By early spring 1910, Baden-Powell reached the conclusion that the Northumbrian Division of the Territorials was so firmly established that his services were no longer needed. On the other hand, the Boy Scouts were moving ahead with such vigour that far more of his time was required to keep the movement on the right track. He and his two travelling inspectors had made a good start in getting local Boy Scout committees established—but the greater part of the country was yet to be covered. Increased travelling and many more conferences lay ahead. If his hopes for scouting were to be fulfilled, the amalgamation of the various splinter groups into the main movement was absolutely necessary. That, too, would require more and yet more of his time than he had hitherto been able to give.

The Scout movement was flourishing because so many adults came forward to further its cause. The least he could do was to give more of his own time, more of his own efforts. The only way this was possible was for him to end his army career, to close the book on his 'first' life, his military life, and dedicate himself to the movement he had founded.

It would be a big wrench for him to take this final step out of the Service. Yet, as he weighed his decision to leave the Army after thirty-four years, he did not mind taking his foot off the military ladder, 'for I had no wish to do any further climbing on it. I was not built for a general. I liked being a regimental officer in personal touch with my men.'

He discussed his plans for the future with his mother and talked them over with Haldane and Lord Roberts, then submitted his request to retire from the Army. Haldane received Baden-Powell's decision with regret although he fully appreciated B-P's motive: 'I feel,' he wrote, 'that this organization of yours has so important a bearing upon the future that probably the greatest service you can render to the country is to devote yourself to it.'

A few days later B-P received a letter from Buckingham Palace. It was from King Edward's secretary:

My dear Baden-Powell, The King was told, incidentally, the other day that you were retiring, and has desired me to write and ask you if this is correct. The King would be sorry to hear if it is the case; but of course you are the best judge of what is best.

Will you send me a line that I can show the King as I am sure he would like to know the reasons which are inducing you to take this extreme step (if the rumour is correct).

I remain yours very sincerely,

ARTHUR DAVIDSON

Baden-Powell sat down and wrote a letter, setting forth in detail the reasoning behind his decision, and sent it off to Buckingham Palace. He was happy, shortly afterwards, to receive his King's assurance that he seemed to have taken the right course. He was less happy to learn from the War Office that the Royal Warrant did not allow a pension for one of his rank retiring at his age. 'My promotion had been so rapid that I was a Lieutenant-General at 50, whereas the warrant did not allow for anyone holding that rank under 62.' Arrangements were, however, eventually made through the King's intercession to grant him a Lieutenant-General's pension.

On 5 May 1910, two days before his retirement went into effect, Baden-Powell went to Buckingham Palace. He was there to pay his respects, as a retiring general, to his King, and to formulate the plans for the royal review of the Boy Scouts which King Edward himself had suggested should take place at Windsor some time during the summer of 1910.

As Baden-Powell was waiting in an ante-room, an equerry came out from the King's chambers. He regretted to have to inform the General that the King was not feeling well. His Majesty would see Sir Robert at a later date—he wanted to assure the General that the June date suggested for the review was agreeable to him.

The following day, although still feeling poorly, the King insisted on getting up and dressing. That afternoon he received the pleasant news that his horse, Witch of the Air, had won at Kempton Park by half a length from the favourite, Queen Tii. In the evening he fainted twice, then lapsed into unconsciousness. He died as Big Ben struck the three-quarter hour after eleven o'clock.

The reign of King Edward VII and the Army career of one of his most devoted generals had come to an end on the same day.

XX

The World Spread of Scouting

Years: 1910–11   Age: 53–54

1

IT did not surprise Baden-Powell that the British dominions, possessions and dependencies should have picked up scouting soon after its appearance in the British Isles—after all, his movement was a British movement meant to appeal to all British boys. But the speed with which scouting spread overseas astonished him. Patrols had sprung up in Canada, Australia and New Zealand in 1908, in India in 1909.

He was more astonished when he discovered that his invention seemed to have the same appeal to boys of other countries as it had to the boys of Britain.

After he told an audience of Chilean educators and boys about scouting on his visit in 1909, Chile had become the first foreign country to take up scouting. Before another year had passed, scouting had spread into neighbouring Argentine and Brazil.

The Scout movement took hold in the United States early in 1910. A Chicago publisher, William D. Boyce, whose tip had been refused by a British Scout who had helped him find his way in a London fog, became so impressed by the boy's attitude that he decided to incorporate a Boy Scouts of America on his return home.

In Europe, without any effort on Baden-Powell's part, scouting had quickly jumped the English Channel and the North Sea. In Belgium, a Royal physician whose son wanted to become a Scout founded the Boy Scouts of Belgium. At about the same time, *Padvinders* made their appearance in Holland and *Éclaireurs* in France. A Danish professor, after a trip to England, gave a lecture on scouting to the boys of a Danish school and the next day eight boys asked the headmaster's permission to start a patrol of *Spejdere*. A young Swedish officer, on a stormy trip on a steamer along the west coast of Sweden, picked up a copy of B-P's

Scouting for Boys, left by a fellow-passenger, decided to translate it into Swedish and became Sweden's first Chief Scout. A British Scout patrol on a walking tour in Germany created an interest among German boys to become *Pfadfinders*. In Russia, the Ministry of Education prepared a translation of Baden-Powell's book for use by the boys of the Russian Empire.

This world spread of scouting gave B-P a great deal of gratification but also a great amount of extra work. Numerous letters reached him at British headquarters from many parts of the world from boys who wanted to join his Scouts. In the beginning he told them simply to live up to the Scout Law and to follow the instructions in *Scouting for Boys*. But it soon became necessary for him to lay down the principle that foreign boys wanting to become Scouts should be members of a national organization of their own country.

Requests for permission to translate *Scouting for Boys* into foreign languages arrived at regular intervals. B-P readily gave his assent. To make the translations legal he asked a fee of one guinea; he was not interested in making money on his book but solely in spreading his scouting scheme.

Before long, he began to receive invitations from different parts of the British Empire and from Scout associations in foreign countries to pay them a visit for the purpose of inspecting his Scouts. The first Empire invitation he accepted came from Canada, the first foreign invitation from the United States of America.

2

For several years there had been agitation in Great Britain to persuade young men to emigrate to Canada. *The Scout* took up the cause. As prizes in its third annual contest it offered the winners a trip to Canada. Of the thousands of boys who entered the contest, sixteen were picked to take the journey under the leadership of Eric Walker of the Headquarters Staff and Captain A. G. Wade, County Secretary for Sussex.

When Lord Grey, B-P's acquaintance from Matabeleland and now Governor-General as well as Chief Scout of Canada, heard of the British Scouts visiting the Dominion, he insisted that Baden-Powell come too. The Canadian Scouts would pay for B-P's ocean journey; the Canadian Railway would give him a free pass.

During the trip across the Atlantic B-P was much impressed with a recent scientific development he found on board: 'One striking feature about the trip is the wireless telegraph through which we are continually in touch with other ships or the shore. The consequence is that a daily newspaper is printed on board and given to every passenger, with the day's latest news by telegraph. It is really wonderful!'

After stopping at Quebec and Montreal, Baden-Powell, his sixteen Scouts and his two leaders boarded the train for the journey across Canada. At Grand Valley, at the foot of the Rockies, B-P said farewell to the British Scouts. There the boys were to camp for a couple of weeks to learn at first hand the kind of life lived by Canadian ranchers, backwoodsmen and Indians, while Baden-Powell, after continuing to the Pacific Coast, returned east, stopping at the main population centres to inspect Canadian Boy Scouts and greet their leaders, to confer with leading authorities and explain to them the aims and methods of the Scout movement.

Back in Quebec, a Canadian officer friend placed an overwhelming temptation in B-P's path: he invited him for a week of camping and fishing in the Canadian wilderness north-west of Ottawa. The prospect of a week's outdoor adventure was too hard to resist. He delayed his scheduled departure from Canada and took to the backwoods.

At a hunting camp at Big Gull Lake he had his first experience of white-water canoeing and portaging, of moose hunting and bass fishing. He was never gripped more firmly by the spell of the outdoors than when he sat by the fire the last night in camp, long after the others had turned in:

> ... a divinely calm velvety night with brilliant stars, moonlit woods, and a deep waiting stillness just broken now and then by the splash of a feeding trout, or the wail of a wildfowl, or, occasionally, the distant moan of a moose—while the fire glowed and smouldered into thin strands of smoke. ...

The next day, back to civilization and off to New York.

Baden-Powell had received reports about the progress of scouting in the United States from Edgar M. Robinson, Senior Secretary of the Y.M.C.A. Committee on Boys' Work and the person mainly responsible for getting American scouting established along the right lines. He had also heard from his old friend Ernest Thompson Seton, who had been elected Chief Scout of the Boy Scouts of America.

He had no real idea of the strength and the scope of the young organization until his day in New York, 23 September. He was received by Robinson, Seton and Dan Beard, the National Scout Commissioner, and taken, as a special treat, to the offices of the *Outlook* magazine to meet Colonel Theodore Roosevelt—the former President of the United States who had agreed to become Honorary Vice-President of the Boy Scouts of America. The main event of B-P's visit was a dinner given to him that evening at the Waldorf-Astoria. He was seated at the main table between

Seton, the Chairman for the occasion, and John D. Rockefeller, Jr., face to face with three hundred representative American citizens, leaders in business and finance, in education and the arts.

After a lively introduction by Seton, Baden-Powell rose to speak. He began by paying a generous tribute to Seton and other American Scout leaders and went on to tell of his experiences in getting scouting under way, of the methods of the Boy Scout scheme, of its aims and values, of

Scouting was the link that tied Baden-Powell's two lives together.

his high hopes for its future in the United States. As he sat down, his speech concluded, the audience rose in a standing ovation.

Among the many foreign letters that greeted B-P on his return to London there was one from the Russian Minister of War in St Petersburg inviting him to visit Russia. B-P hadn't been in Russia since he was there with his brother in 1886. Curious to learn what changes had taken place, he decided to spend the New Year there.

On the last day of 1910 he strolled through the streets of St Petersburg. Snow had fallen during the night, 'all wheeled vehicles had ceased to run and everywhere sledges were dashing about'. The city looked much as it had looked twenty-four years before, 'except that the shops are very much modernized and the tea houses are now restaurants or electric cinematograph theatres. Crowds of prosperous-looking people in the street indicate a middle class growing up in St Petersburg.'

On 2 January, B-P went by train to Czarskoe Selo where he was ushered into the study of Czar Nicholas II. To Baden-Powell, the Czar looked very much like his own King George V, but paler and more tired-looking and with lighter hair. 'There was no ceremony about him: he shook hands and, speaking in very good English, asked me about my visit and then went on to talk about the Boy Scouts.' The Czar had himself read *Scouting for Boys* and had himself ordered it to be translated into Russian. The first school that had taken up scouting was located in South Russia, and the Czar had the boys brought up to Czarskoe Selo so that he could inspect them, thereby encouraging other schools to start the scouting programme. The Czar asked B-P about progress in other countries, 'after which we parted, having had a very cheery talk (no one else present) of over half an hour'.

In Moscow Baden-Powell was entertained by the Russian Boy Scout Committee to dinner and was informed of the steady growth of the Russian movement—Moscow alone had more than three thousand Scouts.

3

Throughout the early months of 1911, much of Baden-Powell's time was taken up with leadership training and the financial problems of the Scout movement. The membership had reached 107,986 boys and leaders, according to the first census taken at the end of 1910. To provide for sound expansion, a thorough training of the leaders in the aims and methods of scouting became more and more imperative.

After discussing the subject with some of his helpers, B-P wrote out the syllabus for the first scoutmasters' training course. He turned the organization of a course in London over to Captain Wade, just appointed to the Headquarters Staff as organizing secretary, but ran the course himself over a three-week period starting on 17 January. The talks by Baden-Powell and his assistants became the basis for future training programmes.

While the movement itself had shown a steady growth, the Headquarters Staff had jumped in three short years from a single man and a single secretary in a single room in Henrietta Street to an office force of twenty-six volunteer and paid staff members in twelve rooms in Victoria Street. A yet larger staff was required to organize and train an ever-increasing membership. And a larger staff meant more money.

The public appeal of 1910 had placed the movement on a sound financial basis. The death of King Edward had temporarily halted it before its goal had been reached. A new start was made in January 1911 at an inaugural banquet which resulted in the course of the evening in promises amounting to over £3,000. Baden-Powell's concern for financing a growing staff was again temporarily relieved. He could resume his promotional efforts and his inspections.

4

On 22 May 1911, at a luncheon party in Lincoln following one of his Boy Scout functions, B-P was seated next to an American lady whom he judged to be a couple of years younger than he. In reality, Juliette Gordon Low was 50 to Baden-Powell's 54. Mrs Low, who was exceedingly deaf and had to use a hearing aid, overcame any difficulty by doing most of the talking herself—and she had much to talk about. She had travelled widely in Europe, in Egypt, in India, in places thoroughly familiar to Baden-Powell. She had many friends in common with the General, among them Lord Mahon, General Sir Archibald Alexander, and Major Neville Smyth, B-P's cousin. She had recently spent several months in Paris sculpting under an excellent French instructor and was continuing her hobby in London under an English teacher.

She had B-P's complete attention. He had himself experimented with sculpting. He had made a couple of pieces while at Malta under the instruction of an Italian teacher, and in 1907 had had a bust he had made of one of his heroes, Captain John Smith of Virginia, exhibited at the Royal Academy. They discussed styles and methods, compared notes on armatures and materials. When Baden-Powell mentioned that he knew Signor Lanteri, the portrait sculptor, Juliette Low became excited. Did he think that Lanteri might take her on as a pupil?

Juliette Low accepted with pleasure an invitation to visit the Baden-Powells. She and B-P went to see Lanteri and talked sculpture before returning to 32 Princes Gate for a very amiable tea presided over by Baden-Powell's mother, with Agnes in attendance.

Mrs Low was intrigued with everything she was shown: B-P's sketch-books and trophies from Africa and India, Agnes's nature collections, the mother's mementoes of her children. They talked about their various interests—one of Mrs Low's was palmistry—but soon the conversation turned to Boy Scouting and Girl Guiding. Mrs Baden-Powell, 87 years of age at the time, said little but listened the more. Mrs Low seemed to be a very pleasant lady—although American, deaf and rather old.

Juliette Low returned to her house in Grosvenor Street with her mind in turmoil. That night she wrote in her diary:

> 30 May, I looked into the lines of his hand, which are very odd and contradictory. The impression he makes on one is equally contradictory. For instance, all of his portraits and all of his writings represent him in action, essentially a man of war, though never has any human given me such a feeling of peace. He rushes from one engagement to another, though he doesn't strike me as restless or

pushed or driven. It may be because in his own mind he is not personally seeking anything. His activities are for mankind and he has, perhaps, eliminated the effort to attain things for himself. . . . To him his own life, as a unit, is apparently unimportant.

During the days that followed, Juliette Low's thoughts continued to be preoccupied with her meeting with Baden-Powell:

1 June, Today in the few moments I have had to myself, my mind has irresistibly dwelt on B-P. A sort of intuition comes over me that he believes I might make more out of my life, and that he has ideas, which if I follow them, will open a more useful sphere of work before me in the future.

Mrs Low, wealthy American expatriate, had reached a point in her existence where she was in desperate need of finding something that would give meaning to her life.

Juliette Low—born Juliette Magill Kinzie Gordon on 31 October 1860— was the daughter of William Washington Gordon II, a well-to-do business- man of Savannah, Georgia.

Within a week of Juliette Low's birth Abraham Lincoln was elected President of the United States. Four months later Georgia and the Southern States had seceded from the Union and had created the Con- federate States. On 12 April 1861, Fort Sumter was bombarded—the Civil War had started. Her father, a true Southerner, signed up in the Confederate forces. He fought through the long, dreary years of the conflict. When the war ended with his cause lost, he was reunited with his family. The family fortune was gone. Energetically, he set out to rebuild it. By the middle 1870s, the Gordon name was again of importance in Savannah.

After the sad war days of her early years, Juliette Gordon had a happy girlhood. She developed into a vivacious and charming young woman, brimful of energy and with a quick wit. Her health was generally good— except for the sadly impaired hearing in one ear caused by the piercing of the eardrum in the lancing of an abscess.

On trips to England in 1882 and 1884 Juliette Gordon met Willy Low, the tall, handsome son of Andrew Low, a Scottish multi-millionaire and one of her father's business associates. When Willy Low told his father that he intended to marry Juliette Gordon, the elder Low readily gave his blessing and settled a sufficient annual income on his son to permit the young couple a comfortable life. His death shortly before their wedding made the couple even wealthier. Soon after her wedding Mrs Low became

The Camp

To test his 'Boy Scouts scheme', Baden-Powell held the world's first Boy Scout camp on Brownsea Island, Poole Harbour, August 1907.

Baden-Powell on his way to the Brownsea Island camp with the four Rodneys and the two Nobles.

B-P in makeshift Scout uniform.

Baden-Powell (right) telling a campfire story during the Boy Scout camp at Humshaugh, August 1908.

The first Girl Scout at Crystal Palace, 1909.

King George V and B-P at the Windsor Rally, 1911.

Olave St Clair Soames at the time she met B-P on their voyage in 1912.

Eighty-nine-year-old Mrs Baden-Powell with her grandson, Peter.

*Sir Robert,
Chief Scout of the
British Empire.*

At Little Mynthurst, 1917: B-P with Heather;
Peter; Olave with Betty.

Lieutenant-General Baden-
Powell at the front, 1916.

The first Wood Badge Course at Gilwell Park in September 1919. At
B-P's right: Francis Gidney. Behind Gidney: Major A. G. Wade.

CLIMAX TWO

The climax event of Baden-Powell's second
life occurred in Olympia, London, at the
closing of the first World Jamboree. On
7 August 1920, the Boy Scouts of the world
proclaimed B-P 'Chief Scout of the World'.

B-P and Prince of Wales, Imperial Jamboree, 1924.

With the Danish King Christian X at the Second World Jamboree. At left: Queen Alexandrine and Lady B-P.

Inspecting the Fourth World Jamboree in Hungary, 1933, with Count Paul Teleki.

B-P with the Duke of Connaught, at opening of Third World Jamboree, 1929.

Chief Scout of the World and World Chief Guide in Australia in 1931.

B-P, the artist, painting a water-colour (notice use of left hand).

B-P, Chief Scout of the World at age 80.

'Now the time has come for me to say good-bye . . .' Baden-Powell bids the Scouts farewell at the closing of the Fifth World Jamboree, Holland, 1937.

The Baden-Powell family, 1940. Gervas and Betty Clay with their daughter Gillian. B-P and Lady Baden-Powell with Robin Clay, son of Gervas and Betty. Peter and Carine Baden-Powell with their son Robert.

deaf in her other ear. A hunting accident ended her riding. Internal disorders undermined her health.

Willy Low had always been a gay blade. He had no intention of allowing a deaf and ailing wife to spoil his fun. He went with male companions to hunt in Africa and India and was seen with female companions in many European pleasure spots. The estrangement between Willy Low and his wife resulted in their separation in 1901. Divorce proceedings were started and dragged on while Juliette Low's health returned and Willy Low's slowly disintegrated. The divorce settlements had not been completed when Juliette Low learned in June 1905 of her husband's death.

After many years of emotional upheaval, Mrs Low could now attempt to rebuild her life.

The day after their visit to Lanteri's studio, Mrs Low sent B-P an invitation for supper. He was not able to go—he was off again on some of his Boy Scout inspections. But he got back in time to join Mrs Low and a few of her friends in a box at the Shakespeare Ball.

During this period London was waiting excitedly for the Coronation of King George V and Queen Mary.

On Coronation Day, 22 June, space on Constitution Hill had been reserved for the Boy Scouts. Baden-Powell, in Scout uniform with shorts and broad-brimmed hat, took his position in front of a hundred picked British Scouts, most of them wearing the life-saving medal, and a Canadian contingent of another hundred.

Just before the final arrangements were completed, three magnificent horses came by. The riders, three military men with nodding plumes and rows of medals, were greeted with enthusiastic cheers from the crowd— they were Lord Wolseley, Lord Roberts and Lord Kitchener. As they came opposite the Scouts, they stopped and saluted, then bent down to shake hands with Baden-Powell and to speak warmly with him for a few minutes, before moving off to take their places in the Coronation procession—while B-P returned to stand with his Scouts to cheer Their Majesties as they passed by.

B-P had been detailed to attend the Thanksgiving Service on 27 June. He decided to use the occasion to repay Mrs Low for her hospitality. He would slip away in the morning to get her and her American companion, Mrs Davis, installed in one of the windows of Mercers' Hall from which they would be able to witness the Royal Procession passing in the street immediately below. He might also be able to secure tickets for the ladies for the service in St Paul's by appealing directly to the Dean.

According to plan, Baden-Powell joined the ladies for breakfast, then drove with them to the City.

> We got out and had to walk one hundred yards [Juliette Low reported to her family], and Baden-Powell was recognized and the whole mass of people along the tour began cheering him. He was in full uniform (13th Hussars) and we walked in the middle of a perfectly empty space in the street—soldiers, two-deep, lining each side and thousands of people on the sidewalks cheering B-P to the echo. I liked it. We got to our places in the Mercers' Hall and then drove to St Paul's Cathedral where the ceremony was touching and solemn and very beautiful.

In Juliette Low, Baden-Powell had found his match in quantity of letter writing.

He had long ago accustomed himself to answer all letters by personal notes immediately upon their receipt, but his correspondence with Mrs Low during the early summer of 1911 turned into a tennis match. He had hardly answered a letter from her before an answer to his answer was posted which in turn required an answer—or at least an acknowledgement since many of the lady's missives were unanswerable.

Mrs Low on her part had found in B-P a person worthy of cultivation. She complimented him on his art work in his sketch-books, chided him coyly about a future Lady Baden-Powell, hinted she had found the right mate for him, sent him analyses of his character based on his handwriting. Her letters amused him—but he considered her character analyses as being well off the mark:

> I am not so unhappy you know [he wrote to her]. I know my weak points and am only thankful that I have managed to get along in spite of them! I think that's the policy for this world: Be glad of what you have got, and not miserable about what you would like to have had, and not over-anxious as to what the future will bring.

Her invitations were another matter. She asked him to supper parties in her London home, suggested that he join her and her friends in her box at the opera, offered him the use of her motor-car. Baden-Powell succeeded in coming for supper one evening and in dropping in at her box another night for a short while, and accepted a ride to Godalming for the Tercentenary Celebrations at Charterhouse—but for the rest had to beg off because of his crowded schedule.

5

The death of King Edward VII had cancelled the royal review of the Boy Scouts scheduled for June 1910 at Windsor. A year later, King George V, who, like his father, had become the Patron of the Boy Scout movement, agreed to carry out the review.

It was of extreme importance to the future of the movement that this Royal Rally should be the greatest possible success. To ensure this, Baden-Powell lined up a small committee of capable men to handle the preparations: General Sir Herbert Plumer, Colonel H. S. Brownrigg, and Percy W. Everett who had become very active in scouting as a county commissioner. The details of managing the affair B-P entrusted to Captain Wade.

On 4 July 1911, the largest and most representative gathering of boys that England had ever seen assembled in Windsor Great Park. They came from every county in England, from Scotland, Ireland, and Wales and were joined by detachments from Malta, Gibraltar and Canada. The final number was close on thirty thousand, plus additional thousands of spectators.

Soon after noon the Scouts began to move from their temporary positions on the nine assembly areas towards the parade ground. Here they formed three semi-circles, one behind the other, each of them twenty-four Scouts deep. It was an amazing sight, with the brilliant sunshine playing on the boys' faces, on their multi-coloured neckerchiefs, on patrol flags and troop banners and Union Jacks.

At three o'clock a hush fell over the large crowd. Baden-Powell, mounted on a black horse, raised his hand and the mass of boys, as one man, came to the alert. A knot of horsemen approached from Windsor Castle. First King George V attended by the Duke of Connaught, Prince Christian, and Prince Alexander of Teck. Then Field-Marshals Lord Roberts and Lord Grenfell, General Sir John French, and two gorgeously attired Indian Maharajahs. And in a carriage behind the horsemen, Queen Mary, Edward, Prince of Wales, and the Royal Princesses. As the procession reached the parade ground the band struck up the National Anthem.

The King beckoned Baden-Powell to his side and, followed by his glittering staff, set off on the tour of inspection. For more than half an hour they wended their way on horseback along the front of each of the columns, each of the semi-circles, greeted wherever they went by tornadoes of cheers.

With the inspection over, the King took his place under the Royal

Standard at the saluting point. Baden-Powell, on his black horse, gave another signal for the most stirring incident of the day—the Grand Rush, invented by B-P for the occasion.

> A sudden roar filled the air, and the whole mighty horseshoe of thirty thousand boys with one impulse leapt forward from either side, rushing as only boys can rush, gathering speed and force as they came, screaming out the rallying cries of their patrols as they swept, a kaleidoscopic mass of colour, with flags fluttering, hats waving, knees glinting, in the great charge towards the King.

There was a gasp from the spectators—it seemed for a moment as if the King would be engulfed in the foaming wave. But no—at a line which none but the Scouts knew, the wave stopped dead, as if suddenly frozen. The tumult died. In the sudden abrupt silence, the Chief Scout called for three cheers for His Majesty.

> Up went a forest of staves and hats, and higher into the sky went the shrill, screaming cheers of the boys in a cry that gripped the throat of every onlooker—'God Save the King'—that apogee of patriotic fervour in young Britain, that surge of enthusiasm to do anything that might be demanded of them in the name of their country and their King.

B-P's eyes were moist. 'That was one of the most thrilling moments of my life!'

6

With the climactic scouting event of the year successfully behind him Baden-Powell felt himself entitled to a working holiday. He would go fishing in Norway for a couple of weeks with an old friend, then follow up on the invitations he had received to review the Scouts of some of the countries of northern Europe.

Just before leaving for Norway he received a letter from Mrs Low inviting him to join her and her party in Scotland for some trout fishing at Lochs in Perthshire, a lodge she had rented. To stay at Lochs on his way north fitted in perfectly with B-P's plans for he could go on to Norway by boat from Scotland.

During his four days there he had several long talks with Juliette Low. He decided on some proselytizing—perhaps Girl Guide leadership would give her life the meaning she sought for it. She agreed to try, starting with the girls in the vicinity of Lochs.

B-P's departure took on the aspect of tragi-comedy. Mrs Low's butler had an attack of delirium tremens and became violent. The only person who could handle him was Baden-Powell, who got the raving butler safely on to a train for London, arranged for the guard to look after him, then left for Norway.

In Copenhagen, Danish Boy Scouts and Girl Guides formed an archway of staves for Baden-Powell's motor to pass through.

On the way home from his holiday Baden-Powell stopped in Christiania and Stockholm, in Copenhagen and Amsterdam and Namur in Belgium. Everywhere hundreds of Scouts turned out to hail him as their Chief.

In Norway he learned of the existence of two separate Boy Scout associations—his coming brought them together. The same was the case in Holland. In Sweden, Dr Sven Hedin, the famous explorer of Tibet, proved to be one of the moving spirits of the Swedish Scout Council. Together, he and Hedin reviewed a Scout parade attended by the Crown Prince and Princess and spent a long afternoon at the Palace discussing scouting with King Oscar II. In Denmark he found the Scouts almost more enthusiastic than English boys: 'After the parade they made an avenue with staves crossed overhead through which we drove in the motor.' In Holland and Belgium he was greatly impressed by the Scout displays put on for him.

These past few days [he wrote to his mother in reporting his trip] have been a very useful winding-up to my holiday. They have enabled me to feel that I have killed two birds with one stone—for while the trip through Norway, Sweden, Denmark, Holland and Belgium has been a most interesting one, it has at the same time put me in touch with the Boy Scout movement in all those countries, which I have found much more advanced than I had thought. . . .

It will become an international movement before long, I do believe!

Baden-Powell was understating the case. Scouting was not becoming an international movement; it already was one. It only waited for the founder to tie the strands together, which he promptly proceeded to do.

The next month Baden-Powell reported on his trip in the British *Headquarters Gazette* and informed his readers: 'In several cases I was urged to start an International Alliance of the various organizations, and these have since been backed by further applications from other countries. For these reasons we propose to start a Foreign Department in our office for the promotion of international touch.'

7

The few hours that Baden-Powell took off from scouting were as fully occupied as the rest.

He was very conscientious about his hereditary membership in the Mercers' Company. He attended the weekly meetings whenever he was in London and accepted assignments turned over to him. The Mercers had made him a Warden of their ancient Company in 1910. In 1911 they elected him to take office the following year as Master, a task that carried with it the Chairmanship of the Governors of St Paul's School—the school that three of his brothers had attended.

In addition to his duties with the Mercers' Company, B-P also did his utmost to keep up his relationships with his old army friends. Every year on Mafeking Day he had dinner with the officers of the defending force and of the relief force, and once a year the South African Constabulary Old Comrades gathered for a reunion. So did the old members of the 5th Dragoon Guards and of the 13th Hussars and B-P made a special point of being present.

In November 1911, he was saddened by the death of his old colonel, Baker Russell, although there was a measure of compensation connected with it. On 9 December, the official *Gazette* carried the news that Baden-Powell had been appointed to the colonelcy of the 13th Hussars.

As 1911 drew to a close B-P was gratified by another achievement.

For more than a year, he and members of his Boy Scouts Council had been at work trying to secure a Royal Charter, which would give the move-ment a special standing in the eyes of the country and would help im-measurably in extending the work. Their petition had been presented to His Majesty in Council. By the end of December the petition had been cleared for the King's signature.

On 4 January 1912, King George V signed the Royal Charter of Incor-poration, ordaining that the petitioners with Baden-Powell as Chairman of the Council, 'shall be one body corporate and politic by the name of The Boy Scouts Association for the primary object of instructing boys of all classes in the principles of discipline, loyalty and good citizenship'.

B-P received the news by radio as he was on the high seas. 'This gives the seal of the highest approval in the land upon our aims and methods,' he commented.

XXI

A Journey of Consequence

Year: 1912   Age: 55

1

AT about this time Baden-Powell had a dream that he duly recorded in one of his books:

> When I arrived at the Gate of Heaven, Saint Peter had a friendly chat with me and, after questioning me a good deal about my doings on Earth, asked:
> 'And how did you like Japan?'
> 'Japan!' I replied. 'I was never in Japan.'
> 'But my dear man,' said Saint Peter, 'what were you doing all your life? Do you suppose you were put into that world, with all its beauties and wonderful countries, merely to sit down in one corner of it and not go abroad and see what God set out for you? Go back, man, and see all you can while yet you have time.'
> I awoke!
> I lost little time in carrying out Peter's timely hint. I went to Japan, and I went to many other parts of the world and tramped and camped in them and thoroughly enjoyed the varying beauties and wonders of each in turn.

Baden-Powell's dream became a reality through an enterprising American impresario, Lee Keedick, who at the early age of 32 was already the aggressive head of a New York lecture bureau.

Keedick was in London during the winter of 1911 to add more notables to his string of lecturers, which had previously included Sir Arthur Conan Doyle, H. G. Wells, G. K. Chesterton and other English celebrities. This time he decided to add Baden-Powell to his galaxy of speakers. He approached B-P with a lucrative offer of an all-expenses-paid trip through America with a guaranteed sum for a series of twenty lectures in that number of major cities. Keedick knew his American lecture audience. What it would want from the famous General Baden-Powell was a heavy dose of his adventures in India and Africa, with a smattering of Boy Scouting thrown in for the sake of those who had taken an interest in this new fad.

It didn't take Baden-Powell long to decide. He had had many requests to return to America after his short visit in 1910 and was curious about the growth of the Boy Scout movement in the United States. Also, the income from the lecture tour would provide him with funds that would make it possible for him to continue from the west coast of America around the world. He would be able to inspect Scouts in many other countries, giving him a chance to promote scouting to a greater extent than before.

The news that Baden-Powell was coming to the United States was greeted with enthusiasm by the national leaders of the young American Boy Scout movement—an enthusiasm that changed to dismay when the Chief Scout Executive of the Boy Scouts of America, the young Washington lawyer, James E. West, learned the terms of the contract signed by Baden-Powell for his tour. The agreement was so iron-clad that it would be impossible for B-P even to attend the Annual Meeting of the American Scout movement. He could not accept any hospitality where he would meet any considerable number of people—luncheons, dinners and other social engagements—without the explicit written consent of the manager of the lecture bureau. Furthermore, West was apprehensive about the effect of Baden-Powell, in his capacity as a British General, lecturing about his war experiences at a time when a vocal minority group in America was insisting that the Scout movement was a cloak for military preparedness.

West wrote to Baden-Powell to find out what could be done about the situation. B-P could do nothing—beyond referring West to Keedick. West met Keedick and proposed to him that the Boy Scouts of America take over his lecture contract with Baden-Powell. Keedick was agreeable —at a price. To him, Baden-Powell's engagement was a commercial enterprise from which he expected to reap a substantial income.

After a number of conferences, Keedick agreed to sub-let Baden-Powell to the American Boy Scout movement. He reserved for himself B-P's first seven lectures in America, from his arrival on 31 January until 9 February. The Boy Scouts could then have him for the remaining thirteen lectures. The compensation to Keedick was underwritten by three wealthy members of the Boy Scouts' Executive Board. The sum was high, but the expenditure was considered justified in view of the expected benefits of focusing public attention upon scouting and presenting the true merits of the movement.

West was jubilant. He immediately sent off to London an intensive programme for Baden-Powell's tour. It included a review of a Boy Scout guard of honour on arrival at every stop where a lecture was to be held, a luncheon by the local civic leaders, a dinner by the mayor of the city or the governor of the state as the case demanded, and an indoor Boy Scout demonstration followed by Baden-Powell's lecture.

B-P put his foot down! He had agreed to a lecture tour, not a whirl of social functions. He had just gone through a few very strenuous years of organizing the British Boy Scouts Association during which he had steadily overtaxed himself. He was willing to do his best to accommodate the Boy Scouts of America and to help promote the movement in the United States. The American leaders, in turn, would have to take his health into consideration. West reluctantly submitted.

2

On the afternoon of 3 January 1912, Donald and Maude Baden-Powell, son and daughter of B-P's late brother George, wished their uncle *bon voyage* as he embarked in the S.S. *Arcadian*—an 8,000-ton steamer formerly employed on mail service between England and Australia but recently converted into a 'cruising yacht *de luxe*' for the tourist traffic to the West Indies and New York.

As soon as the ship was well out of Southampton Water, Baden-Powell looked over the passenger list. A few names were familiar—some Government officials returning to duty in the West Indies and Central America, a couple of writers, and people like himself in search of sunshine and travel adventure. Under the letter 'L' he came upon 'Mr A. M. Low, Mrs Low, Mrs Low and maid. . . .' Obviously a printer's error—there would certainly only be one Mrs Low accompanying Mr A. M.

The first morning out B-P strolled the long promenade deck that extended the full length of the ship. There was a stiff breeze blowing. The ship was rolling and only a few passengers were on deck. As he walked along, he noticed two ladies ahead of him. He recognized one of them as Miss Hildabert Rodewald, a friend of his family in London. He did not know the other, yet there was something vaguely familiar about her. He must have met her somewhere. He searched his memory. No. . . . and yet . . . then he remembered: her gait, that quick determined gait. He couldn't be wrong.

As the ladies turned and came towards him Baden-Powell took off his yachting cap in greeting. Miss Rodewald held out a gloved hand.

'General,' she said, 'I want you to meet a friend of mine, Miss Olave Soames.'

The General bowed. 'Delighted!' His eyes swept approvingly over the young lady's smiling face with the frank, brown eyes.

Now to find out if he had remembered correctly. He charged the young lady with living in London. Wrong. She lived in Dorset.

'But you have a brown and white spaniel?'

'Yes.' The lady showed surprise.

'And you have been in London? Near Knightsbridge Barracks?'

'Yes, two years ago.'

It was the same girl—the girl whose gait he had noticed as he was hurrying one day through Kensington Gardens towards the Barracks. She was the same girl who had walked in a way which, according to his notions of human characteristics, had shown her 'to be possessed of honesty of purpose and common sense as well as a spirit of adventure'.

When other friends of Miss Rodewald appeared on the scene, she excused herself, leaving Baden-Powell and Olave Soames alone. They quickly found things to talk about as they slowly walked the deck of the rolling ship. Miss Soames had, of course, heard of Baden-Powell. She had followed his career ever since the days of the Boer War when, as a 10-year-old girl, she, like millions of other Britons, had bought and worn a button with his portrait. They discovered that they shared 22 February as a birthday with each other and with a famous American, George Washington. They were both interested in music, art, nature, sport and especially horses and dogs. The subjects for conversation seemed inexhaustible.

They sat down in deck-chairs and were provided by the deck steward with steamer rugs against the January chilliness. They were so deep in conversation that they hardly noticed what was happening around them, and only the signal announcing the approaching dinner-hour made them interrupt their conversation.

That evening, at Captain Custance's table, Baden-Powell was introduced to a group of selected guests including Harold Soames, the father of Olave.

Soames was a tall, slim, well-to-do Englishman, only a few years older than Baden-Powell. He had inherited a large brewing business from his father and had tended it successfully for a number of years before retiring at an early age to devote his time to travel, architecture, painting and gardening. He was now on his annual search for sun and warmth. Soames knew the General by reputation and had heard of B-P's artistic abilities. The two men soon found themselves engaged in a vivid discussion about art and happily discovered that their common speciality was water-colours.

The following day the movement of the ship became smoother. Passengers who had previously kept to their cabins ventured out on deck.

Baden-Powell was greeted most heartily by one of them: Mrs Juliette Low.

She had a ready explanation for her presence on board. She had originally planned to go to Rome for the winter but had changed her mind because she had learned that her business affairs in Colombia needed looking into. But now that Baden-Powell was here, he would be able to help her decide what steps she should take to get Girl Guiding established in the United States. She had made up her mind to get a company under way in Savannah the moment she returned home.

Although B-P had hoped to steer clear of any discussions about scouting and guiding during the trip, this was an impossibility with Mrs Low on deck whenever the weather was good. She was determined to dedicate the rest of her life to found and to foster, in the United States, the female branch of Baden-Powell's movement and needed all the advice he could give her.

The weather again turned rough, with a strong head wind and lumpy seas. Again the deck was almost deserted, except for the more determined travellers.

Olave Soames made her appearance on deck, alone. Baden-Powell joined her. They strolled the deck in spite of the ship's pitching, then relaxed in deck-chairs. Miss Soames had an eager interest in every subject that arose and her young enthusiasm drew him out. He surprised himself by telling her about thoughts and feelings he had never before confided to anyone else. Her laughter was contagious, her seriousness deeply moving. He had never met anybody quite like her before.

When, a few days later, Olave Soames agreed to serve on the committee organizing a concert, she turned to B-P for assistance. The rehearsal in the forenoon was very satisfactory and the rest of the day simply 'glorious', according to Olave's diary: 'Had B-P to myself all day, till 11 p.m. Such interesting conversation on religion, etc., sitting aft watching phosphorus balls of light whilst other people dance.' And the next day: 'Do sports and win potato race in intervals between sitting with B-P on the top deck. Yes, I'm up against it.'

Once, at a gathering of officer comrades, when B-P scoffed about the idea of ever getting married, a friend of his, 'Ginger' Gordon of the 15th Hussars, had warned him: 'You'll get it in the neck one day when you least expect it, old boy!'

The day had arrived!

From the moment Baden-Powell met Olave, his mind was filled with thoughts of her. His whole being was stirred as it had never been before. Was she his fate? Was she the kind of girl his mother meant for him when she had occasionally advised him to find a 'young woman'?

The pros and cons began to line themselves up in his mind. She was so young—22 to his 54. But so had his mother been young when she married —21 to his father's 49. He had heavy financial obligations in regard to 32 Princes Gate. But counting up all the family income there should be enough left to manage another establishment. He would have less freedom to look after his Boy Scouts. But a young vigorous wife might be just the helpmate he needed.

As the *Arcadian* ploughed its way across the Atlantic and into the Caribbean Sea, Olave Soames entered each day's outstanding events in her diary:

> Wednesday, 17 January, Up before dawn just to see him and kiss him. See Venezuela coast in dim distance. . . . Small talks with various people and the beloved Scout is always there. He gives me a photo album and sketches.
> Sunday, 21 January, Frightfully hot. Arrive at Colon. Boy Scouts to meet him of course.
> Tuesday, 23 January, Visit Panama Canal. Sail at two. Out to sea and she pitches like anything, but, oh, I'm so happy all day with him. He sketches away and I talk and we laugh together. Even when we try to be serious the imp of mirth steps in. We feel and think alike about everything. Perfect bliss.

When the *Arcadian* reached Kingston, Olave had come to the end of the journey. Harold Soames and his daughter were scheduled to spend the next few weeks in Jamaica.

During the day the ship stayed in port, Mr Soames, Olave and B-P joined some of the other tourists for a sight-seeing trip 'in a rather bumpy motor over a very bumpy road'.

After dinner that night Olave went for a stroll. So did Baden-Powell. He 'happened' to overtake her on the way to the harbour. The evening was warm. They sat down close to each other on the edge of one of the piers, dangling their toes over the water. They spoke gaily for a while, then fell silent. The parting in the morning lay heavily on their minds.

Baden-Powell was particularly troubled. For the next months he would be travelling farther and farther away from the girl he wanted. Was he to lose her again? If only. . . . In his desperation he blurted out, 'Why don't

you come with me? Why don't we get Captain Custance to marry us?'
And knew immediately that he had suggested an impossibility.

The next morning Baden-Powell was up early. He picked up his set of
water-colours and went to sketch the palm trees near the pier where Olave
and he had sat the previous night. Back at the hotel he looked for her but
did not find her. He wrote a note, included it with the sketches and gave
them to the porter to deliver to Miss Soames.

He had left the hotel and was on his way to the ship when he spotted
her in front of him on the road. He hurried to catch up with her. She
was not alone. The best he could manage was to shake hands with a
most casual 'Well—good-bye'.

The moment the *Arcadian* steamed out of Kingston Harbour bound for
New York, Baden-Powell sat down at the writing-desk in the ship's lounge
and wrote his first letter to Olave Soames:

> 26 January 1912, It is much worse than I had expected, to be on
> board—and no you to be found. It is exactly the feeling I had when
> my two mates had been killed in Matabeleland—one kept looking
> round expecting to see them as usual at the camp fire—whereas, they
> were dead ... the stitches in my heart tighten as I remember there is
> no little friend on board. ...

3

When the *Arcadian* docked in New York Harbour on 31 January, Baden-
Powell stepped down the gangway into the clutches of a dozen reporters,
into the lenses of as many photographers, and into the waiting arms of
his lecture manager and the American Chief Scout Executive and a guard
of honour of forty New York Scouts.

A 14-year-old Brooklyn Boy Scout, Billy Walker, wearing the Life-
saving Medal for having rescued another boy from drowning, saluted
Baden-Powell and presented him with a letter of welcome from the
President of the United States. B-P took the letter and shook Billy's hand
to the accompaniment of clicking camera shutters. There were calls of
'One more please!' and yet more. At last Baden-Powell turned his back
on the photographers ('They could not understand why I didn't want any
more of it!') and was whisked off to the Waldorf-Astoria by his reception
committee.

During the next eight days, under the aegis of Keedick, Baden-Powell
lectured at large audiences in Boston, Montclair, New Jersey, Washington,
D.C., Detroit, Chicago, and Pittsburgh. He managed the hurried travelling and his lecturing with comparative ease. His main problem was that

his steps all along the way were dogged by the energetic James E. West whose big objective was to have B-P's visit everywhere count as strongly as possible towards the future success of the Boy Scout movement in America.

B-P found himself in triple jeopardy. West had alerted city and state officials as well as local Boy Scout executive boards of the coming of the British Chief Scout and the Founder of the Boy Scout movement, and everywhere the British consuls rushed into the act. Wherever Baden-Powell arrived he was greeted by the very kind of official reception he had refused to consider and became involved in formal and informal luncheons and dinners arranged without his consent.

He somehow carried through the first week's intensive programme, shunted round from place to place with no rest and little sleep because of night travel. He participated, although reluctantly, in certain social functions that could not have been cancelled without detriment to American scouting—such as a dinner for a select group of New York financiers, a luncheon at the Boston City Club presided over by the Lieutenant-Governor of Massachusetts, a tea with the Andrew Carnegies in New York, and a reception by President William Howard Taft in the White House.

On 9 February, Keedick turned his lecturer over to the Boy Scouts of America as the main attraction of the Second Annual Meeting at the Hotel Astor in New York. Here, in the evening, he faced 'a splendid audience' of six hundred leading New York men and women at a dinner presided over by Gifford Pinchot, the former Chief of the United States Forestry Service.

The next day, five thousand Boy Scouts from New York, New Jersey and Connecticut, assembled in the Seventy-first Regiment Armory, showed him, in a three-hour demonstration, what American Scouts could do. When he stepped into their midst, at the end of the performance, the cheers rose around him and continued unabated for five minutes. B-P was deeply impressed with the reception of these American boys. 'They received me,' he wrote to his mother, 'with greater enthusiasm than if they had been British boys. I have never heard such cheering! So they do appreciate one.'

A luncheon at Sagamore Hill the next day with Theodore Roosevelt was another highly satisfactory affair. The General and the former President of the United States had many interests in common and much to talk about—although the conversation was quite one-sided: 'Roosevelt, very cheery, genial host did all the talking on every kind of subject,' B-P noted in his diary. 'Very interesting, full of vitality and force. He was like a boy in his enthusiasm over African hunting. He talked ravenously the whole time we were there telling us how *he* had made the Panama Canal, etc.'

Baden-Powell's journey westward was hardly, as he had hoped, 'a leisurely one'. Again and again he pleaded his health, attempting to evade social functions thrust upon him. And again and again he got caught by West asking to make exceptions. He was rewarded by the fact that everywhere he went local Scouts and officials and the general public turned up in great numbers and received him warmly and enthusiastically.

Only in one American city—Portland, Oregon—did he encounter a demonstration of antagonism. An afternoon speech to a group of school-boys in the city's main auditorium was interrupted repeatedly by hecklers railing against scouting as 'a military movement run by a general'. They proclaimed themselves anti-militarists of the I.W.W. (Independent Workers of the World), a branch of Socialists. In the evening, the same group picketed the hotel where B-P was to deliver his main lecture of the day, flaunting placards on which Baden-Powell's 'K.C.B.' had been turned into 'King's Chief Butcher', and distributing leaflets purporting to be a true exposition of the Boy Scout movement.

The heckling and picketing gave the Portland morning papers an occasion to write about 'the outrageous insult on the part of the Socialist Party to the Boy Scouts in general and to Baden-Powell personally' and to decry the incident as 'a disgrace to the citizens and authorities in Portland who allowed it'.

Baden-Powell took the occurrence philosophically. To a member of the Oregon Socialist Party who had sent him a letter apologizing for the insults that had been directed at him, he wrote: 'I don't mind these but I, too, felt sorry that they were made because I know that these men were misinformed as to what we are trying to do for them, and that they did not know me as the Socialists at home do.' As far as B-P was concerned, the incident was closed.

4

In spite of the busy schedule of his American tour, B-P found time to write a couple of letters a week to Olave Soames—often long ones. She answered them with letters that were full of news and encouragement for his exacting tasks, and brimming over with her feelings for him.

Most of his letters were gay and non-committal, yet full of his yearning for her:

9 February 1912, You keep turning up in such funny places. Why do you do it? In the middle of watching a steel ingot being cast at

Carnegie's works in Pittsburgh—there you were enjoying the wonderful glare, bang, rattle and roar, just as much as I was. When I was in
the middle of a speech at luncheon yesterday, when I was reviewing
Boy Scouts, when I was stamping about the platform waiting for the
night express with the thermometer at 15° below zero . . . when I
was—oh well—I'd just like to know when or where you didn't show
up. . . .
19 February, Thank you so much for those sweet birthday wishes.
They are good to get and I am really thankful—and as you say it is
splendid our hitting off the same day in starting life—and then the
way you persist in not noticing any difference in the year makes the
stitches in my heart strain. . . . You say I am pulling your leg when I
said you would probably have forgotten by the 22nd that you had a
twin—well, you see much might have happened in the interval—and
besides, I never pull legs. I wouldn't be so forward. I merely
'elongate a limb'—I'm nothing if not proper.

In numerous letters he told Olave of his experiences, of interesting sights,
interesting people. In many of them he expressed the wish that she might
be with him:

Nearing San Francisco, 5 March, Oh! Why aren't you here at this
moment? Running through the Sierra Nevada—how silly of you!
The line keeps twisting and turning among the mountain spurs and
precipices, through splendid fir forests, all in deep, clotted fresh
snow. . . .
Oh! In the few minutes that I have been writing we have run out
of the snow into quite a different world. Thickly wooded hills and
valleys, bright red earth, very blue distant hills—charming chalets,
life everywhere, after hours in the wilderness. . . .
Oh! Fruit trees all in blossom!! For goodness' sake come and
look! Isn't it good? There's a house—just the spot—such a view—
and a dog scampering about the lawn, a trout-looking stream below
and a quaint little dovecote made like a little house on its pole. . . .

And then, suddenly, in the middle of March, at the end of his American
tour, B-P sent a letter to Olave that spoke of a dream that couldn't come
true, of a bubble that had burst. A letter from home had caught up with
him, and all his castles were collapsing. His mother told him of her concern about keeping up 32 Princes Gate, of added expenses, of the inability
of Warington and Baden to help, of Frank coming home, more ill than
when he left, from a stay in southern France that was meant to have

improved his health. She asked him to increase his annual contribution to her and to his home.

B-P poured out his soul to Olave, giving her a dozen reasons why he could not marry anyone, telling her of his obligations to his mother, his sister, to the upkeep of the family home. He would only have enough money of his own to be able to 'keep a dog'.

He was in a sombre mood as he boarded the S.S. *Minnesota* of the Great Northern Steamship Company at Seattle for Japan.

5

On 2 April, as his ship entered Yokohama Harbour, a decorated steam launch circled the ship and the cry of 'Baden-Powell! Baden-Powell!' resounded over the calm water. A boatful of Japanese Scouts and Scouts from the British colony had come out to welcome the Chief Scout and to escort him in.

Baden-Powell had arrived at the height of cherry-blossom time, at the height of the pilgrimages to the shrines of the Shoguns, the thousand images of Kwannon, the Daibutsu Buddha, the tombs of the forty-six Ronins. Everywhere he turned were subjects for his water-colour brush —men and women in multi-coloured costumes, rickshaw men in blue with black mushroom-shaped hats, streets with decorated houses, long streamers with Japanese letters moving in the breeze, paper lanterns, and first, and foremost, the temples. The scores of water-colours that B-P painted during his short stay in Japan show to excellent advantage his eye for colour and composition and his lively sense of humour.

On to China—another land that Baden-Powell had longed to visit. But China of 1912 was different from the country he had originally hoped to find. The revolution of 1911 had deposed the infant Manchu emperor, and the country was still in the throes of violent upheaval. A journey into the interior of China was out of the question. B-P could only hope to get a slight impression of the vast country by a peek through some of the ports on the China Sea at which his ship stopped.

He had little chance during the short stop he made at Tsingtau, ceded to the Germans on a long lease as compensation for the murder of the German ambassador during the Boxer Rebellion in 1899.

He came closer to the real China at Shanghai, his next stop. After the usual reception and review of British Scouts, he expressed a desire to see the Chinese part of the city. He was told that such a visit was not altogether safe in the present unsettled state of affairs. Nevertheless he was provided with two guides—a European and a Chinese detective—with whom he walked through the narrow alleys of the old city, stopping from time to time to do a bit of sketching.

In Hong Kong the sense of danger was equally strong. The port was full of steamships of many nations with the continual movement among them of tugs, steam launches and picturesque Chinese junks and sampans, 'while quietly guarding them lay four or five grim, grey men-of-war with the White Ensign of Great Britain floating in the breeze'. When the Governor of Hong Kong arranged for Baden-Powell to go up-river to Canton, B-P noticed a number of bullet holes in the bulwarks of their ship, received in the fighting between the Imperial troops and the Revolutionists.

In Canton, again, he felt the concern of the small European community. A smart-looking British gunboat was anchored off the green wooded island of Sameen, the part of Canton in which the Europeans lived, 'just now in a state of defence because of the unsettled state of the Chinese.'

Baden-Powell left China wondering what the future might hold in store: 'One of the greatest authorities on the Chinese, a good judge of people there, stated two years ago that there would be no fear of a revolution in eighteen years. How wrong he proved—it had come in eighteen months! Nobody knows what is before the Chinese. They may suddenly take it into their heads that they would like more territory.' If that were the aim of the Chinese, B-P was convinced that 'they would look around for the weakest people and the most desirable country.' But he was equally certain that 'if they found that a country they looked at was ready to defend itself, they would hesitate. . . .'

From China, B-P continued south-eastward, calling at Manila where scouting was already well established among the Filipino boys and the sons of American military personnel. Then onward with short stops at various German colonies on the Pacific islands of the Caroline and Pelew groups and on to New Guinea.

6

Soon after his official reception at Government House in Sydney, Australia, a package of accumulated mail was placed in B-P's hands. He opened the package and hurriedly riffled through the letters. It was there—the letter he had hoped to receive from Olave in answer to his note of almost a month before. His spirit brightened as he read her letter. Olave brushed aside all his arguments, told him to find out exactly what expense was involved in the running of 32 Princes Gate and insisted that a way could be found to solve his worries.

During the first break in the numerous appointments that had been arranged for him, B-P sat down to write to Olave:

> 19 May, You know—while I hate 'business letters'—yours sent you up higher than ever in my estimation. You've so much more sense than I should have guessed (flattering of me!), although I had an inkling that way from a certain characteristic of your brow (very personal, ain't I?).
>
> I know that I ought not to have written to you as I did, but then I just write things to you as they occur to my mind. I was at that time full of those confounded cons and I just rattled them down as they occurred to me, without pausing to think. Do please forgive. I am trying to find out how things promise at home. . . .

At the same time that he mailed the letter to Olave, he sent another off to his mother asking for a definite estimate of what the household expenses of No. 32 amounted to—and hinting, for the first time, of plans for the future:

> It would be a most valuable guide to me—especially in making up my own estimate as to my ability to afford to get married, supposing that a lady only moderately rich, but otherwise desirable, should cross my path! So if the cost of running Number 32 has been made out, and the income with which it is met, I should be glad to see it when I get home, and I shall then know how to trim my sails.

With his money concern pushed aside until his return to England, his letters to Olave took on their previous gaiety. His main thoughts now were of getting the trip over so that he could see her again.

B-P's seven-week journey through Australia and New Zealand became a succession of triumphant receptions and demonstrations. Old and young competed in showing him honour and respect.

To the older people, to the Government officials and to the military, it was the arrival, after twelve years, of the 'Hero of Mafeking'. Australia and New Zealand had showered him with gifts and honours following the raising of the siege, but from a distance. Now the populace had the chance to do it again in person. To the younger people it was their Chief come to inspect them, come to see for himself how well they were carrying out his scheme.

He soon learned that a violent discussion in regard to youth training was going on all around. The Australians and the New Zealanders had looked askance for more than fifty years at the 'yellow peril', starting in the middle of the nineteenth century, when there had been a large influx of Chinese coolie labour. The defeat of China in 1895 and of Russia in

1905 by Japan had created further apprehension. Since then there had been evidence of Japanese expansionist tendencies and even of Japanese espionage along the coast of Australia. Alarmed at the situation, Australia had adopted conscription and universal training for home defence in 1909 for all men above the age of 18. Cadet training for youngsters of 16 and over had followed. The question now was whether military training should be introduced into the schools.

Baden-Powell was called upon to present his opinion based on his military experience and his work with boys.

He spoke out strongly and to the point. 'I have come to Australia by way of China and Japan,' he said. 'The head men of those countries are highly civilized, but the rank and file—and there are millions of them—are still at a backward stage. It is easy to see what might happen if the head men of those nations, seeking for colonies and for seas for commerce, tried to gain them by force with the backing of hordes of uncivilized men who would stop at nothing.'

He commended the Australians on preparing themselves to defend their homes. 'But,' he warned them, 'I have long since found out that drill does not make a soldier. It is necessary to develop the intelligence of the men, and to instil in them a sense of "playing the game" before exposing them to drill. There are better things to teach boys in school than military drill—above all, discipline is absolutely necessary.' And that is where, he suggested, the Boy Scout movement could be made useful to Australia. 'The movement will bring out the boy and make a man of him by giving him a sense of duty. By then—and only then—will he be ready to take the polish of military drill that the country's defence requires.'

In addition to lecturing and advising on educational matters, Baden-Powell used his time in Australia to get to know the land and the people. He accepted the hospitality of governors and bush hands, of colonels and sheep farmers, of educationists and Scout people and, while in Victoria, went to pay his respects to Dame Nellie Melba, the famous Australian soprano, in her retirement. He found her 'digging weeds in her garden and enjoying it.'

He had a very strenuous and hurried time 'down under', but, as he wrote to his mother:

> I think I have done some useful work in the course of it—and at any rate I enjoyed it immensely. It taught me a lot—and it cost me nothing at all—and it has been grand schooling for the staff at home in doing without me which will let me take things more easily there when I come back. And that will be quite soon now.
>
> And then I must get married and settle down!

7

Baden-Powell's reception in Australia and New Zealand had been enthusiastic, his reception in Africa was overwhelming. He got his first taste of it at Durban in Natal, where he was received on landing by a large crowd of townspeople, welcomed by the Mayor, hailed by the Boy Scouts, dined by city and Government officials, and invited on the first aeroplane flight of his life: 'One scarcely knew when the machine left the ground but presently one saw that the ground was a long way down below—one waved to little pigmy people right down under one. It was delightful. I was quite sorry when it was over.'

At Pietermaritzburg and Ladysmith and at every station in the Transvaal, Boy Scouts and former members of the now disbanded South African Constabulary were on hand, in the glaring sun, to greet him.

At Johannesburg he stepped out of the railway coach to find a mass of people all over the station and on the roof and in surrounding trees:

> Mayor ... defence officers covered with uniforms and medals ...
> police by the hundred ... three hundred Boy Scouts ... fifty-four of
> the Mafeking garrison ... deputation of two hundred ex-Constabu-
> lary men. Bands—ladies—cheers. For nearly an hour I was going
> around shaking hands, lumpy in the throat as could be. Then there
> was a sudden heave—and just the sensation of aeroplaning—and I
> was being carried above the heads of the crowd.
>
> I had it once before, that feeling, after the war, and I remembered
> how a kind man held my pockets shut to prevent valuables falling out.
> That's all that occurred to my numbed brain. And so I clutched my
> pockets tight myself so my valuable little possessions should not be
> lost. . . .

The next day he was off for Pretoria for another great reception and for an important interview with General Jan C. Smuts, the Minister of Defence, to discuss the place of the Boy Scout movement in the South African defences. Smuts assured him that he would depend heavily on the Scout organization for assistance in the development of the cadet branch of his defence scheme.

8

On his way home in the S.S. *Balmoral Castle*, Baden-Powell summarized the activities of his world trip. He had delivered forty-one lectures, made sixty-three speeches, given sixty-nine Scout addresses. He had talked for 73 hours 33 minutes to somewhat more than seventy thousand people— 70,280 he estimated. He could only hope that his words had taken hold, that some of them, at least, had inspired boys and men to take up his scouting scheme, and carry it forward.

What he had seen had far exceeded his most optimistic hopes. Scouting in America had already grown to amazing proportions. Scouting in Japan was on the way. And every British colony and territory had embraced the movement.

He had travelled round the world and everywhere scouting itself had preceded him. With God's help and the efforts of men of good will it had a chance to grow into a genuine brotherhood of boys of all the countries of the world, all creeds, all colours and all classes.

He arrived home on Saturday, 24 August 1912, stayed for the week-end at 32 Princes Gate and on Tuesday left London again—not for Olave Soames's home at Parkstone, Dorset, but for Norway with Donald Baden-Powell for a fishing trip he had promised the boy when he said good-bye to him at Southampton almost eight months before.

Olave Soames had known all along of B-P's promise to take his nephew to Norway when he got home. She approved of his wanting to do a fatherly act to the fatherless boy. But while she understood what was in her Robin's mind, her father did not.

Immediately upon her return from her Caribbean journey, Olave had told her mother of her love for Baden-Powell and her determination to marry him, but only after B-P had again set foot on English soil did Olave confide in her father. Mr Soames fumed. Was she serious? Had Baden-Powell committed himself? What manner of man was this— leaving for Norway instead of paying his compliments to his daughter and himself? Did no one—not even a suitor—respect a father any more? He rushed a letter off to Baden-Powell inviting him in no uncertain terms to come to his home, Gray Rigg near Parkstone, Dorset, immediately upon his return from Norway, which he understood was to be on Friday the 13th.

Baden-Powell had planned on returning to England on the 13th, expecting to catch the steamer at Christiania (now Oslo) on 11 September. But when he and Donald arrived, they learned that every berth in the ship was taken. Fortunately, B-P knew the captain. He appealed to him personally, 'asking for a hole or corner of any kind—and the first officer very kindly gave up his cabin to Donald and myself'.

In London, the very thought of having to appear as a suitor before Olave's father made B-P feel nervous—with the result that he cut himself shaving and missed his train to Parkstone. He arrived several hours late to find Olave there to meet him. She drove him to her home and turned him over to her father for a man-to-man talk in Harold Soames's study.

The next morning B-P wrote to his mother from the home of his bride-to-be:

> Dearest Mother, I have been wondering what to give you as a birthday present, but I think I've got one now that will please you (as I hope and believe)—and that is a daughter-in-law for you!
>
> Olave Soames whom I met on board the *Arcadian* travelling with her father promises to make a very good one. I hope you will like her half as much as I do. She has only one fault (and both George and Frank told me that in getting a wife you must overlook a fault or two if she is on the whole what you want). Her fault is that she is young, but she has an old head on her shoulders and is clever and wise and very bright and cheery. . . .
>
> So I came here . . . last night to dine and sleep, and to have a talk with her father . . . I must tell you all about it when I get back on Monday—and get your consent and good wishes.

The 55-year-old General and Hero of Mafeking felt two feet tall when he sat before his mother. This was the first time he had kept an important secret from her in all the years since he was a child. His usual easy manner of speaking left him, but his mother encouraged him with 'little detective questions' to tell her about Olave. When he had had his say, she sat quietly before asking very gently, 'Is she rather small?'

B-P 'was cruel enough', as he reported to Olave later, 'to squirgle and to hem and haw till the dear old lady had begun to picture a slightly hunch-backed deformity before I told her that the dear girl was as tall as I was. . . . So she is at present delighted with the dominant idea that however plain you may be, you are very cheery and bright. . . .'

Mother Baden-Powell had a chance to find out for herself. On the Wednesday following the Gray Rigg week-end, Olave came up to London for tea with B-P's mother, his sister Agnes and his three brothers.

9

The news that their beloved Chief Scout was to be married around Christmas was greeted with general enthusiasm by his Boy Scouts. Only one small Scout expressed his disapproval in a pathetic letter to his hero:

> I am dreadfully disappointed in you. I have often thought to myself 'How glad I am that the Chief Scout is not married, because if he was he could never do all these ripping things for boys.' And now you are going to do it. It is the last thing I should have expected of you. Of course, you won't be able to keep on with the Scouts the same as

before, because your wife will want you, and everything will fall through. I think it is awfully selfish of you.

Baden-Powell tried to reassure the boy through one of his weekly articles in *The Scout*:

My future bride is as keen about scouting as I am. She will help me in the work, so that my marriage instead of taking me from the movement will bring in another assistant to it, and one who loves the Scouts as they, I am sure, will love her so soon as they get to know her.

The Scout who had written proved to represent a tiny minority. Practically everyone else decided to celebrate Baden-Powell's forthcoming wedding. Without telling B-P, his old Army comrades and his associates in scouting set the wheels in motion to turn the occasion into a major festival, a great ceremonial. Details of their plans began to make their appearance in the daily press: 'A large congregation of Army and Navy men will assemble for the ceremony. . . .' 'A guard of honour of Boy Scouts will surround the bride's home and link up with the church. . . .' 'The two hundred thousand Boy Scouts in the United Kingdom will contribute one penny each towards the purchase of a gift to be selected by the Chief Scout himself. . . .'

The proposed arrangements were getting out of hand. Neither B-P nor Olave and her family desired the attendant publicity. Olave's suggestion of eloping was vetoed by the family. Instead, another solution was decided upon.

On 30 October 1912, the customary mid-day Holy Communion was celebrated in St Peter's Church, Parkstone, Dorset. With the service over, the communicants departed. Soon after, a motor-car drove up a short distance from St Peter's. The passengers entered the church unobserved through the vestry. A moment later, another car arrived and dropped its passengers. They walked quietly into the church. The vicar of St Peter's, the Reverend the Honourable R. E. Adderley greeted the wedding party, with Canon Inman at his side.

The bride was dressed in a pale blue costume with a hat to match. She was given in marriage by her father, Harold Soames, and was attended by Agnes Baden-Powell, sister of the bridegroom. The bridegroom wore a dark-blue lounge suit. His brother Major Baden Baden-Powell acted as his best man. He was attended by an old Army friend, Major-General R. G. Kekewich, C.B., the defender of Kimberley in the Boer War. Only four others were in the wedding party: Olave's mother and brother

Arthur, her brother-in-law Robert Davidson and Miss Sie Bower, a close friend of the family.

By mutual consent the service was the simplest possible, without music. But as soon as it was over the church bells rang in honour of the occasion.

The newly married couple said good-bye to the wedding party and drove off to Bournemouth to catch the two o'clock train for London. They arrived at Waterloo shortly before seven and drove directly to 35 Rutland Court, where B-P had rented a flat.

The Hero of Mafeking, the famous Lieutenant-General Sir Robert S. S. Baden-Powell, K.C.B., K.C.V.O., had become a married man at last and Olave St Clair Soames had become Lady Baden-Powell.

XXII

The End of an Era

Years: 1912–14   Age: 55–57

1

FROM the moment of their wedding Olave watched her husband's health with much care. Although he had seemed cheerful enough and had greatly benefited from a seventeen-day honeymoon at Roch Castle in Pembrokeshire, by courtesy of Lord and Lady St Davids, to Olave her Robin did not seem quite himself. He admitted to severe headaches but tried to joke them out of existence. When he was hit by an attack of his recurrent African Fever, Olave sent him to bed and called the doctor. She was a young bride with no intentions of becoming a young widow.

For the first time since early childhood, B-P found himself pampered. He had often suffered from piercing headaches, and malaria and other tropical fevers had caused repeated bouts of illness. But he had refused to give in to them, claiming that he had too much to do. Even when a pounding head made it almost impossible for him to see straight, he forced himself to carry through an engagement.

He had, for the most part, managed to escape the attention and ministrations of his mother and sister at home but he couldn't escape the searching eyes and the concern of a devoted wife. Her decisions in regard to his health became law.

The doctor agreed with Olave's diagnosis that B-P needed rest and recommended that his patient get away from the cold of London for a while. The Baden-Powells decided on Algiers. There they could depend on good weather and B-P would have a chance to show Olave some of the places he had visited long ago. But before they left there was another matter to be attended to.

Scores of B-P's and Olave's friends had expressed a desire to meet the newly-weds. The two of them wondered how it could be arranged. The problem was solved by Baden-Powell's old Guild throwing open the Mercers' Hall for a belated wedding reception on the afternoon of 17 December.

Nearly three hundred guests turned up to be greeted by a guard of honour of West London Boy Scouts and entertained by a Scout choir singing carols. The wedding presents were displayed in one of the reception

The Baden-Powells spent their honeymoon camping in Algiers.

rooms, but the gift of the Boy Scouts to their Chief and his wife was missing. Almost a hundred thousand Scouts had contributed a penny each towards a 20 h.p. Standard motor-car, but it was not ready for delivery. It still had to be painted in the Scouts' colours of dark green with yellow trim and to have the Scout badge and motto added.

At last they were off. After the customary sight-seeing around the city of Algiers with the obligatory tour of the Kasbah the Baden-Powells went inland by way of Constantine and Batna to El Outaya. Here they rented camping equipment, bought food, hired two Arab guides ('or guards, for they were fully armed'), secured two mules and set off through the mountains. 'We were soon camped out on the desert, far from human habitation, in the glorious sunshine of North Africa.' At night, although the air was cold, they put their beds outside the tent and slept under the stars. Ten days later they arrived at El Kantara, their camping expedition at an end.

That night, Olave jotted in her diary, 'Sorry it is over—it was good' and added triumphantly 'I am built for camp as my Beloved is!' And B-P with a great sigh of relief—this had been Olave's first camping experience —reported to his mother:

> Olave is a perfect wonder in camp—thoroughly enjoys the life and is as good as a backwoodsman at it. She is a splendid walker, a good Scout—never loses her way. . . . She conforms her ideas so fully to mine that we have already become exactly alike—and though she has ideas and opinions of her own they tally with mine—and she looks after me like a mother, absolutely spoils me.
>
> You were so right, my dear Ma, when you said one ought to marry a young woman.

They celebrated their first joint birthday (22 February) together on board ship on the way back to England. And then they were home and yet not home. They had made up their minds that London was not for them, that they wanted to live in the country in a house of their own.

2

They found a house to their taste in Ewhurst Place—a large red-brick building outside the village of Robertsbridge in East Sussex, with wide lawns and a view of both Bodiam Castle in the Rother Valley and the rolling hills of Sussex and Kent. The Baden-Powells rented the house and moved in in April.

It was a thoroughly suitable place for them. There was space in the large rooms for displaying B-P's hunting trophies and gifts bestowed on him after Mafeking, for hanging some of his best water-colours, and for exhibiting some of the presents sent him by admiring Scouts from many parts of the globe. There were dens for working and rooms for relaxing. Baden-Powell could at last get some of the rest his doctor had prescribed.

One of his publishers, Herbert Jenkins, described B-P's idea of resting after having spent a few days at Ewhurst:

> This process of 'resting' is not without its elements of originality and interest. It consists of rising between the hours of 5 and 6 a.m. and, after a cup of tea, devoting himself to a bewildering correspondence; and, with the exception of a walk and an occasional excursion with his gun, or a motor run, correspondence, administration and a thousand other urgent things occupy him throughout the day. There are innumerable dashes up to town and back again. In the intervals he writes books with both hands, for he is ambidextrous, contributes

to magazines, is the life and soul of everything he touches, and incidentally forgets nothing, although he never makes a note.

Whenever B-P went up to London on one of his 'innumerable business dashes' he usually took Olave with him. They often wound up the day at a play—the theatre was another interest they shared.

On one of these dashes, on top of a London bus, Olave informed her husband that they were going to have a child. She had been to see the doctor. They were both overjoyed with the prospect and, then and there, decided on the name of the boy (it had to be a boy!): Peter, from Barrie's *Peter Pan* which they had seen and enjoyed only a few months before.

Shortly after, they proudly told the family the exciting news. Warington also had news for the family: Stephe's getting married had given him the courage to take the big step himself. Hilda Farmer, his sweetheart of nearly twenty years, would become his wife in September.

Peter timed his arrival perfectly. He came into the world on his parents' first wedding anniversary.

But the day that should have been unmitigated joy for the Baden-Powell family had its touch of sadness. Instead of staying at home to enjoy the advent of his heir B-P had to rush up to London for the funeral of his brother George's widow—Frances Baden-Powell, the mother of Donald and Maud. Death had come as a release since for several years Frances had been ill, crippled and deaf.

On his return home in the evening from the funeral B-P was greeted by more than two hundred telegrams congratulating him on the birth of his son. One of them came from his old friend the Duke of Connaught, now the Governor-General of Canada, offering to be the boy's godfather.

The boy was baptized on 14 February 1914 at St Peter's Church, Parkstone, the same church in which his parents had been married. He was christened Arthur (for the Duke) Robert (for his father) Peter (for the boy who never grows up). After the ceremony Peter was carried before a guard of honour of more than three hundred Scouts, then taken to London and placed on the lap of his paternal grandmother. She held him firmly, tenderly, as over the years she had held her own ten children and the three grandchildren previously presented to her.

On 3 September 1914, Mrs Baden-Powell would be 90. Her four surviving sons and her daughter debated how to celebrate this important milestone in her life, but they had not counted on their mother. The old lady set herself against any celebration whatever. They had their work to do, she told them, and they could honour her best on her birthday by carrying on with what they were in duty bound to do. Furthermore, the excitement might not be good for her since she felt very tired recently. She just might, as a matter of fact, spend most of the day in bed.

The children obeyed their mother's wishes and Mrs Baden-Powell spent her ninetieth birthday quietly among the mementoes of her long life. Among them was a small slip of paper, kept for so many years, with her father's, the Admiral's, handwriting on it:

From Papa to Henrietta Smyth on her Birthday, 3 September 1832

> Since now you've turned the age of eight,
> Improve, my dear, and pray sit straight.
>   May each revolving year produce
>   The good to which our cares conduce;
> So may each birthday, each excel,
> And find you always passing well,
>   Until you reach four score and ten—
>   And who knows what may happen then?

'. . . four score and ten—and who knows what may happen then.' The answer was not long in coming.

A month later, she fell seriously ill. The two doctors who were called in held out no hope for her survival. Henrietta Grace Baden-Powell lingered for a few days, then slipped away peacefully on 13 October. She was laid to rest at the side of the husband she had mourned for more than half a century. At her funeral, one of the family members was missing. Florence, Frank's wife had come down with pneumonia. She died four days after her mother-in-law.

His mother's death was a great blow to Baden-Powell. The alliance between his mother and himself, 'of the nature of a loving comradeship', had come to an end. In spite of her advanced age her mind had been sharp to the last. He had often told his Scouts that he owed everything he had become to his mother. He was happy in the knowledge that she had watched his work prosper, that she had had the joy before she passed away of seeing him established in his own home, with a loving wife and with a son to carry on the name of Baden-Powell.

3

The two years that followed B-P's trip round the world had been as eventful for the Scout movement as for the Baden-Powell family.

With the Crystal Palace Rally of 1909 and the Windsor Rally of 1911, a pattern had been established calling for a major Scout event every two years to stir up public interest and to give excitement to the participants.

Each of the previous events had been one-day affairs. Perhaps, with 1913 at hand, the time had come for planning for a longer and more varied activity. The outcome of the deliberations of Baden-Powell and his associates was a decision to invite the Scouts of the British Empire for an Imperial Scout Exhibition to be held at Bingley Hall, Birmingham, from 2 July to 9 July 1913. The Scouts participating in the public exhibits and demonstrations would be camped for the week at Perry Hall Park, a few miles outside the city.

The event was vigorously promoted. Troops and patrols were encouraged to come to Birmingham, or, if they couldn't come themselves, to send their handicrafts and models to be exhibited. At the same time, Baden-Powell invited each of the Scout associations established in foreign countries to send a representative or a patrol to Birmingham as the guests of their British brother Scouts.

The camp was scheduled to house five thousand boys for the one-week period in large bell tents set up in company streets, but shortly before the opening day, more than six thousand Scouts had signed up. The organizers were forced to appeal to the people of the surrounding countryside to permit the overflow of Scouts to pitch their tents in private gardens, or to sleep in nearby 'summer arbours, coach-houses and lofts.'

The exhibition in vast Bingley Hall was opened on 2 July before a capacity crowd by Prince Alexander of Teck, one of Baden-Powell's old comrades-in-arms from Matabele war days.

This was the first time that a public demonstration had been attempted to show the multitude of activities within the scouting programme. In addition to the scoutcraft skills of the outdoors—hiking and camping— every proficiency badge subject was on display, ranging from Carpenter to Starman, from Farmer to Printer, from Basket-worker to Missioner. In the arena and in surrounding booths, Scouts who had earned the Pioneer's badge were building bridges and signal towers; Cooks were cooking, Signallers signalled; Cyclists cycled; Firemen put out fires; Ambulance-men gave first aid while still other Scouts demonstrated the physical fitness side of scouting through wrestling and boxing, gymnastics and Swedish drill.

On the Friday of the Exhibition, a big Sea Scout display was staged at the Edgbaston Reservoir, with the Chief Sea Scout, Admiral Lord Charles Beresford, in charge. In spite of the wet and blustery afternoon the boys carried out an ambitious programme. There were swimming and boating races, and 'sailors' from a sinking ship were brought ashore with the aid of rocket apparatus and breeches buoy.

The biggest event of the week was the Rally on Saturday 5 July when an estimated eighteen thousand Scouts gathered in Perry Hall Park, the six thousand Scouts in camp augmented for the day by twice as many more from counties near and far. The programme followed closely the programme of the Windsor Rally, with His Royal Highness Prince Arthur of Connaught representing King George V. A new feature had, however, been added. The imperial aspect of the occasion had been enlarged into an international one. Mingling with the British Scouts from every part of the United Kingdom and from Canada, Australia, South Africa, India and Gibraltar, were patrols or representatives from an even dozen foreign countries: France, Belgium, Holland, Spain, Italy, Sweden, Norway, Denmark, Austria (with Scouts from Bohemia and Austrian Poland), Hungary, China, and the United States.

B-P came away from the Birmingham Exhibition with increased faith in the possibilities in his movement for fostering a world-wide spirit of comradeship:

> It needs no great stretch of the imagination to see in this the promise of a closer bond between ourselves and our Empire across the Seas, and a stronger guarantee of future peace between nations when their men begin to look upon each other as members of one brotherhood instead of as hereditary enemies.

The Birmingham Exhibition had received wide and favourable publicity. Baden-Powell decided that the time was ripe for an appeal to the British people for help in establishing an Endowment Fund that would, once and for all, keep the Boy Scouts Association solvent and enable it to do its work effectively. He set the goal at a quarter of a million pounds.

The public solicitation was opened by the Duke of Connaught who, returned from Canada, had accepted Baden-Powell's invitation to become the President of the Boy Scouts. The campaign moved ahead well under a strong committee with Eric Walker its energetic secretary. A great part of its success was due to Baden-Powell's personal efforts. Even before the public launching he had privately obtained gifts and pledges to the tune of £20,000. Now he went out on a tour of the country to collect further funds, speaking at scores of public meetings and inspecting rallies of Scouts wherever he went. As if all this were not enough to occupy his time, B-P was elected Master of the Mercers' Company, a high honour which carried with it a great deal of responsibility and involved his attendance at numerous committee meetings and official functions.

With almost a year and a half of concentrated work behind him, B-P was now looking forward to taking Olave with him to Norway for two weeks of camping, fishing and sketching. After this, the Chief Scout and his wife were due to sail for Cape Town in the early autumn as the heads of the Scout movement in South Africa were anxious for him to pay a visit there, and B-P was equally anxious to go.

But a bullet pumped into the body of an Austrian archduke on 28 June, by a Serbian nationalist, changed the plans of the Baden-Powells—as it did those of the rest of the world.

Weathering The Storm

<hr>

Years: 1914–20   Age: 57–63

1

FOR an entire month the spark struck in the small Bosnian town of Sarajevo smouldered. On 28 July it burst into flame with Austria declaring war on Serbia. During the weeks that followed, the flame turned into a holocaust with Germany declaring war on Russia and France and Great Britain going to war against Germany for violating the neutrality of Belgium. That the crisis should have come to a head during an August Bank Holiday was a remarkable fulfilment of the prediction Baden-Powell had made six years earlier at Newcastle before the 'Terriers'.

As soon as events pointed to war, B-P rushed off telegrams to all Boy Scout county commissioners in Great Britain asking them to mobilize their Scouts for immediate action and to place them at the disposal of the authorities. At the same time he sent a telegram to the War Office offering the services of the Boy Scouts. It was the story of the Mafeking Cadets all over again:

> Just as the boys of Mafeking were utilized to take the lighter work of men in order that these might be released to the more arduous duties, so can Scouts now give valuable assistance to the State at home— and for this their training and organization have already to a great extent fitted them.

Even before Britain's formal declaration of war, Scouts went to work guarding bridges, culverts and telegraph lines against possible sabotage by German spies. Military and civilian authorities throughout the country called upon Scouts to act as messengers and orderlies. In London alone two thousand Scouts were put to use by the police. The day after war was declared, hundreds of Sea Scout troops patrolled the British shores on coast-watching service.

Baden-Powell had no illusion about being called into active military service himself. He knew that, having retired, he could not expect to be brought back over the heads of serving generals. Besides, Lord Kitchener had entered Asquith's Cabinet as Secretary of State for War and Kitchener had nothing but disdain for Haldane's Territorial Army and for all those who had worked to establish it. He regarded the Territorials as amateurs with a play-boy spirit. The new 'Kitchener Armies' would be professional forces.

When Baden-Powell, on 10 August, called at the War Office to offer his services, Lord Kitchener surprised his old friend by greeting him with a hearty: 'What a splendid thing this war is for you!'

Baden-Powell protested that he didn't see it that way since he was on the Retired List.

'I don't mean you personally,' Kitchener explained, 'I mean for the Scouts. The scoutmaster can now show the boys the real meaning and value of their training, and the boys can see it for themselves.'

That was a point with which B-P could agree and a good opening for his interview with Kitchener. He was pleased to be able to report to the War Secretary that 'The Boy Scouts are now ready in all counties and are already at work in several, in numbers of not less than a thousand in each county, in assisting the local defence, civil and municipal authorities.' Apart from the Scouts he could further report that a number of ex-South African Constabulary officers and men had applied to him, volunteering to join a corps if he were raising one. 'If it is desired that such a force should be raised I could probably get a lot together.' If this proposition was not feasible, he would, he suggested, 'make a good corporal'.

Kitchener did not want an irregular corps and was certain that he would have all the corporals he would need. The Scouts were another matter. As president of the North London Boy Scouts he knew what these boys could do. It was he who had charged the Scouts of Britain to continue their scouting into their manhood years under the rallying phrase of 'Once a Scout always a Scout!' He also knew that only their beloved Chief Scout could inspire them to their finest potential. He told Baden-Powell that he could think of no task more important for him at present than to carry on with his Boy Scouts. 'So I came home very bucked!' B-P confided to his diary.

Throughout the war, through his writings and his personal appearances, Baden-Powell kept in touch with his Scouts and their leaders, challenging them, suggesting things for them to do in the service of their country, keeping them informed of what other Scouts were doing.

The Scouts of Britain spent millions of boy-hours on war work in an astonishing number of capacities. Among other things they patrolled railway lines, acted as messengers in Government offices, assisted at hospitals, collected scrap, harvested flax, and sounded the All Clear bugle calls after air raids.

Of all the multitudinous services performed by British Boy Scouts during the four long years of World War I, the coast-guarding of the Sea Scouts along the shores of Britain proved of greatest significance. The work was tough and never-ending, day in and day out, night after night in all weathers. To keep up the spirit of the boys, Baden-Powell visited as many of their stations as he could manage. Everywhere he found the Sea Scouts, 'the men of the second line', carrying on faithfully and effectively. He took immense pride in 'these youthful watchers, earnest and untiring, rising like men to the responsibilities placed upon them'.

During the early days of the war, Baden-Powell had to give much of his time and attention to the Boy Scout Headquarters in London. Daily, more and more requests arrived from national and local government sources for Scouts to be used in war service; and daily, fewer and fewer staff members were left to handle the requests and to carry out the rest of the work. Colonel Ulick de Burgh was recalled to his regiment. Captain Wade left for the Army, Eric Walker for training for what was to become the Royal Flying Corps. All the other able-bodied men on the Headquarters Staff joined the forces. B-P was kept busy finding men to fill their places.

It was not only at headquarters that the manpower situation was becoming critical. Most of the county commissioners left for the front, so did large numbers of scoutmasters. In many instances, their places were taken by men not called up for war service because of age or health. In numerous cases, wives or sweethearts of departing soldier-scoutmasters took on the task that had meant so much to their menfolk.

For the rest, the patrol system that Baden-Powell had built into his scouting scheme did the job. The boys themselves carried on in their patrols under their self-chosen patrol leaders. Where, previously, conferences for adult Scout leaders had been the custom, now conferences for patrol leaders became the order of the day. B-P took to the road again speaking before large crowds of boy leaders, charging them to train their patrols and to forge ahead in scouting with their boys.

Instead of tottering, as some pessimists had predicted, the Scout movement grew stronger as the war progressed. More and more boys joined. The Scout uniform became the coveted proof for thousands of boys that they, too, like their fathers and older brothers, were serving in the war effort, were doing their part for King and country.

2

Early in 1915, the 13th Hussars were sent to the front. Sir John French, now a Field-Marshal and Commander-in-Chief of the British Expeditionary Force, invited Baden-Powell, as the regiment's Honorary Colonel, to come to France to inspect his men. B-P jumped at the chance and sailed from Folkestone on 27 March for a ten-day visit to the front. After meeting with French's staff at the British Headquarters at St Omer, Baden-Powell was driven along the front over roads with their trees felled or ravaged by shell fire, through towns and villages with half of their buildings in ruins. Everywhere soldiers by the thousand were moving up to the trenches.

Beyond Armentières he had a chance to see life as it was lived in an advanced trench, 'a narrow ditch, banked with sandbags or boards and brushwood on both sides . . . crowded with men, all very dirty, cooking their food over buckets punched with holes with fires inside them'. They seemed astonishingly cheerful: 'When a bullet smacked the top of the trench and then "bizzed" on angrily they called to the Germans "No good—try another!"' At a sentry post B-P stopped to scan the German line through a periscope. The enemy trench was only about a hundred yards away—'with its mass of staked and barbed wire along the front of it, and lines of sandbags making its parapet, with the peaceful country of woods and villages and churches beyond it, and the muddy, crumpled figure of a dead German in the foreground'.

Two lines of trenches from the English Channel to the Swiss border, with a shell-pocked no man's land between them, and hundreds of thousands of men locked in tactical immobility. Baden-Powell thought back to Mafeking days, to the trenches in the Brickfields. War hadn't changed much in fourteen years except in magnitude.

After driving through ruined Ypres and stopping at Poperinghe to see General Plumer ('red-faced and smiling as usual'), Baden-Powell arrived at Roncq where he was welcomed by the officers and men of the 13th Hussars drawn up for his inspection. 'It was a pleasure to see them once more, in four strong squadrons and a machine-gun section looking very business-like . . . but all except about half a dozen were new to me.'

On his way back to le Havre, B-P stopped at hospitals along the route to visit patients and dropped in at a score of the Y.M.C.A. recreation huts distributed among the British base camps. He came away from the huts strongly impressed with their importance to the welfare and morale of the soldiers. But many more were needed! Here was a war project into which he could throw his efforts, a project with a direct impact on the men at the front.

An episode during the First World War, sketched at the front by B-P.

Upon his return to London, B-P quickly persuaded the Mercers' Company to finance the construction of a recreation hut in France. The Company left it to him to make all arrangements for the building of it and for manning it with Boy Scout volunteers. His early efforts resulted in the opening of the Mercers' Arms on 21 July 1915, with a troop of French Boy Scouts acting as a guard of honour.

Baden-Powell was back in France in October to open another hut. This time he took Olave with him. She had not been able to join him before for another child had been on the way. It was a girl, born 1 June and christened Heather Grace. Now, with Peter and baby Heather safely established with their maternal grandmother at Gray Rigg, Olave had her first chance to take up active war work. She had her mind set on spending three months as a barmaid, with other women volunteers, in one of the recreation huts. She went to work in the Mercers' Arms while B-P went to see Plumer about more huts for the Second Army and returned to England to collect funds for building them.

He was back in France again in November, this time to find out what huts were needed for the Third Army. His old friend General Allenby took him on a personally conducted tour of his area to pick the locations. And so, back to England for more fund raising and back to France for opening another hut at Étaples with a hall large enough to hold a thousand soldiers, the first of six financed solely by Scout and Guide contributions.

Baden-Powell's repeated trips to France came to the attention of German Intelligence. The trips were even more suspect after the appearance of B-P's best-selling booklet *Quick Training for War*, which sold 65,000 copies in the first month, and his larger volume telling of his spying experiences in war and peace, *My Adventures as a Spy*. Each of the tricks described in his 'Q.T.', as the booklet was popularly called, and each of the spying stunts of *My Adventures* might well fit whatever the renowned hero of the last major war might be doing in this one.

The rumours made their rounds throughout Germany that B-P was inside the borders of the *Vaterland* working as Britain's master spy. The Germans went to considerable trouble to find the elusive Baden-Powell. One story had it that he had been spotted in Berlin, 'cat-burglaring' a war office building disguised as a chimney sweep. Another story was that he had almost been caught after a daring spying jaunt but had escaped across the Baltic and had been brought home from refuge in Sweden on an English destroyer.

None of the reports about B-P's supposed spying activities was ever denied by the British War Office. On the contrary, the Intelligence Department happily assisted in spreading the rumours. But the tales of B-P's alleged World War I spying were all false. Baden-Powell did no spying in World War I. He had too many other things to do.

3

Inspections and training courses, fund-raising and recruiting speeches, letters and articles formed his daily routine outside his work in France. In addition the expansion of the Scout movement and planning for the future beyond the war were much in his mind.

First on his list of projects was a plan for dealing with boys below the minimum Scout age of 11. The need for such a plan was becoming increasingly urgent. When first considered, it was mostly a matter of finding a way of providing for the youngsters who wanted to join because their older brothers had joined, who wanted to share in the fun the others were having. As the war went on, a further consideration was the necessity of dealing constructively with the up-surge of juvenile delinquency caused by the turbulence of the times. Some child psychologists were pointing out that the tendency toward delinquency began around the age of 8. If

Scouting's character-training purposes were to be attained, its programme would have to take in boys of that age.

Previous efforts in working with younger boys had not been successful. Some Boy Scout troops had tried to accept younger boys as Junior Scouts but always with disastrous results. The troops had disintegrated, the older boys having no wish to mingle with the kids and the kids being unable to keep up with the older boys in their vigorous scouting activities.

Baden-Powell had already had the problem of a younger-boy programme studied by Percy Everett in the autumn of 1913, and Everett had prepared a set of 'Suggested Rules for Junior Scouts' which he submitted to the Chief Scout for amendments.

> The name Junior Scouts will never do as a permanent name [B-P commented]. I never thought of keeping it—but it does for preliminary use as explaining the movement. We must invent a name that will appeal to the small boys. . . . I had originally in my mind 'Wolf Cubs', or 'Cubs', or 'Colts', or 'Young Scouts'.

After further amendments and changes, a set of rules for 'Wolf Cubs, or Young Scouts' was developed and published in the January 1914 issue of the *Headquarters Gazette* with the promise that a new book by the Chief Scout on the subject was shortly to be published.

Even though the rules opened the door for further experimentation, Baden-Powell was not too happy about them. The activities they suggested amounted to little more than watered-down Boy Scouting. The younger boy, he felt, deserved something that would be peculiarly his own, something that would be fun to him and yet mould him into a real boy.

To make headway B-P knew that he would have to find a theme round which a suitable programme could be built. And suddenly he realized that he had it in Rudyard Kipling's *Jungle Books*, the tales of Mowgli, the man-child, growing up among the wolves . . . obeying the wise Akela, the old Wolf . . . learning the law of the jungle from easy-going Baloo, the bear . . . hunting with silent Bagheera, the panther. Here was a story that all young boys should know, a hook on which B-P realized that he would be able to hang a multitude of activities and ideals.

He wrote to Kipling for the author's permission to base a programme for younger boys on *The Jungle Books*. Kipling, a good friend of scouting from its earliest days, the author of the official Boy Scout song and the father of a Scout, immediately gave his consent.

Baden-Powell's book explaining his new scheme for younger boys— *The Wolf Cub's Handbook*—was published on 2 December 1916. On 16 December, B-P's Wolf Cubs under the new programme made their first public appearance at Caxton Hall before about two hundred educationists, with a display by a group of boys and an address by B-P.

Wolf Cubbing quickly assumed major proportions. In spite of war-time conditions, the new branch of the Boy Scout movement prospered. At the end of the first full year, 1917, close to thirty thousand youngsters had become Wolf Cubs in the British Isles alone. B-P had set another snowball rolling.

4

As the war continued, Baden-Powell became more and more disturbed about the Girl Guides, the female counterparts of the Boy Scouts.

After having turned the Girl Guides over to Agnes Baden-Powell to handle and after helping her prepare the Girl Guide handbook *How Girls Can Help Build up the Empire*, he had left it to his sister and her committee to carry on while he concentrated his efforts on getting the Boy Scouts firmly established. Things hadn't worked out quite as well with the Girl Guides as he had expected. Agnes as president and, in quick succession, three different chairmen of what amounted to Agnes's private 'executive committee' had not given the new girls' movement the strong and imaginative leadership he had hoped for. The Y.W.C.A., on the other hand, had realized the value of Girl Guiding in its work and had moved vigorously forward establishing companies and recruiting leaders. While Agnes's Girl Guide movement had remained poorly organized its Y.W.C.A. counterpart was forging ahead.

In the autumn of 1914, Baden-Powell received an urgent letter from Mrs W. J. Benson of the Executive Committee of the Girl Guides to come to the rescue of the Association. Agnes, Mrs Benson felt, was selling out to the Y.W.C.A., had practically told that organization that it might as well take over the Girl Guides. B-P rushed up to London for a conference with Agnes and her president. Mrs Benson's diagnosis of the situation appeared to be correct. If the Girl Guides Association was to continue as the main body, a reorganization was called for. B-P decided to see to it that it got one.

He worked out suggestions for a complete reorganization and for securing an urgently needed Charter of Incorporation, then met the Girl Guide Committee to explain the steps that had to be taken. In spite of difficulties with Agnes and with several members of the committee, B-P persevered and eventually persuaded the majority of the members to adopt his views.

On 24 September 1915, entirely through B-P's efforts and persistence, the Girl Guides Association was granted a Charter of Incorporation, giving it the Government's official recognition as an established movement.

Under the provisions of the Charter, the original President's Advisory Committee was changed into a Council and greatly expanded. The new Council, at its first meeting, elected a strong Executive Committee to carry on the work. It insisted on Baden-Powell himself assuming the post of Chairman, with Agnes Baden-Powell retaining her title as President.

And so, while working to keep the war efforts of his Boy Scouts at a high pitch, B-P was faced with the further responsibility of strengthening the Girl Guides Association. The immediate, most urgent task before him was the recruiting and training of local commissioners.

Olave Baden-Powell had worked steadily at her husband's side in his efforts to straighten out the Girl Guide situation. An offer of help she had extended to the original Girl Guide Committee in 1914 had been brushed aside. A renewed offer was promptly accepted by the new committee. Sussex, where she lived, had no county commissioner. She received her warrant in June 1916 and threw herself into the task with all the energy and enthusiasm of her twenty-seven years. She established a model organization for her county, visiting all the existing Girl Guide companies and secured a full complement of local commissioners.

With the blessing of the Executive Committee she next set out to extend her efforts beyond her own county. While B-P was at one desk, his wife was at another writing to people all over the country, urging them to take up Girl Guide work. The results were impressive.

In October 1916, the Baden-Powells took part in the first Girl Guide Commissioners Conference at Matlock in Derbyshire. One of the main speeches, on County Organization, was given by Lady Baden-Powell. The soundness of her suggestions was appreciated by all her listeners and her verve and easy humour were a refreshing change from the dryness and lack of enterprise that had so long characterized the Girl Guide movement.

One of the important outcomes of the conference was a unanimous resolution recommending to the Executive Committee the establishment of the office of a Chief Commissioner and asking that it be entrusted to Lady Baden-Powell who, in the estimation of the commissioners, 'alone could fulfil this office in such a way as to give us the guidance and support which are essential for the further continuance and progress of our work'. The resolution was placed before the Girl Guides' Executive Committee on 26 October and passed without a dissenting vote.

Olave swung into action to secure commissioners and committees for all counties of Great Britain and to help establish a strong and efficient Girl Guides Association. Within eighteen months, her title of Chief Commissioner was changed to Chief Guide as more descriptive of her responsibilities. Her work during this period was interrupted only once: by the birth of another child, Betty St. Clair, born on 16 April 1917.

Agnes's Girl Guide handbook, *How Girls Can Help Build up the Empire*, was due for reprinting and possible revision. As Baden-Powell re-read the book he realized that as far as the Girl Guides were concerned the world seemed to have stood still for five years. His sister's book might have filled the needs when published in the long, long ago of 1912, but in 1917 it was utterly out of date. The old-fashioned ideas about what women, young and old, could and should do had changed immeasurably with the war. Agnes's Victorian viewpoint which shone through every paragraph of *How Girls Can Help* was a thing of the past. A completely different approach was required in a handbook that was to lead girls of Britain successfully into the post-war world. Since Agnes obviously was not able to write this new book, Baden-Powell took it on himself.

B-P's *Girl Guiding* made its appearance in February 1918. It went further than he had originally intended. In addition to dealing with girls in the 11 to 14 years of age bracket, the book established a programme for their younger sisters whom he called Brownies—from the story of *The Brownies* by Juliana Horatia Ewing—and for an older-girl branch of Senior Guides.

5

World events moved fast during early 1918. The war, after months of stalemate, was rising in a final crescendo. In February Russia was knocked out. On 21 March the great German offensive began. Day after day reports reached England telling of German successes, of the Allies falling back eight miles here, seven miles there, of Allied guns by the hundred and prisoners by the thousand falling into German hands. March . . . April . . . May . . . June. And then, on 18 July, the turning of the tide with the combined attacks of British, French, and American forces pushing the enemy back. Soon after, the Germans were in retreat everywhere. July . . . August . . . September . . . the end of the war was in sight.

The last week of September, Baden-Powell was called to the office of the Ministry of·Information. The ministry thought it desirable for B-P to go to France and Spain. His attendance had been requested for a parade in Paris and his appearance in Madrid, at this moment, in his capacity as founder of the Boy Scout movement, might have a salutary effect in helping to counter a wave of pro-German propaganda being feverishly pushed throughout Spain.

On 20 October, B-P was in Paris, standing in front of the Hôtel de Ville in the midst of a large group of officials, military and civilian, witnessing a march past of detachments of all the Allies before President Poincaré. The soldiers were followed by seven hundred French Boy Scouts who passed with cheers for their president and Clemenceau, the Marshal of France, who was at his side. The Scouts were being honoured by their government; for the service performed by the *Éclaireurs* of France during four long years had been just as valuable to the war effort as that of their British brother Scouts.

In Madrid, Baden-Powell was met by General Primo de Rivera and representatives of the Spanish Boy Scout movement. His many public appearances were covered thoroughly and favourably by the Spanish press. So was his luncheon with King Alfonso and his English-born Queen Victoria Eugenie. The King used the opportunity to explain to B-P the reasons why Spain had stayed out of the war and to impress upon him that, as far as Spain was concerned, 'there is only one country which we desire should hold the command of the sea—and that is Great Britain'.

Baden-Powell reached home on 10 November after a Channel crossing during which 'all had to wear life-belts—the last time in the war!' He was back with his family when the news spread from house to house the next morning that the Armistice had been signed at last, that 'the war to end all wars' had ended.

6

The day after Armistice Day B-P took Olave house hunting. They had had a marvellous four years at Ewhurst Place where their three children had been born, but the house had proved inconvenient for London. For a while they lived in another rented home near Horley in Surrey: Little Mynthurst Farm. Now the time had come for them to settle down permanently in a home of their home.

Even before B-P went to Spain the two Baden-Powells had been out looking for a house, armed with Orders to View from several agents. Their quest had not been easy. Because of war-time restrictions on motoring they had had to travel by train and bicycle over many weary miles. So far their hunt had been in vain.

Now they began again, this time into the beautiful countryside of Hampshire, a county convenient to London and yet with the completely rural landscape they both loved. For themselves, as well as for their three children, they wished for the peace and quiet of rural England, with the delights of gardening, walking, fishing and the keeping of dogs and ponies.

They had heard of several houses for sale not too far from Godalming which was near Charterhouse, B-P's old school. They took their bicycles by train to Farnham, then pedalled along the narrow lanes. None of the houses was suitable. They continued to Bentley, where they stopped to eat their picnic lunch at the entrance to a long wooded drive to a house with a For Sale sign in front. Before continuing on their way, they decided to see what was 'round the corner of the drive'. There was their house, just what they wanted—the size, the looks, the setting, the view, everything they were seeking.

The maid-servant, reluctantly in the owner's absence, permitted them to come inside to look over the fairly modern, red-brick house. They rode back to the station in brilliant moonlight fully determined that this was to be their home. Within a month it was—thanks to careful financial negotiations with a kindly bank, B-P's share from the sale of 32 Princes Gate and the generous response from Olave's father to her call for assistance.

On 29 January 1919, the Baden-Powells moved into their new home. They changed its name from the sombre Blackacre to Pax Hill, Pax for the Armistice Week in which it was found and Hill for the challenge to Look Wide from the eminence of its location.

The Baden-Powells had hardly established themselves in Pax Hill before they were planning to leave it for a while. Throughout the war B-P had been in contact with national Boy Scout and Girl Guide associations round the world—but only by correspondence. Now, with travelling again possible, invitations arrived for him and Lady Baden-Powell to come visiting.

Mrs Juliette Low was among the first to send an invitation. Much had happened since she had last seen the Baden-Powells. From the first small company of Girl Scouts she had formed in Savannah after her home-coming in 1912, the movement had spread throughout the United States. Its membership was booming but would become even larger and grow even faster if the Baden-Powells were to come to Washington for the National Girl Scout Council Meeting in May 1919, as the guests of the Girl Scouts.

The Baden-Powells paid a hectic visit of a little more than three weeks to Canada and the United States. They distributed their time and efforts equally between the Girl Scouts and Boy Scouts, B-P alone delivering forty addresses in twenty-three days.

This was Olave's first trip to America. She was treated with great deference not only as the wife of the founder of scouting but also as Chief Guide of Great Britain. Her speeches were almost as numerous as her husband's. B-P was proud. In just a few years Olave had blossomed out of her original shyness into an excellent speaker with a strong and arresting personality and the ability to speak with authority on any aspect of Boy Scouting and Girl Guiding—or Girl Scouting, as Mrs Low and her com-mittee insisted on calling their American movement, to Baden-Powell's dismay. He was still of the opinion that the girls should have a distinctive name of their own instead of capitalizing on that of the boys.

7

With the purchase of Pax Hill one of Baden-Powell's dreams for himself and his family had come true; at last they had a home that was truly their own. Soon after, one of B-P's dreams for his Boy Scout movement was fulfilled; the Boy Scouts Association was given a national training ground.

Late in 1918, a Scottish district commissioner, W. F. deBois Maclaren (no relation to 'The Boy' McLaren), of Rosneath in Dumbartonshire, had become interested in the plight of the Scouts of East London who had no place to go camping. He approached Baden-Powell with an offer to present a camp site within easy reach of East London to the Boy Scouts Association. In discussing this generous offer with Maclaren, B-P suggested that the gift would be of even greater value if the site could also be used as a training centre for scoutmasters. Maclaren acquiesced.

B-P put some of the members of the Headquarters Staff and some commissioners to work to find a suitable place. They searched the vicinity of London and finally came upon Gilwell Park, a derelict estate with a ramshackle manor house built in the 1790s and fifty-seven overgrown acres of woodland. It would need a lot of repair but its position was perfect. It lay near Chingford in Essex, and bordered on Epping Forest. On 31 January 1919, Maclaren agreed to its purchase.

During spring and early summer, a number of Scout troops camped on the new site and cleared the grounds. On 26 July, at a ribbon-cutting ceremony with Baden-Powell officiating, Gilwell became the property of the Boy Scouts Association. The first Camp Chief, appointed by B-P, was Francis Gidney, an imaginative leader with wide experience in scouting.

Baden-Powell himself developed the details of the training course for scoutmasters along lines he had laid down as early as 1913. It was to consist of three parts: a theoretical part covering the fundamentals of scouting as explained in his book, *Aids to Scoutmastership*; a practical part of a week in camp; and an administrative part in the form of the scoutmaster's performance in his own troop.

The first scoutmasters' training camp held at Gilwell started on 8 September. It followed the pattern B-P had used with boys on Brownsea twelve years before. The patrol system was again put to the test with the nineteen participants divided into patrols and living a patrol life. The instruction also took the same form as on Brownsea. Each day a new subject was introduced and covered in demonstrations, practices and games. The Matabele koodoo horn that had called the boys into action on Brownsea was used for all signals.

What should these men be given as a token of having finished their training camp? The usual and obvious thing would be some kind of certificate, but B-P did not care for certificates. He rummaged among his trophies and souvenirs for a suggestion and pulled out the long string of wooden beads he had found in Dinizulu's deserted hut in the Ceza bush during the Zulu War in 1888. He presented each man who had taken part in the camp with one of the beads.

These simple wooden beads signifying the completion of the training course soon became one of the most highly prized possessions a scoutmaster could want. The beads gave the training its name of the Wood Badge Course. When Dinizulu's original beads ran out, the Gilwell training staff whittled others to keep up the tradition established by B-P.

8

Following the triumph of the Birmingham Exhibition in 1913, Baden-Powell felt that it would be of great value to the Scout movement to continue the practice of calling his Scouts together for some spectacular activity every two years. Unfortunately, because of the war, all plans for an event in 1915 had to be cancelled. In the summer of 1916, Baden-Powell appointed a planning committee and sent a provisional prospectus for a 1917 event to Percy Everett, the Secretary, for consideration.

The terms 'rally' or 'exhibition' no longer suited Baden-Powell. Something more picturesque was required. From out of his subconscious, possibly placed there on one of his trips to America, he pulled the word 'jamboree'.

'But you can't possibly use that word for a Boy Scout event!' someone told him.

'And why not?' Baden-Powell wanted to know.

'Have you looked it up in the dictionary?' B-P hadn't. Now he did:

> **jamboree** (jam-bō-rē′), n. [A slang word, prob. arbitrary.] A carousal; a noisy drinking bout; a spree; hence, any noisy merrymaking. [Slang.]

Although its dictionary definition was not particularly dignified, B-P happened to like the word, and with no better suggestion forthcoming, 'jamboree' it was.

The jamboree committee held its first meeting on 26 July 1916, and decided 'that an Imperial and International Jamboree shall be held in 1918—provided the war is over in 1917'. That optimistic hope was not fulfilled. By November, Baden-Powell was forced to cancel all thoughts of a 1918 jamboree: 'We are obliged regretfully to put it off until happier times are in sight.'

The happier times arrived with the Armistice in November 1918. B-P reactivated the jamboree committee and made public the plans for holding a jamboree in 1920—'the jamboree, be it understood, meaning an exhibition of work done by Scouts together with demonstrations of their activities, with displays, rallies and competitions both indoors and out-of-doors'.

After long discussion about a suitable site, the jamboree committee, at a meeting in 1919, agreed that the location of the Jamboree would be Olympia, a huge glass-roofed exhibition hall in the heart of London, in which large crowds of spectators could be accommodated. Baden-Powell, as Chief Scout and director of the whole undertaking, placed the job of Organizing Secretary in the hands of A. G. Wade, returned with the rank of major from the Salonika campaign. He further appointed a director for each of the twenty-nine departments involved in staging the Jamboree.

The promotion for the participation of British Scouts was started in their official publications. Thousands of circulars, handbills, and advertising stamps were showered upon the general public. Besides, Baden-Powell arranged for Hubert S. Martin, the recently appointed International Commissioner, to extend invitations to Scout associations throughout the world.

Before long, Martin reported himself completely overwhelmed with the enthusiasm he had met. Twenty-one countries, in addition to British dominions and colonies overseas, accepted the invitations to send representatives, ranging from two from Japan and four from Siam to four hundred from the Netherlands.

Planning and preparation for the Jamboree went ahead smoothly. With his firm belief in decentralization, Baden-Powell let all his directors proceed without interference on his part. Whatever suggestions he felt called upon to make were passed through his secretary, Miss Eileen Nugent, to Major Wade. They dealt mostly with programme items.

> Wade, I want very much to encourage (1) Acting, (2) Shakespeare reading. Do you think we could offer a prize for the best performance of an act from any play by Shakespeare by members of any two troops in co-operation . . . or of a troop of Scouts and a company of Girl Guides? RBP.

> Wade, I think we should add a competition in staves and give prizes for the best decorated staff. Also for the best camping apparatus ideas. RBP.

24

Wade, We must devise some outlandish form of diploma to award as prizes at the Jamboree. Suggest that we issue wooden totems and leather diplomas as rewards—nothing of intrinsic value. RBP.

Wade, Provide a river in the arena for building bridges over. RBP.

Wade managed to take care of Baden-Powell's requests, including the river and only had to give up on one: 'I cannot find a hole or corner in Olympia for Shakespeare plays,' he reported regretfully. The close co-operation between B-P's private secretary and the Jamboree's organizing secretary had an unexpected result. B-P was one day informed that Major Wade and Miss Nugent planned to get married as soon as the Jamboree was over. Major Wade had actually proposed to Miss Nugent in a taxi while taking her from Olympia to St Pancras Station.

With more and still more registrations pouring in from Scouts wanting to take part in the Jamboree, the problem of sleeping them became acute. It was finally solved by quartering 1,050 performing Scouts at Olympia, where they would be on hand to take part in the daily displays, and by camping the remaining 5,000 in the Old Deer Park, Richmond, within an easy train or bus journey of Olympia.

On the afternoon of 30 July, the stalls of Olympia were packed with an audience of some ten thousand expectant people. They were confronted by an immense dark-green curtain hung along one side of the great 325-foot-long arena. For a while they were entertained by the singing and whistling of a chorus made up of five hundred London Scouts. At exactly 2.30 p.m., a Scout band struck up the National Anthem as the Duke of Connaught and Princess Mary, in Girl Guide uniform, entered the Royal Box, followed by Baden-Powell and Olave, Peter and Heather, and a group of ambassadors and Government officials. The Duke had come to open the Jamboree on behalf of His Majesty, King George V.

At a bugle signal, the huge drop curtain rose. There was an excited gasp from the audience. The whole side of the vast hall was filled with a vivid landscape out of the dream scenes of a boy's imagination. Far to the left an old three-decked pirate ship out of *Treasure Island* was set against a rolling sea and a rock-girt island scene; to the extreme right rose a dense tropical forest out of *The Jungle Books*, with primitive huts and log-houses; and in the middle was a rocky mountain pass leading up into the rafters of Olympia.

A roll of drums, a rousing march—and the youth of the world began to wend its way over the pass and down the mountain slope to the thundering applause of the audience. First came the American Scout orchestra from Denver, Colorado, followed by a group of American Indians in magnificent war bonnets. Team upon team of Scouts, straight-backed, proud behind their nations' flags, streamed down the ramp, round the arena and out, leaving a lump in the throat of practically every spectator.

For a moment the arena was empty. Suddenly it was filled again with hundreds of Scouts in vigorous motion, act upon act depicting the programme of scouting.

After the arena performance, the audience scattered into the annexes of Olympia where hundreds of scoutcraft skills were on exhibit in rows of booths. Olympia was a teeming mass of people that night until at last the lights went out and the doors closed, leaving 1,050 Scouts inside the huge building to drop off to sleep after a happy and thrilling day.

The next eight days were among the most exciting and exhausting in Baden-Powell's life. Every day he attended special lunches and conferences and was present at one or both of the daily arena performances. Twice during the Jamboree Week he visited the Scouts encamped in the Old Deer Park. On the Sunday, at Olympia, he joined twelve thousand worshippers for the Thanksgiving Service conducted by the Archbishop of York.

Throughout the week Baden-Powell's elation grew, his satisfaction deepened as the performance of the boys became more finished and the enthusiasm of the public mounted. The press accounts changed from routine reportings into raves. The first Boy Scout International Jamboree was an unqualified success.

It reached its climax on the closing night.

Things had been happening behind the stage during the last day of the Jamboree. In small and larger groups the leaders of the foreign contingents had been conferring. They had talked about Baden-Powell, about some way of showing him the gratitude of their boys and themselves, of a way of honouring the founder of scouting. The night before, at the end of their pageant, the Boy Scouts of America had placed an Indian war bonnet on B-P's head and proclaimed him Chief Lone-pine-on-the-skyline. Might it be appropriate and feasible to incorporate a similar, yet different, proclamation into the repeat performance of the American pageant, chosen as the last item of the closing night's arena performance?

The leaders turned to one of their number, the American Chief Scout Executive, James E. West, to act as spokesman for all of them. West went to Major Wade and told him of the leaders' proposal. The Organizing Secretary readily consented to have the idea carried out on condition that the proclamation be part of the closing pageant and did not involve further rehearsing.

Climax Two

Just before seven o'clock on 7 August 1920, B-P and Lady Baden-Powell took their seats in the Royal Box among the Chief Scouts of the countries participating in the Jamboree. Then, with the usual punctuality, the performance started. The programme was made up of the items that had proved of greatest interest during the past week.

A score of British troops put on a fitness show of vigorous camp activities and exercises. Five hundred Wolf Cubs turned the arena into a bedlam of confusion and then, as if by magic, formed a large, orderly circle and raised the roof in a resounding Grand Howl. The last championships were decided, in trek-cart obstacle racing and in tug of war, with Danish teams winning both of them. The Boy Scouts of America contingent staged their spectacular Indian show, with a war dance that called forth thunderous applause from the audience.

The American display ended with a short pageant that was to lead into the closing of the Jamboree. From either end of the arena, troops representing Britain and the United States approached each other. They were preceded by two girls dressed symbolically as Britannia and Columbia. As they reached the centre of the arena, they embraced, then mounted a dais and sat down on gilt chairs.

A moment's silence was followed by the tramp of many feet as the Scouts of the world wound their way down into the arena, deployed, and marched to their allotted places. When the whole arena was a sea of Scouts, Britannia and Columbia moved towards the Royal Box. Baden-Powell saluted them, then joined them to walk across the arena through an impressive and colourful lane of the flags of all the nations represented at the Jamboree.

Mounting the highest tier of the dais, he turned and faced the great gathering. The moment had come for him to close the Jamboree, to bid the Scouts good-bye. But before he knew what was happening, he heard a clear boyish voice proclaim aloud 'We, the Scouts of the World, salute you, Sir Robert Baden-Powell—Chief Scout of the World!'

Suddenly, the standard bearers in front of the dais dipped their nations' flags in his honour and from all sides, the cheering of the crowd, of his Scouts, engulfed him.

Chief Scout of the World! B-P hesitated, taken completely aback. As he slowly raised his hand in the Scout sign, the cheering abruptly ceased. There were a few seconds of impressive silence before his voice rang out with its accustomed force to the farthest corners of the building:

Brother Scouts, I ask you to make a solemn choice. Differences exist between the peoples of the world in thought and sentiment, just as they do in language and physique. The war has taught us that if one nation tries to impose its particular will upon others, cruel reaction is bound to follow. The Jamboree has taught us that if we exercise mutual forbearance and give-and-take, then there is sympathy and harmony. If it be your will, let us go forth from here determined that we will develop among ourselves and our boys that comradeship, through the world-wide spirit of the Scout brotherhood, so that we may help to develop peace and happiness in the world and good will among men. Brother Scouts, answer me—will you join me in this endeavour?

A thundering shout answered him: 'Yes!'

'God speed you in your work', Baden-Powell concluded. 'And fare you well.'

B-P stepped down from the dais and came to the Scout salute in the middle of the arena. The melancholy notes of the 'Last Post' sounded in the large hall, and the whole audience rose to its feet while a huge laurel wreath was raised on the flagstaff at the end of the arena in memory of the Scouts of all nations who had died in the war.

The American Scout band struck up 'Auld Lang Syne'. The Scouts of Britain and America crossed their arms and joined hands with their friends to the right and the left and broke into song: 'Should auld acquaintance be forgot. . . .' Their brother Scouts, not quite knowing what was happening, looked on for a moment, then did what the others had done. Up and down the arena the chains formed, then spread to the audience. Everywhere arms were linked as friends bade each other good-bye.

There was only one lonely figure in the whole, vast building: the Chief Scout standing in the middle of the arena. The feeling of isolation was too much for him. He dove into the front rank of the contingent nearest to him and linked hands with two young American brother Scouts.

With the last notes of the song, the evening's programme was officially over, but the boys didn't want it to end. They took over for a completely spontaneous programme of their own.

B-P had just returned to the Royal Box when a thunder of cheering swept the hall. It swelled in volume with every second that passed. Louder and louder it grew, until it became a deafening roar. For several minutes the boys stood and cheered with all their attention directed at the slender figure standing at the Scout salute high above them, until, at last, a Scout was sent up into the Royal Box with a message that if the Chief Scout did not return to the arena he would be fetched.

Baden-Powell stepped down into the arena again, He was instantly seized by four hefty scouts, mounted shoulder-high and carried in triumph among the frenzied boys. Twice before, he had had the same experience of being chaired. Then, he had tried to protect the contents of his pockets. This time he did not have that concern. He relaxed and let himself be carried through the surging throng, trying to shake every hand that gripped his fingers.

After a triumphant journey round the arena, he was carried back again to the Royal Box. In the arena there was pandemonium still, with Scout hats flying through the air to the accompaniment of cheering, cheering, cheering.

A single bugle note.

The cheering subsided. Short commands in many languages rang through the hall. Quickly the Scouts formed into lines by contingents and marched out of the arena past Baden-Powell, standing at his post until the last Scout had left.

The first Boy Scouts International Jamboree had reached its glorious end.

XXIV

The Chief Scout of The World

Years: 1920–29   Age: 63–72

1

FROM his earliest boyhood days everything had tended towards that day in August 1920 when Baden-Powell became the Chief Scout of the World. His hiking and sailing with his brothers . . . his camping and riding in Africa and India . . . his training of men in reconnaissance and scouting . . . his Mafeking experience that had made him a hero to his countrymen . . . his contact with the founder of the Boys' Brigade . . . his decision to develop a 'scheme' to strengthen the physical and moral fibre of the boyhood of Britain . . . his sacrifice in retiring from the Army . . . his writing ability . . . his artistic skill. Each item was like a piece in a jigsaw puzzle, interlocking pieces from which the final picture emerged: B-P, Chief Scout of the World.

In the early development of his Boy Scouts scheme Baden-Powell's Victorian upbringing had caused him to concern himself exclusively with the welfare of the boys of the British Empire, using scouting as a means 'for consolidating our Empire by the development of personal sympathy and sense of comradeship between the manhood of all the different overseas States and the Mother Country'. When he discovered the hold his scheme was taking among boys of other countries, his concern widened to include the boyhood of all the world. He arrived at the conviction that the principle of brotherhood he was expounding for the boys of the Empire might 'extend its influence for good among those who will be the men of the different nations within the next few years'.

The long war of 1914–18 had held in abeyance the realization of this dream of a League of Youth. Now, because others had shared his dream, such an international league had been realized.

Two days before the opening of the Jamboree B-P had convened a Conference on International Questions in Olympia to discuss common problems with representatives of the countries taking part. By unanimous vote it had been decided to hold similar conferences biennially in the future and to establish a central information bureau to co-ordinate world scouting. France had offered to act as host for the next conference in Paris and Britain had agreed to house an international bureau in London.

Throughout this first informal conference Baden-Powell had tried to keep himself and his own ideas in the background but had found that the others did not want it that way. They accepted him as their logical head to guide them, to inspire them, to exert on them his unifying influence. And the boys, in proclaiming him Chief Scout of the World, placed their stamp of approval on their leader's decision.

Baden-Powell was eager to get an International Bureau established at the earliest possible moment. He took up the problems of financing it with Hubert Martin, the British International Commissioner. And suddenly the problem was a problem no longer. It was the old story all over again of bread cast upon the waters.

During the war years, a young girl of enormously winning personality had stormed through the United Kingdom and the United States drumming up money for the Red Cross and for the Scottish Women's Hospital. Her success in charming dollars out of her audiences had been so great that Kathleen Burke had become known to the press of two continents as the Million Dollar Girl. After the war Miss Burke dropped in at Boy Scout Headquarters to see Hubert Martin, who, in his every-day capacity as Chief Passport Officer of Great Britain had arranged her trip to America. She had come to offer her services to scouting. After telling her of the need for helping Scout associations that had been disrupted by the war, Martin—woman-shy bachelor that he was—turned her over to Miss Nugent, B-P's private secretary.

Nothing further was heard of Miss Burke until a year later she showed up in Olympia for the Jamboree as Mrs Frederick F. Peabody, accompanied by her husband, a wealthy American she had met on a post-war visit to the United States. At the conclusion of the Jamboree, B-P received a letter from Peabody. The American told him of the thrill he had experienced on seeing the 'March of the Nations' and intimated that he was interested in finding out more about the international aspects of scouting.

At a luncheon on 24 September, Peabody listened to Baden-Powell's and Hubert Martin's ideas about world scouting and then almost stunned his two guests by offering 'to finance the International Central Bureau at £2,500 per annum', until it should be self-supporting. After all the details were settled, Mrs Peabody turned to Martin with a smile. 'See what comes of being kind to a little Irish nurse,' she said.

Office space was leased in the British Boy Scouts Association's new head-quarters at 25 Buckingham Palace Road. A small staff was engaged, and Hubert Martin agreed to take on the position of Honorary Director. The Boy Scouts International Bureau came into existence on 11 October 1920. In January 1921, it published the first issue of its quarterly magazine, dubbed *Jamboree* by Baden-Powell.

While Baden-Powell's League of Youth was becoming an established reality, another league, the League of Nations, was taking its first stumbling steps.

During the war, a number of far-seeing politicians had begun to look forward to the time when hostilities would end. Somehow, they realized, if war was to be prevented in the future there must be a concert of nations. The idea of using war for solving disputes among quarrelling nations must be outlawed, armaments must be decreased throughout the world, secret diplomacy must be abandoned, and nations must learn to co-operate with each other in some kind of organization. The term League of Nations made its appearance in 1915 and was heard more and more often as the war progressed. In January 1918, President Woodrow Wilson expounded his Fourteen Points for a League and called for a 'general association of nations'. The Peace Conference, convened after the war, took up the question. On 28 April 1919, the Conference, by unanimous decision, adopted the Covenant of the League of Nations.

Baden-Powell carefully watched the creation of the League of Nations. He recognized it as an important step in the direction of stamping out the evils of war. He felt that if the League were to succeed it must possess a soul, and that the Boy Scout and Girl Guide movements might play an important part in fostering the objectives of the League.

A field of immense possibilities has become opened to us [B-P wrote in the first issue of *Jamboree*]. While we are building, each for the good of our country, our own individual national associations of Boy Scouts and Girl Guides as a school of young citizens let us keep ever before us the still greater aim of promoting the comradeship with our brother Scouts in other lands.

In this way we may help in no mean degree to bring about the mutual unity and good will which will make the world an assured home of peace, happiness and prosperity for all.

While in general accord with the purposes of the League of Nations B-P felt concern over its organizational structure. The League seemed to him quickly to become a vast debating committee of representatives of different countries, each zealously and jealously watching the interests of his own particular nation. To B-P's way of thinking, it should, instead, have taken the form of a group of experts meeting in consultation for the purpose of bringing about the good of all mankind.

He wanted the Boy Scouts' international co-operation to be organized the way he thought the League of Nations should have been. When, therefore, at the Second International Boy Scout Conference in Paris, an International Committee of nine members was being formed to act on behalf of the Conference between its biennial meetings, Baden-Powell urged that the individual members be chosen not as representatives of any country but solely on the basis of their own qualifications, their character and their Scout knowledge. The Conference followed his advice. The newly elected International Committee, at its first meeting, selected Baden-Powell, by acclamation, its permanent Chairman.

2

After the crowded days of the Olympia Jamboree, Baden-Powell was looking forward to settling down at Pax Hill to a quiet country life in the midst of his family. His hopes were soon disappointed.

Scouting had come to India in 1909, but only for British-born and Anglo-Indian boys of mixed English and Indian parentage. The Government of India had expressly forbidden Indian boys to join the Boy Scouts Association, giving for its astonishing reason that 'Scouting might train them to become revolutionaries'.

The boys of India wanted scouting. If they couldn't get it inside the officially recognized association because of Government meddling, they could get it outside by forming their own unofficial groups. A few of these had been established before World War I. With the agitation for self-government that swept the country after the war they sprang into being all over India. By 1920 all provinces and several individual States had their own Indian Scout organizations, in addition to those established on a national scale, such as the Indian Boy Scouts Association headed by the controversial Englishwoman and disciple of Gandhi, Mrs Annie Besant.

In August 1920, Major Alfred Pickford, a member of the Indian Legislative Assembly and Chief Commissioner of Scouts for India, had called a conference in Calcutta to attempt to achieve a measure of correlation among the conflicting groups. The conferences had had only limited success and had mainly shown how difficult it would be to arrive at a common understanding, Pickford reached the conclusion that only Baden-Powell could reconcile the various factions. He prevailed upon the Viceroy, Lord Chelmsford, to invite Baden-Powell to come to India. B-P gladly accepted on the condition that he could bring his wife to help to straighten out the Girl Guide situation.

From the moment Baden-Powell landed at Apollo Bunder in the harbour of Bombay, at the same spot on which he had first stepped ashore in India as a young sub-lieutenant, he was subject to more spontaneous youthful adulation than he had ever experienced before. The glorification reached one of its highest points in Calcutta at a big rally staged by John Skinner Wilson, 'a particularly sympathetic and broad-minded District Scout Commissioner', who, in his professional life, was Senior Deputy Commissioner of Police for Calcutta.

Throughout the whole tour of India, wherever the Baden-Powells stopped, B-P met and held conferences with the leading authorities inside and outside the movement, getting their views. When, at Madras, Baden-Powell joined the leaders of the different organizations at the conference, it was not difficult for him 'to enter with all sympathy into the points which they put forward'. Before the meeting was over, agreement had been reached to blend the British and Indian Scouts into a single association. 'We who had sat down to the table as a meeting of representative heads rose at the end of it a united band of brother Scouts.'

Baden-Powell himself proclaimed the amalgamation that afternoon at a rally of fifteen hundred Scouts. To signify the agreement in a spectacular fashion, Mrs Besant, 'picturesque in native costume', stepped out and took the Scout promise on behalf of all the leaders before B-P himself.

> It is a tribute to Sir Robert Baden-Powell's spirit of compromise and accommodation [one of the Indian leaders wrote afterwards], that in that difficult year—1921—when questions of national ideals and values evoked touchy responses from leaders of Indian organizations, the first steps towards forming an all-India association could be taken.

On their return journey, Baden-Powell learned that his brother Warington had taken seriously ill. As soon as he and Olave reached London they went directly to Chelsea Court to see him and were relieved at finding him in good spirits although very weak. Their relief was short-lived. The following Sunday, the 73-year-old Warington had a relapse. At noon the next day—24 April 1921—B-P's oldest brother died, leaving another break in the ranks of the Baden-Powell family.

After the funeral, B-P returned to Pax Hill for a happy reunion with the children. He was truly home now, with no major undertakings or journeys in the immediate offing.

3

During the twenty years the Baden-Powells lived at Pax Hill, it was not only a real home for B-P and Olave and their three growing children, it was also the centre from which the spirit of world scouting emanated. It was a place of pilgrimage for thousands of people connected with scouting all over the world. For twenty years an endless stream of letters and notes, articles and sketches and books flowed out from Pax Hill for furthering and strengthening the Boy Scout and Girl Guide movements. The quantity and quality would have been remarkable for a writer in his thirties or forties dedicated solely to writing. It was phenomenal for a man in his sixties and seventies for whom writing and sketching were only part-time work. The volume was possible only because of Baden-Powell's extraordinary self-discipline and powers of concentration.

His working day began early, about 5 a.m., a pattern he had been forced to adopt during his Army service in India where everything had to be done before the heat of the day intervened. He had discovered that in England, as in India, 'there is nothing like the early morning for getting over your work'. His mind was fresh and clear after a good night's rest, the house was still, and there were no telephone interruptions or callers to interfere.

An even more important reason for his early rising was that he needed the extra time for accomplishing the tasks he had set for himself.

> Mind you [he wrote], if you only take an hour extra per day it means three hundred and sixty-five hours per annum, or three weeks longer of waking time than your average neighbours get. . . .
>
> Personally, I reckon to get thirteen months of life into each year instead of twelve.

So, summer and winter, B-P rose early, silently, went down to his study, made himself a cup of tea and started to work. At seven or half past he laid down his pen or brush and went upstairs to bathe and dress. By then, Olave was up and about, and the two set off for their customary walk through the Hampshire countryside accompanied by their two Labradors. Upon their return, they had breakfast with the whole family and whatever guests might be staying at Pax.

> The Chiefs were good breakfasters [according to B-P's private secretary, the former Eileen Nugent, who now, as the wife of Major A. G. Wade lived in a cottage in nearby Bentley village]. They could sit at leisure enjoying their food and their mail, which nearly always contained something of interest. The letters would be thrown across the table to me, sometimes with a pencilled note, more often with just

a comment. Anything which had to be thought out or dictated would then be gathered up, and we repaired to the study. . . .

With the morning mail out of the way, Baden-Powell could return to his desk, provided he had what he called a 'free day': a day without a Scout conference, or a Mercers' meeting in London, or a rally he had to attend in some part of the United Kingdom. While Olave took up her Girl Guide correspondence at her own desk in the drawing-room, B-P worked on the project of the moment. By the time a few people had telephoned or had called, the hour for lunch would be at hand. In the afternoon of a 'free day' there might be another walk with the dogs, and at five o'clock the evening mail would have arrived with new problems to be dealt with.

If the weather was suitable, Baden-Powell generally spent an afternoon hour or two in the garden. Whenever he could spare the time he was out tending his roses; until far into the late autumn, roses from his own garden filled the bowl he liked to have on his desk.

Unlike most other English houses where lunch and dinner were the main family gatherings of the day, tea was the biggest occasion in the B-P household, offering time for relaxation and sharing the events of the day.

In the evening, B-P might be finishing up a task or he might join the rest of the family for a game or for a discussion. If there were guests, he might show a film he had taken on one of his journeys. About ten o'clock he would excuse himself with the comment that he had a 'few things to do' the following day.

4

The childhood world of the three Baden-Powell children was composed of nurseries and nurses, of playhouses and governesses, of ponies and dogs, of rabbits and pigeons and other pets.

Peter, the spitting image of his father as a child, was turning into a sturdy boy after a delicate childhood. Heather, a freckled redhead like her brother, was the tomboy of the family with much of her father's daring. In contrast with the others, Betty, with her black hair and fair skin, resembled her mother in both looks and temperament.

B-P and Olave spent as much time as they could with their children. They picnicked with them in spring on the banks of the River Wey in the valley below Pax, camped with them in summer in the counties of southern England, went blackberrying in the autumn along the hedgerows of Bentley, searched the woods for mistletoe and holly at Christmas-time. The cavalryman in B-P was especially happy at seeing the interest they took in horsemanship. Each had a pony to catch in the field, to saddle and to care for. All three enjoyed riding, although it was Heather rather than

Peter who was the born equestrian, sitting her horse the way her father sat his and becoming the best jumper of the three.

From time to time, watching the growth of his children, Baden-Powell speculated on what might happen to them if he should die. He was old for a father. He had been 56 when his first child, Peter, was born, and 60 when the last, Betty, came into the world. He was particularly concerned about Peter since he felt that a boy needed a father to stand by him and give

Peter 'off on service, in heavy marching order, mounted'.

him advice. To provide this fatherly advice in case of his death, B-P wrote a series of letters to Peter and placed them in sealed and numbered envelopes, one of which was to be given to Peter each year on his birthday.

The most important of these letters to Peter was written on 22 March 1922. It was intended for a birthday more than seven years in the future.

> My dear old Pete, I have just finished a very long letter to you for you to read when you are 16.
> It is my book *Rovering to Success*. It is mainly made up of things that I should like to have told you—but as they apply also to other boys growing into manhood I have published them for all to read.
> But I want you especially to read the book and be guided by it.
> It contains a lot of information and advice that I badly needed as a young man—but I had no father to give it to me. He died when I was 3.
> Your father will be dead, I expect, when you are 16—but let that book help you in my place. Will you?
>
> Your loving,
> DAD

Of all his many books—and Baden-Powell wrote more than thirty—
Rovering to Success is the best written and the best edited. 'He took
immense trouble over this book', Eileen Wade recalled, 'writing and re-
writing, asking advice and suggestions from many people and often
adopting their suggestions.'

Rovering to Success is a book for young men on how to achieve success
in life—not the success of wealth or fame but the success of happiness,
'the only true success'. It was also Baden-Powell's proposed solution to the
'older-boy problem' in scouting, his design for a programme for 'Senior
Scouts' whom he called 'Rovers', hence the word 'Rovering' in the title.
The title, incidentally, did not particularly appeal to Herbert Jenkins, the
book's publisher—he suggested, tongue in cheek, that the book would sell
many more copies if it were called *Women, Wine, and Cuckoos*, the headings
of three of the chapters.

The problem of keeping the older boy in scouting had concerned Baden-
Powell for several years. At scoutmasters' and commissioners' conferences
he had put forward various ideas on 'Retaining and Training the Senior
Scout'. In 1917, he had established a Senior Scout Section but the timing
had proved wrong and no definite programme had been forthcoming.

With the end of the war and the return to Scout Headquarters of Colonel
Ulick de Burgh from active war service, things began to look up. B-P
discussed his latest ideas with de Burgh and together they worked out the
details of the Rover scheme. Experiments throughout Britain during
1920 and 1921 seemed to indicate that they were on the right track. With
the publication of *Rovering to Success* on 14 June 1922, the older-boy
branch of the Scout movement came into its own—'a Brotherhood of the
Open Air and Service'.

When Peter was 9, he left home for boarding school. Soon after, Heather
and Betty also departed for boarding school. So that the family could be
together during school holidays B-P and Olave did their utmost to arrange
their absences from home to coincide with the periods when the children
were away. They didn't always manage, for summer was the time when
Scouts and Guides were best able to gather for rallies or camps and the
adult leaders could most easily congregate for conferences. As the children
grew older, their father and mother did their best to make it up to them by
taking them on some of their trips.

5

During the 1920s, one major scouting event followed another—some of
them of an Imperial character, others of an international nature. In all of
them, Baden-Powell was involved.

When, for instance, the Prince of Wales was returning to England from his highly publicized world tour in 1922, B-P got the idea of giving the Royal Chief Scout of Wales a special Boy Scout 'Welcome Home'. The idea developed into a 'Posse of Welcome', held on the large grounds surrounding the Alexandra Palace in North London. Upon arriving on the ground the Prince was taken in hand by Peter Baden-Powell, in Wolf Cub uniform, and led to a large 'council rock' where he received a piercing Grand Howl from the throats of nineteen thousand enthusiastic, green-capped Cubs. The hush of the silence that followed was as surprising as the loudness of the Howl. It was broken only by the Prince's greeting, heard by all the boys by means of one of the earliest uses of a public address system loaned by the Marconi Company.

From the Wolf Cubs the Prince was brought to another part of the park to witness the overwhelming rush of thirty-two thousand Boy Scouts surging toward him with waving flags and banners, in a re-enactment of the famous Windsor Rally for the Prince's father more than ten years before.

The Posse of Welcome was hardly over before the plans were being formulated for the British Empire Exhibition at Wembley, which was to open in 1924. Sir Henry MacMahon, Chairman of the Stadium Committee, approached B-P with the suggestion of holding a great Imperial Boy Scout Rally or Jamboree in conjunction with it. The idea seemed feasible and was accepted by the Boy Scouts Executive Committee. The work of Organizing Secretary was turned over to Major Wade who had done such an outstanding job for the Olympia Jamboree.

For almost two weeks in the summer of 1924, ten thousand Scouts from Great Britain and approximately two thousand more from the dominions and the colonies camped at Wembley Paddocks, half a mile from the Exhibition grounds, the largest Boy Scout camp ever held up to that time.

This Imperial Jamboree was plagued by abominable weather, but it had extraordinary Royal Patronage to make up for the rain and the gales: one ruling King and two future Kings took part in the proceedings. Before the formal opening, Baden-Powell introduced the Overseas Scouts to King George V at a parade in the Riding School of Buckingham Palace. During the camp, the Prince of Wales, the future King Edward VIII, braved the mud to participate in a camp fire sing-song with B-P as his host. And the Duke of York, the future King George VI, attended a rally of six thousand Wolf Cubs at which Rudyard Kipling, for the first time, had a chance to see how Baden-Powell had made the characters of his *Jungle Books* come alive.

The Girl Guides also registered a claim on Baden-Powell in the summer of 1924, requiring his services for opening the first World Camp of Girl Guides at Foxlease Park, the new training grounds of the British Girl Guides.

Soon after the Boy Scouts had secured Gilwell Park, Baden-Powell had started to agitate for a similar centre for the Girl Guides. And as in the case of the boys, a centre for the girls had suddenly materialized. In 1922, a wealthy American woman, Mrs Anne Archbold Sanderson, offered her property in the New Forest, Foxlease Park, to the Girl Guides Association to commemorate the marriage of Princess Mary, President of the Girl Guides since 1920.

There had been some concern that the Association might not be able to accept the gift, that its finances would not suffice for the upkeep of such a large place. The problem was solved in surprising fashion by a telephone call to B-P from Buckingham Palace at ten in the morning of his and Olave's joint birthday, 22 February 1922. The call was to inform him that Princess Mary had decided to give to the Girl Guides £6,000 out of her wedding present from the Empire's girls and women named Mary. Their gift had been unexpectedly large, and the Princess had refused to allow more than a certain amount to be spent on herself. The surplus, she had determined, was to go to the Guides to make it possible for them to have their training centre.

In the summer of 1924, Foxlease was ready for its first major camp, and both of the Baden-Powells came to take part in it. They visited each of the camps of the eleven hundred girls and joined the Girl Guides and Girl Scouts of twenty-eight nationalities at their international camp fire.

After the big summer events in England, the Baden-Powells went to Denmark for the Second International Jamboree, taking their Wolf Cub son along for Peter's first trip abroad.

The Jamboree camp, organized by the Danish Scout leaders, met with Baden-Powell's highest approval. It was pitched on a grassy plain surrounded by ancient beech trees in Ermelunden, a forest a few miles north of Copenhagen. Unlike the first Jamboree at which Scouts had been quartered in dormitories at Olympia or in military bell tents at Richmond and fed by a catering firm, the Danish leaders had based the second Jamboree in Denmark squarely on B-P's own kind of scouting, as expounded in *Scouting for Boys*. The boys, organized in troops and patrols, had brought their own equipment, had pitched their own camp, were cooking their own meals, were taking part in special scoutcraft events. Close to five thousand Scouts from twenty-four nations and a large number of British colonies were living together through sun and rain in a genuine Boy Scout camp, mingling with each other, making friends with each other, using 'jamboreese' for communication when they didn't know each other's language. The pattern established in Denmark became the pattern for all future world Jamborees.

On the day of Baden-Powell's arrival, the whole Jamboree gathered at the Copenhagen stadium for a parade to honour their Chief and for a public exhibition of the world's scoutcraft activities. In spite of a drenching downpour, an enthusiastic crowd of Copenhageners filled every seat of the vast open-air structure and remained faithfully until the last country had put on its part of the display. The Scouts, soaked to the skin, marched back to camp through the streets of Copenhagen, singing in the rain.

The weather was no better on the closing day when Denmark's King Christian X and Queen Alexandrine, accompanied by B-P and Olave, reviewed all the Scouts at a Royal parade. 'I have seen great numbers of Scouts in my life,' B-P said in his speech, 'but I have never seen any as wet as you!'

For three days after the Jamboree, Scout leaders from thirty-four nations met in the Council Chambers of Copenhagen's Town Hall to share their experiences, discuss their problems, deliberate the future of scouting. To two official observers from the League of Nations it was an astonishing performance. No speaker, no voter on final resolutions spoke on behalf of his own country but on behalf of the good of the world Scout movement as a whole as he saw it. Baden-Powell had expected to see 'Scout Spirit' at work at the conference but the reality gave even more hope for the future than he had thought possible.

Early in 1926, the Boy Scouts of America invited Baden-Powell to come to the United States in April so that they might present him with the first Silver Buffalo, a new award 'for distinguished service to boyhood'. As soon as he had accepted, Juliette Low asked him and Olave to take part in another special occasion involving the Girl Scouts.

On 30 April, B-P and Olave were entertained at the White House by Calvin Coolidge and Mrs Coolidge. That same evening B-P and the President of the United States were together again at the speakers' table of the National Council of the Boy Scouts of America. Both of them spoke to the crowd of two thousand: 'President Coolidge gave a long address on Boy Scouts and then retired: I gave another three-quarter hour harangue.'

Pleased as B-P was to have Silver Buffalo Number One hung around his neck on its red-and-white silk ribbon, he was even happier when he found out that Silver Buffalo Number Two was awarded

> *To the Unknown Scout Whose Faithfulness in the*
> *Performance of the Daily Good Turn Brought the*
> *Scout Movement to the United States of America*

On a bleak autumn night in 1909, an English Boy Scout had guided an American publisher to his destination through the fog of London and had refused a tip for his service. Now, seventeen years later, this simple Good Turn that had had such far-reaching effects received the highest recognition that American scouting had to offer. Since there was no boy grown into man around whose neck to hang a small silver buffalo on a silk ribbon, the award to the Unknown Scout took the form of a statuette of a buffalo to be erected at Gilwell Park.

The Girl Scout event to which Mrs Low had invited the Baden-Powells became Juliette Low's crowning glory. The single company of Girl Scouts she had founded in 1912 had grown into an American movement of more than a hundred and fifty thousand girls and leaders. She had worked untiringly for the friendship of Girl Scouts and Girl Guides around the world and had persuaded the International Council of Girl Guides and Girl Scouts to hold the Fourth World Camp in the United States, at the Girl Scouts' Camp Edith Macy at Briarcliff, New York.

As Juliette Low guided the Baden-Powells through the camp, she told them that she felt she could die happy now. She had seen her life become worth while and her wish had come true of witnessing international scouting flourishing on her own soil.

Very few people at the time were aware how seriously ill Juliette Low was, for her spirit and her energy seemed as strong as ever. But she was death-marked in the summer of 1926. She succumbed to cancer the following winter, her work done.

The Baden-Powells' trip to South Africa the autumn and winter of 1926–27 was entirely different from their American experience. In the United States, they had been the guests of two firmly established organizations; in South Africa, the Boy Scout and Girl Guide movements were still in a state of flux. Also, the Baden-Powells decided to make their South African sojourn a family occasion. Since they would be gone for more than half a year, they took Peter, Heather and Betty with them and placed them in Cape Town schools while they themselves went travelling and inspecting.

This was B-P's ninth trip to Africa. When he landed at Cape Town in 1896, B-P had come as a Victorian colonel imbued with all the traditions of Her Majesty's Army to help suppress the revolt of a tribe of rebellious Africans. In 1899 he had been sent out to protect a British colony against the inroads of other whites. This time he had come, not to fight but to promote brotherhood, not as a British officer to uphold the British Empire but as the Chief Scout of the World intent on helping boys to become better citizens of their Motherland, the Union of South Africa, and of their Brotherland, the whole world.

Wherever he had the chance in his extensive travels throughout South Africa, Baden-Powell preached the non-political, non-military, non-sectarian aspects of scouting and the importance of Dutch and British co-operation in the training of the country's youth. Even though he came away with the feeling that he had partly succeeded in his efforts to dispel some of the Dutch mistrust of scouting and had given an impetus to the spread of the movement, he knew the road ahead was still long and thorny.

6

There was much discussion in scouting circles about the date and place of the Third International Jamboree. Some of the delegates to the Fourth International Conference in Switzerland in 1926 had urged that a clash with the 1928 Olympic Games should be avoided. Others pointed out that 1929 would be the twenty-first anniversary of scouting as an organized movement and suggested that the Jamboree would be an appropriate occasion for celebrating this important milestone. Czechoslovakia, Hungary and Holland invited the world's Scouts to meet in their countries. But others held that the coming-of-age of scouting should be celebrated in the country where the movement was born. It was finally decided to hold the third Jamboree in England in 1929.

Before the celebration of the twenty-first anniversary of the movement was undertaken, there was another twenty-first anniversary to celebrate, that of the 1907 camp on Brownsea where the acorn had been planted that had grown into the sturdy oak of scouting.

Baden-Powell put Mrs Wade to work tracing the boys who had camped with him on Brownsea, and he himself sent out the invitations. They discovered that four of the boys had been killed during World War I, that one had succumbed afterwards from war-time gas poisoning, that three more had since died. Four had settled abroad. Twelve boys would be absent. So would Baden-Powell's assistant at the camp, his old friend 'The Boy' McLaren who had died in 1924.

On 28 July 1928, the Baden-Powells entertained the ten remaining Brownsea boys, now grown into men, at a luncheon at Pax Hill. They were joined by Percy W. Everett who had been with them during the last days of their camp and had afterwards become one of B-P's staunchest helpers. They enjoyed a 'cheery lunch' with a number of 'small speeches'. They had much to talk about. Twenty-one years had been a long time. The world had become a different world.

The preparations for the Third World Jamboree were progressing smoothly. The Mayor and Corporation of Birkenhead had offered Arrowe Park,

By 1929, the acorn of Brownsea Island had become the oak of Scouting.

five miles from the city, as a camp site. The park was a mile long and half a mile wide, and filled with undulating woods. Fifteen thousand Scouts from forty-two countries and from all parts of the Empire and fifteen thousand from the home counties would be in attendance. Visiting British Scouts who could not be included in the allotted quota would be accommodated in nearby auxiliary camps.

A few months before the Jamboree, Olave was approached in secret by Scout Headquarters. A collection had been started for Scouts from all over the world to contribute one penny each towards a gift to their Chief. What kind of gift would he like? Olave promised to find out.

She brought up the subject on an appropriate occasion.

'What would I like? Nothing!' B-P said. 'I have everything I want.'

But Olave pressed him further. 'Think again,' she said. 'You certainly must want something.'

B-P thought it over. Then he remembered. 'Oh yes,' he said, 'I do need some new braces.'

Six days before the official opening of the Jamboree, Baden-Powell went up from Pax Hill to Birkenhead to greet the foreign delegations as they arrived. To act as his A.D.C., 'watchdog' and 'nurse' he took with him John Skinner Wilson, who, as Commissioner for Calcutta, had so impressed B-P on his visit to India in 1921. Wilson had retired from the Calcutta Police Department in 1922, had returned to England in 1923, and had immediately been grabbed by Baden-Powell for the job of turning Gilwell Park into a truly international training centre for world scouting.

The next couple of days Baden-Powell traversed the camp by car and on foot, enjoying the brilliant summer weather and the sight of the arriving Scouts.

On Sunday morning 28 July the long drought broke with a gentle rain that increased during the day. B-P's old car, 'Jimmy', broke down in the middle of the camp and had to be towed to a garage. Baden-Powell continued his inspection of camp in gum boots. And then: 'Gale and rain in the night—alas for the Jamboree!'

The Opening Day of the Third World Jamboree started with heavy rain; but by the appointed hour, when the Duke of Connaught, in his capacity of President of the British Boy Scouts Association, opened the Jamboree with Baden-Powell at his side, the weather had turned 'windy and fine'.

B-P had brought with him to Arrowe Park the old koodoo horn of Matabele War days he had used to awaken the campers at Brownsea for the world's first Boy Scout camp and to open the first scoutmasters' course at Gilwell Park. Now he lifted it to his lips to blow a blast that would reverberate over the vast parade ground in front of him. But in his excited state, his lips refused to do his bidding. The sound of the horn was only a feeble 'pffft'.

Nevertheless, as if called to action by the koodoo horn, the March Past got under way, with contingent upon contingent swinging by the saluting base, with the flags of practically every civilized country in the world snapping in the brisk wind, with the grandstand's thousands of onlookers greeting each nation with enthusiastic applause. For almost an hour the Scouts marched by—boys black, brown, yellow, red, white, most of them in the familiar uniform designed so long ago by Baden-Powell, with shorts and broad-brimmed hats, but also some in the native costumes of their homelands to add extra colour to the proceedings.

After the Duke had left, Baden-Powell had a highly emotional session with Olave, his secretary, Eileen Wade, and John Skinner Wilson.

The upheaval had started the day before when Mrs Wade had arrived at Arrowe Park from Pax Hill with a batch of mail and had triumphantly placed a letter in his hands.. He had read it quickly before shattering his usual calm with the unusual exclamation of 'Damn!' followed by an emphatic, 'Well, I suppose I can refuse it'.

The letter, from the office of Ramsay MacDonald, the Prime Minister, informed him that it had been proposed to His Majesty the King that a peerage should be conferred on B-P on the occasion of the Jamboree.

Baden-Powell did not want it. He had always been against the idea of hereditary titles and if he had been against the baronetcy conferred on him in 1923, he was even more determinedly against the barony. He thought it too much of an honour for himself and too much of a burden on his descendants. He told his wife of his inclination to refuse it and Olave heartily agreed.

The Duke of Connaught thought otherwise when he arrived to open the Jamboree. He advised B-P that, whether he liked it or not, he must take it for the sake of the movement.

Mrs Wade and Wilson used the same argument when they discussed the subject with B-P and Olave. 'You cannot refuse it—you have deserved it . . . it is an honour to the movement as well . . . it will mean a great boost for scouting . . . it will give further inspiration to all leaders in scouting. . . .'

Baden-Powell was in tears before those close to him persuaded him to accept the proffered peerage. When he finally agreed he said, 'This is for scouting, not for me.'

Wilson quickly drafted a telegram of acceptance to the Prime Minister. After showing it to Baden-Powell, who brushed it aside with a curt 'Do as you damned well like!' he dashed to the camp post office to send it before B-P could change his mind.

When he returned, he and Eileen Wade did their utmost to change Baden-Powell's solemn mood by coming up with the most ludicrous suggestions for the territorial designation that customarily follows the name of a peer. Soon B-P smiled as he joined in their game. Then he got serious again. The name could not be Mafeking, he decided, although to most people that would have been the logical choice. He did not want a place connected with his military life. The place name should stand for scouting, not for British scouting alone but for world scouting.

'Gilwell Park has become an international scouting centre', he finally said, 'I think I should like to be called Lord Baden-Powell of Gilwell. But this is not for me to decide—it is for the International Committee to tell me what title they would like me to adopt.'

Wilson immediately went to see the International Committee, in session in another part of the building.

Half an hour later [Wilson wrote afterwards], Hubert Martin, the then Director of the International Bureau, placed a paper in my hand which conveyed the congratulations of the International Committee, their pride in being informed in advance of the others and in being consulted by their Chief. It also carried their humble suggestion that he should adopt as his title: Lord Baden-Powell of Gilwell. And so it was.

Two days later, in clearing weather, the Prince of Wales read a letter from his father, King George V, to the assembled Scouts from all over the world:

It has given me great pleasure to mark this signal event in your history by conferring a peerage on the Chief Scout. Ever since its inception he has been the mainspring of this great adventure, from its small and almost humble beginning until today, when you number nearly two million in your ranks. The recognition of his valuable services to the cause will be welcomed by all who realize the importance of training the world's youth both in mind and body. . . .

GEORGE, R. I.

The announcement of this new honour to their beloved Chief Scout of the World was greeted with tumultuous cheering by the Jamboree Scouts. It was obvious that the King's tribute had the boys' whole-hearted approval.

After a short respite of a pleasant day, the weather again turned vile:

Saturday, 3 August, Gale and showers.
Sunday, 4 August, Wind and heavy rain squalls. The camp a sea of mud.
Monday, 5 August, After a gale, fairly fine. Big crowd visited the Jamboree: about forty thousand. . . .

The arena was a morass of oozey clay, the camp roads a mire of soupy mud through which waded and slid and skidded the thousands of Scouts and the thousands of visitors who had come to see this amazing Jamboree, now popularly known as the 'Mudboree'.

In spite of mud and rain and gales, morale was high, health excellent. The Scouts braved every obstacle to visit each other throughout the camp, to swap badges, to make friends. The camp became a huge family party, with its presiding genius, the Chief Scout, mingling with his followers, covering the whole area on horseback.

At last, the rains let up and a spell of dry weather set in.

On 10 August, following the arena performance in front of sixty thousand visitors, Baden-Powell and his family were invited to step to the saluting platform. As they took their places, a Rolls Royce with a caravan trailer attached rolled into the empty space below them. Christian Holm, President of the Danish Boy Scouts, joined the Baden-Powells on the platform. In a short speech he told how the Boy Scouts of the world had contributed a penny each for a remembrance to their Chief and asked Baden-Powell to accept their gift of the Rolls, the trailer, a portrait of B-P painted by David Jagger and a cheque for £2,800.

B-P had a new automobile to take the place of broken-down 'Jimmy' but not the braces he had wished for.

He got his braces, nevertheless, before the Jamboree was over, by courtesy of the Irish contingent. Their leader, George S. Childs, had scoured the surrounding territory and had located a pair of beautifully gaudy braces, green in colour and strong enough to serve as a mooring rope. They were wrapped up and presented with appropriate ceremony. B-P was greatly amused as he unpacked the parcel and saw the braces. He hung them around his neck like a mayoral chain of office.

'Now I have everything I want in this world,' he said.

XXV

Lord Baden-Powell of Gilwell

Years: 1929–37   Age: 72–80

1

KING GEORGE V had made B-P the Lord Baden-Powell of Gilwell. A light-hearted ceremony at Gilwell Park and a solemn one in the House of Lords made the title completely official.

Gilwell Park was growing up. Ten years had passed since it was presented to the Boy Scouts as a training centre. During the Jamboree, it had become more truly international than ever before, with numerous foreign participants staying to take the Wood Badge Course at its fountainhead. Although still young, Gilwell had become a place of firmly established traditions—among them a yearly reunion for those who had completed the training.

B-P, with his family, was invited to the Gilwell Reunion of 1929 to be recognized 'on taking possession of his lands after the Highland manner—a long way after!'

At the evening camp fire, in the presence of nearly three hundred Scouters, a white wand and an immense sword were presented to B-P and the 'ancestry' of the Chief Scout was proclaimed. 'Those very ancestors' were summoned 'from the misty past' to testify to Baden-Powell's right to his title. They made their appearance one by one to the notes of a Danish Viking horn: the Amoeba in its bowl, the Monkey off his tree, the Piltdown Man with his 'microscopic brain', the woad-stained early Briton, the armoured Knight, and the modern Boy Scout—all acted by some of the 'stoutest' men in the movement.

A more formal ceremony took place on 30 October when Baden-Powell on his seventeenth wedding anniversary and Peter's sixteenth birthday, was introduced to the House of Lords by two of his Boy Scout commissioners, Lord Hampton and Lord Glentanar.

It was a fearful adventure [he wrote to Peter, now a pupil at Charter-house]. It meant a procession into the House with Black Rod, Garter King of Arms, two Barons and other officials. I had to wear a red gown and cocked hat and bow a dozen times at different corners of the Chamber, etc.

B-P survived the ordeal of introduction into the House of Lords but only rarely afterwards attended the sessions of Parliament. While he had reluctantly accepted the title as an honour extended to the Boy Scout movement, he had no intention of getting himself or his movement involved in politics.

Many years before, while still in South Africa at the end of the Boer War, B-P had received a cable from England from a politically-minded friend asking him to stand for Parliament. Baden-Powell's answering telegram had abruptly stopped any further solicitation. 'Delighted,' he had cabled back. 'Which side?'

At that time he was a military man abhorring all politicians. He had not changed his mind since. 'From what I know of them, I would not trust an ordinary politician with my grandmother's toothbrush. This world seems divided into talkers and doers. There are too many talkers. The doer is the man we need—the man whose vision is not limited by narrow party considerations.'

2

Before becoming the Lord Baden-Powell of Gilwell, B-P had done a great deal of travelling on behalf of his vision of the world as a 'Brotherland' through scouting. He did even more afterwards, causing a correspondent to *The Scouter* to chide him for spending so much time away from home.

B-P answered the letter-writer through his monthly column in the same magazine.

I notice [he wrote] that one correspondent has remarked that 'during one of his brief visits to the United Kingdom', the Chief Scout did so and so.

Yes, it does look rather that way, and I must apologize for my frequent absence from the Old Country—but there are reasons. For one thing, the Old Country is not the only country in the world, and I am supposed to be World Chief Scout. The world is rather large in size, and it takes time to get from end to end of it.

There have been calls for me to come to various points, in order to help them in their organization or progress. Moreover, I am not entirely unconnected with the Girl Guide Movement....

So there you are!

Luckily for Baden-Powell, his wife was just as excited about travelling as he was and her reasons suddenly became as imperative as his.

In the summer of 1930, while Baden-Powell travelled to Switzerland for a meeting of the Boy Scouts International Committee, Olave went to Foxlease for another World Conference of Girl Guides. The Guides had followed the example of the Scouts in establishing an International Bureau and an International Committee. Both had functioned satisfactorily but a woman of decided leadership ability to provide guidance and inspiration was missing. The Conference solved the problem by unanimously choosing Lady Baden-Powell, Chief Guide of the World. She carried the magic name of Baden-Powell, the founder of Girl Guiding and Girl Scouting, but that alone would not have been enough. She also had the personality, the drive, the dedication, the thorough understanding of guiding that made her the obvious choice.

Baden-Powell congratulated himself, as he had had occasion to do so many times before, on having been clever enough, in 1912, to marry Olave. He had taken a gamble, of course, by marrying, at 55, a girl of 23. He had picked her for his true love, for his wife and for his children's mother. He could not have known or even imagined that she would be the perfect travelling companion, the perfect co-worker in the cause he had created, the perfect female counterpart to himself in the leadership of the movements he had founded.

Things had worked out miraculously well. And so, wherever Lord Baden-Powell travelled as Chief Scout of the World, Lady Baden-Powell went with him as Chief Guide of the World. With Olave to carry the burden of the Girl Guides and the Girl Scouts of the world, B-P could concentrate as never before on the Boy Scouts.

3

With the approach of Baden-Powell's seventy-fifth birthday, two publishers got the idea of suggesting to him that this was an appropriate time for him to write his autobiography for serialization and book publication. The Northcliffe papers were interested in running the Baden-Powell story first as a newspaper feature, Pearsons as a series of magazine articles. With B-P's close friendship with Pearsons' Percy Everett—now Sir Percy, knighted for his services to his country through scouting—Pearsons won.

B-P developed a suggested outline and discussed it with Everett who arranged for the final terms of the sale of the book, not only to his own company but also to an American publishing house. With the contracts signed, B-P's two publishers began to hound him for the manuscript just as he was ready to start off with Olave on a promised visit to Australia.

Baden-Powell decided that a world tour by ship might be the perfect opportunity for writing an autobiography, especially since he was to be accompanied by so expert a secretary and typist as Olave. He collected his source material and packed it in a number of boxes, including the tin dispatch-box that had served him so well in developing *Pigsticking* and *Scouting for Boys*.

Every day during the trip across the North Atlantic, through the Panama Canal and across the Pacific, the two Baden-Powells spent several hours sorting out diary entries and sketching out incidents. In New Zealand and Australia they put the book aside while they inspected their Scouts and their Guides and explained the importance of the two movements to the general public.

After leaving Australia, they resumed their literary endeavours across the Indian Ocean and, after a hasty tour of South Africa, picked up the book again as they continued northward along the west coast of Africa back to England. By the time the two Chiefs reached home, B-P had the whole book roughed out and several of the chapters in first draft. However there were still a long task and a great number of obstacles to overcome before the book would be completed.

Baden-Powell managed to meet his deadline by working overtime between Scout and Guide rallies in various parts of England . . . between meetings of the Mercers, the 13th Hussars, the Old Carthusians, the Mafeking Defenders, the Bentley Fly-Fishing Club . . . between reports for *The Times* and articles for the *Daily Mail* . . . between weekly and monthly articles for the Scout magazines, and letters, letters, and still more letters.

Other things also kept him, physically and emotionally, away from his book writing. Within the short stretch of only a few months he was faced with the deaths and funerals of Olave's mother and his own Aunt Connie, of his old friends Lord Methuen and Viscount Plumer.

The Baden-Powell autobiography, *Lessons from the Varsity of Life*, appeared first serially in *Pearson's Magazine*, then in book form with more than a hundred pen-and-ink drawings by the author. The book is a 'casually built-up autobiography', as *The Times* pointed out in a very friendly review, or, as B-P himself more correctly described it: a 'sort of hotch-potch or plum-pudding'. It is a book of people and places, of anecdotes thrown together without regard to chronology under such headings as 'Sports' and 'Acting', 'Soldiering', 'Spying and Scouting'. Only in certain chapters—on the Siege of Mafeking and the development of the Boy Scout and Girl Guide movements, for instance—does any semblance of continuity occur. The book is not literature any more than *Scouting for Boys* was literature but it is typically Baden-Powell:

entertaining, witty, happy-go-lucky, with an undertone of idealism and earnest challenge, told in the simple style and easy language with which B-P was always able to enthral his audiences.

4

By the early 1930s, the Rover movement for young men that B-P had started in the twenties had prospered in many countries in Europe. During the 1929 World Jamboree, it had been decided to call the Rovers together for a world gathering, or a 'Moot' as Baden-Powell dubbed it. A logical place for this First World Rover Moot was Kandersteg in Switzerland.

Kandersteg in the beautiful Kander valley of the Bernese Oberland had become another centre of world scouting with the dedication of an International Scout Chalet in 1923. The Swiss Chief Scout, Major W. de Bonstetten, had long had a dream of such a centre. He found it in the form of a large chalet built to house the engineers and workmen constructing the Loetschberg tunnel that was to connect Berne with Milan. When the tunnel was completed, the abandoned building was put up for sale. Vigorously backed by Baden-Powell, de Bonstetten persuaded a number of Scout enthusiasts from Switzerland, Holland, England and the United States to join in purchasing the chalet. The surrounding area was bought as camp grounds with money contributed by Mortimer L. Schiff, American financier and International Commissioner of the Boy Scouts of America.

At Kandersteg, two thousand six hundred Rovers from twenty-two nations, Rover Peter Baden-Powell among them, forged yet another link towards Baden-Powell's dream of a world-wide brotherland of scouting. In the past, the large international gatherings in which B-P had taken part had been rallies and camps for boys, planned and organized and run by adults. This was different, for the Rovers, young men in their late teens and early twenties, were planning their programme together and carrying it out together. The result confirmed Baden-Powell's deep conviction that young people, growing up in the spirit of scouting and given the chance to co-operate, could be depended upon to live peaceably together in their maturity.

The Kandersteg Rover Moot was followed two years later by the Fourth World Jamboree, when twenty-five thousand Scouts from thirty-two countries pitched their camp in the park surrounding the former Royal castle at Gödöllö in Hungary, the favourite summer residence of the ill-fated Empress Elizabeth.

Baden-Powell was not feeling well when he arrived at Gödöllö. His head was aching, his back was bothering him. After a drive through the camp with the Jamboree camp chief, Count Paul Teleki, he retired early to a suite in the large castle placed at his disposal by the Regent of Hungary, Admiral Horthy.

The next day, for the opening of the Jamboree, the Regent and Baden-Powell proceeded together to the Jamboree arena. The air was full of music—bands playing and Scouts singing on their way to the big parade.

> And it *was* a big one [B-P wrote to Olave that evening when the opening ceremony was mercifully behind him], rather like Arrowe Park. The Regent took me there, he in full uniform riding a White Arab and I mounted on a very nice black horse—mounted, yes, but the job was to mount. However, a low wall nearby gave me the means. We walked our horses half a mile to the rally ground and there were thousands of Scouts drawn up in two lines from end to end of the plain. His Highness galloped to the front of the line and I with him, but it was real agony. I held my back with one hand and the horse with the other. Then an endless walk up and down the lines— then, to my horror and renewed agony, a gallop across the plain to the saluting point in front of the grandstand. There we dismounted —or were supposed to, but I just couldn't. I got a couple of grooms to sort of lift me down! Then came an endless march past! A wonderful show of all the nations. It took over an hour in a nasty cold wind, the Regent and I standing on a small dais. We both addressed the boys through loudspeakers. At the end we went up into the grandstand and there was a run of all the boys yelling their hearts out.

The programme of the Fourth World Jamboree was similar to the programme of all previous Jamborees, but one day, the Hungarians surprised their foreign visitors by staging a unique parade of their own. Twenty thousand country officials and merchants, land owners and peasants, people of every walk of life, men and women, boys and girls, in national dress, led by the High Sheriff of Gödöllö, walked by the dais where Baden-Powell was standing, throwing bouquets towards him till the ground was covered with flowers.

When the remarkable demonstration was over and B-P stepped down from the dais to get into his car, one of the peasant women made her way through the crowd around him and pressed a tremendous spray of flowers into his arms. As he received it with a smile and a Köszönöm—Hungarian for 'Thank you'—the woman suddenly bent down, impulsively seized his hand in both her coarse hands and kissed it again and again, while tears streamed down her cheeks.

I have heard the Chief laugh off many a tribute [Wilson wrote many years after in recollecting the incident], but he was completely silent in the car for a long time after that one, for he recognized sincerity when he saw it.

Baden-Powell had hardly returned to Pax Hill before he was off to the Baltic countries on a trip that had started from a casual remark made by Olave at the World Girl Guide Camp in Poland the summer before. In her enthusiasm over the camp she had said to one of the British Guiders, 'I wish I could take a whole group of you along to see some of these camps— a whole shipload of you!'

And the Guider had said, 'Why don't you?'

The idea had stuck in Olave's mind. Back in England she discussed it with her husband. They investigated the possibility of a Baltic cruise for the Boy Scout and Girl Guide leaders and found it completely feasible. Percy Everett was put to work organizing the trip, while Hubert Martin made the arrangements with the foreign associations involved. On 12 August, the S.S. *Calgaric* steamed eastward with six hundred and twenty Scouters and Guiders for a seventeen-day tour.

The cruise accomplished its main aim of bringing British leaders into personal touch with their counterparts in the countries along the Baltic Sea. It did far more than that, for in each country, the presence of the Chief Scout of the World and the Chief Guide of the World gave new impetus to scouting and guiding and caused the leaders of the different nations, many of them previously uncommitted to scouting, to take a public stand behind B-P's movement.

5

Baden-Powell had a special reason for being happy over the success of the cruise of the S.S. *Calgaric*. What he had seen had been a partial consolation for an expectation destroyed. When he last visited Eastern Europe in 1911, a strong Boy Scout movement was developing in Russia. It had come to naught, dissolved by the leaders of the 1917 Revolution. Totalitarianism and scouting are by their very natures incompatible.

But out of World War I had come freedom to some of the countries that had been under the Russian yoke. In Poland and Lithuania, Latvia, Estonia and Finland, scouting had taken a vigorous hold. In each of them, Baden-Powell, his wife and their large party were honoured and given a rapturous reception. In Poland they were welcomed by the Minister of Education on behalf of President Pilsudski. The President of Lithuania joined them for a camp meal. The President of Latvia received them at the presidential palace. The Head of the Estonian Government attended their camp fire. And in Finland, Field-Marshal Baron Mannerheim was on hand to greet them on their arrival in Helsingfors.

Baden-Powell was learning that the type of totalitarianism made no difference. Fascism was just as intolerant towards scouting as communism was. In Italy, the Italian Boy Scout Association felt the heavy hand of Mussolini. For a few years after his ascendancy to power he suffered the Boy Scouts, but only until he had worked out a youth programme of his own. In 1927, he absorbed the Scout movement into his own *Balilla* and *Avanguardisti* programme for younger and older boys.

On a trip to Rome in 1933, Baden-Powell was disappointed in his hopes of softening Mussolini's attitude towards scouting. The Italian dictator left no doubt in B-P's mind that scouting was dead as far as Italy was concerned, that Mussolini's own movement, as part of the national youth education, was there to stay. Anyway, Mussolini intimated, Baden-Powell should be very happy because the Italian movement was definitely patterned on that of the Boy Scouts, although, as he insisted, in an 'improved' version.

When Baden-Powell demurred, Mussolini asked him what objections he might have. B-P replied that the *Balilla* was an official instead of a voluntary organization; that it aimed at partisan nationalism instead of wider international good feeling; that it was purely physical, without any spiritual balance; and that it developed mass cohesion instead of individual character.

Mussolini had an answer to each of Baden-Powell's points. As far as the boys were concerned, he insisted, joining was voluntary but, 'of course, for the parent it is different. They feel the moral obligation for their sons to join the *Balilla*'. The development of an intense nationalist spirit was essential for Italians as a first step before they could consider the feelings of other nations. Courage was the only spiritual quality needed. Consolidation rather than individualism was necessary to make Italy strong.

> The *Balilla* movement is as yet in its infancy [Baden-Powell wrote in his confidential report], but when the organization of the training is complete, within the next two or three years, and practically every boy in the land comes through it from childhood up to manhood, I think it cannot fail to make a big difference in the physical and moral health of the nation. But much depends on Mussolini being alive to see it through since it is his child. The important point to us is that it is an experiment in applying Scout training to the national education.

Yet another effect of dictatorship upon scouting was in evidence at the 1933 Jamboree in Hungary at which Baden-Powell had expected to see a large delegation of German Boy Scouts. More than a thousand had signed up to attend. In the middle of June, however, Adolph Hitler had appointed the young Baldur von Schirach *Jugendführer des Deutschen Reiches* (Youth-Leader of Germany). Von Schirach's first action, under his new authority, was to abolish all existing German youth organizations, including all Scout troops, and to proclaim the *Hitler-Jugend* the one and only youth movement for Germany's boys and girls.

During the next few years, the *Hitler-Jugend* made a great show of trying to make friends with the youth of other countries through camping clubs, cycling clubs, school journeys. A number of boys of the *Hitler-Jugend* visited England, hiking its highways and byways in small bands. And within Germany itself, the *Hitler-Jugend* made an effort to entertain Scout troops travelling through the German countryside or passing through the German *Vaterland* on their way to a camp in some other country.

As a national organization, the British Boy Scouts Association stayed aloof in the matter, although some of its leaders advocated a decree against fraternizing. Baden-Powell, for once, was not certain of the proper approach. His belief that world peace could only be assured if the young people of all countries came to know each other as friends suggested to him that an effort should be made to befriend the boys of the *Hitler-Jugend*. On the other hand, Hitler's astonishing mesmeric hold on the youth of Germany and his indoctrination methods made B-P wonder.

While he was still considering the position to take, Baden-Powell was suddenly invited to tea at the German Embassy. He was made most welcome by German Ambassador Joachim von Ribbentrop and Baldur von Schirach. They spent a very pleasant afternoon hour discussing how to bring the youth of their two countries together.

To Baden-Powell, it was his meeting with Mussolini all over again. The two Germans told their British guest of the great debt the *Hitler-Jugend* owed to his pioneering work in the youth field. As in the case of the Italian *Balilla*, Germany's youth leaders had taken the best features of scouting and had adapted the programme to fit German conditions and current mentality. There was no reason in the world, the Germans insisted, why Germany's *Hitler-Jugend* and Britain's Boy Scouts should not be the best of friends. B-P came away from his meeting with von Ribbentrop and von Schirach unconvinced.

6

Baden-Powell had returned from the exertions of the *Calgaric* cruise not only tired but ill. He had had plenty of warning of trouble brewing. Early in January 1933 his doctor had diagnosed an 'enlarged prostate gland but not needing operation' and had told his patient 'to stay quiet, no exercise, keep warm'. Later the same month, the doctor ordered B-P to 'knock off more work in the future' and to 'take things very easy'. A trip to the Mediterranean had helped him; the Jamboree and the cruise had helped him not at all. A severe case of sciatica developed and, early in December, an internal haemorrhage was accompanied by severe pains. B-P's doctor sent him to bed.

After that, events happened fast. On Christmas Day Baden-Powell had word that his brother Frank had died after a long illness. On New Year's Day his daughter Betty was rushed to the nursing home in Farnham for an emergency appendectomy. The following day Baden-Powell was speeded to London by ambulance and admitted to the King Edward VII Hospital for Officers. The next morning he underwent the first of two operations for the removal of the prostate gland.

Olave and Peter were waiting at the hospital while the operation was performed. When they were assured that it had been successful they went to a nearby hotel for the night. But, in Olave's case, not to sleep. In packing her husband's suitcase the day before she had seen, as usual, the large sealed envelope that was always at the bottom of B-P's bag on long journeys. Before, it had seemed just part of the luggage and had hardly registered in her mind. It did now—with terrifying clarity. The envelope, in her husband's distinctive handwriting, carried the legend: 'In the event of my death. . . .'

The second operation, on 20 January, was followed by an agonizingly slow improvement in B-P's condition. A sudden relapse set in, with days of grim suspense, of blood transfusions and semi-conscious periods, of *rigors* lasting an hour at a time. Daily hospital bulletins kept the public informed about the famous patient's condition.

Finally a slow turn for the better . . . with flowers and telegrams and letters pouring in to cheer him on his seventy-seventh birthday . . . with his sitting up in bed on 24 February for the first time in eight weeks . . . with an ambulance taking him home to Pax Hill on the 'wonderful golden glorious morning' of 8 March.

During Baden-Powell's illness, preparations had been progressing for another Good Will Voyage of Scouters and Guiders during the Easter Holidays, this one to the Mediterranean. The question was now, 'Will the Chief be going?' B-P was determined to go. At the very last moment, his doctors gave their consent on condition that he travelled as an invalid, that he stayed on the ship when in port, that he took no part in the planned activities.

B-P lived up to his doctors' demands. He spent most of the time 'lolling in the sunshine' on the deck of the S.S. *Adriatic*, watching Olave setting off with six hundred and eighty Scouters and Guiders for excursions and rallies wherever the ship stopped. He came home rested and sunburned and greatly improved in health, but was again warned to take things easy.

How could he? His long illness and convalescence had left him far behind in what he felt he must accomplish. Before long he was as hard at work as ever.

Even while bedridden after a serious operation in 1934, B-P kept his sense of humour. (*Design of Thank-You card sent to his well-wishers.*)

7

In a lecture Baden-Powell had delivered at University College a short while before his illness, he had expressed one of the points of his life philosophy:

> For my part I have habitually given myself three more years to go, and that makes me hurry up and get things done and get all the enjoyment I can out of life, because in three years' time it might be too late. That is a very good incentive, because some day it will come true. In the meantime it makes you burst along and get all you can out of life.

The idea of 'three more years' was very much in his mind as he now planned for the future.

Baden-Powell opened the year 1935 by reviewing more than ten thousand Scouts and Guides, marching past him under a bright blue Australian summer sky. Before his illness, Baden-Powell had promised the Boy Scouts of Australia that he would be on hand for the opening of the first Jamboree of the Southern Hemisphere at Frankston, near Melbourne, during the Christmas and New Year holidays. At the same time, the Australian Girl Guides had extended an invitation to the World Chief Guide. Since they would be half way round the globe, the Baden-Powells decided they might as well continue eastward back to England. They invited Heather and Betty to join them in this world tour as 'secretaries'. Peter would be cheated out of it. He had finished his schooling in England and had left home to join the British South African Mounted Police in Southern Rhodesia.

If Baden-Powell's doctors had known the schedule to which their patient would be exposed they might not willingly have given their assent to his journey. Since this would be his last visit to a great number of countries, Baden-Powell was intent on making the most of his time at scores of stops along the route.

The idea of holding an international gathering of Boy Scouts in Australia had been criticized as an 'absurdity' in part of the Australian press. There had been some anxiety about the sort of reception 'the coloured folk' might get in a country where the Asiatic question was causing heated discussion. But when the boys started to arrive, all apprehension disappeared for all of them were Scouts together.

One of Baden-Powell's main reasons for undertaking the long trip to Australia had been to find out 'how far Eastern races have grasped the ideals of scouting, and how far they mix with the European and Australian elements'. He left the Jamboree and Australia with the 'inspiring conviction that scouting and guiding so long as they are applied by understanding leaders, have to a large extent their appeal and their effect on boys and girls of whatever race whether their environment is tropical or Arctic, highly civilized or primitive and rough'.

> East and West certainly met on equal footing and on good terms as brother Scouts [he could report in an article in *The Times*], so that at the end of the fortnight never the twain wanted to part.

B-P's reason for going home by way of Canada was not ethnical but theological. The founder of scouting had been concerned from the very beginning of the movement by the fact that, in some countries, separate associations had sprung up along sectarian lines. He had worked for many years for co-ordination and amalgamation and had, to a great extent, succeeded. But in the early 1930s, particularly, there had again been talk, in various quarters, of Roman Catholics breaking away from established national associations and forming their own Scout organizations.

To secure a weapon for fighting this tendency B-P had sought, and was granted, an audience with his Holiness, Pope Pius XI, during his visit to Rome in 1933. On 2 March 1933, Baden-Powell and Olave were taken to the Vatican by the British Chargé d'Affaires to the Papal Court, J. Kirkpatrick, for a personal audience. Pope Pius showed his great interest and close knowledge of the Scout and Guide programmes by asking the two Chiefs a number of questions about their progress.

> His Holiness [Baden-Powell reported after the audience] said that he fully approved the movement; that he considered scouting and guiding 'a magnificent work', and looked upon the movement in its disregard of differences of class and creed and race as 'a great family carrying out the ideal of unity', and in parting he wished us success.

While the Pope's endorsement had had a salutary effect in a number of European countries, in Canada a separate organization of French-speaking Roman Catholic Scouts had been formed. Baden-Powell spent several days in Quebec discussing the situation with the leaders of the Catholic hierarchy and of the Canadian Boy Scouts. After a 'cheery talk' with Cardinal Villeneuve, an affiliation was established of the *Scoutes Catholiques de la Province de Quebéc* under the Canadian General Boy Scout Council. It was with great relief that Baden-Powell countersigned the agreement.

Another major problem in world scouting lay in South Africa. B-P, more than most people, was aware of the 'colour question' that existed there. He had had a chance during his long life and his many years in Africa to follow its emergence. In the early days he had himself fought against the Zulus and the Matabele and the Mashonas when they were wild 'savages' fighting for their land and what they conceived to be their rights. He had seen their tribal system of stern discipline, self-control and respect for authority broken down with the introduction of European rule with little to take its place. He had seen warriors leaving their kraals and hunters their veld to become workers in mines and cities, 'with freedom from any moral restraints and with all the temptation and vices of the underworld of civilization thrust upon them without their having received any education in character for facing them'. He had also seen the 'colour question' further complicated by the fact that in addition to the indigenous Africans, large numbers of 'coloured' people had been born and had grown up out of mixed marriages. He had furthermore seen the increase into a strong minority of the descendants of emigrants from India.

Because of this perplexing 'colour question' and the prejudices that went with it scouting in South Africa, so far, had been confined to Dutch and

British whites. Baden-Powell had grieved that, in the land he loved best after England, the policy that scouting should be open to all boys 'regardless of class, creed or colour' was not heeded.

But while the policy of scouting had not been accepted by the South African whites, scouting itself had been accepted by the non-white. The Pathfinders—of whom B-P had seen a few when he last visited Africa—had flourished. Numerous 'coloured' Scout units had been formed. Many Indians had started their own kind of unrecognized scouting.

At a conference of the Union Scout Council of South Africa in the Town Hall of Durban, 25 and 26 February 1936, the whole question of scouting and its relation to all South African boys came up for consideration and solution. Under B-P's guidance, the various pros and cons were thoroughly discussed in 'excellent temper and in the true Scout spirit of fairness and wide outlook'.

After two days of earnest deliberation the Council adopted a scheme of federation whereby three parallel branches of the Scout movement were officially authorized in addition to the parent organization. Pathfinder Boy Scouts for African boys, Coloured Boy Scouts and Indian Boy Scouts, each section a self-governing unit, were all to be registered under the control of the Council. The arrangement was not all that Baden-Powell could have hoped for but it was more than he had expected. It was a foundation to build on.

8

The trip to South Africa of Baden-Powell and Olave, accompanied by Heather and Betty, had several unexpected results.

Early on their trip, after two weeks of hectic activities with Boy Scouts and Girl Guides and Government officials, they had called a halt and had gone to Kenya to stay with Eric Walker at Nyeri, the same Walker who had been one of B-P's travelling inspectors in 1908. Walker had had an adventurous life since leaving his Scout job in 1914 to join the services, later to become a member of the Royal Flying Corps. He had travelled widely, had earned a substantial amount of money in Canada and Africa, and was now the manager of The Outspan, a highly successful hotel in Nyeri.

The Baden-Powells were completely enthralled by Walker's unique hotel.

> Never could we have imagined a more perfect place [Olave wrote home to Eileen Wade]. Exquisite view over forty miles of wild Africa and the snow-covered peak of Mount Kenya beyond—just indescribably lovely.

And this hotel is unique as we each have our own sort of little house with verandah, looking on to a garden ABLAZE with cannas, roses, salvias, Madonna lilies, geraniums, arum lillies, stocks and snap-dragons, and besides that all the lovely tropical things like jacaranda, flamboyant tree, etc. QUITE DIVINE—and with the comfort of electric light, water laid on, and blazing sun by day; and cool (with fire and blankets on the bed) at night. It is absolutely perfect.

The Outspan proved the ideal place for both relaxation and work—for writing letters and articles, and, in B-P's case, for sketching and painting.

About ten miles from the hotel Walker had built a tree house high above the ground in a tremendous old wild fig tree standing in solitary majesty in an open glade. This house—Tree Tops—was, in reality, a two-roomed bungalow surrounded by a balcony. Visitors climbed the thirty-foot ladder leading up to it at sunset and stayed for the night, watching the wild animals coming to drink in the salty pools below. B-P and Olave spent 'a most thrilling and enjoyable night' at Tree Tops, watching from sunset to 2 a.m. when the moon set, then again from five o'clock. They saw dozens of different buck, pigs, possums and eleven rhinos. Heather and Betty had even better luck the following night: 'Two big elephants came so close that B. was able to spit on them!'

Having tasted the thrill of seeing the wild life, the Baden-Powells were eager for more. They quickly fell in with Walker when he suggested a week's safari into the no man's land between Kenya and Abyssinia, a hundred miles north-east of Nyeri. Walker sent a truck ahead with camping gear and porters, then followed with the Baden-Powells in his own car. They ran through a herd of giraffe on the way and arrived at their destination, the small 'Ngare 'Ndare river, to find their camp already pitched.

For the next four days they made excursions from their base camp into the surrounding landscape which, ordinarily dry and bare and brown desert, was at that time green and lush with recent rains. Baden-Powell did a lot of shooting, not as formerly with a gun but with a motion picture camera given him by George Eastman of Kodak fame. He filled reel upon reel with shots of zebra and giraffe, impala and oryx, gazelle and dik dik, wart hog and baboon, stork and crane and marabout, but was disappointed in finding no lion.

In the evenings, the party gathered round a camp fire until the mos-quitoes became too bothersome and drove them into their screened tents.

Back to The Outspan and to packing for the resumption of the journey. 'But we'll be back,' B-P told Walker. 'Next winter, perhaps.' A dream for the future had entered his mind.

The following day the Baden-Powells boarded a plane in Nyeri. Nine days later, on 24 December, Olave went to bed with 'a ghastly head aching and temperature 102'. B-P came down with a high temperature the day after— 'a *jolly* Christmas Day'. They both had malaria, the result of mosquito bites suffered on the safari.

None of the thousands of Scouts at the first South African Jamboree realized, from the way the Chief Scout of the World mounted the speakers' platform, that it was a seriously ill man who had come to greet them. And no-one listening to B-P's speech, broadcast throughout the Empire, could possibly have imagined that that ringing challenge, in that resonant voice, was given by a 79-year old man who had defied his doctor in order not to disappoint his Scouts.

Back in bed after the opening of the Jamboree, B-P stayed there for the next two weeks, reading a little and listening to the radio over which he heard the news of the death of King George V and the accession to the throne of King Edward VIII.

By the beginning of February B-P was 'feeling wonderfully better already'. His doctor permitted him to get up but prescribed further rest. He interrupted his enforced vacation only to attend the Union Scout Council Conference in Durban. With the conference completed and his health somewhat regained, Baden-Powell, his wife and two daughters took a leisurely trip to some of the South African landmarks that had played a role in his life.

Although B-P tried to take life easily during this family trip he only partially succeeded. In every major locality in which they stopped they ran into the inevitable receptions and rallies and conferences. By the time they were ready for the return journey back home to England, the thought of taking a 'stopping boat' and calling at half a dozen ports along the west coast of Africa, from the Congo to Sierra Leone, seemed just too much for Baden-Powell. And yet, the Scouts in those places were expecting him . . . B-P's doctor made up his mind for him. The return journey was shifted to a mail boat going directly from Cape Town to London.

The weather was pleasant the whole way home. So was the company on board. Baden-Powell and Olave had a lot of good conversation with fellow passengers, among them a Mr and Mrs Gerard Clay, going home with their son who was on leave from his Colonial Service job in Northern Rhodesia. Heather and Betty were rarely in sight as they were enjoying themselves in the company of a group of young people.

Eric Walker of The Outspan was not the only one of B-P's first two 'travelling inspectors' from 1909 who had made out well. The other, W. B. Wakefield, had also made a success of his life and work. In 1936, he presented Great Tower Plantation, two hundred and fifty acres of wild country on the eastern side of Lake Windermere, to the Boy Scouts as a camp site and a National Training Ground for Woodcraft and Backwoodsmanship.

When it was dedicated in Baden-Powell's presence on 17 August, B-P's mind was not on the ceremonies. He was thinking of the three letters that had arrived in the morning mail. The first was from his wife. It told him that Betty was head-over-heels in love with Gervas Charles Robert Clay, her constant companion on the boat coming home from Africa. Olave enumerated a number of reasons in favour of an engagement between Betty and Gervas. The clincher was 'It would be odd if history repeated itself too in the sort of romance of their meeting on board ship and having the same birthday like us!' The second was from Betty telling her father of her love for Gervas. The third was from Gervas Clay. 'May I come and talk to you about her when you come back next week . . . I hope you will let me ask you for your permission to marry her one day.'

B-P rushed home from Windermere. As soon as he got to Pax Hill, he was met by Betty announcing that she was not only intent on becoming engaged but on getting married at once. The day after, Gervas Clay arrived to talk over the prospects in Northern Rhodesia for Betty and himself. He was due to leave England on 26 September to get back on his job and he hoped that Baden-Powell would give his blessing and let him marry Betty without delay so that his return journey might be their honeymoon.

The wedding took place on a perfect day in September, with the Dean of Westminster, an old Carthusian friend of Baden-Powell's, performing the ceremony. After a reception on the lawns of Pax Hill, Betty and Gervas Clay sailed for Africa.

Such was the power of a mosquito bite. If B-P's malaria had not forced him to cancel the voyage up Africa's west coast and to sail home direct from Cape Town, Betty and Gervas probably would never have met.

9

1937—the year that Baden-Powell reached 80—became the culminating year in a long and varied life. He started it with a journey to India, the country where his career had begun.

The Boy Scout movement there had grown to such strength that the leaders, confident of success, had planned an All-India Jamboree. They invited the Chief Scout of the World to join them and B-P gladly agreed to come, in spite of the long journey and the great exertion that would be required of him. He was eager to see for himself how scouting had prospered in India. In addition to meeting his Scouts he would be able to see his old regiment for the last time.

On 3 February, outside Delhi, Baden-Powell was greeted by four thousand Scouts from all parts of India. 'Wild Baluchis met quieter Bengalis', he noted afterwards, 'the Nagas (sons of the headhunters of Assam) chummed up with the boys of Bombay, the Pathans of the Punjab with the Burmese. It was a wonderfully mixed pudding.'

Following the Jamboree, Baden-Powell took the train north. After a ride of almost twenty-four hours he arrived in the town of Risalpur in the North West Frontier Province, half a hundred miles east of the Khyber Pass. He was back again with the 13th Hussars, now combined with the 18th.

It was a marvellous homecoming for him. He spent his eightieth birthday in the bosom of his old regiment, reciting to the new young Hussars some of the old stories and old traditions, and reviewing a mounted parade of the regiment. 'I felt forty years younger on the spot,' B-P wrote after the parade. 'It was for me my last mounted parade.'

It was also the last mounted parade for the regiment. That autumn the 13th/18th Hussars were motorized and turned into what Baden-Powell called 'a kind of steam perambulator'.

On two occasions early in 1937, Baden-Powell and the movement he had founded were honoured by King George VI who had ascended the throne on the abdication of his brother.

The first took place on 25 April, the Sunday closest to St George's Day which was also the International Boy Scout Day. After a lunch *en famille* at Windsor Castle with the King and Queen Elizabeth, Queen Mary, the Queen Mother, and the two small Princesses, Elizabeth and Margaret, the whole party proceeded to the Quadrangle of the Castle. Here the King reviewed the parade of a thousand Scouts who had earned the King's Scout badge or the award for life-saving. It was an annual event that had been established by King George's father three years before and was now perpetuated by the son.

The second occasion that placed Baden-Powell face to face with his King was even more important. The Coronation Honours, announced in connexion with the Coronation of King George VI and Queen Elizabeth, had included the name of Baden-Powell. B-P was awarded the Order of Merit, one of the most coveted of all British awards and held by only twenty-four living persons. Previously, among the men Baden-Powell knew and admired, Wolseley, Roberts and Haldane had received the award. On 24 May, Baden-Powell was asked to appear at Buckingham Palace. Here, after 'a charming ten-minute talk' in the King's study, King

George invested B-P privately with the Order 'in appreciation of his valuable services to the Empire'.

Less than two month's later, another honour was Baden-Powell's. A number of years before, a Dutch banker, J. G. D. Wateler, had decreed in his will that the annual income from all his property should be awarded to the person 'who had rendered the most valuable services to the cause of peace, or had contributed to finding means of combating war'. On 8 July, the Board of the Carnegie Institute announced that the Wateler Peace Prize for 1937 had been awarded to the Chief Scout, Lord Baden-Powell, 'for his services to World Peace and promoting international good will through the Scout movement'. In addition to the honour, the Prize carried with it a monetary reward of £2,100.

But the greatest honour that came to Baden-Powell during that climactic year of his life—an honour even greater than a King's to bestow on behalf of a nation, or an institute's on behalf of a philanthropist—was the accolade of the millions of boys around the world who had experienced the joy of scouting. It found its expression through their representatives at the Fifth World Jamboree at Vogelenzang, near Bloemendaal, Holland.

On 31 July, Baden-Powell took his place beside Queen Wilhelmina of the Netherlands in the Royal Box of the Jamboree arena. They were surrounded by members of the Dutch Cabinet and the ambassadors of a score of countries. Behind them and to the left and right, along the three sides of the arena, the grandstands were packed with an estimated twenty thousand spectators.

On the stroke of two o'clock the most impressive event of all Jamborees got under way with the March Past of the nations. Seventeen years had passed since Baden-Powell had first seen the Scouts of the world on parade, since the memorable opening night of the Olympia Jamboree. He had witnessed many other Marches Past since then in many parts of the world. Each one had thrilled him. But this one was different for he was old now, very old, and the sands of time were running out.

The music swelled. And there they came, the countries of the world in alphabetical order according to Dutch spelling. *Amerika* first—a thousand Americans waving miniature Stars and Stripes in salute as they passed the Royal Box. . . . Armenia next—boys without a country, but with a flag of orange, red and blue waving over them. . . . A large delegation from Belgium, Holland's neighbour country. . . . A small delegation from China, of only a dozen Scouts, but getting as much applause as the large contingents. . . . Danish Scouts behind their country's red flag with the white cross. . . . A half a hundred Egyptians with red tarbooshes on their heads.

England—and by 'England', according to Dutch vocabulary, was meant the whole British Empire—eight thousand boys from every point of the compass, the largest British contingent ever to leave the home shores.

Unconsciously, Baden-Powell checked off the places as the boys marched by. He hadn't missed one. On his travels he had visited each of the places from which the boys had come, he had seen their older brothers, or perhaps their fathers, on their home ground.

And still they came. Estonia behind the sombre white, blue and black flag. . . . Finland with the quaint blue-and-white skull-caps. . . . Fifteen hundred Scouts from France. . . . Greece with some of the boys in national costume. . . . Five hundred Hungarians with plumes of wild grass waving in their hats. Iran . . . Japan . . . Jugoslavia . . . Latvia . . . Liechtenstein . . . Lithuania . . . Luxembourg . . . Mexico making its first appearance at a World Jamboree. . . . Norway in green uniforms . . . Austria (*Oostenrijk* in Dutch) in white stockings that made tanned knees look even more tanned. . . .

Again Baden-Powell's memories drifted back to the countries from which these boys had come. Some he had visited recently, others many years ago. A few he had failed to visit but now the boys had come to him.

Still they marched. Poland in long, flowing capes . . . Roumanian Scouts with their arms raised in the ancient Roman salute . . . Syria in blue helmets . . . Siam with black hats pinned up at one side with gold tiger-head brooches . . . Czechoslovakia, Iceland and Sweden (*Tsjecho-Slovakije, Ysland and Zweden*) . . . Switzerland (*Zwitserland*), dressed in *lederhosen*, bringing up the rear of the foreign contingents. Finally column upon column of Dutch Scouts—first from the vast-flung colonies, then from every corner of Holland—with flags waving and the audience shouting its approval.

After a hundred minutes the grand parade was over. For a moment the large arena was empty. Suddenly a bugle signal and the roar of twenty-six thousand Scouts storming into the field in one surging, cheering mass of youth. Another signal and twenty-six thousand Scouts falling silent to listen to the message of welcome from the Queen of the Netherlands. As she finished, the notes of the *Wilhelmus*, the Dutch national anthem, rang over the field, and everyone came to attention.

The cheers broke loose once more. Someone started the chant of 'B . . . P . . . B . . . P . . . B . . . P!' and in a moment the whole arena resounded with the chant. Flags were waved high, hats thrown in the air. Here they were, the boys of the world, standing shoulder to shoulder as friends, with the one thought of paying homage to their Chief.

Hero worship? Of course. But also something else, something far more lasting, something much deeper. The boys did not see in the small figure before them an old man to be venerated. To them he was a youngster like themselves, a friend with a spirit as youthful as their own, a man who had brought them together and bound them together, a giver of gifts supreme. Their cheering was their way of expressing their thanks. It engulfed Baden-Powell and never abated until he had led Queen Wilhelmina to her car and had driven off himself with Olave to the camp site that had been set aside for him.

B-P had stood up during the whole long afternoon programme. He was physically and mentally tired, as well as emotionally drained. It had been a glorious day. 'But,' Olave insisted, 'you must rest.'

There was little rest for Baden-Powell for the ten days of the Jamboree. He visited every part of the large camp, not so much for his own sake as for that of the boys. For a couple of hours each day he had himself driven through the camp in his car, slowly so that the boys could gather round it, could follow, could stretch out their hands to their Chief. For several more hours each day he was in his large tent chatting with Scouters from many parts of the world, listening to their problems, encouraging, giving them a new spirit and increased enthusiasm. Or he was in the grandstand in the arena witnessing the performances of the different countries or participating in a Girl Guide rally, a Wolf Cub display, a Sea Scout exhibition, a Gilwell Reunion.

Olave tried to slow her husband down and Wilson from Gilwell, again acting as the Chief's 'watchdog', tried to do the same. They made B-P rest between engagements and sent him to bed early. Although tired, B-P felt exhilarated and remarkably fit.

He spent much of his time the last morning of the Jamboree planning the speech he would make that afternoon. He rested until two o'clock when the car drove up before his tent to take him to the final rally.

From the Royal Box, where he sat with Olave at his side, the arena looked magnificent. The nations' flags waved over the crowded grandstands. In the middle a large replica of the Jacob's Staff, the emblem of the Jamboree, had been erected.

At 2.30 the Scouts made their entry. Instead of marching round the arena and out, as they had done on the opening day, this time the contingents kept moving round and round in an ever tighter gigantic spiral until the whole arena was a wheeling mass of Scouts. At last, with all the Jamboree participants in the arena, the movement ceased. A lane was formed from the Royal Box to a platform in the centre of the arena and the Scouts sat down.

Baden-Powell stepped from the Royal Box, passed down the lane and took his stand on the platform. Looking out over the vast gathering, the Chief spoke. It was the same, full-throated, resonant voice that had thrilled Scouts at other Jamborees. Age had neither muted it nor altered its timbre:

> The emblem of our Jamboree is the Jacob's Staff. This was the instrument by which the navigators in the old days found their ways across the sea. Let it also for us today be an instrument of guidance in our life. It bears the Cross which for all who are Christian points the way —but it is also a cross with many arms: they are held out to embrace many creeds. Those eight arms, together with the head and foot of the emblem, remind us of our ten-fold Scout Law.

Baden-Powell beckoned to a representative of each of the countries present at the Jamboree to step forward. To each he gave a wooden replica of a Jacob's Staff to take home as an emblem of good will.

When all the countries had received the Jamboree emblem from the Chief Scout's hands, Baden-Powell again addressed the Scouts:

> The time has come for me to say good-bye. You know that many of us will never meet again in this world. I am in my eighty-first year and am nearing the end of my life. Most of you are at the beginning, and I want your lives to be happy and successful. You can make them so by doing your best to carry out the Scout Law all your days, whatever your station and wherever you are.
>
> I want you all to preserve the badge of the Jamboree on your uniform. . . . It will be a reminder of the happy times you have had here in camp; it will remind you to take the ten points of the Scout Law as your guide in life; and it will remind you of the many friends to whom you have held out the hand of friendship and so helped through good will to bring about God's reign of peace among men.
>
> Now good-bye. God bless you all!

His voice faltered. He halted. Then took off his broad-brimmed Scout hat and swung it overhead in a wave of farewell.

'God bless you!' he repeated—and his voice was again strong . . . and young. . . .

EPILOGUE

FEW pioneers live long enough to see
what they have done;
Most men are glad if they can leave
the world a single son;
Did ever man, before he died, see
such a dream come true?
Did any leave so many living
monuments as you?

A. P. HERBERT

XXVI

The Last Years

Years: 1937–41   Age: 80–83

1

BADEN-POWELL came home from the inspiring experience of the Jamboree to a bitter-sweet autumn. While in Holland he had received word from Agnes that Baden was seriously ill. As soon as he got back to England, B-P rushed to Baden's bedside. He was shocked on seeing the condition of his 77-year-old brother. Baden had had a heart attack. He was extremely weak and in need of continual care. Baden-Powell went to see his brother every few days, driving from Pax Hill in Hampshire to Sevenoaks in Kent. Baden grew progressively weaker. He died on 3 October and was buried on 7 October with the full military honours of his old regiment, the Scots Guards.

Baden was gone. Of the whole flock of them only Agnes and B-P were still alive.

For a while B-P's spirit was low. It soared again on 30 October when he and Olave celebrated their twenty-fifth wedding anniversary. From early morning gifts and letters and telegrams poured into Pax Hill. Two telegrams were especially welcome. One from Southern Rhodesia from Peter who had married a South African girl, Carine Boardman, the year before and had presented B-P with his first grandson and namesake; the other from Northern Rhodesia from Betty who had given him his first granddaughter only four months before.

The Silver Wedding was celebrated all over again three days later at a dinner party in London of three hundred Scouters and Guiders. Princess Mary, President of the Girl Guides Association, took the chair and unveiled the gifts of the Scouts and Guides, the Wolf Cubs and the Brownies of the world to their Chiefs: silver galore plus a cheque for £2,600 to be used 'for some of those domestic wants that are always felt in a household, such as the provision of a toothbrush'.

409

27A

The cheque was useful when Baden-Powell and Olave set sail on 25 November to spend the Christmas Holidays at Nyeri in Kenya with Eric and Bettie Walker. They had fallen in love with The Outspan. They arrived on 22 December, after stopping at a dozen places on the way and settled down in 'lovely quarters, with fires burning, everything ready. Such a haven after our journey!'

B-P was not himself. He had caught a chill off Aden which had given him a touch of lumbago and bronchitis. His first nights at The Outspan were 'horrible, wakeful'. In the daytime he was 'headachy, with a severe cough'. When the headaches persisted, Olave called a doctor.

On New Year's Day 1938, the Nyeri doctor gave Baden-Powell a thorough examination. He found his pulse good, his blood pressure satisfactory, his lungs all right, his bronchitis much improved. One thing was definitely wrong, 'a tired heart from overwork'. A specialist brought in from Nairobi confirmed the diagnosis, prescribed pills and injections and 'advised a long rest, no work for a year. Heart not diseased, should recover for all practical purposes (including fishing)'.

B-P was somewhat shamefaced during the examination:

> When the doctor asked me my history of the past twelve months and heard the recapitulation of my programme in India, the Coronation, the World Jamboree, our Silver Wedding, and the Scout rallies en route to East Africa, he remarked something to the effect that if I was 81 and had not learned sense by now, I deserved all the ills that fell upon me.

There is an old African legend about the majestic bull elephant. When he realizes that death is near, he returns deep into the darkest jungle. There he dies hidden from the world.

Baden-Powell looked to the future with equanimity. He had lived two lives—one as a soldier, the second in scouting. Now he was beginning his 'third volume, the nature of whose contents would largely depend on the condition in which the doctors turned me out'.

After writing home to Lord Somers, whom he had appointed Deputy Chief Scout of Great Britain, and telling him to carry on, he spoke to Eric Walker about an idea that he and Olave had had since they first visited him the year before. They wanted to build a small home for themselves at The Outspan. It would be another Pax Hill, but a much smaller Pax: a 'Pax, too' or 'Pax No. 2' or 'Paxtu'—a Swahili word meaning 'complete'. It would be paid for by the money that had been presented to them for their Silver Wedding.

Walker was more than willing. He developed plans for a small, comfortable bungalow with a garden and a view. 'We'll have it ready in the
autumn,' he assured his old friend and mentor.

B-P was beginning to fret. He felt guilty in his unaccustomed and unwanted leisure. There were loose ends to be tied up in England, there were

Baden-Powell's last home: Paxtu at The Outspan, Nyeri, Kenya.

promises to be kept. After three long months of convalescence the doctor
passed him for the sea journey to England.

He spent a quiet summer at Pax, writing articles, sorting out old papers
('So much waste paper goes into our furnace for heating the wing these
days that there is always hot water there!'), developing ideas, seeing
his co-workers in scouting and discussing with them the future of the
movement.

Another Cruise of Good Will had been arranged for August. This time
it was to Iceland, Norway, Denmark and Belgium. B-P had promised
that he would come along if at all possible. He kept that promise. The
five hundred Scouters and Guiders on the *Orduna* saw little of him, but his
very presence was an inspiration to them. As the ship stopped in different
ports, Baden-Powell came to the rail to wave to the thousands of Scouts
and Guides who had come to see him and to hail him as their Chief,
although he did not leave the boat.

On 25 October he bid 'Good-bye to Pax'. Two days later he left England for the last time with his beloved Olave at his side.

2

Eric Walker had been true to his word. When the Baden-Powells arrived at The Outspan, they found their new home awaiting them. 'Delightful house beyond all our expectations.' In the distance the top of Mount Kenya 'peeped through the clouds of sunset to welcome us'. They were home.

For the first time in their many married years, B-P and Olave were completely alone together, without the interference and interruption of thousands of people. 'We are utterly and supremely happy here,' Olave wrote to her children, 'and almost every other minute we keep saying to each other how heavenly it is and how lucky we are to be here.'

For the first time in B-P's life he was not under pressure of deadlines he must meet, appointments he must keep, conferences he must attend, rallies he must review, of things that needed to be done. When he finally accepted the fact that his enforced retirement was permanent, he pushed all anxiety aside and choked off all qualms of his conscience telling him he must do this and that.

He could not be idle, though. When he no longer felt ill, he had a block and paper at his side at all times, so he could scribble things. He established a bird bath and a bird feeder in front of his verandah and spent hours watching the bright-coloured birds that descended on them. He adopted a couple of hyrax as pets and greatly enjoyed their antics.

When he was well enough again to walk in the garden, to take short motor trips, to spend an occasional night at Tree Tops, he started to write up his experiences with African 'birds and beasts' and to make sketches and water-colours of the animals he saw on his excursions. Most of his articles he sent home to England where they were published in the *Daily Mail* or in *The Scout*. They were afterwards collected and edited by Eileen Wade and published in book form with reproductions of some of the water-colours: *Birds and Beasts in Africa, Paddle Your Own Canoe*, and *More Sketches of Kenya*.

3

In 1939, Baden-Powell, the Chief Scout of the World, without his know-ledge was nominated for the Nobel Peace Prize as the person 'who in 1938 and for thirty years previously "has most and best promoted the fraternity of nations and the abolishment or diminution of the standing armies and the formation and increase of peace congresses" through the Boy Scout movement'.

No Peace Prize was awarded in the autumn of 1939 for there was no peace in the world. Hitler had marched!

Baden-Powell had worked for more than three decades to diminish the chance of war, by establishing friendships among the boys and the girls of the world. He had held no illusions that this alone would do the job as long as the statesmen of the world had not caught the same spirit. He was convinced that, in the end, what he stood for would prevail.

He could not help thinking of the perversion of the prediction he had made as he closed the Holland Jamboree: 'Many of us will never meet again in this world.' He had meant that he would not be there, yet here he was still alive while many of the boys of the Jamboree were giving their lives for their countries.

Baden-Powell's first reaction to the outbreak of war was to write to Lord Somers, offering to return to England if his services were needed. Somers assured him that they were not, that the Boy Scouts of Britain were living up to every expectation the country had of them. B-P resigned himself, although reluctantly, to continue his quiet life at 'Paxtu'.

> I have been pruning roses in my garden here in Kenya [he wrote home to the British Scouters]. Not a very high-class job of service in war-time! I am not proud of it, but it is all I am allowed of outdoor exercise by my doctor. At any rate, pruning has its moral for us Scouters. I had cut some of the plants to such an extent that I feared I had overdone it and possibly killed them, but not a bit of it. With our alternate sunshine and rain, they are all sending out fine, strong shoots and are coming to bloom better than ever, thanks to the operation.
>
> So it will be in our Scout rose garden. The war has pruned our movement by taking away the Scouters and Rovers, and has scattered many of the Scouts as evacuees in various parts of the Kingdom. In many cases the Nazis have pruned the local bushes down to the very ground, and have tried to replace them with other plants, such as Hitler Youth and *Balilla*. But the roots are still there!
>
> When the spring-time of peace returns, in God's good time, the plants will put out their new shoots in greater strength and profusion than ever, and vitalized by the test they have gone through, they will very materially help restore the glory of their respective national gardens.

In February 1940, Peter in Southern Rhodesia and Gervas in Northern Rhodesia managed to get leave at the same time. They went north to

Nyeri—Peter and Carine with little Robert, Betty and Gervas with Gillian and with Robin Baden, born on his parents' joint birthday the year before. The days they stayed at The Outspan were some of the happiest in B-P's life. He wished Heather could have been there to complete the family. But Heather had joined the Army and had also become engaged; she could only pay her parents a flying visit.

In the early spring of 1940, the war broke into full fury with Denmark and Norway invaded, with Holland and Belgium overrun, with the British armies being rescued at Dunkirk, with Hitler before Paris, with the threat of bombs over London.

Baden-Powell and Olave, father and mother, thought much of Heather during those days, doing her war service, having found the man of her choice but not knowing how and when they could get married. With the war news getting grimmer and grimmer, B-P and Olave decided to brush aside all old-fashioned notions of the 'proper' formalities. There was no use for the young people 'to wait and wait for nobody knows how long'. So they cabled to Heather:

> Airmail suspension delays correspondence otherwise had intended writing that owing changed war conditions and directly John is in His Majesty's Service we agree immediate announcement of engagement and marriage if you desire. Good luck dear and courage in facing war duties. All loving thoughts.

Heather Baden-Powell and John King had a quiet wedding in Bentley, on 24 June, in the same church where Betty had been married three years before. The bells that had pealed at her sister's wedding were silent by official decree at Heather's; the pealing of church bells was the alarm signal that Germany had invaded England.

4

In September 1940, Baden-Powell had a relapse. The doctor in checking his heart found it 'awfully tired'. He even warned Olave that this might be 'the beginning of the last lap and nobody can tell how long he may live—weeks?—months?—but not years'. To the surprise of everyone, the patient rallied. A week later he walked round the garden with his pet hyrax on the leash.

Baden-Powell knew that the end was in sight. On one of Olave's occasional short absences on Girl Guide business in Nairobi, he got out his old battered suitcase and took out the long envelope that carried his instruction 'In the event of my death. . . .' He opened the envelope and extracted the sheets it contained. He read them carefully, almost tore them up, then thought better of it. Instead of throwing them out and inserting a new letter, he would simply add a new message to the old. The old one, written at the front in France during World War I, on a day when German aeroplanes were sweeping overhead, still conveyed his deepest feelings:

Étaples, 21 January 1916

Dindo darling, I look on it this way if you were to get killed before me: I feel that one must always pay for what you get in this world and if it is something very good you must naturally expect to pay the more heavily for it. The question comes—is the good worth the cost?

That question has often occurred to me when I have found myself more and more in love with you—more and more bound to you. I have realized, only in part perhaps, how awful will be the break when it comes (as some day it has to come for one of us). I have asked myself, would it be better to live as some couples do, on easy terms of friendship so that when the parting comes it is not so knock-down a blow to the survivor? But my answer has been NO—this glorious love between us is worth any shock that can come later. It is such absolute and continuous happiness, so long as it lasts, that it gives life a different character altogether: and to have had the few years of it that we have had is well worth any temporary pang of sorrow that may (and has got to) come at the end. So if the blow has to fall on me I feel that by Being Prepared for it in this way I shall be able to bear it in looking on it as the price I have naturally got to pay for having had the best and happiest life that any man ever had. And I shall still have part of you with me in the dear children—and they will help to fill the empty place.

But if all this happens you won't see this note—you will only get it if the converse happens—that is if I go first. But it applies equally to you. Will you see it in the same light? . . .

Now, almost a quarter of a century later, B-P pulled out a sheet of Outspan Hotel paper and wrote slowly, in a handwriting that was still clear although wavery:

Dindo darling, I don't know whether my increasing and unaccountable weakness of the last few weeks may mean the beginning of the end for me, but if so I don't mind personally—it is only the natural thing. I have arrived at the time of life for passing on.

I have had a most extraordinarily happy life, most especially in those last twenty-seven years of it which you have made it so heavenly and successful for me. I don't think I have frittered away much of my time while alive. It is good to think that in addition to my keen soldiering our efforts for the boys and girls have been successful beyond all expectation. It is good to feel that our youngsters are all happily married and established in life.

The world has been awfully good to me and in a way I am sorry to leave it and all its interest, but I have reached the stage where I can be of no use other than as a looker-on so it is right that I should go.

But what is more to me than all the world is you my darling. The fact of having to leave you is the one pang that haunts me—not only on my own account but more especially because it will mean a terrible break in your own life. One thing that comforts me is that you are so sensible that you will see it in its right proportion as a natural thing that had to come, and you will face the ordeal with courage during its short spell, till time heals the wound.

I am glad to think that you have the best form of consolation before you in the shape of plenty of work with the Guides. Also you have the great love of your children and their children to help you.

Your sorrow would be the only regret I should have in dying: if I know that you will not let it grieve you unduly I shall die all the happier, my D,

Your BIN

And there were other letters that must be written:

TO BOY SCOUTS: Dear Scouts, If you have ever seen the play *Peter Pan* you will remember how the pirate chief was always making his dying speech because he was afraid that possibly when the time came for him to die he might not have time to get it off his chest. It is much the same with me . . .

TO GIRL GUIDES: My Dear Guides, This is just a farewell note to you, the last that you will have from me. It is just to remind you when I have passed on that your business in life is to be happy and to make others happy. . . .

In November Baden-Powell had another set-back with occasionally good periods. He drifted into December in a tedious monotony of existence that was not quite 'life'. He and Olave had a strange, unreal sort of Christmas. He stayed in bed indoors most of the day, then got up into an arm-chair for a while to hear his King's speech to the Empire.

As 1940 waned so did the life of Baden-Powell.

Olave was at his bedside continuously, tending to his wants, sharing the hours of the day-and-night watch over him with a kindly trained Sister and noting sadly in her diary each day's occurrences:

29 December 1940, My poor dear very gloomy and feels he is not improving—and though I pooh-pooh this, in my heart I feel the same and he is not getting any better this last day or two. Actually I like looking after him alone at nights, and he only rang me up four times, and I fuddle round him.

30 December, Not a very good night last night and he had a sharp pain in his side most of the night. Sent for Dr Doig. Suddenly he said he was feeling cold, and I put on a blanket, and then he began to shiver and shiver and had a horrible *rigor* again. Dr Doig arrived in the middle of it and injected Coramine, and he pulled round again fairly quickly.

The New Year, 1941, began badly. Daily the pains and the *rigors* returned. Olave sat silently at her Robin's side watching him grow weaker and weaker. He did not want to talk or be read to. And yet, on 6 January, when she told him the news that had come over the radio, of an Italian defeat at Bardia, he nodded his head in understanding.

The minutes were ticking off towards the end. Olave recorded their passing—then slowly closed her diary:

7 January, My darling slept most of the day. After dinner, Sister Ray, sitting there, said he seemed suddenly much worse, and he might not live through the night even. He was breathing heavily and quite unconscious, and only moved his hand now and then. I just cannot believe the end is coming. Went to bed and dropped off to sleep.

8 January, At 2.30 Sister woke me, saying 'He is going'. I went to his room and just sat by his bed and watched the dear darling's life ebbing away. He was quite unconscious and still, breathing slowly and rather in gusts, white and thin. Sister Ray sat at the other side of the bed holding his pulse—just flickering.

About 5.00 I thought he would still live the day through and went back to bed to get warm. I kissed his dear forehead and Sister Ray stayed by him. And as I lay listening she suddenly came at 5.45— 'He is gone'.

He looked so sweet and perfect in death as he was in life—utterly, utterly noble and good and dear and wonderful, great and faultless.

Scout trail sign: '*I have gone home.*'

Si monumentum requiris, circumspice.

SOURCES AND NOTES

GENERAL SOURCES: THE WRITINGS OF BADEN-POWELL

BOOKS BY BADEN-POWELL

1884 *Reconnaissance and Scouting*
1885 *Cavalry Instruction*
1889 *Pigsticking or Hoghunting*
 (1923 Re-issue: *Pig-Sticking or Hog-Hunting*)
1896 *The Downfall of Prempeh*
1897 *The Matabele Campaign*
1899 *Aids to Scouting for N.C.O.s and Men*
1900 *Sport in War*
1901 *Notes and Instructions for the South African Constabulary*
1907 *Sketches in Mafeking and East Africa*
1908 *Scouting for Boys*, in six parts
 Scouting for Boys, complete edition
  (1911 Canadian edition: *The Canadian Boy Scout*)
  (1923 Indian edition: *Scouting for Boys in India*)
  (1932 Boys' edition)
  (1942 Memorial edition)
  (1946 Definitive 'World Brotherhood Edition', edited by William Hillcourt)
1909 *Yarns for Boy Scouts*
1910 *Scouting Games*
1912 *Handbook for Girl Guides*
 (in collaboration with Agnes Baden-Powell)
1913 *Boy Scouts Beyond the Seas*
1914 *Quick Training for War*
1915 *Indian Memories*
 My Adventures as a Spy
  (1924 Re-issue: *The Adventures of a Spy*)
1916 *Young Knights of the Empire*
 The Wolf Cub's Handbook
1918 *Girl Guiding*
1919 *Aids to Scoutmastership*
 (1944 Definitive 'World Brotherhood Edition', edited by William Hillcourt)
1921 *What Scouts can Do*
 An Old Wolf's Favourites
1922 *Rovering to Success*
1927 *Life's Snags and How to Meet Them*
1929 *Scouting and Youth Movements*
1933 *Lessons from the Varsity of Life*
1934 *Adventures and Accidents*
1935 *Scouting Round the World*
1936 *Adventuring to Manhood*
1937 *African Adventures*
1938 *Birds and Beasts of Africa*
1939 *Paddle Your Own Canoe*
1940 *More Sketches of Kenya*

COLLECTIONS OF BADEN-POWELL ARTICLES

1923 *Blazing the Trail:* Being wise saws and modern instances from the works of the Chief Scout. Collected by Laura Holt

SPECIFIC SOURCES AND NOTES

LIFE NUMBER ONE

Page 1 'In those days B-P's fame . . .': quoted from Winston Churchill's *Great Contemporaries* by permission of the publisher, Odhams Press Ltd.

I THE SEVENTH SON—1857–70

The main source of this chapter is a scrapbook entitled 'Archives'. It contains a great number of family portraits, early pen-and-ink sketches and water-colours by the young Stephe, as well as his birth certificate, school reports, and earliest letters.

Although in most countries where the memory of B-P is kept green his name is pronounced Ba'd'n Pou'l, Baden-Powell himself gave the 'proper' pronunciation in a piece of doggerel:

> Man, matron, maiden,
> Please call it Baden.
> Further for Powell,
> Rhyme it with Noel

Subdivision § 1. Page 3 Funeral of Professor Powell on 16 June 1860: from privately printed 32-page pamphlet, *Notices of the Life of the late Rev. Baden Powell, N.A.*, with a List of His Publications. 4 Henrietta Grace's financial problems: letters and diary notes in possession of Lady Baden-Powell and Donald Baden-Powell, specifically of Sept. (undated), 23 Oct. and 5 Nov. 1869; March (undated) and 2 June 1870; 4 Apr. 1873. Letter of 29 Jan. 1889 describes various legacies received. Details also from the wills of Baden Powell of Speldhurst (1844). Eleanor Powell (1878), Susanna Powell (1878), Charles Powell (1885), William Henry Smyth (1864), and Ann Smyth (1870)—all made available to author by Registrar of Wills, Somerset House, London.

§ 2. Pages 4–6 Courtship of Professor Baden Powell: Henrietta Grace's journal December 1845–April 1847, in possession of Donald Baden-Powell. 6 Baden Powell's marriages and children: *Pedigree of the Powell family*, compiled and edited by Edward Powell (1891). 7 The birthplace of B-P at 6 Stanhope Street, Paddington (later changed to 11 Stanhope Terrace, W.2.) was demolished in 1959 to make room for new houses. 7–8 A complete listing of the Rev. Baden Powell's writings is found in the pamphlet *Notices of the Life*. 8 Furore over *Essays and Reviews:* Andrew Dickson White's *A History of the Warfare of Science with Theology in Christendom.* (The other six authors of essays were Dr Frederick Temple, Headmaster of Rugby; Dr Rowland Williams; the Rev. H. B. Wilson; C. W. Goodwin; the Rev. Mark Pattison; Professor Benjamin Jowett of Oxford. The two authors prosecuted and later reinstated were Williams and Wilson.)

§ 3. Page 8 Guests of the Powells: letters in possession of Lady B-P.

§ 4. Page 9 Thackeray episode and communal cash-box: Harold Begbie's report of interview with Henrietta Grace in *Pall Mall Magazine*, April 1900, afterwards included in Begbie's book *The Story of Baden-Powell.*

§ 5. Page 10 History and genealogy of Powell family: *Pedigree of the Powell Family.* 10–11 Life and accomplishments of Professor Baden Powell: *Directory of National Biography* and *Notices of the Life.* (Baden Powell's influence on the teachings at Oxford University are set forth in W. Tuckwell's books *Reminiscences of Oxford* and *Pretractarian Oxford.*) 11–12 History of early Smyth family was pieced together by author with the assistance of Commander Dacre H. W. Smyth, son of one of B-P's cousins. (A story, occasionally heard, asserting that B-P descended from Captain John Smith, the Elizabethan adventurer and leader of the Virginia colonists, is completely without foundation: John Smith died a childless bachelor.)—Details on Benjamin Smyth: *History of Sussex and Warren Counties*, compiled by James P. Snell; also his will, made available to author by Superior Court of the State of New Jersey. **12–13** The adventures of Joseph Brewer Palmer Smyth: handwritten transcript in New York Public Library of the original at the British Museum of *Memorials to the Commissioners appointed by Act of Congress for Enquiring into the Loss and Services of the American Loyalists*. (A short résumé of these proceedings is found in E. A. Jones' *The Loyalists of New Jersey*.) **13** Life and work of William Henry Smyth: *Directory of National Biography* and pamphlet *Synopsis of Published and Privately-Printed Works by Admiral W. H. Smyth, K.S.F., D.C.L.*, 1864. (That Admiral Smyth was an astronomer of importance may be deduced from the fact that when the features of the moon were given names, one of the 'seas' was named for the admiral: *Mare Smythii*—'Smyth's Sea'—according to article 'Who's Who on the Moon' in Vol. 34, Part 1 of *Memoirs of the British Astronomical Association*. *Mare Smythii* is located near the edge of the moon and extends onto the hidden side, as shown on the Russian Lunik photograph.)

§ 6. Page **14** 'My dear Mama . . .'; letter* March (undated) 1863. —Walk with grandfather: article by B-P in *The Scout* 3 Aug. 1940. **15** Stephe's "Law's": from original in 'Archives'.—'Oh Law! . . .': letter from Admiral Smyth 3 Mar. 1865 in 'Archives'.—Summer excursions: notes and sketches in 'Archives', including Stephe's first lithograph (St Sebastian 1868).

§ 7. Page **16** Information about B-P's brothers: *Dictionary of National Biography*.— Ruskin incident: article by Harold Begbie in *Pall Mall Gazette* Apr. 1900. (Ruskin invited Mrs Powell to bring Stephe for a visit to his home, 'Denmark Hill', in April 1866.) **17** Gil Blas illustrations: originals in 'Archives'.—Name change: announced in *Daily News* 23 Sept. 1869. **18** 'Old Mrs Hyphen' nickname reported by Jane Baden-Powell. (On 20 May 1902 the Baden-Powell family received Royal Licence regulating the name and enrolling it in the College of Arms.)—Stephe at Rose Hill School: bills for board and tuition in 'Archives'; also letter from Mrs Sarah Alpee 28 Aug. 1868.— 'A stranger and a worm . . .' B-P article in *The Scouter*, Jan. 1928.—Supposed 'unhealthiness' of St Paul's School: letter from Henrietta Grace June (undated) 1869. **19** Fettes School: notification, acceptance of Stephe 30 June, and Alex. W. Potts' regrets in letter 13 Aug. 1870: in 'Archives'.—'That in thus exercising my trust . . .': letter from Duke of Marlborough 22 June 1870.

II CHARTERHOUSE BOY—1870–76

Subdivision § 1. Pages **20–1** Stephe at Charterhouse: letter (undated, approx. 1923) from his Upper, E. H. Parry, to Eileen Wade. **20–2** History of Charterhouse: A. H. Tod's *Charterhouse*, presented to author by Dr B. W. M. Young, Headmaster, Charterhouse.

§ 2. Page **22** Experience with music master: autobiography manuscript. **22–23** Shrove Tuesday lemon-peel fight: general description in Tod's *Charterhouse*; Stephe's involvement described in articles by Harold Begbie in *Pall Mall Gazette* Apr. 1900 and by 'An Old Carthusian' in *Daily Telegraph* 19 May 1900. **23** Ditty blessing memory of Sutton: *London*, edited by Charles Knight.

§ 3. Page **24** Personality and work of headmaster: *William Haig Brown of Charterhouse*—Written by Some of His Pupils and Edited by His Son Harold E. Haig Brown. —Battle with Smithfield boys: *Indian Memories*. **25** Haig Brown's recollection of Stephe's helpfulness: *Daily News* interview (undated) 1900. **25–26** Removal to Godalming: Tod's *Charterhouse*.

§ 4. Page **26** 'Your son's ability . . .'; letter from Dr Haig Brown 11 Aug. 1871. —School reports: quoted from originals in 'Archives'.—'Badden Povvell! . . .'; B-P article in *Officers' Training Corps Gazette* Nov. 1925. **27** Stephe as goalkeeper and

---

* NOTE. In these 'Sources and Notes', the word 'letter' followed by a date refers to a letter from B-P to his mother of that date, unless otherwise specifically indicated.

marksman: Tod's *Charterhouse*.—Haig Brown's views on play-acting: *Lessons from Varsity*.—Stephe's first stage appearances (in *To Parents and Guardians*) took place 13, 14 and 15 May 1872, according to E. H. Parry's letter to Eileen Wade.—Further theatrical appearances: clippings in 'Archives'. **28** 'On one occasion . . .': interview with Dr Haig Brown, *Daily News* (undated) 1900.—'The Druids': B-P sketches in 'Archives'; also *The Greyfriar* 1914.

§ 5. Page **29** The Copse: description sent to author by Graham Leask, Scoutmaster of Godalming Troop.—'It was here . . .': *Lessons from Varsity*.—'What I picked up . . .': *Life's Snags*.

§ 6. Page **30** Hiking experiences with brothers: B-P article in *The Scout*, No. 1, Vol. 1, page 1, 18 Apr. 1908. **30–31** Sailing trip with brothers: *What Scouts Can Do*. **31** Experiences in English Channel: *Adventures and Accidents*.

§ 7. Page **31** Stephe as monitor: article by 'An Old Carthusian' in *Daily Telegraph* 19 May 1900. **32** Turned down by Balliol (20 Apr. 1876) and Christ Church (11 May): *Indian Memories*.—Signed up as *'scholares . . .'*: receipt for dues, entrance fee and caution money paid to University of Oxford 12 May 1876. **33** Requirements for Open Competitive Examination: Extracts from Civil Service regulations relative to 'Examination of Candidates for First Appointments to Cavalry and Infantry, July 1876.' —News of results of examination: *Lessons from Varsity*.—Score of examination: 'Table of Successful Candidates, Civil Service Commission Appendix to Report 1876,' secured for author from Somerset House, London, by Brigadier E. Mockler-Ferryman. **34** 'I assure you . . .': letter from Dean Liddell 15 Oct. 1876.—'It makes me almost think . . .': letter from Dr Jowell 28 Oct.—'Stephe is actually . . .': exclamation written by Henrietta Grace on back of envelope in which Stephe received his orders. (During his whole military life, Baden-Powell considered the date when he entered the Army, 11 Sept., more important than his birthday, 22 Feb.)

III A SUBALTERN IN INDIA—1876–78

Subdivision § 1. Page **36** Information about *Serapis*: *Indian Memories*.—'Swinging all the fellows . . .': letter 30 Oct. 1876.—'Have you ever . . .': letter 17 Nov.—'Dreary scene . . .': letter 19 Nov. **37** Theatrical performances on board: letters 12 and 17 Nov., 4 Dec.—'A new way of living . . .'': letter 30 Nov.—Arrival in Bombay: *Indian Memories*.

§ 2. Page **38** 'No regular town . . .': letter 24 Dec. 1876.—Number of servants: letter 31 Jan. 1877. **39** Cholera belt episode: *Quick Training for War*. **39–40** Initial training: *Indian Memories*. **40** 'I have altogether . . .': letters 13 Apr. and 25 May. **40–1** Story of Hercules: *Old Wolf's Favourites*.

§ 3. Pages **41–2** B-P's theatrical experiences: *Indian Memories*.—Theatrical review: *Lucknow Times* 10 Feb. 1877. **42** First meeting with Roberts: *Indian Memories*. (In this book B-P mistakenly places the meeting at Simla at a much later date. He actually met Roberts at Lucknow 26 Feb. 1877, according to letter 2 Mar.)

§ 4. Page **42** 'Shouted out the words . . .': letter 5 Sept. 1877.—Attempts to sign up for famine work: letter 12 Sept. **43** 'At dinner eat little . . .': letter 23 Sept. 1878.— Result of examination: letters 29 July and 6 Aug.—Visit to Baden Henry: letter 16 June. **44** Theatrical performances at Simla: letters 7 and 15 July. —'Liver medicine . . .': 23 Sept.—'I am getting to dislike . . .': letter 4 Oct. **44–5** Medical board review certified by Edson Fairland, Staff Surgeon of the 13th Hussars. **45** 'I thought your illustrations . . .': *Indian Memories*. (The general who kept B-P's sketches was Sir Cranford Chamberlayne.)—'Mark the coincidence . . .': letter 29 Nov.

IV THE HUSSAR IN ACTION—1879–84

Subdivision § 1. Page **46** Description of 8, St George's Place: letters between 2 Oct. 1880 and 13 Nov. 1884.—'When you are old . . .'; Henrietta Grace's letter of 24 Mar. 1884, initialled by Warington, George, Frank, Stephe, and Baden. **48** Visits to family:

mementoes in 'Archives'.—Doings of 'Skakers': B-P water-colours in 'Archives'.—B-P's theatre-going: Begbie in *Pall Mall Gazette*, after interview with B-P's mother, 1900.

§ 2. Pages **49–50** Background of Afghanistan situation: *Indian Memories*, Lord Roberts' *Forty-One Years in India*, S. Gopal's *The Viceroyalty of Lord Ripon* 1880–84. **49–50** School of Musketry: information about B-P's experience at 109th Course supplied to author by Captain W. E. Whitburn of Small Arms Wing, School of Infantry, Hythe, Kent.

§ 3. Pages **50–1** Trip to India: letters 10 and 28 Oct., 6 and 11 Nov. 1880. **51** First meeting with 'The Boy' McLaren: *Indian Memories*. **51–2** Trip to Kandahar: letter 24 Dec. **52** Characterization of Baker Russell: autobiography manuscript and *Indian Memories*. **52–3** Trip to Maiwand 28–30 Dec.: letter 2 Jan. 1881; also *Indian Memories*. **53** Blame for Maiwand débâcle: letter to George 19 May.—'I enjoy this awfully . . .' and 'At dusk we go . . .': letter 30 Jan. **54** Performing 'general': autobiography manuscript. (Lord Wolseley is supposed to have been the model for the major-general in the Gilbert and Sullivan song.)—'But there was always the danger . . .': *Paddle Your Own Canoe*. **55** Departure from Kandahar: letter 29 Apr.; also *Indian Memories*. —Gun wound: letters 29 Apr. 6 and 14 May, 9 June. (The accident happened around 20 Apr.; bullet was located 14 May, cut out 31 May.) **56** 'We are getting to know . . .': letter 8 Sept.—'The long-prayed-for moment . . .': letter 5 Nov.—'Bloater': letter 18 Dec.

§ 4. Page **56** Duties at Muttra: letters 15 Jan. and 29 July 1882, 21 May 1883.—Honours of polo team: letter 5 Mar. 1883. **57** Pigsticking details: *Pigsticking or Hoghunting*. (This book, republished in a revised edition in 1924, is still considered the standard work on the subject.)—First try at pigsticking 5 Jan. 1882: letter 8 Jan. **57–8** Kadir Cup race: letter 14 Apr. 1883.

§ 5. Page **58** Literary production of B-P's brothers: *Dictionary of National Biography*. **59** Request for advice: letter to George 28 June 1883.—'Even if it did not sell . . .': letter to George 28 Apr. 1884. (Manuscript of *Reconnaissance and Scouting* was sent to Clowes 18 July.)—'Grouping events': letter 5 Sept. 1883. **60** Duke's dinner with 13th Hussars: letter to George 25 Dec.—'Under the Distinguished Patronage . . .': hand-bill 5 Feb. 1884.—'We had one splendid run . . .': *Indian Memories*; also reported in *The Times* Feb. 1884. **61** 'So that the General . . .': letter 8 Mar. **61–2** B-P's advice on handling young ladies: letters 20 Mar. and 19 July. **62** 'I am beginning to feel . . .': letter 24 Aug. **63** Experience as locomotive driver: *Indian Memories*.

V SERVICE IN AFRICA—1884–85

Subdivision § 1. Pages **64–7** British-Boer relationships: *'The Times' History of the War in South Africa*, vols I–V, edited by L. C. M. Amery; *South Africa and the Transvaal War*, vols I–VI, by Louis Creswicke; *Inside Africa*, by John Gunther.

§ 2. Page **67** 'It's no good wishing . . .': letter to Warington 3 Mar. 1885.—Work on *Pigsticking*: letters 6 Jan. and 11 May **67–8** Work on *Cavalry Instruction*: letters 26 Jan. and 28 Feb. (B-P sent off 'last lectures' on 23 Mar.) **68** Poor facilities for polo: letter to Baden 13 May.—B-P's 100-mile ride: letter to George 2 Feb. (The ride took place on 28 Jan.)—Drakensberg expedition: letters 6 Apr. and 5 May; also *Lessons from Varsity*.

§ 3. Page **70** Shooting trip: diary 10 July–7 Sept. 1885.—*M'hlalapanzi* experience: diary 27 July; also more detailed in *Paddle Your Own Canoe*. **71** Departure: 13th Hussars left Natal 30 Sept.

VI ON BOTH SIDES OF THE CHANNEL—1886–87

Subdivision § 1. Page **72** Getting re-established in England: letters from Dec. 1885 to May 1886.—Inspection by General Wood: autobiography manuscript.

§ 2. Page **73** Visit to Armstrong works: diary 13 Feb. 1886.—Experience at Spandau: letters to George 12 and 13 Aug.; also *My Adventures as a Spy*. **74** Spying at Krasnoe

Selo: diary 21–26 Aug.; also *My Adventures as a Spy*. **75** 'We found out . . .': letter to George 28 Aug.
§ 3. Pages **75–6** Bismarck's 'war crisis': *Encyclopaedia Britannica*. **76** Trip to expected war front: diary 10–20 Jan. 1887.
§ 4. Page **77** B-P's part in tournament: handbill for performances 30 July and 1 Aug. 1887. **77–8** Experiences with Nordenfelt and Wolseley: autobiography manuscript. **77** Adoption of Nordenfelt machine gun: *The Times* 20 Sept.—'Dear Captain . . .': letter from Wolseley 28 Oct. **78** Aldershot experience: autobiography manuscript. (B-P received award of £100 from War Office 19 Apr. 1891.)—General Smyth's earlier offer: letter 13 July 1883.—B-P's departure: *Lessons from Varsity*.

VII AFRICA AGAIN—1888–89

Subdivision § 1. Pages **79–80** B-P's life and work at the Cape: letters 24 Jan., 5, 15 and 20 Feb. 1888. **79** Characterization of Sir Hercules Robinson: *Lessons from Varsity*.
§ 2. Pages **80–1** Zululand situation: autobiography manuscript, J. Y. Gibson's *The Story of the Zulus*, *Encyclopædia Britannica*. **81–4** Zululand expedition: diary 22 June–12 Sept. 1888; also letters to George 22 and 28 July, 3, 9 and 17 Aug. **82** Allenby's part in expedition: Raymond Savage's *Allenby of Armageddon*.—Meeting with John Dunn's Zulu warriors 8 July: *Lessons from Varsity*.—*Eengonyama* chorus: *Scouting for Boys*. **83** Dinizulu's beads were found 10 Dec. (Beresford Webb in his book *Scouting Achievements* quotes B-P as having stated, 'In the hut which had been put up for Dinizulu to live in, I found, among other things, his necklace of wooden beads.') **84** 'Another example . . .': *Lessons from Varsity*.
§ 3. Page **85** War Office telegram: 19 Oct. 1888.—Sending-off of *Pigsticking* manuscript: letter to George 12 Nov. (Galley proofs were received by B-P approx. 20 Dec. and returned 30 Dec.)—'The government here . . .': letter to George 12 Feb. 1889.—General Smyth's refusal: letter from Smyth 29 Mar. **85–6** Big-game expedition: diary 6–19 Apr.
§ 4. Page **86** Work at Government House: letter 19 May 1889.—Illness: letter 24 June.—'We think his attack . . .': letter from General Smyth to B-P's mother 31 July. **87** B-P's meeting with Sir Francis: letter 16 Sept.—'We put him up . . .': letter 26 Oct.
§ 5. Page **87** Swaziland problem: B-P's résumé, 'Swaziland, Its Past, Present and Future,' a manuscript report of 28 pages; also B-P article 'Sketches from Swaziland' in *The Graphic* 25 Jan. 1890 and *Encyclopædia Britannica*. **88** Meeting with Kruger: autobiography manuscript. **90** Details of Swaziland expedition and quotes: diary 24 Oct.–4 Dec. 1889.
§ 6. Page **91** 'My dear Stephie . . .': letter from General Smyth 17 Dec. 1889.—'Did I do rightly?': letter 29 Dec.

VIII MEDITERRANEAN INTERLUDE—1890–95

Subdivision § 1. Page **92** B-P's work on Malta: letters 25 Feb., 9 and 24 Mar., 24 Apr., 24 May 1890. **92–3** B-P's daydream: *Matabele Campaign*. **93** 'My dear George . . .': letter from de Winton to George 12 May.—'The family may rest easy . . .': letter from General Smyth to George 12 May.—'You can't picture . . .': letter 9 June. Decision to try for Staff College: letters to George 23 May and 12 Oct.
§ 2. Page **94** Background history of Malta: *Malta* by H. Bowen-Jones, J. C. Dewdhey and W. B. Fisher; Maturin M. Balloy's *The Story of Malta*.—Archaeological expeditions: letters 5 Oct. 1890 and 3 Apr. 1891.—'He told us . . .': letter to George 26 June 1890.—Efforts on behalf of Malta garrison: *Malta Times* 31 Mar. 1893; also letter from Lady Smyth to Eileen Wade 24 Feb. 1924.—'Week after week . . .': *Malta Chronicle* 11 Apr. 1893. **95** The 'Poultice' story: *Lessons from Varsity*.—Polo playing and hunting: *Lessons from Varsity*.—Malta cart: letter 5 Aug. 1890. **96** Experiences with female companions: letters 31 Aug. 1890 and 14 Dec. 1891.

28

§ 3. Page **96** Appointment as Intelligence Officer: letter 31 Aug. 1890. **96–7** Bizerta port and opinion of 'experts': *Pall Mall Gazette* 2 Aug. 1893.—Experiences in North Africa: three sketchbooks—18–30 Dec. 1890, 5–14 Apr. 1891, 5–17 Nov. 1891. **97** 'With their enormous military budget . . .': letter from Wolseley 25 Jan. 1891. **97–8** Experiences on Dalmation coast: sketchbook 29 Oct.–11 Nov. 1891: also *My Adventures as a Spy.* **97–100** Experiences in Austria, Italy and Turkey: sketchbook 30 July–17 Sept. 1891; also *My Adventures as a Spy* and B-P article "How I Saw the Austrian Manoeuvres' in *Daily Chronicle* 26 Sept. **99** Experiences at the Italian manoeuvres: sketchbook 29 July–1 Sept. 1892; also *My Adventures as a Spy* and B-P article in *Army and Navy Gazette* 24 Sept. 1892.

§ 4. Page **101** 'Those beastly Maltese politics . . .': letter 17 Oct. 1892.—Concern over future: letter to George 17 Oct.—Sir Henry's advice: letter 6 June.—Sir Baker Russell's advice: letter 11 Mar. 1893.—Telegram from War Office: 20 Apr.—'Everyone in the Army . . .': *Malta Chronicale* 24 Apr. **102** 'The more I think . . .': letter 3 Mar. (Later in 1893 George bought a sea-going yacht, the *Otaria.* George and Frances invited B-P to join them for a Mediterranean cruise off the shores of Italy, Albania and Greece which he took from 5 Jan. to 9 Feb. 1894.)

§ 5. Page **102** Reception at Ballincollig: letter 24 June 1893. **102–3** Description and quotes in regard to Irish manoeuvres: autobiography manuscript. (In September 1893, B-P joined Sir Baker Russell and his staff for the Berkshire manoeuvres near Lambourn, as brigade-major to Colonel John French, later to become Field Marshal and Earl of Ypres.) **103** 'I am afraid . . .': letter to George 13 Mar. 1894. **103–4** Earnings: letter 2 Dec. 1893 and 28 Jan. 1895. **104** Telegram from *The Graphic*: 12 Nov. 1895.—Telegram from War Office: 14 Nov.—Interview with Wolseley: *Lessons from Varsity.*

IX ASHANTI EXPEDITION—1895–96

The main source of this chapter is Baden-Powell's book *The Downfall of Prempeh-Ashanti Campaign 1895–96*, developed from articles by B-P to *Daily Chronicle, Daily Graphic,* and *The Graphic.* The quotes are from *The Downfall* except as explained in the following.

Subdivision § 1. Pages **105–7** Background material on history of Gold Coast and Ashanti Wars: Sections I and II of B-P's *The Downfall of Prempeh* and Sir George Baden-Powell's 'Policy and Wealth in Ashanti' in the same book, W. W. Claridge's *A History of the Gold Coast and Ashanti,* W. E. D. Ward's *A History of Ghana,* F. M. Bourret's *The Gold Coast,* Edwin W. Smith's *The Golden Stool,* Paul Redmayne's *Gold Coast to Ghana,* John Gunther's *Inside Africa.* **107** Ashanti war chant: B-P article in *Jamboree* April 1923. (Garnet Wolseley explained meaning of chant in his book *The Story of a Soldier's Life.*) Joseph Chamberlain's speech: quoted in *The Downfall of Prempeh.*

§ 2. Page **108** Organization and work of levy: B-P article 'The Native Levy in the Ashanti Expedition, 1895–96' in *Journal of the Royal United Service Institution* March 1896.

§ 3. Page **110** 'A smile and a stick . . .': compare this with Theodore Roosevelt's 'Speak softly and carry a big stick' in his speech 2 Sept. 1901. (According to Burton Stevenson's *The Home Book of Quotations,* Roosevelt described his slogan as being 'a West African proverb'.) **112** Word 'fetish': supposedly of Portuguese origin—*feitiços,* charms, sorcery. **112–13** Bekwai experience 3–5 Jan. 1896: expanded version in B-P's article 'Bush Strategy' in *Cornhill Magazine* June 1924, reprinted in *Adventures and Accidents.*

§ 4. Pages **113–14** Entry into Kumasi: *The Downfall of Prempeh.* (An apocryphal story, circulated among Boy Scouts, attempts to explain that B-P got the idea for using the left hand for the Scout handshake from a friendly Ashanti chief putting down his shield and, thus undefended, trustingly offering his left hand in friendship. This story runs counter to all available evidence.) **116** Capture of Prempeh's chiefs: expanded version in *Adventures and Accidents*. **117** Search of Bantama: letter to commanding officer 20 Jan. 1896.—Fetish bowl: B-P article 'The Fetish Bowl of the Ashanti' in *Sunday Pictorial* 25 Mar. 1924. (The bowl was presented to the Royal United Service Institution in Whitehall, London.)

§ 5. Page **118** Experience with tobacco: letter 21 Dec. 1895; also *Yarns to Boy Scouts*.—'When I got on board . . .': letter 11 Feb. 1896.—Confusion at return of *Cormandel*: *Lessons from Varsity*.

X THE MATABELE RISING—1896

The main sources of this chapter are Baden-Powell's 'Matabeleland Diary' and his book *The Matabele Campaign* 1896 developed from this diary. Where at all feasible the quotes are from the diary pages written on the spot, rather than from the edited book version. In certain instances, other sources have been used, as follows:

Subdivision § 1. Page **120** B-P's newspaper scoop: letter 8 Mar. 1896.—Giving up book idea: letter 8 Mar. **121** 'The lucre was offered . . .': letter to Lady Smyth 3 Apr.—Conditions in Belfast: autobiography manuscript. **122** Trip from England to Bulawayo: letters 22, 23, 25, 30 May and 20 June.

§ 2. Pages **122–6** Background material on the Matabele War and Cecil Rhodes involvement: Lewis Michell's *The Life of the Rt Hon. Cecil Rhodes*, J. G. Donald's *Rhodes—a Life*, Sarah Gertrude Millin's *Rhodes*, Howard Hensman's *Cecil Rhodes*, Vere Stent's *Some Incidents in the Life of Cecil Rhodes*, Stuart Cloete's *Against These Three* (Rhodes, Lobengula, Kruger). **124** Lord Knutsford's letter: J. E. J. Green's *Rhodes Goes North*.

§ 3. Pages **126–9** Work at Bulawayo: diary June 1896. (B-P's scouting expedition with Burnham 12–14 June was described by Major Frederick Russell Burnham in 1944 in his book *Taking Chances*, presented to author by the major's son Roderick Burnham.)

§ 4. Pages **130–2** Experiences with Grootboom 26 June–14 July 1896: related by B-P in several versions—among them in his books *Aids to Scouting*, *My Adventures as a Spy*, *Accidents and Adventures*, *Life's Snags*. **131** Skirt dance: B-P article 'I Owe My Life to Skirt-Dancing' in *Sunday Pictorial* 11 Mar. 1934.

§ 5. Pages **132–4** Plumer's work and B-P's association with it: *The Matabele Campaign*, Herbert Plumer's own book *An Irregular Corps in Matabeleland*, Frank W. Sykes' *With Plumer in Matabeleland*, D. T. Laing's *The Matabele Rebellion*. **134** Capture of Umzava: diary 4 Aug. 1896. (In addition to B-P, Plumer and Sykes tell of Umzava's being taken prisoner and brought to the British camp. Plumer—like B-P—speaks of her as Inyanda's mother; so does Hans Sauer in *The Story of the Cape to Cairo Railway* and Robert Clarmont Witt in his article 'Personal Recollections of Cecil Rhodes' in *Nineteenth Century and After* May 1902. Sykes, Sauer, Witt and B-P agree that she was Lobengula's stepmother as one of the wives of his father who is variously named M'silikatsi, Mosilikatsi, Umziligazi and Umzilikatze. None of Rhodes' biographers— all of them basing their reports of the *indaba* on Vere Stent's account—have anything to say about the capture of Umzava, although they are all aware of her importance.)— Vere Stent's quote: *Some Incidents in the Life of Cecil Rhodes*. Plumer's quote: *An Irregular Corps in Matabeleland*.

§ 6. Page **135** Setting-up of 'dodge': diary 10 Aug. 1896; letter 23 Aug. 1896. **135–6** Working of 'dodge': letter to Agnes 15 Aug.; also Plumer's *An Irregular Corps* and Sykes' *With Plumer*. **136** Listing of 'white chiefs': *The Matabele Campaign*.—Cost of military operations: Millin's *Rhodes*. **137** Rhodes' nickname: Vere Stent in *The Cape Times* 24 Aug. 1896.—B-P's concern in regard to *indaba*: autobiography manuscript.—'That we give them . . .': letter 31 Aug. **138** 'It was, undoubtedly . . .': Plumer in *An Irregular Corps*.

§ 7. Pages **138–41** Details of this subdivision and all quotes: B-P's 'Matabeleland Diary.' **140** Finding of koodoo horn: note dictated by B-P to his secretary 1929. **141** Wedza's stronghold: letter to George 18 Oct. 1896.

§ 8. Page **141** Lord Rosmead: the former Sir Hercules Robinson returned to the

Cape in 1895.—Defence in Uwini case and Carrington's letter: autobiography manuscript.
§ 9. Page 142 Rhodes' nickname: *The Matabele Campaign.*—'He is always thinking
. . .': diary 22 Nov. 1896. 143 'I am sorry to find . . .': diary 17 Dec. 144 'A most
interesting shipload . . .': diary 6 Jan. 1897.—Olive Schreiner incident: S. C. Cronwright-Schreiner's book about his wife, *The Life of Olive Schreiner.*

XI A COMMAND IN INDIA—1897–99

The main source of this chapter is B-P's book *Indian Memories*. The manuscript
of his autobiography contains a number of further details; so do his letters to his mother
and his sketchbooks.
§ 1. Page 145 'The departure would have to come . . .': letter 7 Mar. 1897. 145–6
Leaving Dublin: *Lessons from Varsity.* 146 'It almost feels . . .': letter 27 Apr.—
Barrack conditions and B-P's efforts to improve them: *Indian Memories.*
§ 2. Page 147 Conditions at North West Frontier: *Indian Memories* and *Encyclopædia Britannica.*—B-P's disappointment: letters 2 Aug. and 23 Sept. 1897.—'We are
having a pheasant shoot . . .': Bindon Blood telegram of 4 Jan. 1898 in *Lessons from
Varsity.* 148 Trip to front: quotes from *Indian Memories.*—'The bravest man . . .':
B-P article in *The Greyfriar* October 1898. 148–9 'We as a nation . . .': *Indian
Memories.*
§ 3. Page 149 'But without individuality . . .': *Lessons from Varsity.*—Ideas on
scout training: B-P's 'Report on the Scouting System 5th Dragoon Guards' submitted
to Asst Adjt Genl Southern Division Camp Delhi, 16 Jan. 1899. 150 'Our colonel does
work us hard . . .': letter 23 June 1897.
§ 4. Page 150 Workings of Simla Amateur Dramatic Club: article 'The Simla A.D.C.'
in *The Times* 16 Dec. 1924. 150–1 Details of *The Geisha* episode: B-P scrapbook.—
Theatrical review: *The Simla News* 1 Sept. 1897. 151 'You may think it an awful waste
. . .': letter 1 Sept.—Molly Seamore's real name was Mabel Turner.—B-P's jitteriness
on resuming pigsticking: *Adventures and Accidents.* 152 Churchill episode: *Indian
Memories.* (Churchill described his meeting with B-P in India in his book *Great
Contemporaries.*)
§ 5. Pages 152–3 Kashmir excursion: *Indian Memories* and six sketchbooks containing scores of water-colour sketches. 153 'I ought to get married . . .': letter 15 Aug.
1898.—'Just as he plunged . . .': *Indian Memories.*—Writing book on scouting:
Kashmir sketchbooks. (*Cavalry Aids to Scouting* was the title by which *Aids to Scouting*
was first announced by the publishers, according to *Morning Post* 27 Oct. 1899.)
§ 6. Page 154 'Poor George . . .': letter 23 Nov. 1898.—Alighar manoeuvres:
quotes from B-P sketchbook 'Cavalry Manoeuvres 1898.'

XII THE START OF THE BOER WAR—1899

Subdivision § 1. Pages 156–7 Interview with Lord Wolseley: *Lessons from Varsity.*
157 B-P's nervousness: special notebook entitled 'Mafeking Notes'.—Farewell to
Charterhouse: interview with Dr Haig Brown in *Daily News* April (undated) 1900.—
'We shan't hear . . .': letter 11 July 1899.
§ 2. Pages 157–8 Events leading up to the Boer War (as well as the war itself):
The Official History of the War in South Africa 1899–1902, L. C. M. Amery, editor;
'*The Times*' *History of the War in South Africa*, vols I–V; Harold Holgate Brown:
War with the Boers, vols I–V; Louis Creswicke: *South Africa and the Transvaal War*,
vols I–VI; Rayne Kruger: *Good-Bye Dolly Gray*; Conan Doyle: *The Great Boer War*;
Edgar Holt: *The Boer War*; C. R. de Wet: *Three Years War.* 158 'Fold my hands in
peace . . .': letter 11 July 1899.
§ 3. Pages 158–9 Experience at the Cape: autobiography manuscript. 158 Meetings
with Rhodes and Hanbury Williams: diary 26 July 1899.—'On arrival then I slept . . .':
'Mafeking Notes'. 159 Meeting staff and deciding strategy: diary. 159–60 Work

during Aug. and Sept.: diary. **160** 'The volunteers keep havering . . .': letter to Hanbury Williams 26 Aug.—Value of Julius Weil and Co.'s stock: Sir Alexander Godley's *Life of an Irish Soldier*.—'I have nearly completed . . .': letter 10 Sept. **161** 'As the strength of that guard . . .': autobiography manuscript.

§ 4. Pages 161–2 B-P's defence dispositions: 'Mafeking Notes'. **161** Experience with FOGBELL vs. FOLKRIGHT: autobiography manuscript.—Apology for mix-up: letter from J. McLane 11 Oct. 1899. **162–3** Arrangements for defence: *Sketches in Mafeking*. **164–5** Dynamite mines: diary 6 Oct. **165** 'With everybody safely indoors . . .': B-P radio speech on BBC reported in *The Listener* 13 Oct. 1937. **165** Underground gallery: *Sketches in Mafeking*.

§ 5. Page 165 Turn-down of *Aids to Scouting*: letter from publisher, W. Thacker 26 June 1899. (Thacker told B-P, 'We should be pleased to bring out the book at your own expense.') **166** Royalty offer: letter from E. Russell Polden of Gale & Polden Ltd 6 Sept.—'I would like to see the proofs . . .': letter to Frank 20 Aug. (According to *Morning Post* 27 Oct. 1899, proofs were sent from the Gale & Polden printing plant at Wellington Works, Aldershot, on 5 Sept. and were received back on 23 Oct. with B-P's notation to publish.)

§ 6. Page 166 Final dispositions: diary. (B-P penetrated into the Transvaal on a night mission on 8 Oct. 1899.)

§ 7. Page 167 B-P's proclamation: Standing Orders. Speech to the Town Guard: J. Emerson Neilly's *Besieged with B-P*. **168** 'Telegram today from Military Secretary . . .' diary 12 Oct.—Nesbit's foolhardiness: diary 13 Oct.—Disposition of dynamite: diary 13 Oct.—'No Boers hurt . . .': diary 15 Oct.

XIII THE SIEGE OF MAFEKING—1899–1900

The main sources of this chapter are B-P's own writings: his extensive Staff Diary 13 October 1899 to 17 May 1900, General Orders of his command, the section on the siege in his book *Sketches in Makeking and East Africa*, his autobiography manuscript, and his occasional letters and special notes. Source material was also provided by the writings of four newspaper correspondents in Mafeking during the siege: J. Angus Hamilton (correspondent to *The Times* and author of *The Siege of Mafeking*); J. Emerson Neilly (correspondent to the *Pall Mall Gazette* and author of *Besieged with B-P*); Major F. D. Baillie (correspondent to the *Morning Post* and author of *Mafeking— A Diary of the Siege*): Vere Stent (correspondent to Reuter's Agency). (D. Grinnell Milne has described the siege in more detail in his book *Baden-Powell in Mafeking*.) In certain instances, other sources have been used, as follows:

Subdivision § 1. Pages 170–1 Census of population and Mafeking's strategic importance: B-P's official 'Résumé of Report on the Siege of Mafeking'. **173** 'Bluff the enemy . . .': extract of Standing Orders. **174** 'First blow . . .,' 'spirit and dash . . .' and 'smartly fought engagement . . .': 'Résumé of Report'. **175** Boer emissary in Mafeking: diary 16 Oct. 1899.—'All well . . .' message: sent 21 Oct. **176** '*Wel Ed Heer* . . .': letter from Cronje 20 Oct. **176** 'To His Honour . . .': letter to Cronje 21 Oct. **177** 'In Zeerust . . .'; diary 20 Oct.

§ 2. Page 177 'A sharp ringing . . .': B-P's 'Mafeking Notes' (manuscript of an apparently unfinished article on the siege). **178–9** Corps of Cadet orderlies: first attempt at assembly 7 Oct., according to B-P diary. **179** Action of 25 Oct.: diary. **179** Fitzclarence attack 27 Oct.: diary. **180–1** Searchlight story: *Lessons from Varsity*. **182** B-P's histrionics: described by Hamilton and Neilly; also by another personality besieged in Mafeking—Lady Sarah Wilson (aunt of Winston Churchill) in her book *African Memories*. Wire entanglements: diary; also B-P radio speech on BBC reported in *The Listener* 13 Oct. 1937.—Cannon Kopje attack 31 Oct.: diary. **183** 'Seeing that we could not . . .': 'Résumé of Report'. **184** B-P's characterizations of Snijman and Botha: *Sketches in Mafeking*. (The Boer spelling of the name Snijman has been preferred to the Anglicized Snyman.)

§ 3. Page **185** B-P's orders to Plumer: diary 22 Dec. 1899. **185–6** Attack on Game Fort 26 Dec.: diary. **186** 'For a moment . . .': Vere Stent in Reuter dispatch. **187** Kaiser-Wilhelm's insistence on 31 Dec. 1899 as last day of the century: Walter Lord's *The Good Years*.

§ 4. Pages **188–9** Finding of 'Lord Nelson' gun: Sir Alexander Godley's *Life of an Irish Soldier*. **189** 'It didn't really . . .': *Sketches in Mafeking*.—Making and firing of 'The Wolf': B-P article in *The Scout* 23 May 1908, reprinted in *Yarns for Boy Scouts* ('The Wolf' is now in the Royal United Service Institution in Whitehall, London.) **190** Note from Roberts and B-P's answer: diary 8 Feb. 1900.—'In Mafeking . . . we were not far behind . . .': *Sketches in Mafeking*.

§ 5. Page **191** Making bank notes: *Lessons from Varsity*. (The notes were to be exchanged for cash if presented within six months after the lifting of the siege. But only a few of them were; people kept them for souvenirs. According to B-P, 'the Government scored at least six thousand pounds and for two years afterwards were calling on me for explanations of what they supposed was faulty bookkeeping which showed us so much to the credit.') **191–3** Mafeking siege stamps: The story of these stamps is of particular interest to philatelists—specifically to 'Scouts-on-Stamps' enthusiasts who consider the Mafeking stamps the incunabula of all 'S-on-S' stamps. The material in this subdivision is based on the reports of three of the persons involved: note from General Sir Alexander Godley to Eileen K. Wade 19 May 1924; letter from Lt. Col. Herbert Greener to B-P 20 Sept. 1926 and articles by Greener 'Mafeking Siege Stamps' in *South Africa* 22 July 1927 and 'Mafeking Siege Stamps' in *Stamp Collecting* 18 May 1929; article by J. V. Howat on 'Mafeking Siege Stamps' in *The South Africa Philatelist* December 1938. The fourth person involved, Lord Edward Cecil, seems never to have expressed himself on the subject. Eventually, 9,108 3d stamps with B-P's portrait (6,072 18½ mm wide, Scott Number 179; 3,036 21 mm wide, Scott Number 180) and 9,480 1d stamps (Scott Number 178) picturing the boy messenger were printed. For a complete description of all Mafeking siege stamps, see Stephen G. Rich's *Philately of the Anglo-Boer War* 1899–1902. For articles on Mafeking bicycle stamps, see 'Plating Mafeking Bicycles', by A. Lichtenstein in *The American Philatelist* January 1949, and 'The First Boy Scout and His Cadet Corps' by Dr K. Freund in *The O.F.S. Philatelic Magazine* August 1957. The printed items on the Mafeking stamps were made available for the author's research by Harry D. Thorsen, Jr., co-founder and past president of Scouts on Stamps Society International. (Some time after the siege, B-P received an objection to the stamps from postal authority in England: for one thing, they were not legal tender, and, for another, they were of no use to collectors as a genuine issue of stamps. B-P brushed the objection aside: 'I felt inclined to reply,' he wrote in *Sketches in Mafeking*, 'that I did not care much for either reason, because they had done their work . . . That they should have become of value to collectors in spite of official objection I did not foresee—if I had I should have kept some myself!' Before the stamps went on public sale, B-P was presented with a couple of stamps with his head on them, precancelled 'MAFEKING—AP 7 1900—C.G.H.') **193** 'I said to one of these boys . . .': *Scouting for Boys*.

§ 6. Page **194** Panzera's bombs: *Lessons from Varsity*.—Brickfields trenches: *Sketches in Mafeking*. **195** McLaren incident: letter 3 Apr. 1900—'You need not feel alarmed . . .': Letter to McLaren 11 Apr.—'Everybody is talking . . .' and 'I have got your book . . .': letter from Agnes 25 Nov. 1899. **196** 'Creaky's' swan-song 11 Apr. 1900: diary.—Telegram from Queen Victoria, dated 1 Apr., arrived 12 Apr.—Message from Lord Roberts, dated 9 Apr., received 20 Apr. **197** '*Dan Kolonel* Baden-Powell . . .': Eloff's letter 29 Apr. translated from original.—'Sir, I beg to thank you . . .': letter to Eloff 30 Apr. (The original of B-P's answer is still in the possession of the Eloff family, according to the *Mafeking Mail* 31 May 1949.)

§ 7. Page **198** Events of 12 May 1900: diary. **199** Message to McLaren: *Sketches in Mafeking* and letter 21 May. **200** Wording of helio message: *Sketches in Mafeking*. B-P awakened by Baden: letter 19 May.

CLIMAX ONE—18 MAY 1900

Pages **202–6** Based on newspaper reports and advertisements (mainly *The Times* 19 and 21 May 1900, and *Daily Telegraph* 19 May) and magazine articles (*Illustrated London News* 19 and 26 May; The *Sphere* 26 May; *Illustrated Weekly News* 26 May). Also privately printed sheet 'London on Mafeking Night' by James R. Fairbairn, Quartermaster-Sergeant, R. A. Aldershot, 21 May 1900.

XIV THE END OF A WAR—1900–03

The main sources of this chapter are B-P's own writings—specifically his Staff Diary 18 May to 5 July 1900, General Orders 18 May to 29 August, 'Résumé of Report on the Siege of Mafeking, Part II Operations in the Transvaal, 18th May to 29th August', and B-P's autobiography manuscript. For background material the same sources were used as for subdivision § 2 of chapter 'The Boer War'.

Subdivision § 1. Page **208** 'I and my whole Empire . . .': telegram from Queen Victoria 19 May 1900. Casualties: 'Résumé of Report'. **209** Letters from all classes of British Life: Mafeking scrapbook prepared by B-P's mother.—'You did splendidly . . .': letter from Wolseley 18 May.—'Azzie and I . . .': letter from mother 24 July.

§ 2. Page **211** Surrender of Piet Kruger: letter to unknown address 16 June 1900.—Reception in Pretoria: autobiography manuscript. **212** 'It was awfully embarrassing . . .' and 'It was a luxury . . .': letter 19 June. **212–13** Churchill's interview with B-P: *London Morning Post*, 27–28–29 June. **212** 'He read it with concentration . . .': Churchill's *Great Contemporaries*. **214** 'I considered (and still do) . . .': letter to Roberts 8 Aug.

§ 3. Page **214** B-P's estimate of de Wet's fame: autobiography manuscript. **215** 'Your note has been received . . .': letter to de Wet 17 Aug. 1900.

§ 4. Page **216** 'I want you to see me . . .': Roberts' telegram quoted from *Lessons from Varsity*. **217** Milner's letters and Roberts' reply: *The Milner Papers*, edited by Cecil Headlam.—Arrival and official reception in Cape Town: *Uitenhage Chronicle* 13 Sept. 1900. **218** 'I do wish . . .': letter 27 June. **218–19** Experience at Groote Schuur and meetings with Milner, Roberts, and Kitchener: autobiography manuscript. **219** Purpose of South African Constabulary: *Notes and Instructions for the S.A.C.* **219–20** Organization of S.A.C.: *Lessons from Varsity.* **221** 'He is an awfully jolly . . .': autobiography manuscript.—'Worst southeaster . . .': letter 19 Dec. **222** *Aids to Scouting* in *Boys of the Empire:* November 1900 to January 1901. (Approximately fifty per cent of *Aids to Scouting* was published in nine instalments in the magazine 'by kind permission of the publishers'.)—'I appeal to the British spirit . . .': *Notes and Instructions for the S.A.C.* **223** Kitchener's plans: sources enumerated in notes for § 2 of chapter 'The Boer War'; also in Philip Magnus' *Kitchener*. **224** 'I have long hoped . . .': report of army doctor 12 July 1901.

§ 5. Page **224** Experiences at Madeira and Southampton: autobiography manuscript.—Itinerary in England: letters 26 July, 14, 20, 25, 28 August 1901. **225** Charterhouse visit: *The Greyfriar* December 1901. **225** Powell luncheon: diary; also letter by A. S. Inge to *The Times* 15 Jan. 1940.—Joseph Chamberlain presentation 6 Nov. 1901: B-P scrapbook.—'Had a long sit-down talk . . .': letter 1 Oct. **226** London experiences: diary 28 and 29 Oct., 9 and 24 Nov. Departure: diary 14 Dec.

§ 6. Page **226** S.A.C. progress: autobiography manuscript. **227** Peace terms: *The Official History of the War in South Africa.* **228** Work of S.A.C. after end of war: autobiography manuscript and *Review of the South African Constabulary* 1900–1908 by Colonel R. S. Curtis, Inspector General S.A.C. (B-P's successor). **229** Distances travelled: diary 2 Sept. 1938.—'Now it only remains . . .': letter 12 Apr. 1902. **229–30** Chamberlain tour: autobiography manuscript. **231** 'The question as to whether . . .': letter to Milner undated, probably 12 Jan. 1903.—'The principal advantage . . .': letter from Milner undated, probably 14 Jan.—'Your extreme get-at-ableness . . .': letter from S.A.C. officer (undated) quoted in autobiography manuscript.

XV INSPECTOR GENERAL—1903–07

Subdivision § 1. Page **232** 'Awful Tuppenny Tube' and 'No. 8 had done its work . . .': letter 27 Oct. 1902.—B-P's feelings about task: autobiography manuscript.

§ 2. Pages **233–4** Trip to the United States: diary 4–28 Apr. 1903. **234** 'Stunning display . . .': letter 16 Apr.—Experience with reporter: diary 28 Apr. **235** 'I have caused your cable . . .': letter from General Henry C. Corbin 22 May.—Apology from editor: letter from H. D. Wright of *The Commercial Advertiser* 4 June.

§ 3. Pages **235–6** B-P in England: diary and autobiography manuscript.

§ 4. Page **236** 'Six schemes carried out . . .' and 'Although their officers . . .': letter 30 Aug. 1903.—'Quite a wonderful sight . . .': letter 2 Sept. **236–7** Kaiser Wilhelm episode: autobiography manuscript. **237** 'The way he did it . . .': letter 1 Sept.

§ 5. Pages **237–8** B-P's achievements: autobiography manuscript. **238** Purpose of *Cavalry Journal*: first issue January 1906.

§ 6. Pages **238** Visit to France: autobiography manuscript.

§ 7. Pages **239–40** Trip to Africa with Duke of Connaught: *Sketches in Mafeking and East Africa*. **239** 'Nothing but hard work . . .': letter 27 Jan. 1906. **240** 'At that hour . . .': letter 25 Feb. **241** 'This country is really . . .': letter 25 Feb.—'I've finished half my book . . .': letter 13 Aug.—'Enough to purchase my first automobile . . .': letter 10 Apr. 1908.

§ 8. Page **242** B-P's interest in Egypt: autobiography manuscript.—Piazzi Smyth's work in Egypt: *Dictionary of National Biography*.—'The ugly little fact . . .': Flinders Petrie's *Seventy Years in Archaeology*.—B-P's first week in Egypt: letter 9 Feb. 1907.— William Petrie and Henrietta Grace: Petrie's *Seventy Years*. **243** 'Tourists are in crowds . . .': letter 15 Feb.—Stay at Khartoum: letters 24 and 25 Feb. **244** Farewell party: *Lessons from Varsity*.—Duke of Connaught's statement: diary 6 May.

LIFE NUMBER TWO

Page **245** 'How lucky for B-P . . .': quoted from Winston Churchill's *Great Contemporaries* by permission of the publisher, Odhams Press Ltd.

XVI THE GENESIS OF AN IDEA—1904–07

Subdivision § 1. Page **247** History and purpose of Boys' Brigade: Roger S. Peacock's *Pioneer of Boyhood—Story of Sir William A. Smith; Encyclopædia Britannica.*—'Finding that some . . .': *Glasgow Weekly Herald* 7 May (?) 1904. **248** 'Seven thousand youngsters . . .': *Glasgow Evening Citizen* 2 May. (*Boys' Brigade Gazette* 1 June gave the actual count as 130 companies with 6,783 officers and boys.)—'That boys would come eagerly . . .': *Lessons from Varsity*. **248–9** Smith's suggestion: *Lessons from Varsity*. **249** 'Boys should try . . .': B-P article in *Boys' Brigade Gazette* 1 June 1904.

§ 2. Pages **249–51** Conditions in England during the early 1900s: G. M. Trevelyan's *History of England*; Arthur Bryant's *English Saga*; R. H. Gretton's *A Modern History of the English People*; R. J. Evans' *The Victorian Age 1815–1914*; André Maurois' *The Edwardian Age*; K. B. Smellie's *Great Britain since 1688*. **251** Report of conditions in London: Charles Booth's *The Life and Labour of London.*—Number of school boys under 'good' influence: Sir John Gorst's *Children of the Nation* and Dr Macnamara's Report, quoted in *Scouting for Boys.*—'Thousands of boys . . .': *Scouting for Boys.*—'Could there be some higher purpose . . .': autobiography manuscript. **252** 'One thing you must learn . . .': letter to Eastbourne boy quoted in *Boy's Own Paper* 19 Jan. 1901.—'Be prepared . . .' and 'Be happy . . .': letter to unnamed 'Dear Sir' 18 Aug. 1902.—'Make up your mind . . .': letter to 'My dear boys' 20 July 1901. **252–3** Letter from Lord Roberts: facsimile in Eileen K. Wade's *Twenty-One Years of Scouting*. (This letter was also submitted as part of B-P's affidavit of 24 May 1918 as referred to under note for § 3, pages **254–5**.) **252** B-P's article 'Scouting for Boys' appeared in 1 June 1906 issue of *Boys' Brigade Gazette*.

§ 3. Pages **253–4** Allenby story: *Lessons from Varsity*. (B-P met Miss Loveday later, on 14 Dec. 1906, at the home of Allenby at Roman Hill House, Colchester. Michael Allenby was killed in World War I.) **254** Charlotte Mason was the founder of the Parents' National Education Union and the author of *Parents and Children*. **254–5** Sources of Scouting scheme: enumerated in B-P's affidavit of 24 May 1918, when he appeared at the American Consulate General, 18, Cavendish Square, London, as witness in case Boy Scouts of America against The United States Boy Scouts before Supreme Court of New York County.

§ 4. Pages **255–6** Life and work of Seton: *Ernest Thompson Seton—A Biographical Sketch Done by Various Hands*. **256** 'It may interest you . . .': letter to Seton 1 Aug. 1906. **257** 'Each camp . . .': diary 30 Oct.—'You will see . . .': letter to Seton 31 Oct.—B-P and Seton association during following months: diary, also letters to Seton made available to the author by Mrs Ernest Thompson Seton.

§ 5. Page **258** Original manuscript of 'Boy Patrols' in possession of British Boy Scouts Association. **259** 'The same causes . . .': source of quotation in W. S. Adams' *Edwardian Portraits*. **260** Four-page circular 'Boy Scouts. A Suggestion' has only two pages of type—the other two pages are blank; first printing has '32 Princes Gate, London SW, May 1907' on page 2.—Ireland itinerary: diary.—Dispatch-box: described in letter 29 Sept. 1907.

§ 6. Pages **261–2** Life and work of C. Arthur Pearson: *Dictionary of National Biography—Twentieth Century*, Sidney Dark's *The Life of Sir Arthur Pearson* and *History of 'The Times'*. **261** Visit to Frensham Place: diary 14 July 1906. **262** Meeting with Pearson: diary.—Work at Dovedale: diary 15–22 June 1907.—B-P's qualms: letter to Seton 17 June.—Meetings with Pearson: diary 25 June, 5, 8, 18, 24, 25 July. **263** Wimbledon Common and Wimbledon Mill: *London*, edited by Charles Knight; also

435

pamphlet prepared by Wimbledon Borough. **262** Work at Mill House: diary 13–23 July. (On 5 July 1948 a tablet was put up at Wimbledon to commemorate B-P's writing there of *Scouting for Boys*: but tablet was placed on the wrong house—on the Wimbledon Mill instead of the Mill House—and carries the wrong year—1908 instead of 1907.) **263** 'I hope to finish . . .': letter 20 July.—Tentative agreement: quoted from original signed 30 July 1907.

XVII THE ISLAND ADVENTURE—1907

Subdivision § 1. Page **264** B-P met Charles van Raalte on 18 May 1907 and characterized him in his diary in three words: 'Bald, bearded, bright'. **264–5** Description and history of Brownsea: *Brownsea Island* by Charles van Raalte, with illustrations by Florence van Raalte; also John Leland's *Itinerary of England* (1535–43), John Hitchin's *The History and Antiquities of the County of Dorset*, R. Thurston Hopkins' *Thomas Hardy's Dorset*. (The term 'Brownsea Island' is somewhat of a redundancy since the name 'Brownsea' already carries the island connotation in the last two letters: Ea— old Danish for island. 'Brownsea' is a contraction of the original 'Bronk's Ea' or 'Brown's Ea'—named, perhaps, for an ancient invader or, as legend has it, for a Bruno who, at the time of Edward the Confessor, was Lord of the Manor of Studland to which the island belonged.) § 2. Page **266** Invitation to Bournemouth Boys' Brigade: facsimile of letter to Henry Robson 19 June 1907 in Eileen K. Wade's *Twenty-One Years of Scouting*.—Invitation to parents: original draft of letter in possession of British Boy Scouts Association.— 'Perhaps you could give me . . .': letter to Henry Robson 19 June. **267** Story of harpoons: told by Alderman Henry Robson at Scouters' Conference at Bournemouth 2 Apr. 1927, as reported in *The Scouter* May 1927. § 3. Page **267** Harvey's recollection told to author in summer of 1960. (A commemorative tablet was placed on the *Hyacinth* in 1947; the boat was stolen from Harvey's Wharf and subsequently found wrecked on the rocks near the Needles, Isle of Wight, June 1953.)—Description of camp site: article by Arthur Broomfield in *The Scouter* July 1957 and author's personal observation 1960 on visit by invitation of owner, 95-year-old Mrs Mary Bonham Christie. (On Mrs Bonham Christie's death in April 1961 her heirs turned the island over to National Trust in lieu of inheritance taxes; it was formally opened to the public on 15 May 1953. Report of camp pitching: *Daily Express* 1 Aug. 1907. **268** B-P's costume: from contemporary photo. (Description and sketches of hat in letter 3 Oct. 1907.) **268–9** Names of boys: list of patrols in *The Scout* 30 May 1908, verified and augmented by the autographs of the participants on a sheet of writing paper, imprinted 'Scouts Camp, Brownsea Island, Poole', dated 7 Aug. 1907. (This sheet, originally given to Mr van Raalte as a souvenir, was presented to the author by Lady de Walden, née Margharita van Raalte.) § 4. Page **269** Use of koodoo horn: letter from Arthur Primmer to author 6 May 1960. **269–70** Details of camp: B-P's 4-page report 'Boy Scouts—A Successful Trial', later included, in abbreviated form, in Part VI of *Scouting for Boys*; also *The Richmond Hill Magazine and Congregational Record CCLXXV*. **270** 'I remember . . .' letter from Arthur Primmer 6 May 1960. **271** Donald's experience: interview with Donald Baden-Powell by author in summer of 1960.—Comment on organization: B-P's report on camp. **271–2** Evening campfire: Percy Everett's *The First Ten Years*. Everett's visit to Brownsea: letter from Everett to B-P 1 Aug. 1907. (In this letter, Everett arranged for himself and Herbert Shaw to arrive Poole Wednesday 7 Aug. and return to London Thursday 8 Aug.) **272** Programme of show 8 Aug. The *Richmond Hill Magazine CCLXXV* and The *Echo* Aug. 9; also in the patrol leaders' own handwriting on letterhead imprinted 'Scouts Camp, Brownsea Island, Poole', presented to the author by Lady de Walden. § 5. Page **272** '*Boy Scouts, A Successful Trial*': published November 1907. **274** 'It was awfully kind . . .': letter to Saxton Noble 10 Aug. 1907 reproduced in *The Scouter* July 1957.—Account of camp: letter to Saxton Noble 28 Aug. reproduced in facsimile with article by Sir Humphrey Noble in *Martins Bank Magazine*, Autumn 1957, sent to the author by Sir Humphrey.

XVIII THE MAKING OF A BEST SELLER—1907-08

Subdivision § 1. Page **275** 'Whether there would be . . .': letter 1 Sept. 1907.—'To take up the training . . .':.letter 2 Sept. **276** Offer to B-P: diary note of meeting with Haldane at War Office 15 Nov.—'Sent "Introduction" to typist (Mr Cavan) to be copied 6 Oct.'—Comments on B-P's 'Notes': letters from Pearson 1 Aug. and 22 Oct. **277** Itinerary of lecture tour: diary.—Move to Mill House: diary 26 Dec.

§ 2. Page **277** Pearson's attempt to secure *The Times: History of 'The Times'* and Sidney Dark's *The Life of Sir Arthur Pearson*. **277-8** Keary's attitude: evident from his letters 1907–08. **278** 'In coming to a formal agreement . . .' and terms of arrangement: letter to Pearson 19 Nov.—Pearson's answer: letter from Pearson 26 Nov. **279** 'I am very sorry . . .': letter to Pearson 29 Nov.—'A bit one-sided . . .': letter to Pearson 3 Dec.—Details of agreement: from original signed 1 Jan. 1908. **279–80** Outcome of Pearson's negotiations for *The Times: History of 'The Times'*.

§ 3. Page **281** Details of B-P's lecture tour: diary. **281-2** Completion of remaining parts of *Scouting for Boys*: letters 13 Jan. 1908 (Part III), 31 Jan. (Part IV), 24 Feb. (Part V), 3 Mar. (Part VI). (In 1947, a retired civil servant called at headquarters of the British Boy Scouts Association with a parcel under his arm. Would anyone be interested in the original manuscript of *Scouting for Boys*? He proved to have been the clerk in the War Office who had typed B-P's manuscript. The material eventually became the property of the Boy Scouts Association. It consists of the holograph, on pieces of paper of all shapes and sizes, of about 27 per cent of the first edition of *Scouting for Boys*, and typescript of approximately 35 per cent.)

§ 4. Pages **281-2** Review of Part I: author's perusal of original first edition copy. **281-3** Publication of the parts of *Scouting for Boys*: Part I, 15 Jan. 1908; Part II, 29 Jan.; Part III, 12 Feb.; Part IV, 26 Feb.; Part V, 11 Mar.; Part VI, 25 Mar. Book reviews: *The Times* 17 Mar.; The *Spectator* 25 Jan.; *Evening Citizen* 18 Jan.; *Daily Graphic* 18 Jan. **283** Announcement of publication of *Scouting for Boys* in book form: inside back cover of Part VI.

XIX A SCHEME BECOMES A MOVEMENT—1908-10

Subdivision § 1. Pages **284-5** Early days of Scouting: author's personal experiences. **286** Goschen Buildings were headquarters of C. Arthur Pearson Ltd.—Herbert Shaw was assigned to the task of editing *The Scout* in Oct. 1907. (Shaw, according to Everett in *The First Ten Years*, had 'vivid recollections' of the Brownsea Island camp from his visit on the island with Everett.)—Review of *The Scout*, No. 1, Vol. 1: author's perusal of original copy. (The early pages of *The Scout* indicate B-P's difficulty in settling on a name for his new movement. In the first issue, 18 Apr. 1908, he calls the movement 'Legion of Boy Scouts'; in the second issue, 25 Apr., it is 'Britain's Boy Scouts'; and in the 12 Dec. issue simply 'The Boy Scouts'.)

§ 2. Page **287** Report of B-P's speech: *Newcastle Daily Journal* 4 May 1908.—B-P's trip to London to see Haldane 4–5 May: diary. **287-8** Debate in Parliament: *The Parliamentary Debates (Authorized Version)*, Fourth Series, Vol. 188, 5–18 May. **288** 'They were pretty rough . . .' and 'barracks square drill . . .': autobiography manuscript.

§ 3. Page **289** Humshaugh Camp: *The Scout* 12 Sept. 1908. B-P's Scout inspections: diary.—B-P's expectations: B-P article in *National Defence Review* February 1909. **290** Message to Scout-interested adults: letter 28 Sept. 1908 quoted in Eileen K. Wade's *Twenty-One Years of Scouting*.—Announcement of two travelling inspectors: memorandum 'Boy Scouts' October 1908.

§ 4. Pages **291-2** Trip to South America: sketchbooks and B-P article in the *Graphic* (reprinted into 16-page pamphlet: 'A Trip to Sunshine'), autobiography manuscript.

291 'In a very nice cabin . . .': letter 19 Feb. 1909.—'Rio was better . . . ': letter 13 Mar.—'When they heard . . .': letter 20 Mar. **292** 'I never saw such people . . .': letter 3 Apr.

§ 5. Page **292** 'The office must be separate . . .': letter to Pearson 21 Jan. 1909. —Fry's invitation: at B-P's visit to Fry's camp 18 Feb.—Buckler's Hard Camp 24 Aug. –4 Sept.: H. G. Elwes' article in *Essex County Standard* 18 Sept. **293** 'Total 250 miles . . .': diary 15 Aug.

§ 6. Pages **293–4** Crystal Palace Rally: *Headquarters Gazette* Oct. 1909. **294** 'It would be difficult . . .': *Public Opinion* 10 Sept.—B-P's first meeting with Girl Scouts: *Lessons from Varsity*. **295** Letter from 'A Would-Be Scout': *Headquarters Gazette* November 1909. **295–6** Description of Girl Guides, choice of name and quote 'Anyone who had come in touch . . .': Rose Kerr's *The Story of the Girl Guides*. **296** 'It is all a part . . .': letter in Leeds newspaper quoted by B-P in *The Scout* 12 Sept. 1908. **296–7** Scouting's alleged socialism or conservatism: 'Letters to Editors' and 'leader columns' in *Manchester Guardian* (among others) 1908–09. **297** Appeal to Irish boys: handbill in B-P scrapbook. **297–8** Scoutmasters' Conference and resolution 4 Sept. 1909: *Headquarters Gazette* October 1909. **298** 'Here come the Brussel Sprouts . . .': Leslie Paul's *Angry Young Man*.

§ 7. Page **298** Invitation to Balmoral: card in B-P scrapbook. **298–9** Balmoral experience: letter 3 Oct. 1909.

§ 8. Page **300** 'Even if the desirable consummation . . .': *Headquarters Gazette* Feb. 1909. **300–1** List of committee and staff members: *Second Annual Report of the Boy Scouts* 23 Jan. 1910. **301** New arrangement with Pearson: letter from J. A. Kyle to C. Arthur Pearson Ltd. 12 Mar. 1910.

§ 9. Page **302** B-P's decision to retire from army and quote 'for I had no wish . . .': autobiography manuscript.—Haldane's regrets: letter from Haldane 13 Jan. 1910.— 'My dear Baden-Powell . . .': letter from Arthur Davidson 13 Jan. **303** Visit to Buckingham Palace May 5: diary.—Death of King Edward VII: André Maurois' *The Edwardian Age*.

XX THE WORLD SPREAD OF SCOUTING—1910–11

Subdivision § 1. Pages **304–5** Growth of World Scouting: *Facts on World Scouting* (pamphlet published by Boy Scouts World Bureau, Ottawa, Canada) and Beresford Webb's *Scouting Achievements*.

§ 2. Page **305** Canadian contest: *The Scout* during spring 1910.—Invitation to B-P to come to Canada: letter from Lord Grey 19 Feb. 1910. **306** Itinerary of Canadian trip: diary.—'A divinely calm velvety night . . .': sketchbook 14–21 Sept. **306–7** New York day: diary, also Seton's journal 23 Sept. **307** B-P's tribute to American Scout leaders: stenographic report of 23 Sept. speech. **307–8** Trip to Russia: sketchbook 27 Dec. 1910 to 5 Jan. 1911. **308** 'There was no ceremony . . .' and 'after which we parted . . .': letter 2 Jan.

§ 3. Page **308** Growth of British Boy Scouting: *Second Annual Report of the Boy Scouts* 23 Jan. 1911.

§ 4. Page **309** B-P's meeting with Mrs Low: diary 22 May 1911. (B-P diary note of 14 May 1930 states 'Met Lord Monson at whose lunch I first met Mrs Low.')—B-P's bust of Captain John Smith was, in the opinion of the *Outlook* 11 May 1907, 'the best work, among the sculpture' at the year's Royal Academy. (B-P later presented one cast of this bust to Charterhouse, another to the Commonwealth of Virginia. A cast of his first sculpture made on Malta—'The Blind Nubian'—is in the possession of Lady B-P.) **310** 'Today in the few moments . . .': Mrs Low's diary of 30 May and 1 June, quoted by her brother G. Arthur Gordon in *Juliette Low and the Girl Scouts*. **310–11** Life of Juliette Low: *Juliette Low and the Girl Scouts* edited by Anne Hyde Choate and Helen Ferris; *Lady from Savannah* by Gladys Denny Shultz and Daisy Gordon Lawrence. **311** Mrs Low's association with B-P: diary; also B-P letters to Mrs Low and Mrs Low's letters to her family in the archives of the University of North Carolina Library,

Chapel Hill, North Carolina (Gordon Family Papers, Southern Historical Collection) and in the Georgia Historical Library of the Georgia Historical Society Museum, Savannah, Georgia (Gordon Collection). 311–12 B-P's arrangements for the ladies: letters to Mrs Low 24 and 27 June. 312 'We got out and had to walk . . .': letter from Mrs Low to 'Dearest Mama' (undated, approx. 30 June 1911).—'I am not so unhappy . . .': letter to Mrs Low 4 July.

§ 5. Page 313 Planning and arrangements for Royal Rally: B-P notes in the possession of Major Wade. 313–14 Windsor Rally: *The Scout* 15 July 1911; also B-P article in *Sunday Pictorial* 22 Apr. 1934 from which quotes are taken.

§ 6. Page 314 Visit to Lochs: diary 5 Aug. 1911 and letter from Mrs Low 'To Mabel' 7 Aug. 314–15 Trouble with Mrs Low's butler: letter to Mrs Low 4 Aug. and letter from Mrs Low 'To Eleanor' 6 Aug. 315–16 Trip to Scandinavia, Holland and Belgium: two volumes of sketchbooks 7–30 Aug. 315 'These past few days . . .': letter 10 Sept. 316 Announcement of Foreign Department: *Headquarters Gazette* October 1911.

§ 7. Page 316 B-P's non-Scouting activities: diary. 316–17 Original petition to secure Royal Charter dated 7 Mar. 1911. 317 'Shall be one body . . .': Royal Charter. —'This gives the seal . . .': letter (undated) quoted in B-P's *Scouts*.

XXI A JOURNEY OF CONSEQUENCE—1912

Baden-Powell described his trip round the world in weekly 'yarns' in *The Scout*. These yarns were later published in book form under the title *Boy Scouts Beyond the Seas—My World Tour*. Numerous other incidents are contained in diary notes, letters, and in sketches and memorabilia in scrapbooks of the trip.

Subdivision § 1. Page 318 'When I arrived at the Gate . . .': *Rovering to Success*. 318–19 Details of contract: from original 'Memorandum of Agreement made this 29th day of August 1911'. 319 Dismay of James E. West: letter from West to B-P 5 Oct. 1911. Agreement telegraphed to B-P on 18 Nov.—B-P's concern: letters to West 24 Nov. and 27 Dec.

§ 2. Page 320 Description of *Arcadian*: B-P scrapbook. (*Arcadian* was turned into a British transport during World War I. It was torpedoed with troops on board by an enemy submarine in the eastern Mediterranean 15 Apr. 1917 and sank in five minutes with a loss of 279 officers and men.)—Passenger list: B-P scrapbook. 321 B-P's first meeting with Olave Soames: diary 4 Jan. 1912 and *Lessons from Varsity*. 321–3 Details of journey provided by Lady B-P in interview with author. 322 B-P's surprise at seeing Mrs Low: diary 5 Jan.—Mrs Low's sudden decision to go to Colombia: letter from Mrs Low to family 15 Dec. 1911. (She changed plans on board; instead of proceeding to Colombia she decided to continue on *Arcadian*, according to letter from Mrs Low to 'Papa and Mama' 23 Jan.)—'Had B-P to myself . . .': Olave Soames' diary 10 Jan.— 'Do sports . . .': Olave Soames, diary 11 Jan.—'Ginger' Gordon's warning: *Lessons from Varsity*. 323 Kingston episode: diary and told by Lady B-P in interview with author. 324 'It is much worse . . .': letter to Olave Soames 26 Jan.

§ 3. Page 324 B-P's reception in New York: *New York World* 31 Jan. 1912.—'They could not understand . . .': diary 31 Jan. 324–6 Tour of the United States: diary 31 Jan.–16 Mar.; also *Third Annual Report of the Boy Scouts of America* (1913). 325 Armory event: *New York Times* 11 Feb.—'They received me . . .': letter 10 Feb.— 'Roosevelt, very cheery . . .': diary 11 Feb. 326 Portland episode: diary and *Portland Journal* 9 Mar.; also B-P article in *Headquarters Gazette* April 1912.—'I don't mind . . .': letter to Dr Campbell 11 Mar.

§ 4. Pages 326–7 Letters quoted from originals. 327–8 B-P's concern: letters to mother and to Olave Soames during April and May.

§ 5. Pages 328–9 Tour of Pacific: diary and sketchbooks. 329 'One of the greatest . . .': B-P speech reported in *Lyttelton* (New Zealand) *Times* 1 June 1912.

§ 6. Page 329 Arrival in Sydney: diary 10 May 1912. 330 'It would be a most . . .': letter 18 May.—Seven-week journey: diary 11 May–5 July. 330–1 Situation in

Australia and B-P's viewpoint: B-P speech reported in the *West Australian* 3 July.
331 'I think I have done . . .': letter 5 July.

§ 7. Page **332** 'One scarcely knew . . .': letter to Olave Soames 20 July 1912.—
'Mayor . . . defence officers . . .': letter to Olave Soames 26 July.—Meeting with
Smuts: diary 26 July.

§ 8. Page **332** Number of talks: tour résumé in 1912 diary. **333** Trip to Norway
with Donald: diary 27 Aug.–13 Sept. and sketchbooks.—'Asking for a hole . . .':
letter 11 Sept.—Arrival at Parkstone: told by Lady B-P in interview. **334** 'Dearest
Mother . . .': letter 14 Sept.—Talk with mother: letter to Olave Soames 17 Sept.

§ 9. Pages **334–5** Boy's letter and B-P's answer: *The Scout* 3 Oct. 1912. **335** Preparations for B-P's wedding: *Daily Graphic* 19 Sept. **335–6** Wedding ceremony: *Bournemouth Guardian* and *Daily Mirror* 31 Oct.

XXII THE END OF AN ERA—1912–14

Subdivision § 1. Page **337** Honeymoon at Roch Castle: letter 1 Nov. 1912. **337–8**
B-P's health and wedding reception: details related by Lady B-P to author. **338** Trip
to Africa: B-P articles in *The Scout*, later included in book *Young Knights of the Empire*.
339 'Sorry it is over . . .': Lady B-P diary 9 Feb. 1913.—'Olave is a perfect wonder
. . .': letter 8 Feb.

§ 2. Page **339** Description of Ewhurst Place from photographs in B-P scrapbooks.
—'This process of "resting" . . .': Herbert Jenkins' article in *Headquarters Gazette*
December 1914. **340** Lady B-P's pregnancy: Lady B-P diary 3 Mar. 1913.—Warington
Baden-Powell married Hilda Farmer on 13 Sept. 1913; they had no children.—Peter's
birth and baptism: diary. **341** Admiral Smyth's poem: quoted from original.—
Tribute to his mother: B-P article in *The Scout* October 1914.

§ 3 Pages **342–3** Birmingham Exhibition: souvenir book *Boy Scouts and What They
Do—Imperial Scout Exhibition 1913*. **343** 'It needs no great stretch . . .': B-P introduction to souvenir book.—Fund drive: *Headquarters Gazette* 1913–14.—Plans for trip
to Norway and South Africa: *Headquarters Gazette* August 1914.

XXIII WEATHERING THE STORM—1914–20

Subdivision § 1. Page **345** 'Just as the boys of Mafeking . . .': letter of preliminary
instructions 'Mobilization of Boy Scouts', quoted in Eileen K. Wade's *Twenty-One
Years of Scouting*. **346** Kitchener's disdain for the Territorials: Philip Magnus'
Kitchener.—Interview with Kitchener: B-P article in *Headquarters Gazette* September
1914.—'The Boy Scouts are now ready . . .': letter to Kitchener 6 Aug. 1914.—'Make
a good corporal . . .': autobiography manuscript.—'Once a Scout . . .': in Kitchener's
speech before Leicestershire Boy Scouts at Coronation Rally April 1911.—'So I came
home very bucked!': diary 10 Aug. **346–7** Report of war activities of the British Boy
Scouts: *'The Times' History and Encyclopædia of the War* Part 213—'The Boy Scouts'.
347 Activities at Headquarters: articles in *Headquarters Gazette* 1914–15.

§ 2. Page **348** Trip to France: special diary 27 Mar.–6 Apr. 1915. **349** Work on
hut: *Headquarters Gazette* November and December 1915. **350** Sales of *Quick Training for War*: diary 24 Aug. and 24 Sept.—Rumours of B-P in Germany: interview with
B-P in the *Star* 27 Mar. 1930.

§ 3. Page **350** Early efforts in regard to programme for younger boys: Percy Everett
in *The First Ten Years*. **351** 'The name "Junior Scouts" . . .': letter to Everett 19 Nov.
1913. **352** Growth of Wolf Cubs: *Annual Report of the Boy Scouts* 1918.

§ 4. Pages **352–4** Reorganization of the Girl Guides: Rose Kerr's *The Story of the
Girl Guides*, Marguerite de Beaumont's *World Adventure*, and Eileen K. Wade's *The
World Chief Guide*.

§ 5. Pages **354–5** Trip to France and Spain: diary 20 Oct.–10 Nov. 1918. **355** Report
about Spain: letter to Lord Stamfordham 13 Nov.—'All had to wear . . .': diary
10 Nov.

§ 6. Pages **355–6** Finding 'Pax Hill': diary and author's interview with Lady B-P. **356** Trip to America: diary 28 Apr.–29 May 1919.

§ 7. Pages **357–8** Story of Gilwell: *The Gilwell Book* published by the British Boy Scouts Association. **357** Contents of training course: quoted from undated draft by B-P.

§ 8. Page **358** 'Jamboree' definition: *The Imperial Dictionary* by Dr Ogilvie and Dr Armandale. (Protest against use of term possibly registered by Charles Chester Branch, Deputy Chief Commissioner.)—First meeting of jamboree committee: *The Jamboree Book* 1920. **359** 'We are obliged . . .': *Headquarters Gazette* November 1917.—'The jamboree, be it understood . . .': *Headquarters Gazette* February 1919. **359–60** Requests to Wade: from originals in the possession of Major Wade. (The close co-operation between the jamboree's organizing secretary and B-P's private secretary had an unexpected result: Major Wade and Miss Nugent decided to get married as soon as the jamboree was over; wedding took place 9 Sept.) **360–1** Events of the jamboree: *The Jamboree Book* 1920 and the author's personal experience. **361** B-P's week: diary. —West's approach to Wade: note from, and author's interview with, Major Wade.

CLIMAX TWO—7 August 1920

Pages **362–4** Closing of jamboree based on author's personal experience, on newspaper reports (*The Times* the *Morning Post* and *Daily Telegraph* 9 Aug. 1920), and on the description in *Headquarters Gazette* 21 Aug. 1920 and in *The Scout Jamboree Book* 1920. The process by which Baden-Powell was proclaimed Chief Scout of the World was pieced together from interviews with or letters from eye-witnesses: Lady Baden-Powell and Major A. G. Wade, Julian Salomon of the United States, Tage Carstensen of Denmark, George S. Childs of Eire—plus the author's personal recollections of the occasion.

XXIV THE CHIEF SCOUT OF THE WORLD—1920–29

Subdivision § 1. Pages **366–7** Start of International Bureau: 'Report to International Conference on Activities of International Bureau, 1922' and J. S. Wilson's *Scouting Round the World*. **366** Story of Kathleen Burke: Eileen K. Wade's *Twenty-Seven Years with Baden-Powell* and interview with Hubert S. Martin in *The Scouter* January 1937. —Invitation to luncheon: letter from Peabody 21 Aug. 1920.—'To finance International Bureau . . .': diary 24 Sept. 1920. **367** Start of League of Nations: *Encyclopædia Britannica*.—'A field of immense possibilities. . .': *Jamboree* January 1921. **368** Second International Boy Scout Conference was held at Sorbonne, Paris, 22–30 July 1922. (Constitution of International Conference was adopted on this occasion.)

§ 2. Page **368** Scouting in India: J. S. Wilson's *Scouting Round the World*. **369** Itinerary of journey: diary 28 Jan.–22 Mar. 1921 and *Headquarters Gazette* June 1921. —'We who had sat down . . .': B-P article in *The Times* 20 May.—'It is a tribute . . .': 'Some Recollections of the Visit of Baden-Powell', manuscript article by Satta Bose, State Commissioner, Bharat Scouts and Guides, West Bengal.—Deathwatch over Warington: diary 18–24 April.

§ 3. Pages **370–1** Life at Pax Hill: Eileen K. Wade's *Twenty-Seven Years with Baden-Powell*; also interviews with Lady B-P and personal experience of author. **370** 'If you only take an hour extra . . .': *Yarns for Boy Scouts*.

§ 4. Pages **371–2** Life of Baden-Powell family: interviews with Lady B-P, Peter (the second Lord Baden-Powell) and Betty Clay, née Baden-Powell. **373** Jenkins' suggestion in regard to book title reported by Lady B-P.—Establishment of Senior Scout Section: *Headquarters Gazette* June 1917.—Peter's boarding school: Mr Pooley's Preparatory School 'Dane Court' at Pyrford.

§ 5. Page **374** B-P's idea of 'posse' first broached in memo to Wade 20 Sept. 1922. Report of 'posse': *Morning Post* 9 Oct. 1922.—Imperial Jamboree: diary 25 July–10 Aug. 1924; also *Imperial Jamboree Souvenir Book*. **375** The securing of Foxlease:

article by Mrs Mark Kerr in *Yorkshire Post* 11 Sept. 1922.—Telephone call on 22 Feb. 1922: diary. **375–6** 2nd World Jamboree in Denmark: B-P article in *The Times* 29 Aug. and author's personal experience. **376** Trip to the United States: diary 21 Apr.– 21 May 1926. **377** The Baden-Powells at Camp Edith Macy with Mrs Low on 13 May: Jane Deeter Rippin's chapter 'Her Dream Comes True' in *Juliette Low and the Girl Scouts*. **377–8** Trip to South Africa: diary 2 Sept. 1926–18 Apr. 1927; printed report *South African Tour* 1926–27; also B-P articles in *The Times* 12 and 13 May 1927.

§ 6. Pages **378** During the years 1927–28, the two Chiefs visited Denmark, Sweden, Norway, Hungary, Gibraltar, Monaco, Algiers, Tangier, Sierra Leone, Canary Islands, Spain, Portugal, Belgium, Luxembourg.—Reunion of Brownsea Island campers: *The Scouter* September 1928. **379** What-kind-of-gift: reported to author by Lady B-P. **380** B-P at 3rd World Jamboree: diary 25 July to 10 Aug. 1929.—Opening day based on author's personal experience. **381** Details of emotional session in regard to peerage based on letters from and author's interviews with three of the people involved—Lady B-P, Eileen K. Wade, J. S. Wilson. **382** 'Half an hour later . . .': J. S. Wilson's *Scouting Round the World*.—'It has given me great pleasure . . .': letter from King George V 2 Aug. **382–3** Details of jamboree: *The Scout Jamboree Book* edited by William Hill-court, and *The World Jamboree of Boy Scouts* 1929 (pamphlet of reprints of articles in *The Times* 31 July to 5 Aug. 1929). **383** Gift of braces: *The Scouter* September 1929 and letter to author from George S. Childs.

XXV LORD BADEN-POWELL OF GILWELL—1929–37

Subdivision § 1. Page **384** Recognition at Gilwell: *The Scouter* October 1929. **385** 'It was a fearful adventure . . .': letter to Peter 30 Oct. 1929.—'Delighted! Which side?': in interview in *Daily Graphic* 25 Feb. 1910.—Opinion of politicians: B-P's message of congratulation to the students of Edinburgh University 1932 on their having 'decided to abandon the pernicious practice of electing their Lord Rector on his political merits'.

§ 2. Page **385** 'I notice that one correspondent . . .': *The Scouter* November 1935. **386** Lady B-P's election as Chief Guide of the World: Eileen K. Wade's *The World Chief Guide* and Marguerite de Beaumont's *World Adventure*.

§ 3. Page **386** Idea for autobiography: diary 3 and 25 Oct. 1930. **387** Writing of autobiography: diary notes 1931–32.

§ 4. Page **388** Description of Kandersteg and Rover Moot: *The Scouter* September 1931; also B-P article in *The Times* 29 Aug. **389** 'And it *was* a big one . . .': letter to Lady B-P 2 Aug. 1933.—Description of 4th World Jamboree from the author's personal experience as recorded in *The Scout Jamboree* 1933 by James E. West and William Hill-court. **390** 'I have heard the Chief . . .': J. S. Wilson in *Scouting Round the World*. —Origin of Good Will Cruises: reported to author by Lady B-P.

§ 5. Pages **390–1** Details of *Calgaric* Cruise: diary 12–29 Aug. 1933 and B-P article in *The Times* 4 Sept. **391** Interview with Mussolini 3 Mar.: B-P manuscript 'Confidential Report to Imperial Headquarters'. **392** Meeting with Ribbentrop and 'Chief Commissioner of *Jugend* movement': diary 19 Nov. 1937. (According to William L. Shirer in *The Rise and Fall of the Third Reich*, two points to be gained by Hitler's projected occupation of Britain were the elimination of the British Boy Scouts and the arrest of Baden-Powell.)

§ 6. Page **392–3** B-P's illness and operation: B-P and Lady B-P diaries December 1933–February 1934.

§ 7. **394** 'For my part . . .': Second Sir Alfred Fripp Lecture delivered by B-P 24 Jan. 1933. **395–7** Trip to Australia, Canada and round the world: B-P articles in *The Scout*, later published as book *Scouting Round the World*. **395** 'Inspiring conviction . . .' and 'East and West . . .': B-P article in *The Times* 5 Aug. 1935. **396** Audience of Pope Pius XI: B-P article in *The Scouter* April 1933.—Affiliation of Canadian Scouts: B-P article in *The Times* 5 Aug. 1935. **396–7** South African trip: B-P article in *The*

Times 3 June 1936. **396** 'With freedom from any moral restraints . . .': B-P article in *The Scouter* April 1936.

§ 8. Page **397** 'Never could we have imagined . . .': letter from Lady B-P to Eileen K. Wade 9 Dec. 1935. **398** Night at 'Tree Tops': B-P article in *Country Life* 11 Apr. 1936. (On 5 Feb. 1952, Princess Elizabeth, with her husband Prince Philip, climbed up the ladder to spend the night at 'Tree Tops'. She climbed down the next morning Queen of England. 'Tree Tops' and the huge fig tree in which it was built were destroyed during the Mau Mau uprising, on 27 May 1954; it has since been rebuilt—on stilts.) **398–9** Safari and illness of the two Chiefs: B-P and Lady B-P diaries.—Experiences in South Africa: B-P article in *The Times* 3 June 1936. **400** Dedication of Great Tower Plantation: *The Scouter* September 1936.—Betty B-P and Gervas Clay romance: letters of 14 and 15 Aug. in B-P scrapbook.—Wedding day: 24 Sept.

§ 9. Page **401** Trip to India: diary and B-P article in *The Times* 22 Apr. 1937.— 'Wild Baluchis met quieter Bengalis . . .': B-P article in *The Scouter* May 1937.—'I felt 40 years younger . . .': B-P article in *The Scouter* March 1941.—B-P meetings with King George VI: diary. **402** Announcement of Wateler Prize: *The Scouter* August 1937 and *Jamboree* October 1937. **402–4** Details of 5th World Jamboree from author's personal experience. **404** B-P's week at jamboree: B-P and Lady B-P diaries. **405** Closing speech: *The Scouter* September 1937.

EPILOGUE

XXVI THE LAST YEARS—1937–41

Page **407** 'Few pioneers . . .': *Jamboree*, 1st Quarter 1941. Quoted from the poem 'To B-P, 12 January 1941' by A. P. Herbert and reprinted from *Let Us Be Glum* by permission of the author. Subdivision § 1. Page **409** Baden's illness and death: diary 4 Aug.–7 Oct. 1937. **409** Silver Wedding reception 2 Nov.: *Country Life* 13 Nov. and *The Scouter* Nov. 1937 **410** 'A tired heart . . .': letter to Frank 21 Jan. 1938.—'When the doctor asked me . . .': B-P article in *The Scouter* March 1938.—'Third volume . . .': diary 1 Jan. 1938. **411** 'So much waste paper . . .': diary 1 Sept. 1938.—*Orduna* Cruise 8–23 Aug.: *The Scouter* September 1938, *The Guider* 22 Sept., and B-P article in *Daily Telegraph* 8 Sept.

§ 2. Page **412** 'Peeped through the clouds . . .': diary 26 Nov. 1938.—'We are utterly . . .': letter from Lady B-P to her children 26 Nov.

§ 3. Page **412** Nobel Peace Prize nomination quoted from pamphlet prepared by Boy Scouts of America, 'Outstanding Achievements of Lord Baden-Powell'. **413** B-P's offer to return home: letter to Lord Somers 16 Sept. 1939.—'I have been pruning roses . . .': B-P article in *The Scouter* October 1940. **413–14** Visit of family: accounts and photographs in B-P scrapbook. **414** Decision in regard to Heather: Lady B-P diary 13 June 1940.—'Airmail suspension delays . . .': cablegram 13 June.—Wedding reported to the Baden-Powells by Mrs Wade in letter 24 June.

§ 4. Page **414** 'The beginning of the last lap . . .': Lady B-P diary 9 Sept. 1940. **415** 'Dindo darling—I look on it . . .': quoted from original letter by B-P written at Etaples 21 Jan. 1916.—'Dindo darling—I don't know . . .': quoted from original letter, undated. **416** B-P's last messages: (B-P placed his 'last messages' in his 'current correspondence' folder, ready for release upon his death.)

L'envoi

The Dean and Chapter of Westminster Abbey offered a place in the Abbey for Baden-Powell, between the graves of the Unknown Warrior and David Livingstone. After careful consideration, the family declined this great honour as not conforming to B-P's expressed wishes. He was buried in the Africa he loved with full military honours accorded to his rank of Lieutenant-General and with a guard of Boy Scouts—European, African and Asian. His grave in the tiny cemetery at Nyeri, Kenya, is marked by a simple stone that carries his name and the Boy Scout trail sign for 'I have gone home'.

'Si monumentum requiris, circumspice'
('If you seek [his] monument, look about you')

This inscription in the floor of Saint Paul's, honouring Sir Christopher Wren, is equally fitting as an epitaph for Baden-Powell. But while Wren's monument was made of stone and mortar, Baden-Powell's is a living one. His 'monument' is that host of an estimated seventy million boys and men and forty million girls and women who have been members of the two movements he founded. His memory is kept alive today in close to one hundred countries round the world by nine million active Boy Scouts and six million active Girl Guides or Girl Scouts.

BADEN-POWELL'S LAST MESSAGES

To BOY SCOUTS: Dear Scouts—If you have ever seen the play, *Peter Pan*, you will remember how the pirate chief was always making his dying speech, because he was afraid that possibly, when the time came for him to die, he might not have time to get it off his chest.

It is much the same with me; and so, although I am not at this moment dying, I shall be doing so one of these days, and I want to send you a parting word of goodbye.

Remember it is the last you will ever hear from me, so think it over.

I have had a most happy life, and I want each one of you to have as happy a life too. I believe that God put us in this jolly world to be happy and enjoy life.

Happiness doesn't come from being rich, nor merely from being successful in your career, nor by self-indulgence.

One step towards happiness is to make yourself healthy and strong while you are a boy, so that you can *be useful*, and so can enjoy life when you are a man.

Nature study will show you how full of beautiful and wonderful things God has made the world for you to enjoy.

Be contented with what you have got, and make the best of it; look on the bright side of things instead of the gloomy one. But the real way to get happiness is by giving out happiness to other people.

Try and leave this world a little better than you found it, and when your turn comes to die you can die happy in feeling that at any rate you have not wasted your time but have *done your best*.

'Be Prepared' in this way, to live happy and to die happy; stick to your Scout Promise always—even after you have ceased to be a boy—and God help you to do it.

Your friend
BADEN-POWELL

To GIRL GUIDES: My Dear Guides, This is just a farewell note to you—the last that you will have from me.

It is just to remind you, when I have passed on, that your business in life is to be happy and to make others happy.

That sounds comfortable and easy, doesn't it?

You begin making other people happy by doing good turns to them. You need not worry about making *yourselves* happy, as you will very soon find that that comes by itself.

When you make other people happy, it makes YOU happy too.

Later on, when you have a home of your own, by making it a bright and cheery one you will make your husband a happy man.

If all homes were bright and cheery there would be fewer public houses, and the men would not want to go out to them but would stay at home.

It may mean hard work for you but will bring its own reward.

Then if you keep your children healthy and clean and busy they will be happy. Happy children love their parents. And there is nothing can give you greater joy than a loving child.

I am sure God means us to be happy in this life. He has given us a world to live in that is full of beauties and wonders, and He has given us not only eyes to see them but minds to understand them—if we only have the sense to look at them in that light.

We can enjoy bright sunshine and glorious views. We can see beauty in the trees and flowers. We can watch with wonder how the seed produces the young plant which grows to a flower which, in its turn, will replace other flowers as they die off.

For, though plants, like people, die, their race does not die away, but new ones are born and grow up to carry on the Creator's plan.

So, do you see, you women are the chosen servants of God in two ways: first to carry on the race, to bring children into the world to replace the men and women who pass away; secondly, to bring happiness into the world by making happy homes and by being yourselves good cheery comrades for your husbands and children.

And that is where you, as Guides, especially come in. By being a 'comrade'—that is, by taking an interest in your husband's work and aspirations—you can help him with your sympathy and suggestions and so be a guide to him. Also, in bringing up your children by strengthening and training their minds and characters, as well as their bodies and health, you will be giving them to the better use and enjoyment of life.

By giving out love and happiness in this way you will gain for yourselves the return love of husband and children—and there is nothing better in this world.

You will find that Heaven is not a kind of happiness somewhere up in the skies after you are dead, but right here and now, in this world, in your own home.

So—guide others to happiness, and you will bring happiness to yourselves; and by doing this you will be doing what God wants of you.

God be with you.
BADEN-POWELL

To MY BROTHER SCOUTERS AND GUIDES: Cecil Rhodes said at the end of his life (and I, in my turn feel the truth of it), 'So much to do and so little time to do it.'

No one can hope to see the consummation, as well as the start, of a big venture within the short span of one life-time.

I have had an extraordinary experience in seeing the development of Scouting from its beginning up to its present stage.

But there is a vast job before it. The Movement is only now getting into its stride. (When I speak of Scouting I include in it Guiding also.)

The one part which I can claim as mine towards promoting the Movement is that I have been lucky enough to find you men and women to form a group of the right stamp who can be relied upon to carry it on to its goal.

You will do well to keep your eyes open, in your turn, for worthy successors to whom you can, with confidence, hand on the torch. Don't let it become a salaried organization: keep it a voluntary movement of patriotic service.

The Movement has already, in the comparatively short period of its existence, established itself onto a wide and so strong a footing as to show most encouraging promise of what may be possible to it in the coming years.

Its aim is to produce healthy, happy, helpful citizens, of both sexes, to eradicate the prevailing narrow self-interest, personal, political, sectarian and national, and to substitute for it a broader spirit of self-sacrifice and service in the cause of humanity; and thus to develop mutual goodwill and co-operation not only within our own country but abroad, between all countries.

Experience shows that this consummation is no idle or fantastic dream, but is a practicable possibility—if we work for it; and it means, when attained, peace, prosperity and happiness for all.

The 'encouraging promise' lies in the fact that the hundreds of thousands of boys and girls who are learning our ideals to-day will be the fathers and mothers of millions in the near future, in whom they will in turn inculcate the same ideals—*provided that these are really and unmistakably impressed upon them by their leaders of to-day*.

Therefore you, who are Scouters and Guiders, are not only doing a great work for your neighbour's children but are also helping in practical fashion to bring to pass God's Kingdom of peace and goodwill upon earth.

So, from my heart, I wish you God-speed in your effort.
BADEN-POWELL

To the GENERAL PUBLIC: My life has been an intensely happy one, not only in my own home circle, but also in the world outside it.

I would like, before I go hence, to say how grateful I am to hundreds—aye thousands —for kindnesses they have rendered to me.

I have been deeply touched from time to time by that jolly goodwill which I have met with from brother Scouts and from fellow subjects of all stations in life throughout the Empire.

Nor has this goodwill been confined merely to fellow countrymen, for men of other nationalities have given me their friendliness in the same way.

It has been due not to anything that I have done for them, since in a great number of cases they have been entire strangers to me; but it has been the expression on their part of the kindliness that lay in their character.

It has helped very largely to making my life the happy one it has been, and for that reason I do hope that that same kindly spirit will be inculcated and developed still more widely in the next generation, so that more lives will be made the happier, and the practice, not merely the precept, of the Christian ideal of peace and goodwill among men may become general.

Looking back on a life of over eighty years, I realize how short life is and how little worth while are anger and political warfare.

The most worth-while thing is to try and put a bit of happiness into the lives of others.

BADEN-POWELL

INDEX

Acland, Dr Alfred 8, 33
Adriatic Cruise 393
Afghanistan 48, 50, 55, 56; B-P in 52–5
Africa, B-P in *see* Algiers, Ashanti,
    Egypt, Gold Coast, Kenya, Matabele-
    land, Natal, Rhodesia, South Africa,
    Swaziland, Tunis, Zululand
Aids to Scouting, by B-P 153, 165, 166,
    195, 196, 222, 248, 253, 254, 257, 260
Aids to Scoutmastership, by B-P 357
Aldershot, B-P at 78
Alexander III 74
Alexander of Teck, Prince 313, 342
Alexander, Sir Archibald 309
Alfonso XIII 355
Algiers, B-P in 97, 337, 338
Allenby, Edmund H. H. (later Field
    Marshal Viscount) 82, 238, 244, 253,
    349
All-India Jamboree 400
American Colonies 11, 12
Argentina 291
Armstrong, Sir William (later Lord) 73
Army Examination 33
Arrowe Park 378
Arthur, Prince, *see* Connaught, Duke of
Ashanti, B-P in 110–18
Ashanti Expedition 105–118
Ashanti Wars 104–7
Australia, B-P in 330–1, 387, 394–5
Austria, B-P in 98, 239

Baden, Susannah 10
Baden-Powell, Agnes (sister) 4, 7, 29,
    35, 46, 86, 195, 222, 232, 295, 309, 335,
    352, 409
Baden-Powell, Baden (brother) 4, 7, 17,
    30, 31, 46, 58, 73, 74, 195, 200, 327,
    335, 409
Baden-Powell, Baden Henry (half-
    brother) 3, 7, 40, 43, 58
Baden-Powell, Betty St Clair (daughter)
    353, 371, 373, 377, 393, 397, 398, 400,
    414
Baden-Powell, Carine (daughter-in-law)
    414
Baden-Powell, Donald (nephew) 266,
    269, 271, 320, 340
Baden-Powell, Florence (sister-in-law)
    229, 341

Baden-Powell, Frances (sister-in-law)
    102, 340
Baden-Powell, Francis (brother) 4, 7, 15,
    16, 18, 29, 32, 46, 58, 166, 195, 229,
    241, 327, 393
Baden-Powell, George (brother) 3, 7, 16,
    18, 29, 30, 32, 46, 53, 58, 59, 69, 79, 80,
    85, 86, 92, 93, 101, 103, 104, 106, 154
Baden-Powell, Gillian (granddaughter)
    414
Baden-Powell, Heather (daughter) 349,
    360, 371, 373, 377, 397, 398, 414
Baden-Powell, Henrietta Grace, (mother)
    17, 18, 19, 30, 33, 34, 35, 46, 47, 86,
    222, 232, 295, 309, 327, 334, 340, 341
Baden-Powell, Maude (niece) 320
Baden-Powell, Olave (wife) 336, 337,
    338–9, 340, 349, 353, 355, 356, 360,
    362, 369, 370, 371, 375, 376, 377, 379,
    380–1, 386–7, 390, 393, 395, 396, 397,
    399, 400, 404, 409, 410, 412–14, 415,
    416, 417 (*see further* Soames, Olave)
Baden-Powell, Peter (son) 340, 349, 360,
    371, 372, 373, 374, 377, 385, 388, 393,
    395, 413
Baden-Powell, Robert (grandson) 409,
    414
Baden-Powell, Robert Stephenson
    Smyth (later Lord Baden-Powell of
    Gilwell). Actor 27, 28, 41, 42, 43, 54,
    94, 102, 150, 182, 326. Artist 16, 17,
    32, 90, 99, 103, 120, 153, 243, 309, 412.
    Ancestors 10–13, 14, 15. Appearance
    20, 47, 404. Author 16, 17, 32, 59,
    67, 103, 120, 153, 166, 281, 351, 354,
    386, 412. Birth 7. Childhood 9–19.
    Children 340, 349, 353, 370–3, 377,
    413–14. Death 417. Education 7, 9,
    18, 21–32. Family life 9, 13–15, 16,
    29–31, 46. Health 18, 44–5, 47, 86,
    138, 337, 393, 404, 410, 412, 414.
    Homes 4, 7, 46, 232, 336, 339, 355,
    356, 410. Love affair 320–36; marri-
    age 336; silver wedding 409. Mili-
    tary appointments 56, 81, 85, 92, 104,
    121, 157, 219, 230, 276, 316. Military
    campaigns: Afghanistan 52–5; Zulu-
    land 81–4, Swaziland 87–9; Ashanti-
    land 105–18; Matabeleland 121–42;
    North West Frontier 147–8; Boer

449